From Coleridge to Gore

A Century of Religious Thought in Britain

From Coleridge to Gore

A Century of Religious Thought in Britain

BERNARD M. G. REARDON

Senior Lecturer in Religious Studies
in the University of Newcastle upon Tyne

Longman

LONGMAN GROUP LIMITED
London

Associated companies, branches and representatives
throughout the world

First published 1971

ISBN 0582 48510. X

Set in Garamond and printed in Great Britain by
Ebenezer Baylis & Son Limited
The Trinity Press, Worcester, and London

In Memoriam S.G.R.

Contents

Contents

Preface

It is a sound principle that an author should have in mind as clearly as may be the public for whom he is writing. My aim in this book has been to meet the needs of students of religious thought in nineteenth-century Britain. In the past these were well served, at any rate for the first sixty years of the period, by V. F. Storr's *The Development of English Theology in the Nineteenth Century*, published as far back as 1913; but the volume has been long out of print and in any case its point of view, as well as its interests and emphases, would today call for some readjustment. L. E. Elliott Binns's *English Thought 1860–1900: The Theological Aspect*, which took up the story where Storr left off, is also, although of more recent date, not now available. And the same has to be said for C. C. J. Webb's admirable *A Study of Religious Thought in England from 1850*. Thus the number of works which can be used with profit as an introduction to this subject has become seriously diminished, a fact of which, as a university teacher, I have been repeatedly reminded by my own pupils. To fill the gap, therefore, is what the present volume attempts to do.

I offer it, however, in all modesty. I have not sought to be original, in the sense of providing either fresh facts or unusual judgments. The scope of my book is too limited to admit the former, had they indeed come to light; and as to the latter, although I have not gone out of my way to conceal my personal views, I consider that from a textbook the student has a right to expect unbiased guidance. My intention has simply been to supply as much detail as space allowed in as objective a way as possible, so enabling the reader to arrive at tentative conclusions of his own. There are aspects of my subject to which I would have liked to pay more attention, but to have done so would have been to make the book even bigger than it is and hence more costly.

My material has had, in fact, to be very selectively treated. I have concentrated on what seems to me to have been of real significance as marking new concerns and pointing to farther horizons. What especially is evident during this period is the awakening consciousness that religious belief poses problems not only as to the truth or otherwise of specific doctrines but in regard to its essential nature, evolution and social utility. Accordingly I have not tried to take account of what may be called the literature of popular religious edification. This in the Victorian age gave satisfaction to a very numerous public, but consideration of it was not to my purpose.

My title, I may add, was suggested by the Archbishop of Canterbury's *From Gore to Temple*, published in 1960, and my own book was in the first instance planned as a kind of forerunner to Dr Ramsey's. But I soon realized that to confine myself to Anglican teaching, for all its domination of the theological scene, would have proved a hampering restriction in view of what I felt to be wanted.

The task I have assigned myself has been one purely of historical survey. As the century passed the issues which were to confront theology in our own time came more and more closely into sight, but the temptation to discuss them in their wider bearing had to be resisted. The historian of thought may permit himself to comment, but he should avoid using historiography as a platform for canvassing his own opinions, a mistake which Storr himself sometimes made. The period with which I have dealt witnessed a general relaxation of the ties of orthodoxy and tradition and a growing appreciation of the variety, complexity and ultimate importance of human interests and values. This, religiously speaking, may have been desirable as well as inevitable. I personally think it was. But I believe also that liberal attitudes in religion have resulted in a loss of that sense of the divine rule and governance in life which through much of the nineteenth century was almost instinctive with a vast number of people in this country, of whatever class of society. The difference between the Victorian era and ours is in this respect greater perhaps than in any other. If to us our grandparents' and greatgrandparents' habitual manner of expression often seems tiresomely religiose and doubtfully sincere it may only be because we fail to understand the force of a conviction which we in this age are unable to share with them.

In selecting a period of history for special study one is always confronted with the problem of limits. To avoid arbitrariness is scarcely possible: the continuum of time has to be broken at some point or other. Coleridge's *Aids to Reflection* was published in 1825, but he was then turned fifty and his contemporaries included Wilberforce and the Evangelical philanthropists, High Churchmen such as van Mildert and Joshua Watson, and liberals like the 'Noetics' of the Oriel Senior Common Room. It is therefore with these that I have appropriately begun my study. To fix a *terminus ad quem*, however, has been more difficult. I have balanced the name of Coleridge with that of Charles Gore, another great Anglican. But the greater part of Gore's career— as a bishop indeed all of it—belongs to this century. Yet as editor of and contributor to *Lux Mundi* he is a very significant figure of the last. I have therefore considered his work as far as his *Dissertations*, beyond which I did not feel justified in going. I have alluded, I admit, to men and books of later date; but this has been only where omission of them would in my view have been a fault. To have made the turn of the century an insurmountable barrier would have been pedantic. Nevertheless the year 1901 marks the start of a new epoch and the close of my inquiry.

BERNARD M. G. REARDON

The University of Newcastle upon Tyne

Introduction

The world we know today, with all its turbulence and ceaseless change, had its birth in the nineteenth century, an age which, viewed now in the lengthening perspective of time, seems to have combined progress with order, experimentation with moral certainty, in a measure unique in history. The recollection of it indeed, as one beholds our troubled contemporary scene, can easily arouse feelings of nostalgia. At heart we long for the same sense of security and confidence. And of no sphere of life is this more deeply so than the religious. The Victorian Church had every appearance of advantage. It boasted distinguished bishops, natural leaders of men; it had learned divines and conscientious parish clergymen; its public voice was heeded, in whatever degree, by all but the utterly heedless or grossly ignorant; its influence on society was a pervasive force for moral good. Nor was Protestant dissent a negligible quantity; on the contrary, its numbers, over the century, grew steadily and its stern conscience was always respected and sometimes feared. Likewise the old religion of Rome, from being at the beginning of our period an all but forgotten sect, increased rapidly as the decades passed, despite prejudice, suspicion and even active hostility, until at the end it had won for itself high prestige and an acknowledged place in the nation's life. From the viewpoint of institutional Christianity the Victorian age was outstanding. For most men, at least among the educated classes, were convinced that religion is a matter of serious concern and that its social recognition is a prime responsibility among a people still claiming the Christian name.

Yet to heighten the contrast between that epoch and our own, tempting though it is, would be a mistake. To whatever century, taking the longest vista, historians may wish to assign the origins of the modern world, the modernity that we all readily identify as such made its *début* then, for the last century was an age not merely of innovation but of revolution.[1] When it began, although the portentous political and social upheaval in France was already more than a decade old, it was still scarcely to be distinguished, in almost any regard, from a period which today can be evoked only by an effort of the imagination working on knowledge studiously garnered. When it ended, the world war of 1914 to 1918 and its immediate product, the Russian Revolution, were, so to say, but a stone's throw off, and Western technology was bestriding the entire globe. In the interval man's knowledge of himself and of his physical environment had immeasurably increased, whereas his faith in another and better world beyond, of which his ancestral religion yet spoke, was far less secure. Moreover, such a world, to a growing multitude of men, seemed not only not very real but not very relevant either. Life here had become so varied and complex, and its potential so much greater, that concern for a hereafter whose blessings looked shadowy beside more proximate and solid goods hardly justified the mental and moral discipline involved.

Our task in the chapters that follow will be to consider a single aspect of the nineteenth century cultural revolution in Britain: that, namely, of informed thought about the Christian religion, it aims and its truth. The epithet is necessary in order to bring the enterprise within manageable limits. What is offered, that is, is not a sociological study. It certainly does not attempt to deal with its subject in *depth*, if by depth is meant the 'grass roots' of popular belief—the religious aspirations and hopes of those who constitute the great majority of the members of any denomination in any age. What it undertakes, rather, is a survey of the manner in which many believers for whom religion was of serious intellectual as well as practical concern sought to understand it in the light of increasing—and unsettling—secular knowledge. This means that little attention will be paid to publications which

---

[1] Thus A. R. Vidler entitles his history of Christianity from 1789 to the present day *The Church in an Age of Revolution* (1961). K. S. Latourette parallels this with his *Christianity in a Revolutionary Age* (1959–63).

simply reiterated traditional Christian doctrine, Catholic or
Protestant, in the traditional way, although for a large number
of people—as it goes without stating—such works, whether
intended for a wider or a narrower public, provided all that they
asked. Interest will be concentrated instead on what was new,
searching and tentative; on what, it may be claimed, was characteristic of the age itself. Hence the room allowed for writings of
a broadly apologetic nature, designed to explain and defend the
accepted creed in its relation to history, science and philosophy;
for it was in the nineteenth century that the studies known as the
history, science and philosophy of religion had their beginnings
and fruitful development. More and more was it apparent that
even those who, despite inevitable questionings and recurrent
doubt, continued to hold to their Christian profession, were
finding it natural to stand aside, as it were, from faith itself and to
view it with at least a degree of detachment and in a critical
spirit. That such an attitude was now judged both possible and
proper emerges clearly from the work of two great Anglicans,
Coleridge in the early decades of the century and Charles Gore in
the last. How far new intellectual approaches to old orthodoxies
were to succeed in vindicating them is not, however, to our purpose to estimate. What we shall be investigating are simply, in a
particular field, the phenomena of continuity within change,
marking as we go what maintains itself in being and what perforce disappears with the years.

At the commencement of the century religious thinking in
Britain was in a state of torpor. The Hanoverian Church, after its
forays against deism, had succumbed to a quiet worldliness, well
content to be untroubled by either overmuch intellectual speculation or 'enthusiastic' piety. Its one great name had been that of
Joseph Butler, whose celebrated apology for revealed religion was
to be a bastion of orthodoxy for generations to come; for although
John Wesley remained to the end of his long life a clergyman of
the establishment, strongly repudiating separatism, the Church
could claim no credit for the movement he led and little exonera-
tion for the breach which eventually occurred. The leading divines
of the period 1790 to 1810—Paley, Watson, Horsley, Porteus—
were all men whose attitudes had been formed in the previous age
and none disclosed the slightest awareness of the new outlook
already evident on the European continent. William Paley,

Introduction

archdeacon of Carlisle,[1] who died in 1805, had won fame with his
Elements of Moral and Political Philosophy (1785), in which virtue
is defined as 'doing good to mankind in obedience to the will of
God and for the sake of everlasting happiness', and still more so
with *Evidences of Christianity*, which appeared in 1794, and the
treatise on *Natural Theology* eight years later. These all in their
day were acclaimed as masterly presentations of the theistic case.
To us their arguments are as frigid and unpersuasive as are the
author's utilitarian ethics. Paley's natural theology is manifestly
not the work of a philosopher, and Hume's writings, as far as the
archdeacon is concerned, might never have seen the light of day.
The focal point of the *Evidences* is the testimony of miracle, from
which the divine origin of Christianity draws its conclusive proof.
Whether the miraculous is a possible conception is a question not
asked: presumably the celestial Watchmaker does as he pleases
with his handiwork. Richard Watson, bishop of Llandaff from
1782 until his death in 1816 (although he preferred to reside on his
Westmorland estates), was mainly interested in church reform,
for the most part equated with anti-popery—revision of the
liturgy in accordance with latitudinarian principles and a loosen-
ing of the bonds of subscription. Samuel Horsley (d. 1806), bishop
successively of St David's, Rochester and St Asaph, was a noted
scholar and preacher, but a stickler for dogmatic rectitude, his
detestation of heretics being matched only by his antipathy to
Methodists and sectaries generally. Let the establishment clergy
but do their duty faithfully, he urged, and 'the moralizing
Unitarian would be left to read his dull lectures to the walls of a
deserted conventicle, and the field preacher would bellow to the
wilderness'. On the other hand, Beilby Porteus, bishop of London
from 1787 to 1809, was both a practical reformist and a warm
sympathizer with evangelicalism within and without the Church.
But he was no theologian.

Nor, it seems, was theology of much concern to Dissenters
either. The Baptists, in the main still loyal to their Calvinist past,
were preoccupied with domestic affairs. Robert Hall, their most
eloquent preacher, was in his younger days an admirer of the
French Revolution and retained a more liberal outlook than was

[1] His other preferments included prebendal stalls at St Paul's and Lincoln cathedrals, and the rich benefice of Bishop Wearmouth in Co. Durham. See Leslie
Stephen in *D.N.B.* 'Paley' (1895).

4

usual among his brethren. The Independents—or Congregationalists, as they later came to be called—were also conservative in
their theological tenets, apart from the unitarian fringe attacked
by John Pye Smith, a tutor at the Homerton Academy and a man
of learning and influence, in his *Letters to Belsham*. Thomas
Belsham, himself a former Independent, had founded the Unitarian Society in 1791 and became, with Joseph Priestley, the sect's
acknowledged leader. He was the author of a book on Christian
evidences, but merely reiterated the arguments of Paley.[1] Christ
he regarded as a divinely guided teacher of heavenly truths,
especially that of a future life with its appropriate rewards and
punishments. The gospel miracles he accepted, on what he believed to be the reliable testimony of inspired witnesses. On the
Old Testament, however, he felt less assured, questioning in
particular the inspiration of Genesis on the ground that it is only
a compilation of ancient documents and not the unitary work of
Moses. The English Presbyterians, professing a wide degree of
tolerance in doctrinal matters, also had strong leanings to unitarianism, whether in an Arian or a Socinian form. But the
Wesleyans were rigorously orthodox, although their one scholar
of eminence, Adam Clarke, was himself generally considered unsound. Suspected of Pelagian tendencies, he certainly denied the
traditional doctrine of the Sonship of Christ, holding that the very
phrase 'Eternal Son' is self-contradictory.

It needs little knowledge of these now remote figures to realize
how isolated, and in its isolation how jejune, English religious
thought then was. It was not until the third decade of the century
that new intellectual pressures began to make themselves felt:
physical science—although in this field British effort was well
forward; a deeper understanding of the significance of history
and of the nature of historical change; the Romantic ethos in
literature and the arts; and, in due course, the philosophical
idealism of Kant and his successors. To these forces must be
added that of political democracy and the democratic spirit.
Yet even after 1830 positive theological reaction was tardy enough.
For long religion had been devoid of intellectual stimulus and was
satisfied to rest on accepted beliefs, a naïve biblicism and the
social prop of the state connection. But the French Revolution
and the ensuing wars spelt the end of an epoch in this as in other

[1] *A Summary View of the Evidences and Practical Importance of the Christian Revelation* (1807).

things and the consequent sense of once more 'living in history', to borrow Arnold Toynbee's phrase, meant that the time sequence itself, as measured in terms of political, social and cultural advance, now entered as a dominant factor into men's estimate of reality. Reason, that is, could no longer stand above the flux of events; life had to be historically viewed. Thus the past, acquiring a new significance, demanded more sophisticated methods of study, methods of which, in Germany, Lessing and Herder had been the pioneers. In fact the nineteenth century may be characterized as the century of History even more than of Science, immense as the latter's progress was to be. At all events the key concept of the whole era, the principle of evolution, was applied by Hegel and the German idealists to human history long before Darwin made signal use of it in biology.

Scientific history was the outcome of the attempt to see the past in its once living movement. Historical facts were henceforth to be presented not in mere fragmentary separation but as parts of an interconnected whole; a whole, moreover, organically related to the present as parent to offspring. The age of rationalism had, of course, not viewed it so, its own procedure being selective and abstract and content with surface impressions. Of any true sentiment for the past or of understanding sympathy with those aspects of it which most conspicuously differ from the present, it had little if any. History might be called on for useful lessons or exposed as a salutary warning, but its intrinsic character was not of interest and was unappreciated. Towards the end of the century, however, a sense of the past as the past and as having an appeal and a significance of its own was already awakened. The ensuing years were to show how the feeling could produce systematic knowledge. Thus the great age of German historical scholarship began, although at first no doubt too much blinkered by metaphysical presuppositions which, for all their apparent usefulness as explanatory categories, hindered rather than helped genuine scientific headway. It was inevitable also that the efforts to recover the past in its true semblance and with the aim of comprehending the laws of historical change should before long be made to include the biblical history and in particular the origins of Christianity, the primary documents of which furnished capital material for the scientific investigator. Here especially, perhaps, was progress impeded by the notion that historiography is really a branch of philosophy and can best yield results when guided by preconceived ideas. This speculative treatment of history was very evident in the work of D. F. Strauss, as too in that of F. C. Baur and other scholars of the Protestant school of Tübingen. Indeed its outcome, in the eyes of the British reading public, only succeeded in giving the 'higher criticism' a bad name, thus retarding its influence. But when historians were able at last to divest themselves of the philosopher's mantle research was at liberty to adopt more profitable methods. The upshot was the development of biblical study on properly scientific lines. This, in the field of Old Testament criticism, was the achievement of such men as Eichhorn, De Wette, Gesenius, Vatke and Ewald, as later of Kuenen, Graf and Wellhausen. But Baur's pre-eminence as a student of the New Testament and the early Church was incontestable, whatever subsequent modifications, often drastic, had to be made in regard to his actual conclusions.

The application of the historical method to Christianity's title-deeds was, however, of more than academic consequence. It had theological implications of far-reaching scope. If the Scriptures were to be examined like any other *corpus* of ancient writings and submitted, as to the circumstances of their composition, to the judgment of investigators whose procedures seemed to require them to lay aside their religious convictions, then what room might be left for the concepts of revelation and inspiration, or what meaning attached to the claim that the Bible possesses unique authority? Further, since the method was genetic, the growth of doctrine and dogma, no less than that of ecclesiastical organization and ritual, would be subject to the same type of scrutiny and the same subtle process of devaluation. Any clear cut distinction between natural and supernatural might well disappear and in the end Christianity itself be seen as no more than a phase in the long course of human civilization. Such risks had none the less to be run. That the researches of the historian would continue, in this realm as in others, was plain, and to ignore them was scarcely more possible than to inhibit them. But the change of attitude to traditional religion which this entailed was something the true nature of which was to be increasingly apparent as time went by. The earlier generation was to blame, we may think, for its timidity in welcoming what it so little understood, but can we say today that its fears were entirely groundless?

The difficulty which historical criticism presented to orthodox faith was its evident refusal to look beyond natural causation to explain events, even those of 'sacred' history. But the scientific historian could not, without abandoning a fundamental postulate of his discipline, attribute any occurrence simply to direct divine intervention. On the contrary, he could not rightly introduce theological categories at all. He might indeed have a philosophical interest, even to the point of attributing history's whole movement to a single operative principle. But such, were it capable of being identified, was necessarily to be understood as inherent in the process itself. Of any transcendental teleology he could as a historian know nothing. Providence and miracle belong to the context of faith, not of science. The result was a division between religion and history such as the theologians of an older day had never contemplated. For them sacred and secular history had been interwoven, and the pattern of the whole, secular as well as sacred, was divinely ordered. But historical criticism could admit faith, if at all, only at a quite different level of interpretation from its own. Certain events might be allowed a 'transcendent' meaning, but in their purely material and temporal aspect they had to be shown to belong to the natural sequence of things. This it was, more than anything else, which gave rise to the immanentism increasingly characteristic of the religious philosophy of the period. It was a tendency to which the nature-mysticism of the early Wordsworth and later on the influence of German idealism afforded corroborative expression.

But the historical method was not only genetic; it was comparative as well. Christian theology was being studied as history, but it had to be seen in relation to other religious traditions too, they likewise being taken not merely as true or false but as aspects of man's spiritual consciousness in all its diverse manifestation. Hence the emergence of what has come to be known, perhaps not altogether happily, as comparative religion. Its beginnings in Britain were amateurish enough. Carlyle, in May 1840, delivered the lecture on Mohammed which appeared in *Heroes and Hero-worship*, whilst one of F. D. Maurice's few works to gain a popular readership was his volume of Boyle lectures, *The Religions of the World*, published in 1846. But the very attempt to describe non-Christian religions objectively betokened a significant change from the attitude of mind which abruptly dismissed them as mere human superstition. The subject was one that aroused public interest, the more so as information about these religions increased. For here was an altogether fresh province of knowledge —in Frazer's words, 'the faith and the practice, the hopes and the ideals, not of two highly gifted races only, but of all mankind'. It was one also, as Jowett sagely predicted, which was to have an immense influence on Christian theology itself.[1] With the work of E. B. Tylor; Robertson Smith—notably his *Religion of the Semites* (1889)—Frazer himself, the first edition of whose *Golden Bough* came out in 1890; of the orientalist, Max Müller, editor of a series of translations. 'The Sacred Books of the East'—'the real history of man', he suggested, 'is the history of religion'—of Edward Caird; F. B. Jevons and Andrew Lang, the whole vast field of research at last came under exploration. But in the light of the new knowledge and with a widened intellectual sympathy resulting from it the accepted view of the absolute uniqueness of Christianity needed qualification. At any rate, even when its distinctiveness and special claims were insisted upon its apparent affinities with other faiths and cults had the almost inevitable effect of causing its authority to be questioned as a wholly God-given revelation of truth.

That a heightened sentiment for the past was a leading feature of the Romantic movement is a commonplace. Yet it was one element only in a complex phenomenon. Romanticism, in literature, music and the visual arts, as likewise in philosophy and theology, defies precise characterization. But in English thought, as compared with German and French, it was, again, a less potent impulse; the national insularity tempered it. Nevertheless the age of Wordsworth, of Coleridge and of Byron—the last-named in many eyes, the very embodiment of the Romantic spirit—could not but be aware of a changing intellectual climate. Reason was quickened, sometimes indeed superseded, by imagination. Coleridge defined it now as 'the power of universal and necessary convictions, the source and substance of truths above sense, and having their evidence in themselves'. The knowledge of truth, for the Romantic mind, was a visionary experience, an intuition or immediate beholding. But vision, intuition, is of its very nature subjective. External proof is irrelevant, even alien to it. 'All the subtleties of metaphysics', wrote Rousseau, 'would

[1] See *The Epistles of St Paul* (1855), ii, p. 186.

not lead me to doubt for a moment the immortality of my soul or a spiritual Providence; I feel it, I believe it, I desire it, I hope for it and will defend it to my last breath.' To this frame of mind a mere calculation of probabilities on the basis of adducible evidence could effect nothing of importance. As Schleiermacher put it: 'The feelings, the feelings alone, provide the elements of religion', an utterance paralleled by Keats's 'I am certain of nothing but the holiness of the Heart's affections and the truth of the Imagination.' Not argument but experience became the foundation of faith, an experience personal, individual and in its ultimate essence incommunicable. Coleridge insisted that what justifies Christianity is a man's own felt need of it. Maurice believed all men to be religious and have only to be made conscious of the fact. The whole trend of nineteenth-century thought was thus a retreat from the view, self-evident to the age of reason, that religion is a body of propositional truths requiring demonstration and that what cannot be so demonstrated may be discarded. No abstract verification of religion but its practical utility was the pertinent criterion. Even in Catholic France it was religion's social function that particularly impressed the more original minds. Chateaubriand's *Le Génie du Christianisme*, published in the spring of 1802, on the eve of Napoleon's concordat with the Vatican, marked the beginning of a new style in apologetics. Philosophically null, it disclosed all the same an emotional thirst for religion which only the living imagination could satisfy.[1] But it was also, in the words of Sainte-Beuve, 'as the rainbow, a brilliant token of reconciliation and alliance between religion and French society'.

In the intellectual approach to Christianity a parting of the ways was signified by the critical philosophy of Immanuel Kant, the counterpart in the sphere of thought to the French Revolution in politics. Old-style rationalism in religion was demolished, although it was the Scotsman Hume who first brought home to the German master that the work needed doing. Things-in-themselves, the *noumena* that lie beyond *phenomena*, we do not and

---

[1] The appeal was frankly aesthetic: 'Le christianisme sera-t-il moins vrai quand il paraîtra plus beau? . . . Sublime par l'antiquité de ses souvenirs, qui remontent au berceau du monde, ineffable dans ses mystères, adorable dans ses sacrements, intéressant dans son histoire, céleste dans sa morale, riche et charmant dans ses pompes, il réclame toutes les sortes de tableaux (*Le Génie du Christianisme*, pt. I. ch. i). Sainte-Beuve saw in Chateaubriand little more than 'a sceptic with a Catholic imagination'.

cannot know, says Kant, because they are outside human experience. At least, when the mind strays beyond its province it at once involves itself in contradictions—in *antinomies*. Freedom and necessity, for example, are each demonstrable, but yet are—mutually inconsistent. Hence any so-called proof reaching out to the supernatural realm is bound to fail. Of the classical arguments for divine existence not only does the ontological harbour a fallacy but the cosmological also, which itself turns upon the ontological; whilst the teleological, despite its obvious appeal, is unable to show that the Creator's attributes are infinite. Yet for Kant these criticisms do not end in pure scepticism. His aim, in his own words, was to abolish knowledge in order to make room for faith, which alone is religion's proper basis. And faith springs from man's moral nature, which testifies certain fundamental truths. That God exists and that man possesses freedom and immortality are to be accepted, that is, as postulates—not theoretical dogmata but presuppositions of an essentially practical import. Although, in other words, morality does not *prove* God's existence the fact that to us moral criteria are inescapable makes such existence a necessary assumption on our part, if the highest good known to man is to be fulfilled. Hence if God is to be discovered at all he must be sought in man's own inner life as a moral being, which is the only real sphere of human freedom. Salvation accordingly consists in that ethical self-realization which is open to every rational creature. It implies no external restraint or arbitrary change in human nature, since in obeying the moral law we but submit to an imperative the reason and justice of which is wholly in accord with our own best judgment. And what universal morality thus dictates religion will interpret as the command of God, the community of all who so recognize it—the 'ethical commonwealth', in Kant's term—providing the requisite environment for the promotion of individual virtue and happiness.

This ethical commonwealth was easily identifiable with what Christian faith understands as the Kingdom of God, or the Church Invisible. Kant's own attitude towards Christianity was determined by his philosophy. He approved it for its approximation, closer than that of any other religion, to the ideal of a purely ethical theology. Christian doctrine presented the deepest moral insights under symbolic form; but the symbolism, to continue to

remain acceptable, had to be interpreted in harmony with morality.
The idea of heaven, for example, is profoundly inspiring, but
duty must be pursued for its own sake and not from hopes of
a celestial reward. The Christ of the gospels Kant saw as an
embodied ideal of moral goodness; not, however, in an absolute sense, since moral man himself, who has the shaping of
all moral idealism, is still in course of development. The real
significance of Jesus stands in the immense influence his
example has exerted upon man's own moral progress, a truth
obscured by preoccupation with metaphysical accounts of his
person.

In these respects Kant's impress upon nineteenth-century
religious thought was to prove indelible. Its outcome is to be
seen, in Germany mainly, but also to some extent in France and
the United States of America, in the teaching of Albrecht Ritschl
and the Liberal Protestant school which he inaugurated. But any
direct influence Kantian philosophy might have had on English
theology, apart from Coleridge, was not extensive, and Ritschlianism certainly had no impact here until near the end of the
century.[1] The influence which did make itself felt, after 1870,
was that rather of Kant's idealist successors, at first as mediated
by T. H. Green, although the Caird brothers certainly went back
to the original fount of the doctrine, to Hegel himself. The
attraction of idealism was in the means of exit it afforded from the
impasse of mechanistic naturalism. In a modified form it 'claimed
supreme worth for self-conscious personality as the only possible
subject for the spiritual activities, knowledge, love and goodness, on which we set the highest value, and as therefore the
only adequate revelation of the ultimate reality which we call
God'.[2] Green's epistemology led him to posit an 'intellectual
principle', a 'self-distinguishing consciousness', an 'eternal
intelligence' as the organizing principle of the universe, even if he
failed to make clear any final distinction between the universe and
the personality which informs it. But in an age when the prestige
of science (conjoined as it often was with a positivistic philosophy
ostensibly based on it) was steadily rising any reasoned assurance

---

[1] Ritschl's principal work, *Justification and Reconciliation*, appeared in an English
translation (by H. R. Mackintosh and A. B. Macauley) in 1900 (2nd edn. 1902). See
the present author's *Liberal Protestantism* (1968).

[2] C. C. J. Webb, *Religious Thought in England from 1850* (1933), p. 112.

that the essential nature of the universe is spiritual was as music in Christian ears, and the theologians who contributed to *Lux Mundi* were glad to make all the use they could of the idealist metaphysic. Moreover, idealism gave to the historical process a full valuation. Kant's thought, progressive in other respects, had been typical of its century in its non-historical character. But Hegel and his school had identified spirit by its historical manifestations. Hence, therefore, the importance they attached to historiography. But the historical process was interpreted also as evolutionary or developmental, an idea which concurred (as it seemed) with Darwinism. Spiritual philosophy and physical science thus might go hand in hand.

For the shadow of physical science alone undoubtedly brought a chill to the hopes and sentiments of orthodox religion. The area of life of which the sciences could now claim to provide exact knowledge was immense and continually growing. Would it in the end assert a dominion over the whole of man's reason and understanding? If so, what would have become of the very different world view described or implied by traditional Christianity? The latter still professed to give sufficient account of man and the universe in terms of divine purpose. But the God hypothesis, as was becoming ever plainer, was one with which science, intent only upon so-called secondary causes, could very properly dispense. Theological or metaphysical control of its conclusions was therefore precluded. Facts must be sought and correlated for their own sake, in the interest of truth itself. Further, autonomy of procedure was clearly leading to unity of view. Nature was seen to be at all levels subject to the operation of the same inherent forces and to be capable of description as a unitary system of law. A clash between religious beliefs and scientific theory was thus inevitable: first, on the question of the Genesis story of the creation, then on Darwinism, especially as propounded by T. H. Huxley, whose respect for the susceptibilities of theologians was minimal, and finally on the doctrine of materialism generally, a philosophy destructive of all spiritual values. The issue of science *versus* religion was most prominent from about 1862 to 1877, when both sides were in the mood for conflict, the theologians from an authoritarian confidence whetted by fear, the scientists (or their publicists) from an exhilaration born of achievement. The struggle was carried on with much bitterness, particularly since the combatants on either hand were making larger assumptions than a cool concern for truth would have warranted. A truce was possible only when it was recognized that the spheres of both were limited. Philosophy contributed not a little to the settlement: in the case of science by pointing out where its bounds might be said to lie, namely in the selectivity and abstractness of its methods; and in that of religion by enhancing its understanding of what the spiritual dimension of life does and does not include. Moreover, as remarked above, the principle of evolution provided a useful area of conceptual common ground. At least, as the century drew to its close, theologians and scientists were no longer merely shouting at one another from opposite sides of a brick wall. Charles Gore even went so far as to claim that if the Darwinian theory had been formulated in the intellectual atmosphere of early Greek Christianity—the Fathers being accustomed to interpret the opening chapters of Genesis allegorically—it would have presented no difficulty for faith.[1]

The aid and succour which idealist philosophy brought to orthodox theology in its confrontation with science was, however, paid for at a price. This, we have noted, was the acceptance, in varying degree, of the idea of the divine immanence. Naturalism could be rejected as inadequate to explain human experience as a whole, or indeed science itself; but the philosophers' conception of nature was such also as to lead them to seek its determining spiritual principle *within* rather than outside nature's own observable processes. On this view the historic doctrines of Christianity demanded reinterpretation as symbolic representations of the inner significance of man's life, in all ages and under all conditions, rather than as factual statements of unique and miraculous events directly expressive of a transcendent divine will. The implication was clear that 'super-naturalism', in the old sense of the word, was now incapable of acceptable restatement, and values whose source had hitherto been located in a world 'other' than this must henceforth be sought within the structures of the here and now. Orthodoxy, in truth, was not prepared to admit the conclusion outright, and its own vigorous revival towards the end of the century was in large part actuated by the genuine conviction that a *super*natural faith could yet be success-

---

[1] *Belief in God* (1921), p. 10. He was not at all sure that even Paley and Darwin were wholly irreconcilable. See *The Incarnation of the Son of God* (1891), p. 31.

fully adapted to the spiritual needs of the age. The assurance was one for which Gore contended all his life, despite a philosophical atmosphere increasingly inhospitable to Christianity's basic postulates. But there could be no disguising the fact that religious belief was under heavy pressure from a cultural environment no longer disposed to derive its valuations from or pin its hopes to an order of things for which the phenomenal world is but a temporary screen.

However, the forces making for change in the religious outlook were not only intellectual; they were also political and social. To some, as to Charles James Fox, or the poet William Wordsworth, the French Revolution had come as a new vision of hope for mankind:

> Bliss was it in that dawn to be alive,
> But to be young was very heaven.

With the setting up of the Terror, on the other hand, and the European war which followed, the movement's appeal waned, even for these enthusiasts. Revolutionary ideals now appeared subversive of all order in society. In particular, the French innovators had shown slender regard for ecclesiastical authority or even for religion itself. Had not the Goddess Reason, in the person of a woman of the Paris streets, been enthroned in the cathedral of Notre Dame? Furthermore, behind the Revolution lay not only deist modes of thought but, in the philosophy of men like Holbach and Cabanis, sheer godless materialism. Thus to sober opinion in England the dreaded name of Jacobin was usually synonymous with atheism. The immediate result was a reawakened concern for the safety of the Church and the maintenance in the nation of a sound Christian profession. Certainly among the rapidly growing industrial population respect for the Church and its clergy was scant enough, to the point of overt hostility. But dislike of the ecclesiastical inheritance was for the most part an expression of a more widely diffused resentment against class-privilege in general than of any real rejection of religion as such. Accordingly in the early decades of the century the Church actually stood higher in public esteem than it had done for a generation or more previously. In its turn the Church, despite its notorious antagonism to reform—the solid opposition of the bishops to the great Reform Bill of 1832 has always been cited as the palmary instance of clerical intransigence—felt the necessity of making some demonstrable response to the needs of the age, and a time of unwonted activity began. Abuses, all too numerous, in the ecclesiastical system were removed; the Ecclesiastical Commission was established in 1835, new churches were built in districts hitherto unprovided for, and Christian responsibility in the matter of popular education was freely recognized. At the outset of Queen Victoria's reign the national Church was astir with a new sense of its obligations and mission, of which the Oxford Movement, in principle anti-liberal though it was, appeared as the timely and challenging utterance.

Yet all this was but a phase, a reaction to an existing situation. Of more permanent significance was the growth over the century of democratic feeling and aspiration. The traditional structure of society, once fear of Jacobinism and revolutionary subversion had begun to abate, became an open question. Distinctions of social class and wealth no longer seemed pre-ordained and unalterable. The liberty on which Englishmen were wont to pride themselves also entailed freedom from the iron restraints of poverty; nor could liberty be fully realized unless equality accompanied it. The prophets and doctrinaires of the new democracy were the Philosophical Radicals—Jeremy Bentham and his disciples, who proceeded on the assumption that it was both possible and necessary to apply disinterested intelligence to social problems. Their principle of the greatest happiness of the greatest number, warmed by the sentiment of a common humanity, was in intention plainly altruistic. The result was the gradual permeation of the public mind with a feeling of social responsibility. Men, it was now realized, possess a natural solidarity, of which the body politic, incorporating and articulating the community's reason and conscience, is alike the expression and ultimate safeguard.

Such ideas could not but have their effect upon religious opinion. The day of individualism, rationalistic or pietistic, was passing, making possible a recovery of the idea of the Church as a collective entity. Indeed, for F. D. Maurice all humanity was one in Christ its Head. Further, even the individual, when seen in the due perspectives of history, was manifestly the product of the social conditions under which his life was lived; conditions not immune therefore to a moral judgment rendered all the more imperative in view of the economic and social problems thrown up by the rapid growth of industrialism. Christian thinkers, that is, felt increasingly obliged to consider man not only as a soul on pilgrimage to heaven but as he is at present, in his determining social and economic relations. It was no fit discipline of the spirit that the body should be arbitrarily deprived of its elementary needs. But the lesson was not easily learned and it took the Church the best part of the century to comprehend on the social plane the full ethical implications of its own gospel. The so-called Christian Socialist movement at the turn of the half-century was an early and single instance of this concern, even if by socialism its promoters meant not an economic doctrine but an ethical ideal: 'the science of partnership among men'.[1]

The main lines of development in religious thought in Britain during the century can be summarily indicated. At the outset, as we already have seen, intellectual interest was at a discount. Influences from the European continent had not yet begun to make themselves felt, and the stagnation of the closing decades of the preceding century continued. In any event men's minds were preoccupied with national affairs. After 1820, however, new trends are clearly discernible. First we have the liberal or 'Noetic' school at Oxford, associated with the Oriel senior common room: rationalizing—hostile observers complained that the place 'stank of logic'—and well aware that increasing historical knowledge would mean the end of some long-cherished illusions, yet sharing also in the narrowness and insularity of their time and place. Next to be noted is the teaching of their Scottish contemporary, Thomas Erskine of Linlathen, which, as against mere 'evidence' theology, made a direct appeal to spiritual experience and the inward testimony of the feelings—a man whose writings Maurice judged to mark 'a crisis in the theological movement of this time'. Thirdly, there was the phenomenon of Coleridge, a genius of astonishing gifts whose achievement, although falling short of promise, was to prove, through his religious philosophy, one of the most potent spiritual influences of the century and who, already in advance of the Oxford Movement, declared it his 'fixed principle' that 'a Christianity without a Church exercising spiritual authority is vanity and dissolution'. The decade 1830 to 1840 saw that Movement's rise, with its call to the national

---

[1] On the later phases of the Christian Social movement see below, pp. 211f. and the appended Note to Ch. XIII.

Church to a renewed understanding of its true status and vocation. Yet for all Tractarianism's *réclame* and apparent novelty its impulse was reactionary and in intellectual terms produced less than what the talents and scholarship of its adherents would seem to have augured. Its strength lay rather in its practical effect on Church life and worship. As a revival of faith within the university of Oxford itself its force was spent by the time of the defection in 1845 of its leader and dominant personality, J. H. Newman. After 1845 changes in the intellectual climate there were unmistakable. Mark Pattison, a Tractarian disillusioned, might subsequently rejoice that the spell of ecclesiasticism had been broken and the university at last set free to go about its proper business—a large measure of reform in the ancient universities was introduced in the 'fifties[1]—but a period was beginning of intellectual questioning and unsettlement: science was confronting devout churchmen with some awkward problems; the Bible, under the searching light of historical criticism, seemed to be losing its authority—to be the work, of God perhaps, but also, more and more patently if the critics were to be believed, of fallible men. Inquiry into the literary history of the Old Testament was disturbing enough, but the publication in 1835 of Strauss's *Leben Jesu*, as still more the English version of it by George Eliot a few years later—W. G. Ward remarked at the time that it was selling more than any other book that had appeared on the market—presented the supreme issue of the New Testament in the shape of an alternative before which traditional belief could not but tremble. Yet it was at this time that Maurice, a conservative by instinct and a theologian in every facet of his thought, stood forth as the unflinching upholder of Christian idealism, even if to many of his contemporaries the obscurity of his utterance also attenuated the relevance of its message. But his influence was to persist and bear fruit later.

In the second half of the century the Christian churches found themselves living in an obviously changed environment. The inescapable presence of physical science, intent on pursuing knowledge by its own tried methods, had to be reckoned with.

[1] The Oxford University Act was passed in 1854, that affecting Cambridge two years later. By the abolition of religious tests at matriculation dissenters were able to be admitted as undergraduates. Such tests were also abolished for most degrees. See F. Warre Cornish, *The English Church in the Nineteenth Century* (1910), i, pp. 306–318.

Criticism of the Scriptures, although it might still appear impious to the majority of churchmen, could not now be disregarded and some attempt to meet it constructively was imperative. *The Origin of Species* was significantly followed, a year later, by *Essays and Reviews*, whilst the controversy which the latter provoked was soon to be further enflamed by Bishop Colenso's idiosyncratic study of the Pentateuch and Joshua. But by the 1870s Christian opinion, or at least its better informed sections, was beginning to accept the facts of the situation. The theory of evolution had to be assimilated, and divines whose loyalty to the creed could not be doubted were learning to approach the Bible in a state of mind less inhibited by dogmatic presuppositions. Meanwhile a new and sophisticated attempt to defend the whole concept of revelation from philosophical attack had been under- taken by a Bampton lecturer, H. L. Mansel, on the seemingly paradoxical basis of complete metaphysical agnosticism, in a way indeed foreshadowing theological trends characteristic of our own day. Nor, in the course of the long theological debate, were the imaginative writers silent. Tennyson voiced both the misgivings of his era and its determination to cling to 'the larger hope'. Browning, fundamentally optimistic, was nevertheless under no illusions as to the gravity of the trial to which religious belief was being subjected. George Eliot, among the *avant-garde* thinkers of the time, was, however, no iconoclast and to the end remained deeply sensitive to the appeal of a faith she had herself early on felt compelled to abandon. In her fashion she was typical of the intellectual dilemma of the age.

The three final decades of the century are marked by an effort to imbue the old orthodoxy with new confidence. The great Cambridge triumvirate, Westcott, Lightfoot and Hort, were the first on the scene, and with their work biblical study in this country was able at last to face comparison with what had been done in Germany. For the most part they were conservatives, Westcott especially so; but their conservatism was one of considered principle, not of lethargy or fear. With the appearance of *Lux Mundi* in 1889 a group of the younger High Churchmen made it clear that the heirs of Tractarianism also were set upon modifying its traditionalism and even giving up positions once judged to be vital. Evolution was made a leading *motif* in their philosophy and the doctrine of biblical inerrancy was frankly jettisoned. By the close of the century the dogmatic stance of the Thirty-nine Articles was widely felt to be an anachronism.[1] Adjustments had to be effected and concessions made at many points. The question now was not whether such a course was permissible but where precisely it could be halted. Gore, the outstanding English theologian of the day, was himself scarcely in two minds. The Scriptures, he held, must be seen to have been in their outward form products of their time and circumstances, and thus with inevitable human limitations attaching to them. But the content of the creed remained and must remain the residuum of faith apart from which Christianity ceases to be orthodox in form or even recognizable in substance. The Broad Church party, moreover, so far from having been 'extinguished by popular clamour', as had been claimed some years earlier, had very arguably succeeded, in the words of a then rising young liberal, Hastings Rashdall, 'in leavening the tone of theological thought and theological temper among the clergy and religious world at large'.[2] By the beginning of the new century Broad Churchmen had become definitely liberal or 'modernist', to use a term then coming into vogue,[3] and was attracting adherents from Evangelicalism, hitherto still solidly conservative.

Outside the established Church the demands of modernity were similarly gaining recognition. The Baptist and Methodist bodies continued to hold the new views in suspicion, but Congregationalism, always more intellectually alert, showed no such hesitation in welcoming them, and men like Fairbairn and, a little later, Forsyth were easily among the best theological minds of the period. In Scotland the century was largely one of movement away from the more or less strict Calvinism of the past, a movement in which the most prominent figure was John McLeod

[1] Already by the terms of the Clerical Subscription Act of 1865 a detailed subscription 'willingly and *ex animo*' to the Articles had been changed to a 'general assent'. A clergyman was now required simply to declare his belief in 'the doctrine of the [United] Church of England [and Ireland], as therein set forth, to be agreeable to the Word of God'. The new form also necessitated an alteration in Canon 36 of the Canons Ecclesiastical. The disestablishment of the Irish Church was carried out by Gladstone in 1869.

[2] P. E. Matheson, *The Life of Hastings Rashdall* (1928), p. 45.

[3] Cf. H. D. A. Major, *English Modernism* (1927), ch. iii, where the author distinguishes between Broad Church, Liberal and Modernist. But the last of these terms was used more precisely of a movement of thought in the Roman Catholic Church, and many Anglican liberals objected to its adoption on that account.

Campbell, who preached an unlimited atonement as the only possible ground for man's assurance of God's absolute love. In the field of biblical study the path of criticism was opened up by William Robertson Smith. Both men paid for their independence by loss of office, ministerial or academic. But by 1900 the intellectual outlook of the Scottish Churches, established and free, had greatly changed, and as in England the old orthodoxy was being either restated or in certain points dropped altogether.

The era of religious thought which we are to survey in the ensuing chapters was thus one of adjustment, slow and at times painful, to intellectual and social conditions of a kind increasingly to render the religious interpretation of life difficult in a way that it had never been before. Religion was no longer conceived as a set of ideas and aspirations which society, or at any rate its more responsible section, was bound to maintain as a matter of conscience. The attitude of faith had now to be defended—explained and if possible justified in terms which to the less sophisticated were bound to seem remote. Indeed the moral prestige of faith passed to science itself, whose primary virtue was intellectual integrity and respect for evidence. 'Agnosticism', it has fairly been said, 'had the temper of the age on its side',[1] especially when retreating credulity, in its last-ditch struggles, appeared to care for nothing beyond its own self-preservation. Yet at times also one kind of dogmatism became the excuse for another: the cocksureness of some representatives, or partisans, of science likewise was uninviting. The impression left on the student of the history of ideas is that at the close of the period the received Christian teaching was finding it necessary to concede so much to its critics as evidently to have undergone a complete transformation. The divine, it could be said, had now to be sought much less in a transcendent Creator, Lawgiver and Judge than in an immanent Power, progressively manifesting itself in the course of the universal process, including man's own advance in cultural self-realization. Theologians and philosophers who were anxious for their responsibility to historic Christianity might endeavour to resist the tendency, and assuredly before the present century was many years old a reaction against it had set in. But the intellectual comprehension of religion and its place in life was profoundly

[1] G. M. Young, *Victorian England* (1936), p. 109.

altered, with the consequence that in our own day the former clear-cut alignments and antagonisms, Catholic and Protestant, High Church and Evangelical, Anglican and Nonconformist, appear less and less consistent or even intelligible. It is a development whose implications are perhaps not wholly reassuring.

Chapter I

The early decades

I. THE EVANGELICALS

'The deepest and most fervid religion in England during the first three decades of this century', wrote Henry Parry Liddon, 'was that of the Evangelicals. The world to come, with the boundless issues of life and death, the infinite value of the one Atonement, the regenerating, purifying, guiding action of God the Holy Spirit in respect of the Christian soul, were preached to our grandfathers with a force and earnestness which are beyond controversy.'[1] As a party within the Church of England the Evangelicals, although the heirs of the religious revival of the preceding century the outcome of which had been the Methodist schism, were loyal adherents of the establishment and the Prayer Book. No doubt, too, they were 'Low' Churchmen, but at the same time they were clearly distinguishable from the Whig Latitudinarians who commonly bore the designation. Always dedicated to charitable causes, they, like the Methodists, nevertheless cultivated the inner life as the spiritual substance of all true religion. In the impression they made on the public mind of their day they were unique, combining as they did an energy for good works with an evangelistic zeal and a personal moral discipline which provoked both admiration and dislike, but rendered indifference impossible. Criticism they certainly encountered: the party, although influential, was not popular. The majority of the clergy resented or distrusted them; not entirely without reason, for the tone of evangelical piety was sometimes distasteful even to men of goodwill.

[1] *The Life of Edward Bouverie Pusey*, ed. Johnston and Wilson (1893–4), i, p. 255.

Preferment, in the early days, eluded them. Henry Ryder, appointed to the see of Gloucester in 1815, was the first to be raised to the episcopate. The bishop of London, Beilby Porteus, was markedly sympathetic, but as a rule his brethren on the bench were chary of ordaining men with known evangelical leanings, whilst the universities, as the experience of Charles Simeon at Cambridge well illustrates, were *milieux* of a kind which no evangelical clergyman was likely to find very congenial. As late even as 1810 the subscription lists of the Church Missionary Society did not include the name of a bishop or peer, and it was difficult for any clerical member of the Society to gain access to a pulpit. The Evangelicals' rise to power—for later the party became very powerful in the Church, to remain so until quite recent years—was gradual. The current of opinion began to flow in their favour chiefly as a result of frank recognition of evangelical virtues and achievements, but also, in the fourth decade of the century, from a reaction to the supposedly Romanizing aims of Tractarianism. For the evangelical teaching was uncompromisingly Protestant and its puritan moral temper fully in accord with a growing seriousness of outlook in the nation at large.

The older generation of Evangelicals, typified by such men as John Newton and Richard Cecil, scarcely survived the age of Wesley himself. The new generation was associated mainly with Clapham, then an outlying London suburb, and with Cambridge, where Simeon, a fellow of King's, was vicar of Holy Trinity. The 'Clapham Sect'—and Sidney Smith's label at once stuck to them—comprised a group of high-principled and energetic men, friends and neighbours united by a shared religious faith and a common philanthropic purpose. A natural leader was the banker, Henry Thornton, member of parliament for Southwark and a tireless promoter of good causes. His nearest neighbour and close friend was William Wilberforce (1759–1833), himself a rich man and a member of parliament also—he was an intimate of William Pitt's—who won renown as the protagonist in the movement for the abolition of the slave trade. Other members of the group were Granville Sharp, Zachary Macaulay—Thomas Babington Macaulay's father—likewise devoted to the anti-slavery campaign, Lord Teignmouth, a former govenor-general of India, and James Stephen, a man in Brougham's opinion of 'the strictest integrity and nicest sense of both honour and justice'. All were

laymen, but they were warmly supported by John Venn, rector of
Clapham from 1792 to 1813. Frequent visitors to the district
included Hannah More (1743–1833), prolific author of edifying
books and pamphlets and a courageous worker for the poor,
insufferably condescending though her social attitudes would now
be judged, and the two outstanding members of the Cambridge
following, Charles Simeon (1759–1836) and Isaac Milner (1751–
1820), the latter president of Queens' College and dean of Carlisle,
a man of respected position in the university and the most
impressive scholar in the party.

The literary organ of the Evangelicals was *The Christian
Observer*, founded in 1802, which did much to publicize their
opinions, but their contribution to theological study was meagre.
Wilberforce's *Practical View*, first published in 1797 and repeatedly
reissued, is representative and in its day had great influence.[1] But
although they are chiefly remembered for their philanthropy,
which made their wealth possible, they were not simply activists.
None of them ever thought of his religion only in terms of
moral endeavour. What moved them was a fervently held if
narrow Bible Protestantism, although their contemporaries often
despised them for the weakness of their theology, with its
alleged lack of intellectual fibre and the conventionalism of its
language. Thus Newman dismissed it as 'but an inchoate state or
stage of a doctrine', whose final resolution would be in rationalism.
But the charge is hardly fair. Evangelical theology was unspecula-
tive certainly, and it had very little to offer in the way of an
ecclesiology, whilst the emotive phrases of the popular evangelism
in which it found expression were apt to sound glib. Yet its
teaching, within its limits, was clear and firm. The very point of
Wilberforce's book was to impress on its readers the need of an
adequate Christian belief. There was much, he feared, in the
religion of people of his own social class—and his words were
addressed to them—which was merely nominal and formal, yet
if the basis of faith was insecurely laid the superstructure was
bound to be precarious. A superficial and complacent moralism,
the notion that 'if, on the whole, our lives be tolerably good, we
shall escape with little or no punishment', would not do. Such an

---

[1] Its full title is *A Practical View of the prevailing Religious System of Professed
Christians in the higher and middle classes in this country contrasted with Real Christianity.*
The book was translated into several languages.

error sprang from an impoverished idea of what the fundamentals of Christianity really are. The 'fruits of holiness', contrary to the popular view, are the effects not the causes of justification and reconciliation. The intrinsic corruption of human nature—'the sense we ought to entertain of our natural misery and helplessness' —the death of Christ, accordingly, as the one satisfaction for human sin, and the converting and sanctifying influence of the Holy Spirit—these are the elemental truths necessary to a real Christian profession. They are not abstruse, and the poor and simple can grasp them often better than the sophisticated. The humblest intelligence may hold to the death of Christ as an atonement for sin and the purchase price of a believer's future happiness.

The Reformation doctrine of justification by faith lay at the root of evangelical piety. The Christian religion was a way of personal salvation, rendered urgent by the presence and power of sin in human life. In the words of John Overton's *True Churchman Ascertained* (1801), a reply to Robert Fellowes's *The Anti-Calvinist*: 'We *can* only teach that every man who is born, considered independent of the grace of God, and in respect to spiritual concerns, is wholly corrupt, utterly impotent, under the wrath of God, and liable to everlasting torments.'[1] Overton indeed, unlike most English Evangelicals of the time, was a pronounced Calvinist, taking the gravest view of man's spiritual incapacity. But even Wilberforce, himself not at all of the Calvinist conviction, followed suit in this matter, believing sincerely that humanity is 'tainted with sin, not slightly and superficially, but radically and to the very core'.[2] This impressed him as the plain teaching of the Church of England, in its Articles even more expressly than in its liturgy. Nothing in this world was so important as the salvation of individual sinners from their sin and its consequences. Good intentions, however, are unavailing; rather must one turn to 'the high mysterious doctrines' professed by 'real' Christians. Wilberforce speaks with warmth of 'the profaneness of . . . treating as matters of subordinate consideration those parts of the system of Christianity, which are so strongly impressed on our reverence by the dignity of the person to whom they relate'. Man's only hope lies in Christ crucified:

[1] Second edition, 1802, p. 157.
[2] *A Practical View*, p. 27.

If we would love Him as affectionately, and rejoice in Him as triumphantly, as the first Christians did, we must learn like them to repose our entire trust in Him, and to adopt the language of the Apostle, 'God forbid that I should glory, save in the cross of our Lord Jesus Christ'.

Thus the atonement is the heart of Christian truth. It was no mere example of self-giving love but a unique event in which, by the substitution of the sinless one for sinners, the just wrath of God was appeased and his attitude to mankind changed. Man himself contributes no more to his redemption than he did to his first creation. To God alone is the praise.

Yet neither is salvation unconditional. To accept or reject it is the sinner's own awful responsibility and he can accept it only by an act of faith beyond all consideration of personal merit. 'You build for eternity', said Isaac Milner, 'on the righteousness of Christ; you renounce for ever, as a foundation of hope, your own righteousness.'[1] A true Christian indeed is one who is moved to believe that Christ died, not to endorse some broad moral principle, but, quite literally, *for him*. It was *his* sin, along with that of all his fellows, which made that holy death necessary. To admit this, out of personal conviction, is the beginning of conversion. Once possessed, the sense of sin is overwhelming. Moral virtues are discounted and one is aware only of mercy received. To suppose therefore that the Evangelicals' works of charity were done from utilitarian motives, in expectation of a heavenly reward, is to misconceive them completely. But good works, it was believed, are rightly taken as evidence of a justified state. They show that the faith professed is a living one. For the sinner to go unrepentant, and so fail to bring forth the fruits of the Spirit, is to await eternal doom. Even a man like Simeon adhered to the doctrine of reprobation without the slightest misgivings. It was sufficient that the Bible should teach it.

The Evangelicals were agreed, then, that the aim of religion is not only to humble the sinner and exalt the Saviour but to promote personal holiness. Sanctification was as much a divine operation as conversion. The two, in fact, were continuous, since conversion, so far from being of necessity instantaneous, is only the start of a process expected to last through life. The nature of holiness was conceived on puritan but not ascetic

[1] *Sermons* (1820), i, p. 207.

lines. Prayer and Bible-reading were vital to it, and regular attendance at Sunday worship was its dutiful expression. Thus G. W. E. Russell recalled from his youth 'an abiding sense of religious responsibility, a self-sacrificing energy in works of mercy, an evangelistic zeal, an aloofness from the world, and a level of saintliness in daily life such as I do not expect to see realized again on earth'.[1] Such testimony may be over-idealistic, but conduct in evangelical households was carefully regulated and a benefiting tone of 'seriousness' or 'earnestness' always looked for. Yet the Thorntons and the Wilberforces and their friends—unworldly men of the world—did not eschew the solid comforts and conveniencies appropriate to their rank in society. Nor were 'innocent' amusements by any means prohibited; it was only that the question of innocence had 'not to be tried', as Wilberforce put it, 'by the loose maxims of worldly morality, but by the spirit of the injunctions of the word of God'. Believers, he said, are not gloomy. 'The Christian relaxes in the temperate use of all the gifts of Providence.' Imagination and taste and genius, and the beauties of creation and works of art, all lie open to him. No doubt the advice was honestly meant, but it cannot be claimed that the Evangelicals displayed much aesthetic sensibility or an interest in liberal culture for its own sake. It was religion that dominated their lives and imposed a kind of ethical stewardship 'for every hour passed and every penny spent'.

The Evangelicals of the early nineteenth century, unlike many of their predecessors in the eighteenth, were not usually Calvinists. Legh Richmond, vicar successively of Brady in the Isle of Wight and Turvey in Bedfordshire, was among those who maintained the tradition in the Church of England, if in a modified form, whilst Overton was probably its doughtiest defender. But by this time the heat had gone out of the controversy.[2] The majority of Evangelicals believed that Christ had died for all men and not

---

[1] *The Household of Faith* (1902), p. 232.

[2] *A Refutation of Calvinism*, by George Tomline, bishop of Winchester, published in 1811, was a somewhat belated though vociferous contribution to the debate. Tomline detested the Calvinist tenets, but he overstates his case when he declares that 'there is not in any part of our Book of Common Prayer, or in our Articles, a single expression, which can fairly be interpreted as asserting or recognizing any one of the peculiar doctrines of Calvinism'. A more judicious examination of the Calvinism of the Articles was made by Richard Laurence, archbishop of Cashel, in his Bampton lectures of 1804.

simply for the elect few and that the appeal of the gospel is universal, a conviction with which their missionary zeal fully accorded. They were genuinely lovers of souls and could not contemplate that any should finally be lost, unless from his own hardness of heart.

The practical basis of evangelical religion was Bible study. Scripture was the Word of God, indeed the very words of God. It was verbally inspired in the sense that every statement in it was divinely authorized and essentially inerrant. The result was a biblicism, not to say a bibliolatry, the effect of which was intellectually benumbing. The sacred pages were treated as an oracle. Not only was critical curiosity about the facts of the Bible's historical origins non-existent; the Evangelicals produced remarkably little in the way of Scripture exegesis. Thomas Horne, who ministered at the Welbeck Chapel in London, wrote an *Introduction to the Critical Study of the Holy Scripture* (1818), but this ponderous enterprise hardly drew its inspiration from Evangelicalism. The best of the party's exegetes was Thomas Scott (1747–1821), whose commentaries were much read and admired. It was Scott of whom Newman records in the *Apologia* that he had made a deeper impression on his mind than any other writer, one 'to whom (humanly speaking) I almost owe my soul'.[1] Nothing else calls for mention.

The Evangelical view of Scripture indicates indeed where the weaknesses of Evangelicalism lay.[2] Intellectually it was narrow and naïvely reactionary. The wider problems of faith and reason did not trouble it and in philosophical theology it had no interest. Such matters, in evangelical eyes, did nothing to advance real religion. Christianity meant the gospel, and the gospel the converting of sinners. It was to be taught and believed to this end and no other. Philosophy, science and the arts were things intrinsically of this world, and of no consequence for eternity.

[1] Scott, who in 1781 succeeded John Newton as curate of Olney, was converted by the latter from Arminianism to Calvinism. His chief work, *The Holy Bible with . . . Notes*, was published in four volumes between 1788 and 1792. Newman himself was brought up in an evangelical household.

[2] Not that the Evangelicals were unique in their exaggerated biblicism. Bishop van Mildert of Durham, for instance—one of the most thoughtful and scholarly churchmen of his time—considered it 'impossible even to imagine a failure, either in judgment or in integrity in the Bible' (*An Inquiry into the General Principles of Scripture Interpretation* (1804), 3rd ed, p. 158.

> To be happy in another life [wrote Isaac Milner], to square all our
> conduct by that object steadily and primarily kept in view; to attend
> to the things of this life only as necessary, not as objects of choice
> ... these are the grand objects in the religion of Jesus.[1]

In any case the practical Christian, faced by the spiritual and moral
condition of the mass of his fellow-men, would have little time
to spare for pursuits that gave no lasting satisfaction and easily
became the occasion for sinful pride. All the same, it is slight
wonder that the evangelical influence, which in time permeated
Victorian society, encouraged philistinism and sometimes
hypocrisy. Popular Protestantism, fundamentalist and illiberal,
identified the Christian ethical ideal with the moral inhibitions of
the middle classes. A reaction therefore was bound to come
about, of which, in their differing ways, Arnold and Pater and
William Morris were to be the mouth-pieces. 'Nothing', observed
Walter Bagehot, 'is more unpleasant than a virtuous person with
a mean mind. A highly developed moral nature, joined to an
undeveloped intellectual nature, an undeveloped artistic nature,
is of necessity repulsive'—severe criticism, and as regards the
best of the Evangelicals hardly applicable. Wilberforce's certainly
was not a mean mind, but the limitations of the evangelical
attitude were very evident even to contemporaries. Moreover, it
also comprised a degree of moral obtuseness which posterity has
been unable to overlook.

Theologically likewise Evangelicalism had its faults, especially
of omission. Of religion as a historical and cultural phenomenon,
to be studied as such, it, needless to say, had no conception. Even
the history of Christianity as a major phase in the education of the
human race did not interest it, whilst the idea of religious development would have appeared irrelevant, if not false. Further,
although themselves loyal members of the Church of England,
the Evangelicals ignored much that was best in the Anglican
inheritance. The importance of conversation was insisted upon,
but little guidance was offered for subsequent spiritual training.[2]
All, it was assumed, that the convert needed was the open Bible.
The result was an excessive individualism; the corporate character
of the religious life, except as it might find expression in common
effort for special ends, was unappreciated. Of the Church as a

---

[1] *Sermons*, ii, p. 260.

[2] Cp. *Remains of Alexander Knox*, ed. Hornby (2nd edn, 1836), i, p. 72.

visible institution having a historic experience continuous ultimately with that of the apostolic age itself the Evangelicals had no real sense: as Gladstone wrote, 'I had been brought up with no notion of the Church as the Church or body of Christ'.[1] The 'Catholic Church' acknowledged in the creed was barely more indeed than an abstract term, and episcopacy merely the accepted form of ecclesiastical government, involving no theological principle. Fellowship in all essentials with Dissenters they did not question, since provided a man was in right relation with God and believed the true gospel it mattered little to what sect or denomination he belonged. The genuinely faithful—Wilberforce's 'real' as distinct from 'nominal' Christians—would spontaneously associate for the promotion of good causes. Thus voluntary societies became typical of evangelical life.[2] The party did not by any means disregard the sacraments, but it cannot be said that its characteristic piety was centred upon them. Baptism and the Lord's Supper were taught as no more than symbolic and commemorative acts, enjoined by Holy Writ. The sober among them might deplore 'enthusiastic' excesses, but they were far from ever adopting High Church positions.[3] Clergymen were simply ministers of the congregation, not the stewards of the mysteries of God. For the Evangelical personal religion, grounded in an intensely held faith in the atonement, was all-important; the Church was but the assembly, for prayer and praise and the hearing of the word of God, of those who possessed it. That they lacked a clearly defined ecclesiology was perhaps the Evangelicals' most signal deficiency. Because of it they gave a ready weapon to the Tractarians.

2. SOME HIGH CHURCHMEN

The evangelical 'Clapham Sect' was to some extent paralleled by a contemporary group of High Churchmen known as the 'Hackney Phalanx', from the district of London where they resided and

[1] W. E. Gladstone ed. (D. C. Lathbury), *Letters on Church and Religion* (1908), i, p. 8.

[2] Of these there were very many. Suffice it to mention the Religious Tract Society (1799), the Church Missionary Society (1799), the British and Foreign Bible Society (1804), the British and Foreign School Society (1807), and the London Society for Promoting Christianity among the Jews (1809).

[3] To suppose otherwise is the error of Ford K. Brown in *The Fathers on the Victorians. The Age of Wilberforce* (1961), pp. 498–506. Cp. David Newsome, 'Father and Sons', in *The Historical Journal*, vi.2 (1963), pp. 295–310.

from which their influence radiated. The designation High Church
was at this time somewhat vague. It was commonly used of such
as were not 'Low Churchmen'—Latitudinarians, that is—or
Evangelicals, and included not only the exponents of 'high'
sacramental views but, more generally, the 'high-and-dry' Church-
and-State men: orthodox, anti-Roman, hostile to Dissent, severely
critical of 'enthusiasm' and Tory in politics. With these latter,
and their numbers were considerable, we are not here concerned,
since to the positive thinking of their age they contributed virtually nothing. As Alexander Knox said of them, they were for
the most part 'men of the world, if not of yesterday', and 'worn
out'. The evangelical revival had conspicuously not touched them.
The Hackney group, however, were spiritually awake and socially
active. The extent of their influence was, furthermore, out of all
proportion to the relative modesty of their social rank. In temper
and outlook they and the type of High Churchmen of whom they
were representative harked back to the ecclesiastical ideals of
the Nonjurors and the Carolines. Politically of the Tory party,
they valued but did not especially stress the State connection and
stood rather for the Church's independence as essentially a
spiritual and not merely a political entity. They were the immediate
forerunners of the Tractarians, whose doctrines and attitudes
they anticipated at almost every point; but unlike the Oxford
High Churchmen of the 'thirties they were not propagandists.
They adhered to their beliefs with a reasoned assurance and
would gladly have had others share them, but they wanted zest
for bold policies, judging that sound opinions require cautious
procedures as well. They were polemical only when forced to
defend their convictions against opponents, whether Latitudinarian, Nonconformist or Roman Catholic. But they respected
theological learning whilst distrusting speculation. Eccentricity
and eclecticism seemed to them likely only to lead to error. At the
same time a man should have an understanding faith, knowing
why and on what authority he believes as he does. Their defensiveness and fear of change may have indicated a defect of spiritual
vitality; Knox, a shrewd observer, himself thought so. Yet, as
the Hackney men prove, they were not indifferent to practical
religion and philanthropy. In their quieter and less obtrusive way
they were as forward in this regard as were the Evangelicals.
It was the advance of liberalism, both political and theological,

which in the fourth decade of the century led High Churchmen to assume a more aggressive tone. The events of 1833 may well be looked on therefore as marking the turning-point in the party's destiny. Yet the novelty of the Tractarian teaching should not be overstated. The Oxford divines did not set out to innovate, as they themselves insisted. Yet in appealing to the example of their seventeenth-century predecessors they were prone to undervalue the clear and consistent church teaching of the generation immediately behind their own. The great difference between them and the older men was that they had come to see the past in a more dramatic light. It was not enough simply to accept traditional doctrines as things always taught; rather their truth was to be *felt*, to be taken to the heart. Hence the younger churchmen could be spoken of, in a way that their elders could not, as (in R. W. Church's phrase) 'the movement party', showing as they did all the self-propagating energy of a genuine spiritual revival. On their lips the term 'catholic' acquired a fresh, almost a revolutionary, significance. The doctrine of the apostolic succession reappeared as a principle to be striven for and with full recognition of its practical implications. What in short the Oxford leaders did for the old High Church theology was to make it into a *cause*, so that endorsement of their opinions became the equivalent of loyalty to the Church itself.

The 'orthodox' party of pre-Tractarian days was not numerous, but it included some prominent men. Its bishops—notably William van Mildert of Durham (1765–1836), Charles Lloyd of Oxford (1784–1820) and Herbert Marsh of Peterborough (1757–1839)—were among the most distinguished on the bench. But, conscientious and learned though they were, their influence was restricted. They offered no challenge to a lax public opinion. Conservation rather than propagation was their watchword, and their teaching, strict in principle, was in presentation unimaginative. Traditionalist by nature, the real trends of the time they scarcely saw.

Apart from the bishops—and the archbishop of Canterbury himself, Manners Sutton, might perhaps be classed with them—the leading members of the party comprised the scholarly Thomas Middleton (1769–1822), who became bishop of Calcutta; the archdeacons Charles Daubeny (1744–1827), a hard-hitting controversialist, and George Cambridge, and John James Watson,

33

the rector of Hackney; Watson's brother-in-law, Henry Handley Norris, also a Hackney incumbent, a man of both means and energy; Norris's gifted father-in-law, Thomas Sikes of Guilsborough, Northants; Hugh James Rose (1795–1838), rector of Hadleigh; and Christopher Wordsworth, brother of the poet and Master of Trinity College, Cambridge. Two stalwarts of the Hackney Phalanx (or 'Clapton Sect', as it was also sometimes called) were, however, laymen—Joshua Watson the rector of Hackney's brother, and William Stevens, both of them retired London merchants and staunch churchmen.[1] A layman, too, was Alexander Knox (1757–1831), a member of the Church of Ireland and the intimate friend and tireless correspondent of Bishop Jebb of Limerick, who himself strongly sympathized with Knox's views. The High Church periodical was *The Christian Remembrancer*, which began publication in 1819.

Distinctive of High Church teaching was the importance it attached to church polity and the sacraments. On these matters Archdeacon Daubeny, whose celebrated *Guide to the Church* came out in 1789, was as rigid as any Anglo-Catholic of a later day. His style of writing, however, may be judged from the statement that 'as the time of our Saviour's departure from the world drew near, the future establishment of His Church appears to have constituted the most interesting subject of His thoughts'.[2] On the apostolical succession he was firm: the Church must have a duly commissioned ministry deriving its authority in direct line from the apostles. Without episcopal government a 'true and lawful Church' indeed does not exist. The priesthood is a divine institution, since 'Christ was in all that the Apostles did'. Sacraments are the 'seals of the divine covenant',[3] but those of Dissenters, who lack a properly constituted ministry, are mere human ordinances, without effect. 'There is a holiness of *office* independent of the holiness of the minister; the former being essential to the validity of the ministerial act.' For the eucharist to be a sacrifice and for the presence therein of Christ to be real it must be celebrated by a priest. Schism in any case is indefensible, unity in the Church's membership being a Christian obligation.

[1] Watson's activities on behalf of Christian missions and popular education—he and Norris were co-founders in 1811 of the National Society—places him in this respect with the keenest of the Evangelicals.

[2] *Guide to the Church* (ed. 1829), p. 6.

[3] *Ibid.*, p. 180.

The civil toleration of dissent is no more than a political expedient, in principle inadmissible. In religion external authority must have the final voice; private judgment is unwarranted, for no man has a right to think otherwise than as God has ordained. The supreme duty of conscience is to recognize divine law as made known by revelation and taught and safeguarded by the Church.

Harsh towards Protestant nonconformity, Daubeny reserved a milder censure for Rome, since she and Canterbury (he claimed) are agreed on essentials. Thus he chides 'indiscriminating' Christians who are 'frightened with the words cross, altar, sacrifice or priest, words peculiarly characteristic of the Christian Church'.[1] But it is the Calvinists who really provoke his anger. Overton's reply, in *The True Churchman Ascertained*, to anti-Calvinist polemic has already been mentioned, but it did not silence the archdeacon, who in *Vindiciae Ecclesiae Anglicanae* (1803) answered both it and Wilberforce's *Practical View*.

Another divine of whom it was said that 'orthodoxy oozed out of his pores, and that he would talk it in his dreams' was, of course, van Mildert, who before his elevation to the episcopate, of which at the time he was the most learned member, had been Regius Professor of divinity at Oxford and both Boyle and Bampton lecturer.[2] He was as emphatic as Daubeny that episcopacy is of the essence of the Church. Sacraments and priesthood are, he held, 'interwoven into the very substance of Christianity and inseparable from its general design'. Dissenters accordingly are outside the Church. Bishop Marsh of Peterborough maintained a similar view, as, too, had the highly respected Horsley of Rochester, who denounced Methodists and 'gloried' in the name of High Churchman.

Thomas Sikes (1767–1834), although he never won preferment and spent his life as a country parson, was a man of strong personality whose opinions were greatly valued—he was known locally as 'the Pope'—and advice widely sought. He is especially remembered as a prophet of the Oxford Movement. What in general the churchmen of his day lacked, he judged, was any real understanding of the doctrine of the *Church* itself, which as an article of the creed was scarcely at all considered. Certain words of

---

[1] *Ibid.*, p. 220.

[2] In 1802–5 (*An Historical View of the Rise and Progress of Infidelity*) and 1814 (*An Inquiry into the General Principles of Scripture Interpretation*) respectively.

his uttered in 1833 and recalled long afterwards by Edward
Bouverie Pusey in a letter to the archbishop of Canterbury,
William Howley, have often been cited but are worth repeating
here in full, in view of their remarkable prescience.

> I seem [he said] to think I can tell you something which you who are
> young may probably live to see. Wherever I go about the country
> I see amongst the clergy a number of very amiable and estimable
> men, many of them much in earnest and wishing to do good. But
> I have observed one universal want in their teaching: the uniform
> suppression of one great truth. There is no account given anywhere,
> so far as I can see, of the one Holy Catholic Church. I think that
> the causes of this suppression have been mainly two. The Church
> has been kept out of sight, partly in consequence of the civil estab-
> lishment of the branch of it which is in this country, and partly
> out of false charity to Dissent. Now this great truth is an article
> of the Creed; and if so, to teach the rest of the Creed to its exclusion
> must be to destroy the 'analogy or proportion of the faith'. This
> cannot be done without the most serious consequences. The doctrine
> is of the last importance, and the principles it involves of immense
> power; and some day, not far distant, it will judicially have its
> reprisals. And whereas the other articles of the Creed seem now to
> have thrown it into the shade, it will seem, when it is brought
> forward, to swallow up the rest. We now hear not a breath about
> the Church; by and by those who live to see it will hear of nothing
> else; and just in proportion perhaps to its present suppression, will
> be its future development. Our confusion nowadays is chiefly owing
> to the want of it; and there will be even more confusion attending
> its revival. The effect of it I even dread to contemplate, especially
> if it come suddenly. And woe betide those, whoever they are, who
> shall, in the course of Providence, have to bring it forward. It ought
> especially of all others to be a matter of catechetical teaching and
> training. The doctrines of the Church Catholic and the privileges
> of Church membership cannot be explained from pulpits; and those
> who will have to explain it will hardly know where they are, or
> which way they are to turn themselves. They will be endlessly
> misrepresented and misunderstood. There will be one great outcry
> of Popery from one end of the country to the other. It will be thrust
> upon minds unprepared, and an uncatechised Church. Some will
> take it up and admire it as a beautiful picture, others will be
> frightened and run away and reject it; and all will want a guidance
> which one hardly knows where they shall find.[1]

[1] H. P. Liddon, *The Life of Edward Bouverie Pusey*, i, p. 257.

It may be that Sikes's statement was somewhat coloured in Pusey's memory from his knowledge of subsequent events, but its substantial accuracy as he records it need not be doubted, even though it would appear to have been hardly fair to much current High Church teaching. The expression, 'an uncatechized Church', conveys precisely the Tractarians' own complaint: churchmen were largely ignorant of and indifferent to their doctrinal heritage. A new religious revival must appeal not to mere sentiment, nor to the primacy of a single article of belief, as did the Evangelicals to the doctrine of the atonement, but to a body of theological principles which the Church of England had in the final resort received from the undivided Church of antiquity.

It remains to speak of Knox, a lay theologian—in those days a rare enough phenomenon in itself—of a singular insight and breadth of sympathy. The ecclesiastically-minded layman is prone to be more, not less, rigid than the cleric. It was not so, however, with this surprising Irishman, Lord Castlereagh's one-time private secretary. A freelance among orthodox churchmen, he was both sure of his principles and consistent in applying them, yet wholly devoid of a spirit of exclusiveness or the controversialist's desire to use truth mainly in order to impale error. High Churchman though he was, he had a profound admiration for John Wesley, with whom he had from time to time corresponded, and was fully in accord with the spiritual ideals of Methodism, if not with its express theology. What his own party needed, he was convinced, was an infusion of the Methodists' fervour. Newman spoke of him as a remarkable instance of 'a man searching for and striking out the truth by himself'. Could we, he added, 'see the scheme of things as angels see it, I fancy we should find he has his place in the growth and restoration (so be it) of Church principles'.[1] Pusey too had a great respect for him, although there is little evidence that the Tractarians in general acknowledged any special debt to him, partly because he and they alike looked back for inspiration to the 'Anglo-Catholic' divines of the seventeenth century, but partly also because there is in Knox's outlook a broad, almost Coleridgean,

---

[1] *Letters and Correspondence of John Henry Newman*, ed. Anne Mozley (1891), ii, p. 93.

quality less to their liking.[1] Knox himself did not live to witness the Oxford Movement, but had he done so his reactions would have been interesting. Archdeacon Daubeny—'a strange kind of clergyman at Bath'—was evidently not a man after his own heart. The fact is that Knox, like F. D. Maurice later, was an individualist, fitting exactly into no party. A reclusive scholar, he preferred, for all his deep regard for the traditions of the Church Catholic, to think for himself.

The fruits of his thought are contained in the four volumes of his *Remains*,[2] and the two further volumes of his correspondence with Bishop Jebb.[3] It is in a letter of the year 1816 on 'The Situation and Prospects of the Established Church' that he criticizes the High Churchmen of his day for their lack of religious feeling and of what he calls 'interior learning'—that instinctive understanding of the needs of the human heart which Wesley and the Evangelicals, despite their defective theology, unquestionably possessed. The High Church critics of Evangelicalism all too often failed, he thought, to appreciate where its strength really lay. The grounds of its personal appeal they should have studied rather than derided. The coldness of their own teaching, characteristic though it was of the times in which they lived, was an impediment to the gospel message and to the extension of the Church's influence on the popular mind. Orthodox doctrine is greatly to be desired, but of itself is no substitute for that 'spiritual view of religion which implies an habitual devotedness to God' such as could be found in Methodism. What Knox judged most likely to arouse the national Church from its prevailing torpor was the growth of liberalism and the spread of an anti-ecclesiastical spirit among the common people. The old-fashioned 'high-and-dry' churchmanship was utterly insufficient for the nation's needs in an age of change and disintegration. Its principles were sound, but the teaching of them lacked all conviction. The party wanted revitalizing, and for this even persecution might

---

[1] Thus Newman's good opinion had definite qualifications. 'He seems to say dangerous things ... I should be unwilling to think him more than an eclectic, though that is bad enough. Froude did not like him. I think his works on the Eucharist have done much good' (from a letter to Robert Wilberforce, dated 9 June 1838. See D. Newsome, *op. cit.* p. 197).

[2] 1834–37.

[3] *Thirty Years' Correspondence between Bishop Jebb and Alexander Knox*, ed. Forster (1836).

not come amiss. What in particular was required was a genuine sentiment for the Church, a lively interest in its history and the continuity of its witness, in its corporate being and in its 'unsurpassed liturgy'. Preaching had sunk to the level of mere routine moralizing: there was 'intellectual pumping' but no 'gushing of the spring'.[1]

A further reason for the all but universal failure among Englishmen to weigh the significance of the word 'catholic' and therefore to attach any substantial meaning to the idea of the Catholic Church was, he considered, the inveterate suspicion of Rome. Rome doubtless was in error in many respects, but she also had preserved vastly more that was true. The answer to the dogma of transubstantiation was not to turn the eucharist into a bare memorial ceremony any more than was the claim to infallibility to be met by every man deciding his own creed.[2] Scripture certainly is the ultimate source of authority in matters of faith, but catholicity rests upon the additional principle of 'the concurrent judgment or tradition of the Church', the *consensus omnium*, the *quod ubique quod semper quod ab omnibus*, which next to Scripture is 'our surest guide'. Knox for his part looks back to the Church of the first centuries for the solid content of Catholic teaching and to the early seventeenth century for that special presentation of it characteristic of the reformed branch of the Catholic Church established in England. At the Reformation the English Church, whilst asserting its right to decide in controversies of faith, also acknowledged its allegiance to an older and wider inheritance, an allegiance 'which reduces all that was done about articles and homilies to such a municipal rank, as to make it, of necessity, but subordinately and conditionally obligatory, even on subscribers.'[3] Thus to call the national Church Protestant is to make do with a very inadequate description. Her body indeed, thanks to the circumstances of her history, may be Lutheran, but her soul is Catholic.

Knox was devoted to the Book of Common Prayer, the spirit and language of which he found entirely congenial because unquestionably Catholic. The viability of the Church of England had lain in its identity of organization and mental character with

---

[1] *Correspondence*, i, p. 14.
[2] *Remains*, i, p. 58.
[3] *Correspondence*, ii, p. 502.

the Church of former ages, the one secured by our 'unbroken episcopacy',[1] the other exemplified by the liturgy—the latter being a standard of doctrine as well as of devotion. He had no quarrel with the Thirty-Nine Articles as such, but denied that they bore the same intrinsic authority as the prayer book. Whereas the former were 'very much human' the latter 'fell little short of divine'.[2] As for the establishment, he esteemed it well enough for its actual, or potential, influence on the life of the nation, but more, he thought, should be understood by the term than the mere state connection, however beneficial. The Church's real strength was in its interior organization. 'An Hierarchical Church has the nature of an Establishment whether it is, or is not, allied with the State.' To this inherent structure state support added little.

Consonant with Knox's hierarchial conception of the Church was his strong sacramentalism. His view of baptism indeed is qualified. He believes that the sacrament may be said to effect regeneration, but in the sense only of contracting indelible relations between God and man, relations which may either be realized or nullified on man's part, to his spiritual loss or gain. In the case of infant baptism the grace bestowed is unconditional: 'Nothing less can be concluded than that a vital germ of all virtuous dispositions and pious affections is implanted in the mind of the baptized infant.' Nevertheless the germ will not grow up of itself, and it does not follow that because a man has been baptized he is in fact regenerate.[3] On the doctrine of the eucharist, however, Knox is remarkably firm. His argument is directed expressly against the eighteenth-century divine, Daniel Waterland, for whom the bread and wine were no more than 'the signs or pledges of concomitant blessing'. But Knox holds that the consecrated symbols are properly to be regarded as themselves vehicles of saving grace and hence as the 'permanent representatives of [Christ's] incarnate Person'.[4] By them God works invisibly in us, even though we cannot explain how. Knox is satisfied that he finds this teaching not only in the Fathers of the early

---

[1] On Knox's opinions in the matter of the apostolical succession see I. Brillioth, *The Anglican Revival* (1925), pp. 46–55.

[2] *Remains*, i, p. 425.

[3] *Ibid.*, i, pp. 488–510.

[4] *Ibid.*, ii, p. 155.

Church but in St Paul himself, and deems it the natural interpretation of Christ's own words.

> Of this supernatural influence I consider the Lord's Supper the divinely constructed conduit: it is the connecting link between earth and heaven, the point where our Redeemer is vitally accessible, 'the same yesterday, today, and for ever'; and when He said, 'This is my body' and 'This is my blood', He made the sacrament, the simple elements (which, wherever thus used, receive the same divine touch and the same efficacious sublimation), to be for ever the vehicle, to all capable receivers, of all that is vitalizing, sanative, purificatory, confirmative, in Himself—in His life, or in His death, His exquisite humanity, or His adorable divinity.

In receiving the sacraments devotional feeling is not necessary. The only impediment to true communication is incapacity:

> The co-operation of mind on the part of the receiver, which in all the common means of edification must be deemed indispensable, was, in the Eucharist, peculiarly and mysteriously superseded; and *capacity* the requisite for the reception of the heavenly blessing.[1]

For the truth is that 'we cannot co-operate in the divine act, because it is so purely divine as to exclude even subordinate co-agency.'

Regarding the inspiration of Scripture Knox avoids any rigid or exclusive theory. Inspiration is given in degree and is not confined to a single age, nor is it entirely lacking even to the heathen. The commonly accepted view, he complains, 'has kept very many back from exercising their judgments on its structure and composition'.[2] Altogether Knox's was an independent and forward-looking intelligence. Not only did he presage Tractarianism, Maurice, too, had in him a worthy forerunner. His influence would assuredly have been greater but for the modesty, or personal disinclination, which inhibited him from making his voice heard in the world by publishing more than he did.

3. LIBERAL OPINION

The liberal theologians of these early decades also compose a group, although from the very nature of liberalism a less clearly defined one. They at any rate did not constitute an ecclesiastical

---

[1] *Ibid.*, ii, p. 280.
[2] *Correspondence*, i, p. 41.

party. At the beginning of the century liberal opinions were generally not much in evidence among churchmen. Conservatism, militant or lethargic, was the mark of the age. Men like Paley and Bishop Watson of Llandaff favoured prayer book revision and the abolition of subscription; otherwise latitudinarianism was in decline. One rather solitary, not to say eccentric, figure is, however, worth noticing, namely Robert Fellowes (1771–1847), a cleric of deistical views. The earlier of his two books, called *Religion without Cant* (1811), is intended to be a defence of the established Church against the objections of Dissenters, but much church doctrine also comes under fire. Original sin, for example, is dismissed as a falsehood for which the Bible itself is not responsible. Man is not by nature depraved and the story of the Fall is no more than an allegory. The Trinity, again, is a mystery beyond human comprehension. The later volume, *The Religion of the Universe*, published in 1836, is pure deism and prefers science to Christianity as a basis for the moral life. True religion is essentially a matter of the rational understanding, of which science is now the ripest fruit. Knowledge of nature in fact is knowledge of God. Miracles, disallowed by science, can have no place in religion. Even prayer rests on a misconception of God's perfection. As for creeds and dogmas, what are they but priestly contrivances fostering superstition? Yet for all its crudity Fellowes's book is of some interest on account of its grasp of the principle of evolution, though the word itself is not mentioned. Geology is right in what it tells us of the immense age of the earth, and the first organisms must have been extremely simple. It is doubtful, moreover, whether man himself represents a special act of creation; although even as a part of nature and the product of secondary causation alone he still is a manifestation of 'divine agency' and the climax of a long providential development. Immortality, finally, is a reasonable belief in view of man's inherent capacities.

Fellowes, as a clergyman of his time, was doubtless an oddity. He was a man of intelligence, but essentially (in biological language) a 'sport'. On the other hand, the nearest thing to a liberal *school* is to be found in the group of Oxford teachers associated with Oriel College and known in their day as 'Noetics', a nickname which, like most such, was not intended to be flattering. To the traditionalists they appeared self-opinionated and brash. Their common disposition was to examine and criticize received beliefs in the light of history and reason. A provost of the college, Edward Copleston (1776–1849), may be said to have been the originator of the group, although his predecessor, Eveleigh, had already shown—what then was rare—a reforming spirit in university affairs. Copleston himself was a man after Eveleigh's own stamp. 'August and commanding', he was a keen judge of intellectual ability, as his appointments to college fellowships proved, and he made a principle of taking the liberal line in most matters. His pupils included some of the best minds of the following generation—Whately, Hampden and Baden-Powell among them. Yet he was not at all an original thinker, or in any sense a theological adventurer, and could fairly be classed as a High Churchman. Although he found no support among the sixteenth-century Reformers for a rigid theory of episcopacy, he believed the Church as a visible institution to be of divine foundation and to possess an inherent authority secured by a ministry having historical continuity with that of apostolic times. What he could not sanction was the view that this continuity ensures the transmission of a special power or virtue, or that ordination confers on the individual minister any distinctly sacerdotal character. His attitude to Tractarianism—'that folly', he dubbed it—was accordingly unsympathetic.

Edward Hawkins (1789–1882), Copleston's successor at Oriel, was no less critical of the new High Church divinity, dismissing the doctrine of the apostolical succession, which he regarded as central to it, as devoid of adequate basis in known historical fact. Episcopacy as the traditional form of church government was one thing; exclusive claims built upon it quite another. Yet his depriving of three such brilliant college tutors as Newman, Hurrell Froude and Robert Wilberforce of their office was prompted, we may suspect, as much by personal jealousy as by conscientious difference of view. In any case Hawkins had little of his predecessor's force of character and was not himself in any marked degree a liberal. 'The Church to teach, the Bible to prove' was a maxim he shared with the Tractarians.

The real inheritor of the liberal tradition was Richard Whately (1787–1863), who joined the Oriel common room in 1811. With his hard-headed trust in the all-sufficiency of reason he was the very type of a 'Noetic', and proud of the influence he believed himself to exert. Religion, he was confident, needed a stiff infusion of the critical spirit. Party bias especially was an obstacle to truth.[1] But although a born questioner, Whately was no rationalist in the sense of refusing to recognize the limits of reason when faced with the mysteries of faith. The fault of too much religious philosophy was, he considered, its glib assumption that the meaning of such words as 'cause', 'time' and 'eternity' is self-evident. Religion pertains to a realm of thought demanding the temper of the scientific investigator more than of the dogmatist. The prime necessity, however, was a renewed study of the Bible, a task the nature and scope of which he sought to indicate in his own *Essay on Some Difficulties in the Writings of St Paul* (1828). In this he takes another look at a vocabulary long familiar in theological debate. What, he asks, is the real significance of terms like 'election', 'law', 'grace', 'justification' and 'imputed righteousness', as distinct from the meanings which centuries of misuse had forced upon them? Let the modern theologian rid himself of his preoccupation and return with an open mind to the text of Scripture itself. A book of the Bible should be read as a whole and with its general character and content in view, not merely picked over for isolated 'texts'. Scripture is not a manual of theology, and definitions and consistency in the use of words are absent. Nor is it of equal revelational value throughout, since much of it has slight bearing on the practical religious life. Certainly revelation has no function to instruct us in the natural sciences. All the same, Whately had little taste for German negations: the errors of one extreme do not validate those of another. Conventional ideas call for re-examination in the light of new knowledge and superstitions have to be dispelled. But the religious spirit will always employ judgment with reverence.

The *Essays* served their turn at a time when biblical studies in this country were in poor shape, but their author, who was never much more than an ecclesiastical publicist, left behind him no book of lasting interest. As a writer he could hit hard, but the sort of thing he was best at is of its nature ephemeral. To Tractarian ideas he was implacably opposed, particularly disliking a reactionary exaltation of the principle of authority. For Newman

[1] The subject of his 1822 Bampton lectures was *The Use and Abuse of Party Feeling in Matters of Religion.*

and his friends the one source of truth was in the past, in church tradition. Reason was distrusted or disparaged, a docile and unquestioning faith extolled. Such a state of mind could lead in the end only to scepticism, or at best to that mere 'reason of the heart', or the paradox of an argued irrationalism, which Coleridge seemed to be proclaiming. For Whately an internal disposition was no substitute for external evidences open to examination by any reasonable inquirer. In some respects, and despite his swash-buckling manner, his own standpoint was very much that of his orthodox contemporaries. He did not reject the dogmatic principle, or institutionalism in religion. His anonymous *Letters on the Church: By an Episcopalian* (1826)[1] describe the Church as 'a body corporate, of divine institution' and even entertain the doctrine of the apostolical succession in so far as it implies a delegated authority and a rightly exercised discipline. The author also disapproves the state establishment: Christ's kingdom is not of this world, and to fulfil its spiritual vocation it must enjoy a freedom with which such political and legal bondage, whatever seeming privileges it may confer, is incompatible. Disestablish-ment, though without the inconvenience of disendowment, ought not to be delayed. Later, however, these opinions underwent modification.[2] One now looks in vain in the Bible for instruction as to the formal constitution of the Church. How actual Christian societies should organize themselves is a matter for historical circumstances to determine, in the light of Christian principles. The Church indeed, like the human race itself, is 'undoubtedly one', but not as a society. Visible unity will be realized only 'in its future existence': hence the designation 'the Universal Church' is a phase only; there is no corresponding reality having a recognizable cohesion or focus of authority, and no existing Christian body justly claims so comprehensive a title. The Jews no doubt did so, and rightly, since they already were one people; but Christians are not in a like situation. Unity is not, at any rate, constituted by the episcopate, as the Tractarians argued, for

---

[1] Whately never admitted, but he also never denied, authorship of the pamphlet. That it came from his pen was generally understood. With the years Whately's atti-tude to the Oxford Movement, and Newman particularly, became increasingly critical. See Jane Whately, *The Life and Correspondence of Richard Whately, D.D., late Archbishop of Dublin* (1866).

[2] See *Essays on Some of the Dangers to Christian Faith which may arise from the Teach-ing or the Conduct of its Professors* (1839), especially Note A to Essay III.

episcopacy has no credentials as the sole legitimate form of ecclesiastical government. Criteria such as this were not laid down by Christ or his apostles, but are simply men's 'unauthorized conjectures'. The truth of the Church's teaching is substantiated only by Scripture. Tradition adds nothing, inasmuch as its own witness depends on Scripture.

Newman, in spite of their mutual estrangement, always admired Whately, who, he said, 'opened my mind, and taught me to think and to use my reason'.[1] But of Whately's close friend, Dr Hampden, he was bitingly critical. Renn Dickson Hampden (1793–1868) was, no doubt, a very controversial figure in the Oxford of the 'thirties. Yet he was a scholar whose distinction only sheer prejudice could have denied. Newman and his followers, however, both denigrated his scholarship and ridiculed the man. That he lacked personal attraction is evident. But the campaign mounted against him in 1836, when Lord Melbourne (on Whately's persuasion) nominated him Regius professor of divinity at Oxford, is an event lying beyond our purview here, fascinating though its details are to the connoisseur of ecclesiastical and academic *causes célèbres*.[2] Hampden, not only then but since, has frequently been underrated,[3] and in any case there is no question of his being a strongly original or influential theologian, nor as a writer does he always succeed in making his meaning clear. Yet he had considerable insight and a prescient sense, far beyond that of most of his critics, of where the religious thinking of the future would tend. A Tory in politics and in his way a firm churchman, he was both astonished and grieved at the animus his opponents displayed against him, not only in 1836 but years later, when he was appointed to the see of Hereford. He assuredly was not by intention the heresiarch he was accused of being, and as a bishop he came to be regarded as a moderate High Churchman, his supposedly heretical opinions

[1] *Apologia pro Vita Sua*, ed. Svaglic (1967), p. 23. Newman adds: 'What he did for me in point of religious opinion, was, first, to teach me the existence of the Church, as a substantive body or corporation; next, to fix in me those anti-Erastian views of Church polity, which were one of the most prominent features of the Tractarian movement' (*op. cit.* p. 24).

[2] For the particulars see W. O. Chadwick, *The Victorian Church*, i (1966), pp. 112–26.

[3] Thus A. O. J. Cockshut, *Religious Controversies of the Nineteenth Century* (1966), p. 102, is satisfied that as a theologian Hampden was 'comparatively unimportant' and in the wake of R. W. Church calls him 'a muddled and inconsistent thinker'.

having by then been forgotten. He himself, in his old age, denounced the heterodoxy of Bishop Colenso.

Hampden, like the rest of the Oriel liberals, believed that in religion as elsewhere critical reason has its rights. The paramount authority of Scripture he never doubted. His Bampton lectures of 1832, which dealt with *The Scholastic Philosophy considered in its Relation to Christian Theology*, were described by him modestly enough as an inquiry into the nature of theological terms.[1] The essential truth of Christianity, he held, is to be distinguished from the particular forms in which history has clothed it and which have been largely moulded by Greek philosophy. The source of dogmas is the Bible, whose content alone is to be received as divine revelation. Theology is necessary for the definition and defence of the faith, but is itself secondary and mutable, a human discipline serving heavenly truth but no integral part of it. The fault of scholasticism had been its infatuation with abstractions and deductive logic, its absorption in mere *reasoning*. The result had been the creation of a vast theological superstructure wrongly identified with the fundamentals of revelation itself. The Church in resisting one kind of rationalism had adopted another, and schemes of doctrine took the place of the living truths they were intended to clarify and safeguard. A return to the Scriptures was the only way out of the speculative mazes into which theology had been led. For Scripture gives us not theories but facts. To the question, however, of what exactly these facts amount to Hampden accords no very clear answer. Does the Bible not teach doctrines, or, as he seems to imply, are the doctrines themselves the 'facts'? If he means only that the doctrinal statements in Scripture are not formal or systematic, that they are presented imaginatively and for practical ends, few would disagree with him. In any case it is a just *caveat* that the Bible should not be read with mistaken presuppositions. Hampden's point was that while Scripture contains the germs of the developed doctrines the development itself, in its historical course, has drawn upon material which is not scriptural. This is not necessarily an illegitimate procedure, but the instructed believer must distinguish the kernel from the husk.

---

[1] Earlier publications of his included *An Essay on the Philosophical Evidence of Christianity* (1827) and an article on 'Thomas Aquinas and the Scholastic Philosophy' contributed to the *Encyclopedia Metropolitana*.

Such general considerations, Hampden maintains, help us to assess the true function and purpose of dogmatic theology, which primarily are negative: its first aim is to exclude error. The Christian religion, by a natural process, 'has been acted on by the force of the human intellect', but the outcome may be distortion as well as clarification. Theology's task is to keep the original deposit intact whilst excluding interpretations which would transform its essential character. But dogma has also a positive role as a bond of social union. Beliefs, to be shared, depend on effective communication, and the institutionalizing of faith is a necessity if the social and cultural environment is not to prove a solvent. Conciliar definitions and their accompanying anathemas are the price to be paid for a requisite service.

Hampden's thesis was not strikingly new, and the lectures provoked no especially hostile criticism until the occasion of his nomination to the divinity professorship, although his pamphlet on *Religious Dissent*, 'with particular reference to the use of religious tests in the University', which appeared in 1834, did give some offence. Here he had argued that Christianity is basically a disposition of will and feeling, not a body of doctrinal formulae, and that purely intellectual criteria ought not therefore to be made a condition of unity among Christians. In view, however, of the Crown's choice of Hampden for high academic office his published opinions could not be overlooked. But Newman's criticisms of them, under the title 'Elucidations of Dr Hampden's Theological Sentiments', was a work of more skill than scruple. Pusey, too, had a good deal to say,[1] noting how heretics invariably quote Scripture in preference to the definitions of the Church. Hampden, although aggrieved and distressed at the way in which he felt himself to have been misrepresented, stood firm.

> It is one thing [he wrote in a letter to Lord John Russell] to endeavour to unfold the theories on which a particular phraseology is employed in the systematic statement of divine truth, and adapted to its purpose, and quite another thing to state that the truths themselves, which that phraseology expresses, are mere theories, or mere opinions, or probable conclusions having no certainty in them. The latter misconstruction belongs to those who have taken it up, it is not mine.

[1] *Dr Hampden's Theological Statements and the Thirty-nine Articles: By a resident member of Convocation.*

In his inaugural lecture as Regius professor, as well as in the preface to a new edition of the Bamptons, he tried to explain the nature and drift of his opinions. The foundation of all his teaching, he protested, was Jesus Christ. Trinitarian doctrine he received in the full sense, as the Church had declared it. The authority of the Scriptures uncontestably was final, but he did not deny that of the Church also: it was simply that ecclesiastical authority cannot challenge biblical. In any event the ultimate criterion of truth is bound to be the reason. On the particular point of the 'facts' of Scripture it was his undoubted intention, he explained, to include also its *doctrines*.

The agitation against Hampden is usually quoted as a prime example of Tractarian bigotry; nevertheless in the eyes of the new Oxford High Churchmen his position was a threat to true belief. The importance he attached to Church tradition and authority seemed to them insufficient. His explanations of his meaning were so far acceptable, but ambiguity was not wholly removed, whilst Pusey scored a hit by showing that the new professor had failed to distinguish between the scholastic theology and that of the early Church fathers. Yet Hampden's book had merit and is to be praised for its grasp of the principle of organic development in Christian doctrine in response to changes in the cultural environment. This the Tractarians, with their static conceptions, did not understand. Newman himself omitted to face the problem until the need to defend post-Tridentine Catholicism compelled him to devise a theory of his own. Again, Hampden's appeal to simplicity in belief and his refusal to identify faith with theology was a plea for religious feeling. He also realized that traditional Christianity would in the light of historical science inevitably come to assume a new aspect. But of its basic truth he declared he had as firm a conviction as had his critics. It was only that in his view a living theology was likely to be a theology awake to its own limitations.

Hampden's *University Sermons* (1848), always forthright and lucid, are a sustained critique of Tractarian ideas, which he saw as Romanism in a fresh guise. Was ecclesiastical tradition really to enjoy an authority parallel with the Bible? The new Oxford divinity, in allowing it the sole right to determine the sense of Scripture in fact accorded it precedence, whereas the witness of the apostolic writers is unique and whatever comes after it must be tested by it. Thought and experience may confirm the scriptural message, but they can neither add to nor alter it. Of itself tradition has no evidential value. Moreover, there is doubt as to where its authentic voice is to be heard. In general councils? In the papacy? There was no more reason, in Hampden's judgment, for believing in the infallibility of the one than of the other. Patristic exegesis has its value, but it, too, has no charisma of inerrancy. The use of theological terms varies from age to age and affords no unquestionable assurance of truth. Newman's doctrine of development also comes in for severe handling: the whole idea of an *unfolding* of religious truth is subject to the necessary proviso that the Church has actually possessed it from the beginning. And this only the Scriptures can demonstrate.

4. THOMAS ARNOLD

The last of the Oriel liberals to be considered here, a figure of greater interest than any of the others, is Thomas Arnold (1795–1842). Educated at Winchester and Corpus Christi College, Oxford, he was elected to an Oriel fellowship in 1815. At the age of thirty-three he became Master of Rugby School, a post his tenure of which was to mark him out as one of the greatest of English educationists. The caricature drawn by Lytton Strachey can at once be dismissed. Maliciously amusing, it is essentially false. But with Arnold the schoolmaster we are not now concerned.[1] As a religious thinker he is most impressive when expounding Scripture, of which he had a penetrative understanding not common in his day. Arnold's devotion to the Bible sprang from his own deep moral seriousness, coupled with an inherited reverence for what all Englishmen then regarded as the word of God. At root it was personal and rather naïve. Arnold did not approach the Bible as a theologian, for theologian he was not, and the philosophical theology then in the ascendant in Germany made no appeal to him: probably he knew little about it. Nor was he interested in the details, or even the methods, of scientific biblical criticism as this, too, was being developed in the German universities. Yet his great respect for the work of Neander, whom he knew personally, sharpened his appreciation of the importance of the critical attitude in biblical study. He is thus to be placed among the earliest of British divines to take

[1] See D. Newsome, *Godliness and Good Learning* (1961), ch. i.

account of the new historical perspectives. Nevertheless his
primary concern was with exegesis, and was motivated by his
unfailing sense of mission as a preacher and teacher. Criticism, he
realized, could not leave the traditional theology unaffected, and
its influence, unless disciplined by religious faith, might be
disastrous. Secure in his own beliefs, he felt it his duty to show
how the results of criticism fortified rather than weakened the
Bible as a witness to divine truth. His published *Sermons* (1829–34)
can still be rated an impressive attempt to uphold the Scriptures in
an age in which the fear was already growing that the biblical
foundations of Christianity were no longer safe.

The proper task of theology, as Arnold judged it, lay in
biblical exposition; but how was it to be performed? The
customary method had involved a culling of isolated texts, as
though the several books had 'all been composed at one time, and
addressed to persons similarly situated'. Obscurities, contradictions and moral stumbling-blocks hence remained unexplained.
What now was required was a historical view, enlarged by the
wider context of other religious and literary traditions, showing
revelation to have been progressive. This necessary discipline did
not imply, however, only a cold detachment, although some there
were for whom, truly enough, 'the Bible has presented itself to
their minds more frequently in connexion with their studies than
with their practice'. But as a book with a history it called for such
aids as historical science could provide; its difference from all
other books was that it contained the words of eternal life. The
theologian's responsibility was its sound interpretation, bringing
out the spiritual meaning as distinct from the merely literal or
historical. The fault of the allegorical method had been to
separate them altogether, in failing to realize that the historical
form is the necessary vehicle for the spiritual truth. Behind the
history, that is, stand certain 'general principles'. With these
prophecy 'is busy', and inasmuch as the particular nations,
persons and events represent the principles 'up to a point, so far
is it concerned also with them'. But their mixed character, as it
embraces and qualifies the judgment of the historian, must
'necessarily lower and qualify the promises and threatenings
of the prophet'. A Messianic prophecy (say) will thus, from the
historian's standpoint, refer to particular historical circumstances,
fairly clearly determinable. But beneath the surface play of far-

C

distant events there lies a deep and permanent truth, addressing itself to men's abiding spiritual wants, 'an answer given by God to the earnest questionings of their nature'. When we perceive the real significance of the prophetic utterance, Arnold contends, we realize that it is not simply predictive, a precise forecast of what is to come. The prophet's teaching is, rather, both a message for his contemporaries, in their own situation, and a truth effective for the future; the latter meaning, however, being latent and possibly unconscious. In so far as a prediction may be fulfilled it will be in substance, not in detail.

The influence of Coleridge upon Arnold's opinions seems here beyond doubt. In January 1835 Arnold wrote to Coleridge's nephew, Mr Justice Coleridge, asking whether he had seen his uncle's 'Letters on Inspiration' and noting their likely bearing on a matter which 'involves so great a shock to existing notions',[1] although he expresses also his own confidence that 'in spite of the fears and clamours of the weak and bigoted' the outcome will be 'the higher exalting and more sure establishing of Christian truth'. Indeed Coleridge's posthumously published *Confessions of an Inquiring Spirit*[2] is anticipated by Arnold in his own 'Essay on the Right Interpretation and Understanding of the Scriptures', which appeared in 1832, in the second volume of his *Sermons*. What Arnold has to say would today, of course, be considered trite, but it must be taken in the context of its time. Revelation, he argues, is progressive, accommodated to men's capacity to receive it. Christ himself 'must often have spoken as a man who possessed no greater knowledge than the men of that time and country'. Further, once it is understood that revelation is adapted to the circumstances of the recipient some at least of the moral problems presented by the Old Testament can be satisfactorily explained. Inspiration is not a guarantee of inerrancy nor does it displace the writer's own personality.

> Inspiration does not raise a man above his own time, nor make him even in respect to that which he utters when inspired, perfect in goodness and wisdom; but it so overrules his language that it shall contain a meaning more than his own mind was conscious of, and this gives it a character of divinity, and a power of perpetual application.

[1] A. P. Stanley, *The Life and Correspondence of Thomas Arnold, D.D.* (ed. 1898), ii, p. 69.
[2] See below, Ch. ii.

But criticism in dealing with the Bible's literary history, is not attempting to settle 'questions of religion' and does not disprove revelation.

Arnold believed that the best critical aid to the study of Scripture is a thorough general education, in particular a knowledge of history, and regretted that on this score the clergy were so often deficient. Arnold was not himself a very erudite man, but he had a breadth of mind which set him above most of his contemporaries.[1] More, he was a deeply convinced Christian who saw all life and experience as ideally related to Christian truth and morality, Thus he believed that society as such ought to be recognizably Christian; that, in the words of his biographer, 'the region of political and national questions, war and peace, oaths and punishments, economy and education, so long considered by good and bad alike as worldly and profane, should be looked upon as the very sphere in which Christian principles are the most applicable'.[2] Such an end, however, could be attained only if Christians themselves were visibly united. The sectarian or party spirit in religion Arnold detested. The historical divisions among Christians were a major source of weakness, especially when they rested on no really basic differences and could be regarded only as matters of opinion. He declared that he himself had one great principle: 'to insist strongly on the differences between Christian and non-Christian, and to sink into nothing the differences between Christian and Christian'.[3] The Church of the future would have to be truly comprehensive, although uncompromising on fundamentals. Dogmatic uniformity, in the nature of the case is an impossible goal and to insist upon it as a condition of unity will only render division permanent. The mark of a Christian, Arnold believed, is a readiness to worship Christ and all who do so may be reckoned members of a genuinely national church. Unitarians present an obvious difficulty, but as long as they are willing in principle to render such worship no pressure need be put on them to define their understanding of Christ's divinity. A

[1] A letter of his son, Matthew, dated 20 February 1869 (addressed to his mother), speaks of his father's 'immense superiority', 'mainly because, owing to his historic sense he was so wonderfully, for his nation, time, and profession, European . . .' See *Letters of Matthew Arnold*, ed. G. W. E. Russell (1895), ii, p. 5.

[2] A. P. Stanley, *op. cit.*, i, p. 126. A projected work of Arnold's on Christian politics was never carried out.

[3] *Ibid.*, p. 223.

formulary like the Thirty-nine Articles should be used positively, to secure agreement, not 'to serve as a test of latent error'.

Arnold in fact had little use for abstract theology. The Athanasian creed presumed to do what cannot be done and ought not to be attempted. The one test of any religion is its efficacy for moral good. God's self-revelation to man has a practical not a theoretical end, and Christian doctrine must be understood accordingly. 'There can be no more fatal error,' he wrote, 'none certainly more at variance with the Scripture model, than to acquaint the mind with the truths of religion in a theoretical form, leaving the application of them to be made afterwards.'[1] The method of Scripture is pragmatic, 'as producing a certain particular moral impression on our minds—not as declaring some positive truth in the nature of things',[2] a statement foreshadowing the argument elaborated many years later by his son in *Literature and Dogma*. The soul draws its nourishment from history more than from doctrines, and theology can easily become faith's enemy. Yet Arnold denied that his views were rationalistic or latitudinarian, and so far from minimizing the importance of church teaching he wished only to give it greater consistency and relevance. But it should be essential teaching, the gospel of truth itself. Subscription to formulae, when necessary, should be taken always in the broadest sense, 'except on points where they were especially interested to be stringent, and to express the opposite of some suspected opinion'. The Articles, subject to this proviso, are to be assumed to exclude 'Romish' doctrines, but they might at a pinch cover tender consciences. What mattered was sympathy with the Church 'in its main faith and feelings'.[3]

It was a cardinal point in Arnold's creed that Church and State have the same essential function and would ideally merge with one another.

> Civil society aims at the highest happiness of man according to the measure of its knowledge. Religious society aims at it truly and

---

[1] *Fragments on Church and State* in *Miscellaneous Works* (1845), Appendix II, p. 34.

[2] Thus God's moral attributes 'are of the last importance, because such as we suppose Him to be morally, such we strive to become ourselves; but opinions as to His nature metaphysically may be wholly unimportant, because they are often of such a kind as to be wholly inoperative upon our spiritual state: they neither advance us in goodness; nor obstruct our progress in it' ('Principles of Church Reform', in *Miscellaneous Works*, p. 325).

[3] Stanley, *op. cit.*, ii, p. 173.

really because it has obtained a complete knowledge of it. Impart then to civil society the knowledge of religious society, and the objects of both will be not only in intention but in fact the same. In other words, religious society is only civil society fully enlightened; the State in its highest perfection becomes the Church.

This was the old Hookerian principle in more modern guise: the Church is (or should be) the State in its religious aspect. Indeed, Arnold thinks that the State's officers actually perform a Christian service and are even in their way Christian ministers, no less than the accredited ministers of the Church. In case of necessity they should be empowered to discharge the latter's duties, including the administration of the sacraments. The Church's organization should be more democratic and rely less on a rigid and arbitrary distinction between clergy and laity.

Arnold had no objection to episcopacy as such, but the great obstacle to the united Church of his dreams was the doctrine of the episcopate as *jure divino* and the only legitimate system of ecclesiastical government, a doctrine which in principle un-churched an immense number of sincere followers of Christ. A just policy would encourage dissenters to return to the fold of a church at last become truly national. That such a Church should also be established was an advantage to society itself, not least in securing the presence throughout the country, in the persons of its territorial clergy, of a body of well-educated men 'whose sole business is to do good of the highest kind'—another echo of Coleridge.

Arnold's views, as set out in his *Principles of Church Reform* (1833), were widely condemned, especially by the clergy. That they should have been is scarcely surprising. His defence was that the times were critical and the situation urgent.

> I cannot [he wrote] get over my sense of the fearful state of public affairs; is it clean hopeless that the Church will come forward and crave to be allowed to reform itself? . . . I can have no confidence in what would be in men like —— but a death-bed repentance. It can only be done effectually by those who have not, through many a year of fair weather, turned a deep ear to the voice of reform, and will not be thought only to obey it because they cannot help it.[1]

His despair of the established Church in its existing condition left him no comfort: no human power, he thought, could save it.

[1] Stanley, *op. cit.*, i, p. 176.

To a friend about to leave for India as a missionary he declared: 'You are going from what bids fair, I fear, to deserve the name of a City of Destruction.' The tone of Arnold's utterances, it has to be said, is apt to be overstrained, and to the great majority of churchmen, not necessarily the complacent, his words gave offence.[1] Moreover, his proposed remedies, extremist and seemingly impractical, afforded no reassurance. Opposition came mainly from the Tractarians. Newman even feigned a wonder whether Arnold was a Christian.[2] But to Arnold in turn Tractarian doctrines were no less repugnant. The doctrine of the apostolic succession he dismissed as a sacerdotalist superstition. 'Bishops confer a *legal* qualification for the ministry, not a real one, whether natural or supernatural.'[3] Were the national Church to succumb to the new Oxford doctrines its essential character, as rooted in Protestantism, would be lost. Newman and his associates, he pointed out, made much of the witness of antiquity, but the evidence to which they appealed was that of the fourth century, not the first. Nor did they stand in the authentic tradition of Anglican divinity, and men like Hooker or Bull or Pearson would not have countenanced their teachings. But Arnold's bitterest attack came in his notorious *Edinburgh Review* article of 1836, written in defence of Hampden, entitled 'The Oxford Malignants'.[4] In this he overreached himself, his tone verging on the hysterical. Were, he proclaimed, 'the pitiful objects' of High Church fanaticism—'the fanaticism of mere foolery'—to be gained, 'they would make no man the wiser or better,—they would lead to no good, intellectual, moral, or spiritual—to no effect, social or religious, except to the changing of sense into silliness, and holiness of heart and life into formality and hypocrisy.' For this outburst Newman never forgave him.

[1] Yet the hardheaded Whately was almost as alarmist. 'Whatever turn things take', he wrote, 'I can see nothing that bodes well to the church establishment; I fear its days are numbered' (E. J. Whately, *The Life and Correspondence of Richard Whately* (1866), i, p. 159).

[2] See *Apologia* (ed. M. Svaglic), p. 42. Also A. Whitridge, *Dr. Arnold of Rugby* (1928), p. 170 n. Newman thought the contents of Arnold's pamphlet 'atrocious' (*Letters*, i, p. 332).

[3] *Principles of Church Reform*, in *Miscellaneous Works*, p. 329.

[4] The actual title was the editor's, not his own. His views on Tractarianism are more carefully stated in the Introduction to the collection of sermons, *Christian Life, its Course, its Hindrances, and its Helps* (1841), and in his discussion of Priesthood in the Appendix to Sermon xi of the third volume of the *Sermons*.

Arnold was not a very profound thinker nor, theologically, a very influential one. The real significance of the Oxford Movement he did not appreciate, whilst his liberalism was of the latitudinarian pattern then going out of date. Yet he left a mark on his times by the sheer force of personal character. His ideal of a national Church 'to Christianize the nation, and introduce the principles of Christianity into men's social and civil relations' was noble. A man of real faith, he was the embodiment of his own declared conviction that Christianity is primarily a way of life, not a creed or confession or speculative system. When he died at the early age of forty-seven his fellow-countrymen knew that a man of the finest moral grain had passed from their midst.

In concluding this chapter there is one more name to list, that of Connop Thirlwall (1797–1874), bishop of St David's for thirty-four years. He was not one of the Oriel group, having taken his degree (in law) at Trinity College, Dublin, but he was closely akin to them in temper and outlook. His lifelong concern was that Christian teaching should take positive account of the changing spirit of the times and the immense advances in human knowledge. Firmly convinced that the critical intelligence cannot be debarred from the religious sphere, he was far from being a narrow rationalist and possessed a rare capacity for seeing both sides of a question. But a keen judgment joined with considerable learning made him a formidable figure among nineteenth-century liberal churchmen. His episcopal charges in particular afford an invaluable commentary on some of the chief intellectual issues of the mid-century, as a clearsighted Christian viewed them. His legal training also stood him in good stead, for he was never misled by irrelevancies or rhetoric. His earliest published work, dating from 1825, when he was still a layman, was his translation of Schleiermacher's *Essay on St Luke*. The great German theologian was even then little known in England, although his name provoked fear. Thirlwall prefaced the book with an introduction of his own, in which he observed that 'it would almost seem as if at Oxford the knowledge of German subjected a divine to the same suspicion of heterodoxy which we know was attached some centuries back to a knowledge of Greek'.[1] His personal opinions, like his choice of author, displayed some courage. Thirlwall was among the few in England

[1] *Translation, with Introduction, of Schleiermacher's Critical Essay on St Luke*, p. ix.

who through proficiency in the German language were familiar with contemporary German thought. His interest in biblical studies was stimulated by acquaintance with the German scholar-diplomat, Baron Bunsen, and by his friendship with Julius Hare (a disciple of Coleridge), with whom he collaborated in a translation of Niebuhr's *History of Rome*. He did not, however, succumb to the fascination of Hegel, then at the height of his fame and influence. On the contrary, his reaction was one of complete antipathy, and the foremost philosopher in Europe he dismissed as an impudent literary quack. Whether this failure in appreciation is to be attributed to unusual insight or simply to an intellectual 'blind spot' opinions will differ.

The bishop's views on the controverted subject of Tractarianism were temperate. Whether the Oxford teachings were or were not compatible with the doctrine of the Church of England was, in the light of history, a matter not easily to be settled. The national Church had from the start aimed at comprehension and hence had tolerated more than one theological tradition. At the time also of the *Essays and Reviews* uproar in the 'sixties Thirlwall struck a balanced attitude. Liberal though he was he felt that the contributors had gone too far and that their book was a potential danger. Yet he had no doubt that the policy of hushing up the more disconcerting implications of biblical criticism was a mistaken one and that when free inquiry was permitted views like theirs were to be expected. They could properly be met only on their own terrain, candidly and with a sufficiency of knowledge. On the point of biblical inspiration he maintained that a critical judgment does not preclude belief that the Scriptures are truly inspired and that their authors had been secured from material error. But 'verbalist' theories were to be rejected, the limits of inspiration not being exactly definable. The pious reader can be sure only that where needed it had been given and may assume that what fell within the writer's own experience or had been related by him on the testimony of inspired witnesses required no special charisma.

It should be evident even from such a relatively brief survey as we have undertaken that English theology during the first three decades of the last century was not nearly as moribund as has sometimes been said. For the Evangelicals, narrowly channelled though their thinking was, religious belief was still a vital force. High Church doctrine too had exponents personally committed to the principles for which they stood; whilst liberal churchmen were already prescient of issues which the future was to render increasingly important. What, on the other hand, was lacking among all parties and groups was a new intellectual and imaginative stimulus. Attitudes were conventional and determined for the most part by traditional alignments. This was true even of the Noetics, who owed more to the eighteenth century than they seem to have realized. Happily new impulses were soon to make themselves felt. Evangelicalism, it is true, was to continue for a good many years yet in an intellectual doldrums, but High Church orthodoxy, without in any way modifying its basic positions, was, under the subtly compulsive leadership of Newman, to acquire a wholly fresh vigour. But for Anglicanism generally another factor had emerged, the effects of which were quickly to become apparent, leaving no party untouched by it. This was the mind of Samuel Taylor Coleridge, to whom we now must turn.

Chapter II

Coleridge

I. THE PHILOSOPHER

It was John Stuart Mill, a man of a totally different disposition and outlook, who, in often-quoted words, described Coleridge as one of 'the two great seminal minds of England of their age', the second, of course, being Jeremy Bentham.[1] 'By Bentham beyond all others', he judged, 'men have been led to ask themselves in regard to any ancient or received opinion, Is it true? and by Coleridge, What is the meaning of it?'[2] The contrast thus noted indicates at once the bias and the strength of both men. Bentham, a rationalist impatient of humbug, was typically a child of the eighteenth century. Coleridge, on the other hand, a poet as well as a critic and philosopher, proclaimed the ideals of a new age of visionary romanticism. That Mill appreciated his genius as perceptively and as generously as he did is no little testimony to the breadth of his own mind. His pithy account of the romantic revolution could hardly, in fact, be bettered. 'The Germano-Coleridgean doctrine', he suggested, expressed the revolt of the human mind against the philosophy of the preceding century: it was 'ontological' because that was 'experimental'; conservative and religious, because that was 'innovative' and infidel; concrete and historical, because that was abstract and metaphysical. The old had been prosaic, the new was poetical.[3] Mill's genuine admiration for Coleridge is beyond doubt: no one of his time, he considered, had 'contributed more to shape the opinions of those

---

[1] *Dissertations and Discussions* (1867), i, p. 330.
[2] *Ibid.*, p. 394.
[3] *Ibid.*, p. 403.

among its younger men, who can be said to have opinions at all'. Yet in his personal philosophy he reveals nothing of Coleridge's influence, and so far as his *Essays on Religion* are concerned the author of *Aids to Reflection* might never have uttered a word on the subject.

The singular originality of Coleridge's genius has its witness in all who studied him closely enough to admit some reflexion of it. One of the earliest of these was Thomas Arnold, who acknowledged Coleridge as 'a very great man indeed, whose equal I know not where to find in England'. Newman, though critical and guarded in his language, was also deeply impressed.[1] Julius Hare, an avowed Coleridgean, recalled in 1848 how twenty years before it was beginning to be said by not a few that the poet-philosopher was 'the true sovereign of modern English thought'.[2] F. D. Maurice, who more, probably, than any other is reckoned an apostle of the Coleridgean teachings, confessed his great debt to Coleridge in the preparation of his own book, *The Kingdom of Christ*, declaring that it was mainly from him that contemporary theology had learned how 'the highest truths are those which are beyond the limits of Experience' and that 'the essential principles of the Reason are those which cannot be proved by syllogisms'.[3] 'The power of perceiving', he added, 'that by the very law of the Reason the Knowledge of God must be *given* to it; that the moment it attempts to create its Maker, it denies itself . . . I must acknowledge that I received from him.'

Always an omnivorous reader, Coleridge possessed a capacity for assimilating ideas which has rarely been equalled. Yet whatever ideas were borrowed they acquired from him a new life and character. A highly idiosyncratic thinker, his opinions show his personality at every turn. What unhappily he lacked was the

[1] In an article on 'The Prospects of the Anglican Church' published in 1838, he wrote: 'And while history in prose and verse was thus made the instrument of Church feelings and opinions (i.e. by Sir Walter Scott), a philosophical basis for the same was under formation in England by a very original thinker (i.e. Coleridge) who, while he indulged a liberty of speculation which no Christian can tolerate, and advanced conclusions which were often heathen rather than Christian, yet after all instilled a higher philosophy into inquiring minds, than they had hitherto been accustomed to accept' (*Essays Critical and Historical*, ed. 1897, p. 268). See also p. 135 below.

[2] See his edition of Sterling's *Essays and Tales*, p. xiv. Hare's own *The Mission of the Comforter* (1846) is dedicated 'To the honoured memory of Samuel Taylor Coleridge, the Christian Philosopher.'

[3] *The Kingdom of Christ* (ed. 1842), p. xxv.

capacity to organize his thinking, or at any rate the literary expression of it, on an extended scale. His writings in consequence are bewilderingly unsystematic. He jumps from point to point, from theme to theme, as the mood, or some inward and personal logic, impels him. But for all his idiosyncrasy and defect of system Coleridge is by no means a confused thinker. The pattern of his doctrine, we may be sure, was clear enough in his own head. What emerged in print, or was scribbled down in his notebooks, is often tantalizingly haphazard and ambiguous, and inconsistencies remain, however patiently the underlying unity may be sought. But to suppose that, in the words of one hostile critic, Coleridge was 'a slothful, pusillanimous dreamer, in whom sincerity, if it ever existed, had been destroyed by the use of laudanum', would be the grossest of errors.[1] Despite the vices which so disorganized his personal life as to render necessary the protective care bestowed upon him over his last years by the admirable Dr Gilman, his intellectual keenness, his acute spiritual sensitivity and his moral integrity are beyond question. For all his weaknesses and failures Coleridge was a soul *naturaliter christiana*.

To separate the many interwoven threads of his philosophy is, then, a task far from easy. He must be read sympathetically and always with the closest attention. At times he is baffling. Often he is tortuous and obscure. Truth comes to him by intermittent flashes of insight. He will pursue an idea for the fascinating prospect that suddenly opens up before him, and then as suddenly abandon it for some other equally alluring. Such is his way, but the reader must take him for what he is and for what he so liberally gives. And the gifts, as in recent years we have come more and more to appreciate, are superlatively rich. Indeed, satisfaction with the much that he did accomplish is qualified only by regret for being without the more which, with a greater self-discipline, he might have accomplished. But a man's nature is not a matter of option. Coleridge is both an astonishing and a dis-

---

[1] A. W. Benn, *The History of English Rationalism in the Nineteenth Century* (1906), i, p. 262f. On the other hand a very favourable critic also admits that Coleridge's 'system'—if it may be so called—'was really a strategy for reconciling conflicting oppositions in his own mind, and it is perfectly obvious that some of his manœuvres were less successful than others'. What matters, however, is 'the rich variety of complex philosophical and religious opinions which filtered through the mind of this genius' (James D. Boulger, *Coleridge as Religious Thinker* (1961), p. 219).

appointing genius. Had his talents been more prosaic his luminous insight might have been less bright. He could have been one of the greatest philosophers of modern times had he submitted his exuberant intelligence—not to mention his personal conduct—to a stricter control. That he did not it is idle to deplore. As it is this country has produced few thinkers of his order, whilst his right to be considered one of the Church of England's most brilliant sons is beyond doubt.

2. REASON AND UNDERSTANDING

In early manhood Coleridge's thinking had been swayed by a mechanistic philosophy. His release from this in the first years of the new century is described at length in the *Biographia Literaria*,[1] where the Hartleian school comes in for some abrasive criticism. His disillusionment with associationist doctrines, therefore, need not detain us. What had attracted him to this philosophy was the simplicity of its explanations: any idea could be reduced to the pattern of its antecedent mental vibrations and every act of will made the product of mechanical force. But by March 1801 he could no longer accept it or 'the irreligious metaphysics of modern infidels' that accompanied it. The human mind, he now saw, is not merely passive but has its own energy and creativity—it is not simply receptive of objects but can in some way be said to enter into them. Hence 'any system built on the passiveness of the mind must be false, as a system'.[2] What in fact he had come to realize was that the mind's constitutional energy is the *will*. Deny this, he thought, and the ground beneath both ethics and theology gives way. Man's fundamental conviction of volitional freedom, his capacity for originative action, are something of which abstract argument has no power to deprive him: 'It is the principle of our personality.' But Coleridge's mechanistic period was over before he had begun to reflect seriously on religious questions and it had no real influence upon his later views. What is of importance was that a heavy impediment had been cast off, once for all. And along with associationism went also the Socinianism he had imbibed from Joseph Priestley, leaving him with the orthodox Christianity in

[1] Chaps. 8 and 9.
[2] *Letters*, ed. E. H. Coleridge (1895), i, p. 352.

which he had been brought up. Having gone the whole hog he was able, as he afterwards put it, 'to come right round to the other side'.[1]

The fact of man's freedom is, then, the basis of a Christian philosophy; but we do not know the meaning of freedom, of a 'responsible will', apart from the law of conscience and the existence of evil: evil, that is, which is essentially such and 'not by accident of outward circumstances, nor derived from its physical consequences, nor from any cause, out of itself'.[2] The law of conscience, like the responsibility of the will, is a 'fact of consciousness', the existence of evil being a 'fact of history'. Thus Coleridge opposes both the necessitarianism of men like Hobbes, and its contrary, the deism of Shaftesbury and his followers:

> In contradiction to their splendid but delusory tenets, I profess a deep conviction that man was and is a *fallen* creature, not by accident of bodily constitution, or any other cause which *human* wisdom in a course of ages might be supposed capable of removing; but as diseased in the *will*, in that will which is the true, and only synonime of the word, I, or the intelligent Self.[3]

In these truths the Christian thinker has his starting-point. To Coleridge they were the postulate of a new type of apologetic.

Just such an apology *Aids to Reflection* was designed to be, and we fail to appreciate either its inherent importance or the nature of its author's procedure—daunting enough to the modern reader who takes up the book without previous warning of what he should expect—unless we relate it to its theological back-ground. When it appeared in 1825 it offered an altogether fresh approach to Christianity as understood in terms of Anglican orthodoxy. Its novelty indeed was too much for its immediate contemporaries, who in the main chose to ignore it. Current religious discussion, in so far as it ventured upon philosophical problems at all, fastened on the 'evidences' of Christianity, chiefly in an attempt to refute the sceptic Hume. Coleridge's aim was to break entirely with these arid and unconvincing methods.

---

[1] *The Table Talk*, ed. H. N. Coleridge, 1835, p. 517, entry for June 23, 1834: 'I think Priestley must be considered the author of modern Unitarianism. I owe, under God, my return to the faith, to my having gone much further than the Unitarians, and so having come round to the other side.'

[2] See *Aids to Reflection* (Bohn's Library ed.), pp. 190f.

[3] *Ibid.*, p. 92.

> I more than fear [he wrote] the prevailing taste for books of Natural
> Theology, Physico-Theology, Demonstrations of God from Nature,
> Evidences of Christianity, and the like. Evidences of Christianity!
> I am weary of the word. Make a man feel the want of it; rouse him,
> if you can, to the self-knowledge of his need of it; and you may
> safely trust to its own Evidence.[1]

For not only was evidence-theology useless—ineffectual for its
own end; it was also false in principle. Its procedure was purely
rationalistic and made no appeal to religious feeling. To the
believer external evidences are unnecessary: he builds his faith
on other grounds; whilst to the philosophically-minded unbeliever
they rest on a mistaken premise. The reader Coleridge sought to
address was the intelligent doubter, especially if he were among
the young, whom the conventional arguments left untouched.
He himself held Christianity to be such a faith as a reasonable man
could reasonably embrace, and that the objections commonly
brought against it may be fully met. But not only was Christianity
reasonable; it is, he was persuaded, the very 'Perfection of Human
Intelligence', the sum and fulfilment of all truths. That there
are many speculative difficulties to be faced he did not deny; but
speculative difficulties, if no more than speculative, can be put
aside, since religious truth is not discoverable by speculation
merely as such. The only substantial objections would be moral,[2]
and for readers sensitive to these he admits a special concern.
Difficulties at the purely intellectual level, that is, do not necessarily
preclude the holding of a reasonable faith, for faith is practical,
not theoretical, and Christianity a life, not a philosophy.[3] To one
who asks for proof Coleridge would simply reply, Try it; the
truth of the Christian religion is self-testifying. 'Ideas, that
derive their origin and substance from the *Moral* Being, and to
the reception of which as true *objectively* (that is, as corresponding
to a *reality* out of the human mind) we are determined by a
practical interest exclusively.'[4]

The basis of faith, then, is not argument but experience, and
deep thinking is attainable only by a man of deep feeling. All truth
is a species of revelation; it cannot be possessed unless the heart
has 'fed' upon it. Christian doctrine, to be meaningful, must be
understood (as we now would say) existentially. In attacking the
current evidence theology his particular target was Paley, whose

[1] *Ibid.*, p. 272.   [2] p. 103.   [3] p. 134.   [4] p. 108.

smug and superficial apologetic was repugnant to him. The author of the *Evidences of Christianity* and the *Principles of Moral and Political Philosophy* was a rationalist appealing to rationalistic criteria in order to impress other rationalists. But Coleridge saw also that the rationalistic method, however misconceived, was specious and popular. Its point was obvious: the average 'intellectual' Christian, persuading himself that his own belief rested on such arguments, assumed that others were to be won over by the same means. *Aids to Reflection* was an attempt to dispel this illusion and put something real in its place. As Coleridge once wrote to Wordsworth, what was needed was a

> general revolution in the modes of developing and disciplining the human mind by the substitution of life and intelligence ... for the philosophy of mechanism, which, in everything that is most worthy of the human intellect, strikes *Death*, and cheats itself by mistaking clear images for distinct conceptions, and which idly demands conceptions where intuitions alone are possible or adequate to the majesty of the Truth.[1]

That such a mechanical philosophy as Paley's should pass, in the universities as among readers generally, for a serious Christian philosophy was a fact which irked Coleridge beyond endurance. He found himself bound 'in conscience to throw the whole force of my intellect in the way of this [Paley's] triumphal car, on which the tutelary genius of modern Idolatry is borne, even at the risk of being crushed under the wheels'.[2] No man ought to be argued into faith, even were it possible. Instead he should be led to feel within himself the vital need of it; and a genuine philosophy of belief would help him to do so. Spiritual things must be spiritually discerned, we learn them through moral experience only.

> The Law of Conscience, and not the Canons of discursive Reasoning, must decide in such cases. At least, the latter have no validity, which the single veto of the former is not sufficient to nullify. The most pious conclusion is here the most legitimate.[3]

The authority of Christianity is to be seen not in logical demonstration, the procedures of which are inapplicable in this realm,

---

[1] *Letters*, ii, p. 649.
[2] *Aids to Reflection*, p. 273.
[3] *Ibid.*, pp. 108f.

but in its power to meet the needs of our humanity. And of this each must judge for himself.

What we must learn to realize, Coleridge teaches, is that spiritual truth is to be apprehended by man only in the fulness of his personal being. It cannot be a matter chiefly of the feelings, as many Evangelicals seemed to suppose. Reason too has its necessary part, for although the mere intellect is unable to make any certain discovery of 'a holy and intelligent cause' it nevertheless may supply a demonstration, in order that no legitimate argument may be drawn from the intellect *against* its truth. Yet the conviction is not to be resisted that religion, as both the cornerstone and the keystone of morality, must have a *moral* origin. At all events the evidence of its doctrines is not, like the truths of abstract science, independent of the will.[1] Faith, rather, is an energy relating to the whole man, 'in each and all of his constituents, faculties and tendencies'.[2]

These considerations bring us to Coleridge's primal distinction between the reason and the understanding, a parallel to the one he draws in aesthetic theory between the fancy and the imagination. Both imagination and reason are, he holds, to be stressed as against the modern mind's infection with 'the contagion of its mechanic philosophy'. Coleridge's conception of reason is peculiar. It does not signify 'reasoning', in the usual sense. The latter he would cover by the word 'understanding'. Reason, he thinks, is essentially 'the organ of the supersensuous', whereas understanding is 'the faculty of judging according to sense'. The one is 'the science of phenomena', the other 'the Power of Universal and necessary Convictions, the Source and Substance of Truths above Sense, and having their evidence in themselves'.[3] Understanding deals with means, reason with ultimate ends. Reason is the eye of the spirit, understanding the mind of the flesh. The latter remains 'commensurate with the experimental notices of the sense from which it is generalized', the former 'either predetermines experience, or avails itself of a past experience to supersede its necessity in all future time'. Reason's capacity is to affirm truths 'which no sense could perceive, nor experiment verify, nor experience confirm'. The understanding,

---

[1] *Biographia Literaria*, ed. J. Shawcross (1907), i, pp. 134f.
[2] *Aids to Reflection* ('An Essay on Faith'), p. 349.
[3] *Ibid.*, p. 143.

needless to say, has a large and a perfectly legitimate use; its concern is with measurement and analysis, abstraction and classification, in short, with the method of natural science. We employ it necessarily and consistently in the affairs of daily life. With reason, however, there is

> an *Intuition* or *im*mediate Beholding, accompanied by a conviction of the necessity and universality of the truth so beholden not derived from the senses, which intuition, when it is *construed* by *pure* sense, gives birth to the Science of Mathematics, and when applied to objects supersensuous or spiritual is the organ of Theology and Philosophy.[1]

The mistake of the age was to suppose that the understanding is competent to treat of what belongs to the sphere of the reason. This confounding of one mode or order of knowledge with another had led to the 'godless revolution' which had installed utilitarianism, determinism and atheist materialism in the place of spiritual religion, or alternatively had reduced spiritual religion to mere rationalism, its mysteries 'cut and squared for the comprehension of the understanding', after the manner of eighteenth-century divinity. Coleridge's whole position is well summarized in a passage in *The Friend*, a weekly paper which he edited from 1809 to 1810.[2] 'The groundwork of all true philosophy', he there says,

> is the full apprehension of the difference between the contemplation of reason, namely that intuition of things which arises when we possess ourselves *as one with the whole* . . . and that which presents itself when . . . we think of ourselves as separated beings, and place nature in antithesis to mind, as object to subject, thing to thought, death to life. (Italics ours.)[3]

In *The Statesman's Manual*—'a Lay Sermon', as he calls it, published in 1816—Coleridge undertakes some further explanation of what he sees the place of reason in religion to be. The two things, religion and reason, he points out, differ only as a twofold application of the same power. Reason is neither sense nor understanding nor imagination, but contains within itself all three,[4]

---

[1] P. 155 n.

[2] It originally comprised twenty-eight numbers. It was reissued in 1812 with supplementary matter; and again, with some new material, in 1818.

[3] Bohn's Library ed., p. 366.

[4] 1839 ed., Appendix B, p. 266.

although it cannot in strictness be described as a faculty, much less a personal property, of any human mind. Religion is 'the consideration of the particular and the individual . . . as it exists and has its being in the universal'. If, in other words, in a too exclusive devotion to the specific and individual religion 'neglects to interpose the contemplation of the universal' it becomes superstition. Even so, it is never an abstract matter. It is born, not made, and thus, being a sort of organism, must grow. As the finite expression of the unity of the infinite Spirit it is 'a broad act of the soul', a life within a life.[1]

It has commonly been assumed that Coleridge owed his distinction between reason and understanding to Kant, and certainly the influence of Kant upon his English admirer's thinking was deep and lasting. Coleridge first became acquainted with the *Critique of Pure Reason* in about 1799 and was forthwith converted. But Kant's was by no means the sole influence. In any case it probably was more formal than material, and 'to have resided', as Shawcross puts it, 'rather in the scientific statement of convictions previously attained than in the acquisition of new truths'.[2] Kant, that is, enabled Coleridge to give intellectual definition to a view already emerging from his reading of the seventeenth century English Platonists and one which remained fundamentally more Platonist than Kantian in its inspiration.[3] As the poet made his way through the writings of men like John Smith, Henry More and Archbishop Leighton he was more and more delighted with a conception of reason differing entirely from the arid intellectualism still current in his day. Rationalist reason appeared to alienate faith altogether; the two principles were virtually antithetical. But as the Cambridge Platonists saw it reason and faith were essentially one; reason indeed was 'the candle of the Lord'. It was not, in Smith's words, a faculty, 'but

[1] *Ibid.*, p. 282.
[2] *Biographia Literaria*, i, p. 198.
[3] The Kantian element in Coleridge's philosophy is especially emphasized by both Rene Wellek (*Kant in England*, 1931), and Elizabeth Winkelmann (*Coleridge und die Kantische Philosophie*, 1933). Wellek finds the combination of the critical Kantian with the mystical Platonist elements to have resulted in a basic inconsistency, and concludes that Coleridge finally 'gave up any attempts at a solution and came to take for granted the dualism of speculation and life, of the head and the heart'. 'At length', he says, 'he seduced the struggling spirit to acquiesce in immediate knowledge and faith, he lured it to enjoy a mere feeling of mystery and to give up the labor of thinking penetration into problems' (*Kant in England*, p. 134).

rather a light, which we enjoy, but the source of which is not in ourselves, nor rightly by any individual to be denominated *mine*'. Reason, as an emanation of the divine, is seen here as the necessary vehicle or medium of spiritual experience at its fullest, as opposed to the merely discursive or reflective function of individual reasoning. Yet it was evident also that the Platonists had no clearly conceived epistemology. 'What they all wanted was a pre-inquisition into the mind, as part organ, part constituent of all knowledge.' They, however, had lived in an older world and did not have to face the type of problem now posed. For them any difficulty of the 'lower' reason could be solved by appeal to a 'higher'. But the work of Locke and Hume had made this expedient impossible. What was needed, Coleridge realized, was a logical propaedeutic, a systematic investigation of the human intellect as such 'which, previously to the weighing and measuring of this or that, begins by assaying the weights, measure, and scales themselves'. This task, envisaged long before by Bacon, had now been accomplished by Kant in his great *Critique*.

Coleridge imbibed Kant with characteristic zest, but the main attraction of Kantianism lay for him in the Transcendental Dialectic. The Aesthetic, he was confident, had shown that the 'understanding' faculty was the legitimate instrument of truth in scientific inquiry; yet the fact was that Coleridge, for all his immense curiosity, was not himself greatly interested in the grounds and scope of scientific knowledge, at least as compared with metaphysical, theological and literary questions. It was not unnatural, therefore, that he should have stressed the negative side of what Kant had said about the understanding, to the neglect of the more positive, dealt with at length in the Transcendental Analytic. What struck him most about Kant's teaching was the principle that the understanding, of its very constitution, is incapable of establishing truth in the realm of metaphysics, ethics and theology. Kant's purpose of supplying a sound philosophical basis for Euclidean geometry and Newtonian physics could well take care of itself, the possibility of scientific knowledge being beyond all doubt. But science, so the Dialectic had demonstrably shown, could not extend its territory into the metaphysical. The processes of the 'pure speculative reason', in Kantian terminology, are not 'synthetic'. Pure reason has no finally satisfying object, since on the great metaphysical issues—

God, the Self, Freedom, Immortality—it arrives only at contradictory conclusions. Metaphysical knowledge is not, therefore, possible. Kant's solution of the difficulty is to distinguish between what he calls the noumenal and the phenomenal. Noumenal ideas are not scientific, but have only a *regulative* force. They are essentially practical: we must act *as if* they were true and valid, even though they cannot be grasped with the scientific understanding. Yet it was this side of Kant's doctrine which most deeply impressed the theologians and philosophers of the nineteenth century, encouraging them, moreover, in the very kind of speculation which on the principles of the critical philosophy was henceforth to be excluded. Coleridge himself was no exception.

For Kant, it seemed to him, had succeeded in delivering the really important truths—the truths of faith and religion—from the thraldom of mere logic. Hume's objections, before which the customary apologetic appeared impotent, had now been met. But was it enough that metaphysical ideas should have only a regulative function, a merely postulated validity? What Coleridge desiderated for them was the ontological reality which they possessed for the Platonists. In contrast, therefore, to the 'understanding'—Kant's pure speculative reason—Coleridge asserted the existence of a 'higher reason' for which the great truths of the spirit were truths indeed, not simply plausible assumptions.[1] Kant's 'practical reason' thus becomes something more than what he himself was content to understand it. For Coleridge 'the Practical Reason alone is Reason in the full and substantial sense'. It is reason 'in its own sphere of perfect freedom; as the source of IDEAS, which Ideas, in their conversation to the responsible Will, become Ultimate Ends'.[2] In other words, the reason is no less valid a means of apprehending truth than is the understanding. Spiritual experience can *know* itself to have an objective ground—without presumably having to render any account of itself in terms of an inappropriate, and perhaps inconvenient, logic. Such at least is the impression that Coleridge's argument often conveys. *Le cœur a ses raisons que la raison ne connaît pas.* Hence the charge that he used Kantian language as a cloak for Platonist doctrine and that his

[1] In this he received further encouragement from the German mystical writer, F. H. Jacobi, for whom reason is the 'eye' wherewith man beholds spiritual realities.
[2] *Aids to Reflection*, p. 277 n.

thought fails to resolve the inconsistency of a fundamental dualism.[1]

So long as we confine ourselves to Coleridge's attempt simply to define what he means by reason the conclusion would indeed seem warranted. Certainly his definitions are not free from ambiguity. A more fruitful approach is to study the *use* which he makes of his distinction when confronted with the actual data of Christian experience. For Coleridge is a religious man in the process of thinking out his faith, and although the relationship between faith and speculative thought may defy precise formulation, in the full context of a living experience the problem assumes a different aspect. Coleridge's religious philosophy is in this sense a practical one. His answers may dismay the rationalist and the dogmatist, but, like Pascal or Newman or Kierkegaard, he was a man for whom any *rationale* of faith must be made in essentially personal terms. To have tried to put it on a purely objective basis would in his view have been a misapplication of the function of the 'understanding'. As he saw it it was something which every man must work out for himself, by resort to criteria which in the long run are peculiar to himself. Herein lies Coleridge's chief significance as a religious thinker, for after him it was impossible to omit the subjective consciousness from any serious discussion of the basic issues of religious belief. And beside him virtually all of his immediate British contemporaries seem to belong to a different intellectual world.

3. CHRISTIAN BELIEF[2]

Turning now to Coleridge's view of the content of religious faith, we find it dominated by his belief in God as a Being with whom man can hold communion. The gravest error of deism—a creed as cheerless as atheism itself—was its denial of an assurance without which we may have a philosophy but not a religion. So far is man from being alien to God that he himself participates in the divine nature.

[1] Cp. Boulger, *Coleridge as Religious Thinker*, p. 84: '[Coleridge's] was an adventure in the meaning of faith, incomprehensible alike to those for whom it implies a retreat into fancy, and for those for whom it implies a steady objectivity.... What he offers is an authentic example of the religious mind reporting a variety of experiences in religion to religious dogma; the validity of this experiment in the strict sense no man can judge.'

[2] For an attempted systematization of Coleridge's mature views on Christian doctrine see J. Robert Barth, *Coleridge and Christian Doctrine* (1969).

Whenever by self-subjection to this universal light, the will of the individual, the *particular* will, has become a will of reason, the man is regenerate, and reason is then the spirit of the regenerated man, whereby the person is capable of a quickening communion with the Divine Spirit.[1]

The mediator, or the effort, connecting 'the misery of the self' with the blessedness of God is *prayer*. But first the reason must be justified in its claim that God really exists as more than an impersonal Absolute. That any fully rational demonstration of this kind is possible Kant had very plausibly disallowed: divine existence is not open to speculative proof. Coleridge agrees, therefore, that faith is the prerequisite. It was in vain, he tells us, that he looked round to discover a vacant place for a *science* whose result had to be the 'knowledge and assertainment' of God. Proofs of divine existence founded either on the senses or on reasonings from them are to be discounted, along with the type of theology which appeals to them. The ever-popular argument from design Coleridge admits to being superficially impressive, but he rejects it as firmly as did Hume; not, however, merely from the consideration that it would prove the existence only of a limited deity, a demiurge, but because to infer that nature's adaptations necessarily imply intelligence in the creative force behind them is to beg the whole question. The conclusion has in fact been assumed as a premise. But although the traditional arguments are too faulty to be of any real service, the exposure of their faults, Coleridge thinks, does not of itself prove that all rational argument in this regard is unavailing. Rather is it that the idea of God is something which, in Lockean phrase, 'cannot be conveyed into the mind' at all. An idea of this order can only be conjured up, or brought into consciousness, by an appropriate experience. The arguments have a certain subjective effectiveness, but the proper task of philosophy is to designate the kind of experience which does induce belief in God and to help remove the obstacles which may impede its full acceptance. Yet when all is said such belief 'could not be intellectually more evident without becoming morally less effective; without counteracting its own end by sacrificing the *life* of faith to the cold mechanism of a worthless because compulsory assent'.[2] Faith, that is, is neither a

[1] *Aids to Reflection*, p. 143.
[2] *Biographia Literaria*, i, p. 136.

matter exclusively of the 'heart', of the emotions, nor of the 'head', the purely intellectual judgment, but is the reasoned belief of a practical man.[1]

Coleridge, then, thought of the God of experience as living and active, and the indwelling light and life of all mankind. But since the divine light lighteth every man no sharp distinction can be drawn between natural religion and revealed. The parcel of truth in any religion is *ipso facto* revealed. That there is a pantheistic tendency here is to be conceded, and other passages in Coleridge's writings having a pantheistic tone can readily be instanced; but the claim that the whole drift of his thought inevitably carried him into pantheism may be dismissed. He had certainly at one time been influenced by Schelling, finding in the latter's *Natur-Philosophie* and *System des Transcendentalen Idealismus* 'a general coincidence' with a good deal in his own thinking, especially Schelling's theory of the imagination, which appeared to confirm his personal aesthetic doctrines. But further consideration awakened a more critical judgment. 'The more I reflect', he wrote, 'the more I am convinced of the gross materialism which underlies the whole system'.[2] Idealistic monism could not be reconciled with Christian dualism. 'In short, Schelling's System and mine stand thus: In the latter there are God and Chaos: in the former an Absolute Somewhat, which is *alternately* both, the rapid legerdemain shifting of which constitutes the delusive appearance of Poles.'[3] The idealist Absolute was impersonal and abstract, whereas for Coleridge personality, in man and in God, is a fact always of supreme value. Schelling's *Ich* was not the living, personal subject, but a mere logical principle, the first step in a system in which a personal deity could have no place. As soon as Coleridge realized this—and his notebooks provide

---

[1] Thus J. H. Muirhead goes so far as to claim that Coleridge's philosophy is 'in a true sense metaphysical rather than mystical'. 'Coleridge was prepared . . . to admit that in the end *omnia in mysteria exeunt*. But he was also prepared to maintain that it is only following our reason that we are able to discover when we come to that end, and to protect ourselves against the mistake, not to say the arrogance, of drawing the line where it happens to suit our prejudices or the desires of our indisciplined hearts' (in *Coleridge Studies by Several Hands*, ed. E. Blunden and E. L. Griggs (1936), p. 197).

[2] See *Biographia Literaria*, i, p. 248 and section vi of Shawcross's Introduction.

[3] Unpublished Notebook 28, ff 30ᵛ–31 (quoted Boulger, p. 108). Coleridge's manuscript notebooks are in the British Museum. On Coleridge's alleged pantheism see T. McFarland, *Coleridge and the Pantheist Tradition* (1969).

copious evidence of the way his thought developed—he fell
back more and more upon a metaphysic of the traditional
Christian kind. God could not be the source of the indubitable
reality of moral evil. The object of faith and worship is not some
sort of *anima mundi*, nor the doctrine of the divine omnipresence,
whatever its difficulties, be expressed simply by the maxim
Jupiter est quodcunque vides, since in Christian theology omnipresence
means that all things are present *to* God, not that they *are* God.
Unless God is truly personal the spiritual experience of man
becomes unintelligible. 'To hesitate to call God a person is like
hesitating to speak of the root which is antecedent to stem and
branches.' The all-important thing about man himself is his
personality; the reality, therefore, that is beyond sense cannot
itself be less than personal. The visible universe *manifests* deity:
God is to be perceived *in* it, by the eye of the spirit. Underlying
both nature and the interpreting mind there is a principle of
identity: that which is known is *like* that which knows it.

> The fact, therefore, that the mind of man in its primary and con-
> stituent forms represents the laws of nature, is a mystery which of
> itself should suffice to make us religious; for it is a problem, of which
> God is the only solution, the one before all, and of all, and through all.[1]

None the less there is a difference between personality as we know
it in ourselves and the personality which we ascribe to God.
Divine personality includes the qualities which belong to ours,
but in a higher degree of perfection. Coleridge even coins a new
word, 'Personeity', to mark the difference.

But he is by no means insensitive to the problem of reconciling
the order of the universe disclosed by science with the idea of
God demanded by the religious consciousness; an idea which
requires belief in providence and renders prayer natural and
meaningful. Such an idea can be sustained by faith, understood
as the *fidelity* or personal adherence of the individual will to the
moral reason. But the question is bound to arise of the connection
of this assurance with *belief*, in the sense of intellectual affirmation.
Coleridge himself thinks that faith so defined does not imply
belief as of necessity. It may exist without it, and even in despite
of it, since faith at its root is an act of volition, a personally
activated submission to that transcendent Will upon which

[1] *The Statesman's Manual*, Appendix B, p. 273.

reason itself ultimately depends. Thus prayer involves the recognition that behind all rational order there is a supreme Volition, or Purpose of God, with which human purposes must ever seek to identify themselves. Acceptance of this divine will, and therefore of the order of providence, is to secure the only conditions under which man can achieve self-fulfilment, rational as well as moral.

> As a light from God directly and immediately such, was necessary in the past instance to actuate the Human Reason, and as it were, to induct and inaugurate it into its legislative capacity & offices, it follows likewise that the Human Reason began in *Faith*; that an insight into the reasonableness of obedience was anterior and antecedent to an insight into the reasonableness of the command to be obeyed; that therefore even from the beginning Man's moral Being had the primacy over the intellectual, and the Light of Reason in the conscience a far higher authority than the Light of Reason in the Understanding.[1]

But man's self-fulfilment cannot be thought of aside from his immortality. Here Coleridge parts company altogether with Kant, for whom the ethical imperative needs no such exterior support. He could not in truth conceive of a 'supreme moral Intelligence' at all unless he also could believe in his own immortality. The alternative would be to accept 'a whole system of apparent means to an end which has no existence'. Give this up, he tells himself, and virtue wants all reason. He could conceive dying a martyr's death, even knowing that death in *his* case would mean annihilation, 'if it were possible to believe that all other human beings were immortal and to be benefited by it'; but emphatically not from any benefit that would affect 'only a set of transitory animals'. 'Boldly should I say: O Nature! I should rather not have been; let that wh. is to come so soon, come now, for what is all the intermediate space, but sense and utter worthlessness?'[2] Such language reveals the force of a conviction greater surely than any ordinary affirmation of orthodox faith. The mind and will of man cannot, of their very nature, remain satisfied with the transient objects of sense, but must reach out to whatever amid ceaseless flux seems to have the character of permanence, to be one, that is, with man's own essential being. Nor can the

[1] From Notebook 26 (quoted Boulger, p. 226).
[2] See J. H. Muirhead, *Coleridge as Philosopher* (1930), pp. 233f.

apparently universal intimation or presentiment of a life hereafter be disregarded. For why should Nature, who normally
fulfils her promises, deceive man, her noblest creation, only in
this? Coleridge is even prepared to press his conviction into the
shape of a logical argument:

> If we assume a graduated scale of assent from the minimum of
> consciousness ... up to the highest imaginable perfection of con-
> sciousness that can exist in a *Creature*, there must be some first
> instance, in which the consciousness survives the metempsychosis of
> the Creature—even as there must be a first, in *which* the consciouness
> becomes *individual* (i.e. proper self-consciousness). Now as this
> latter takes place *first* in Man, there is every reason to suppose and
> none to deny, Man will be the first instance of the former likewise.[1]

Whatever be thought of this argument, it at least testifies to
Coleridge's belief that what we find ourselves obliged to think is
unlikely to have no purchase at all on reality.

> Immortality! [he elsewhere exclaims] What is (it) but the impossi-
> bility of believing the contrary? ... The moment that the soul
> affirms, I Am, it asserts, I cannot cease to be. For the I Am owns no
> antecedent, *it* is an act of Absolute Spontaneity and of absolute
> necessity. No cause existing why it *is*, no cause can be imagined why
> it should cease to be. It is an impossible thought so long as I Am is
> affirmed.[2]

The nature of the belief, as Coleridge held it, thus stands revealed:
the intellectual argument is at every point underpinned by the
emotional assurance; or rather, the two together compose a
single structure of reasoned, but nonetheless impelled, self-
commitment. Coleridge would have to concede, of course, that the
idea of immortality, merely as an abstract speculation, is quite
undemonstrable. But he does not allow that rightly it can be
so stated. On the contrary, it is a 'preassumption' at the root of
every primal hope, fear and action. When, however, it becomes a
specific article of Christian faith it acquires a further aspect: not
that simply of a life to come and a future state, 'but *what* each
individual soul may hope for itself therein; and on what grounds'.
It is a state which has become 'an object of aspiration and fervent
desire, and a source of thanksgiving and exceeding great joy',

[1] Notebook 26, ff 45–45ᵛ.
[2] Notebook 39, f 37ᵛ.

already, moreover, to be anticipated in this world, in the life of grace.

If for Coleridge religion was the highest activity of the human spirit, in Christianity it reached its apex. The Christian religion teaches man two things: the worthlessness of a life given over merely to the senses, and the true meaning and vocation of human existence. Thus the two great principles or 'moments' of Christian doctrine are original sin and redemption. Any suggestion, however, that in embracing Christian orthodoxy Coleridge abandoned the rational quest of the philosopher would be misleading. His mind was by native constitution an enquiring one, ever seeking to discover, to correlate and to explain. On the one hand he could not deny the plain facts of his experience, but on the other, his interpretation of them always strove for expression in intellectual terms. That much would necessarily remain mysterious he freely admitted, since the mystery is inherent in the facts themselves. Original sin undoubtedly is mysterious, yet not so intransigently as to defy the probings of philosophy. The notion of hereditary sin Coleridge dismissed as 'a monstrous fiction'. The seat of moral evil is in the will; and an evil common to all must have a ground common to all. But unless this evil ground, unthinkably, originates in the divine will, it must be referred to the will of man. So much Coleridge tells us in *Aids to Reflection*; but his concern there is simply practical and religious. In his unpublished notebooks he attempts to search the mystery by the light of his metaphysic. In the earlier work, that is, he gives us the doctrine in terms that any man could refer back to his own experience. The subsequent discussion, by contrast, is daringly speculative. Yet from the one position to the other there is a smooth and natural transition, and further proof if needed of the basic unity of Coleridge's thought, for all the fragmentaries of its expression.

The essence of sin, he holds, resides in the subjection of the individual will to an alien control and the repudiation of its own true law. We should not blame Adam for it—here Coleridge finds the traditional Christian concepts uniformly unsatisfactory—but the will that is in every one of us. For 'every man is the adequate representative of all men'. Each may be described as a 'separated finite', that which is not God nor yet with God. When the individual will is in harmony with the Absolute Will it is in positive 'potency'. Its negative potency consists in its ability to act for itself: in other words, to yield the possibility of evil.[1] Such negative potency has its maximum realization in the 'Apostasy of Satan', but partially also in the sin of mankind. Where the will *wills* its autonomy—of which, again, the devil is the supreme symbol—it falls into original sin. But with man all such self-willing, being only partial, involves an inherent contradiction, since the capacity for redemption remains, a capacity revealed in man's potentiality for good as well as evil. Hence the possibility is open to him of a restored harmony with the Absolute Will. Yet it is only too obvious that the will *per se* cannot effect this restoration: its self-contradiction always limits it to the selfish ends presented to it by its separation from the Absolute. Help therefore is needed from without, from a mediator or redeemer.

If sin is disobedience to the true law of one's being in pursuit of natural appetites, redemption, on the other hand, is achieved by a willing return to this law and the resumption of the freedom which it confers. It is a new birth in the spirit, although how so is a 'transcendent Mystery'; but its results are 'Sanctification from Sin, and liberation from the inherent and penal consequences of sin in the World to come, with all the means and processes of Sanctification by the Word and the Spirit'. The 'Agent' in redemption is the incarnate Son of God—'tempted, agonizing, crucified, submitting to death, resurgent, communicant of His Spirit, ascendant'. Yet for all this Coleridge does not appear to have been greatly interested in the problem of the historicity of the gospels. The broad facts he accepted; but rather, it seems, as marking what had come to pass by God's eternal purpose. It is hardly surprising, therefore, in view of this attitude, that he should have dwelt comparatively little upon the doctrine of the incarnation itself, central though it is in all traditional theology. He is credited indeed with the opinion that the 'law of God and the great

---

[1] Cp. Notebook 31, f 33 (quoted Boulger, pp. 153f.): 'For pure Evil what is it but Will that would manifest itself as Will, not in Being [Ἑτερότης] not in Intelligence (therefore formless)—not in union or Communion, the contrary therefore of Life, even eternal Death. . . . It is the creaturely will which instead of quenching itself in the Light and the Form, to be the Warmth [of Life] and the Procession [of Love]; and so resolve itself into the Will of the One, it would quench the Light of the Form, and shrink inward, if so it might itself remain the One, by recoiling from the One—and find a centre by centrifuge—and thus in the Self-love, it becomes Hate and the lust full of Hate—and in the striving to be one (instead of striving after and toward the One) it becomes the infinite Many.'

principles of the Christian religion would have been the same had Christ never assumed humanity'.[1] Hence, too, his lack of concern over the question of miracles. In fact, as touching the human life of Christ Coleridge is persistently evasive, perhaps because the difficulties it involves appeared to him incapable of satisfactory treatment. Yet in one of his notebooks he asks, concerning Jesus's ignorance of temporal matters, whether the repugnance to such a supposition is not

> grounded in the habit of the Christian world since the Arian controversy of directing their thoughts so exclusively to the Son of God in his character of co-eternal Deity as to lose sight of the *Son of Man*, and to forget that the Son of Mary, in whom the Word ἐσκήνωσεν (=tabernacled), was still *the Man*, Jesus.[2]

He even applies to the problem his distinction between reason and understanding:

> The human understanding is in each individual united with the Reason in one and the same person, and yet cannot comprehend the Reason which shines down into it; for if it did it would cease to be Understanding . . .[3] Who [he goes on to ask], 'will dare assert that the Gospel represents *Jesus* as omniscient in his personal consciousness as Jesus? Jesus knew that the Son of God was the *true* and proper ground of his Being—which was to him what our Reason is to us . . .[4]

He confessed to himself, however, that the only right thing to be done in face of the difficulties was to 'walk humbly and seek Light by Prayer'.[5]

Thus, then, does Coleridge find Christianity to be necessary. It is a necessity for the human spirit itself if it is to be saved from the destructive pressures of all 'mechanic' philosophies. But in claiming this he also conscientiously avoids the fundamentalist attitudes of contemporary orthodoxy, according to which revelation and the order of grace are miraculous divine *interpositions* upon the order of nature and reason. It is the universal and abiding need of man, in all his parts and potentialities, which religion exists to serve. From this the question of its truth is

[1] *Letters, Conversations and Recollections of S. T. Coleridge*, ed. Allsop (1836).
[2] Notebook 35, ff 19ᵛ–20.
[3] *Ibid.*
[4] Notebook 37, ff 19ᵛ–20.
[5] Notebook 25, ff 21–21ᵛ.

inseparable. No theology, therefore, which sees God and humanity in terms of a radical mutual 'alterity' can be satisfactory. To understand what Christianity essentially is we must view it as a growth, a becoming, a progression. It is history, and history under the form of moral freedom, in which alone its 'idea' can be realized. Hence it is not simply the Scriptures which prove the divine origin of the Christian religion, but the 'progressive and still continuing fulfilment of the assurance of a few fishermen that both their own religion and the religion of their conquerors should be superseded by the faith of a man recently and ignominiously executed'. In other words, the existence of the Church itself is the required proof, had the apostles indeed left no scriptures behind them.

4. THE BIBLE

But Coleridge for all his metaphysical interest did not overlook the Scriptures, and his posthumously published *Confessions of an Inquiring Spirit*[1] was among the first books to challenge public opinion in this country with a plea for a new and more perceptive approach to the Bible as a whole. He certainly was among the few to have any firsthand acquaintance with contemporary German investigations in this field. For during his stay in Germany from 1798 to 1799 he read Eichhorn's *Introduction to the New Testament*, and made a close study of the writings of Wilhelm Gottfried Lessing, including the latter's edition of the Wolfenbüttel Fragments of Reimarus, former professor of oriental languages at Hamburg. The operative principle of biblical criticism became clear to him from Eichhorn, but it was from Lessing, by whose ideas he was deeply impressed, that he learned to appreciate history as a developmental process. The outcome of these influences was that he achieved a more intelligent grasp of the nature and implications of the biblical problem than was possessed by any other Englishman of his time. Not that he personally acquired any special degree of technical knowledge as a biblical scholar; nor that he ever felt called upon to offer the detailed conclusions of such scholarship to the general reader. Here, too,

---

[1] The first edition, by H. N. Coleridge, appeared in 1840. A reprint of the third edition, 1853 (with J. H. Green's introduction and a note by Sara Coleridge), was issued in 1956. It is edited by H. St J. Hart.

his own role was rather that of the Christian apologist trying to meet the increasing difficulties which historical criticism raised for the received belief that the Bible is a book uniquely inspired and authoritative.

Coleridge's special purpose in the *Confessions* is to show that the customary 'literalist' theory of inspiration is unsatisfactory in itself and in any case untenable when confronted with the facts of the Bible's literary history. He argues that a broader, more historical conception of it not only will not diminish but will actually enhance its inherent spiritual value. To be rightly appreciated the Bible must be read like any other book; but the reader with his mind thus open will soon come to realize that in reality it is *not* like any other book and that its appeal is entirely its own, since more fully than any other does it meet the needs of man's spiritual being. The Bible, that is to say, like Christianity itself, is its own sufficient evidence.

> In every generation, and wheresoever the light of Revelation has shone, men of all ranks, conditions, and states of mind have found in this volume a correspondent for every movement towards the Better felt in their own hearts.[1]

The final test, as always, is that of personal experience.

> With such purposes, with such feelings, have I perused the books of the Old and New Testaments,—each book as a whole, and also as an integral part. And need I say that I have met everywhere more or less copious sources of truth, and power, and purifying impulses;— that I have found words for my inmost thoughts, songs for my joy, utterances for my hidden griefs, and pleadings for my shame and feebleness?[2]

In short, he declares, whatever *finds* me, bears witness for itself that it has proceeded from the Holy Spirit. But this conviction is not merely a subjective reaction. It implies that although Scripture truly is a revelation of God from without, the knowledge it conveys has to be assimilated to that which a man has within him. To read the Bible spiritually, therefore, is a living experience of which divine word and personal faith are the constituents; for 'as much of reality, as much of objective truth, as the Scriptures communicate to the subjective experiences of the Believer, so

---

[1] *Confessions*, ed. Hart, p. 68.
[2] *Ibid.*, p. 42.

much of present life, of living and effective import' do these experiences in turn give to the letter of the Scriptures. The familiar notion that the Bible was divinely dictated, requiring as it does the corollary that all its parts are equally inspired, really makes this impossible. This doctrine Coleridge maintains—and it was the doctrine all but unanimously held by Christians in this country at the time—simply petrifies the whole body of Holy Writ with all its harmonies and symmetrical gradations.

> This breathing organism, this *panharmonicum*, which I had seen stand on its feet as a man, and with a man's voice given to it, the Doctrine in question turns at once into a colossal Memnon's head, a hollow passage for a voice, a voice that mocks the voices of many men, and speaks in their names, and yet is but one voice, and the same;—and no man uttered it, and never in human heart was it conceived.[1]

The Bible, however, is not a unity, nor homogeneous, but a body of literature in varying stages of development, some of it primitive, some of it highly advanced; whilst inspiration properly signifies 'the actuating influence of the Holy Spirit' in quickening the writer's entire personality, thus rendering it more perceptive of spiritual truth.

Coleridge saw plainly that the traditional view, when examined, throws up insuperable difficulties. It demands in effect that the Bible from cover to cover be read as a transcript of the pronouncements of an infallible intelligence. Yet Scripture itself nowhere advances such a claim. Further, once the character of infallibility is attributed to it there can be no admission of degree; it extends to all matters, physical no less than spiritual. Hence every statement, whatever its content, must be taken as unequivocally true, and the curses of the Psalmist are no less 'inspired' than the Beatitudes of the gospel. On the other hand, if you distinguish between infallible truth and its fallible expression where exactly is the dividing line to be drawn? For what is the *criterion* of infallibility? The fear that criticism will destroy the authority of the Bible can be met, Coleridge believes, by appeal to the general drift and tenor of the Scriptures. Indeed,

> the more tranquilly an inquirer takes up the Bible as he would any other body of ancient writings, the livelier and steadier will be his

[1] *Ibid.*, p. 52.

impressions of its superiority to all other books, till at length all other books and all other knowledge will be valuable in his eyes in proportion as they help him to a better understanding of his Bible.[1]

And he personally confesses to the reader how 'difficulty after difficulty has been overcome from the time that I began to study the Scriptures with free and unboding spirit, under the conviction that my faith in the incarnate Word and His Gospel was secure, whatever the result might be'.[2]

Coleridge was ahead of the vast majority of his fellow-countrymen in his perception both of what criticism would mean for traditional attitudes towards the Bible and of how also the genuine worth and authority of Scripture are to be vindicated. His 'literary and spiritual insight placed him', it has been well said, 'upon a point of vantage from which he could overlook the nineteenth-century country in front of him, and reply in advance to all that the *Zeitgeist* thereafter would bring forward.'[3] Assuredly much of the bitter and futile controversy about the rival authorities of religion and science could have been avoided if the argument of the *Confessions* had been more deeply pondered by both the churchmen and the scientists of the generation following. The book, brief though it is, is a work of capital importance. Its appeal, as always with Coleridge, is to the spirit as against any merely mechanical adherence to the letter; only when spiritual things are spiritually judged can criticism of the letter be usefully pursued. Wisely, he bids his reader not to be 'an Infidel on the score of what other men think fit to include in their Christianity'. The Christian religion is constituted not by the Bible but by Christ and the truth revealed through him, the proof of its divine authority being its fitness to our nature and its needs; and, as Coleridge himself puts it, 'the clearness and cogency of the proof' is 'proportionate to the degree of self-knowledge in each individual hearer'. The Bible, beyond any doubt, is 'true and holy' in consideration of its declared aims and purposes, and for all who seek truth with humility of spirit a sure guide.

5. CHURCH AND STATE

One more aspect of Coleridge's far-ranging thought remains to be

[1] *Ibid.*, p. 75.
[2] p. 63.
[3] Basil Willey, *Nineteenth Century Studies* (1949), p. 40.

discussed. With his political opinions in general we are not here concerned, but his mature reflexions on the relations of church and society, set forth in his essay on *The Constitution of the Church and State*,[1] are of immediate relevance. The strands of his thought are always so tightly interwoven that seldom if ever can any one of his characteristic ideas be properly assessed apart from the others. Thus for him there could be no politics without a religious reference, and no religion without political implicates. No other writer of his day, in this country, possessed anything approaching either his philosophical detachment or the instinctive sympathy for the task he set himself in this treatise. His purpose is the basic one of examining the 'ideas' of both Church and State in respect of their essential functions. By 'idea', however, he means not an abstraction from the given historical conditions but a conception determined by a knowledge of objectives. Hence an idea may be true without its ever having had an historical embodiment. He cites in illustration the notion of the Social Contract, which was never an historical event yet is none the less valid as a symbol of that 'ever-originating social contract' apart from which society could not maintain its existence. It is, in a word, a necessary *regulative* idea, comparable, as a 'truth-power' of the reason, with such other regulative ideas as those of God, freedom, will and the values we call absolute. These life itself requires, however short the understanding may fall in its effort to provide them with a sufficient rational foundation, or indeed however little we are able to realize them in action. 'Ideas', Coleridge insists, 'correspond to substantial beings, to objects the actual subsistence of which is implied in their idea, though only by the idea revealable.' So when we turn to the idea of the State we discover that two equally requisite but evidently opposing principles or interests must be held in balance: *permanence* and *progression*. The former is represented by the landed classes, the latter by the mercantile and professional. Both are reflected in the British constitution, which secures such a balance without its ever having been expressly devised to do so.

That it was by no means a perfect balance Coleridge knew well enough. In his own day, as he points out, the landed classes

---

[1] Published in 1829. Coleridge's influence is to be detected in W. E. Gladstone's early work on *The State in its Relations with the Church*, first published in 1838, in which some affinity with Maurice's views is also evident. See Appendix III below.

enjoyed an excess of power and influence relative to the monied interests, whereas the health of the body politic as a whole demands the adequate representation of every vital and energetic element in society. But it is the failure of the 'third estate' of the realm, the Church, to counterbalance these two which seems to him the great social defect of the age. The true function of the third estate is of a National Church whose responsibility is 'to secure and improve that civilization, without which the nation could be neither permanent nor progressive'.[1] Its purpose, in fact, is nothing less than the promotion of 'the harmonious development of those qualities and faculties that characterize our humanity'. The State is concerned with citizenship, the Church with the powers and instincts which constitute the man, and 'we must be men in order to be citizens'. But by the National Church Coleridge does not mean either the Church of Christ, in the high theological sense, or the Church of England as an established institution. His view is a good deal wider, and what he wishes us to understand by it is perhaps not altogether easy to grasp. The National Church, as he envisages it, comprehends the sum of the nation's cultural and spiritual resources—'all the so-called liberal arts and sciences, the possession and application of which constitute the civilization of a country, as well as the theological' —and is composed of what he rather oddly calls 'The Clerisy', the entire body of 'clerical persons', that is, whose *raison d'être* is to safeguard, develop and disseminate the spiritual and cultural heritage as a whole. It thus will consist not only of the clergy, as the specifically ministerial order in the Church, but also of the learned of all denominations and professions, expert in their several fields. The former Coleridge views from a sociological standpoint. The Church's chief function, under this aspect, was not primarily that of teaching religion but of providing, in the parish clergyman, 'a resident guide, guardian and instructor' throughout the land. This the existing establishment fulfilled with only qualified success, but the machinery itself, and the opportunity of enlarging it, already existed.

Coleridge's fear was that in an epoch of rapid technological advance the higher values of civilized life would be neglected or destroyed. 'We live under the dynasty of the understanding, and this is its golden age.' *Means* in plenty were being put at men's

[1] *The Constitution of the Church and State* (ed. 1839), p. 4.

disposal—'With these the age, this favoured land, teems'; but there was a remarkable uncertainty as to ultimate *ends*. When, he asks, shall we seek for information concerning these? Material prosperity does not automatically bring happiness and the production of greater wealth may also cause greater poverty. Education, synonymous with instruction, would, he also foresaw, become increasingly secular:

> Knowledge being power, those attainments, which give a man the power of doing what he wishes in order to obtain what he desires, are alone to be considered knowledge, or to be admitted into the scheme of national education;[1]

whilst the Church itself, amid dissent and unbelief, would be reduced to the status of a sect.

The Christian Church in relation to the National Church was for Coleridge 'a blessed accident'—a singular phrase which he explains as meaning that 'Christianity is an aid and instrument which no State had a right to expect'. It certainly is not a kingdom of this world, nor an estate of any realm, but 'the appointed opposite to them all collectively—the sustaining, correcting, befriending opposite of the World; the compensating counter-force to the inherent and inevitable evils and defects of the State, as a State'.[2] But it is neither invisible nor secret; on the contrary, it is visible and militant. Yet it has no local centre of unity, and no visible head or sovereign. Nor in any sense ought it to be described as an institution over against and rivalling the State. It offers, that is to say, no alternative organization of human society, but only a corrective to the evils arising within it. Its 'paramount aim and object' is another world; not a world to come exclusively, but 'likewise another world' to that which now is and to the concerns of which alone the epithet 'spiritual' can be applied without a mischievous abuse of the word.[3] Finally, the Christian Church is of its nature universal. It is neither Anglican, Gallican nor Roman, neither Latin nor Greek. In England there exists a 'Catholic and Apostolic Church', which he himself would prefer to call simply the Church, or Catholic Church, of Christ *in* England. The Roman Church plainly is not national, but neither

[1] *Ibid.*, p. 66.
[2] pp. 124f.
[3] p. 12.

is it universal. The English Church, still standing in an authentic tradition, is the best adapted to the needs of Englishmen.

The significance of Coleridge's genius rests in its many-sidedness. As a philosophical thinker he is always stimulating and often profound, even though his place in the textbooks of modern philosophy is not prominent. Insatiable in the pursuit of truth, his mind was perhaps too eclectic. He has aptly been called 'the first of the great nineteenth century "thinkers" rather than a philosopher in the strict technical sense'.[1] His concern was with the spiritual life of man in its widest range, so that theology, philosophy, politics, social theory and aesthetics are severally viewed by him as the intellectual aspects of a single existential reality. To English theology he gave what certainly it most needed, a broader horizon and a wholly fresh inspiration, doing for it indeed, in his way, what Schleiermacher in different circumstances did for theology in Germany. Rationalism, deism, evangelicalism, high-and-dry traditionalism—all were either dead or in need of an infusion of fresh spiritual or intellectual life. Coleridge's thinking struck out new paths, which he followed with a degree of spiritual concentration, an awareness of essential problems and a personal if idiosyncratic self-dedication for which his times, in this country at least, afford no parallel. It could be said that from Coleridge it is but a step to Kierkegaard and modern existentialism. Like the Danish thinker he came to see Christianity in an entirely new perspective. Conventional Church teaching suddenly acquired the depth and urgency of life itself. Truth was something to be 'done' and not merely argued about. Religion was an expression of the nature of man himself, in all its complexity, a yearning of the soul which only the ultimate assurance of God could satisfy. As Coleridge interprets them the great dogmas of faith—the incarnation, the atonement, the trinity, original sin—are not simply theoretical propositions but regulative and practical norms of experience. As theoretical principles alone they would be inexplicable, whereas accepted in the full context of man's moral nature they are a revelation of a mystery, a form of being rather than a system of knowledge. 'Too soon', Coleridge warns his Christian readers, 'did the Doctors of

[1] G. Hough, 'Coleridge and the Victorians', in *The English Mind*, ed. H. S. Davies and G. Watson (1964), p. 178.

the Church forget that the *heart*, the *moral* nature, was the beginning and the end; and that truth, knowledge, and insight were comprehended in its expansion.'[1] The Christian religion is not a theory or a speculation, but a life; not a philosophy of life but a process of living, proved in the act.

Coleridge's direct influence is apparent in Thomas Arnold, in Julius Hare, in F. W. Robertson, and above all in F. D. Maurice, as possibly too in Newman.[2] Yet his true rank and importance as a religious teacher was not really appreciated until more recently, and with the study of his unpublished writings. Today his frequent anticipations of the modern standpoint seem of an almost uncanny appositeness. As a purely literary figure he has, of course, received his meed of praise, perhaps even in excess when the tribute has been accompanied by expressions of regret that so fine a poetic imagination should eventually have run to waste in a desert of metaphysical ruminations. But Coleridge was not merely a poet *manqué* whose intellectual energy had therefore to cast about for some new and congenial outlet. Had he possessed a more sustained architechtonic gift, a more evident ability to control and direct the flood of his often paradoxical thought, he might have been the greatest original theologian this country has ever produced, as well as one of its foremost philosophers. As it is his very failures are such that beside them other men's successes look meagre.

---

[1] *Aids to Reflection*, p. 126.
[2] See below, p. 135.

Chapter III

The Oxford Movement

I. THE INWARDNESS OF RELIGION

The story of the Oxford Movement has so often been told that it needs no further repetition here, the main course of events being familiar.[1] Nor is it part of our task to assess its influence on the Church's life and worship, all-pervasive though this has been. Our concern, after a brief glance at the movement's causes, will be to review the underlying principles which in the given context make up its particular contribution to the religious thought of the century. The subject is a large one and our study of it must necessarily be concentrated.[2] But first, why did the movement occur, and occur when it did?

It arose from a variety of circumstances, political as well as theological. The era was one of reform. A spirit was abroad no longer tolerant of old abuses and injustices. The Test and Corporation Acts, by then indeed an insult rather than an injury to those against whom they discriminated, had been repealed in 1828. The Roman Catholic emancipation measure, though hotly disputed, passed into law the following year. In 1832 came the great Bill for parliamentary reform, to which the national Church, not least as represented by its bishops, was in solid opposition: 'In every village', the Whigs complained, 'we had the black recruiting-sergeant against us.' Before many months had gone by clerical fears were endorsed by the government's proposal to

---

[1] R. W. Church's classic account in *The Oxford Movement: Twelve Years 1833–1845* (1891) is still the best.

[2] Of the theology of the movement Brilioth's *The Anglican Revival* is unsurpassed as a detailed study. A useful collection of extracts from Tractarian writings is included in Owen Chadwick, *The Mind of the Oxford Movement* (1960).

abolish ten out of the twenty-two bishoprics of the Church of Ireland, a measure which in view of the actual situation in Ireland was neither unreasonable nor inappropriate. To High Churchmen, however, rootedly Tory and deeply apprehensive of the growing 'march-of-mind' liberalism, it seemed to portend only one result: a relaxation of the age-old bond of sympathy which held Church and State together in a Christian realm and an increasing likelihood that the former would find itself yoked with a partner whose ends and purposes might cover much that to a sound churchman would be repugnant. Parliament could now no longer be taken as voicing ecclesiastical opinion with any degree of certainty. Yet it retained, by virtue of the establishment, complete control over ecclesiastical affairs. It was the Irish Church Bill which gave John Keble the theme for the assize sermon which he preached in the university church at Oxford on 14 July 1833, and to which he accorded the alarmist title of 'National Apostasy'—an event which has usually been regarded as setting the Oxford Movement on its way.[1]

A more insidious danger, however, was felt to be liberalism in religious teaching. Not only was the old faith being questioned, the Bible was exposed to critical examination and its inspiration, in some quarters, impugned. For men like Arnold, the Church, it thus followed, was merely a human institution, to be reorganized on new lines as conditions might require. Why, it could be asked, as Arnold himself had done, should not different opinions, rites and ceremonies be brought together in a single Christian body coextensive as far as possible with the entire nation? Exclusiveness, promoted by 'the anti-Christ of priesthood', had no place in Christ's own fellowship. To Newman such views were anathema. The very spring of liberalism was the antidogmatic principle, or the notion that a man's creed was his own affair, about which others had no business to vex either themselves or him.[2] In face of this the Evangelicals' zeal was of itself impotent. At any rate as

---

[1] Such was Newman's view, as stated in the *Apologia* (ed. Svaglic), p. 43 (cp. also *Letters*, i, p. 380 and *Correspondence of John Henry Newman*, edited at the Birmingham Oratory, 1917, p. 316). Others did not necessarily share it. See F. L. Cross (1933), *John Henry Newman*, Appendix iv, 'The Myth of July 14, 1833', pp. 162f.

[2] *Apologia*, p. 54: 'My battle was with liberalism; by liberalism I mean the antidogmatic principle and its developments. This was the first point on which I was certain . . . From the age of fifteen dogma has been the fundamental principle of my religion.'

D*

High Churchmen judged them the Evangelical party's lack of doctrinal platform meant that against such a philosophy mere emotional individualism had no foothold. The liberal menace could be met only by recourse to the historic teachings of Catholic Christianity which the Church of England, despite the Reformation, had preserved in its formularies and which the best of its divines had never sought to minimize. Hence the Oxford school of the 1830s were far from claiming to be innovators. Their business was not to invent anything but to recall men to ancient truths that had for too long been overlooked or had ceased, in an age of indifference, to stir the pulses of faith. To preach these truths became therefore a mission. An urgent work was to be done, the doing of which demanded not only learning and fixity of principle—for such, as we have seen, were by no means wanting among many churchmen—but for the personal dedication and commitment which alone would arouse merely nominal Christians from spiritual lethargy and arm them to resist the forces under which all religious belief might in the end crumble. 'I do not', declared Newman in an article written some years after the movement began, 'I do not shrink from uttering my firm conviction that it would be a gain to the country were it vastly more superstitious, more bigoted, more gloomy, more fierce in its religion than at present it shows itself.'[1]

Yet the historian today, as he looks back upon the movement over more than a century of time, can view it in a larger perspective than either the political or the theological. Seen thus it appears as an aspect of the general cultural renaissance denoted by the word romanticism. Newman himself, in the *Apologia*, spoke of 'a spirit afloat' thirty years previously. What precisely this spirit was is not easy to define. Romanticism was curiously complex in manifestation and affected many areas of thought and action: literature, scholarship, philosophy, the arts and religion all reflected it. Essentially it was a protest against rationalism and formalism, alike in art and in life. Its ideals might have very varied utterance, but always freedom and spontaneity were deemed the vital conditions of their pursuit. Self-expression in all its modes required for authenticity immediacy of feeling, originality of insight, and liberty of imagination. Truth was to be found not in prescribed formulae or in abstract argument but in the direct

[1] 'The State of Religious Parties', in *The British Critic*, April 1839.

apprehensions of personal experience. If we are to understand the deeper significance of the Oxford Movement this latter consideration is of special importance. The teachings of the Oxford divines in their own day and since has often been superficially judged. It was absurd to see in the new High Churchmanship, as did Arnold, the 'mere foolery' of a dress, a ritual, a name, or a ceremony. It would be only a little less wrong to think that Tractarianism was no more than a reactionary insistence upon dogma and tradition for their own sake. In some respects the movement was reactionary, as in its proclaimed hostility to 'liberalism'. But always the appeal to the letter was made in the interest of the spirit. The past which these men venerated was no enshrined corpse but, however idealized their conception of it, a living and active principle, a spur to the imagination and the feelings. Religion as they saw it was not simply a matter of doctrines and rites, but of the life of prayer and worship, the sense of eternity, the discipline of the self's wayward desires. Dogma, like ritual and ascetic practice, existed solely to promote it. Experience was the necessary test. A merely 'notional' assent to religious truth could know nothing of what such truth really is, for the fundamental testimony is that of conscience. Tractarianism, whatever its shortcomings, was rightly described by the most brilliant of its leaders as 'a spiritual awakening of spiritual wants'. True to the romantic impulse, which in other regards it might deplore, it was an assertion of the claims of the creative spirit as against externalism, routine or the cold mechanism of logical reason.

2. THE CATHOLICITY OF THE ENGLISH CHURCH

Thus the Oxford Movement gave to the old High Church theology what Alexander Knox believed it so much needed: interiority and spiritual warmth. Herein lay its vital difference. Bishop van Mildert might have spoken of the apostolical succession with as clear a grasp of its principle as did Newman in the first of the *Tracts for the Times*. But with Newman the idea takes wing. The very creed becomes a banner unfurled in the wind. Traditionary institutions and orthodox principles exist only that men may find the way of sanctity and have the divine life within themselves. Not that the Tractarians did not insist on inherited

93

forms and sound professions: on the contrary, men like Dr
Pusey and William Palmer were dedicated to their maintenance.
But even if its concern for orthodoxy tended to be obsessive the
long-term effect of the movement was a change in the whole
ethos of English religious life. Upon the theological and philosophical thought of the age it left a mark much less distinct. The
fact is indicative of where the true strength of the movement lay
and the grounds of any just appraisal of its achievement.

Tractarianism, then, was a genuine revival of the spirit, arousing
in its adherents a sense of elation. The disciples of Newman
displayed all the enthusiastic energy of new hopes and purposes.
Their cause imbued them with confidence. Mere antiquarianism or
the praise of things past could not have done this. The Oxford
divines believed themselves to be addressing the supreme need
of their times. The decorous, torpid Protestantism commonly
identified with the national religion could do nothing, they
believed, to stem the advancing tide of irreligion. The Church
establishment in its existing condition was a deplorable compromise with worldliness. It had lost its sense of spiritual direction
and failed to teach with the authority that belonged to it. If the
Church was to fulfil its apostolic commission and restore to the
lives of the people an awareness of the presence and claims of the
invisible and eternal, then it must recover the Catholic heritage
which still was its by right. But to do so would mean re-emphasiz-
ing the fact that the Church of England, although reformed,
was not 'Protestant' and that if its real identity was to be disclosed
traditions of faith and polity which Calvinism, Erastianism and
latitudinarianism had overlaid would have once more to be put
before the world. Faced with this grave vocation the party could
spare no time for the outward appurtenances of religion. The
immediate task was to underpin and strengthen the doctrinal
foundations; and the doctrines which called for the clearest
reassertion were those of the supernatural authority of the Church
and of the efficacy of sacramental grace.

If the Church of England should continue to look on such
teachings only as 'Romish' then plainly it had misunderstood
its own nature and status; and if to stress them seemed to de-
Protestantize it, then let the work of de-Protestantizing be carried
out regardless of the opposition it might incur. This emphatically
was Hurrell Froude's conviction. Froude, Newman's close friend

and in its early days the movement's *enfant terrible*—he died in 1836, at the age of 33—declared that he had come to 'hate the Reformation and the Reformers more and more'.[1] He confessed that for nothing would he abuse the Roman Church *as a Church* 'except for excommunicating us'. 'We are', he announced, 'Catholics without Popery, and Church of England men without Protestantism.'[2] His words are the theory of the *via media* in a nutshell. The national Church was not what she was popularly supposed to be, as her wisest teachers had always made clear. In avoiding one kind of error she had not heeled over into another. She had providentially chosen a middle course, and to pursue it was her divine destiny here on earth. But if in the past mistaken emphases for which many of the sixteenth-century Reformers themselves were responsible—had obscured this truth it was up to the men of a later age to readjust the balance. As Froude aphoristically put it: 'The Reformation was a limb badly set—it must be broken again in order to be righted.' The resetting might indeed be painful. The actions of those whose task it was to carry it out would be misunderstood. Not only were Catholicism and Popery synonymous in the popular mind, but some assumptions that had for generations passed unquestioned would now be challenged. 'The Bible and the Bible alone' might well be the religion of Protestants, but it was not and could not be the religion of the Church, whose own primary teaching office was an inalienable responsibility. Again, the State connexion, far from being a spiritual privilege, had rather proved to be an Egyptian bondage. The imagined 'purity' of English Protestant Christianity was only a meagre reduction or paring down of a once richer truth, as the Church's poverty in saints regrettably testified. The Reformers were not wholly at fault, but their doctrine was one-sided and sometimes false, whilst they themselves had too often been politically minded timeservers.

[1] Froude's *Remains*, edited by Keble and Newman, were published in 1838–9 Unfortunately the book did much to swell the movement's adverse press. 'The world', as Dean Church puts it, 'was shocked by what seemed [Froude's] amazing audacity both of thought and expression about a number of things and persons which it was customary to regard as almost beyond the reach of criticism.' 'Whether', he adds, 'on general grounds [the editors] were wise in startling and vexing friends, and putting fresh weapons into the hands of opponents by their frank disclosure of so unconventional a character, is a question which may have more than one answer' (*op. cit.*, pp. 42f.).

[2] *Remains*, i, pp. 389, 395, 404.

Such was the polemic of Tractarianism. But its theory of the *Via Media* was capable of a more positive shape: namely, to exhibit the Church of England as a true branch of the Church Catholic, with the Churches of Rome and of Constantinople as coordinate branches—a position argued with much force by Newman in his *Prophetical Office of the Church* (1837).[1] This work appeals in support of the theory to the 'Anglo-Catholicism' of divines like Andrewes, Laud, Hammond, Butler and Wilson. Newman's three essential 'points' are dogma, the sacramental system and anti-Romanism (the maintenance, that is, of the 'Catholic' claim of the English Church against the familiar objections of Rome). In basic matters indeed the Church stands with Rome: in both systems, it is contended, the same creeds are acknowledged; both hold certain doctrines as unconditionally necessary to salvation: the trinity, the incarnation and the atonement; both believe in original sin and the need of regeneration, in the supernatural grace of the sacraments and in the apostolical succession; both teach the eternity of a future punishment. Further, if the two Churches are so far united on fundamentals they are 'also one and the same in such plain consequences as were contained in those fundamentals and in such natural observances as outwardly represented them'.[2] Newman goes on:

> It was an Anglican principle that 'the abuse of a thing doth not take away the lawful use of it'; and an Anglican Canon of 1603 had declared that the English Church had no purpose to forsake all that was held in the Churches of Italy, France, and Spain, and reverenced those ceremonies and particular points which were Apostolic. Excepting then such exceptional matters, as are implied in this avowal, whether they were many or few, all these Churches are evidently to be considered as one with the Anglican. The Catholic Church in all lands had been one from the first for many centuries; then, various portions had followed their own way to the injury, but not to the destruction, whether of truth or of charity. These portions or branches were mainly three:—The Greek, Latin, and

[1] The full title is: *Lectures on the Prophetical Office of the Church viewed relatively to Romanism and Popular Protestantism*. This able book is outstanding among Tractarian publications. F. L. Cross calls it 'a magnificent apology for what may be termed the Anglican ethos' (*op. cit.*, p. 70). Christopher Dawson, a Roman Catholic, thinks that it 'perhaps still remains the best justification for the essential Anglican position' (*The Spirit of the Oxford Movement*, 1933, p. 102).

[2] *Apologia*, ed. Svaglic, p. 72.

Anglican. Each of these inherited the early undivided Church *in solido* as its own possession. Each was identical with that early undivided Church, and in the unity of that Church it had unity with the other branches.[1]

The three branches thus agreed together in all but their later accidental errors. The Anglican Church was one with the Church of the middle ages. 'The Church of the twelfth century was the Church of the nineteenth', and Dr Howley[2] sat in the seat of St Thomas the Martyr. Anglicans ought to be indulgent to Rome, even though Rome teaches much which they would not wish to adopt. 'By very reason of our protest, which we had made, we could agree to differ.'

The Oxford leaders—and Newman at that time not less so than the rest—were entirely convinced of the controversial strength of their position. Their views, they had no doubt, were not novel and a weighty tradition supported them. The great defect of the national Church was that so many of its members had forgotten or had chosen to disregard its true character and constitution. What had now to be upheld were, first, the Church's apostolic descent as the real ground of its authority, and secondly, the dependent principle that the sacraments, not preaching, are the covenanted sources of divine grace.

The apostolic theory was advanced by Newman in the very first of the *Tracts*, published along with others on 9 September 1833. The authority of the Church's ministry rested not, as commonly supposed, on legal status or popularity or temporal distinctions but on Christ's original commission to his apostles, who in turn had commissioned by the laying on of hands those who should succeed them. Thus by a constantly repeated rite the sacred gift had been 'handed down to our present bishops, who have appointed us as their assistants, and in some sense representatives'. Such was the meaning of the doctrine which, it was claimed, is inherent in the ordination service itself. 'Make much of it', Newman exhorted his clerical readers. 'Show your value of it. Keep it before your minds as an honourable badge, far higher than that of secular responsibility, or cultivation, or polish, or learning, or rank, which gives you a hearing with the many.'

[1] *Ibid.*
[2] William Howley was archbishop of Canterbury from 1828 until 1848. With Newman's opinions, however, he himself had no sympathy.

This implied that the kind of veneration and devotion ordinarily felt by Protestants for the Scriptures was now to be extended to the Church. 'The Church Catholic is our mother.'[1] She had the right and duty to teach, appealing to Scripture in vindication of her teaching.[2] But the doctrine of the apostolic succession was vital to that of the Church. Without the succession there would have been no Church, or no true Church. The threefold ministry of bishops, priests and deacons, in lineal descent from the apostles themselves, is constitutive of a sacred order apart from which real sacraments, as distinct from merely external signs, the *simulacra* of sacraments, could not exist. As Newman put it in the fourth of the *Tracts*:

> The Holy Feast on our Saviour's sacrifice, which all confess to be 'generally necessary for salvation', was intended by Him to be constantly conveyed through the hands of commissioned persons. Except, therefore, we can show such warrant, we cannot be sure that our hands convey the sacrifice. We cannot be sure that souls are worthily prepared ... are partakers of the Body and Blood of Christ.

The reason for the English Church's authentic standing in Christendom is the fact of its possession of the unbroken historic succession. Public position and influence are of themselves insufficient. Although the life of the non-episcopal bodies may flourish by God's 'uncovenanted mercies', churches, and Catholic, in the proper sense they are not.

Yet what was it to be Catholic, in the proper sense? How far could the Church of England itself lay just claim to Catholic status? That it was a 'true' church was guaranteed by the episcopal succession. The reverence of Anglican teachers for the witness of antiquity could be demonstrated. It also could be argued that on doubtful points the Church would defer to that witness instead of to the Reformers 'as the ultimate exponent' of its meaning. Yet on the face of it the contents of the Articles called for some measure of explanation. Their Protestant character seemed obvious and as a Protestant manifesto they had always in fact been taken. In particular how did they stand to the prayer book? Is not the latter to be read in their light? To this problem Newman was later to address

[1] *The Prophetical Office of the Church* (ed. 1838), p. 314.
[2] J. H. Newman, *The Arians of the Fourth Century* (1833), p. 55.

himself with all the resourcefulness of a supple dialectic as well as the fixed determination to defend a controversial position of the validity of which he was sincerely convinced. His solution we shall have to return to in a moment. But the Tractarian conception of the Church was itself undergoing some revision as a result of a deepening sacramentalism. Catholicity, it appeared, might be interpreted either statically, as residing essentially in a form of order, or dynamically, as an 'extension' of the incarnation, the means whereby the life of the eternal Christ is imparted to every new generation of believers. For the 'Catholic' the sacraments, and especially the eucharist, focus his faith and piety, and are the point at which Christ, in symbolic guise, comes to meet him. In Newman's eloquent words:

> Christ shines through the sacraments, as through transparent bodies, without impediment. He is the Light and Life of the Church, acting through it, dispensing of His fulness, knitting and compacting together every part of it; and these its Mysteries are not mere outward-signs, but (as it were) effluences of grace developing themselves in external forms, as Angels might do when they appeared to men. He has touched them and breathed upon them; and thenceforth they have a virtue residing in them, which issues forth and encircles them round, till the eye of faith sees in them no element of matter at all.[1]

Thus the Church is the Body of Christ in no merely figurative way. It lives because he lives. It is the expression of his mind. In a real sense it 'incarnates' him here on earth. But this means that the Church, because alive with the life of its divine founder and master, can and must 'grow'. It looks forward to the future as well as back to the past. Its authority is not simply traditionary but intrinsic. As Newman pointed out in reply to critics of Tractarian 'antiquarianism', the Fathers are not to be imitated for imitation's sake—a servility 'likely to prevent the age from developing Church principles so freely as it might otherwise do'. Nineteenth-century men had to be men of their own century, not of the fourth; nor, and the inference is plain, of the sixteenth either. Hence in the English Church's growing realization of its Catholic heritage the marks of such a temporary vicissitude as the Reformation must be judged of less account than formerly. If one inquires what doctrines are fundamental the question, Newman answers,

[1] *Parochial Sermons*, iii, p. 302.

is not what is necessary to be believed by *this particular person or that*, since none but God can decide 'what compass of faith is required by given individuals', but what doctrines the Church Catholic teaches indefectibly, or enforces as a condition of communion, or rescues from the scrutiny of private judgment—in a word, what doctrines are the foundation of the Church. To find them, to discover what that common faith is which the Church 'now holds everywhere as the original deposit', one must turn to the creed, in which all branches of the Church agree.[1]

A local confession of faith, therefore, or a mere set of 'articles of religion', can beside this universal formulary be no more than a temporary particularization of Christian truth. It was thus, Newman contended, that the famous Anglican confession of 1571, to which the clergy were obliged to make *ex animo* subscription, was to be understood. Its terms were certainly not sacrosanct, and in any case its purpose, as its ambiguous phrases disclose, was to comprehend rather than exclude. Catholicism, accordingly, it was never intended to shun. To interpret the Articles in a manner favourable to Calvinism or even latitudinarianism was usual enough; but was it not also demonstrable that they were not only not contradictory of the witness of the early Church but likewise not opposed to Catholic doctrine down the ages, being incompatible, that is, with 'the dominant errors of Rome' alone? To attempt such a demonstration was Newman's aim in the notorious *Tract 90*, published in 1841.[2] To be merely polemical was not his intention, nor was it his purpose to declare what the Articles ought to be taken to mean. Nor again was he

---

[1] *The Prophetical Office of the Church*, pp. 264f.

[2] The enterprise was not without precedent. To show that the Articles were patient of a Catholic interpretation had been undertaken as long ago as 1634 by Christopher Davenport—known after his conversion to Roman Catholicism as Sancta Clara—in a work printed at Lyons entitled *Deus, Natura, Gratia, sive Tractatus de Praedestinatione, de Meritis, et peccatorum remissione, seu de Justificatione, et denique de Sanctorum Invocatione*. A supplement to the main treatise is described as a *Paraphrastica Expositio reliquorum Articulorum Confessionis Anglicanae*, the purpose of which is stated as: 'Articuli Confessionis Anglicanae paraphrastica exponuntur, et quantum cum veritate compossibiles reddi possunt, perlustrantur.' An English translation of this *Expositio*, by F. G. Lee, was published in 1865. Sancta Clara's arguments are ingenious but seldom plausible. Like Newman he distinguishes Roman doctrine proper from popular misconceptions of it, although unlike Newman he attributes these to Rome's critics, not to Catholics themselves. It is not clear that at the time of writing *Tract 90* Newman was familiar with Sancta Clara's work. On Davenport see G. G. Perry in *D.N.B.*

concerned to inquire what might or might not have been in the minds of those who framed them. His sole interest was to examine how far the language of the formulary could be read in accordance with the faith of the Church Universal without doing violence to its grammatical and literal sense. He was himself, he considered, doing no more than had been done by adherents of other ecclesi-, astical parties on behalf of their own beliefs. He simply was objecting that the Articles 'need not be so closed as the received method of teaching closes them, and ought not to be for the sake of many persons'. Were their meaning to be confined to the Protestant interpretation alone the risk would be incurred of driving such persons into the Church of Rome, when on an 'open' view of the said Articles, and one historically quite justifiable, they could remain loyal members of the Church of England.[1] But this further twist to the theory of the *Via Media* was more than Anglican opinion as a whole was ready to countenance. Newman was bitterly attacked. Many even of his sympathizers voiced their misgivings. Oxford officialdom accused him of evading rather than explaining the sense of the formulary and reconciling subscription to it with the adoption of errors which it was expressly designed to prevent. 'It was a crisis', observes Church, 'in which much might have been usefully said, if there had been any one to say it. . . . But it seemed as if the opportunity must not be lost for striking a blow.'[2] Not surprisingly the effect on the author was to cause him, in time, to reconsider the basic assumptions of the argument which he had so carefully elaborated. Was the Church of the *Via Media* after all nothing more than what at first he had thought it, a 'paper Church'? By 1842 he was, as he phrased it years later, 'on his death-bed' so far as the Church of

---

[1] The exact title of *Tract 90* was: *Remarks on Certain Passages in the Thirty-Nine Articles*, the Articles discussed being 6 and 20, 11, 12 and 13, 19, 21, 22, 25, 28, 31, 32, 35, and 37. 'Our present scope', the author explained, 'is merely to show that while our Prayer Book is acknowledged on all hands to be of Catholic origin, our Articles also, the offspring of an un-Catholic age, are, through God's good providence, to say the least, not un-Catholic, and may be subscribed by those who aim at being Catholic in heart and doctrine.' He ended with the statement: 'The Protestant Confession was drawn up with the purpose of including Catholics, and Catholics now will not be excluded. What was an economy in the reformers, is a protection to us. What would have been a perplexity to us then, is a perplexity to Protestants now. We could not then have found fault with their words: they cannot now repudiate our meaning.' On the controversy in Oxford see Owen Chadwick, *The Victorian Church*, i, pp. 181–9.

[2] *The Oxford Movement*, p. 291.

England was concerned. The entire notion of the English establishment as a true part of 'the Church Catholic and Apostolic, set up from the beginning', revealed itself to him as an illusion. The establishment had a life of a sort, assuredly; but it was not Catholic life. It was essentially Protestant, Erastian and national. The very idea of the supernatural was alien to it. Christ's Kingdom, as Englishmen saw it, was a kingdom very much of this world, and one over which parliament exercised a plenary authority. The establishment simply kept back 'those doctrines which, to the eye of faith, give real substance to religion'.

The full force of Newman's disillusionment did not, however, find vent until the publication in 1850—five years after his secession to Rome—of his lectures *On the Difficulties felt by Anglicans in Catholic Teaching*, where traces of a lingering personal resentment are not absent. Thus in allusion to the Gorham dispute he could say:

> The Evangelical party, who in former years had the nerve to fix the charge of dishonesty on the explanations of the Thirty-nine Articles, put forward by their opponents, could all the while be cherishing in their own breasts an interpretation of the Baptismal Service, simply contrary to its most luminous declarations.[1]

Yet the memory of his Anglican days was still something he treasured, and the experience of grace which he then knew, and which countless others continued to know, might not, he realized, be gainsaid:

> Cannot I too look back on many years past, and many events, in which I myself experienced what is now your confidence? Can I forget the happy life I have led all my days, with no cares, no anxieties worth remembering; without desolateness, or fever of thought, or gloom of mind, or doubt of God's love to me, and providence over me? . . . O my dear brethren, my Anglican friends, I easily give you credit for what I have experienced myself.[2]

The trouble was that although individual Christians might and undoubtedly did show the workings of God's grace within them,

[1] *Op. cit.*, p. 20.
[2] *Ibid.*, pp. 71f.

yet, apart from the divinely authenticated ordinances, it was not *safe*—the word is Newman's own—consciously to do so. Quality of life is not the guarantee of soundness of doctrine. Only in a Church which is unquestionably Catholic is there real assurance of salvation.

But Newman's personal rejection of Anglicanism as a true 'middle way', although influencing the rank and file among a large number of his followers, did not deter the other Oxford leaders. Dr Pusey's solid if unimaginative learning strongly upheld the idea. John Keble had no doubts at all. The High Church party rallied after Newman's defection and the doctrine that Anglicanism presents an authentically 'Catholic' form of Christianity, avoiding alike the unwarranted accretions of Rome and the manifest deficiencies of Protestantism, lived on to gain, as the years went by, ever larger acceptance with a new generation of Anglicans as the true account of their Church's historic character and claim. For although it may have been the case, in part at least, that, as Mark Pattison complained, 'the Tractarians desolated Oxford life, and suspended for an indefinite period all science, humane letters, and the first stirrings of intellectual freedom which had moved in the bosom of Oxford',[1] the Church of England became increasingly in outward appearance what the Tractarians had insisted that it is in principle. And however it may have failed to stem the tide of liberalism and the nation's growing secularization the established Church at the end of the century was in every aspect a very different thing from what it had been at the beginning. To that extent the work initiated by the Oxford divines was accomplished. Whether they would have approved the result it is idle to speculate. Events have their own logic and those who deliberately set them in train rarely foresee their course.

3. ORTHODOXY AND HOLINESS

Newman, beyond question, was the movement's presiding genius and the sincerity of the compliments he paid to others as he looked back on a scene from which, after much heartsearching, he himself had chosen to withdraw do not hide the fact. Quite apart from his great personal influence in the immediate circle

[1] *Memoirs* (1885), p. 101.

of his followers, he was easily the movement's leading publicist, with his unrivalled gifts as a writer. But the *Tracts* were not his work only. Out of a total of ninety he was responsible for twenty-nine. Keble wrote eight, Pusey seven, three of which (nos. 67–69), on baptism, make up a weighty volume. The rest were from various hands—Froude's, Perceval's, Isaac Williams's and J. W. Bowden's chiefly. Not all were original compositions: eighteen were reprints of the works of old authors such as Wilson, Cosin Beveridge, Bull and Ussher. The public reception of the tracts also varied. The evangelical *Record* was generally critical. But among the parish clergy, to whom in the main they were addressed, widespread curiosity was aroused. 'They fell', says Church, 'on a time of profound and inexcusable ignorance on the subjects they discussed, and they did not spare it.'[1] Pusey records that 'the Tracts found an echo everywhere. Friends started up like armed men from the ground. I only dreaded our being too popular.'[2] On the other hand, some were in the position of Charles Kingsley, who confessed that his own heart 'strangely yearned towards them from the first', but that he soon realized that the Oxford writings contained only half-truths. Arnold, as we saw, entirely deplored them and poured scorn on the ideas they were seeking to promote. The episcopal reaction was for the most part cool. One or two bishops seem to have been genuinely puzzled by them; others, like Sumner of Winchester, were mildly appreciative. Sooner or later the charge of Romanism was inevitable. The theological knowledge was, in Church's judgment, 'wanting which would have been familiar with the broad line of difference between what is Catholic and what is especially Roman'.[3]

Were, in fact, the views expressed in them really in accord with Church doctrine, as embodied in the liturgy and articles and in the writings of representative Anglican divines? The question cannot properly be answered without regard to historical conditions. The Church's formularies might well enshrine Catholic principles, as an impressive body of earlier Anglican theology testified that they did. Hooker, the Carolines, the Non-jurors and contemporary High Churchmen like van Mildert, Joshua Watson

[1] *The Oxford Movement*, p. 120. The tracts were at first circulated privately and the earliest of them were anonymous.
[2] Liddon, *Life of Pusey*, i, p. 259.
[3] *Ibid.*, p. 121.

and Alexander Knox had never looked on the national Church in a purely 'Protestant' light, Protestant though it indubitably was in regard to Rome herself. But the average Englishman saw it otherwise. For the Church of England stood for what he believed to be Bible Christianity in opposition to the errors of Popery, that ill-defined but always emotive word. It was this uninstructed mass opinion which the Tractarians believed it their mission ultimately to convert. The task, however, was immense. Prejudice against all 'Catholic' notions was deep-rooted and ignorance might prove invincible. The kind of language that came so easily to their own lips —'priest', 'absolution', 'apostolic succession', the word 'Catholic' itself even—had for the great majority of churchgoers an alien and sinister sound. The new Oxford theologians could of course cite prayerbook authority for employing it and might exercise great care in explaining what it meant, but public feeling on these matters had its own assurances, which were of a contrary nature. Moreover, such feeling was increasingly to be reflected in episcopal pronouncements, notably those of John Bird Sumner, bishop of Chester and subsequently archbishop of Canterbury, who in 1838 spoke out against the 'undermining of the foundations of our Protestant Church by men who dwell within her walls'.

Tractarian belief in the Church as a divine institution had for corollary an insistence on strictness in adhering to the received doctrines. With these men orthodoxy was not only a principle but a passion, liberalism and dissent alike representing, in their different ways, grave declensions from the truth. Several of the tracts took the form of *catenae*, lengthy extracts from the Fathers or from High Church divines of the past to show how certain teachings—that on the eucharistic sacrifice, for example—are rightly to be held by loyal members of the Church of England. Similarly Keble's *The Christian Year*, the publication of which in 1827, rather than his 1833 sermon, could as plausibly be taken as marking the real start of the movement, was deliberately composed with the aim of expressing Church doctrine in verse of 'a sober standard of feeling'.[1] Their author's sermon *On the Baptismal Offices* and his later *Treatise on Eucharistic Adoration* are imbued with the same concern. Pusey, despite his early, tentative interest

---

[1] Newman thought the poems 'exquisite' (*Letters*, i, p. 165). But Keble's own estimate of them was unfeignedly modest.

in German rationalism, remained a monument of orthodoxy,[1] abjuring all idea that he and his friends taught peculiar doctrines'.

In any case the purpose of the tracts was practical and popular, and as a rule technical theology was avoided. The intention of all the writers was soundness of doctrine and simplicity. Questions of ritual and ceremonial were not dealt with. Tractarian practice continued to be 'low'—Newman, for instance, always celebrated holy communion at the north end of the table, Pusey maintaining that the times were not ripe for anything more than the needful reassertion of Catholic principles and that attention paid to the externals of worship would only compromise the teaching of essentials.[2] Frederick Oakeley, who later became a Roman Catholic, seems to have been the first to interest himself in such matters. 'We are for carrying out', he wrote in an article in the movement's organ, *The British Critic*[3], 'the symbolic principle in our own Church to the utmost extent which is consistent with the duty of obedience to the rubric.' If ornaments in churches should to some appear trivial, let them be reminded 'that care about minutiae is the peculiar mark of an intense and reverent affection'. There was, he thought, 'something quite revolting in the idea of dealing with the subject of External Religion as a matter of mere taste'. The subsequent growth of ritualism in the parishes was in fact an obvious practical development of the Tractarian ecclesiology and sacramental doctrine.

One tract which, rather surprisingly, aroused a good deal of adverse comment was Isaac Williams's *On Reserve in Communicating Religious Knowledge*, no. 80 in the series, described by Church as 'a protest against the coarseness and shallowness which threw the most sacred words about at random in loud and declamatory appeals'; a protest, in short, against much current evangelical preaching. The use of the term 'reserve', however, caused alarm. Did it not mean a holding back of the full truth of the saving gospel? Worse still, it suggested devious ways—priestcraft and

---

[1] His *Historical Inquiry into the Probable Causes of the Rationalistic Character lately predominant in the Theology of Germany*, in which he displayed considerable knowledge of the contemporary intellectual scene in that country, was published in 1828.

[2] He thought it 'beginning at the wrong end for ministers to deck their persons; our own plain dresses are more in keeping with the state of our Church, which is one of humiliation'. For this reason he deprecated the attempt to restore 'the richer style of vestments' used in Edward VI's reign. See Liddon, *Life of Pusey*, ii, pp. 142–5.

[3] January–April 1840, p. 270.

Jesuitry. Thus innocently, for Williams was a man of a singularly modest and retiring disposition, did the unfortunate author provoke suspicion not only as to his own motives but towards the movement as a whole, a suspicion which was never to be allayed, and to which *Tract 90* appeared to supply the most devastating confirmation. But there was nothing at all of a prevaricating spirit among the tract writers. They were simply careful of their language. 'Prune thy words', wrote Newman, 'the thoughts control'

> That o'er thee swell and throng;
> That they will condense within thy soul,
>   And change to purpose strong.

The Church's doctrine filled them with awe, for soundness of creed was the road to personal holiness. The Tractarians' moralism, as has been particularly stressed by modern commentators, was in some respects the most striking thing about them. 'Be ye perfect', they would have said, 'even as your Father in heaven is perfect.' The profoundest mysteries of the faith—and no doctrine was more profound or mysterious than the atonement—were not in their judgment to be exhibited indiscriminately before minds unchastened by moral discipline. The articles of the Christian creed, wrote Williams, 'contain great sacred truths of the very highest possible importance that we should know; but if we attempt to arrive at any knowledge of them by speculation, or any other mode but that of practical obedience, that knowledge is withheld, and we are punished for the attempt'.

The note the Tractarians struck in their sermons was consistently one of moral severity. A recent writer indeed detects in the work of all of them 'an undercurrent of pessimism and gloom'.[1] Thus Newman gave to one of his earliest published sermons, preached in August 1826, the title 'Holiness necessary for future blessedness', whilst in another, of June 1825, he declared that 'the whole history of redemption . . . attests the necessity of holiness in order to attain salvation'. In a Whitsun address of 1831 he warned his hearers that 'our ascended Saviour, who is on God's right hand, and sends down from thence God's Spirit, is to be feared greatly, even amid His gracious consolations', reminding them of the apostle's words, 'Work out your own

[1] David Newsome, *Godliness and Good Learning*, p. 180.

salvation with fear and trembling.' Again, many years later, in September 1842, he speaks of the danger of attempting one aspect of the Christian character while neglecting another: 'Religion has two sides, a severe side, and a beautiful; and we shall be sure to swerve from the narrow way which leads to life, if we indulge ourselves in what is beautiful, while we put aside what is severe.'[1] Pusey likewise says that everything may, and does, minister to heaven or hell:

> We are, day by day, and hour by hour, influenced by everything around us; rising or falling, sinking or recovering, receiving impressions which are to last for ever; taking colour and mould from everything which passes around us and in us, and not less because unperceived; each touch slight, as impressed by an invisible spiritual hand, but, in itself, not the less, rather the more lasting, since what we are yielding ourselves to is, in the end, the finger of God or the touch of Satan.[2]

If, therefore, certain doctrines seem to make religion gloomy and even repulsive, it is because, in Newman's words, it 'must ever be difficult for those who neglect it'.

> All things that we have to learn are difficult at first, and our duties to God, and to man for His sake, are peculiarly difficult, because they call upon us to take up a new life, and quit the love of this world for the next. It cannot be avoided; we must fear and be in sorrow, before we can rejoice. The Gospel must be a burden before it comforts and brings us peace. . . . Religion is in itself at first a weariness to the worldly mind, and it requires an effort and a self-denial in everyone who honestly determines to be religious.[3]

It is the duty of a Christian to witness to God and to glorify him, to be as a light on a hill, through evil report and good report; the evil report and good report being indeed less of his own making than the natural consequence of the Christian profession itself. Such admonitions, on Tractarian lips, were far from being the stock-in-trade of conventional pulpit utterance. These men believed wholeheartedly in their message and practised it in their daily lives. For the world they cared nothing. They despised its comforts and set little or no value on its honours. They did not

---

[1] *Sermons bearing on Subjects of the Day* ('Feasting in Captivity') (ed. 1918), p. 391.
[2] *Parochial Sermons* (1869), iii, p. 431.
[3] *Parochial Sermons* (1837–42), i, p. 26.

aim at popularity, nor seek social advancement—which most of them never in any case obtained. Newman believed that 'the Church itself is always hated and calumniated by the world', since Christians, in actually thwarting the world's pride and selfishness, are inevitably disliked by the world. This intense moral earnestness was for the Oxford divines the acid test of a genuine religious conviction. Beside it A. P. Stanley's remark, echoing Arnold, on 'the trivial elements which produced so much excitement' is itself trivial.[1]

In view of this strong moral *motif* in Tractarianism it is scarcely surprising that the Evangelicals at first saw little to object to in it, apart from its doctrine of the ministry. 'holiness rather than peace', which Newman took as motto, had been a principle of Thomas Scott, the Calvinist Bible commentator, to whom, 'humanly speaking', Newman confessed he almost owed his soul.[2] Long after, in 1851, Robert Wilberforce, a son of the great philanthropist, recalled in a charge to the clergy of his archdeaconry that

> during the first quarter of the century men were roused from slumber and wakened to earnestness; the next period gave them an external object on which to expend the zeal that had been enkindled. For it must be observed . . . that these movements, though distinct, were not repugnant. On the contrary, persons who had been most influenced by the one, often entered most readily upon the other. . . . So then the second movement was a sort of consequence of the first.[3]

The leaders of the Oxford Movement were, then, as intent upon moral commitment as were any of its Evangelical or Broad Church critics. In this indeed they were Englishmen typical of their age and social class. They had, moreover, assiduously read

---

[1] Mr Newsome calls attention to this same note of severity in the parochial sermons of H. E. Manning, afterwards archbishop of Westminster and cardinal. In the first volume, for example, there are addresses bearing such titles as 'Salvation a Difficult Work' and 'A severe Life necessary for Christ's followers'. 'To all mankind, as fallen men,' says the preacher, 'the way of life is not more blessed than it is arduous. . . . There must pass on each a deep and searching change. And this change, though it be wrought in us of God, is wrought through our striving. It is no easy task to gird up the energies of our moral nature to a perpetual struggle. . . . It is a hard thing to be a Christian.' See Newsome, *op. cit.*, pp. 207f.

[2] *Apologia*, ed. Svaglic, p. 18.

[3] R. I. Wilberforce, *A Charge to the Clergy of the East Riding, delivered at the Ordinary Visitation* (1851), pp. 10f (quoted Newsome, *ibid.*, p. 14).

their Bishop Butler, by whom Newman in particular was profoundly influenced and in a way that reinforced the strong ethical predisposition imparted to him by his own evangelical upbringing. To all of them the ground of religion, especially of a religion whose teaching authority was the Bible, lay in the moral consciousness. The heightening of religious sensibility, a deepened understanding of religious doctrine, depended in the first instance upon obedience to the law of conscience. Not, of course, that grace was only secondary, for without grace the soul could make no progress in the saving knowledge of God. Rather, as Newman expressed it, 'the grace promised us is given, not that we may know more, but that we may do better'[1]—advance farther along the path of sanctification, in the more studied performance of our duty to God and man. It was in fact this very moralism which sharpened the Tractarians' criticism of the evangelical theology. For the Evangelicals' emphasis on soteriology led them, in the classical Protestant manner, to disparage man's inherent moral capacity, although without it the preaching of repentance itself could hardly have much meaning; as also to lose sight of the wider significance of that *incarnation* of the Son of God whence the death on Calvary necessarily drew its efficacy. Christ's assumption of humanity was, in truth, 'a higher gift than grace', being the pledge of

> God's presence and His very self
> And essence all divine.

This incarnationalist *motif* in Tractarian thought was to reveal its broader implications in the work of a subsequent generation of High Churchmen; but its immediate result was an enhanced appreciation of the sacramental means whereby the divine life is communicated to the believer and an insistence upon his gradual conformation to the moral pattern of Christ's own supreme example.

A main reason why Isaac Williams's tract *On Reserve* had offended evangelical susceptibilities was, as we have noted, its objection to any exploitation of the mystery of the atonement. 'The highest and most sacred of all Christian doctrines', he wrote, 'is to be brought before and pressed home to all persons indiscriminately, and most especially to those who are leading

[1] *Parochial Sermons*, i, p. 234.

unchristian lives.' The only fitting approach to religion is through holiness of life; otherwise superstition is the outcome, as in the tendency of Roman Catholicism to substitute the Virgin Mary for God in ritual and devotion—a plain illustration, he thinks, of the way in which 'the natural heart lowers the object of its worship to its own frailty'. The risk of idolatry in the case of the atonement was in suggesting that acceptance by 'faith' of the merits of Christ's death is alone sufficient and that moral obedience may be dispensed with, whereas conscience is our first and always necessary guide: 'There is no one living but to whom Wisdom speaks, a voice that tells him of something better which he ought to do than what he does. . . . Until he follows this voice, the higher and better wisdom is hid from him.'

Mankind's innate moral sense was for all the Tractarians the threshold of the knowledge of God. So far they recognized a divine revelation outside the Bible, a revelation which Christian doctrine itself presupposes. Further, Christian doctrine could not properly be understood until its moral dimension had been fully realized. Thus Hurrell Froude could admit that although he assented to the damnatory clauses of the Athanasian creed as affirming no more than Scripture itself teaches, yet he did so with difficulty since it seemed to him axiomatic that no opinion *as such* can be the object of God's wrath or favour. If an opinion is condemned it is because it involves 'something moral as its effect or cause, or both'.[1] Again, the same writer, in an address significantly entitled 'The Gospel as the Completion of Natural Religion', states his belief that the only possible way of comprehending the doctrines of the trinity and incarnation and of profiting by them, 'or, indeed, by entering at all into their meaning', is by leading that sort of life which they are intended to help us in leading. Referring again to the Athanasian creed, he goes on to say:

> We must ask ourselves, not 'Am I thoroughly convinced and certain that these mysterious doctrines are true?' for that is a matter over which we can have no control; we cannot feel certain by trying to feel ever so much; and God will not require of us impossibilities. But what we must ask ourselves is this: 'Is my conduct such as it *would be* if I was thoroughly convinced of them? In the first place, do I act as if I believed God to be my Father, and my neighbour

[1] *Remains*, i, p. 117.

to be my brothers?' That is, 'do I believe in earthly things?'[1] and, secondly, 'as to heavenly things, do I endeavour with all my might and with all my soul, and with all my strength, to *follow and obey* the Lord Jesus Christ *as* my Saviour and my God?'[2]

Newman is no less explicit. In an Oxford University sermon preached in 1830 on 'The Influence of Natural and Revealed Religion Respectively' he considers the knowledge of the divine order which may be attained apart from an express revelation, and observes that:

> Such is the large and practical religious creed attainable (as it appears from the extant works of heathen writers) by a vigorous mind which rightly works upon itself under (what may be called) the Dispensation of Paganism. It may even be questioned whether there be any essential character of Scripture doctrine which is without its place in this moral revelation. For here is the belief in a principle exterior to the mind to which it is instinctively drawn, infinitely exalted, perfect, incomprehensible; here is the surmise of a judgment to come; the knowledge of an unbounded benevolence, wisdom, and power, as traced in the visible creation, and of moral laws unlimited in their operation; further, there is something of hope respecting the availableness of repentance, so far (that is) as suffices for religious thought; lastly, there is an insight into the rule of duty increasing with the earnestness with which obedience to that rule is cultivated.[3]

From this it ensues that the heathen are not in danger of perishing in so far as they follow the 'secret voice' of conscience within them. On the other hand, to arguments for natural religion based merely on the evidences of design in nature Newman was less sympathetic. To a believer in God such evidences might be beautiful and interesting, 'but where men have not already recognized God's voice within them ineffective, and this, moreover, from some unsoundness in the intellectual basis of the argument'.[4] It is the same indeed with history itself. Of God's existence Newman is as certain as he is of his own; but the

[1] The reference is to John iii, 2.

[2] The Tractarians, it appears, had not read Kant, but there are Kantian overtones in such a passage as that quoted. Religious doctrines are to be understood as essentially practical and moral. It is a view, moreover, which anticipates the religious pragmatism of the Catholic Modernists, especially E. Le Roy, who describes a dogma as 'une prescription d'ordre pratique, une règle de conduite pratique' (*Dogme et Critique*, 1907, p. 23).

[3] *Oxford University Sermons* (1843), ed. 1892, p. 21.

[4] Concerning Newman's distrust of rational proofs in religion see below, ch. IV

world, as he looked out on it, filled him, as he afterwards confessed in one of the most memorable passages he ever wrote, with 'unspeakable distress'. It seemed to him to give the lie to a truth of which his own whole being was full.

> The effect upon me is, in consequence, as a matter of necessity, as confusing as if it denied that I am in existence myself. If I looked into a mirror, and did not see my face, I should have the sort of feeling which actually comes upon me, when I look into this busy world and see no reflection of its creator.

But this conviction was inescapable only because of the voice of conscience—that 'aboriginal Vicar of Christ', as he called it— inside him. Save for this minatory counsellor, speaking so authoritatively as it did, he might, he says, have been 'an atheist, or a pantheist, or a polytheist'. The spectacle of the world as it is is 'nothing else than the prophet's scroll, full of "lamentations, and mourning, and woe" '.[1]

But the Oxford Movement's profound moralism received perhaps its most insistent expression in the work of William George Ward (1812–82), a fellow of Balliol and a tutor in philosophy, who eventually, like Newman, left the Church of England for that of Rome. Ward in earlier days had been a disciple of Arnold, whose moral earnestness made a strong appeal to him. What he sought, and in Arnold (it seemed) had discovered, was a 'wholesome antidote' to all mere formalism in religion, whether as the old-fashioned Protestant cult of respectability or the new, romantic antiquarianism. Plainly Arnold was a man to be trusted, and Ward, with his natural capacity for philosophical thinking, was willing to give him his trust; but, as his son and biographer, Wilfrid Ward, relates, 'on hearing Newman preach for the first time he found in his tone and teaching all and more than all of that exalted ethical character which had won him to Dr Arnold'.

> The devotion to antique rule, the love of unreal supernatural legend, the advocacy of superstitious rites as all-important, which had in his mind been the essence of Newmanism, did not appear at all, and the idea of holiness as the one aim was the pervading spirit of the whole sermon.[2]

[1] *Apologia*, pp. 216f.
[2] *W. G. Ward and the Oxford Movement* (2nd ed., 1890), p. 79.

In comparison with the doctrines to be heard from the pulpit of St Mary's church Arnoldism clearly 'stopped short', at every turn. Intellectually it stopped short, for the principle of free critical inquiry which Arnold extolled appeared to lead to scepticism rather than faith. Practically, too, it stopped short: as a way of religion it kept the supernatural at a distance. Likewise, ethically it stopped short: 'It had no saints. It watered Christianity down to what seemed more practicable to the average Christian than Christ's own teaching.'[1] Thus the reflection passed Ward's mind, as he considered whither the consistent application of latitudinarian principles might lead, that there may yet prove to be 'some indissoluble connection between the plenitude of doctrine and the highest morality'. If so, then belief could not be simply a matter of the intellect, a rational balancing of pros and cons. Its true genesis, rather as under Newman's guidance he was coming to see more and more plainly, was in obedience to conscience. Obedience is primary, knowledge secondary. Men see God by being pure in heart; they do not become pure in heart by seeing God. 'He who learns the truth from argument or mere trust in men may lose it again by argument or by trust in men; but he who learns it by obedience can lose it only by disobedience.'[2]

This view was re-emphasized in Ward's main work, *The Ideal of a Christian Church*, published in 1844, a year before his conversion to Rome.[3] It seemed to the author that the Protestant doctrine of justification *sola fide* ignored the truth that 'careful moral discipline is the necessary foundation, whereon alone Christian faith can be reared'.[4]

> To do what is right because it is right, and from a motive of duty, is the highest and noblest of all habits ... far nobler than the doing what is right out of gratitude for free pardon.[5]

[1] *Ibid.*, p. 86.

[2] *Ibid.*, p. 77.

[3] The book was formally condemned, on 13 February 1845, by the university of Oxford, and its author deprived of his degrees. See Church, *The Oxford Movement*, pp. 38off. 'The 13th of February', Church adds, 'was not only the final defeat and conclusion of the first stage of the movement. It was the birthday of the modern Liberalism of Oxford' (*ibid.*, p. 393).

[4] *The Ideal of a Christian Church*, p. vii.

[5] *Ibid.*, p. 301.

In any case the intellect should never be permitted to replace conscience as the arbiter of religious truth. The one faculty to be visited by divine grace is the sense of duty.[1]

> If conscience [he averred] be not on all moral and religious subjects paramount, then it does not really exist; if it do not exist, we have no reason whatever, nay, no power whatever to believe in God,

pointing out that Auguste Comte's atheism was grounded in his very denial that such a faculty exists. Again, in a passage cited by his biographer, remarkably reminiscent of Coleridge, Ward maintains that whereas the knowledge of phenomena is obtained by the intellect, knowledge of realities comes from the conscience; the one by inquiry, the other by obedience. The former, he thinks, 'tends to pride', the latter 'indispensably requires and infallibly increases humility'.[2] Nevertheless, if the one vitally important principle is the absolute supremacy of conscience, the other—and here we have the presiding thesis of his book—is 'the high sacredness of hereditary religion'. For conscience needs to be educated if private idiosyncrasies are not to pervert its judgment. To fulfil the role of universal moral educator a visible Church is a necessity; a merely unseen one would be 'a very sorry antagonist against so very visible a world'. As he wrote to Pusey:

> The more a person feels his deficiency in the apprehension of unseen things, the more painfully he feels the want of so consoling and impressive an image of a visible Church as even Rome displays; the more difficult he finds his contest with his old nature; the more he regrets that he has not been trained from the first in regular confession; the more he misses the practical rules of conduct in which Roman books of devotion abound, drawn from the stores, which they have retained, of traditional teaching; the more he misses the guidance of a priest carefully trained with a view to the confessional.[3]

The Ideal might and did appear to many as '*Tract* 90 writ large', and the goal towards which its author was heading was plain enough; but always it is the Church and the externals of religion as ministering to and promoting personal sanctity which is the core of his argument.

---

[1] *Ibid.*, p. 204.
[2] Wilfred Ward, *op. cit.*, p. 258.
[3] *Ibid.*, p. 183.

4. JUSTIFICATION AND SANCTIFICATION

The stress on inwardness characteristic of the movement is manifest in its understanding of the doctrine of justification. Newman's lectures on this subject, published in 1838, may well be considered the most important contribution to dogmatic theology to have come from the Tractarian school. Their purport was to show that the teaching laid down in the Thirty-nine Articles is by no means irreconcilable with Catholic doctrine on the priesthood and sacraments. The lectures are not indeed among their author's most arresting works, but they make up a treatise of unquestionable learning and penetration. The true doctrine, he thinks, steers a middle course between the Lutheran and the Roman.

> Whether we say we are justified by faith or by works or by Sacraments, all these mean but this one doctrine, that we are justified by grace, given through the Sacraments, impetrated by faith, manifested in works.[1]

He then examines some of the diverse views that have from time to time been held. Of these the first asserts that we are justified directly upon the holiness and good works wrought in us *through* Christ's merits by the Spirit. This he calls the 'high Roman view'. Its opposite is the 'high Protestant', which insists that Christ's merits and righteousness, imputed to us, become the immediate cause of our justification, superseding everything else in the eye of the heavenly judge. Between these extremes fall two further views, the one holding that we are justified 'directly upon our holiness and works *under* the covenant of Christ's merits', the other 'that our faith is mercifully appointed as the substitute for perfect holiness, and thus as the interposing and acceptable principle between us and God'. Whether these doctrines really are but differing forms of what is commonly considered the High Church view among Anglicans—as Newman himself believes —is open to question. But his clear purpose is to oppose both the Roman doctrine (as he understands it), which, although maintaining that the atonement wrought on man's behalf by Christ is the only ground of good works, nevertheless denies the need of a continual imputation of Christ's merits to make good the defects of man's actual obedience, and the Protestant doctrine (again as he understands it), which, in putting all the weight on

[1] *Lectures on Justification*, p. 348.

the imputation of Christ's merits as the substitute for man's failure in obedience, seems to deny the need for any subsequent effort after the maximum holiness on his part, and even to suspect the wish for such holiness as in some way casting doubt on the sufficiency of Christ's sacrifice. As between these poles more stress or less may be placed on the respective roles of faith and works, so long as we regard works as effective only because springing from a faith made possible by the grace of Christ.

What in his treatment of this subject Newman was basically concerned to establish is that to be 'justified' means for the believer an intrinsic 'newness of life', and not merely, as the Evangelicals taught, a forensic attributing of Christ's own holiness to one who is himself 'vile'. Sacramental incorporation into the mystical Body of Christ involves *gratia infusa*, an actual *impartation* of the righteousness of Christ. A mere imputing and not an imparting of that righteousness is but a 'joyless shadow' of the glorious reality. Not that Newman himself knew nothing directly of a conversion experience. As related in the *Apologia*, he had as a youth undergone just such an experience, of which he was still, at the time of writing (1864), 'more certain than that he had hands and feet'.[1] But by the time he delivered the lectures on justification he had embraced opinions very different from those in which he had been nurtured. Conversion experiences of the evangelical type now appeared to him to rely far too much on feelings of confidence, or, as the term was, an 'assurance' of salvation. By contrast the Tractarians were too conscious of their unworthiness and of the need for perpetual moral vigilance. As Pusey expressed it in his own book on *Justification*, published in 1853:

> It is easy to deceive ourselves as to our deeds, if we will but look into our consciences by the light of the law of God. It is easy to say 'Lord, Lord'; it is *not* easy, but of the power of the grace of God, to 'deny ourselves and take up our cross and follow Him.' . . . It is *not* easy, amid the fire of passion within, the manifold force of temptation without, the delusive pleasure dancing before our eyes, the treachery of our own hearts, to be 'dead to the world, that we may live to God'.

---

[1] He was fifteen years of age at the time, but the experience was not a predominantly emotional one. See H. Tristram, *John Henry Newman Autobiographical Writings* (1957), pp. 79f, 172.

The evangelicals, for all their talk about sin, were apt to be smug. This difference of view, however, was only one aspect of a deeper-lying difference of theological emphasis. In Christ, so the Tractarians believed, a man at once finds a new quality of life. He has become one with the Risen Christ and no longer is a mere suppliant at the cross of the Crucified. On this Newman is explicit:

> If the Resurrection be the means by which the Atonement is applied to each of us, if it be our justification, if in it are conveyed all the gifts of grace and glory which Christ has purchased for us, if it be the commencement of His giving Himself to us for a spiritual sustenance, of His feeding us with that Bread which has already been perfected on the Cross and is now a medicine of immortality,[1] it is that very doctrine which is most immediate to us, in which Christ most clearly approaches us, from which we gain life and out of which issue our hopes and duties.[2]

It is strange, reading these statements, to recall that the common charge against the Tractarians, then and later, was of 'medievalism' and preoccupation with externals. What in their sight mattered above all else was the soul's inner state, whilst in their faith in the resurrection they drew inspiration less from the cross-centred piety of the middle ages than from antiquity. Thus sanctification—the continuing growth in holiness—more than justification, at least when the latter is isolated as the supreme 'moment' in the process of the soul's regeneration, is the heart of their religious concern. Even in their eucharistic theology attention fastens upon the presence rather than the sacrifice, upon communion rather than propitiation. The 'special joy' of the eucharist to the believer, as more than a simple commemoration of Christ's redemptive acts or a showing forth of his death or a spiritual strengthening and refreshment, is that it is 'the Redeemer's very broken Body' and 'His Blood, which was shed for the remission of his sins'.[3] There is, of course, no question of a *transubstantiation*. What was bread remains bread, and what was wine remains wine. 'We need no carnal, earthly, visible, miracle to convince us of the Presence of the Lord Incarnate.' But 'He who is at the right hand of God, manifests himself in that Holy Sacrament as really and fully as

---

[1] The allusion is to Ignatius' φάρμακον ἀθανασίας (*Ephesians*, 20).

[2] *Lectures on Justification*, pp. 254f.

[3] E. B. Pusey, *University Sermons* (1859), pp. 18f.

if He were visibly there'.[1] In communion the faithful recipient of the sacramental grace becomes spiritually one with Christ himself.

A like conviction explains the importance to the Tractarians of the doctrine of baptismal regeneration. This had been a point of controversy between them and their critics from the beginning. Evangelicals did not identify baptism with conversion, by which alone, as they saw it, the sinner could be said to be regenerate. A rite administered to infants, however fitting in its way, gives no assurance as to the spiritual and moral quality of the recipient's subsequent life as an adult, and one who showed none of the influences of religion could not with propriety be described as 'born again'. Yet the Church's baptismal service seems clearly to affirm that the baptized as such are regenerate, and it was upon this evident meaning of the Prayer Book language that the Oxford school built its case.[2] They saw nothing either superstitious or mechanical in the idea that an infant child should so be described. For what is given in baptism, they held, is nothing less than the new life of the Risen Lord. This it is which makes possible a real and not merely an imputed holiness and provides the incentive as well as the means of a progressive sanctification. The baptized has more and more to become what in spiritual *status* he already is, learning to contemplate himself, so Newman, explains, not as he is in himself, but as he is 'in the Eternal God'.

> Fall down in astonishment at the glories which are around thee and in thee, poured to and fro in such a wonderful way that thou art (as it were) dissolved into the Kingdom of God, and art as if thou hadst nought to do but to contemplate and feed upon that great vision.[3]

All the necessary exactness of obedience, the anxiety about failing, the pain of self-denial, the watchfulness and zeal and self-chastisement, do not interfere with this vision of faith. Moreover, the baptized does not stand alone, even though fortified by the resources of grace within him. For by the sacrament he becomes a member of the Church, Christ's Body. He is now as by right a citizen of a new realm of faith, hope and love.

[1] J. H. Newman, *Parochial Sermons*, iv, p. 167ff.
[2] See below, Appendix I: The Gorham Judgment.
[3] Newman, *op. cit.*, p. 166.

This teaching is brought out with special fervour by Pusey, who has been aptly called the *doctor mysticus* of the movement. He was not indeed among its most compelling preachers—of Newman's pulpit magnetism he had nothing; but when his mind turns to the mystery of the unity of God and man wrought by the redemption his utterance becomes rapturous:

> Oh the blessedness beyond all thought! Unutterable riches of the mercy of God, to be for ever not our own, but to be His, His by creation, His by redemption, His by re-creation, but His too by His indwelling, His life, His love, His glory, His light, His wisdom, His immortality within us; yea, all but His infinitely, and that the endless object of our contemplation, never cloying, never exhausted, because He is infinite. . . .[1]

Yet for all the learning and the moral energy which the leaders of the movement were together able to command, its contribution to religious thought cannot, in the end, be deemed very great. Newman, of course, must be excepted, even though it appear unfair to make an exception so large—he was after all, until 1845, its leading figure. But Newman throughout his life, Catholic as well as Anglican, was deeply concerned with the basic problem of belief to a degree, to which other Tractarians—unless we exclude his disciple, Ward—were not. For that reason alone he requires separate discussion. Whilst being beyond question the movement's greatest personal force he always stood, in some manner, a little apart from it, as not wholly of it. But if the 'mind' of the movement is to be taken to mean the doctrine of the *Tracts*—and the identification is one which the tract-writers themselves would have endorsed—then it cannot be said that it denoted anything creatively new or, for the future, important. The Oxford divines were no more in the forefront of theological advance than were the Evangelicals. The doctrines which they rehabilitated, of the authority and catholicity of the Church, and the sacramentalism which accompanied these, were to have potent influence upon the life of the Church of England and her daughter churches of the Anglican communion in general, as indeed upon churches outside the Anglican world. But this influence affected the piety, the religious ethos, of the Anglican Church, more than its wider theological outlook. That Church

---

[1] *Parochial Sermons*, iii, pp. 422f.

now learned to think of itself, in no formal or nominal sense merely, as Catholic; the once complacently accepted designation of Protestant seemed more and more to be inadequate and misleading. Tractarian revivalism, however, intellectually speaking, pointed to no new horizons. Advances in scientific knowledge, in biblical criticism and in philosophical speculation were viewed with either indifference or distrust. Yet the spirit of reaction in a party which even in its early career showed promise of becoming the most vigorous and influential within the established Church could not prevail indefinitely. The men of the ensuing generations felt less need to erect bulwarks against the tide of change, anxious though they were that the treasures of an ancient and irreplaceable heritage of faith should not be lost. These were the men who, more than forty years after Newman's secession, were to explore the possibility of a Catholic theology fixed no doubt in its principles 'yet ever yielding up new meanings even from its central depths, in the light of other knowledge and human development'. The manifesto of this new phase in Anglican thought was a volume significantly entitled *Lux Mundi*. But of this it must remain to speak in a later chapter.

Chapter IV

John Henry Newman

I. THE TRACTARIAN LEADERS

The Oxford Movement was not the creation of a single mind, however fertile, any more than, contrariwise, it was the planned procedure of a closely organized group. Each of its leading figures brought to it a distinctive personality and a particular aptitude and point of view. Such diversity inevitably entailed differences of emphasis and judgment or idiosyncrasies that resisted the mould of a united purpose and resolve. Keble was very unlike Hurrell Froude; the characters of Newman and Pusey stood in signal contrast to each other; between Isaac Williams and W. G. Ward there may seem almost no affinity of either aim or temper. Yet the Movement as a whole appeared to its more hostile critics as nothing less than conspiratorial alike in its designs and its methods; and even the presentday historian is at once made aware of its strong sense of an agreed purpose and a shared enthusiasm, enough to give it a still live interest, despite the remoteness of its antiquated teachings.

The special dispositions of the protagonists call at this point for some notice. John Keble (1792–1866), whom Newman looked on as the Movement's 'true and primary author', nevertheless possessed few of the characteristics usually associated with the leadership of a radical party. Mildness and modesty he had almost to a fault. Even Dean Church, who admired him greatly, admitted that there was nothing in him to foreshadow the role he was to assume in a bold and influential movement. 'He was absolutely without ambition.' He hated show and mistrusted excitement. Popularity he shunned. Even to exercise influence, at any rate consciously, he had no care. 'He had deliberately chosen the *fallentis semita vitae*, and to be what his father had been, a faithful and contented country parson, was all that he desired.' Not a man of many friends, or a party chief, he was distinguished, however, by qualities of mind and heart which won him the deep regard of those who knew him best.[1] That he had intellectual gifts of no mean order the brilliance of his youthful academic career demonstrates, and as a scholar his edition of the works of Hooker has done him lasting credit. But forcefulness, novelty, even the customary artifices of pulpit rhetoric, he avoided. Ecclesiastically he was rather narrow, 'an old-fashioned English Churchman, with great veneration for the Church and its bishops, and a great dislike of Rome, Dissent and Methodism'.[2] Yet he was not without spirit. The subdued tone, the personal diffidence, indicated no weakness in his adherence to principles. Unquestionably he was a source of personal strength to the Movement in its early days, and it is impossible to think of it without recalling him. His positive contribution to its thought, on the other hand, is not easy to determine. Even the famous sermon on 'National Apostasy' proclaims nothing new or arresting, and is little more than a *rechauffé* of the unimaginative 'political' High Churchmanship of his father's generation. Keble, in fact, was a power in the Movement more by what he himself was, as an embodiment of its moral idealism and sober piety, than by his writings, with the single exception of *The Christian Year*. He was the pure type of the Christian gentleman and country pastor devoted to his flock. As such he stands for what the Movement essentially was, a revival of practical religion and the re-creation of the Anglican clerical ideal. An imaginative intelligence his was not. It is said that the advice he once gave a friend—could it have been Newman?—was 'Don't be original'.

Nearest to Keble in character and outlook was his pupil, Isaac Williams (1802–65), although oddly enough he was the author, as we have seen, of what turned out to be one of the most controversial of the *Tracts*. He too preferred the obscurity of his rural parish. Church says of him that he caught from Keble 'two characteristic habits of mind—a strong depreciation of mere

[1] R. W. Church, *The Oxford Movement*, pp. 23–7. See G. Battiscombe, *John Keble: a Study in Limitations* (1963).
[2] Church, *ibid.*, p. 26.

intellect compared with the less showy excellencies of faithfulness to conscience and duty; and a horror and hatred of everything that seemed like display or the desire of applause or of immediate effect'. But he notes also that 'it seemed sometimes as if in preaching or talking he aimed at being dull and clumsy'. His churchmanship was identical with Keble's. He came to know Newman well, but confessed that from the first he saw in him what he learned to look upon as the greatest of dangers—'the preponderance of intellect among the elements of character and as the guide of life'.[1]

Richard Hurrell Froude, in the early days of the Movement Newman's most intimate friend and the original link between the latter and Keble, was a man of a very different temperament. 'Froude', Newman remarks, 'was a bold rider, as on horseback, so also in his speculations.' Hugh James Rose noted that 'he did not seem to be afraid of inferences'. Church found in him 'a man of great gifts, with much that was most attractive and noble', but sensed that 'joined with this there was originally in his character a vein of perversity and mischief, always in danger of breaking out, and with which he kept up a long and painful struggle'.[2] What inspired him was a roseate vision of the middle ages. The establishment, so much revered by elder churchmen, he wholly despised. 'Let us tell the truth, and shame the devil; let us give up a *National* Church and have a *real* one.'[3] The Reformation he considered a disaster; it had introduced 'a spirit of lawlessness', of which liberalism was the latest offspring. What he longed for himself was the restoration of England's 'ancient religion', a second and better Reformation, inspired by the teachings of the age not of Cranmer but of Laud. 'Never', he declared, 'would he call the Holy Eucharist "the Lord's Supper", nor God's Priests "ministers of the word", or the Altar "the Lord's Table" '. Remarks like these were readily quoted by critics of the Movement from his *Remains*, much of the contents of which from his private journal, would have been better left unpublished. But its author was a chronically sick man. With better physical health his live and vigorous intelligence would have lent added weight to the Movement intellectually, although it is hardly to be doubted that he would have followed Newman to Rome rather than remain behind with the stolid if cautious Pusey.

[1] *Ibid.*, p. 72. [2] p. 36. [3] Quoted by Church, *ibid.*, p. 54.

For Pusey (born 1800), though never the Movement's leader in the way that Newman had been, proved to be its mainstay and guide after the latter's defection, as well as a pillar of strength to it in its beginnings. Newman deeply respected his learning, his immense diligence and above all his 'simple devotion to the cause of religion'. Pusey, he wrote in the *Apologia,* 'gave us a position and a name'.[1] The professorship of Hebrew, and the canonry of Christ Church which accompanied it and which he held from 1828 until his death in 1882, secured him a respected status in the university. He was also well-to-do, generous, and through his family connections influential. In Newman's judgment—here, surely, clouded by excess of modesty—he gave a form and personality to what without him had been 'a sort of mob'. Church more realistically describes him as the Movement's 'second head, in close sympathy with its original leader, but in many ways very different from him', providing it with a guarantee for its stability and steadfastness. 'An inflexible patience, a serene composure, a meek, resolute self-possession, was the habit of his mind, and never deserted him in the most trying days.'[2] Newman, however, was right in seeing in Pusey a man of large designs and sanguine disposition, unafraid of others and haunted by no intellectual perplexities. But he was not a theologian in an original or speculative sense. His mind was no more venturesome than Keble's, and the kind of gifts which make for great leadership he did not possess. He was pre-eminently a scholar, laborious and painstaking, but—and especially in his later years—astonishingly lacking in critical judgment. His contributions to the *Tracts* were of outstanding erudition (and sometimes bulk), but their propaganda value was less than that of the often brief but always shrewdly aimed pamphlets of Newman.

Pusey in all things was a conservative. He wished only that the soundly 'Catholic' doctrines inherited from the past should be perpetuated in or restored to the Church's current teaching. His distinctive contribution to the Movement was in the extent to which he created its spiritual tone. In addition to his translation and adaptation of foreign books of devotion and his pioneering work in the revival of the religious life in the Church of England he gave to the traditional teaching itself a new quality of spiritual fervour. That this at times is somewhat forced and the demand

[1] Ed. Svaglic, p. 64.   [2] Church, *op. cit.*, p. 134.

for personal effort overpressed has to be recognized. Pusey's nature was scrupulous to excess and he in practice attached too little weight to the joy and peace of believing. But in this respect his attitude characterizes the Movement as a whole. Severe always in his moral judgment, his weakness lay in his shortness of intellectual vision, in his lack of understanding of his own times, his failure to see what most lesser men saw plainly, his rigidity in positions adopted once for all, his frequent credulity. His own name provided a sobriquet for the Movement whose leadership, after the departure of Newman, inevitably devolved upon him.

2. NEWMAN'S PERSONALITY

But the dynamism of the Oxford Movement came, beyond all question, from the man who after twelve years of untiring work on its behalf found it necessary in conscience to abandon it and to leave the Church of which by now he was the most brilliant and controversial member. Yet as a thinker John Henry Newman (1801–90) is by no means easy to classify. He was not—as he himself readily acknowledged—a theologian in the narrower, professional sense, in spite of the learning displayed in the *Lectures on Justification*. He possessed a mind of great dialectical force and subtlety, and wrote much on questions of philosophical interest; but of technical philosophy he knew little and held it in no high esteem. For church history he had an abiding concern, but for all the labour bestowed on *The Arians of the Fourth Century* (1833) he was not a scholar-historian to be ranked with others of the kind, then and since. Throughout his long career a wide range of subjects caught his attention and to all of them he brought a keen and critical intelligence. As the author of *The Dream of Gerontius* (1866) and part-author of *Lyra Apostolica* (1836)[1] he could claim to be a poet, if a minor one. To the literature of educational theory he contributed, in his *The Idea of a University Defined and Illustrated* (1873),[2] what has since

[1] *Verses on Religious Subjects* was published in Dublin in 1853. Most of the poems in that collection, as of the earlier book, were republished in *Verses on Various Occasions* (1868).

[2] This volume contains the Dublin *Discourses on the Scope and Nature of University Education*, dated 1852. The first English edition was published in 1859 under the title *The Scope and Nature of University Education*, in which the first and second discourses were combined and the fifth omitted.

become a classic. As a controversialist he possessed a skill which few have ever rivalled. As a preacher he commanded an eloquence that captivated all who heard him, however dubious the doctrine of which it was the vehicle.[1] His literary output as a whole was immense; he wrote ceaselessly. Physically somewhat frail, he was endowed with an interior strength which neither external trials nor the tensions of a mind always exercised at stretch ever overcame. Although by nature or defect of training he may have lacked the specialist qualifications that confer eminence on many men far less gifted than he, his talents were raised to the plane of genius by the compelling force of his personality, one whose magnetism is evidenced not only by the indelible impression it left upon his contemporaries, but also by the fascination it continues to hold even in a world to which his ideals are now for the most part scarcely intelligible. He is, probably, the outstanding religious figure of his century, with the sole exception of Kierkegaard, a man of whom he himself had doubtless never heard. And as with Kierkegaard, it is posterity which has come to realize the full force and capacity of his genius. In his lifetime he was, save among his friends, undervalued, both in the ministry he relinquished and in that he afterwards embraced. Today, however, we are able to see him in a whiter light. Not only is the charm of his curiously elusive character still felt by us both in his writings, public and private, and in the recorded reminiscences of those who knew him in the flesh;[2] his attempted solution of those problems of religious faith to which his mind repeatedly returned, though we can discern well enough the

[1] 'His afternoon sermons at St Mary's', wrote the Presbyterian, Principal Tulloch —to quote one witness only among many—'became a spiritual power. They deserved to be so. Here he is at his best, away from the fields of history and of controversy, searching the heart with the light of his spiritual genius, or melting it to tenderness with the music of his exquisite language. All his strength and little of his weakness, his insight, his subtlety, his pathos, his love of souls, his marvellous play of dramatic as well as spiritual faculty, his fervour without excitement, his audacity without offence or sophistical aggression, appear in his sermons. He was a preacher as other men are poets or orators' (John Tulloch, *Movements of Religious Thought in the Nineteenth Century*, 1885, p. 114).

[2] Even Mark Pattison, whose *Memoirs* leave no doubt about their author's antipathy to Tractarianism, could write to Newman himself in old age: 'The veneration and affection wh. I felt for you at the time you left us are in no way diminished & however remote my intellectual standpoint may now be from that which I presume to be your own. I can still truly say that I have learnt more from you than from anyone else with whom I have ever been in contact.' See M. Trevor, *Newman: Light in Winter* (1962), p. 620.

reasons for its failure, is nevertheless such as to render the problems themselves only the more engrossing. The spiritual experience of so energetic and subtle an intelligence is striking enough in itself to make us continue to examine it for its possible underlying truth, or at the very least to study with deepened sympathy the psychological milieu of so intense a moral conviction. If in the end Newman's positive teachings leave us incredulous, the man himself still fascinates an age whose foreshadowings within his own he always feared and consistently denounced.

Newman, let us repeat, was far from being an academic thinker. Yet when we have considered his role as an ecclesiastical leader and publicist he remains, upon questions of religious belief, an authority whose opinions demand attention. For more, often, is to be learned from the process of his thinking, even when he is wrong, than from the acceptable conclusions of most others. The reason for this is that Newman's thought, like Pascal's is the outcome and expression of great spiritual travail. It is the distillation of a living experience. Here, we recognize at once, the man and his philosophy are an indivisible unity. But his strength is also his weakness. Apart from the experience the philosophy collapses, since in the final reckoning it is not a philosophy at all but a personal apology. His preoccupation, his bias, is not with reasons valid in logic but with the actual workings of the human mind as he knows it from introspection. He is the skilled analyst of the nature of religious belief itself, not of the grounds that would make it intrinsically acceptable. That is why, fundamentally, he is not a systematic thinker. He identifies himself, properly enough, with the Church's tradition of doctrine, but once he has stepped aside, so to speak, from this framework he attaches slight importance to system or even, it would seem, to consistency of argument.[1] Of his fellow-Catholics who criticized his *Grammar of Assent* he declared: 'Let those who think I ought to be answered ... first master the great difficulty, the great problem, and then, if they don't like my way of meeting it, find another. Syllogizing

---

[1] His apologetic can at times be reckless. He writes, for instance, concerning transubstantiation: 'I cannot, indeed, prove it; I cannot tell how it is; but I say, "Why should it not be? What's to hinder it? What do I know of substance or matter? Just as much as the greatest philosophers—and that is nothing at all.". . . The Catholic doctrine leaves phenomena alone: ... it deals with what no one on earth knows anything about—the material substances themselves' (*Apologia*, ed. Svaglic, p. 215).

won't meet it.' Syllogizing, he felt, would never meet the profounder difficulties of religious faith. Belief arises out of life, draws its strength and its colour from life, pertains always to life. Arguments do not create it nor systems authenticate it.

It is evident that Newman's thinking lacked architechtonic power. 'A more inspiring teacher', remarked F. J. A. Hort, 'it would be difficult to find, but the power of building up was not one of his gifts.'[1] In order to write easily he needed, as he himself confessed, a definite *call*. The occasion, the impulse, had to come from without; he could then respond to it—the case of Kingsley's challenge is the signal example—with all the vigour of his nature. But deliberate system-building was not in his genius. As he reflected at the close of his *Prophetical Office of the Church*, 'the thought, with which we entered on the subject, is apt to recur, when the excitement of the inquiry has subsided, and weariness has succeeded, that what has been said is but a dream, the wanton exercise, rather than the practical conclusions, of the intellect'.

> Such [he goes on] is the feeling of minds unversed in the disappointments of the world, incredulous how much it has of promise, how little of substance; what intricacy and confusion beset the most certain truths; how much must be taken on trust, in order to be possessed; how little can be realized except by an effort of the will; how great a part of enjoyment lies in resignation.

No doctrine, indeed, is quite to be separated from the man who teaches it, certainly no moral doctrine. But with Newman the truism attains to a new level of truth. Often the specially revealing phrase—'What intricacy and confusion beset the most certain truths', 'How little can be realized except by an effort of the will' —can do more to reconcile us to his viewpoint than will his set arguments, with the impression these sometimes convey of artifice and even sophistry. Newman's writings—sermon, treatise, private letter, polemical pamphlet—not only instruct or exhort or amuse; they have the added power of the work of art to create *empathy*, to move the reader to enter into the author's own frame of mind, to share his hopes and disappointments. The student of Newman's philosophy must therefore be prepared to approach it not only critically—for criticism has little difficulty in exposing its evasions and inconsistencies—but with personal understanding. *Cor ad cor loquitur*.

[1] A. F. Hort, *The Life and Letters of F. J. A. Hort* (1896), ii, p. 424.

3. THE NATURE OF BELIEF

Newman's religious convictions began to take shape in boyhood, under the influence of a Calvinistic evangelicalism, and the note of austerity in his teaching which persisted through life may in part at least be attributable to this. As a youth, he relates, he readily accepted the doctrine of final perseverance, believing that his adolescent conversion would last into the next life and that he was elected to eternal glory. He retained this Calvinist tenet until the age of twenty, when, he tells us, it gradually faded away. But he thought that it had had some influence on his opinions, notably in the direction of certain 'childish imaginations' such as the sense of isolation from surrounding objects, confirming him in his curious distrust of the reality of material phenomena and—in his own often quoted words—'making me rest in the thought of two and two only absolute and luminously self-evident beings, myself and my Creator'.[1] Another early and permanent conviction was that of the necessary place of dogma in religion. From the age of fifteen, he avers, dogma had been to him an essential principle: religion as a mere sentiment was 'a dream and a mockery'. Liberalism accordingly, as 'the anti-dogmatic principle and its developments', was real religion's most insidious foe. For without its authoritative dogmas Christianity is but a mirage. Yet the statement seems hardly to accord with what Newman himself repeatedly says about the nature of faith. If the essence of religion lies in its positive doctrines then clearly these must be held as propositions completely and accurately true; and it was in seeking an authority for the traditional Christian doctrinal system in its most articulate form that Newman eventually found refuge in the Roman Catholic Church, which alone could speak with a voice not only firm but infallible. On this showing religion and its intellectual expression were for him one. Yet his reflections on faith constantly tend away from such intellectualism. A rational faith, he says in one of his *Oxford University Sermons*, need not mean more than that belief is consonant with right reason in the abstract, *not* that it results from it in the particular case. But if the act of faith is only partially rational, and therefore on grounds of strict reason inexplicable, why should we demand of dogma an exact and sufficient rendering of the *content* of faith? The dis-

[1] *Apologia*, p. 18.

crepancy here is a fault that runs through the whole of Newman's thinking and accounts, arguably, for its pervasive ambiguity, despite the verbal skill with which it is set forth. Newman was not, let it again be said, a philosopher attempting an objective analysis of the rationale of religious belief. His purpose, almost always, was practical and apologetic—to build up and defend the faith. What Wilfrid Ward says of the Oxford school generally is particularly true of him: namely, that it was treating, not like the liberals, of the science of evidence, but of the art of religious knowledge.[1] Furthermore, in Newman's case, at any rate after 1845, this was religious knowledge as propounded by the only body on earth that could do so with an indefeasible authority. For what his arguments present is an account both of the way of faith and of the only satisfactory goal to which, in his view, it will lead. But it is this also which vitiates it as a properly rational defence of faith, since the goal is presupposed at starting. Hence faith becomes a realm of its own, to which reason has no clear right of access. It is, however, thus only, Newman would assure us, that doubt can be resolved into certitude, reason being always a devious guide. For a man of Newman's peculiar temperament such a position may prove possible, if not indeed the only resort. But for one who puts higher store by reason than did the author of *A Grammar of Assent* such a device cannot succeed and the grounds of doubt will remain.

Basically Newman's theory of belief was not changed by his conversion to Rome. He was ill at ease with the conventional Catholic apologetic, choosing in this field to follow his own path—an independence which in time brought him into some disfavour with ecclesiastical authority. The process of argument so elaborately deployed in the Roman *Grammar*—at the time of its publication in 1870 he had been a Catholic for about twenty-five years—is already to be found in the Anglican *Sermons*.[2] In considering it, therefore, and here we are at once in the mid stream of Newman's religious philosophy, we must begin with the latter. At the very outset we meet with the claim that faith is independent

[1] Wilfred Ward, *W. G. Ward and the Oxford Movement*, i, p. 392.

[2] Newman observed in a letter of August 1870, to Aubrey de Vere: 'As to my Essay on Assent, it is on a subject which has teased me for these twenty or thirty years.' See Wilfred Ward, *The Life of John Henry Cardinal Newman* (1912), ii, p. 245. But perhaps most readers will prefer the more tentative and exploratory approach adopted in the earlier book.

of reason, to the extent at least that, as an internal habit or act, it is not the consequence of a preliminary rational inquiry but has its own special basis.[1] Faith, again, does not require evidence so strong as that needed for rational conviction, since it is mainly swayed by 'antecedent considerations'—by previous notices, prepossessions and prejudices ('in a good sense of the word')—whereas reason demands direct and definite proof. Faith moreover is 'a principle of action, and action does not allow time for minute and finished investigations'. It is the reasoning of a religious mind, or of what Scripture calls a right or renewed heart, acting upon presumptions rather than evidence. In this matter there are in fact two distinct processes: the original process itself, and the secondary one of investigating such reasoning. All men reason, says Newman, for to reason is nothing more than to gain truth from truth, without the intervention of sense; but all men do not *reflect* upon their reasoning, much less reflect truly and accurately enough to do justice to their own meaning. They do so only in proportion to their abilities. 'In other words, all men have a reason, but not all men can give a reason.' Thus the distinction resolves itself into one between unconscious and conscious reasoning, or reason implicit and explicit; and too often are they confounded. 'Clearness in argument certainly is not indispensable to reasoning well. Accuracy in stating doctrine or principles is not essential to feeling and acting on them.' The actual process of reasoning is therefore something complete in itself and independent. The analysis that may follow is merely an account of it and makes neither the conclusion correct nor the inferences rational. Indeed to render sufficient account of one's implicit reasoning may be impossible, no analysis being subtle and delicate enough to represent adequately the state of mind under which one believes or the subjects of belief as they are presented to one's thoughts. 'Is it not hopeless', Newman asks, 'to expect that the most diligent and anxious investigation can end in more than giving some very rude description of the living mind and its feelings, thoughts, and reasonings?'[2] In moral and religious inquiries the arguments formally stated are in truth symbols of the real grounds rather than the grounds themselves.[3]

[1] *Oxford University Sermons* (ed. 1892), p. 184.
[2] *Ibid.*, pp. 267f.
[3] p. 275.

Hence the conclusion is reached that the reasoning and opinions which are involved in the act of faith are latent and implicit, and that although the reflecting mind is able to invest them with some definite and methodical form faith nevertheless is complete without this reflective faculty, which may often be more of an obstacle than an aid.

Plainly, then, if the proof of Christianity, by Scripture or any other means, is of this subtle kind it will not be exhibited to advantage in formal exposition. And the danger is that writers on Christian 'evidences' or scriptural 'proofs' will always be tempted to press their case too far or to oversystematize. Religious arguments are not like mathematical demonstrations, to be followed passively and by attending only to what is stated and admitting nothing but what is urged. On the contrary, what they really demand is a certain *disposition* in the inquirer—'an active, ready, candid, and docile mind, which can throw itself into what is said, neglect verbal difficulties, and pursue and carry out principles'. But here we are in the *personal* sphere, the world of faith, which is not simply intellectual assent but an engagement of the whole moral personality. Thus in the *Prophetical Office* Newman points out that faith differs from opinion in considering God's 'being, government, and will as a matter of personal interest and importance to us, not the degree of light or darkness in which it perceives the truth concerning them'. Like Coleridge, he is unimpressed by evidence-theology, aimed only at the logical reason. To him it is typical of the preceding century, 'a time when love was cold'. As a general rule, he thinks, religious minds embrace the gospel chiefly on 'the great antecedent probability of a Revelation' and the suitableness of that gospel to meet their needs, whilst on irreligious minds evidences are thrown away. Further, considerations which are of no practical purpose tend to divert men from the true view of religion and lead them to think that faith is largely the result of argument: 'For is not this the error, the common and fatal error, of the world, to think itself a judge of Religious Truth without preparation of the heart?' In its schools the ways to truth are looked on as open to all men, at all times, regardless of personal disposition. Truth there is to be approached 'without homage'. In religion, however, it is otherwise. Here it is antecedent probability that determines, and antecedent probability involves a personal judgment. Probability

133

of itself may indeed prove nothing; but, equally, facts of themselves persuade no one. Probability is to fact as the soul is to the body, and although mere presumptions may have no force, mere facts have no warmth. 'A mutilated and defective evidence suffices for persuasion, where the heart is alive; but dead evidences, however perfect, can but create a dead faith. Thus in the presence of faith reason bows and retires; or rather, in words already quoted, faith is itself *the reasoning of a religious mind*. Such a mind holds the gospel to be probable because it has a strong love for it, even when the testimony is weak. Moreover, so far from faith being the reasoning of a poorly-equipped mind, as its critics object, it is really that of a divinely enlightened one. For 'as reason with its great conclusions is confessedly a higher instrument than Sense with its secure premises, so Faith rises above Reason in its subject-matter more than it falls below it in the obscurity of its process.'[1]

If faith is a mode of thinking that is commonly dismissed as irrational and therefore despicable—'till the event confirms it'— it is because the real and substantial grounds of inference lie in the character of the individual mind itself and in its general view of things—above all in its actual impressions concerning God's will and the anticipations derived from its own inbred wishes. Hence it is of the essence of faith that it should be an *antecedent* judgment or presumption. Newman allows, of course, that some safeguard is needed which will secure it from becoming mere superstition or fanaticism; but such safeguard is not simply the reason, nor—as liberal opinion contends—is it education. The real safeguard, he insists, is 'a right state of heart', a sound moral disposition. 'It is holiness, or dutifulness, or the new creation, or the spiritual mind, however we word it, which is the quickening and illuminating principle of true faith, giving it eyes, hands, and feet.'[2] In short, it is love which forms it 'out of the rude chaos into an image of Christ', or what the scholastic theology calls *fides formata charitate*—as distinct from the Lutheran conception of a bare *fides informis*, an act or attitude of mind which in itself has no moral content.

Newman's whole idea of faith is thus of something intrinsically personal, an expression of the *totus homo*. The weakness of reason, taken in the abstract, is that it is impersonal. At this point the

[1] *Ibid.*, pp. 198, 200, 203, 216.   [2] *Ibid.*, pp. 218, 229, 234.

resemblance of his thinking to Coleridge's is very apparent. For both men faith enlists the entire self, of which the individual's particular bent, aptitude, characteristics and circumstances form a necessary part. Their use of words obviously differs. Newman takes the eighteenth-century view of reason as *ratiocination*, a meaning much closer to Coleridge's *understanding*. What Coleridge himself connotes by reason, however, is more akin to Newman's *faith*, which itself includes reason as a kind of inner guiding principle—

> a presumption, yet not a mere chance conjecture,—a moving forward, yet not of excitement or of passion,— a moving forward in the twilight, yet not without clue or direction,—a movement from something known to something unknown, but kept in the narrow path of truth by the Law of dutifulness which inhabits it, the Light of Heaven, which animates and guides it.[1]

It is only by faith indeed—by this essentially personal attitude and insight—that the believer comes to recognize personality in God himself. Natural religion teaches God's unity, power and majesty, and even his wisdom, goodness and moral governance, but little or nothing in regard to his personal being.[2] The philosopher, Newman says, aspires towards a divine *principle*, the Christian towards a divine *agent*.[3] The vital thing in truly religious experience is the testimony of conscience. The marks of design in creation say nothing of God to one who does not already believe in him, a fact which suggests that any attempt to prove divine existence from purely rational as distinct from moral considerations is misguided.[4] In the end it is only the spiritual mind that

---

[1] *Ibid.*, p. 245.

[2] See Sermon ii, 'The Influence of Natural and Revealed Religion Respectively', dating from April 1830. 'Conscience', Newman says, 'is the essential principle and sanction of Religion in the mind'; but even conscience, though it seems 'to point in a certain direction as a witness for the real moral locality (so to speak) of the unseen God', affords no certain argument 'for a Governor and Judge, distinct from the moral system itself', to those who dispute its informations (pp. 18, 23). Newman states, by the way, that at the time he made this observation he was not acquainted with Coleridge's writings and in particular 'a remarkable passage' in the *Biographia Literaria*, 'in which several portions of this Sermon are anticipated'. See H. F. Davis, 'Was Newman a disciple of Coleridge?', in *The Dublin Review*, October 1945.

[3] *Oxford University Sermons*, p. 28.

[4] *Ibid.*, p. 70. Cf Sermon x, 'Faith and Reason, contrasted as Habits of Mind': 'It is indeed a great question whether Atheism is not as philosophically consistent with the phenomena of the physical world, taken by themselves, as the doctrine of a creative and governing Power' (p. 194).

can judge spiritually. As Newman put it in a letter to W. G. Ward,
'the religious mind sees much which is invisible to the irreligious.
They have not the same evidence before them.'[1] It is not that either
the intelligence or the honesty of the sceptic's actual reasoning is in
doubt; what signifies is his lack of spiritual training, preventing
him from recognizing certain data, or a special aspect of things,
which, had he perceived them, he would have had to take into
account. That he should have failed to do this—where, it may be,
a quite uneducated believer will have made no such omission—is
a matter for serious reflexion, and none can lightly pass judgment
on him. But to Newman the inference is plain that whatever a man
believes or does not believe will depend, not only on considerations that are external and rational, but on his whole mental
constitution and character—upon an antecedent disposition—
for which, however, he is not himself without moral responsibility.

4. THE '*Grammar of Assent*'

We now must turn to what is probably Newman's most carefully
contrived work, his *Essay in Aid of a Grammar of Assent*, a study
of the psychology of belief the interest and value of which time
has still not dissipated. Its insight into the processes of the human
mind is extraordinarily subtle, whilst as a piece of literary
exposition it is the product of a master hand. Yet it is a difficult
book to read, demanding close attention. Many have found it
sophistical, and if its real purpose is misunderstood sophistical it
undoubtedly appears. For whatever Newman himself conceived
his purpose to be in writing it, his procedure throughout is
directed by his own profound concern with the actual conditions
under which religious faith arises. Again, his temperamental
egocentricity ensures that his approach is consistently personal
and individualist. The process of 'assent' is, naturally enough,
given a generalized form, but the model for it, one cannot help
feeling, is the author's own mind. What indeed 'right' reasoning
is—how the intellect 'ought' to operate in its quest of truth—is an
inquiry which he does not pursue. We must, he seems to say, take
the understanding as it is, as we ourselves are introspectively
familiar with it. What use the instrument of reason can be put to
is determined by its native constitution. It has no 'law' beyond

[1] Wilfrid Ward, *The Life of John Henry Cardinal Newman*, ii, p. 247.

its own intrinsic character. This sweeping prescription of the inquirer's task once made, the only profitable thing to do is to examine *how* men—ordinary men—do reason, and in particular how they attain to religious conviction or certitude.

> That [Newman says] is to be accounted a normal operation of our nature which men in general do actually instance; that is a law of our minds, which is exemplified in action on a large scale, whether *a priori* it ought to be a law or no. Our hoping is a proof that hope, as such, is not an extravagance; and our possession of certitude is a proof that it is not a weakness or an absurdity to be certain. How it comes about that we *can* be certain is not for me to determine; for me it is sufficient that certitude is felt. . . . It is unmeaning in us to find fault with our own nature, which is nothing else than we ourselves, instead of using it according to the use of which it ordinarily admits. We must appeal to man himself, as a fact, and not to any antecedent theory, in order to find what is the law of his mind as regards Inference and Belief. . . . If, then, such an appeal does bear me out in deciding, as I have done, that the course of inference is ever more or less obscure, while belief is ever distinct and definite,—and yet that what is in its nature thus absolute does in fact follow upon what in outward manifestation is thus complex, indirect and recondite, what is left but to take things as they are, and resign ourselves to what we find? That is, instead of devising, what cannot be, some sufficient science of reasoning which may compel certitude in concrete conclusions, to confess that there is no ultimate test of truth besides the testimony borne to truth by the mind itself; and that this phenomenon, perplexing as we may find it, is a normal and inevitable characteristic of the mental constitution of a being like man on such a stage as the world.[1]

It is not, of course, that Newman is content merely to conclude that what a man actually does believe, because his mind happens so to 'work', is on that account true. In principle at least he distinguishes between 'reasons', or causes, of belief and the grounds that would justify it. The trouble is that in practice the distinction is blurred and an analysis of the act of faith becomes its sufficient validation. The word used in the book's title—*assent*—is therefore important. For this, very plainly, is its author's real interest. What he seeks to show is how such assent may be unconditional; as amounting, that is, to a state of complete mental certitude. Locke's view, that assent admits of degrees, he

[1] *Grammar of Assent*, pp. 344–350.

flatly rejects. Once an assent is made it allows of no qualification. Whatever we may or may not be certain of we at least are certain of our uncertainty. The mind cannot rest in mere probabilities; it wants not only to know but to *know* that it knows. Truth, to give the satisfaction of the truth, must be held *as such*. And undeniably men do achieve assurance of this kind, in a vast number of matters. The mark of certitude is a 'feeling of satisfaction and self-gratulation, of intellectual security arising out of a sense of success, attainment, possession, finality, as regards the matter which has been in question'. In this respect it exactly parallels conscience. As a conscientious deed is attended by a self-approval such as it alone can create, so certitude is united to 'a sentiment *sui generis* in which it lives and is manifested', although in fact the two are unrelated. It is simply that as the performance of what is right is distinguished by 'religious peace', so the attainment of what is true is attended by a sense of intellectual security.

But here an obvious question occurs: how far, namely, do confident feelings amount to anything more than subjective assurance? Does my being personally convinced that what I believe is true provide reason enough for someone else to accept it as the truth also? I may, after all, come to change my mind. Newman sees this quite clearly, and allows that certitude does not admit of an interior, immediate test sufficient to discriminate it from false assurance. But he argues that an adequate criterion of its genuineness lies in its 'indefectibility'. For a man, in other words, to lose his conviction on a given point is proof that he has not really been certain of it. 'Certitude', says Newman, 'ought to stand all trials, or it is not certitude.' Its every office is 'to cherish and maintain its object', its lot and duty 'to sustain rude shocks in maintenance of it without being damaged by them'. But again the question is: How does one know that the new conviction will prove more durable than the old? The fact that a man now holds an opinion which contradicts a former one is no guarantee of his present and final possession of the truth. Yet to this quite unsubtle objection Newman really gives no answer. For if in matters of faith and morals it is the authority of the Church which alone produces the ultimate guarantee then the entire argument is at once removed to another plane and all previous considerations cease to be relevant.

The basis, as we have seen, of Newman's whole position is that the very foundation of religion is conscience. Here he undoubtedly was powerfully influenced by Bishop Butler, of whose solemn utterance one repeatedly catches an echo in Newman's own writings. The study of the *Analogy*, he himself tells us, marked 'an era' in his religious opinions. Nevertheless this all-pervading moralism was rooted in his character. Whatever other certainties may in the end have eluded him, the conviction that in the depths of the moral consciousness he truly heard God speak was inexpugnable. 'Even philosophers, who have been antagonists on other points, agree in recognizing the inward voice of that solemn Monitor, personal, peremptory, unargumentative, irresponsible, minatory, definitive.'[1] It was this rocklike assurance of moral values which gave to Newman's own faith grounds that could never be questioned. It was not a matter to be argued for or about, but to be taken as immediate evidence of the existence and presence of a divine Person:

> If, as is the case, we feel responsibility, are ashamed, are frightened, at times transgressing the voice of conscience, this implies that there is One to whom we are responsible, before whom we are ashamed, whose claims upon us we fear. If, on doing wrong, we feel the same tearful, broken-hearted sorrow which overwhelms us on our hurting a mother; if, on doing right, we enjoy the same serenity of mind, the same soothing, satisfactory delight which follows us on receiving praise from a father, we certainly have within us the image of some person, to whom our love and veneration look, in whose smile we find happiness, for whom we yearn, towards whom we direct our pleadings, in whose anger we are troubled, and waste away. These feelings in us are such as require for their exciting cause an intelligent being: ... 'The wicked flees, where no one pursueth;' then why does he flee? whence his terror? Who is it that he sees in solitude, in darkness, in the hidden chambers of his heart? If the cause of these emotions does not belong to this visible world, the Object to which his perception is directed must be Supernatural and Divine; and this the phenomena of Conscience, as a dictate, avail to impress the imagination with the picture of a Supreme Governor, a judge, holy, just, powerful, all-seeing, retributive, and is the creative principle of religion, as the Moral Sense is the principle of ethics.[2]

The entire passage from which the foregoing is cited is intensely illuminating. As Bremond says, whereas so many other Christian

[1] *Ibid.*, p. 123.
[2] *Ibid.*, pp. 109f.

thinkers require religion to be the foundation of conscience, Newman make conscience the foundation of religion.[1] Conscience is more indeed than the foundation of mere natural religion. In his own vivid phrase, it is 'the aboriginal Vicar of Christ'. Revelation itself has its primary authentication here. Once you recognize the origin of conscience you are bound, Newman seems to say, to recognize its scope also. All Christian truth rests ultimately on conscience for its testimony and cannot be apprehended apart from it. Even 'Apostolical Order' is an ethical principle 'or it is not worth much'.[2]

This it was—but, it would appear, this only—which for Newman rendered God's existence a certainty. He repeatedly declared —and we cannot for one moment doubt his word—that it was impossible for him to believe in his own existence without believing 'in Him who lives as a personal, all-seeing, all-judging being in my conscience'. As soon, however, as he tried to put the reasons for this certainty into logical shape he ran into difficulty. When he looked outside of himself—at nature, at history—he beheld nothing that could give him convincing assurance. Without the guiding light within, the phenomena of the physical world could as easily point to atheism as to faith; and as for the world of human society, arguments drawn from it might indeed have real force, 'but they do not warm me, or enlighten me: they do not take away the winter of my desolation, . . . or make my moral being rejoice'.[3] Back, then, to one's own inner experience, to one's fundamental spiritual instincts! Here, plainly, Newman stands with Coleridge. But Coleridge's was a speculative mind, Newman's was not. He distrusted speculation, as he distrusted the metaphysics which rested on it. Take that road and the

---

[1] Henri Bremond, *The Mystery of Newman* (trans. H. C. Corrance, 1907), p. 333.

[2] But Bremond is right in saying that we should avoid the error of trying to present Newman as a mystic, 'in the rigorous sense of the word'. 'He does not claim that each perception of a moral truth brings him directly into touch with the Absolute. His conscience says nothing else to him except "Do this; do not do that"; but by an inevitable association he immediately regards each of these commands or prohibitions as the infallible expression of the will of God in Three Persons, of the Incarnate Word. Thus each of the affirmations of his conscience is, if I may say so, charged with dogmas. And I know well that it does often so happen; but what is extraordinary enough is that it should never have occurred to Newman to dissociate, in thought, such distinct elements, and that this indirect experience of God should always have had for him, if not the delight, at least the certitude of an immediate experience and of a vision face to face' (*Op. cit.*, pp. 333f).

[3] *Apologia* (ed. Svaglic), p. 217.

certainties of life begin to crumble. If belief is to be justified—
and the *Grammar of Assent*, as we have remarked, is a highly-
wrought and sophisticated attempt at such justification—then it
must be so not by objective 'proofs' which bypass conscience but
by examining the subjective conditions under which belief actually
arises. Behind it, of course, is the assumption that God has so
constituted man's mind as to make it possible for him to attain
truth. Our belief may accordingly be trusted even though we
fail to render full account of it. But to most minds the assumption
will seem the very point at issue.

Yet the odd thing is that although Newman's argument
depends on this assumption, reason remains for him suspect and
the world it essays to interpret ambiguous. Hence, therefore, the
further assumption that first principles are beyond dispute; that,
to cite his own words, 'the initial truths of divine knowledge
ought to be viewed as parallel to the initial truths of secular; as the
latter are certain, so too are the former'.[1] In this regard human and
divine knowledge resemble one another. Each of them opens out
into a large field of mere opinion, but in both the primary
principles, the general, fundamental or cardinal truths, are
immutable. These are the principles, the truths, by which man is
bound to live, in the spiritual order as in the temporal. They are
not a matter of mere probability:

> It is on no probability that we are constantly receiving the informa-
> tion and dictates of sense and memory, of our intellectual instincts,
> of the moral sense, and of the logical faculty. It is on no probability
> that we receive the generalizations of science, and the great outlines
> of history. These are certain truths; and from them each of us forms
> his own judgments and directs his own course.[2]

Likewise with regard to the 'world invisible and future'. Of 'our
Maker, His attributes, His providences, acts, works, and will',
we have, claims Newman, a direct and conscious knowledge.
But he also makes the striking assertion that beyond this knowledge lies 'the large domain of theology, metaphysics, and
ethics, on which it is not allowed to us to advance beyond
probabilities, or to attain to more than an opinion'.[3] His meaning
here, it must be said, is unclear. Is not the knowledge of God and

[1] *Grammar of Assent* p. 237.
[2] *Ibid.*, p. 239.
[3] *Ibid.*, pp. 239f.

his attributes, providences, and so forth precisely the matter with which theology does affect to deal? But Newman's words seem to imply that, while we have a deep-seated intuitive or instinctive knowledge of God, any attempt to rationalize this knowledge in the style of traditional Christian metaphysics immediately brings us on uncertain ground, ground becoming more and more uncertain the farther we move from the initial (and unarguable) assurances. It is these last, as the immediate and spontaneous deliverances of experience, which for Newman constitute the substance of religion; and the whole long argument of the *Grammar of Assent*—moving and subtle always, if in the end question-begging—is simply a plea on behalf of the beliefs by which a man of faith lives but of which the full logical structure cannot in the nature of things be articulated. But it is best to let this author speak for himself:

> First, we know from experience that beliefs may endure without the presence of the inferential acts upon which they were originally elicited. It is plain that, as life goes on, we are not only inwardly formed and changed by the accession of habits, but we are also enriched by a great multitude of beliefs and opinions, and that on a variety of subjects. These, held, as some of them are, almost as first principles, constitute as it were the furniture and clothing of the mind. Sometimes we are fully conscious of them; sometimes they are implicit, or only now and then come directly before our reflective faculty. Still they are beliefs, and when we first admitted them we had some kind of reason, slight or strong, recognized or not, for doing so. However, whatever those reasons were, even if we ever realized them, we have long since forgotten them. Whether it was the authority of others, or our own observation, or our reading, or our reflections which became the warrant of our belief, anyhow we received the matters in question into our minds, and gave them a place there. We believed them and we still believe, though we have forgotten what the warrant was. At present they are self-sustained in our minds, and have been so for long years. They are in no sense 'conclusions', and imply no process of reasoning. Here, then, is the case where belief stands out as distinct from inference.[1]

And what is true of belief affirmed is true, too, of belief lost. Good arguments do not necessarily preserve it or restore it, any more than they create it. Probability, according to Bishop Butler,

[1] *Ibid.*, p. 167.

is the guide of life; but on basic things one does not live by probabilities merely:

> Life is not long enough for a religion of inferences; we shall never have done beginning if we determine to begin with proof. . . . Resolve to *believe* nothing, and you must prove your proofs and analyse your elements, sinking farther and farther, and finding 'in the lowest depth a lower deep', till you come to the broad bosom of scepticism . . .

Some assumptions doubtless are better than others. But knowledge of premises and the inferences made upon premises—this is not to *live*. 'Life is for action: to act you must assume, and that assumption is faith.'[1]

Hence the all-importance of assurance, of certitude; and the mark of certitude is the mind's spontaneous and prompt rejection of whatever appears incompatible with the truth which it believes itself to hold. 'No man is certain of a truth who can endure the thought of the fact of its contradictory existing or occurring.' Psychologically indeed this may be true; and as a piece of psychological analysis the successive chapters of the *Grammar* are, we repeat, extraordinarily acute. That process of hidden or telescoped inference which Newman calls the Illative Sense, defined as 'the personal action of the ratiocinative faculty', is unquestionably the mode by which men's conclusions on very many matters are actually reached.[2] As he well observes, it has its function in the beginning, middle and end of all verbal discussion and inquiry. Where, however, he surely goes wrong is in maintaining that the illative sense is *nothing else* than a personal gift or acquisition and that it supplies 'no common measure between mind and mind'. The individual, truly enough, may not be able to assign specific reasons for his beliefs, but what Newman overlooks are the logical connections between individual reasoning, subject as it quite obviously is to personal conditions, and the general reasoning of the race. If the individual cannot produce and may not be aware of the evidence on which his opinions rest, that evidence nonetheless does exist and is producible. However difficult it may be to give exact definition to this general reason or collective understanding, it altogether transcends the workings

[1] *Ibid.*, pp. 94f.

[2] *Ibid.*, p. 345. Newman further defines it as 'the reasoning faculty, as exercised by gifted, or by educated or otherwise well-prepared minds' (p. 361).

of the individual mind and furnishes it with both a guide and a corrective. I may have a complete conviction that a belief of mine is true, but if it happens to conflict with what the vast majority of men take to be the case then it behoves me to reconsider the grounds of my belief with the utmost possible care. To fail to do so is to foster ignorance and fanaticism. Newman certainly was not ignorant, nor was he a fanatic, but his preoccupation with the mental states of the individual was the outcome of an intense personal autocentrism. Again and again, one feels, when he is speaking of man in general he really is alluding to one very unusual man—himself.

But what Newman could not bring to the question, by any process of doubt, was his own spiritual instinct. He yearned for God; and his conscience gave him what seemed to be an immediate assurance of God. In face of this assurance and to meet this yearning mere reasoning offered nothing that would in any way either strengthen the one or assuage the other. On the contrary, its action was all too likely to be corrosive. For with all his own tireless reasoning, channelled into countless books and sermons and papers, Newman in ultimate matters distrusted reason. Even theological doctrines, as the artifacts of human intelligence—albeit working on the data of revelation—do not, he seems to say, take us beyond probabilities, beyond what in the last resort is mere opinion. Such can be *known* to be true only when enunciated by authority. Increasingly during his Anglican career Newman sensed the need of authority. The Church of England, with its discordant voices, evidently lacked it. Yet the assumption that, if it were the Creator's purpose to retain in the world a knowledge of himself, 'so definite and distinct as to be proof against the energy of human scepticism', he would have introduced therein a power having infallibility in religious matters, seemed wholly warrantable. The conviction thus grew in him that not only an authority but an infallible authority actually existed which would restrain men's liberty of thought, in itself one of the greatest of their natural gifts, in order to rescue it from its own suicidal excess—'a working instrument, in the course of human affairs, for smiting hard and throwing back the immense energy of the aggressive intellect'. Rome, he was becoming confident, would be found right in the end. Moreover, the Church was a great historical fact, a vast and impressive reality. Christianity was a *Revelatio revelata,* a definite message from God to man distinctly conveyed by his chosen instruments and to be received as such; hence to be positively acknowledged, embraced and maintained as true, on the grounds only of its being divine, *'not as on intrinsic grounds* nor as probably true, or partially true, but as absolutely certain knowledge, certain in a sense in which nothing else can be certain, because it comes from Him who neither can deceive nor be deceived'.[1] Thus doubt might be crushed by infallible authority and certitude made indefectible by the centuries-old witness of the Catholic Church. Only so could the ever-questioning voice of reason be silenced. But even the most sympathetic observer of the cardinal's spiritual pilgrimage is likely to feel that his certainties are something of a façade and that behind them the 'aggressive intellect' still pursued its destructive work.[2] And although he told the world so much about himself, in the *Apologia* and elsewhere, there remained, the reader is moved to conclude, an inner chamber of his mind—as perhaps of his personal emotions also—whose door he never opened to others.

5. THE DEVELOPMENT OF DOCTRINE

But what of the charge against Rome, brought by all Protestants, that she had added to the original deposit of the apostolic faith doctrines for which Scripture provides no evidence or justification? Could the Roman Church afford guarantees of truth if she herself had so manifestly defaulted in her obligation to teach truth? The objection was a grave one. Were it to be successfully sustained—and it had been urged continuously since the sixteenth century or earlier—Rome's authority would inevitably have been impaired, and at the bar of Scripture itself. The issue was one which, for a man in Newman's position, could not be evaded and to its effective resolution he devoted much care and ingenuity in a work composed by him on the very eve of his reception into the Roman Catholic Church—the *Essay on the Development of Doctrine,* published towards the end of 1845. Of greater intrinsic interest than even the *Grammar of Assent,* it is no exaggeration to describe

---

[1] *Ibid.,* p. 387.
[2] Cp. James Martineau's remark: 'His certainties are on the surface, and his insecurities below' ('Personal influences on Present Theology', in *Essays, Reviews and Addresses* (1890–1), i, p. 234).

it as one of the most significant books of its century; significant, however, less for its positive arguments, which are neither very plausible nor consistent, as for its method of approach to the whole problem of Christian doctrine in its relation to the New Testament. The idea of development as applied to this sphere was, for British theology, completely novel. In Germany it was already familiar: for the Hegelian philosophy development was a master concept, whilst the growth, in the German universities, of scientific historical study, far ahead of anything of the sort here, had clearly established the principle of continuous change as a means of correlating and interpreting historical phenomena. The developmental idea had even been employed, in the interpretation of Catholic doctrine, by J. A. Möhler (1796–1838), of the Catholic faculty at Tübingen, in his book on *Symbolism*, published in 1832, a work which Newman himself acknowledges in his introductory chapter.[1] Möhler's essay is indeed an anticipation of Newman's, without, however, evincing very much of the latter's originality or suggestiveness. From the date of the publication of Newman's work fifteen years were to elapse before the appearance of Darwin's treatise on *The Origin of Species*, yet the theological essay foreshadows Darwin's procedure in the biological sphere in its grasp—if, unhappily, only intermittent—of the basic principles of organic evolution and environmental influence. Like so much of what Newman wrote it seems pregnant with ideas the broader scope and implications of which the author

[1] An English translation of Möhler's *Symbolik* came out in 1843, but there is no evidence of Newman's having used it in writing his *Essay*. From what he says it would seem that he had not even read it. Nevertheless Möhler's view, stated in an earlier book on Church unity (*Die Einheit in der Kirche*, 1825), that 'Christianity does not consist in expressions, in forms, in phrases', but is 'an interior life, a holy force', its various dogmas having validity 'only in so far as they express the substance which is presupposed', would certainly have appealed to him. (On Möhler's work generally see E. Vermeil, *Jean-Adam Möhler et l'école catholique de Tubingue, 1815–1840* and J. R. Geiselmann, *Lebendiger Glaube aus geheiligter Uberlieferung. Der Grundgedanke der Theologie J. A. Möhlers und der katholischen Tübinger Schule*, 1942). It is also very doubtful whether Newman owed much to Dionysius Petavius (Denis Pétau) (1583–1652), the French Jesuit theologian and historian of doctrine, who long before Möhler's time had introduced the idea of development into Catholic theology. Petavius's criticism of the early Church Fathers rests less on an understanding of their theological immaturity, as judged by later standards, than on his hostility to Platonism in any shape or form. Professor Owen Chadwick, although he allows that Newman must have studied Petavius (along with Bishop Bull's answer to his criticisms), considers that he had only 'an insignificant part in Newman's mind' (*From Bossuet to Newman*, p. 59), an opinion with which the present writer agrees.

himself did not fully realize, ideas, moreover, of which others were destined to make more radical use later.

Newman's purpose, in the first instance at least, was overtly apologetic. He was propounding 'a hypothesis to account for a difficulty'.[1] By now he was well aware of his own leaning towards Rome, but the problem created by Rome's apparent innovations upon the teachings of the early Church, to which he hitherto had looked for authoritative guidance, was one which had to be grappled with. That ancient touchstone of catholicity, the Vincentian Canon—*quod semper, quod ubique, quod ab omnibus creditum est*—plainly could not be made to countenance the more specifically Roman doctrines and practices; although to this stock Protestant objection he might, he judged, reply with a *tu quoque*: 'Whatever be historical Christianity, it is not Protestantism. If ever there was a safe truth, it is this.'[2] The appeal, then, to the universal witness of Christendom would not do, for what one age deemed orthodox had, in another, become heresy. Likewise inadmissible is the notion of a *disciplina arcani*—of truths, that is, which, although known from the beginning, have been disclosed by authority only gradually, in the interests of 'reserve' or 'economy'—for 'the variations continue beyond the time when it is conceivable that the discipline was in force'.[3] Other criteria had therefore to be adduced. The postulates of his own theory he stated thus: firstly,

> The increase and expansion of the Christian creed and ritual, and the variations which have attended the process in the case of the individual writers and Churches, are the necessary attendants on any philosophy or polity which takes possession of the intellect and heart and has any wide or extended dominion;

secondly,

> From the nature of the human mind, time is necessary for the full comprehension and perfection of great ideas;

and thirdly,

> The highest and most wonderful truths, though communicated to the world once and for all by inspired teachers, could not be comprehended all at once by the recipients, but, as received and transmitted by minds not inspired and through media which were human,

---

[1] *Esaay on the Development of Doctrine*, p. 27.
[2] *Ibid.*, p. 5.
[3] *Ibid.*, pp. 26f.

have required only the longer time and deeper thought for their full elucidation.[1]

These principles allow of and require a genuine development in the Church's doctrines, involving the emergence of truths till then unknown or at least unrecognized. Yet it can, Newman holds, be shown that these new truths, for all their apparent novelty, are intimately connected with what had gone before, represent no strange and unwarranted departure, and are no mere corruption or decadence, but are of a piece with what the Church has ever held and taught and thus serve to vindicate 'the reasonableness of every decision of Rome'.

For, it is patently the development of *Rome* that Newman is intent upon explaining and justifying. Always it is the Roman Church's massive historical presence which impresses him. It cannot then but be, he persuades himself, that what has occurred under Rome's virtually universal aegis must be right. For he is obliged to admit and to insist on her immense power of survival and revival and on the awe-inspiring coherence of her teaching. This intrusion of the sheer *fact* of Roman Catholicism is for him the really potent consideration, before which Protestant objections spend their force in vain.

If, Christianity being from heaven, all that is necessarily involved in it, and is evolved from it, is from heaven, and if, on the other hand, large accretions actually do exist, professing to be its true and legitimate results, our first impression naturally is, that these must be the very developments which they profess to be. Moreover, the very scale on which they have been made, their high antiquity yet present promise, their gradual formation yet precision, their harmonious order, dispose the imagination most forcibly towards the belief that a teaching so consistent with itself, so well balanced, so young and so old, not obsolete after so many centuries, but vigorous and progressive still, is the very development contemplated in the Divine scheme.

The providential outcome must be accepted or rejected as a whole; attenuation will only enfeeble it—one cannot pick and choose. And such is the coherence of the scheme that to accept any single part of it entails, 'by a stern logical necessity', acceptance of the entirety.[2] Nor is this all: behind Newman's reasoning

[1] *Ibid.*, p. 29.
[2] *Essay*, ed. 1906, pp. 93f.

there is a further assumption. For if, he maintains, the Christian doctrine as originally taught admits of true and important developments, then that in itself is a strong argument in favour of a 'dispensation' having been supplied for putting the seal of authority on those developments. But this is nothing other than the principle of the infallibility of the Church. Nay, 'the common sense of mankind' suggests, he tells us, that the very idea of revelation implies 'a present informer and guide, and that an infallible one'.[1]

It thus becomes evident how far Newman's conclusion is predetermined by his initial assumptions. What the Roman Church is, he decides, must be what the Church of Christ in its historic evolution was divinely intended to be, inasmuch as it has been preserved from actual error by its God-given infallibility. Nevertheless he recognizes that history witnesses to other developments within Christianity and feels accordingly that both the legitimacy of the Roman and the illegitimacy of the non-Roman call for demonstration by means of certain empirical tests. These, seven in number, Newman lists as: preservation of the type, continuity of principles, power of assimilation, early anticipation, logical sequence, preservative additions and chronic continuance. Christianity he sees as an 'idea', and, he points out, an idea not only modifies but is modified or at least influenced by the state of things in which it is carried out, and is dependent in various ways on the circumstances which surround it. It is this process which constitutes its development. It also is a living process because, unlike the working out of a mathematical theorem on paper, it takes place in the minds of men, using them as instruments and becoming dependent on them in doing so.

> Its development proceeds quickly or slowly; the order of succession in its separate stages is irregular; it will show differently in a small sphere of action and in an extended; it may be interrupted, retarded, mutilated, distorted, by external violence; it may be enfeebled by the effort of ridding itself of domestic foes; it may be impeded and swayed or even absorbed by counter energetic ideas; it may be coloured by the received tone of thought into which it comes, or depraved by the intrusion of foreign principles, or at length shattered by the development of some original fault within it.[2]

[1] *Essay*, p. 125.
[2] *Ibid.*, p. 38

Yet whatever the risk of corruption from intercourse with the world around it such risk, Newman contends, must be endured if the idea is to be properly understood and fully exhibited. Indeed all that he says, in a general way, concerning the growth and development of an idea, so clearly governed as it is by organic imagery, is admirable. Contemporary critics of the *Essay* even objected to it for its supposed modernism—it was, said one, 'German infidelity communicated in the music and perfume of St Peter's . . . Strauss in the garment and rope of the Franciscan.'[1] Unfortunately the progress of Newman's own insight as the argument unfolds fails to live up to promise. The point to be ascertained, he reflects, is the unity and identity of the idea with itself through all the stages of its evolution, from first to last. To guarantee this unity and identity, he says, it must be seen to be *one*, alike in type, principles and assimilative power; one also in logical consecutiveness, in the witness of its earlier phases to its later and in the protection which its later extend to its earlier, as finally in its union of vigour with continuance, in its tenacity. Thus he arrives at his seven tests. But in applying them a change occurs in the whole conception of development: the organic gives place to the logical. For example, regarding his fifth test—logical sequence—he explains that he means 'to give instances of one doctrine leading to another; so that if the former be admitted, the latter can hardly be denied, and the latter can hardly be called a corruption without reflecting on the former'.[2] Newman's difficulty, it is apparent, is that of *precluding* those developments which have not issued in modern Roman Catholicism and which, therefore, on his theory are inadmissible; and it is fairly certain that later in life he more or less assimilated his own view to the 'logical' theory approved by Roman theologians, according to which the whole corpus of dogmas had been held in substance by the Church since apostolic times, though not necessarily in the precise terms in which they

[1] In *Fraser's Magazine*, 1846, pp. 256, 265. In response to the 'liberalizing' charge—brought by, among others, so judicious a thinker as J. B. Mozley—F. L. Cross has shown clearly what Newman's real purpose was—that, namely, of resolving a 'concrete theological dilemma'. See 'Newman and the Doctrine of Development', in *The Church Quarterly Review*, January 1933.

[2] *Essay*, p. 397. It has been observed of these tests that 'it is not too much to say that it is impossible to conceive a corruption of the Gospel which could not be brought under one or other of them' (Alfred Fawkes, *Studies in Modernism*, 1913, p. 277).

were eventually promulgated. In fact this conception was already present in the original *Essay*, controlling the author's use of the seven tests, since he may well have realized that in the hands of others their application might lead to very different results. But, as ever with Newman, it is not the argumentation as such which moves the reader, but the personal motives that sustain it.

For in the end it is the man himself who rivets the attention of posterity. The ideas and ideals to which Newman dedicated himself throughout his long career, first as an Anglican and then as a Roman Catholic, were backward-looking and reactionary even in his own times. Not that he had no interest in the age or its concerns, or that he did not read widely. But there is truth in Mark Pattison's comment that 'the force of his dialectic and the beauty of his rhetorical exposition were such that one's eye and ear were charmed, and one never thought of inquiring on how narrow a basis of philosophical culture his great gifts were expended'.[1] His wariness of reason led him into intellectual positions which even to his warmest sympathizers looked precarious. Gladstone remarked that 'he places Christianity on the edge of a precipice, from whence a bold and strong hand would throw it over'. Manning, in his Anglican days at least, thought the *Essay on Development* sophistical, and was 'persuaded that Bishop Butler, if he were alive, would in his quiet way tear the whole argument into shreds'.[2] Thomas Huxley suggested that 'a primer of infidelity' could be compiled from the great divine's works. Certainly as a Roman priest Newman was looked on by his ecclesiastical superiors as insufficiently conservative and lacking in the requisite spirit of intransigence. Manning noted in a letter to a correspondent in Rome that

> he has become the centre of those who hold low views about the Holy See, are anti-Roman, cold and silent—to say no more—about the Temporal Power, national, English, critical of Catholic devotions, and always on the lower side ... I see much danger of an English Catholicism, of which Newman is the highest type. It is the old, Anglican, patristic, literary, Oxford tone transplanted into the Church. It takes the line of deprecating exaggerations, foreign devotions, Ultramontanism, anti-national sympathies. In one word it is worldly Catholicism, and it will have the world on its side.[3]

[1] *Memoirs*, p. 210.
[2] See E. S. Purcell, *The Life of Cardinal Manning* (1895), i, pp. 311f.
[3] *Ibid.*, ii, p. 322.

But not only was his 'tone' inadequate; his meaning also was dubious: 'Newman miscet et confundit omnia', was the common Vatican opinion. Years later the leaders of the Modernist movement condemned by Pius X readily acknowledged their own debt to him. Thus Loisy, who recalls that he in 1896 was reading Newman with enthusiasm, judged him 'the most open-minded theologian the Church had had since Origen'.[1] Tyrrell thought that in his notion of an 'idea' as a spiritual force rather than an intellectual concept Newman had identified himself with the modern as contrasted with the scholastic mind. 'It is the weapon that Modernists have taken from him and turned against much of that system in whose defence he had framed it.'[2] There are indeed passages in the *Essay on Development* any one of which the Modernists might have taken as the epigraph of a collective manifesto. Thus we may read that 'one cause of corruption in religion is the refusal to follow the course of doctrine as it moves on, and an obstinacy in the notions of the past'; or that 'a power of development is a proof of life, not only in its essay, but in its success; for a mere formula either does not expand or is shattered in expanding. A living idea becomes many, yet remains one.' That Newman himself either did not see, or seeing turned away from, the implications of his own doctrine, can in no wise be held to mitigate the significance his thought was to have for a future generation. Doubtless had he lived to read the works of some who claimed his inspiration he would have been scandalized. But for all his introspection and critical self-analysis he could never conceal, in even his most considered utterances, the Janus-image in which his mind was naturally cast.

6. W. G. WARD AND J. B. MOZLEY

William George Ward, Newman's ardent follower, was himself what Newman was not, namely, a philosopher *à metier*. James Martineau, a good judge, testified to his 'singular metaphysical

---

[1] A. F. Loisy, *Mémoires pour servir à l'histoire religieuse de notre temps* (1930–1), i, pp. 421, 426. Loisy examined Newman's theory of development in an article in the *Revue de clergé français* of 1 December 1899, and found it superior to those of Harnack and Auguste Sabatier. He remarks: 'La théologie catholique a eu de nos jours le grand docteur dont elle avait besoin.' But 'il lui a manqué peut-être quelques disciples' (*op. cit.*, p. 20).

[2] *Christianity at the Cross Roads* (1910), p. 33.

acuteness',[1] whilst W. H. Hutton's description is of one who might still today be regarded as the typical Oxford philosopher: 'He never seemed to see the half-lights of a question at all. There was no penumbra in his mind, or, at least, what he could not grasp clearly he treated as if he could not apprehend at all.'[2] Even Mill thought that in replying to Ward's criticisms of his own philosophy he was answering 'the best that is likely to be said by any future champion'.[3] Here then for certain were a mind and interests very different from Newman's. As Church put it, 'Mr Newman's ideas gave him material, not only for argument but for thought. The lectures and sermons at St Mary's subdued and led him captive'.[4] But Ward had felt the pull of Rome sooner and, at first, more surely than his master. As was clear from the *Ideal of a Christian Church*, he immensely admired the Roman Church's power and capacity to teach with authority, its explicit doctrine of the supernatural, its sacramentalism, and its spiritual discipline and ethos. Rome could produce saints; the Church of England could, or did, not. But what in Protestantism he especially objected to was—to quote Church again—its 'ostentatious separation of justification from morality, with all its theological refinements and fictions'.[5] It was, we have seen, Newman's own deeper moralism which drew Ward away from so earnest a moralist as Thomas Arnold. No mere antiquarian ritualism but the idea of holiness was what impressively emerged from Newman's teaching. Thus Ward himself came more and more to believe that moral discipline alone is the real foundation of faith. The notion in particular of making the intellect rather than conscience the arbiter of moral and religious truth was abhorrent to him; and repeatedly in his book one comes across passages in which Newman's insistence on a right state of heart receives still sharper emphasis. The sense of duty, we are told, is 'the one faculty which is visited by divine grace, and which under that grace leads us onward to salvation'.[6] It was customary, he points out, to talk as though the gospel were in some way a *reversal* of the natural law rather than—what it is—

---

[1] See Wilfrid Ward, *William George Ward and the Catholic Revival* (1893), p. 312.
[2] *Ibid.*, p. 304.
[3] Wilfrid Ward, *William George Ward and the Oxford Movement* (1889), 2nd ed., p. 273.
[4] R. W. Church, *The Oxford Movement*, p. 340.
[5] *Ibid.*, p. 342.
[6] *The Ideal of a Christian Church*, p. 204.

solely and exclusively its *complement*.[1] Luther's great error was in denying or disparaging this principle, although Ward concedes a certain virtue to the continental Reformers in having at least followed their consciences, whereas the motivation of their English counterparts was largely political. Later in the book he writes that:

> The priest of a country parish will endeavour to lay his foundation within the heart of his flock; he will not consider any attendance of theirs on Divine Service, even the most regular, even (if so be) daily as well as on Sunday, to be any real security for so much as the beginning of a truly Christian life. It is the feeling of *accountableness* throughout the day, the habitual thought of judgment to come, the careful regulation of thought, words, and actions, which he will impress on his flock as the one thing needful. Their presence in church may be useful as giving him the power to address them, but he will use that power for the very purpose of impressing on their mind that the true religion must have its spring from *within*.[2]

Such a passage, from a work intended to exalt as the ideal of a Christian Church one strongly resembling the actuality, so its author believed, of the Church of Rome, might well have astonished its Protestant readers. Yet it is typical of the prevailing attitude of the Oxford divines—'Holiness', in Newman's aphorism, 'before Peace'.

But although Ward shared with Newman a common standpoint on the relations between faith and the moral consciousness, he did not follow him in the attempt to work out a new and more amenable type of apologetic. As an Anglican Newman had been liberalism's firmest opponent, yet as a Roman Catholic he acquired, paradoxically, the reputation of being himself a liberal. This no doubt rested on a misunderstanding. In a number of respects he was less liberal than Acton or Richard Simpson, for example. But he disliked the kind of arguments with which Catholicism was wont to be defended and wished to put something in their place that would bring the non-Catholic closer to the springs of Catholic religious experience. Ward, on the other hand, was satisfied with things as they were, and was stubbornly opposed to the liberalizing trends which in some quarters were beginning to make

[1] *Ibid.*, p. 248.
[2] *Ibid.*, p. 438.

themselves felt.[1] The Church, with the long record of its saints, had proved itself an incomparable training ground of Christian souls, and the task of reason, once the Church's authority is accepted, could only be to defend what that authority had laid down and the tradition which witnesses to it. He did indeed welcome *The Grammar of Assent*, since its basic position was after all what he had himself always been contending for. But for all his acuteness Ward was without the imaginative genius that led Newman, whether in the English Church or the Roman, towards horizons distant from and strange to either communion as it then was.

In concluding this chapter some mention is due of Newman's brother-in-law, James Bowling Mozley (1813–78), who occupied the Regius professorship of divinity at Oxford from 1871 until his death. Church considered him as, after Newman, 'the most forcible and impressive of the Oxford writers'. For some ten years he was joint editor of *The Christian Remembrancer* in close association with Newman. Yet the event of 1845 left him unshaken. The leader's step, he shortly afterwards wrote, 'was not unforeseen; but when it is come those who knew him feel the fact as a real change within them—feel as if they were entering upon a fresh stage of their own life. May that very change turn to their profit, and discipline them by its hardness!'[2] Discipline of mind was an essential part of Mozley's character and personal loyalties did not deter him from pursuing the truth as he saw it. As time went by he carried his Tractarianism with a notable difference. The Gorham judgment in particular caused him to revise some of his earlier opinions, his newer views being expressed in a series of monographs bearing the respective titles, *On the Augustinian Doctrine of Predestination* (1855), *On Primitive Doctrine of Baptismal Regeneration* (1856) and *A Review of the Baptismal Controversy* (1862).[3] All show a decidedly Augustinian bent. Mozley's best work, however, is probably his Bampton lectures of 1865, *On Miracles*. In this he is mainly interested in the basic issue of the credibility of the miraculous. That miracles are credible he argues with considerable skill, denying (after Hume)

---

[1] On the liberal tendency in nineteenth century English Catholicism see Appendix II below.

[2] *The Christian Remembrancer*, January 1846, p. 167 (quoted Church, *op. cit.* p. 404.)

[3] See below, Appendix I.

that the uniformity of nature is either a self-evident or a demonstrable truth, although for very many minds it is an irresistible belief. But in order to know it as a rational principle one would need to be completely conversant with the ultimate structure of the world. If, however, the principle of uniformity is not rational, in the rigorous sense of the word, then neither is belief in miracle irrational. In any case the dogmatism of Mill and of *Essays and Reviews* in this matter was without warrant.[1]

Of interest, too, is Mozley's treatment of what he calls 'mysterious truths', such as original sin, the atonement and the trinity. These, he says, are truths 'which agree with human reason in a large and general way',[2] and hence are recognizable as truth, although a full understanding of them is not open to us. There are things, that is, as to which we are not totally ignorant of what they affirm but of which also we have no complete or rationally adequate conception. In philosophy they include the ideas of substance, cause, mind or spirit, power and infinity. In dealing with them, therefore, we have to be circumspect, refraining from logical inferences or practical conclusions that offend the moral sense. This is (or should be) evident in the instance of such doctrines as original sin and predestination, where logic seemingly demands that vast numbers of human beings can expect only perdition. The idea behind these doctrines is a sound one, but it has to be offset by a counter-truth no less necessary. And the fact that a doctrine cannot be stated with full logical consistency does not imply that it cannot be believed. The truth we seek in religion is something essentially that 'we feel and react after rather than intellectually apprehend'.[3] We receive it by faith, an attitude of mind by no means non-rational but at the same time not amounting to intellectual certitude; for faith has often to endure paradox—the admission of apparently conflicting principles—where an attempt at a compromise acceptable to reason fails to do justice to the spiritual experience in which all theological doctrine claims to be grounded. Divine revelation, moreover, poses

---

[1] R. W. Church reviewed the lectures in *The Times* for 5 June 1866 and suggested that 'the way in which the subject of Miracles has been treated, and the place which they have had in our discussions, will remain a characteristic feature of both the religious and philosophical tendencies of thought among us' (*Occasional Papers*, 1897, ii, pp. 82ff.).

[2] *Lectures and Other Theological Papers* (1883), p. 102.

[3] *Op. cit.* p. 114.

difficulties from the very fact that it is progressive. Thus the Old Testament sometimes commands actions which in the context of a deeper spiritual understanding would not have been done or commanded, but which in the circumstances prevailing at the time were of necessity the best. But Mozley's width of sympathy did not extend to the new Broad Church liberalism represented by *Essays and Reviews*[1] or even by A. P. Stanley. He was astonished that the latter seemed unable to recognize the immensity of the difference between a religion with miracle and one without it,[2] whilst of the ideas canvassed in the famous volume of 1860 he could foresee no consequence, in the event of their dissemination among the masses, than 'simple infidelity and indeed atheism'.[3] On the other hand his criticism, in *The Theory of Development*, dating from 1878, of Newman's treatment of the concept was little less severe. Reason here has its proper rights and obligations. Granting that a divine revelation has been vouchsafed, is it not, he asks, more reasonable to suppose that for its interpretation and application men have, after all, been left to their own power of judgment?

[1] See below, ch. X.
[2] *Letters of J. B. Mozley* ed. Anne Mozley, (1884), p. 260.
[3] *Ibid.*, p. 250.

Chapter V

F. D. Maurice (1) The Kingdom of Christ

I. THE COLERIDGEAN INFLUENCE: J. C. HARE

The influence of Coleridge on the religious thought of the early Victorian age is a fact beyond all question. Yet to particularize—to indicate where precisely, and how, it proved itself—is somewhat less easy. The Tractarians certainly were not impervious to it, but were chary of acknowledging any debt. Newman admitted the force of Coleridge's insight, if he also deprecated the boldness of his speculations. One, however, who some years before the first of the *Tracts* was to make its appearance could write that 'My fixed principle is: that a Christianity without a Church exercising spiritual authority is vanity and delusion. And my belief is, that when Popery is rushing in on us like an inundation the nation will find it to be so',[1] had already pointed the way the new generation of High Churchmen was to follow. Nevertheless it is not to the Oxford school that we have to look for the Coleridgean teaching's most visible fruits. Rather is it to those who, if in a markedly different spirit, carried on the more exploratory thinking of the Noetics: notably J. C. Hare and F. D. Maurice, although A. P. Stanley, Rowland Williams, John Sterling, F. J. A. Hort and possibly even Dean Church should be counted among them. Maurice confessed how much he himself owed to the poet-philosopher in the Dedication to *The Kingdom of Christ*, even

---

[1] *Aids to Reflection*, p. 295.

though he elsewhere prefers to adopt a more guarded tone.[1] Hare's regard for Coleridge is sufficiently explicit in the dedication prefacing a volume of his sermons, *The Mission of the Comforter*, published in 1846 'to the honoured memory of Samuel Taylor Coleridge, the Christian philosopher, who through dark and winding paths of speculation was led to the light in order that others by his guidance might reach that light, without passing through the darkness', and who, in particular, had helped him, the author, 'to discern the sacred concord and unity of human and divine truth'. For what Coleridge had done for these men was to guide them into new ways of understanding Christianity, to show them indeed new approaches to the whole problem of truth in the spiritual and moral realm. In Hare and Maurice—as also in Maurice's Scottish friend and mentor, Thomas Erskine—the traditional Church teaching acquired a new philosophical depth, away from the shallows of so much current controversy and ecclesiastical partisanship.

Julius Charles Hare (1795–1855) was born in Italy and spent most of his early life there and in Germany. His knowledge of the German language was thorough and he was well versed in German literature and scholarship, an accomplishment rare among the churchmen of his day. With the aid of Connop Thirlwall he translated Niebuhr's *History of Rome*, but in philosophical interests he was more strongly drawn towards contemporary German idealism than his sceptical collaborator, who disliked it. Educated at Trinity College, Cambridge, and for a time a fellow there, he subsequently held the living of Hurstmonceux in Sussex and was appointed archdeacon of Lewes. Among his pupils at Trinity were

---

[1] Thus in his Introduction to Hare's *Charges* (1856) he spoke of those who ultimately experienced a discontent from intercourse with Coleridge. 'They had', he said, 'felt for him the passionate devotion which earnest and generous minds always feel towards one from whom they have received great spiritual benefits; their devotion had become idolatrous, and they demanded from the idol that which it could not bestow.' But he recognized as well that there were some who 'welcomed the voice of a man who said to them, "What you are feeling after is that Father's house which the men of old-time spoke of. It was not a cunningly devised fable of theirs, that their Father and yours is seeking to bring back his children to himself: these struggles and failures of yours confirm their words." Beneath all strange mystical utterances—beneath those tetrads which might or might not be useful as scientific expositions of a truth lying beyond the senses and the intellect—they hear this practical message from, they saw that he could not have received it or proclaimed it unless the whole man within him had passed through a tremendous convulsion' (J. C. Hare, *Charges*, i, pp. xxff.).

Maurice and John Sterling, who afterwards was his assistant curate at Hurstmonceux. Both were to remain his lifelong friends, and for both he had a high admiration, especially for Maurice— 'the greatest mind since Plato' was his enthusiastic verdict— although Maurice on his own admission owed much more to the older man's teaching of the classics than to his theology. In fact Maurice's characteristic doctrines are scarcely to be found in Hare's writings.[1] The latter's own published work consists of collections of sermons—notably *The Victory of Faith* (1840), as well as the already mentioned *Mission of the Comforter*—and three volumes of his archidiaconal charges (1856), in which he ranged over matters of all kinds, from controversial theology to unsightly church stoves,[2] and a series of 'Vindications' of writers whom he thought to have been often misunderstood and misrepresented. Of these last the paper on Luther is outstanding.[3]

Hare belonged to no church party, although his personal sympathies lay with the Evangelicals, from whom, however, he differed sharply both on the question of biblical inspiration and on the central evangelical doctrines of the atonement and justification by faith. Theories of satisfaction and expiation he rejected, maintaining that the Jewish sacrifices, on which they were founded, embodied the idea not of penal suffering but of the sacrifice of the carnal will. It was of this that Christ's own sacrifice on the cross provided the supreme instance. Faith too, he considered, involves more than belief in the particular merits of the Lord's atoning death: a broader attitude of trust in and gratitude for the love of God revealed in the incarnate life as a whole. But

[1] 'When', says Maurice in his introduction to Hare's *Charges* (p. viii), 'we met again many years after, my theological convictions had already been formed by a discipline very different, I should imagine, from any to which he was subjected; they were not altered in substance, nor, so far as I know, even in colour, by any intercourse I had with him. But to his lectures on Sophocles and Plato, I can trace the most permanent effect on my character, and on all my modes of contemplating subjects, natural, human, and divine.' But Maurice did acknowledge his indebtedness to Hare for his ideas on sacrifice. See *The Life of Frederick Denison Maurice*, by Frederick Maurice (1884), ii, pp. 504–7.

[2] The unsigned introductory memoir of the author is by Maurice himself.

[3] In another he took up the cudgels on behalf of Dr Hampden, whose nomination to the see of Hereford aroused bitter opposition from among the clergy. Dr Vidler finds Hare's sermons 'practically unreadable' (*F. D. Maurice and Company* 1966, p. 228); even Stanley thought them, as pulpit discourses, 'needlessly long and provokingly inappropriate' (see *The Quarterly Review*, June 1855, p. 11), but praises the Charges—justly—for their intelligence and vigour of style.

if he criticized current evangelical theology he also had little good
to say of Tractarianism, in which he saw an exaggerated sacramentalism, an over-rigid conception of the ministry and in general
such excessive veneration of the past as could only inhibit the
appreciation of new truth. His in fact was the type of mind for
which dogmatism is always uncongenial. The depths of revelation,
it seemed to him, were not to be plumbed by shallow definitions.
Divisions among Christians that sprang only from differences of
theological interpretation were to be deplored. Truth, he felt,
does not issue from mere polemic; it would too soon be 'twisted
about and distorted' to suit the polemist's aims. 'It swells out to a
huge bulk, and absorbs all other truths, or hides them from our
view.' As Maurice said of him, 'he felt himself called to bear a
continual witness against those who confound the crushing of
opponents with the assertion of principles; he believed that every
party triumph is an injury to the whole Church, and an especial
injury to the party which wins the triumph'.[1] Ecclesiastically he
was a liberal, desiring the revival of Convocation and wishing to
see more powers conferred on the laity in the administration of
church affairs. A man of wide reading and sane outlook, his
opinions were constantly sought and always valued. Above all
he had the courage of sometimes unpopular convictions and was
a ready opponent of injustice in whatever quarter.[2]

Hare's conception of faith closely resembles Coleridge's, but
he seems to have reached it by way of his own study of Kant and
before the publication of *Aids to Reflection*. Reason, he thinks, is in
its highest sense a function of the whole personality, and faith
accordingly an expression of it. Thus:

> Every genuine act of Faith is the act of the whole man, not of his
> Understanding alone, not of his Affections alone, not of his Will
> alone, but of all three in their central aboriginal unity. It proceeds
> from the inmost depths of the soul, from beyond that firmament of

---

[1] Introduction to Hare's *Charges*, p. lxi.

[2] As in both his spirited defence of Hampden and his reply to an article—anonymous, but known to be from the pen of William Palmer—in *The English Review* for
December 1848, entitled 'On Tendencies towards the Subversion of Faith' and
attacking a number of contemporary writers, including Hare himself. The reply
took the form of a lengthy 'Letter' to the editor and was published as a pamphlet of
over seventy pages. Hare was especially concerned to protect the reputation of
Sterling who, in his last years and in the grip of a mortal disease, had given up
orthodox Christian belief.

consciousness, whereby the waters under the firmament are divided from the waters above the firmament. It is the act of that living principle which constitutes each man's individual, continuous, immortal personality.[1]

Religious truth must be seen in the light of human need and human experience. Hence the continuing necessity of doctrinal restatement, since fresh insights require new modes of expression. Much avoidable strife and tension within the Church had been caused by clinging to obsolete forms no longer adaptable to men's enlarging knowledge. Revelation itself has again and again been identified with a particular dogmatic system. The Bible, however, clearly shows how truth is originally conveyed to men; not, that is, abstract doctrinal schemes but in terms of concrete example or, at least, of principles capable of more than one formulation. 'A living faith seeks unity, which implies diversity, and manifests itself therein: whereas a notional faith imposes and exacts uniformity, without which it has no ground to stand on.'[2] His own religious outlook was, moreover, essentially Christocentric. Christ is the only true fulfilment of man's spiritual longings and aspirations, and in him alone do the truths which other religions were seeking after find their real validation. But Christ must be known as a *person*, in a vital experience. He is not merely the residual fact of a methodically sceptical historical inquiry after the manner of Strauss, nor the founder of a self-justifying system of ethics. For Christianity *is* Christ; he himself is the truth which he proclaimed, truth indeed which cannot be known except as personally realized in him. He is the Truth *because* he is the Way and the Life.

2. THE THEOLOGIAN'S VOCATION

Frederick Denison Maurice (1805–72) was arguably the most original theological thinker that the nineteenth century produced in this country. His originality was, in fact, too much for the majority of his contemporaries. In October 1853 the Council of King's College, London, felt it, in view of the tenor of his teaching, 'to be their painful duty to declare that the continuance of Professor Maurice's connection with the College as one of its

[1] *The Victory of Faith*, pp. 37f.
[2] *Ibid.*, p. 74.

Professors would be seriously detrimental to its usefulness', and he was dismissed. At the other end of the spectrum, John Stuart Mill thought more intellectual power was wasted in him than in anybody else of his time. 'Few of them', he continued, 'had so much to waste.'

> Great powers of generalization, rare ingenuity and subtlety, and a wide perception of important and obvious truths, served him not for putting something better into the place of the worthless heap of received opinions on the great subjects of thought, but for proving to his own mind that the Church of England had known everything from the first, and that all the truths on the ground of which the Church and orthodoxy had been attacked [many of which he saw as clearly as anyone] are not only consistent with the Thirty-Nine Articles, but were better understood and expressed in these Articles than by anyone who rejects them.[1]

Carlyle, who knew Maurice well, while reflecting that he 'ought to esteem his way of thought at its full worth', nevertheless confessed that hitherto he had found it 'mainly moonshine and *Spitzfindigkeit*.[2] J. B. Mozley considered he had not 'a clear idea in his head'.[3] Benjamin Jowett saw in him undoubtedly 'a great man and a disinterested nature', but otherwise 'misty and confused', and dismissed his writings as not worth reading.[4] Yet James Martineau, the Unitarian scholar and one of the most perceptive among observers of the contemporary intellectual scene, held that 'for consistency and completeness of thought, and precision in the use of language, it would be difficult to find his superior among living theologians'.[5] Gladstone admitted to finding him, intellectually, 'a good deal of an enigma', but he also admired him as 'a spiritual splendour'.[6]

What then did his pupils think of him? It seems, highly, if with inevitable puzzlement. In the words of a recent historian:

> His face was noble and his expression reverent. He exalted his hearers, but he could not make them understand what he said. In

[1] *Autobiography* (1867), p. 153.
[2] *New Letters of Thomas Carlyle* (1904), ed. A. Carlyle, i, p. 29. But Maurice could be equally caustic upon Carlyle's own 'silly rant about the great bosom of nature.' See *The Life of Frederick Denison Maurice*, i, pp. 282f.
[3] *Letters of J. B. Mozley*, p. 222.
[4] E. Abbott and L. Campbell, *The Life and Letters of Benjamin Jowett* (1899), ii, p. 45.
[5] *Essays, Reviews and Addresses*, i, p. 258.
[6] *Life*, ii, p. 208.

lecturing or preaching he visibly reached upwards towards God, pouring forth words, contorting himself and his language, passionate for truth yet believing truth to be found only in hints and shadows. His better students loved him. His worse students abandoned the exhausting effort and ragged his lectures. Whether his students were better or worse, they could make nothing of the notes they took from his lips. But a lofty purpose and a reverent mien did better for some of them than information or coherence. They could see and feel the grandeur and mystery of truth.[1]

What, at least, emerges from such diverse comment is that Maurice was the sort of man which it is impossible to classify. He fits into no clear intellectual category, even as he belonged to no ecclesiastical party. He evidently had great gifts both of mind and character, as, equally evidently, he lacked the power of effective verbal self-expression. Perhaps also there is something a trifle absurd about him, a high-principled fatuity, a defect of that worldly wisdom (not untouched by disillusionment) which adds the needed salt to inspiration; as certainly, too, a lack of self-critical humour, a quality indeed with which the Victorians generally were not over-well served. But for all the faults of Maurice's published works—and the *Life* (1884) by his son, Sir Frederick Maurice, conveys a far better picture of the man than do his own often laboured productions—his thinking has a range, prescience and depth which gives it permanent value. It can be studied today for its intrinsic and not only its period interest.

The unconventionality of Maurice's opinions, for his times, is unquestionable. He stood quite alone. He had affinities with the Evangelicals, the Broad Churchmen and the Tractarians, each in turn. Yet clearly he belongs to no school or party or following. Neither, on the other hand, is he a purveyor of mere novelties. On this he was himself emphatic. 'But while', he wrote, 'I utterly disclaim *novelty* . . . there is a sense in which I earnestly desire to be original.'

> An original man is not one who invents—not one who refuses to learn from others. I say, boldly, no original man ever did that. But he is one who does not take words and phrases at second hand; who asks what they signify; who does not feel that they are his, or that he has a right to use them till he knows what they signify.[2]

[1] Owen Chadwick, *The Victorian Church*, Part i (1966), p. 349.
[2] *The Doctrine of Sacrifice deduced from the Scriptures* (1879), pp. xf.

Maurice assuredly was one who did not take words and phrases at second hand without making them his own, interpreting them in the light of his personal thinking and experience and impressing on them the mark of his distinctive outlook. So ready was he to borrow from whatever source appeared to him fruitful that he even incurred the charge of eclecticism and of wanting any real principle of coherence in his teaching. But eclecticism, like novelty for novelty's sake, he absolutely abjured. Nothing, he thought, was so emasculating. Better far was 'the keen mountain misty air of Calvinism', or anything else, 'however biting', that would stir to action.[1]

Although, then, the eclectic standpoint was not to his liking, that of the mere system-builder was even less so. Theological systems were anathema to him. Construct one, he declared, and the very gifts and qualities which otherwise would serve the investigation of truth at once become its greatest hindrance. For in system-building, elements which not only are different but often also disparate have to be made to fit in with one another. 'Dexterity is shown, not in detecting facts, but in cutting them square.'[2] The Bible contains no system, nor for that matter do the creeds or the Prayer Book. The Bible records the history of God's acts towards men, not of men's thoughts about God.[3] The creed always has been a statement for the people, something which the 'schoolman' cannot and dares not meddle with.[4] And as for the Book of Common Prayer, it was not its merits as a literary composition which endeared it to him—'I never never called it "an excellent liturgy" in my life'—but the fact that, more than any other book after the Bible, it helped him to understand the love of God and man.[5] Yet even systems have their use and Maurice could not believe that any of them exists without serving some good.[6] Had he indeed possessed one of his own he might perhaps have succeeded in making himself more intelligible. Intellectual schemes, once grasped in their organizing principle,

<hr/>

[1] *Life*, i, p. 339. See also, e.g., *The Kingdom of Christ* (ed. A. R. Vidler, on the basis of the 2nd ed., 1842), i, pp. 178–82, and ii, p. 330.
[2] *Lectures on the Ecclesiastical History of the First and Second Centuries* (1854), p. 22.
[3] *Ibid.* p. 2.
[4] *The Prayer Book . . . and The Lord's Prayer* (1880), p. 147. This publication comprises two collections of sermons.
[5] *Life*, i, 512.
[6] *The Kingdom of Christ*, i, p. 68.

remain in the mind and help to give meaning to whatever data are related to them. Maurice, however, had no skill of this order. He preferred to wait for the light as it might come to him, distrusting fixed assumptions. The attainment of truth was the all-important thing, and for this a man had to be ready 'to be detected in error'—a virtue which resolute systematizers do not easily acquire—and to be certain that 'God's meaning is infinitely larger than ours, and that other men may perceive an aspect of it which we do not perceive'.[1] But because Maurice steered clear of theological schemes it is not to be assumed that he was without method or respect for logic. Logic could be a tyrannical mistress, but as a handmaid she is ever necessary; whilst apart from method (always to be distinguished from system) life, freedom and variety (which system opposes) cannot exist.[2]

Maurice sought always to present the truth as he himself saw it; but because truth has many aspects its consistency is not invariably evident. Hence the confusion that often arose in his readers' minds and the adverse impression he created upon the unsympathetic or impatient. Moreover, he was not helped by his literary style, which is without grace and often repetitive and rambling. His sentences become tangled, their sense obscured by a cumbersome piling up of phrases. It was his practice, especially in his later works, to dictate, with results far from happy, since the manuscripts were sent to press without adequate revision. Unquestionably his shortcomings as a writer, prolific though he was, have prevented due appreciation of his standing as a theological thinker. It was said of him that in conversation he was apt to exhaust his interlocutor, and most readers have found his books certainly no less taxing. His reputation nevertheless grew steadily, reaching its zenith in the 1890s, only to fall precipitously in the early decades of the present century. Within the last generation, however, interest in his intellectual achievement has revived, and we now see him for the remarkable, and possibly the great, theologian that he was.

For it was primarily as a theologian that Maurice saw himself, and such he claimed to be. His social reformism, for which he has usually been remembered, is really an aspect of his theology and an expression of one of its fundamental principles. At the beginning

---

[1] *The Claims of the Bible and of Science* (1863), pp. 30f.
[2] *The Kingdom of Christ*, i, p. 236.

of the second volume of his *Moral and Metaphysical Theology*[1] he says that it will be evident to his reader that 'I have felt as a theologian, thought as a theologian, written as a theologian'. All other subjects were in his mind connected with theology and ultimately subordinate to it. But he explains also that he uses the word in its old sense as of that which concerns the being and nature of God, pointing out that he means by it God's self-relevation to men, 'not any pious or religious sentiments which men may have respecting God'.[2] Nor, be it added, did he take theology, even as thus defined, in a merely formal way. The knowledge of God, he held, comes to men in experience, is indeed their basal experience. Not only is it the coping-stone of knowledge, the presiding element in the universe of man's thought, but the one foundation on which all else stands. He even said that in his opinion the name *theology* would better be exchanged for that of God, in that God himself is the root from which human life and society as well as nature itself are derived.

It was from this viewpoint that Maurice approached the problems of economics and politics. Society was not to be re-created 'by arrangements of ours' but regenerated, rather, 'by finding the law and ground of its order and harmony, the only secret of its existence', in God.[3] In short, to be a theologian was to be a prophet, a man *en rapport* with God and speaking directly as from God. The prophet in the Old Testament is not a systematizer of men's reflections about God, and he never speaks of his experience with detachment, *as* an experience; he does not enunciate a doctrine; he is not, in that sense, a teacher at all. He repeats what God himself utters. Similarly the theologian's role is one of witness—of witness to a Being who, moreover, is not remote from the common interests of mankind; for the world which God made and governs must by that very fact be the theologian's immediate concern, the highest theology being that most closely connected with 'the commonest practical life'. Maurice was convinced that theology would never be more than a *hortus siccus* of schoolmen until carried down into the air of nations and humanity. Worse, politics itself would be simply a ground on which 'despots and democrats, and the tools of both',

---

[1] Published posthumously in 1882.
[2] *Op. cit.*, p. ix.
[3] *Life*, ii, pp. 136f.

play with the morality and happiness of their fellow-beings unless 'we seek again for the ground of them in the nature and purposes of the Eternal God'.[1] His views as a Christian socialist are only an attempt to apply basic Christian principles, and to regard him as in the main a social thinker is to misunderstand him. It is fairly to be claimed, of course, that his social doctrine has a particularly historical significance, and in this respect he was undoubtedly a pioneer among churchmen. He himself, however, would have given this side of his teaching, for all its importance and urgency, a subsidiary place. His own view was that the theologian can speak to men convincingly, even on non-theological matters, only when he addresses them *as* a theologian.

> If [he wrote] I consider what I say I believe, if I determine to hold that fast, I may discover that I have in theology a much broader as well as a firmer meeting-ground with men as men, with men of all kinds and professions, of all modes and habits of thought, with men who attack my convictions, with men who are indifferent about their own convictions, than any maxims of trade, of convenience, of modern civilization, of modern tolerance, can supply me with.[2]

Wise words, we may say, which theologians of any age should lay to heart. For when men hearken, as they think, to a prophet, it is the prophet's authentic message which they ought to be able to hear, not simply information they themselves could have given him. Unhappily in Maurice's own case, though his intentions were sound, the 'prophetic' character of his discourse was sometimes of a kind to darken counsel. His actual phrases can often be telling, whereas his meaning is elusive. But unlike many prophets he has been lucky in that his admirers have since done him the service of making his thoughts clearer.

3. 'THE KINGDOM OF CHRIST'

It has been said that Maurice's teaching draws its inspiration as much from Plato as from the Christian Scriptures. Thus a Victorian critic, the Methodist theologian J. H. Rigg, stigmatized it as 'Platonism in gown and cassock', and argued that Maurice's doctrine of creation is emanationist—all reality exists in the mind of the Logos, so that the distinction between divine and human

[1] *The Gospel of St John* (1885), p. 475.
[2] *The Conflict of Good and Evil in Our Day* (1865), p. 182.

becomes blurred—whilst his doctrine of redemption, in minimizing the significance of Christ's actual historicity, tends to treat the Saviour as an abstraction or a merely impersonal spiritual influence.[1] Maurice said himself that he had never taken up a dialogue of Plato's without getting more from it than from any other book not in the Bible.[2] But the Platonizing charge is easily exaggerated. Maurice, like a great many other Christian teachers from the Alexandrians onwards, found in the ancient Greek thinker a major source of intellectual and spiritual stimulus. In his own instance it was the truth-seeking quality in Plato's writings that especially stirred him. To quote his own words:

> It was the necessary consequence of Plato's situation, and of the task which had been committed to him, that he was always seeking for principles. The most simple everyday facts puzzled him; nothing that human beings were interested in was beneath his attention; but then it was the meaning of these things, the truth implied in them, which he was continually inquiring after. He found the commonest word that men speak, the commonest act that men do, unintelligible, except by the light which comes from another region than that in which they are habitually dwèlling.[3]

This quality he did not find in Aristotle, the collector, arranger and classifier *par excellence* of facts, the framer of definitions. What attracted him in the Platonist philosophy was its abiding sense of the eternal and unchanging behind the surface-show of everyday things, an ultimate reality in which alone man can gain satisfaction and rest. Yet it is Plato's method of inquiry which was the effective influence. Plato taught him to examine his own ideas, his own terms. And this, he claims, was also Christ's procedure.

> I find Him beginning His pilgrimage on earth as a questioner . . . I find Him sanctioning that as His own sound method of detecting falsehood and laziness, and of urging men to seek truth that they may find it.[4]

Rigg's specific objections to Maurice's 'Neo-Platonism' need not detain us. He quite certainly overstates his case. Sufficient is it to say that Maurice's Platonism is to be seen in his general attitude

---

[1] See *Modern Anglican Theology*, published in 1859.
[2] *Life*, ii, p. 37.
[3] *Moral and Metaphysical Philosophy*, i, p. 180.
[4] *What is Revelation?*, p. 29.

to truth rather than in any express attempt to recast Christian doctrine in a particular philosophical mould.

His earliest theological work, *Subscription No Bondage*,[1] was a defence of the obligation of subscribing to the Thirty-nine Articles on matriculation in the university of Oxford. He had himself been brought up in Unitarianism—his father was a minister of the sect—and when at Cambridge the fact that he was not a member of the Church of England was a bar to his proceeding to a degree. When later he became an Anglican and entered Exeter College, Oxford, the requirement of subscription to a detailed theological formulary did not, however, trouble him. The act he considered to be no more than a declaration of the terms on which the university professed to teach its students and they in turn agreed to learn. It was fairer, he thought, to declare those terms openly than to conceal them, and in any case the Articles were in his judgment a not unfitting introduction, *being* theological, to a general education to science both humane and physical. Further, they might contribute to the reconciling of what is positive in the teaching of all Christian sects. This was a point of view entirely congenial to the Tractarians and seemed on the face of it to place him among their friends. But strong believer in the Church though Maurice was, the Tractarian rigidity repelled him. By nature he was not a party man, however broad the party's professions, and the exclusiveness of Newman and his followers towards Dissenters repelled him. That he was not for them nor they for him soon became evident. The realization of this, so far as he was concerned, came on his reading of Pusey's tract on baptism. This sacrament, as the Movement party saw it, was an instantaneously transforming act instead of, as he himself conceived it, a witness to the abiding truth of God's communion with man, the spiritual fact of the living presence of Christ in the life of humanity. For the basic principle of Maurice's theology was his conviction of the *nearness* of God. The Almighty is not a supreme governing Power, remote and impersonal, but the loving Father of mankind. As such he has revealed himself in the past and is ever waiting to do so in the present. Christ indeed, as Christians are bound to believe, was a full and final revelation

---

[1] Published in 1835 under the pseudonym of Rusticus, it bore the subtitle: 'On the Practical Advantages afforded by the Thirty-Nine Articles on matriculation in the University of Oxford'.

of the divine; but the imparting of that revelation to men is a continuing process. What above all they should learn from it is that they are already *in* Christ, and therefore, through him, in God. 'Except', Maurice once said, 'I could address *all kinds of people* as members of Christ and children of God, I could not address them at all.'[1] Man as such is a member of Christ and a child of God; baptism does not make him so. Maurice was emphatic that man does not by baptism or faith or any other process acquire a new character, in the sense of certain inherent qualities and properties not before possessed. If he does become a 'new creature' it is as having already been created anew by Christ, of having been grafted into him and become an inheritor of his life. Hence if baptism gives a man 'the filial name and the filial privilege' it is because Christ has first vindicated that name and privilege for all human beings, by himself assuming their flesh. But it confers no separate grace on any creature.

> It can only say: 'Thou belongest to the head of thy race; thou art a member of His Body; thou dost not merely carry about with thee that divided nature which thou hast inherited from the first Adam—a nature doomed to death, with death stamped upon it—thou hast the nature of the Divine Son, thou art united to Him in whom is life, and from whom the life of thee and of all creatures comes.[2]

Hence, too, although Maurice fully shared the Tractarians' belief in the Church as a divine society—as he was also at one with them in his recognition of its marks of identity—he could not endorse that aspect of their doctrine which pressed its separateness from either the Christian sects or the world without. Neither the world nor the sects *were* the Church, yet they were not without their special witness to the truth, distorted or one-sided in presentation though it might be.

Maurice, however, could not accept the common criticism of the Oxford Movement that it was preoccupied with 'forms'. On the contrary, he was convinced it was a movement not towards fanaticism but away from it.

> It arose, I believe, [he afterwards wrote] from a strong and deep feeling, that if forms exist at all they must have meaning in them,

---

[1] *Life*, ii, p. 236 (italics ours).
[2] *Sermons preached in Lincoln's Inn Chapel* (1891), i, p. 81.

otherwise they are shams and delusions. They did exist; by the Evangelical party they were regarded as useful accessories to personal devotion, in Oxford [i.e. by old-fashioned High Churchmen] they were regarded with antiquarian and traditional homage. The acknowledgement of them, as possessing present worth, as being the witnesses of an actual connexion between man and the invisible world, of an actual fellowship between man and man, was wanting to both.

And he adds:

To recover this conviction was to recover that which is the great principle of social faith, the principle that we exist in a permanent communion which was not created by human hands, and cannot be destroyed by them.[1]

The doctrine of the human race as itself both created and redeemed in Christ its Head and King is central to Maurice's whole teaching. Mankind, he says, stands not in Adam but in Christ,[2] and his proper constitution is his constitution in Christ.[3] All men, therefore, are God's adopted sons, a relationship which existed in Christ before all worlds and was manifested when he came in the flesh. What we have to do is to claim it, looking on ourselves as God himself sees us. For man was created in the divine image; man, that is, as a kind, and individual man only so far as he is the member of a kind;[4] though if we are to behold that image in its true likeness we must do so as it is in Christ, the Man who is God's perfect likeness.[5]

Men are told that they are made in the image of God: how it could be they knew not. Here is His express image, not shewn in the heaven above, nor in the earth beneath, but in a man. In Him creation has subsisted, in spite of all the elements of confusion and discord within it . . . In Him we find how humanity has been a holy thing, though each man felt himself to be unholy.[6]

[1] From an open letter, 'On Right and Wrong methods of supporting Protestantism', dated 1843, to the Evangelical leader and philanthropist, Lord Ashley, afterwards Earl of Shaftesbury.
[2] *Life*, ii, p. 358.
[3] *The Church a Family* (1850), p. 46.
[4] *Sermons preached in Lincoln's Inn Chapel* (1891), ii, p. 51.
[5] *Ibid.*, iii, p. 31.
[6] *The Epistles to the Hebrews* (1846), p. 29. This work also contains a preface in which the author discusses Newman's theory of development.

Again:

> The principle that man was made in the image of God, is not a principle which was true for Adam and false for us. It is the principle upon which the race was constituted and can never cease to be constituted.[1]

Maurice's objection to the traditional presentation of Christian doctrine concerned what seemed to him to be its false basis. Theology, Catholic and Protestant alike, made its starting-point the Fall, so that Christ's incarnation and death, despite St Paul's language about the mystery of Christ as the ground of all things in heaven and earth, were commonly regarded only as provisions against its more or less catastrophic effects. What had always been insisted on was the fact of man's depravity. 'The Fall of Adam—not the union of the Father and the Son, nor the creation of the world in Christ—is set before men in both divisions of Christendom as practically the ground of their creed.'[2] That it was this doctrine which lent force to the evangelical preaching Maurice readily allowed, and without the evangelical rekindling of it the faith of the English people would, he thought, utterly have died. Yet as he saw it 'it made the sinful man and not the God of all Grace the foundation of Christian theology'.[3] What the Christian theologian had to decide was upon what ground humanity really rests, whether upon the fall or upon redemption. Put thus, Maurice held, there could be only one possible answer, and this the Christian conception of God itself dictates.

Not that Maurice entertained any less grave view of sin than did Evangelicals, or for that matter High Churchmen, although

---

[1] *The Patriarchs and Lawgivers of the Old Testament* (1890), p. 56.

[2] *The Conflict of Good and Evil in Our Day*, p. 170.

[3] *Theological Essays* (3rd ed., 1853), p. xvi. In this, of course, the Evangelicals were simply following the doctrine of the sixteenth century Reformers. 'In the Calvinistic bodies from the first, and in the Lutheran so far as they caught the purely Protestant complexion, the idea of the Incarnation was deposed from the place which it occupied in the older divinity of the Church. The state and constitution of humanity was determined by the fall; it was only the pure, elect body, which had concern in the *redemption*; that redemption, therefore, could only be contemplated as a means devised by God for delivering a certain portion of his creatures from the law of death, to which the race was subjected' (*The Kingdom of Christ*, i, p. 126). William Wilberforce had declared that the corruption of human nature 'lies at the very root of all true Religion', and 'is eminently the basis and groundwork of Christianity' (*A Practical View*, p. 24).

he has been criticized for doing so.[1] Man, he believed, is a child of God, surely; but he is a wayward child, and his actual estate is a sad decline from his true and original one. The power of evil in human life and the horror of its consequences no just view can mitigate. Besides, Maurice was himself a man of keenly sensitive conscience. 'How hard', he exclaims, speaking of the clause 'Deliver us from evil', in the Lord's Prayer,

> how hard, when evil is above, beneath, within, when it faces you in the world, and scares you in the closet, when you hear it saying in your heart, and saying in every one else, 'Our name is Legion', when sometimes you seem to be carrying the world's sins upon yourself . . . oh how hard, most hard, to think that such a prayer as this is not another of the cheats and self-delusion in which we have worn out our existence.[2]

In fact, sin is so grievous and its effects so manifest that it is vital for man to know the truth about himself and whether it is Christ or the devil who is master. The joy of the Christian gospel is that it proclaims Christ to be men's lord. It shows us why the life of man is not vanity, in that it is drawn from the life of the Son of God himself, in whom alone is life and light. Man's existence becomes a vain show only as and when he seeks his good elsewhere than in the one source of all good, when he looks for the satisfaction of his being 'in the things which he is to rule, not in the Lord who rules him'.[3] Herein also is the essential difference between the believer and the non-believer; but it is a difference 'not about the *fact*, but precisely in the belief *on* the fact'. For the truth is—Maurice re-emphasizes it—that every man is in Christ, whereas the condemnation of every man is that he will not own the truth, will not *act* the truth. The gospel is simply the full discovery of him who is 'the Living Centre of the Universe' and the assertion that all men are related to him as member to head.

Does this then mean that there is no standing and no function for the Church as such and distinct from the whole race? It certainly is not Maurice's meaning and the answer he would have given to the question is plainly stated in the *Theological Essays*.[4]

[1] See R. H. Hutton, *Criticisms of Contemporary Thought and Thinkers* (1894), p. 88.
[2] *The Prayer Book . . . and The Lord's Prayer*, pp. 318f.
[3] *Sermons preached in Lincoln's Inn Chapel*, iii, p. 90.
[4] A new edition, by E. F. Carpenter, was published in 1957.

The world, he there says, contains the elements of which the Church is composed. In the Church these elements are penetrated by a uniting, reconciling power. The Church is to be thought of, therefore, as human society in its *normal* state, whereas the world is the same society in an irregular and abnormal state. 'The world is the Church without God; the Church is the world restored to its relation with God, taken back by Him into the state for which He created it.'[1] To this conception of the Church Maurice devotes what is probably his most important book and the one in which he comes closest to a systematic exposition of his views: namely, *The Kingdom of Christ; or Hints on the Principles, Ordinances, and Constitution of the Catholic Church, in letters to a member of the Society of Friends*, the first edition of which appeared in 1838.[2] In this his aim is to present a constructive doctrine by taking full account of the kind of objections to the Catholic idea which might be made by, in turn, a Quaker, an orthodox Protestant, a Unitarian and a contemporary rationalist—an enterprise he carries out with remarkable insight and understanding. He seeks to affirm the positive principle in each, freely acknowledging whatever validity it possesses, while at the same time showing how, when this positive principle is over-emphasized and made the basis of an entire system, it rapidly becomes a major error. Then, having considered a number of such systems, he looks for those signs of a 'spiritual and universal Kingdom' by which they could be transcended. That such a Kingdom exists is, he claims, beyond all doubt: it is constituted by the whole body of Christ's witnesses, of all 'who through God's mercy' have heard the gospel of Christ, confessed it to be true and assumed the privilege of belonging to his Church. The signs or marks of this society are the sacraments: baptism and the eucharist, the creeds, the liturgy or forms of worship, the episcopate and the Scriptures.

4. THE MARKS OF THE CHURCH

Maurice's review of opinions, the merits of which he acknowledges whilst deploring their exclusiveness, is characterized by a sympathy so large as to astonish, when the reader is mindful of the

---

[1] *Theological Essays*, p. 403.

[2] The second and considerably revised edition of 1842 carries a dedication to Coleridge's son, Derwent. It is this edition which was republished in 1958 by A. R. Vidler, in two volumes.

controversial clamour of the decade in which his volume saw the light. His efforts to understand may even at times seem laboured, but his criticisms, when voiced, are penetrating. The Quaker, for example, in failing to appreciate the significance of the incarnation is apt to lose sight of the distinctiveness of the sacred and so allow his vision to become secularized. Similarly the Protestant, in making a shibboleth of justification by faith, loses sight of Christ himself as the Justifier in his preoccupation with the experience of being justified.[1] The Unitarian, again, makes much of the God of love, but in denying the incarnate misses what was really the supreme manifestation of that love. In all these failures Maurice sees the consequences of system-building: distortion. Rome's great fault is its obsession with system, in both its doctrines and its practice, filling the place between the believer and Christ with, on the one hand, abstract theologizing, and on the other a mere mechanism for locating an absent Saviour.

The principle of a divine society Maurice finds in Scripture. 'Everyone who reads the Old Testament must perceive that the idea of a covenant of God with a certain people is that which presides in it.'[2] Divine election, however, was not exclusive: the choice of one people was to be for the blessing of all. Israel was the Church of God, first as a family, then as a nation in which king, priest and prophet, law, temple and sacrifice are elements of an integral whole—a way of approach to the ecclesiological doctrine in which Maurice—and again we must bear in mind the period in which he wrote—displays signal originality. For the Christian Church as it has existed in history has its essential principles already disclosed in the Bible. It is a holy nation, a people of God; and as Israel of old had the appropriate signs of its corporate life and calling so too has the Church. To present Maurice's account of these signs is in effect to expose the lineaments of his entire theology. But to him the obvious implication of the idea of the Church as the one people of God, called and redeemed in Christ, is its condemnation of sectarianism. Maurice, as we have said, detested the sectarian spirit with which religion in his day was rife. That sects come into existence on admissible pretexts and with the best of intentions he did not deny. Often

[1] Cf. *Life*, i, p. 139: 'Are there not some people who preach Faith instead of preaching Christ?'
[2] *The Kingdom of Christ*, i, p. 237.

enough they bear genuine witness to truth. Nevertheless, the sectarian impulse, especially since the Reformation, has more and more driven out the old faith and has led people to think 'that the Church must be either a mere world, or else a narrow, self-willed confederation; that it must either cease to be a spiritual body, or cease to be a universal one'.[1] In any case sectarianism does not necessarily imply purity: 'Every experiment to make bodies holy by cutting off the supposed unholy portions from the rest, has proved the more unsuccessful and abortive, the more consistently and perseveringly it has been pursued.'[2] Besides, it encourages bigotry: when any sect or school becomes dominant it changes too easily from a witness to Christ to a witness to itself, while the once vital convictions of its founders pass into dead actions and unmeaning phraseology. It is largely by its opposition to other schools that it retains any energy of its own.[3] Indeed on this topic Maurice is perhaps prone to overstate. The appearance of a sect may have been a historical necessity if some aspect of the truth were not to be forgotten altogether. But in the main his protest was salutary.

Maurice's view of the basic meaning of baptism we have already noted. The rite is a declaration of what man redeemed actually is: a child of God; and it bids him live as such. It is of the baptized accordingly that the Church consists.

> Baptism asserts for each man that he is taken into union with a divine Person, and by virtue of that union is emancipated from his evil *Nature*. But this assertion rests upon another, that there is a society for mankind which is constituted and held together in that Person, and that he who enters this society is emancipated from the *world*—the society which is bound together in the acknowledgement of, and subjection to, the evil, selfish tendencies of each man's nature.[4]

But if baptism is the sign of man's redeemed state as such, the eucharist is the sign of his communion with God in the largest and fullest sense of the word. It testifies that 'a living and perpetual communion has been established between God and man; between earth and heaven; between all spiritual creatures; that the

[1] *The Church a Family* (1850), p. 15.
[2] *Sermons preached in Lincoln's Inn Chapel*, ii, 23.
[3] *Life*, ii, p. 444.
[4] *The Kingdom of Christ*, i, p. 279.

bond of this communion is that body and blood which is the Son of God and the Son of Man offered up to His Father, in fulfilment of His will, in manifestation of His love'. It is the sacrament of his continual presence with his universal family, testifying to each man his own place in that family, and his share in its blessings. It is 'the pledge and spring of a renewed life', and the assurance that that life is his own eternal life.[1] Further, it shows that by the use of material elements men's bodies are redeemed as well as their souls. Maurice speaks of the eucharist in traditional language as both sacrifice and presence, though by presence he does not mean a *descent* of Christ into the consecrated elements, but rather a taking of them into Christ's glorified body. The presence is truly 'real'—faith does not create it—for the words of institution mean what they say. But what those words referred to when first uttered was the Lord's *risen and ascended* body, not that present with the disciples at the Last Supper. So, too, the sacrificial aspect of the eucharist lies in its being a celebration of the completed sacrifice of Christ.

> I have maintained [Maurice writes] that because the sacrifice had once for all accomplished the object of bringing our race, constituted and redeemed in Christ, into a state of acceptance and union with God, therefore it was most fitting that there should be an act whereby we are admitted into the blessings thus claimed and secured to us.[2]

Such an act the eucharist is. It registers the truth that without a sacrifice for sins there could be no communion between God and his creatures.

> Until One appeared who said, 'Lo! I come, in the volume of the book it is written, to do thy will, O God'—until He offered up Himself as a perfect and well-pleasing sacrifice to God, how could there be perfect contentment in the mind of a holy and loving Being, how could a perfect communion exist between Him and men?

That is why the Church teaches the necessity of a real and spiritual sacrifice to the atonement of God and his creatures, a sacrifice offered and accepted once for all for the sins of men. Further, Maurice sees in the eucharist the centre of Christian unity, a rite which 'keeps doctrines from perpetual clashing with each other, and men from being the slaves of doctrines',[3] a boldly paradoxical

[1] Cf. *The Prayer Book . . . and The Lord's Prayer* pp. 230ff.
[2] *The Kingdom of Christ*, ii, p. 71.
[3] *The Kingdom of Christ* (1838 ed.), i, p. 315.

idea, one may think, in view of the bitter disputes to which the problem of its theological interpretation has given rise. But it is the rite itself, not men's arguments about it, for which Maurice makes his claim. For what Christ has here embodied in a living feast is 'the complete idea of the Kingdom, which we, looking at things partially, from different sides, through the prejudices and false colourings of particular times and places, are continually reducing under some name, notion, or formula of ours'.[1]

The creed Maurice connects directly with baptism, as the Christian's open acknowledgement of what he believes his spiritual status to be. 'The name into which we are adopted there, is the name we confess here.'[2] It thus is a declaration of basic faith; it is not a summary of doctrine nor a statement of theological opinion.

On this point Maurice is very explicit. In the creed, he says, 'a man is speaking'. The form of it is, *I believe*. That which is believed in is not a certain scheme of divinity, but a name: a Father who has made the heaven and the earth; his Son, our Lord, who has been conceived and born, has died and been buried and has gone down into hell, who has ascended and is now at the right hand of God, and who will come to judge the world; a Holy Spirit who has established a holy and universal Church, who fashions men into a communion of saints, who is the witness and power whereby they receive forgiveness of sins, who will quicken their mortal bodies and bring them to everlasting life. Maurice's point is that faith is directed not to a doctrine but to a *person*. The creed takes us beyond doctrinal schemes; and whereas they divide it unites. This, he maintains, is true even of the Nicene creed, in spite of the circumstances of its origin. For that confession, too, is an affirmation of belief in a name rather than mere notions and it differs from the Apostles' creed only in that it unites with 'a declaration of the divine relations with men, a declaration of the relations in the Godhead'.[3] That it is a confession of the Church and not a statement for the use of theologians alone is a matter for rejoicing. Both creeds are a 'defence of the Scriptures and the poor man against the attempt of the doctors to confuse the one and to rob the other'. Without them the ordinary believer would be at the mercy of the experts.

[1] *The Kingdom of Christ*, ii, p. 69.
[2] *Ibid.*, p. 20.   [3] *Ibid.*, p. 143.

So also with the liturgy. Forms of worship are 'one of the clear and indispensable signs of a spiritual and universal fellowship'.[1] Here continuity is of positive value and antiquity has special authority. 'The prayers written in the first ages of Christianity are in general more free, more reverent, more universal, than those which have been poured forth since.'[2] Prayer itself is a natural human activity, but there is nothing unnatural in its regulation. In any case a society needs *common* prayer, not simply prayer adapted to special temperaments and moods.

> Prayer is meant to be an expression of the wants of humanity, uttered through one Head and Lord of man; individuals, if they would pray really and spiritually, must learn to take part in the speech and music of humanity, and not to isolate themselves in phrases and discords of their own.[3]

In common worship men lose their self-enclosed individualism and take the ground which they all share of being justified and redeemed in Christ.

Maurice now turns to the Church's ministry as his next principle of catholicity. The ministry is part of the Church's necessary structure. Christ intended his Church to be bodied forth in certain permanent and universal institutions. A permanent ministry would be a means of declaring his will and dispensing his blessings to the faithful as a whole. Its essence is service, not of a minority but of mankind generally, the Church's task being 'to remould the world, not to make a world for herself'. The original ministry was of course the apostolate, as we learn from the gospels and the Acts; the former relate the apostles' call as individuals, the latter tells us how at Pentecost they became a society, not of their own founding but of Christ's. How exactly the historic ministry emerged from the apostolate Maurice admits to be unclear. But the question at issue is whether or not any office corresponding in essentials to the New Testament conception of ministry was to be continued in the Church. 'The common opinion is, that by the perpetuation of this office the Church has been perpetuated; the connection of different ages with each other realized; the wholeness and unity of the body declared.' Changes have over the centuries taken place in it, but none of them of a kind to affect either its nature or its object.[4] Certainly the main constituent of

---

[1] *Ibid.*, p. 40.   [2] *Ibid.*, p. 45.   [3] *Ibid.*, p. 221.   [4] *Ibid.*, pp. 128f.

the Church's polity is the episcopate. Bishops have the direct commission of Christ, as much as did the original holders of the apostolic office. What they expressed is the universal, diffusive, cosmopolitan element in the Church's constitution, which without them would lose its literally 'catholic' character. Maurice even speaks of 'the necessity for Apostolic Succession and Episcopal Ordination'; but he makes it clear that, unlike the Tractarians, he does not imply by this that Christian communions which lack them are not of the Church. Catholicity is a matter of degree; though some Churches may want its fulness they yet have it in a measure and sufficiently. A national Church, moreover, is in no way incompatible with the Catholic ideal. On the contrary, it is the Church's duty to address the nation as such. The Ten Commandments were given to the people of Israel. A national Church, accordingly, is one which exists to purify and elevate the national mind, to impress on it the grandeur of law and of the source whence it comes and to warn it that 'all false ways are ruinous ways, and that truth is the only stability of our time or of any time'. The Church of England, Maurice was convinced, is at once Catholic and national; and in its national aspect Protestant. For Protestant and Catholic are not antithetic principles: the gospel itself has both a Catholic and a Protestant side and justice cannot be done to either one of them when the other is abandoned. The lessons of both have to be learned.

Finally there are the Scriptures. And here it has to be said that Maurice was somewhat behind his own times rather than, as in most other matters, ahead of them. The critical study of the Bible, as already developed in Germany, was beginning to make an impact on opinion in this country. Strauss's *Leben Jesu*, in George Eliot's translation, made its English debut in 1846.[1] Darwin's *Origin of Species*, with its sinister implications for traditional views on biblical inspiration, the *Essays and Reviews* volume and Colenso's *Commentary* all appeared when Maurice was in mid-career and aroused immense controversy. In these matters, however, he felt himself on alien ground. His knowledge of science was negligible—he had no interest in it—while his own attitude to the Bible was markedly conservative. In any case what he sought from Scripture was *religious* truth. Of *Essays and Reviews* he confessed to feeling how hopeless it was to expect any 'theology

[1] See below, ch. X.

or humanity' from it. 'One can only hope that the discussion may
lead us to seek a deeper foundation than the essayists or their
opponents appear to deem necessary.'[1] For himself the authority
of the Bible remained absolute. Scripture was to be looked at less
in its parts than as a whole, and as a whole it was of God. This did
not mean simply that it was *inspired* by God, and anyhow divine
inspiration was not to be taken in a narrow, verbalist sense. Every
man who does the work that he is set to do may believe that he is
inspired with a power to do that work. 'Inspiration is not a
strange, anomalous fact; it is the proper law and order of the
world.' The question, therefore, is not whether the biblical writers
were divinely inspired *as* writers, but whether they were in a
certain position and appointed to a certain work.[2] Thus what
makes the Bible inspired is essentially the character of its contents.
Its authority rests on the uniqueness of these. 'We declare that
there is a book, which so far as it fulfils its idea, becomes the key
by which all books may be interpreted, that which translates them
into significance and determines the value and position of each.'[3]
But the unquestionable truth of its inspiration does not guarantee
it against error. Nor does the Bible stand on its own, for the
Church is its interpreter. Church and Bible have a mutual
relationship. 'The Church exists as a fact, the Bible shows what
that fact means. The Bible is a fact, the Church shows what the
fact means.'[4] The written word and the living society are interdependent because the written word is subject to the living
society, and *vice versa*. In Scripture 'the circumstances and relations
of ordinary life are exhibited as the ladder through which God is
guiding man up to a knowledge of Himself.'[5] It is concerned indeed with the transcendent, the supernatural, but *through* the relations of ordinary daily life. Hence Maurice's stress on the Bible
as a *history*, since it is the history of the establishment of God's
universal Kingdom. But if this history be all-important *as*
history then the question of its authenticity is surely insistent.
And here Maurice's touch becomes less certain. The fact is that
he was impatient of historical inquiries generally; they too
easily tended, he thought, to the neglect of the really vital matter
of the Bible's theological content. For his part he was content to

[1] *Life*, ii, p. 384.
[2] *The Kingdom of Christ*, ii, p. 162.
[3] *Ibid.*, p. 167.   [4] *Ibid.*, p. 178.   [5] *Ibid.*, p. 153.

be a traditionalist, although he recognizes that such difficulties as the obvious discrepancies between the four gospels do exist.[1] Criticism, no doubt had its place. It could discourse about documents, their origin and their purpose; but he himself was far more concerned with what the Scriptures teach, which in the last resort does not depend on the precise historicity of the facts stated.

> If the gospel is a Divine message to mankind it *cannot* depend for the proof of its veracity, for its influence over men, upon any theories about the composition of the books which contain it, upon any arguments about their authenticity or inspiration, upon any definitions which we can give of the words 'Authenticity' and 'Inspiration'.[2]

His own method of interpretation was similarly straightforward. The real question was what the biblical doctrine means as a whole; a mere culling of proof texts in support of a preconceived theological system was worse than useless, Scripture not being a collection of logical propositions or exactly defined articles of faith. Nor did he favour the allegorical or typological method. It is the events themselves that are significant, not the supposed analogies which a misguided ingenuity brings to them. Besides, he feared—by no means unreasonably, as much modern typological exegesis has made us aware—that the method is apt to beget a feeling that the Bible is not 'a real book containing a history of actual men'. He does not say that the Old Testament is without types of the New. On the contrary, because the patriarchs were real men, made in God's image, Maurice felt bound to regard them 'as showing forth some aspect of His life whom I recognize as the express image of God's person'. Indeed the Old and New Testaments constitute a unity. To read them in continuous order is to witness the drawing aside, as it were, of a series of veils, the final stage being one which discloses the full atonement of God and man, the complete revelation of God's name, hitherto denied or concealed by sin. Miracles, lastly, as attestations of this divine revelation, are not mere prodigies,

---

[1] Cp. *The Unity of the New Testament* (1854), p. 244: 'With respect to the times, it seems quite clear that each Evangelist is always ready to sacrifice mere chronology to that order or succession of events which most revealed his purpose. In the short period of our Lord's ministry there are certain great land-marks, such as the Temptation, the Transfiguration, the Entry into Jerusalem, which all observe. Within those land-marks they follow the bent and course of thought which the Spirit has given to each; they group events according to another than a time order.'

[2] *The Kingdom of Christ*, i, p. xxxii.

exceptions to a divinely established rule, but manifestations of it. They were demonstrations that spiritual power is superior to mechanical, that the world is subject to God and not to chance or nature, that, in short, 'there is an order'.[1]

Before concluding our remarks on Maurice's attitude to the Bible as a constituent or mark of the Church some notice, necessarily brief, should also be taken of his other writings relating to Scripture. So far from neglecting biblical theology, as he has occasionally been accused of doing, Maurice was in fact wholly preoccupied with it. His *The Claims of the Bible and Science*, for example, is a series of letters on the Colenso controversy.[2] Maurice allows the rights of historical criticism in principle but strongly contests Colenso's view that because numerous inconsistencies and inaccuracies can be found in the biblical history it is therefore as history unreliable and properly to be used only as a source for 'religious ideas'. Religious ideas there certainly are, and they are important; but of greater importance are the events themselves, the basic authenticity of which criticism has not destroyed, any more than the deficiencies of Herodotus cast doubt on the battle of Salamis. For whatever the shortcomings of the biblical historian the event of the Exodus itself, a fact of determining significance for Israel's whole subsequent life and destiny, is unchallengeable. The really important issue is unaffected by points of detail. Even the traditional Mosaic authorship is not essential, for Moses was a fallible human figure, and upon a mere man, however inspired, divine truth ultimately does not depend. Maurice's own account of what is or is not historical does not, admittedly, make altogether reassuring reading, but historical insight was not his special talent. He firmly upholds a principle—that the Bible relates the acts of God in history— although his way of doing so is naïve and fumbling. As Dr A. M. Ramsey justly observes,

> He was, for all the clumsiness of his handling of the problem of history, putting his finger upon an important point concerning the nature of history and historical evidence. It *is* valid for a great event, that a nation's literature and religious experience took a certain shape, and that an event must be postulated such as created this shape.[3]

[1] *Ibid.*, ii, p. 172.
[2] See below, ch. X.
[3] *F. D. Maurice and the Conflicts of Modern Theology*, (1951) p. 89.

What in all his extensive writings on the Bible Maurice aimed at doing was to bring out the fundamental sense of Scripture as the self-disclosure of God to men. In this he is an early fore-runner of that revival of concern for biblical theology as such which has been so conspicuous a feature of the theological development in our own century. Of his other books in this field, *Patriarchs and Lawgivers of the Old Testament*, which did not appear until 1890, many years after his death, is probably the most satisfactory. But Maurice's work generally is replete with biblical teaching, interpreted in accordance with his characteristic stand-point. Always it is the mighty acts of God in history upon which the student of the Bible must fix his gaze. It is with these, not with 'religion', that the sacred book deals.[1] Nor for certain are they arbitrary inventions, but assertions of the divine sovereignty, proofs of the abiding reality of God's Kingdom. The particular sequence of these acts is a progressive revelation of the divine justice as it operates in and upon human affairs, the culminating event being the coming of Christ, the *Christus Consummator* in whom that Kingdom is fully and finally established. Thus Law points forward to Gospel, as Gospel in turn presupposes Law, since he who is Creator is also Redeemer, and will, at the appointed time, be likewise Judge.

---

[1] 'Religion' Maurice thought 'a peculiarly ambiguous' word, 'and one that is likely to continue ambiguous, because we connect it habitually with the study and treatment of the Bible, though the Bible itself gives us no help in ascertaining the force of the word.' Unfortunately, 'we have been dosing our people with religion when what they want is not this but the living God'. See *What is Revelation?*, pp. 239f., and *Life*, i, p. 369.

Chapter VI

F. D. Maurice (2) Theology and Life

1. 'THEOLOGICAL ESSAYS'

Even Maurice's warmest admirers have tended to regard his *Theological Essays* (1853) as among the least admirable of his works, a book tiresomely disputatious and ill-written. R. W. Church complained of its 'tormenting indistinctness'. Professor Chadwick describes it as 'filled with literary head-scratching'.

> Maurice [he says] engaged ghostly objectors in vehement dialogue. The tone was intense, the inspiration jerky. He waded along a stream of rhetorical questions and littered the banks with parentheses, dashes, inversions, notes of exclamation. The reader is battered and fatigued by the demand to feel indignation on subjects where he did not know himself to feel anything; unable to grasp the author's meaning while seeing that this meaning is life and death to the author.[1]

The description is colourful but apt. To plough through these essays is a task which only the most dedicated or industrious student is likely to accomplish. Yet it is an important book—indeed an indispensable—for the comprehension of Maurice's

---

[1] Owen Chadwick, *The Victorian Church*, i, p. 545. The truth is that Maurice wrote far too much. It is estimated that his published writings extend to more than 16,300 octavo pages and comprise nearly 5 million words. 'Could I have guided Maurice's pen', observed his publisher, Alexander Macmillan, 'I would have published about three books for him instead of thirty.' See Charles Morgan, *The House of Macmillan* (1843–1943), p. 36. Maurice's pen simply ran away with him before he had got his thoughts in order.

views on a variety of themes. It is addressed to Unitarians, and the writer, pursuing his favourite method, goes far in the concessions he is willing to make to his readers' susceptibilities. But the section which most offended Anglicans—for there also was much else in the book which did so—was one near the end, on everlasting punishment. The Council of King's College, London, at which institution Maurice was then a professor, took great exception to it, condemned the entire volume as calculated to unsettle the minds of the students, and forthwith relieved the author of his academic duties.

The trouble was that he had trampled on an all but universal religion assumption of his day: namely, that 'eternal' meant everlasting, and in particular that eternal punishment meant dereliction and torment without end. It was not that he himself believed in universal salvation, or, still less, that the love of God could simply ignore sin. 'I have no faith', he confessed, 'in man's theory of a Universal Restitution.' But to his essentially Johannine and Platonist cast of mind eternal life consisted in the knowledge of God; he could not think of it merely as an extension of personal existence into an unending future. His own conception, he explained, was founded on St John xvii, 3: 'This is life eternal, that they should know thee, the one true God, and him whom thou hast sent, even Jesus Christ.' Eternity is something 'outside of' time, an attribute of God's very being. Yet to live 'eternally' is also a possibility for human life in this world, and is the beginning of salvation. On the other hand, *not* to know God, to suffer the alienation from God which sin encompasses, is dire loss and spiritual death. But here too the idea of duration in time is an irrelevance: separation from God cannot be measured in temporal terms. The divine righteousness condemns sin—eternally; but the divine love ever struggles to overcome sin in the individual, and its efforts are not to be thought of as curtailed by the cessation of earthly existence. The return of the prodigal, in this life or any other, is always possible and always desired by the Father in heaven.

> I cannot [he declared in a letter to F. J. A. Hort] speak of God punishing for a number of years, and then ceasing to punish, or of the wicked expiating their crimes by a certain amount of penalties. The idea of a rebel will is, to those who know themselves what it is, far too awful for such arrangements as these . . . I know that we may

struggle with the light, that we may choose death. But I know also that love does overcome this rebellion.[1]

Thus impenitence at death does not necessarily imply the soul's damnation or consignment to everlasting torments. That men can go on resisting the divine entreaties is not to be doubted.

I dare not pronounce what are the possibilities of resistance in a human will to the loving will of God. There are times when they seem to me (thinking of myself more than others) almost infinite. But I know there is something which must be infinite in the abyss of love beyond the abyss of death. More than that I cannot know, but God knows—I leave myself and all to Him.[2]

Unfortunately Maurice's standpoint in this dark matter was one which was not easily appreciated even by more sophisticated minds. The theology of divine rewards and punishments was generally looked on as a necessary prop for morality. Maurice, it seemed, had denied hell, and with this potent sanction removed what might the moral consequences not be? King's College, after all, had the welfare of its pupils to consider.

The most discerning of Maurice's critics was J. B. Mozley. Mozley acknowledged Maurice's 'prophetic' bent of mind and that his strength lay in force of conviction more than in skill in argument. He realized that the conception of eternity as 'pure existence' was for Maurice a vital truth; but it was one extremely difficult even for the trained intelligence to grasp, 'and our Lord was addressing not philosophers but simple people when He gave His stern warnings about future reward and punishment'. That at least was a religious teaching which the plain man could understand. Moreover, the finest theological minds—and he cites St Thomas Aquinas—had defined eternal life not without reference to a temporal duration as a *conditio interminabilis*. In any case, Maurice's contention that he was interpreting the Church's formularies in their *intended* sense was mere special pleading.[3] Mozley's own conclusion was that King's had done 'a substantial duty to the Church and the nation in suppressing a teaching that immediatley interferes with the very foundation of religion and

[1] *Life*, ii, p. 15. Hort himself remarks on 'the small number of even thoughtful men at Cambridge who were able to recognize the distinction between time and eternity'. See *Life*, i, p. 266.

[2] *Theological Essays*, p. 406.

[3] *Essays Historical and Theological*, ii, pp. 256ff.

morals'.[1] It is one which to the modern mind is likely to appear illiberal and absurd, but it indicates how far Christian opinion even in the last century was wedded to the idea that religious beliefs and moral conduct stand in direct relationship, and that where the former were wrong the latter could not be right.

On the extent to which Maurice's doctrine is genuinely biblical there is more room for debate. Eternity in the Bible is thought of in temporal terms, although the Johannine eschatology approximates more closely to the Hellenic conception. And it was the Johannine view, interpreted with a Platonist bias, which appealed to Maurice's own religious temper and outlook.[2]

A further aspect of Maurice's teaching sharply criticized by his contemporaries bore on the theory of the atonement, since here again it seemed to run counter to deeply entrenched beliefs. Sin, and the cross as God's remedy for sin, were the staple of Victorian preaching. To the Evangelicals in particular the atonement was the heart of the gospel, and to this doctrine a chapter in the *Theological Essays* is devoted, although Maurice's own position is more fully expounded in his *Doctrine of Sacrifice*, a volume of carefully considered sermons published in 1879. In the essay he inveighs against the manner in which this profound mystery of the faith was all too commonly presented. The death of Christ was not, he argued, penal, nor did the satisfaction Christ rendered consist only in his dying, a denial which must have appeared to

---

[1] *Letters*, p. 298. But Maurice's views on eternal punishment were the ostensible rather than the real reason for his dismissal. The real reason was political: his connection with the Christian Socialist movement, especially in the person of Charles Kingsley. Sir Benjamin Brodie, a member of King's College Council, wrote to C. J. Hare: 'It would have been much better if [Maurice] had avoided connecting himself with the Christian Socialists, and discussing questions on which it is plain that persons having great influence in the college would be at variance with him' (*Life*, ii, p. 198f.). The Principal of King's, Dr Jelf, himself advised Maurice openly to disavow Kingsley. See *Life*, ii, 80.

[2] It is nevertheless the fact that Maurice was a good deal influenced by the millenarianism of the Rev. J. A. Stephenson, rector of Lympsham, whose assistant curate he was for a time. See *Life*, i, p. 167 and pp. 147–52 (Maurice's own 'Memoir' of Stephenson). Stephenson held that the events leading to the destruction of Jerusalem in A.D. 70 'were nothing less than the actual manifestation of Christ's kingdom, the actual establishment of a communion between the two worlds, the creation of a new heaven and a new earth' (p. 150). This idea is resumed by Maurice himself in his lectures on the Apocalypse, one of his favourite books in the Bible. 'I believe the Apocalypse,' he once said, 'to be the book which will at last be found to remove most veils from this mystery [the Trinity], as well as from the meaning of all the previous Bible history, and from the course of God's government of the world from the beginning to the end' (*Life*, ii, p. 354).

commit the author to the 'exemplarist' view suggested by the words of St John's gospel (xii, 32): 'I, if I be lifted up, will draw all men unto me.' However, to repeat the teaching of Abelard was not at all Maurice's intention. In *The Kingdom of Christ* he had already expressed a conviction which no traditionalist could have quarrelled with:

> Without a sacrifice for sins [he there wrote] there could be no communion between God and His creatures. His sacrifice removes those impediments to the communion, which the blood of bulls and goats, sacrifices of mere arbitrary appointment, though precious as instruments of moral and spiritual education, could not possibly have removed. Until One appeared who said, 'Lo! I come, in the volume of the book it is written, to do thy will, O God'—until He offered up Himself as a perfect and well-pleasing sacrifice to God, how could there be perfect contentment in the mind of a holy and loving Being, how could a perfect communion exist between Him and man?

Hence the Church teaches that 'a sacrifice, a real and spiritual sacrifice', was necessary to the atonement of God and His creatures, and that it was offered up 'once and for all, and was accepted for the sins of men'.[1] On this the *Theological Essays* are no less explicit:

> Since nowhere is the contrast between infinite Love and Infinite Evil brought before us as it is there, we have the fullest right to affirm that the cross exhibits the wrath of God against sin, and the endurance of that wrath by the well-beloved Son. For wrath against that which is unlovely is not the counteracting force to love, but the attribute of it. Without it love would be a name, and not a reality.

As love Christ himself saw it, and so endured it; nor was he willing that it should end before it had effected its full loving purpose. 'The endurance of that wrath was the proof that He bore in the truest and strictest sense the sins of the world, feeling them with that anguish with which only a perfectly pure and holy Being, who is also a perfectly sympathizing and gracious Being, can feel the sins of others.' Complete suffering with and for sin is possible only in one who himself is completely free from it.

That the cross is thus an exhibition of God's wrath against sin is

---

[1] *The Kingdom of Christ* (1838 ed), i, pp. 272f.

evidently, then, as firm a conviction of Maurice's own as of any Evangelical of his day. He even speaks of the atonement as a 'transaction'. But he also is most careful to point out that, in presenting the doctrine, the theologian or preacher must remember that whatever is good and right *is* God's will; that the Son is ever one with the Father and that his whole incarnate life was a submission to that will and thus a revelation of it; that Christ's work rescued humanity from death and the devil, not from a vengeful deity; and that the cross removes sin itself and not simply the penalties of sin. The satisfaction rendered by the offering of God's own holiness and love constituted 'the only complete sacrifice ever offered'. Was not this, Maurice asks, 'in the highest sense, Atonement'?

Nonetheless his views caused disquiet and provoked some severe comment. He had failed to stress the penal motive, and his meaning in any case was obscure. For in this as in other respects the Maurician theology tries to draw distinctions evidently of great significance to its author but a good deal less than clear to his readers. And do his objections to the prevailing theory imply that he himself saw the atonement only in a moralistic light? So at least it was inferred. But any assiduous student of Maurice is struck, rather, by his traditionalism in this matter. Christ, he believed, assuredly did bear the penalty of mankind's sin, yet not only *as* a penalty. The Saviour, in his death as in his life, was utterly obedient to the Father's will, not indeed as under constraint but in a spirit of wholly self-giving love. Hence in bearing the penalty of sin he did so not as sinful mankind's substitute but as his *representative*. His act is both Godward and manward, an accomplishment as man and for man of what man himself could not do. The theory as Maurice propounds it is no doubt insufficiently lucid, is even to some extent confused. But this, as often, was the consequence, for a man whose power of self-expression was inferior to the originality of his thinking, of an attempt to avoid extreme positions on either hand as both alike erroneous. His teaching, however, was the notable precursor of some later attempts at a more satisfactory interpretation of the doctrine within the framework of an integral orthodoxy.

The Doctrine of Sacrifice takes a wider view of the sacrificial theme, although the field is always strictly biblical. Sacrifice in the Old Testament is first dealt with: the offerings of Cain and

Abel, of Noah, Abraham and Moses are considered in turn. It all makes strange enough reading today, since the author's standpoint is innocently precritical. But interest is sustained by the theological exegesis. Sacrifice is seen as a divine ordinance, not a human means for cajoling deity, and as such man offers it in thankful self-submission and self-dedication. The difference between the two attitudes is shown in the respective oblations of Cain and Abel, the one fearful and self-seeking, the other self-lessly obedient. Noah's sacrifice is that of a man who feels himself to be God's instrument in furthering the divine purpose. His action assumes 'eternal right in the ruler of the universe' and that 'all caprice has come from man in his struggle to be an independent being'. Abraham's, again, is a testimony of selflessness and thankfulness, the offering of the dearest thing he possessed, for in offering his son he also offered himself. It is the same, Maurice contends, with the Passover, with the sacrifices of the Law, and with the self-offering of David, the last conspicuously so. David has nothing to render but himself in his utter humiliation, and thus is open to receive what God alone can give him, a right and a true spirit. In this way his example discloses the real as distinct from the merely legal meaning of sacrifice: that it is man's offering of *himself* and not simply of his belongings, for whereas the latter can be surrendered without ultimate cost the former is total. Only when David had made this full oblation was he in a restored state, in the state in which God intended him to be, as 'a dependent creature, a trusting creature, capable of receiving his Maker's image'.[1]

When Maurice turns to the New Testament he finds the teaching of the Old worked out in the clearest and most explicit manner. It now is seen as a revelation of the very nature of God himself: sacrifice has its ground in the divine being, as manifested in that perfect unity of will and substance between the Son and the Father which is the only possible source of the obedience and fellowship of a new, restored humanity. Sacrifice, therefore—and the point is typically Maurician—is not simply an expedient, a device for dealing with sin, but is 'implied in the very original of the universe', in the divine obedience of the Son 'before the worlds were'. 'In the latter days', however, its particular purpose is to take away sin, sin and sacrifice now being 'the eternal

[1] *The Doctrine of Sacrifice deduced from the Scriptures*, p. 100.

opposites'.[1] How the power of sin was in fact overcome Maurice attempts to show in terms of Scripture itself. The truth he is especially concerned to stress is that he who knew not sin deliberately identified himself *with* the sinner. The meaning conveyed in this Pauline idea appeared to him much richer than the usual teaching about Christ's taking the punishment of sin in man's stead. The latter conveyed 'no impression of the sense, the taste, the anguish of sin, which St Paul would have us think of, as realized by the Son of God—a sense, a taste, an anguish which are not only compatible with the not knowing sin, but would be impossible in any one who did not know it'.[2] In Christ's sacrifice God defeated both sin and death. By it men learn that sacrifice, not selfishness, is the law or principle of their being, for through it they are transformed after his likeness.

> The giving up of His Son to take upon Him their flesh and blood, to enter their sorrows, to feel and suffer their sins; that is, '*to be made sin*'; the perfect sympathy of the Son with His loving will towards His creatures, His entire sympathy with them, and union with them; His endurance, in His inmost heart and spirit, of that evil which He abhorred; this is God's method of reconciliation; by this He speaks to the sinful will of man; by this He redeems it, raises it, restores it.[3]

Hence the presentation of the one perfect and sufficient sacrifice to the Father and its continual thanksgiving is the central act of all worship, as of all fellowship among men.

Maurice's views as set out in these addresses, as in the *Essays* before them, did not find favour. His biblical interpretations are often indeed subjective, even wilful. A more serious accusation was that he had blurred the line between the divine and the human. Christ's action in identifying himself with man seemed to be directed to the latter rather than to God, and to have been, in the final count, a process of enlightenment rather than an effective renewal of corrupted human nature. R. S. Candlish, for example, in his *Examination of Mr Maurice's Theological Essays* (1854), objected: 'If the Gospel is to tell me, not that I must and that I may become what I am not—but only that I ought to know what I already am —then there can be no occasion for any radical renovation or revolution in my moral being. All that is needed is that I shall be

[1] *Ibid.*, p. 118.
[2] *Ibid.*, p. 188.
[3] *Ibid.*, p. 192.

informed and persuaded; not that I must be converted, created anew.'[1] And he added that throughout Maurice's book there was 'a careful and consistent disavowal of anything being really done by God'.[2] But Maurice's correction of the popular evangelical view was necessary and timely, a reminder of the too frequently forgotten New Testament teaching that God was in Christ reconciling the *world* unto himself; whilst his elevation of the principle of self-sacrifice to a level of universal moral significance, thus uniting the theological motifs of atonement and creation, has been of profound moral consequence for modern Christian thinking. Beside it the strictures of Maurice's critics appear narrow and antiquated.

2. CHURCH, STATE, AND SOCIETY

Not always, however, was it misunderstanding and criticism that Maurice encountered. With his Boyle lectures of 1846 on *The Religions of the World*, in which he deals with the relationship of Christianity to other great faiths, he gained an undoubted popular success. Here he rejects the idea that the essential truth of all religions has been found when each has been stripped of its distinctive features. Such a result, he holds, would be merely an abstraction without any real spiritual substance or appeal. Better is it to look for what is positive in them and compare this with Christianity in order to discover whether in the latter this positive element is not present in fuller measure. His contention is that in Christ is the wholeness of truth of which other faiths reveal only partial expressions. The right procedure for the overseas missionary therefore becomes clear: it is to show not that the religion of the people is false but that what is true in it is more richly exhibited in Christ. For God makes himself known, in varying ways and degrees, to all who genuinely seek him. If a man looks into his own soul he will learn there that God is love and so will understand how Christ is the supreme revelation of that love. But can such an individual and personal apprehension of truth be conveyed to another? How can the Christian's claim for Christ be proved to have universal validity? Maurice weighs these questions, yet he is convinced that fundamentally all men have the same spiritual needs, aspirations and ideals, and that these are of a

[1] *Op. cit.*, p. 27. [2] *Ibid.* p. 35.

kind that only the faith of Christ can meet. Christ is in fact, as some
of the early Christian Fathers taught, the divine Logos in every
man. 'The postulate of the Bible is that man could not be what he
is, if God did not hold converse with him; that this is his distinction from other creatures; that this is the root of all that he
knows, the ground of what is right and reasonable in him.'[1]

Is this, as some objected, merely the reduction of the Christian
dogma to a vague Platonism or a high-minded sentimentalism?
Maurice's language, admittedly, is often unguarded and effusive,
but the charge is scarcely fair. Certainly he had no intention of
watering down the express teaching of the creeds, the value of
which he argued at length in *The Kingdom of Christ*. The creeds
testify to a fact of Christian experience which cannot be gainsaid: that Christians have found in Christ, uniquely, the Way, the
Truth and the Life. The religion of personal feeling, 'subjective
religion', thus points to what is objectively real, that in Christ God
himself became incarnate. All the great religious thinkers of
whatever race and time carry some witness to truth; but only one
of them *is* the truth, so far as it is possible for one man to embody
it. It is this which is asserted in the doctrine of Christ's divinity, a
doctrine that does not deny but rather affirms whatever is of God
in the beliefs of the heathen. Christ is always *Consummator*. As
Maurice puts it in his lectures on the Epistle to the Hebrews,
published in the same year as *The Religions of the World*:

> The revelation of God . . . is truly the unveiling of Himself. First,
> He speaks in that which is most distant from Him, the mere things
> He has formed; then in men whom He created to rule over these
> things; lastly, in Him who by the eternal law is the inheritor of all
> things, in whom and for whom they were created. The order of the
> world, the succession of the ages, spoke of the permanence of God.
> Here he speaks in Him by whom He framed the order of the world,
> the succession of times.[2]

It was this profound assurance of his that God's revelation of
himself to man is a real self-disclosure, albeit 'in divers manners',
that forced him into public repudiation of the ideas of Professor
Mansel of Oxford.[3]

The theme which runs through all Maurice's work is that of the

[1] *The Doctrine of Sacrifice*, p. 4.
[2] *Op. cit.*, p. 28.
[3] See below, ch. VII.

universality of the divine rule and sovereignty. The world, mankind, is not to be made God's; it *is* God's. He created it and he has redeemed it. As Maurice expressed it in a letter to J. M. Ludlow: 'The Kingdom of Heaven is to me the great practical existing reality which is to renew the earth and make it a habitation for blessed Spirits instead of Demons. To preach the Gospel of that Kingdom; the fact that it is among us and is not to be set up at all, is my calling and business.'[1] But as God is Lord of the whole so is he of its parts. The task of theology, as Maurice saw it, is to comprehend man in his secular endeavours no less than in his spiritual vocation. Human society in its natural constitution is divisible into the family and the nation. Of these the former is the first great bulwark which God has provided against the domination of the senses and of the purely external world, and to be the sphere in which personality, as distinct from mere individuality, is developed. It is in the family that the meaning of authority and obedience is learned. Positive law therefore presupposes the family relationships as its basis; relationships which express, in the simplest form, the necessary dependence of human beings on one another. Undervalue the family and other types of human association will certainly come to be overvalued. But next in order to the family is the nation. Here a man discovers that he is under law and has personal responsibility. Personality thus finds a still wider field for its development. Under the law of the national community 'each man is taken apart from every other. Each one is met with a "Thou". The Law is over families, but is addressed to everyone who hears it separately, without reference to his ancestors or his descendants.'[2] Of the highest importance in this respect is language, which is the inheritance of the national community; for language is a primary mode of communication and the means of distinguishing truth from falsehood. In short, in the life of one's nation one learns to be, in the fullest sense, a *person*.

But the bond, Maurice now proceeds to argue, which holds society together as a community of persons is no bare abstraction or impersonal scheme of law, but the will of a supreme Person. Indeed to regard the basis of human society as something

[1] See Cambridge University Library, Additional Manuscripts 7348, art. 8, no. 65. It is dated 24 September (1852).

[2] *Social Morality*, 2nd ed, pp. 124f. These Cambridge lectures, first published in 1869, contain a well-balanced statement of Maurice's doctrine on the nature and constitution of human society.

impersonal and abstract is to undermine the personal relationship which subsists between all its members. In other words, the foundation of the national community is a *divine* Person; which means that the nation can never be looked on as a purely secular society. That it is so, Maurice concedes, many Christians themselves suppose. He, however, solemnly denies it.

> If by 'secular' is meant that which belongs to the fashion of a particular age—that which shuts out the acknowledgement of the permanent and the eternal—that, I grant, is hostile to Christian faith, that is the 'evil world' against which we are to fight. But one of the greatest weapons which God has given us in our conflict with this enemy—whether it invites us to worship the conceits of our own age, or of some departed age—is the assurance that the Nation has lived, lives now, and will live in Him, who was, and is, and is to come.[1]

The pattern of national life is provided, Maurice believed, by the history of the Jews. As God had dealt with them so will he deal with all other peoples.

But does not the Church of Christ obliterate national differences? By no means, Maurice thinks; on the contrary, it enables the different nations each to acquire an enhanced strength and distinctiveness of character. The Church, in the shape of a national institution, would itself participate in this distinctiveness, as it would in turn promote it. It was the misfortune of the Jews in the time of Christ to have gone far towards losing their sense of nationhood and to have become, rather, a collection of covetous individuals moved by the spirit of the sect or the faction more than by the conviction of a common origin, land and Lord. National characteristics are therefore good. It is a false universalism which would depreciate them, just as it was a vicious sectarianism or party fractiousness which would weaken them by its divisions. A nation conscious of its nationhood, so Maurice considered, thereby had its faith in God fortified.

> Let us be sure that if we would ever see a real family of nations, such as the prophets believed would one day emerge out of the chaos they saw around them, a family of nations which shall own God as their Father and Christ as their elder Brother, this must come from each nation maintaining its integrity and unity.[2]

[1] *The Ground and Object of Hope for Mankind* (1868), p. 46.
[2] *Sermons on the Sabbath Day, on the Character of the Warrior, and on the Interpretation of History* (1853), pp. 93f.

Plainly, in so thinking, Maurice was living before the era of modern secularist nationalism, but he founded his belief, naïve as it may seem to us now, on the witness of Israel. For the fact that Israel was called by God *as a nation* is a token of the similar calling of every other nation. He therefore thought that an Englishman has as much right to speak of his own nation as holy as had the Hebrew prophets of theirs. It is holy 'in virtue of God's calling', and its members are unholy in so far as they deny this calling and the kind of unity it implies. Hence also the citizen of one land must respect the citizens of every other; they are in a like position with himself, as having the same advantages and obligations. Thus the spirit of an exclusive nationalism is condemned, even if 'no man has ever done good to mankind who was not a patriot'.[1]

By a nation or a state—he uses the two words as equivalents—Maurice understands 'a body connected in a particular locality, united in the acknowledgement of a certain law, which each member of this body must obey, or suffer for its isolation'; but a body also 'recognizing a supreme and invisible Being as the author and sanction of this law'. It is an essential part of the state's function to promote the moral and spiritual welfare of its citizens. Church and State are both requisite to the constitution of man; nay, 'a State is as much a witness for God one way as a Church is a witness for Him in another way'.[2] The State is in fact as much God's creation as the Church. But if this is so what is their exact relationship? Wherein do they differ? Further, what is the relation between national churches and the Church Universal? Maurice's answer is that since Church and State alike have their respective places in the divine purpose their functions are complementary and the one needs the other. This is why the State is not a merely secular institution. It even has claims on the citizen's conscience which the Church itself cannot make, and it bears a witness—in the field of justice, for example—over and above the Church's. Without the State the Church is 'necessarily a maimed and imperfect thing', not simply because it lacks material means and coercive powers, but because 'God hath

---

[1] Cf. *The Kingdom of Christ* (1838 ed), iii, p. 377.

[2] *Ibid.*, pp. 13f. For a similar view stated by W. E. Gladstone, see Appendix III below.

ordained an eternal connection between the law, which is embodied in the State, and the religious, life-giving principle which is embodied in the Church, so that one shall always sigh and cry till it has found the other to be its mate'.[1] In sum:

> We distinguish most carefully between that which is spiritual and that which is legal, that which is ecclesiastical and that which is national, that which concerns the knowledge and cultivation of the good, and that which concerns the suppression of the evil. But we say that one of these, as much as the other, is to be referred to God.[2]

When Church and State are united, as in the nature of things they should be, law and gospel can cooperate. Both are opposed to human selfishness, the State through legal safeguards, the Church by its persuasive doctrine and example. Love and justice therefore are not, as Christians sometimes have asserted, antagonistic principles. Love needs justice as its instrument. The Kingdom of Christ finds a measure of articulation and definition in the kingdoms of men. Church and State, accordingly, have to learn from each other, in mutual accommodation. The State, that is to say, as equated with the *nation*; for Maurice considers the relation a positive and fruitful one only in the case of the nation-state. It could not have been realized under the conditions of the Roman empire, nor of the medieval polity. These amorphous agglomerations of peoples did not and could not possess the moral 'personality' which Maurice discovers in the nation proper. Indeed he goes to extreme lengths in his personalization of the State as a society of which, so he claims, we can predicate 'spiritual conditions and spiritual emotions', and which can repent and be reformed as truly as can any individual.

Nevertheless of the virtues of populist democracy Maurice was not by any means convinced. The will of the majority seemed to him neither well informed nor, as a rule, wisely exercised, and certainly deserved no flattery. The sovereign people has no more right than an individual autocrat to do what it pleases. For the danger in the one case as in the other is love of power for its own sake, a craving to which Demos is no stranger. On this point Maurice expressed his mind forcibly to J. M. Ludlow after the assassination of Abraham Lincoln:

[1] *Ibid.*, p. 106.   [2] p. 389.

As to democracy, I regard Lincoln's inauguration speech as the grandest return from the democracy of the Declaration of Independence to the theocracy of the Pilgrim Fathers that I might have seen anywhere. I always hoped that might be the effect of the war on the best Americans. I never dreamed of seeing it expressed officially in such language as that. And it was not merely the old Calvinistic theocracy—the divinity *minus* humanity. In so far as it recognized the Divine vengeance for the wrongs of the coloured race, it implied a Christ as Head of the human race. I should count it a treason to Lincoln's memory to relapse into the other kind of speech, as we must do if we call the other people to sympathize with him as a democrat. The horror of democracy which you impute to me is a horror in the interests of the people. I believe the Sovereign has been great in so far as he or she confessed a ministry—ignominious so far as they have been aristocrats or oligarchs. I apply the same maxim to the larger class. If they will accept the franchise as a ministry, be it as high as it may, as a calling, I shall rejoice. If they grasp at any power merely as a power, I believe the voice of Demos will be the devil's voice and not God's.[1]

And as for the cant phrase about 'the greatest happiness of the greatest number', he confessed that he could not understand it. What measure would one have of it? Indeed what *was* happiness, and how was its maximum distribution to be ascertained? Ask the masses what they consider happiness and the answer might well be 'something profoundly low and swinish'.[2] And not only was the democratic principle one of devaluation, it was a direct threat to freedom. Destroy a hierarchical society, having sovereign divinity as its apex, and the probability is that rule will fall into the hands of some minority despotism holding the great body of the population in servitude, moral, political, and perhaps even physical.[3] Maurice, 'socialist' though he professed himself to be, was a firm believer in monarchy and aristocracy, providing each was mindful of its obligation to minister. There was nothing amiss with the principle of either. Even the different political parties stood respectively for truths which are not *per se* antagonistic. Reconciliation was possible and desirable, for the total public good.

[1] *Life*, ii, p. 497.
[2] *The Workman and the Franchise: Chapters from English History on the Representation and Education of the People* (1866), p. 202.
[3] *Life*, ii, p. 129.

The responsibility of a national church is one of witness to the law of God before all estates of the realm. It exists to purify and elevate the nation's mind, to remind those whose power and duty it is to frame and administer the laws both of the significance of law and of the ruin to which false ways must inevitably lead. Thus the Church's function in respect of the nation is one essentially of education.[1] As being itself a national institution the Church can discharge this function, whereas mere sects cannot—an argument cogent enough when the Church comprises, at any rate nominally, the vast bulk of the population, but obviously implausible where the religious loyalties of the people are divided among a number of numerically comparable denominations. That educa-tion, therefore, is a primary responsibility of the State as such Maurice had eventually to admit. But he also believed that the State can meet its task, in face of every kind of enemy to the common life, only with the active assistance of the various denominations. In any event, the fact that prevailing conditions impeded the national Church from performing the work which ideally it ought to do was no reason for its not doing what it could.

Humanly speaking the Church's call is to be 'the life-giving energy to every body in the midst of which she dwells'.[2] The Church of a single nation, however, is the token of the bond that unites the citizens of all nations: namely, their universal relation-ship to an invisible Person, supreme over all men. This it can do as the local embodiment, locally characterized, of the Church which is catholic, worldwide, 'the same in all countries and all ages'. For the Catholic principle to Maurice is essentially that of universality. A nation may be Protestant; it cannot be 'Catholic'. Protestantism's strength lies in its emphasis on individual responsibility and a personal relation to God; Catholicism's in the importance it attributes to society as such and the individual's role in society. Neither the one nor the other ought to be re-pudiated nor its truth forgotten. Indeed 'we have to learn Protestantism again as well as Catholicism'.[3] Both are indispens-able to the life of a Christian society.

Hence Maurice's admiration of the Church of England. It was

---

[1] See his early work, *Has the Church, or the State, the Power to Educate the Nation?*, published in 1839.
[2] *The Kingdom of Christ*, ii, p. 254.
[3] *Life*, i, p. 357.

at once Catholic and Protestant. But by this he meant something rather different from the Tractarian apologetic. The idea of a *via media* did not appeal to him; it suggested compromise, and the Church is not a compromise between Catholicism and Protestantism. 'Compromise must always tend to the impairment of moral vigour, and to the perplexity of conscience, if it is anything else than a confession of the completeness of truth, and of the incompleteness of our apprehension of it.'[1] So far from the Church's pursuing a tenuous middle course between two clear and solidly based but antagonistic positions, it is 'most Catholic', Maurice judged, when 'most Protestant'. The argument looks like one of those paradoxes by which he was apt to confuse, if not himself, at all events his readers. His implication seems, however, to be that the Church's good is not secured by a little Catholicism here offset by a touch of Protestantism there, the inclusion of *this* necessitating the exclusion of *that*. Catholicism and Protestantism are to be combined in their fullest vitality, in their utmost concentration. The Tractarian view was not acceptable, despite the fact that Maurice repeatedly uses language having a Tractarian ring, because it was a limited and a limiting conception. He himself was content to look upon the national church as a part or branch of the true Church, but the systems advocated by the ecclesiastical parties, 'whether called Evangelical, Liberal, Catholic, or purely Anglican', were manmade, 'of the earth, earthy', although each had some particular truth in its grasp. Happily and providentially, the English reformers of the sixteenth century had avoided the system-mongering of their continental counterparts, whether or not they had fully realized what they were doing. The Church of England, as it emerged from the Reformation, was a Church more concerned with life than with precise and exigent schemes of doctrine. Accordingly 'that peculiar character which God has given us, enables us, if we do not slight the mercy, to understand the difference between a church and a system, better perhaps than any of our neighbours can'. And he adds, as though prescient of the Anglican part in the ecumenical dialogue of the century to come:

> Our position, rightly used, gives us a power of assisting them in realizing the blessings of their own. By refusing to unite with them

[1] *Ibid.*, ii, p. 392.

on the ground of any of their systems, by seeking to unite with them on the grounds of the universal Church, we teach them wherein lies their strength and their weakness.[1]

Not that Maurice was in any wise blind to the defects of the establishment as it then was. He admitted its 'corruption', its 'evil condition'—thanks in no small part to its deliberate cultivation of the sectarian feeling within its own bosom. But having himself been brought up in a sect he had learned to value the *ethos* of a *church*, whatever its faults. For as a church it had a wider platform of truth than any of the dissenting bodies, and was perhaps less arrogant and intolerant. He firmly believed, however, as he wrote in *Subscription No Bondage*, that unity would bring a profounder apprehension of the truth, since truth itself suffers from the absence of unity.

3. CHRISTIAN SOCIALISM

Until the revival, after the second world war, of interest in Maurice as a theologian he was chiefly remembered as the protagonist of Christian Socialism. This was a mistake. Maurice first and foremost was a theological thinker, an ideologue. In his own day he was thought to have had his head too much in the clouds and to have been a dreamer of intellectual dreams whose practical significance was none too evident. When, therefore, the theology came to be disregarded its author's work as a social theorist, more readily comprehensible, retained its appeal. Nevertheless the social theory stemmed from the theology and was its natural expression. 'Christ', he insisted, 'came to establish a kingdom, not to proclaim a set of opinions. Every man entering this kingdom becomes interested in all its relations, members, circumstances; he cannot separate himself in any wise from them; he cannot establish a life or interest apart from theirs.'[2] Theology is a matter of life, not merely of contemplation, and there can be no cleavage in principle between religion and the secular order. Indeed, as we have seen, Maurice could recognize no secular order exclusively as such. It was mankind as a whole whom Christ came to redeem and whose head he now is. In consequence every aspect of man's being is related to Christ and thus falls within the

[1] *The Kingdom of Christ*, ii, p. 343.
[2] *Ibid.*, (1838 ed), iii, 387.

Christian purview. The conviction was one which deepened the sensitivity of Maurice's naturally sensitive social conscience. And to the condition of the labouring classes in the 1840s only the totally insensitive could remain indifferent. The collapse of Chartism made the need for some kind of social action imperative, and Christian opinion, by virtue of its professed principles, was the obvious force to give stimulus and if possible to provide leadership.

Yet Maurice himself could never have been the effective leader of a political or social movement. He was a man of the strongest moral feeling, but constitutionally an 'intellectual' lacking in practical talent.[1] The issue, however, he saw in the sharpest outline: the condition of the poor was a fact to appal, but it did not lie in the unalterable nature of things; it was the outcome of wrong economic relations, a state of remediable social injustice. A false economy, with its resulting social evils, rested on the principle of competition, whereas what society desperately needed was the principle of cooperation. The Church, accordingly, was bidden to assert 'an actual living community under Christ, in which no man has a right to call anything that he has his own, but in which there is spiritual fellowship and practical cooperation'. That the task, were it to have positive effect, would be of immense difficulty he was under no illusion.

> I believe [he wrote] whoever enters on this path must lay his account with opposition, active or passive, from all quarters, must eagerly welcome and set down for fair gain all tokens of sympathy, must have no confidence in himself; must cultivate entire confidence in God and in the certainty of His purposes. It will and must be a long battle, in which many, even standard-bearers, will fall. But the issue is not to be doubted; let us work and trust for it.[2]

It was an undertaking, unfortunately, for which churchmen of whatever party were ill-prepared. The Evangelicals had behind them a great record of organized charitable endeavour, which was

---

[1] He could never overcome his dislike of the mere machinery of social action. 'I should have to go into a long personal history', he wrote to Ludlow, 'if I undertook to explain how the dread of Societies, Clubs, Leagues, has grown up in me, how I have fought with it and often wished to overcome it, how it has returned again and again upon me with evidence which I cannot doubt, of being a divine not a diabolical inspiration' (from a MS letter of 24 November 1849 in the Cambridge University Library, Additional Manuscripts 7348, art. 8, no. 19).

[2] *Life*, ii, pp. 9f.

continued in the unceasing efforts of Lord Shaftesbury to promote legislation for the removal of specific social evils. Intellectually, however, they were not abreast of their times, the trend of which they feared and failed to comprehend. As C. E. Raven says:

> On its intellectual side the Evangelical movement was not only hampered in the acceptance of new ideas but driven into opposition to them. . . . The democratic and liberalizing tendencies in politics were naturally combined with liberal views upon literary and historical subjects, and particularly so in religion, because the dominant theory laid stress upon just those elements of Old Testament teaching, the conception of the monarchy as a thing of divine decree and the insistence upon submission to law, which the reformers were driven to dispute.[1]

Such was no less true of the Tractarians. Chartism was something altogether beyond the ken of most of their sympathizers. From the Oxford of Newman and Pusey the new industrial world was too distant and the subjects which dominated the former's thinking seemed to have no more bearing upon it than had it upon them,[2] even though it be true that the Oxford Movement, along with Coleridge and Arnold, 'stood for a reaction against individualism through their emphasis upon the organic and historical character of society'.[3] But none of them questioned the basis of class privilege or the gross disparities in economic status between different sections of society which everywhere prevailed. In any case, for the most part, as G. C. Binyon puts it, 'the supernatural character of the Church made public life, in their eyes, an alien, secular, hostile region rather than a field for Christian action'.[4] By contrast Maurice felt that as a theologian simply it was his business 'to dig, to shew that economy and politics must have a ground "beneath themselves" ', that 'society'—and here he declared his opposition to the utilitarians and other secularizing reformers—'is not to be made anew by arrangements of ours, but is to be regenerated by finding the law and ground of its harmony, the only secret of its existence, in God . . . All my future course must be regulated on this principle, or on no principle at all' [5]

[1] *Christian Socialism, 1848–1854* (1920), pp. 13f.
[2] Cp. E. L. Woodward, *The Age of Reform* (2nd ed., 1962), p. 493.
[3] V. A. Demant, *Religion and the Decline of Capitalism* (1952), p. 53.
[4] *The Christian Socialist Movement in England* (1931), p. 64.
[5] *Life*, ii, p. 137.

At heart, then, Maurice distrusted democracy and feared political action of any sort as an instrument of Christian moral idealism. The leader of a *party* of Christian Socialists he had, therefore, no wish to be; nor could he have been so, his antipathy to all 'systems' being too deeply entrenched. Certainly he desired to see socialism Christianized and Christianity 'socialized'. But how this should be done, apart from theological and moral instruction, he never indicates. As he afterwards said, 'they found that I regarded the knowledge of God the key to all other as that which connected knowledge with life. They found that I accepted the Bible as the interpretation of the history of mankind.'[1] Maurice's notion of a Christian society hence remained essentially idealistic and doctrinaire. His generalizations, as statements of basic principle, are unexceptionable, but their practical applications are left in suspense. He boldly supported the socialist cause with his pen, and for educational ventures he had great enthusiasm, but the only practical scheme in which he joined with full consent was the Producers' Associations. Fortunately for the prospects of the social movement Maurice had friends whose talents were more pragmatic. Of these, the first easily, was John Malcolm Ludlow (1821–1911), a barrister and a man with considerable understanding of the requirements of effective political action. Educated in France, he was closely associated with socialist and revolutionary groups in Paris, where he had personal acquaintance with working-class conditions. With the hopes and aspirations of the 1848 he was in warm sympathy. From Paris he wrote to Maurice at the time 'to express his conviction that Socialism was a real and very great power which had acquired an unmistakable hold not merely on the fancies but on the consciences of the Parisian workmen, and that it must be Christianized or it would shake Christianity to its foundations, precisely because it appealed to the higher and not to the lower instincts of the men'.[2] To which Maurice replied, characteristically, that 'the necessity of an English theological reformation as a means of averting an English political revolution and of bringing what is good in foreign revolutions to know itself', had been more and more pressing upon his mind. The upshot was a decision, taken along with Charles Kingsley (1819–1875), to bring out a new series of 'Tracts for the Times' in the

[1] *Ibid.*, i, p. 493. [2] i, p. 458.

shape of a penny journal to be called *Politics for the People*. This particular enterprise lasted for only a few months, but the views expressed were always to the point, especially when Ludlow was their author. For Ludlow was radical and clearheaded. He cared nothing for the susceptibilities of the traditional political parties, believed in a massive extension of the franchise—although he was opposed to universal suffrage—and favoured large increases in direct taxation.

Kingsley, under the *nom de plume* of 'Parson Lot', assumed the role of fire-eating journalist. His only quarrel with the Charter, he declared, was that it did not go far enough. The Bible was a book, not to keep the poor in order, but to admonish the rich; it was throughout, and not in a few places only, the true 'Reformers' Guide'.[1] The idea of religion as an opiate for the people infuriated him. Instead it should be an exhortation, a challenge, a stimulus. The Church, he wanted his readers to believe, was in support of popular aspirations.[2] But on the whole *Politics for the People*, amateurish and somewhat inept in its editing, did not provide reading matter of a type to reach the masses. The Chartists themselves suspected the motives behind it. Yet it did some good in showing that barriers of class and education were not insurmountable.

Kingsley's position is not altogether easy to assess. His bark was loud, but did he do more than make a noise? Undoubtedly he was better informed than Maurice about the real condition of the

[1] *Charles Kingsley. His Letters and Memories of his Life* (ed. by his wife) (1877), i, p. 115.

[2] An example of Kingsley's journalistic style was the placard, displayed in the London streets on 12 April, 1848, which proclaimed: 'Workmen of England! You say that you are wronged. Many of you are wronged, and many besides yourselves know it. . . . You have more friends than you think for. Friends who expect nothing from you, but who love you because you are their brothers, and who fear God, and therefore dare not neglect you. His children . . . You may disbelieve them, insult them—you cannot stop them working for you. You think the Charter would make you free—would to God that it would! The Charter is not bad; if the men who use it are not bad. But will the Charter free you from slavery to ten pound bribes? Slavery to gin and beer? Slavery to every spouter who flatters your self-conceit, and stirs up bitterness and headlong rage in you? Will the Charter cure that? Friends, you want more than Acts of Parliament can give you. The Almighty God, and Jesus Christ, the Poor Man, who died for poor men, will bring it about for you, though all the Mammonites of the earth were against you. A nobler day is dawning for England, a day of freedom, science, industry. There will be no true freedom without virtue, no true science without religion, no true industry without the fear of God, and love to your fellow-citizens' (*Life*, i, 156f.).

English labourer, especially in the country. But he gives the impression of being a man chiefly of words. His many enthusiasms tended to run away with him. He lashed out in all directions indiscriminately and often inconsistently. But he had the born writer's gift for telling statement, as in his famous 'Cheap Clothes and Nasty', which he contributed to *Tracts by Christian Socialists*, a series planned by Ludlow.

It was in connection with this latter venture that Maurice, in January 1850, publicly accepted the designation 'Christian Socialist'. It committed him, he said, 'to the conflict we must engage in sooner or later with the unsocial Christians and the unchristian socialists'.[1] The same year also saw the publication of another periodical, actually called *The Christian Socialist*, the first number of which appeared in November. Ludlow was its founder and sole editor. Maurice indeed was dubious about it, so that Ludlow had a free hand. Its standpoint was serious and always consistently maintained, its aim being to present a view of society both Christian and Socialist. For Christianity, it was argued, had become too ecclesiastical, too cloistered, and needed to find its way back to the world proclaiming God's sovereignty over every sphere of man's life. The Christian gospel, in other words, must express itself in social action and organization, the appropriate form of which, for the present age, is socialism, which alone has a convincing message for the worker, The alternative to a Christian socialism was a godless one, and a godless socialism could have no permanence inasmuch as socialist organization, to be effective, must have such a moral basis as only a religious faith can provide. But Ludlow was in no doubt that by socialism he *meant* socialism —State control of the economy. *Laissez-faire* had to be ended and the profit motive curbed; failing which low wages and unemployment would certainly continue. In his estimation a society economically free—competition being of its essence—was bound to involve a clash of interests between employer and workmen. Meanwhile the struggle between capitalism and labour could be mitigated by the creation of producers' associations or co-operatives, in which labour itself owns the capital and uses it to its own advantage. For this purpose funds had to be raised, and another member of the group, Vansittart Neale, a man of abounding goodwill and considerable practical ability, made over a large

[1] *Life*, ii, p. 235.

part of his personal fortune to the cause. It was the beginning, in fact, of the vast cooperative movement as we know it today, Ludlow being mainly responsible for the Industrial and Provident Societies Act of 1852, which gave legal protection to all cooperative societies. Moreover, these associations were to prove a school of citizenship and a means of preparing workers for the responsibility of the franchise. But socialist though he was Ludlow was by no means committed to ideas of economic and social equality. Such in his view would have meant communism. In any case, what he stood for was a *Christian* society no less than a socialist, and in a Christian society the Church would have the role of leadership.

The question, however, was whether the existing religious bodies were capable of assuming it; and of this Ludlow was not confident. The established Church, unquestionably, was far too undemocratic. What he wanted was—to use his own phrase—an 'Americanized' church, self-governing and with a large element of lay control. It was only, he believed, a church of this type— strikingly different from the legally and socially hidebound institution which the Church of England then was—which could possibly win over the working masses. Ludlow was in truth a convinced radical. In himself a quiet, rather shy man, he nevertheless saw clearly what the situation demanded; whereas Maurice, who was generally regarded as the head of the movement, was uneasy when confronted with practical measures. He greatly respected Ludlow and tried to imbibe his opinions; it was simply that Ludlow's consistent practicality, which realized the need of a party organization, did not accord with Maurice's unpractical idealism, his 'Platonistic dreams about an Order, a Kingdom & a Beauty, self-realized in their own eternity'.[1] Maurice unquestionably wished to Christianize socialism, and, in a sense, to socialize Christianity; but he had no desire 'to Christian-socialize the universe'. His feelings towards the movement cooled, therefore. Further, his ejection from his King's College professorship, as we have seen, was not the consequence of his theological convictions alone; he was identified as the leader of a group whose activities

[1] The words are Ludlow's, who went on to complain that such dreams 'so put to shame all pretended earthly counterparts that it becomes labour lost to attempt anything like an earthly realization of them'. See a MS letter to Maurice of 13 September [1853] in the Cambridge University Library (Additional Manuscripts 7348, art. 17, no. 3).

were arousing sharp criticism, particularly in the influential
Quarterly and *Edinburgh* reviews, representing Tory and Whig
respectively, and the militantly evangelical *Record*. Maurice was
not and could never have become a political radical. But he was
considered to entertain too many notions of a potentially subversive kind for the tender minds of his students to be exposed
any longer to his teaching. Kingsley's ardour also waned,
following a somewhat ranting sermon on 'The Message of the
Church to the Labouring Man' which he delivered in a London
church in June 1851 and for which he was publicly rebuked by the
vicar, the Rev. G. S. Drew. He had already poured much of his
reformist enthusiasm into a novel, *Alton Locke*, published in the
late summer or autumn of 1850, laying about him manfully whenever he espied (as he supposed) an enemy of social justice. But
by 1855 his attitude was changing. In the prefaces to the subsequent editions of the book his tone became noticeably reserved
and even apologetic. Evidently his opinions of earlier years were
now embarrassing him. The faith also grew shaky of yet another
prominent supporter of the movement, Thomas Hughes, of
Tom Brown's Schooldays fame: Christians of a socialistic turn of mind
worked better, he thought, as individuals than in concert. Neale,
too, did not see eye to eye with Ludlow, about either the movement's economic socialism or its agressive Christianity. Thus by
1854 it had virtually petered out. Ludlow was disappointed and
not a little disillusioned, and Maurice turned to education as
providing a better way.

For education was a necessary means to the promotion and
dissemination of truth. The outcome—although the actual scheme
was of Ludlow's devising—was the foundation of the Working
Men's College in Great Ormond Street, London, followed by
similar institutions in the provinces. The London college opened
at the end of October 1854, with 120 students and the former
King's professor as its principal, the latter assisted not only by
others of the Christian Socialist group, Neale and Hughes among
them, but by Ruskin and Dante Gabriel Rossetti as well. The
venture was, however, the expression of Christian Socialist zeal and
with the movement's eventual demise its own fortunes declined.

The Christian Socialist enterprise had lasted for some six
years. It failed for want of a clearsighted and viable policy. Ludlow
could have given it this, but Maurice's concern was for the

theological fundamentals, whilst Kingsley, although a publicist of talent, was too little of a thinker and in any case mistook verbosity for action. Hughes had not much more than a warm heart, and Neale was essentially a private philanthropist, neither socialist nor particularly Christian. Yet their efforts were not wholly un-availing and certainly were timely. Hitherto the Church had stood aloof from all such aims, when not actually resisting them. Maurice and his friends, besides asserting workingmen's right of association for a positive social purpose, had pricked the nation's social conscience. No longer could thoughtful Christians be content to ignore the human aspect of the Industrial Revolution. The wage-earner was seen as having social rights of his own and not simply as the helpless object of middle-class condescension and charity. From now on churchmen increasingly were to feel themselves at one with the worker in his struggle for a better place in society, both economically and politically. A discussion had been started which could not be allowed to drop. The very abuse which the Christian Socialists met with was itself a grotesque compliment to their intentions. In G. C. Binyon's judgment it was largely through Ludlow's influence that 'there has been in England, and particularly in the Anglican Church, a development, unparalleled in any other country or Church, of a theology consonant with the principles and ideals of Socialism, tending at once to infuse religion with a social purpose and fulfil social inspiration by religious faith'.[1] The tribute here paid to one in particular of the group may fairly be shared among them all.

After 1854 Christian social concern in this country took a variety of paths. One was the way of the ritualist priests in the slums, of men like Lowder and Mackonochie. (The Wellclose Square mission, in the East End of London, had received active support from the Christian Socialists, notably in the formation of a working-men's club and institute.) But they were not social theorists, only Christian humanitarians and zealots for 'Catholic' truth, bringing Tractarian ideals to the world of the urban poor. Another was that of H. C. Shuttleworth, a ritualist likewise and rector of St Nicholas Cole Abbey, besides being a professor at King's College. He perhaps had more of conscious principle behind him. 'Poverty', he declared, 'is not a mysterious dispensation of Providence, which, for some inscrutable reason, is the stern

[1] *Op. cit.*, p. 84.

lot of the majority of our race; but an evil brought about by causes which can be remedied, an evil to be fought against and ultimately destroyed.'[1] Working with him at Cole Abbey was Thomas Hancock, whose published sermons, *The Pulpit and the Press*, sometimes bore revolutionary-sounding titles—'The Social Carcase and the anti-social Vultures', 'The Hymn of the Social Revolution' (i.e. the Magnificat), or 'Labour Day and the Red Flag'. Best remembered of them, however, was Stewart Headlam (1847–1924), founder in 1877 of the Guild of St Matthew, a society in which Maurician and Tractarian ideals were united in an alliance with principles avowedly socialist. Headlam's aim was to break down the barrier of prejudice between radical social thinkers on the one hand and the always conservative Church on the other without in any way compromising in the matter of strict High Church teaching and practice. That the Guild would welcome the introduction of state socialism was made plain in 1884. A resolution was also adopted which proclaimed that:

> Whereas the present contrast between the great body of the workers who produce much and consume little, and of those classes which produce little and consume much, is contrary to the Christian doctrines of brotherhood and justice, this meeting urges upon all churchmen the duty of supporting such measures as will tend—(*a*) To restore to the people the value which they give to the land; (*b*) To bring about a better distribution of the wealth created by labour; (*c*) To give the whole body of the people a voice in their own government; (*d*) To abolish false standards of worth and dignity.[2]

Headlam himself was a man of generous and unconventional sympathies, whose quixotic sorties in the field of social amelioration occasionally landed him in trouble with ecclesiastical authority. He had been an undergraduate at Cambridge during the years when Maurice held a professorship there, and relates that it was Maurice's theological teaching which first attracted him.

> He believed in the old term theology, and disliked any substitution for it of the word religion. It is easy to imagine what good news his teaching as to eternal life and eternal punishment was to such of us as had been terrified by the reiteration of the doctrine that half the world or more was condemned to future torment.

[1] *Vox Clamantium*, p. 39.
[2] Binyon, *op. cit.*, p. 143.

And he adds that 'it was from the doctrines of the Incarnation and the Atonement that he derived what unifies his social teaching'.[1]

4. LAST YEARS

Maurice was throughout his life a controversial figure. He would not retreat before an issue upon which he felt strongly. This was further demonstrated by his famous but in some respects unfortunate dispute with Mansel about the nature of divine revelation, and in his impulsive intervention in the Colenso controversy a few years later. But his public reputation was by that time well established. Sir Thomas Acland had written to him:

> For more than a quarter of a century you have been helping Englishmen to see through the theories and systems which have been invented to prop up, restore, develop or narrow the ancient edifice of their national Church; and, amidst ceaseless contumely and misrepresentation levelled against yourself, you have striven to teach, as Alexander Knox and S. T. Coleridge taught before you, that the Bible and the Church of England can best bear witness for their own truth, and for God's providence, against infidelity and pantheism.[2]

Maurice was never a man simply to let matters take their course, to shrug his shoulders, to pass by on the other side. His role was that always of Mr Valiant-for-Truth, even if his assumption of it was sometimes as naïve as it was sincere. There certainly was nothing of the complacent optimist about him. The technological process on which his era prided itself, whilst bringing much good, might also, he feared, create new problems of human self-alienation. 'Are we to live', he asked, 'in an age in which every mechanical facility for communication between man and man is multiplied ten-thousandfold, only that the inward isolation, the separation of those who meet continually, may be increased in a far greater measure?'[3] And although he could foresee 'a terrible breaking down of notions, opinions, even of most precious beliefs, an overthrow of what we call our religion—a convulsion

---

[1] See F. G. Bettany, *Stewart Headlam: a Biography* (1926), p. 20. On the after history of the Christian social movement see Peter d'A. Jones, *The Christian Socialist Revival, 1877–1914* (1968).

[2] *Life*, ii, p. 541.

[3] *Sermons preached in Lincoln's Inn Chapel*, v, 24.

far greater than that of the sixteenth century—in our way to reformation and unity',[1] yet that such reformation and unity would in the end be achieved he did not permit himself to doubt, since his consistent belief in Christ's actual headship of the human race banished any lurking pessimism at the thought of mankind's terrestrial future.

Maurice's last years were spent partly in the incumbency of St Peter's, Vere Street, preaching Sunday by Sunday to a very varied congregation, partly—from 1866—as professor of moral philosophy at Cambridge. The professorship afforded him great satisfaction, and the two volumes of lectures on conscience[2] and on social morality[3] respectively are the harvest of this academic Indian summer. Perhaps his closest disciple was F. J. A. Hort. Hort had studied *The Kingdom of Christ* when still an undergraduate and had been deeply impressed by it. 'Though I proceed', he then wrote, 'very slowly indeed with it, every day seems to bring out more clearly to my mind the truth, wisdom, scripturality, and above all unity of Maurice's baptismal scheme.'[4] Later in life he readily admitted to the powerful influence Maurice's writings had had upon him and how he owed to them, as it seemed to him, 'a firm and full hold of the Christian faith'.[5] This influence is especially evident in his own Hulsean lectures of 1871 entitled *The Way, the Truth, the Life*. Hort's intimate friend and colleague B. F. Westcott, was likewise a Maurician in his sympathies, particularly in the field of social doctrine, but in his case the imprint was not received uncritically.[6] He seems to have been afraid lest Maurice's influence would impair his own originality.[7]

---

[1] *Life*, ii, p. 354.

[2] *Conscience: Lectures on Casuistry delivered in the University of Cambridge* (1868).

[3] *Social Morality: twenty-one lectures delivered in the University of Cambridge* (1869).

[4] A. F. Hort, *The Life and Letters of Fenton John Anthony Hort*, i, p. 67.

[5] *Ibid.*, i, p. 155.

[6] i, p. 222.

[7] Westcott, it would appear, had never read Maurice extensively. It has even been said that, for the reason suggested, he had confined his attention to only one book (see, e.g., W. Moore Ede, *The Modern Churchman* (December 1933), pp. 527 f.). That this literally was so may well be doubted. But the one book of Maurice's which affected him potently was *Social Morality*, of which he wrote in the preface to his own *Social Aspects of Christianity*: 'Few books can teach nobler lessons; and I should find it hard to say how much I owe to it directly and by suggestion' (p. xii). When in 1884 he read the two volumes of the *Life* he told Llewelyn Davies that he had never before known how deep was his sympathy with most of Maurice's characteristic thoughts. 'It is most refreshing to read such a book, such a life' (A. Westcott, *Life and Letters of Brooke Foss Westcott* (1903), ii, p. 37).

Towards the end of the century interest in Maurice waned. A main reason for this was the growing preoccupation with critical biblical study. Serious attention to the problem of the Bible's literary history and authenticity, belated as it was in this country, had become a necessity, and until the problem had been squarely faced the task of theology proper, as distinct from its ancillary studies, was bound to be halted. Of the import of critical considerations Maurice appeared to have been little aware, so that his teaching, in itself none too lucid, now took on an old-fashioned look. In recent years this phase of neglect has passed and his thought has undergone a process of revaluation. It still indeed is difficult to believe that the original writings will ever themselves again attract readers beyond the circle of professed students of his period. Today the essence of the Maurician doctrine needs to be distilled. But orthodox religion, and Anglicanism in particular, has in modern times seldom been served by a body of ideas so consistently recognizable as the utterance of a mind profoundly Christian in all its convictions.

Chapter VII

The Limits of Religious Knowledge

1. THE MAURICIAN SPIRIT: FREDERIC MYERS AND F. W. ROBERTSON

Two Anglican divines, contemporaries of Maurice, who in a number of ways shared his standpoint, were Frederic Myers (1811–51), practically the whole of whose life was spent as incumbent of a Lakeland parish—he was perpetual curate of St John's, Keswick, from 1838 until his death—and Frederick William Robertson (1816–53), who, from 1847 until his own very premature death at the age of thirty-seven, ministered at Trinity Chapel, Brighton, where in a short time he won national fame as a preacher of outstanding ability. Myers, who deliberately chose a life of seclusion amid the mountain scenery he loved so well, did not permit his *Catholic Thoughts on the Bible and Theology* to be published during his lifetime. Its four successive parts, dealing respectively with the Church, the Church of England, the Bible and Theology, were printed and circulated privately, the first in 1834 and the rest at intervals from 1841 to 1848. It did not appear as a whole until 1873, when edited by Myers's friend, Bishop Ewing. A new edition, with an introduction by the author's son, F. W. H. Myers, the classical scholar, came out ten years later.[1] But by this time its opinions had lost their novelty and it

---

[1] F. W. H. Myers suffered many changes in his religious outlook, his final position being antagonistic to Christianity in any form. A pioneer in the field of psychical research, his *Human Personality and its Survival of Bodily Death* was published posthumously in 1903.

failed to make the impression it certainly would have done had it been given wider publicity a generation sooner. For its time it was a remarkable book, perceptive, lucid and independent in its judgments.

Myers united a genuinely religious disposition with a cool reason and refused to be hurried out of mind by current enthusiasms and controversies. He realized that the intellectual climate was fast changing and that immediate interests would before long be displaced by others, probably of more permanent significance. The advent of historical criticism would, he saw, inevitably alter the traditional basis of theology. The English theological tradition in particular would, he thought, suffer grave disturbance from its impact, since English theology was beyond all others 'textual, verbal, every way literal'—not, that is, as simply based on biblical principles but as essentially constructed out of biblical elements. It was rigid and it was insular. Myers himself believed that no sharp line of division could be drawn between the human and the divine. They coexist, the one implicit in the other, in individual experience, in history, in Scripture itself, and it is impossible to say with absolute assurance that *this* is of God, *that* of man. Hence it is that what from one aspect is seen as man's quest of truth becomes, from another, God's revelation of it. Hence, too, the impossibility of a theory of biblical inspiration which would elevate it above human error. His own view he describes negatively as neither 'literal' nor 'rational'; but, positively, he felt that if the divine permeates human life through and through, then the ways of God, to be understood, must be sought over a far broader area than the dogmatically recognized channels of revelation alone. The divine action takes the form rather of a continuous providence than a series of miraculous interventions. Its method is progressive and its ends are not always obvious at any given point in time. The Bible, which in any case must be set against the vaster background of world history, is not itself revelation but the record of revelation, revelation indeed of a multiple kind, culminating in the person of Jesus Christ, by whose standard all that preceded must be viewed and judged. And the record, it is now apparent, is the work of fallible men.

Myers goes on to argue that theology is not in any strict sense a science. What exactly our knowledge of God and man may be, our knowledge of man himself, let alone of the transcendent God, does not allow us to affirm, in the terms of a closed system. The Bible itself is no body of schematized doctrine, any more than it furnishes the answers to all the many and various questions which perplex us today. This is not to say that systems of theology are illegitimate: Christians will naturally and rightly go on trying to construct them; but their legitimacy depends on two conditions. First, it must always be remembered that human speculations are not to be equated with the original truth of revelation, and that the former have in comparison with the latter only a relative and provisional value; and secondly, as following from this, that theology is a progressive discipline, changing with the growth in human knowledge over many fields and being ever open to revision in the light of altered circumstances and wider experience. For no sooner has a theological system been devised than it may have to be modified, perhaps drastically. 'We must make', Myers says, 'the base of our theology as broad and deep as Fact and Truth of all kinds, and build it up with materials as everlasting as the experience and necessities and aspirations of the human soul.'[1] But if theology is not revelation *simpliciter* neither is it religion. 'Religion is a spirit—Theology only a creed.' Religion continues, though theologies may come and go. The Bible is a religious book, but we search it in vain for doctrines formally expounded. Its appeal is to conscience and to the heart. The New Testament epistles come nearest to theology in explicit statement, but chiefly so where they have the special circumstances of the Jewish people in mind. Yet Christianity is not moralism only, a bare code of ethics. It is centred upon and animated by a Person. The truth of Christ which it proclaims is one therefore of underlying principle and not merely of correct dogma; its test is life more than logic. The doctrinal expression of what the Christian believes about Christ may be less or more adequate, but the real criterion is the sense of personal relationship with him.

On the customary appeal to evidences Myers is unhappy. In regard to miracles he considers their probative value to have been greatly over-estimated. It is revelation which justifies them rather than they revelation. And as for prophecy its true nature has been misunderstood. It is not simply predictive, 'the form of an Image of History thrown from the Future upon the Present'; a

[1] *Catholic Thoughts* (1879 ed), p. 187.

more authentic view is that of 'a germinal principle continually reproducing itself in the Future'.[1] Regarding the Church the 'Primary Idea' is that of 'a Brotherhood of men worshipping Christ as their revelation of the Highest'. 'Equality of spiritual privilege', moreover, is so characteristic of its constitution that the existence of a priestly caste would necessarily destroy it. Later in the century such views had gained currency and hence appeared less challenging. When first set down, however, they were ahead of their time.

F. W. Robertson was akin to Myers in spirit and ideas. Essentially he was that comparatively rare phenomenon, a preacher who is also a teacher. The sermon, not the treatise, was his natural medium. Yet his pulpit style, effective as it was, bore well the transposition into cold print. He was keenly aware of the spiritual needs of his age and recognized also that the traditional Christian attitudes could no longer fully meet them. Nevertheless he was a firm believer in the traditional faith and in its power to respond to the deepest wants of men in all ages. His own position was 'broad', but like Maurice he was not a party man. Dogma was a necessity, but the presentation of religion ought not to be dogmatic, for the appeal of religion is not to the intellect alone but to the 'whole man'. In his own teaching, he said, his aim was to establish truth rather than merely to destroy error, whilst holding that truth itself is made up of opposing propositions and not to be thought of only as a *via media* between them. Again, since spiritual things are spiritually discerned, they should be taught 'suggestively'. Finally, we should learn that even in what is evil there is a 'soul of goodness'[2]. Not that Robertson would tolerate vagueness, a fault for which he criticized the American theologian, Horace Bushnell, finding him 'shadowy' and objecting that he did not 'sufficiently show that dogmas express eternal verities', that they are 'what a mathematician might call approximative formulas to truth'.

In this spirit I always ask—what does that dogma mean? Not what did it mean on the lips of those who spoke it? How, in my language,

[1] *Ibid.* p. 311.
[2] See Stopford Brooke, *The Life and Letters of F. W. Robertson* (1865), ii, pp. 160f.; cp. also pp. 102 and 106. Faith, he stated in a sermon of 1849, is not assent to a credal formula but 'the broad principle of saving trust in God, above all misgiving', 'a living for the invisible instead of the seen' (*Sermons*, 4th ser., 1886, p. 141).

H*

> can I put into form the underlying truth, in correcter form if possible,
> but only in approximative form after all? In this way purgatory,
> absolution, Mariolatry, become to me fossils, not lies.[1]

Thus no dogmatic statement can be final: it is in principle
liable to revision in the light of fresh knowledge or deeper
understanding. Christian doctrine must be progressive and the
Christian teacher keep an open mind. Hence the danger of
ecclesiastical parties and 'schools', which tend to narrowness and
rigidity. 'Do not tremble [he wrote] at difficulties and shoreless
expanses of truth, if you feel drifting into them. God's truth must
be boundless. Tractarians and Evangelicals suppose that it is a
pond which you can walk round and say, "I hold the truth". . . .
Dare to be alone with God.' This frame of mind meant that
Robertson, like Maurice, hated systems. They constricted. Far
better was it to teach doctrines—and Robertson's own sermons
are full of doctrinal content—in their organic relation to life than
with a view merely to their coherence in a closed scheme. Suggest,
he repeatedly urges, do not dogmatize.

Robertson's theology was intensely Christocentric. But his
principle here is that the mystery of Christ's person must be
approached through the historic fact of his humanity. The thought
of God can become meaningful to man only through the visible
life of the incarnate. As the perfection of humanity Christ is the
complete antidote to despair at the existing state of human
nature. The note struck is distinctly Maurician:

> Christ was the Son of God. But remember in what sense He ever used
> this name—Son of God because Son of Man. He claims Sonship in
> virtue of His Humanity. Now, in the whole previous revelation
> through the Prophets, etc. one thing was implied—only through
> man can God be known; only through a perfect man, perfectly
> revealed. Hence He came, 'the brightness of His Father's Glory, the
> *express image* of His person'. Christ then must be loved as Son of Man
> before He can be adored as Son of God. In personal love and
> adoration of Christ the Christian religion consists, not in correct
> morality, or in correct doctrines, but in homage to the King.[2]

[1] *Life and Letters*, ii, p. 40. Cp. what Robertson says in his confirmation class
catechism: '*Q*. Why is correct faith necessary to salvation? *A*. Because what we
believe becomes our character, forms part of us, and character is salvation or damnation; what we *are*, that is, our *heaven* or our *hell*. Every sin bears its own punishment'
(*ibid.*, p. 295).
[2] *Ibid.*, p. 40.

One main reason, Robertson thinks, why belief in Christ's
divinity was waning was that they who held it had petrified it into
a theological dogma without life or warmth. 'How are we then to
get back this belief in the Son of God?' His answer has an almost
Ritschlian sound: it can no longer be imposed by ecclesiastical
authority, the day of which is over; begin, then, as the Bible
begins, with Christ the Son of Man. The end will indeed be
adoration. But to adore Christ is not simply to call him God, to
cry 'Lord, Lord'. 'Adoration is the mightiest love the soul can
give—call it by what name you will. Many a Unitarian, as
Channing,[1] has adored, calling it only admiration; and many an
orthodox Christian, calling Christ God with most accurate
theology, has given Him only a cool intellectual homage.'[2] Hence,
too, the idea of presenting Christian truth positively and not
simply in the negative mode of contradicting error, which
produces not 'converts to Christ, but only controversialists'.
Controversy fastens on what is adventitious and temporary,
hiding the real substance of truth.

It is in this positive spirit likewise that the great controversial
issues between Protestantism and Rome must be broached.

> Purgatory, Mariolatry, Absolution, Apostolical Succession, Seven
> Sacraments instead of two, Transubstantiation, Baptismal Re-
> generation, Invocation of Saints—each is based upon a truth; but
> crystallized into form, petrified into dogmas, they are false.
> Endeavour to trace the meaning contained in Romish institutions:
> do not meet them with anathemas. Discover what the Roman
> Catholic means, translate to him his longing, interpret to him what
> he wants. I can conceive no more blessed work than this for the
> man of large heart and clear, vigorous intellect.[3]

On the vexed question of the eucharistic presence Robertson
again differs from both the Dissenter and the Romanist, whilst
also rejecting a mere compromise.

> In opposition to the Dissenting view, it *is* Christ's body and blood
> received; in opposition to the Romanist's view *it is not* Christ's body
> and blood to those who receive it unworthily. We do not go between

---

[1] The American theologian, William Emery Channing, who died in 1847. In his
day he came to be considered a Unitarian, but he believed Christ to have been at
once the perfect revelation of God and the living ideal of humanity.

[2] *Life and Letters*, ii, pp. 169–71.

[3] *Ibid.*, p. 161.

the two. Each of these opposite statements of the Dissenter or of the Roman Catholic are truths, and we retain them. It is not merely bread and wine: it is, spiritually, Christ's body and blood: God present spiritually, not materially, to those who receive it worthily— i.e. to the faithful. It is not Christ's body and blood to those on whose feelings and conduct it does not tell.[1]

So also with the eucharistic sacrifice. The Romanist is right in principle, wrong in his application of the principle. As for the doctrine of purgatory, the 'ultra-Protestant' utterly denies it. 'But the law of the universe is progress.'

Is there no more pain for the redeemed? Is there nothing good in store for the bad? . . . Here, then, we have the principle of purgatory. I have stated this hypothetically; the Roman Catholic states it as a dogma. Our fate is decided here. This is said rigorously by the ultra-Protestant. *So it is*; there is the Protestant truth. The Romanist states the opposite truth, and says, 'Our destiny is determined beyond the grave.' So long as either is a positive statement of a truth, it is right; but the moment either denies the truth of the other it becomes a falsehood.[2]

In the matter of baptism Robertson's ideas, as propounded in his two sermons on the subject, approximate closely to Maurice's. The sacrament, he holds, does not *make* men children of God, but only declares them to be so, the great truth being that all men are born into the world as children of God by right. Neither the sacramental action not the recipient's faith (or that of his sponsors) is needed to bring this about. It is a fact, whether we believe it or not. The Tractarian doctrine of a new kind of human nature created at baptism seemed to him magical, as indeed did the evangelical, which differed from it only in confining the efficacy of the sacrament to select cases. Robertson approved the Gorham judgment not because he thought Gorham right but because it left the question open.

It is not surprising, therefore, that, again like Maurice, he should have stood apart from the ecclesiastical parties. The dogmatic positions they insisted on maintaining required the rejection of those of their opponents. The language of religion, however, is poetic rather than logical. This conviction governed his hermeneutics: in the words of his biographer, 'he did not choose his

[1] *Ibid.*, p. 162.   [2] *Ibid.*, p. 163.

text in order to wring a doctrine out of it, but he penetrated to its centre, and seized the principle it contained. It was the kernel, not the shell, for which he cared.'[1] Hence the breadth of Robertson's appeal as a preacher. He addressed himself to the ordinary man, ignorant or impatient of theological niceties. Yet he paid for the largeness of his views with the bitter opposition of some influential persons in Brighton. His sympathies with the working class were suspect and he was attacked in the press for sharing the socialist opinions of Maurice and Kingsley. That he actually held such views he denied. 'It seems to me', he wrote, ' a great mistake to lead the working-classes to suppose that by any means independent of their own energy, moral improvement, and self-restraint, their condition can be permanently altered.' He disagreed with Kingsley's economic notions—'what he says of the accumulation of capital is vague and declamatory'—and thought that cooperation could not long replace competition without becoming competition itself, 'between bodies instead of individuals'. 'If we were all Christians in fact as well as by right, the difficulty would be at an end; but I do not think that the attempts which begin with society instead of the individual, will any of them solve the question.'[2] Yet he was most anxious that 'sympathy should be felt, or rather candour extended, towards the exaggerations of generous and unselfish men like Kingsley, whose warmth, even when wrong, is a higher thing than the correctness of cold hearts'. In any event Christianity would have to come in to balance and modify political economy.

2. H. L. MANSEL

A contemporary theologian with whom Maurice found himself very much at odds was Henry Longueville Mansel (1820–71), afterwards dean of St Paul's. Yet in the light of the present day Mansel stands out as one of the most original religious thinkers of the century. What he taught was that the transcendent God, by virtue of his transcendence—if the word be taken seriously— must in himself be unknown and unknowable, a doctrine evidently in flat contradiction of beliefs to which Maurice adhered passionately. Mansel's views were fully and lucidly stated in his Bampton lectures for 1858, entitled *The Limits of Religious*

[1] *Ibid.*, p. 165. [2] *Ibid.*, pp. 7f.

Knowledge Examined. These discourses without doubt brought a wholly fresh interest to a series of lecture-sermons which over the years had as a rule sunk to the level of a verbose if well-meaning conventionalism. Mansel himself, who at the time of their delivery was Waynflete professor of moral and metaphysical philosophy at Oxford, was esteemed by the undergraduates as perhaps the best teacher in the university, and welcomed in senior common rooms as one of the liveliest and wittiest of its conversationalists. But behind the verbal brilliance was a keen and well-informed mind and an unusual point of view. The lectures attracted to the university church such a congregation as had scarcely been seen there since the days of Newman. Not that their style was in any sense popular. Mansel stuck throughout to a close-textured argument with no concession to pulpit appeal. Many among his audience found him incomprehensible; others, understanding him well enough, demurred at what he had to say. One elderly don remarked that he 'most certainly never expected to live to hear atheism preached in St Mary's church', as he had done that morning. Yet Mansel's theology was undeviatingly orthodox and his intentions unimpeachable: his sole aim was to defend Christianity from the attacks of a sceptical philosophy. At a time when J. S. Mill was reputed the first philosopher in the land such a defence was widely considered urgent. The Tractarian enthusiasm had waned, at any rate in Oxford, and the party's leading figure, Dr Pusey, was looked on as a conservative among conservatives. A new apologetic was necessary, countering reason with reason. When, therefore, Mansel's lectures were published they were widely acclaimed, for all their admitted difficulty, as a brilliant and successful attempt to supply precisely this. Even the now elderly Keble praised the book as a 'treasure'. The religious press generally hailed it as a triumph and a severe blow to the opponents of Christian faith. Many readers judged its author to have given the final answer to the objections of unbelief. Yet it stung Maurice into violent reaction and thus precipitated the bitterest controversy of his life. Unfortunately his reply, *What is Revelation?*, is one of his least praiseworthy efforts and in the ensuing exchanges with the Oxford theologian he was routed almost with ignominy.

Mansel's work still merits serious attention. He himself was well read in German theology and philosophy, the trend of which, to judge from his Aristophanic lampoon, *Phrontisterion*, he heartily disliked.[1] But to understand his own position one must first consider its relation to the teachings of the Scottish philosopher, Sir William Hamilton (1788–1856), a quotation from whom appears on the title-page of the lectures as printed: 'No difficulty emerges in theology which had not previously emerged in philosophy.' Accompanying this is another, from Bishop Berkeley: 'The objections made to faith are by no means an effect of knowledge, but proceed rather from an ignorance of what knowledge is.' Hamilton, who from 1836 had been professor of logic and metaphysics at Edinburgh, was in his time one of the most prominent figures in British philosophy. Yet he wrote little for publication and his *Lectures on Metaphysics and Logic* did not appear until some years (1859–61) after his death. For a while, however,

---

[1] The Teutonic theologians figure thus:

> Theologians we,
> Deep thinkers and free,
> From the land of the new Divinity;
> Where critics hunt for the sense sublime,
> Hidden in texts of the olden time,
> Which none but the sage can see.

> Where Strauss shall teach you how Martyrs died
> For a moral idea personified,
> A myth and a symbol, which vulgar sense
> Received for historic evidence.
> Where Bauer can prove that true Theology
> Is special and general Anthropology,
> And the essence of worship is only to find
> The realized God in the human mind,
> Where Feuerbach shows how religion began,
> From the deified feelings and wants of man,
> And the Deity owned by the mind reflective,
> Is Human Consciousness made objective.
> Presbyters, bend,
> Bishops, attend;
> The Bible's a myth from beginning to end . . .

The philosophers are treated with no less gusto:

> With deep intuition and mystic rite
> We worship the Absolute-Infinite,
> The Universe-Ego, the Plenary-Void,
> The Subject-Object identified,
> The great Nothing-Something, the Being-Thought,
> That mouldeth the mass of Chaotic Nought,
> Whose beginning unended and end unbegun
> Is the One that is All and the All that is One.

his influence was considerable. What impressed Mansel so deeply was his 'philosophy of the conditioned', as he called it. Mental and material existence, Hamilton argues, are incompatibles; but this should not be taken to exclude their union in a common and more ultimate source or ground. Disparate though mind and matter are, they nevertheless are relative to each other, a fact which establishes the connection as well as the distinction between them. Hamilton accordingly maintains that not only are the respective qualities of mind and matter relative to something which transcends them, they are known *only* in correlation, each with the other. Thus when a fact is said to be known it is so only as limited or conditioned by other facts known in conjunction with it. Knowledge, in a word, is of the *conditioned* alone. The unconditioned is unknown and unknowable. But what is conditioned necessarily implies the unconditioned as its complement or ground: at least, it implies its existence, albeit only as the negative of the relative and conditioned. Being, that is, can be known by us only *as* the conditioned; yet at the same time we cannot avoid positing unconditioned being, even though in itself unknowable or known only negatively as complementary to the conditioned.

Hamilton did not himself apply his doctrine to the basic problems of theology, but he did suggest that such application might be fruitful, citing with evident approval 'the declarations of a pious philosophy: "A God understood would be no God at all"; "To think that God is, as we can think him to be, is blasphemy" '.[1] His own philosophy, he thought, might prove 'the most useful auxiliary to theology'.[2] To Mansel, whose thinking had been shaped in the Hamiltonian mould, the wider application was the obvious next step.[3] He launches his argument with the proposition that 'the primary and proper object of criticism is not Religion, natural or revealed, but the human mind in its relation to Religion'.[4] In other words, no attempt at a rational theology can be made without a prior examination of the nature and scope

---

[1] *Discussions on Philosophy, Literature and Education* (1853), p. 15*n*.

[2] *Ibid.*, p. 621. 'A world', he writes, 'of false, and pestilent, and presumptuous reasoning, by which philosophy and theology are now equally discredited, would be at once abolished, in the recognition of this rule of prudent nescience.'

[3] Mansel's other philosophical writings include *Prolegomena Logica* (1851) and *The Philosophy of the Conditioned* (1866). His work on *The Gnostic Heresies* (1875, ed. J. B. Lightfoot), which even now has not entirely lost its usefulness, was the product of his interests as an ecclesiastical historian.

[4] *The Limits of Religious Knowledge Examined*, p. 16.

of the reason itself. As Mansel sees it there are two extremes between which religious philosophy oscillates; these he identifies as, respectively, rationalism and dogmatism. To all seeming they are antagonistic, indeed irreconcilable, yet they both rest upon a common assumption. For the dogmatist, like the rationalist, is the architect of a philosophical system, the materials of which, 'the pre-existing statements of Scripture', whilst said to have been given by a higher authority, are nevertheless pieced together into systematic form and provided with a philosophical basis. In so doing, however, the dogmatist places them on a new and merely human foundation. Similarly by rationalism is meant a system whose final test of truth is afforded by the direct assent of the human consciousness, whether as logical deduction, moral judgment or religious intuition. The rationalist, Mansel points out, is as such not bound to maintain that this has actually been imparted. It is only that he assigns to some superior tribunal the right of determining what is essential to religion and what is not, that tribunal being the rational human consciousness. Thus both attitudes look to the same end: dogmatism tries to force reason into conformity with revelation, rationalism revelation into agreement with reason. Either seeks to produce a coincidence between belief and thought and to eliminate mystery.

> In relation to the actual condition of religious truth, as communicated by Holy Scripture, Dogmatism and Rationalism may be considered as severally representing, the one the spirit which adds to the word of God and the other that which diminishes from it.[1]

Whether a complete system of revealed theology could have been divinely conveyed to men, one thing at least is certain in Mansel's view, that such a system is not given in the revelation which we possess. If it is to exist at all it must be constructed out of it by human interpretation; and it is in the way they set about this that dogmatism and rationalism exhibit their most striking contrasts. The one accepts the original disclosure and adds to it from various sources and by various means; the other aims at a similar coherence, 'not by filling up supposed deficiencies, but by paring down supposed excrescences'. At first sight the two systems may seem to represent the respective claims of faith and reason; but in fact this is not so, for faith, properly so called, is not constructive

[1] *Ibid.*, p. 4. See K. D. Freeman, *The Role of Reason in Religion: a Study of Henry Mansel* (1969).

but receptive, whilst 'the disciples of the Rationalist are not necessarily the disciples of reason'. But the one, in striving to elevate reason to the point occupied by revelation, and the other in reducing revelation to the level of reason, have alike prejudged or neglected a previous and necessary inquiry, whether there are not 'definite and discernible limits to the province of reason itself', be it exercised 'for advocacy or for criticism'.[1]

Those, Mansel warns, who accept revelation should be extremely careful of the kind of assistance they seek from reason. There is doubtless a union of philosophy with religion in which each contributes to the support of the other; but there is one also which, in appearing to support them, in fact only preys upon and weakens the life of both. Thus the attempt to defend the doctrine of the incarnation on the assumptions of a philosophical realist, like Robert Wilberforce in his treatise on dogma,[2] only associates a fundamental Christian truth with a highly questionable speculation of medieval metaphysics.

> What does theology gain by this employment of a weapon which may at any moment be turned against her? Does it make one whit clearer to our understandings that mysterious twofold nature of the one Christ, very God and very Man? By no means. It was a truth above human comprehension before; and it remains a truth above human comprehension still. We believe that Christ is both God and Man; for this is revealed to us. We know not how it is so; for this is not revealed; and we can learn it in no other way. Theology gains nothing; but she is in danger of losing everything. Her most precious truths are cut from the anchor which held them firm, and cast upon the waters of philosophical speculation, to float hither and thither with the ever-shifting waves of thought.

And what in turn does philosophy gain? Nothing, says Mansel. 'The problems which she has a native right to sift to the uttermost are taken out of the field of free discussion, and fenced about with religious doctrines which it is heresy to call in question.'[3]

What, then, is the scope of human reason? Can it on its own account achieve any knowledge of God at all? If the philosophers,

---

[1] *Ibid.*, p. 7.

[2] Robert Wilberforce (1802–57), second son of the great Evangelical anti-slavery campaigner, became a Roman Catholic in 1854. In his Anglican (and Tractarian) days he published works on the doctrines of the incarnation (1848) and the eucharist (1853). See E. R. Fairweather, *The Oxford Movement* (1964), pp. 283–367; and cp. D. Newsome, *The Parting of Friends* (1966), pp. 370–383.

[3] *The Limits of Religious Knowledge Examined*, p. 10.

Mansel thinks, had been less ready to assume the possibility of a purely rational science, they would have spared themselves the illusions of both idealism and scepticism. More profitable would have been the investigation of the *subject* of religion, the human mind itself, since the mental conditions which determine the character of a philosophy of religion must be the same as those which determine that of philosophy in general. Hence the limits of philosophy in general, if limits they are, will be those of religious philosophy also. And we find, when we consider the matter, that consciousness is subject to certain quite inescapable conditions. To be conscious we must be conscious of *something*, and this can only be known for what it is by being distinguished from what it is *not*. But distinction is, of necessity, limitation. Obviously therefore the infinite cannot as such be distinguished from the finite by the absence of any quality which the finite possesses, as this would imply limitation. Thus a consciousness of the infinite as such necessarily involves a self-contradiction. On this showing no positive conception of the infinite is possible. To the human mind it is a negative concept only, an assertion of the absence of the conditions under which thought is possible. Similarly impossible is it for us to conceive the Absolute, since a further condition of consciousness is *relationship*. There must be both a subject and an object; the destruction of either is the destruction of consciousness itself. A consciousness of the Absolute is as self-contradictory as a consciousness of the Infinite.

> To be conscious of the Absolute as such, we must know that an object, which is given in relation to our consciousness, is identical with one which exists in its own nature, out of all relation to consciousness. But to know this identity, we must be able to compare the two together; and such a comparison is itself a contradiction.[1]

Even if it were possible to know the Absolute we still could not know that it *is* the Absolute. All knowledge is perforce relative, and what a thing may be like *out of* consciousness no mode of consciousness can tell us. The Absolute, like the Infinite, is a term void of positive content. Its sole use is to deny the relationship by which thought is constituted.

A third condition of consciousness, Mansel points out, is that of succession and duration in time. Whatever succeeds something else and is distinguishable from it is necessarily apprehended as

[1] *Ibid.*, p. 52.

finite, on the principle already established. This applies to anything conceived of as having existence in time. No *temporal* object, accordingly, can be regarded as exhibiting or representing the true nature of an infinite being. Thus creation, in the ultimate or absolute sense, is inconceivable by us, inasmuch as time cannot in fact be thought of as limited: to conceive a first or a last moment of time would be to conceive a consciousness into which time enters, preceded or followed by one from which it is absent. Equally inconceivable, on the other hand, is an infinite succession in time, for this too could not be bounded by time and so could only be apprehended by a mind 'outside' time. 'Clogged', says Mansel, 'by these counter impossibilities of thought, two opposite speculations have in vain struggled to find articulate utterance, the one for the hypothesis of an endless duration of finite changes, the other for that of an existence prior to duration itself.'[1] Because of this theologians have adduced the idea that God exists outside time and that in him there is no distinction of either past, present or future. This indeed may be true, Mansel concedes, but if so it makes God utterly inconceivable by us, who exist only in time. To know God by transcending time would be to become God.[2]

But these considerations will at once be seen to have an important bearing on the problem of divine personality. That God is personal Mansel holds, of course, to be vital to religion.

> The various mental attributes which we ascribe to God, Benevolence, Holiness, Justice, Wisdom, for example, can be conceived by us only as existing in a benevolent and just and wise Being, who is not identical with any of his attributes, but the common subject of them all;—in one word, in a *Person*.[3]

But personality as we conceive it is essentially a limitation and a relation. This undoubtedly is the case with our own personalities, and it is from them that all our representative notions of personality are derived. Hence to speak of an absolute and infinite Person is to use language of an object which under the conditions

---

[1] *Ibid.*, p. 57.

[2] Mansel had already used this argument elsewhere. In a paper entitled 'Man's conception of eternity' he wrote: 'To conceive an Eternal Being, I must have experienced a consciousness out of time, i.e. a consciousness other than human in its constitution. The Term Eternity, in this sense, expresses not a conception, but the negation of a conception, the acknowledgement of the possible existence of a Being concerning whose consciousness we can only make the negative assertion that it is not like our consciousness' (*Letters, Lectures and Reviews*, 1873, p. 111).

[3] *The Limits of Religious Knowledge Examined*, p. 59.

of human thought is simply inconceivable. Is it not then wholly inappropriate to speak of God in personal terms? Ought we not to confine our description of him to the impersonal and abstract? By no means. 'Personality, with all its limitations, though far from exhibiting the absolute nature of God as He is, is yet truer, grander, and more elevating, more religious, than those barren, vague, meaningless abstractions which men babble about nothing under the name of the Infinite.'[1] Personality is in fact the highest category known to us. It is by consciousness alone that we can assert God's existence or offer him service. 'It is only by conceiving Him as a Conscious Being, that we can stand in any religious relation to Him at all; that we can form such a representation of Him as is demanded by our spiritual wants, insufficient though it be to satisfy our intellectual curiosity.' But this clearly puts us in a philosophical dilemma. We are obliged both to think of God as personal and to believe that he is infinite, and the two representations are irreconcilable. The dilemma, however, is purely one for thought; it does not follow that it implies any impossibility in the absolute nature of God. The apparent contradiction, that is, is only the inevitable consequence of the attempt on the part of the human thinker to transcend the boundaries of his own consciousness. It proves that there are limits to man's power of thought, but no more. And such limitation is as true of metaphysical thinking as of religious, for although the mere expression, the 'infinite', when regarded as indicating only the negation of limitation—and hence of conceivability—is not contradictory in itself, it becomes so the moment we apply it in reasoning to any object of thought. In short, every object of consciousness is, *eo ipso*, finite, even the allegedly infinite. Thus contradiction is inescapable.

By no subterfuge can philosophy, Mansel argues, avoid the admission that the absolute and infinite are beyond its grasp. Hegelians may contend that the foundation for a knowledge of the infinite must be laid in a point beyond consciousness; but a system which starts from this assumption postulates its own failure at the outset. Consciousness, reason, is used as an instrument to prove that consciousness, rationality, is a delusion. The upshot must be that the terms 'absolute' and 'infinite', like 'the inconceivable' and 'the imperceptible', are merely names indicating not a possible

[1] *Ibid.*, p. 61.

object of thought but one that would be exempt from the conditions apart from which human thought would be impossible. Moreover, if the difficulties of faith are seen really to be difficulties in philosophy itself and inseparable from speculation of any kind, whether religious or irreligious, the Christian will do well to shun the allurements of a philosophical theology.

> Speculations which end in unbelief are often commenced in a believing spirit. It is painful, but at the same time instructive, to trace the gradual process by which an unstable disciple often tears off strip by strip the wedding garment of his faith—scarce conscious the while of his own increasing nakedness—and to mark how the language of Christian belief may remain almost untouched, when the substance and life have departed from it.[1]

Mansel now takes the argument a step forward by showing how in fact those elements in the human consciousness which form the basis of religion and from which positive religious ideas are originally derived require of their very nature belief in a personal deity. Religious thought, he says, is the outcome of two fundamental feelings: the sense of dependence and the sense of moral obligation. It is to these twin data of the inner consciousness that the two great outward acts by which religion has usually been manifested among men are to be attributed, namely prayer and expiation. Neither feeling yields a direct intuition of God, but both provide some intimation of his presence. They point towards a personal being who as a free agent hears and can answer prayer, and as a moral governor is the source and author of the moral law within us. As the immediate sources of mankind's knowledge of God they cannot, so Mansel claims, be set aside by the mere negative abstractions of the so-called philosophy of the unconditioned. But because consciousness of a personal deity is not in itself an intuition of the absolute and infinite we are led to the conviction that behind this positive conception of God as *personal* there nevertheless remains a mystery which in our present state of knowledge we cannot penetrate. Once more are we thrown back on the distinction already established between a belief in the *fact* and a conception of its *manner*; as also upon the paradox that it is our rational duty to believe in that which we are unable to understand.

[1] *Ibid.*, pp. 70f.

But how is the difficulty to be resolved if religious belief is not to be dismissed out of hand as an impossible attempt to comprehend the incomprehensible? Mansel replies that although we cannot contemplate God in his absolute nature we at least can view him in the perspective of his own self-revelation. If, that is, we cannot for the reasons noted have a *speculative* knowledge of God, revelation does furnish us with *regulative* ideas of the divine sufficient to direct our practice although not to satisfy our intellect. 'Guided by this, the only true philosophy of Religion, man is content to practise where he is unable to speculate. He acts, as one who must give account of his conduct: he prays, believing that his prayer will be answered.' Mansel, it should be observed, is careful to define his terms. By a speculative concept is meant, he explains, a conception derived from

> an immediate perception or other intuition of the object conceived, as when I form a notion of human seeing or hearing, or of human anger or pity, from my actual experience of these modes of consciousness in myself; and a speculative truth is a truth expressed by means of such conceptions. A regulative conception, on the other hand, is a conception derived, not from the immediate perception or intuition of the object itself, but from that of something else, supposed more or less nearly to resemble it; and a *regulative truth* is a truth expressed by means of such conceptions.[1]

Thus the language we use of God, as when we speak of his hearing or seeing, or feeling anger or pity, is analogical only, borrowed from that of human consciousness and indicative of divine attributes of which we have no immediate apprehension in themselves. But in this again, Mansel contends, the theologian is in no different case from the philosopher, for whom, as already shown, the attempt to arrive at absolutely first and unconditional principles involves him in apparent contradictions, with the result that he is bound to acquiesce in ideas which he practically assumes and acts upon as true without his being able to conceive how in principle they are true, ideas which necessarily imply the existence of a mysterious and inconceivable reality beyond themselves. (How, for instance, are we to solve the age-old problems of liberty and necessity, or of unity and plurality, or of the nature of space and time?) And when we turn from natural

[1] *Ibid.*, pp. xivf.

theology to revealed we discover that precisely the same considerations hold good.

> In no respect is the Theology of the Bible, as contrasted with the mythologies of human invention, more remarkable than in the manner in which it recognizes and adapts itself to that complex and self-limiting constitution of the human mind, which man's wisdom finds so difficult to acknowledge.[1]

Take for example, says Mansel, the dogma of the person of Christ. To philosophical theologians this has been a major stumbling-block. Despising the historical and particular they have sought refuge, like Hegel, in the empty abstractions of an impersonal idea. But the result has been a 'metaphysical caricature' of the Christian doctrine.

> It is for this philosophical idea, so superior to all history and fact—this necessary process of the unconscious and impersonal Infinite—that we are to sacrifice that blessed miracle of Divine Love and Mercy, by which the Son of God, of His own free act and will, took man's nature upon Him for man's redemption.[2]

Let philosophy say what she will, Mansel exclaims, it is the consciousness of the deep wants of our nature which really turns us to religion. 'It is by adapting His Revelation to those wants that God graciously condescends to satisfy them.' Salvation comes not through man's speculation but from God's revelation. And revelation takes the form of what man is able to understand and appropriate to his uses.

Accordingly it is to the idea of revelation that Mansel now turns his attention, and in particular to those features of it which have been attacked as contrary to reason, whether speculative or moral. But, he contends, the weapon which assails exhibits its own weakness in the act of assailing. 'If there is error or imperfection in the essential forms of human thought it must adhere to the thought criticizing, no less than to the thought criticized.' The alternatives facing us therefore are either total scepticism, 'which destroys itself in believing that nothing is to be believed', or else the simple recognition that reason, in thus criticizing, has transcended its legitimate province. In the latter case inquiry must be

[1] *Ibid.*, p. 106.
[2] *Ibid.*, pp. 114f. Mansel concedes that Strauss at least was consistent in his rejection of the gospel's historicity.

shifted to another field and belief determined partly by the internal character of the doctrines themselves, partly by the evidence producible in favour of their asserted origin as a fact. Talk of the so-called contradictions between reason and revelation is thus out of place, since to know if two ideas really are contradictory it is necessary to have a positive and distinct conception of both as they are in themselves; whereas in fact we have no such conceptions of the divine *per se*, only an imperfect representation through its analogy to the finite. The question to be answered —and it is fundamental—is that of the value of the conceptions we form of the divine in their highest development. Are they exact representations of divinity, yielding conclusions of scientific certainty, comparable with those of mathematics or the physical sciences, or are they merely approximate representations, leading only to probabilities such as may be balanced and modified by counter-probabilities of another kind? To Mansel it is evident that they are the latter, not the former. Theology is not a science inasmuch as we can have no properly rational knowledge of its object. Religious knowledge rests only on analogical reasoning, which furnishes nothing more than probabilities varying, it may be, from slight presumptions up to moral certainties, but whose weight in any given case can be determined only by comparison with other evidences. Hence the whole elaborate structure of metaphysical reasoning about ultimate reality stands revealed for the empty shell it is.

> Let religion begin where it will, it must begin with that which is above Reason. What then do we gain by that parsimony of belief which strives to deal out the Infinite in infinitesimal fragments, and to erect the largest possible superstructure of deduction upon the smallest possible foundation of faith? We gain just this: that we forsake an incomprehensible doctrine, which rests upon the word of God, for one equally incomprehensible which rests upon the word of man. Religion, to be a relation between God and man at all, must rest on belief in the Infinite, and also on a belief in the Finite; for if we deny the first, there is no God; and if we deny the second, there is no Man. But the coexistence of the Infinite and the Finite, in any manner whatever, is inconceivable by reason; and the only ground that can be taken for accepting one respresentation of it, rather than another, is that one is revealed, and another is not revealed.[1]

[1] *Ibid.*, pp. 128f.

In a word, the knowledge of God depends exclusively on revelation. A 'religion within the limits of pure reason' is a figment. Mansel allows, however, that reason, although fallible, is not worthless in this realm. Where no revelation has been given it is man's only guide; and where one exists—real or supposed—it still may sift the evidences on which it rests, its role being to expose the pretences of a false revelation and aid in the interpretation of a true one. But a revelation attested by sufficient evidence is always superior to reason and is entitled to correct the errors to which reason is liable.

The forms, Mansel thinks, in which a revelation may be conveyed are of two kinds, 'presentative' and 'representative'. The one implies that man has the capacity to receive it and the capability of constructing a *science* of the divine, which he in fact has not. A 'representative' revelation, on the other hand, imparts knowledge through symbols relating to human experience. That it should be more or less anthropomorphic in character does not trouble him. On the contrary, he boldly defends anthropomorphism and derides the 'morbid horror' which the philosophers have of it. 'Fools, to dream that man can escape from himself, that human reason can draw aught but a human portrait of God! They do but substitute a marred and multilated humanity for one exalted and entire.'[1]

When, however, he comes to discuss the actual content of revelation Mansel's radicalism is suddenly transformed into the strictest conservatism. Revealed truth is in the Bible and nowhere else. And the truth of the Bible is accepted by us on external evidences. The 'crying evil' of the present day in religious controversy is the neglect or contempt of these, and the first step towards the establishment of a sound religious philosophy would be their restoration to a fitting place in the theological system.[2] Evidences of a merely internal kind, though not without value of a sort, are, as regards the divine origin of the Christian religion, purely negative. They may in certain instances indicate that a religion has *not* come from God, but in no case are they sufficient to prove that it has. 'Where the doctrine is beyond the power of human reason to discover, it can be accepted only as resting on the authority of the teacher who proclaimed it; and that authority must then be guaranteed by the external evidence

[1] *Ibid.*, p. 12.   [2] *Ibid.*, p. 165.

of superhuman mission.'[1] The external evidences in question are
of course the usual ones of prophecy and miracle, to which may be
added the fact of the rise and progress of Christianity in history.
In face of them the only question to be decided is whether one is
or is not prepared to affirm that Jesus of Nazareth was an
impostor, an enthusiast or merely a mythical invention. Indeed,
Mansel insists that there can be no compromise or qualification
here. The choice is all or nothing; the Christian religion cannot be
taken up piecemeal. Admit a single objection and the whole is
discredited, since an objection which proves anything proves
everything.

> If the teaching of Christ is in any one thing not the teaching of God,
> it is in all things the teaching of men: its doctrines are subject to all
> the imperfections inseparable from man's sinfulness and ignorance:
> its effects must be such as can fully be accounted for as the result of
> man's wisdom, with all its weakness and error.

To criticize Christ's teaching in any particular, therefore, is both
impious and futile. Even those features of the Old Testament
revelation which many Christians have found morally objectionable must be accepted. A revelation, no doubt, which men do
consider of questionable morality may not in fact be of divine
origin at all, but the moral difficulty does not in itself disprove it,
for human morality is a relative not an absolute valuation. In any
case he who imposed the moral law—as man understands it—may
also suspend it. Here once more religious knowledge must
recognize its limits. In his moral attributes no less than in the rest
of his infinite being God's judgments are unsearchable and his
ways past finding out. All faith can do is confront this truth and
submit humbly and gratefully to the authority whence alone the
knowledge of salvation is to be had.

3. THE MEANING OF REVELATION

There is no denying the brilliance of Mansel's venture. To many
it seemed the final answer to all rationalist attacks on Christianity.
Moreover, to reread the book today is to encounter a remarkable
anticipation of some recent developments in theological thought.
Here already is the denial of metaphysics and metaphysical
theology on the ground that what lies outside human experience

[1] *Ibid.*, p. 155.

cannot be humanly described; the contention, accordingly, that religious language is and must be anthropomorphic in expression and symbolic in function; the assertion that there is no knowledge of God apart from the exclusive revelation which he himself has vouchsafed to man in Christ; the claim that Scripture is beyond criticism in terms of merely human philosophy. It is an argument that draws its force from its very extremism. Christianity is all or it is nothing. It is wholly true or else wholly false. It must be accepted or rejected *in toto*.[1] Further, the argument at least appears to reduce the knowledge of God to a series of propositions, instructive, useful, indeed true and necessary for their practical purpose, but in themselves incapable of drawing aside the veil which must ever hide the divine from human sight, Again, although the sticklers for orthodoxy may have rejoiced over them, are not the Manselian principles really a solvent of all theology, as Herbert Spencer maintained? The Cambridge theologian, F. J. A. Hort, certainly saw no reason for rejoicing. Mansel, he wrote,

> holds the doctrine of universal nescience more consciously and clearly than I suppose any other Englishman; a just Nemesis on Butler's probabilities! ...(What a very juiceless and indigestible morsel it must be to its orthodox admirers. It is clear, vigorous, and not often unfair; only a big lie from beginning to end.)[2]

It was, however, Maurice to whom Mansel's arguments gave greatest provocation.[3] His indignation overflowed. Mansel, it seemed to him, had substituted religion and even mere theology for God. On the Bampton lecturer's showing the believer could never know God as a reality; he could only know *about* him, in the shape of such limited, 'regulative' truths as have been providentially disclosed. God himself is unknown, and virtually unknowable. Thus faith is to be sited only on the void of agnosticism. It was to this effect that he replied, with such confused vehemence,

[1] W. R. Matthews recalls a sentence in Hobbes's *Leviathan* (ch. 32) which says the same thing in words characteristically homely and blunt: 'It is with the mysteries of our religion as with some wholesome pills for the sick, which, swallowed whole, have the virtue to cure, but chewed are for the most part cast up again without effect.' See *The Religious Philosophy of Dean Mansel* (1956), p. 18.

[2] A. F. Hort, *The Life and Letters of F. J. A. Hort*, i, pp. 398 and 402.

[3] J. S. Mill also was somewhat scandalized by Mansel's a-moral biblicism, which drew from him, in his *Examination of Sir William Hamilton's Philosophy*, the famous comment: 'I will call no being good who is not what *I* mean when I apply that epithet to my fellow-creatures, and if such a being can sentence me to hell for not so calling him, to hell I will go.'

in *What is Revelation?* (1859). Confused indeed the book is. Never skilful in purely literary artifice, Maurice here let his anger get the better of his judgment. The very form of the work—a collection of sermons on the Epiphany (in themselves quite admirable), *plus*, for the larger part of it, a series of involved and tedious 'Letters to a student of Theology'—presented a depressing contrast to the shapeliness and elegance of Mansel's treatise. The tone of it is often clumsily sarcastic, whilst the device of representing himself, a professional theologian after all, as only a plain man 'roughing it in the world' and confronting as best he can—like the supposititious neophyte whom he addresses—the subtle equivocations of this Oxford schoolman was a controversial trick of dubious honesty. Even Maurice's staunchest defenders are driven to admit that *What is Revelation?* could scarcely have offered a worse account of its author's case. For Maurice assuredly had a case. Mansel's thesis not only ran clean contrary to some of his deepest convictions; it appeared superficial, sophistical and lacking in the spirit of genuine religion. For divine revelation was not a matter of propositions or forms of words merely, but of the unveiling, as it were, of a *person*—'and that Person the ground and Archetype of men, the source of all life and goodness in men—not to the eye but to the very man himself, to the Conscience, Heart, Will, Reason, which God has created to know Him, and be like Him'. Maurice goes on:

> Now if this idea of Revelation has been changed for another that is wholly unlike it—if by Revelation *we* understand certain communications made to us by God, and which we cannot dispense with, because the very constitution which he has given us makes us incapable of knowing Him as He is, because by no possibility can there be an unveiling or disclosure of His own nature, or character, or purposes to us, the whole subject must be contemplated by us, and must be presented to others, in an aspect which it never assumes in St Paul's writings and discourses, or in any part of the Old and New Testament. So that we are in the strange predicament of men fighting with prodigious zeal and prowess on behalf of the authority of books which, the moment we take them from their shelves and examine their contents, are found to set at nought the hypothesis upon which we have rested our apology for them. In establishing the necessity for *a* Revelation, we have done what we can to confute *the* Revelation of which these books testify.[1]

[1] *What is Revelation?* pp. 54f.

Maurice's position is that if Mansel is right then the Bible is a deception; for the latter speaks in terms of persons not propositions, living examples, not regulative principles. Take, says Mansel, the doctrine of the incarnation, which is absolutely central to Christianity. 'We believe that Christ is both God and Man, for that is revealed to us. We know not how He is so, for this is not revealed, and we can learn it in no other way.' Maurice's comment is that no attempt is made by the lecturer to present the doctrine as an interpretation of Christ in his *impact upon men*. Rather is it 'an additional, a hard, an insoluble difficulty, which we must receive in addition to all other difficulties, because God commands us in His book to receive it. We are left by this amazing revelation—that He who was the express Image of the Father, was made man and dwelt among us—just where we were before'.[1] Mansel drew, moreover, the conventional distinction between natural and revealed religion, Christianity, the revealed religion, being as it were superimposed upon the former. Maurice could not allow this. Natural reason and revelation are not, he held, two diverse ways of acquiring knowledge of God. On the contrary, all that men can possibly know of God comes from him and thus must be thought of as revealed. Scripture, he contended, assumes it to be the normal condition of man that he should receive communications from God. Indeed according to biblical teaching man could not be what he is if God did not hold converse with him—a fact which distinguishes him from all other creatures. St Paul certainly did not say that whereas the Jews had received a revelation the Gentiles were without one, for he expressly maintains that God did reveal his own righteousness in the conscience of the Gentile and that the sin of those who worshipped the creature more than the Creator consisted in their 'not *liking* to retain God in their knowledge'.[2] Maurice—although he does not use the terms—does distinguish between general and particular modes of revelation. The divine is revealed through nature, through the life of man and through the incarnation. But revelation under whatever mode points always to the centre. First, God speaks in what is most distant from him, in the mere things that he has formed; then in the human beings created by him to rule over these things; and finally, in him 'who by the eternal law

[1] *Ibid.*, pp. 220f.
[2] *Sermons preached in Lincoln's Inn Chapel*, i, p. 125.

is the inheritor of all things, in whom and for whom they were created'. Always it is the disclosure of the inmost personality of God which has constituted the goal of the whole process. To represent revelation therefore as only an imparting of propositions that can be used but never really understood is to travesty the divine action. Mansel was concerned with a system of theology, whereas Maurice detested all such systems, regarding them as a barrier not a bridge between man and God. The Bampton lecturer was meeting rationalism with rationalism and denying the inherent possibilities of faith. The theologian's proper task is not to construct a watertight intellectual scheme but to proclaim God's self-manifestation in Christ.

> He comes with this Gospel to mankind. So far as he is asserting, he is a dogmatist. But he does not rest his assertion upon his own judgment or upon the judgment of ages; he addresses it to the conscience, heart, reason of mankind. He leaves God to justify it in His own way, by the sorrows, needs, sins, contradictions of men. He desires only that the news should go forth with no force but its own. He can trust who had promised His Spirit of Truth to guide us into all Truth. Dogmatism and Rationalism cannot be reconciled in words; the verbal middle between them is feebler than either, destructive of what is good in both. Here is the living, real, uniting Mean between them . . . God declaring Himself to His creatures in a Man, that the creature may rise to a full knowledge of Him.[1]

Mansel countered Maurice's strictures in a characteristically skilful *Examination* of them, to which Maurice in turn retorted in a *Sequel to the Inquiry, What is Revelation?* This restates his position in a more moderate way, but without showing any clearer understanding of what Mansel was about. For the trouble with *What is Revelation?*, quite apart from its misjudged form and ill-tempered expression, is its evident incomprehension of the problem which *The Limits of Religious Knowledge Examined* was trying to tackle. Maurice had all the prophet's sense of the 'immediacy' of the divine in human life. God, he was convinced, *can* be known, because all life testifies to the fact. The whole idea of a *Deus absconditus*, concealed rather than revealed by a set of theological propositions which man has to adapt as best he may to the

---

[1] *What is Revelation?*, pp. 232f.

purposes of living—for such basically was Maurice's reading of Mansel's book—was one which seemed to him to evacuate religion of any real significance. For religion concerns facts, not doctrines. Thus he writes:

> If the doctrine of the Atonement was not false as a doctrine, as an opinion, there must have been an actual Reconciliation between God and His creatures in the person of His Son. If the doctrine of the Incarnation was not false as a doctrine, the Eternal Son must have actually come forth from the Eternal Father, and have taken human flesh, and have dwelt among men; the nature and glory of the Eternal God must have come forth in the man, so that He could say, '*He that hath seen me hath seen the Father*'. You and I had to determine whether, *in this sense*, we could receive the Incarnation and Atonement—whether, *in this sense*, we could proclaim them to men. For if we called on any human being to receive them as doctrines, and yet did not set them forth as facts, it seemed that we were committing a huge injustice to our fellows, deceiving our own selves, violating the trust we had received from God.[1]

Mansel himself was strongly opposed to the idea of theology as a purely speculative system, but felt it necessary to examine the question of religious knowledge viewed simply as such. This was an inquiry which did not at all interest Maurice and for which he saw no need. It was an instance of the plain man's impatience with the philosopher, when the latter deliberately raises doubts about what the former supposes is self-evidently true. But because the Bible does not envisage any philosophical question as to *how* God can be known or what kind of propositions, logically speaking, they are in which man's thought about God is cast, it does not follow that the inquiry is misguided and useless. Maurice did not get to grips with Mansel's arguments in that he did not understand the principles on which they were advanced. Failing this, he could only trounce their author for his culpable wrong-headedness. As has been amusingly said: 'The controversy resembles what one might imagine to have taken place had a discussion ever happened between Aristotle and one of the Minor Prophets.'[2] But the issue between them remains perhaps the most important that the theologian has to face and in our own day has become the centre of debate.

[1] *Ibid.*, p. 235.
[2] Matthews, *op. cit.*, p. 18.

4. BROAD CHURCH TENDENCIES: MILMAN, STANLEY AND
MARK PATTISON

A distinguished contemporary of Maurice's, who also belonged to
no party or school but whose scholarship was among the best the
Church of England produced in his generation, was Henry Hunt
Milman, dean of St Paul's from 1849 until his death in 1868, when
he was succeeded there by Mansel.[1] Chronologically—he was born
in 1791—as in outlook, he could be classed with the Oriel
Noetics. Yet he was not connected with them and neither
Whately nor Hampden was a man after his own heart. His
interest was in history, to the study of which he brought a critical
spirit and a signal literary gift. His Bampton lectures of 1827, on
*The Character and Conduct of the Apostles considered as Evidence of
Christianity*, were conventional enough and drew no special
comment, but his *History of the Jews*, published a couple of years
later in three small volumes in 'The Family Library' series, was a
bombshell. *The Dictionary of National Biography* even calls it 'epoch-
making', although denying it any 'extraordinary merit'. Milman,
of course, was no great historian by German standards and his
work cannot in learning and scientific thoroughness be compared
with that of Ewald. But unlike most English clergymen of the time
he was well aware of what the German scholars were doing and
his own book had, in the circumstances, the virtue of originality.
His approach to his subject was detached, with no overt design
either to edify his readers or to defend traditional views. The
Hebrews are regarded as one among the many ancient peoples and
hence to be studied by the same methods of research as they.
Certainly no Old Testament history was to be exempt from the
principles of criticism, which could be shown to yield results in
this field as justifiable as in any other. But what afterwards was to
become commonplace to all students of the biblical records was
looked on in those early days almost as a profanity. To the vast
majority of churchmen the Old Testament carried supernatural
credentials which placed it beyond criticism. Milman, however,
was dubious of much biblical supernaturalism and entertained the

---

[1] Tulloch went so far as to say that 'in combination of pure genius with learning,
of sweep of thought with picturesque and powerful variety of literary culture and
expression, he has always seemed to me by far the first of modern English churchmen' (*op. cit.*, p. 80).

I

possibility of naturalistic explanations, for instance the pestilential wind which he suggested as the cause of the destruction of Sennacherib's army, or the inflammable bituminous soil which could have burned Sodom and Gomorrah. Hardly less offensive to traditional sentiment was his use of expressions like 'Eastern sheik' or 'Emir' in reference to Abraham, or his 'frank' characterizations of other Hebrew worthies. Archbishop Ussher's chronology was entirely discarded. 'All kinds of numbers are uncertain in ancient MSS, and have been subject to much greater corruption than any other part of the text.'[1] A good deal of the biblical language—the story in Joshua of the sun standing still was cited in point—is poetical, not literally factual.

The History of the Jews was a pioneer work in this country and its aim was popular. But it was bitterly attacked as rationalistic and 'German' and likely to undermine the authority of Scripture. The publishers took fright and suspended further issue of the book. Milman hit back, but he had no zest for controversy and (it is said) came in the end to wish that the Jews were with the Egyptians at the bottom of the Red Sea.[2] He insisted that he was saying nothing which had not been said before by persons whose views were considered unimpeachable. 'If', he declared, 'I am driven to it I will show them'—his critics—'not whence I have derived my notion of the miracles, but where precisely the same explanations are to be found—in Bishop Mant and Dr D'Oyley's *Bible*—and if I am forced I will print them in parallel columns.'[3]

The value of Milman's history lies in its imaginative feeling for its subject. He sought to depict the figures of the Old Testament as true flesh and blood and in authentic life-situations. But contemporary piety was not prepared for such an exercise in realism. Milman was not at all a rationalist. He was simply protesting against lifeless conventionalism in dealing with the scriptures, together with the habit of treating them as a mere repository of sacred 'texts'; and he judged that the historian was well equipped to help distinguish what is essential in religion from what is no more than local and temporary. His best work, however, came later: first, an edition of Gibbon's *Decline and Fall* (1838–39),

---

[1] See the Preface to the edition of 1863.

[2] Quoted in Smiles's *Memoirs of John Murray*, ii, p. 301.

[3] *Ibid.*, p. 300. Mant was bishop of Killaloe and a Bampton lecturer (1812). Both he and Archdeacon D'Oyley were High Churchmen.

and then a *Life* of the master-historian which indicated the direction the author's own studies were taking. A *History of Christianity from the Birth of Christ to the Abolition of Paganism in the Roman Empire* followed in 1840. Here Milman was on safer ground. Protestant susceptibilities were not hurt by disclosure of the sometimes all too human instruments by which ancient Christendom had been built up. At least only Tractarians took umbrage. But the crowning achievement of his career was his *History of Latin Christianity* (1854–55), his most ambitious undertaking and one in which the influence of Gibbon is apparent. Yet Milman's work, although treating of the same great theme, is entirely different from the older historian's. His concern is not with the decline of a secular empire but with the rise of a spiritual one; whilst it scarcely needs remarking that for all his talent as a writer he was manifestly not a second Gibbon. Yet the fact that a comparison of the nineteenth-century history with that bequeathed by the eighteenth is by no means inappropriate is itself testimony to what Milman achieved. It is not too much to say that in this book historical scholarship in the Church of England proved its maturity.

But the typical Broad Churchman of the period is Arthur Penrhyn Stanley (1815–81), for many years dean of Westminster and still perhaps the most notable in the succession of occupants of that office. His purpose, like that of Thomas Arnold, whose pupil and biographer he was—his *Life* of Arnold appeared in 1844—was 'the enlargement of the Church', a phrase used at his installation at Westminster in 1864. The establishment he valued as the foundation of a national Christianity, and he sought to make of the Abbey church itself a symbol of the comprehensiveness he desired. Among those invited by him to speak there were Max Müller, a layman, and Principals Caird and Tulloch, both of them ministers of the Church of Scotland. Keble, Pusey and Liddon were also asked, but the latter alone could bring himself to accept, and then only after considerable hesitation. In Convocation Stanley opposed the continued public use of the Athanasian Creed, favoured a relaxation of the terms of clerical subscription, and hurried to the defence of *Essays and Reviews*, and even of Bishop Colenso. But he also spoke up on behalf of ritualist clergymen who were either being prosecuted at law or having their church services broken up by protesting mobs. He conspicuously had the courage of his broad convictions, whatever criticism their expression might bring down on him, as when he invited a Unitarian, Dr Vance Smith, to holy communion in the Abbey. That he was in any way a theologian of depth or penetration can hardly, however, be claimed and his high-minded innocency sometimes verged on the naïve. But like Milman he possessed a lively historical imagination, even if accuracy was apt to elude him. His *Commentary on St Paul's Epistles to the Corinthians*, published in 1855, is readable enough, but even in its own day was scarcely a handbook for the serious student. He was better at popular history, as in his lectures on the history of the Eastern Church (1861)—still worth perusal—or on that of the Jewish Church (1863-65), or historical travelogues such as *Sinai and Palestine* (1856). All these books have a certain charm, 'period' though it now is. Their chief fault is an excess of colour, a too florid eloquence.

Stanley's most permanently valuable literary enterprise remains the *Life* of Arnold, upon which he spent two years of unremitting toil. Happily Arnold was no more complex a character than his biographer; had he been the latter might well have found the task beyond him. But with the revered headmaster of Rugby he was on ground he knew: Arnold's opinions and interests were very largely his own also. And he avoided—what the biographer of Dr Pusey flagrantly did not—a superfluity of detail.

One last figure stands to be noticed here, a man of very different character from the large-hearted dean, namely Mark Pattison (1813-84), rector of Lincoln College, Oxford, from 1861 until his death. Oxford, or England, had at the time few men of equal learning. Indeed so absorbed in learning was he that in the event he published little. To know everything that could be known, *totum scibile*, seems to have been his ruling passion, a kind of mystical experience.[1] But apart from his eccentricity of temperament—at the age of thirty-eight, when disappointed at not gaining the headship of his college, he turned himself into a misanthropic recluse ('A blank, dumb despair filled me; a chronic heartache took possession of me, perceptible even through sleep')—he is best remembered for his work on Isaac Casaubon (1875), in

[1] See J. Sparrow, *Mark Pattison and the Idea of a University* (1967). On Pattison's rectorship at Lincoln College, Oxford, see V. H. H. Green, *Oxford Common Room* (1957), pp. 203–216.

which his knowledge of Renaissance humanism had full display.

His single but remarkable contribution to theological debate—
he was essentially a scholar and critic, not a theologian—was his
paper in *Essays and Reviews* entitled 'Tendencies of religious
thought in England, 1688–1750', outstanding among the chapters
in that volume.[1] As an inquiry into the nature of deism—the
causes which led to its rise, as afterwards to its decay—it remains
as good as anything that has ever been written on the subject.
Upon the truth of the issues under discussion the author himself
evinces no opinion; he is wholly detached and dispassionate. His
role is that of a historian of ideas, in which field of study he was a
pioneer. Had he been more a prolific as well as fastidious writer
he would have been among the pre-eminent in this type of
scholarship. He treats of his chosen period—his essay has little to
do with the matters generally dealt with in the volume—with
insight and candour. 'We have not yet learned, in this country', he
declared, 'to write our ecclesiastical history on any better footing
than that of praising up the party, in or out of the Church, to
which we happen to belong.'[2] From being in his earlier years a
warm sympathizer with Tractarianism he had become its bitter
critic, looking on it as the incarnation of secretarian partisanship.[3]
The principle of continuity had to be recognized: the present is
what the past has made it. The whole process must be seen as a
living thing, and when the history of theology is so studied it will
cease to be 'an unmeaning frostwork of dogma, out of all relation
to the actual history of man'. Let the Church of England, then,
beware and avoid the petrifaction that has overtaken Rome.
Mere defensiveness, moreover, will not suffice.[4] Advocacy belongs
to the law court and should be rigorously eschewed by the
theologian. 'If theological argument forgets the judge and
assumes the advocate, or betrays the least bias to one side, the

---

[1] See below, ch. X.

[2] *Essays and Reviews*, p. 308.

[3] Pattison describes himself as having been 'a declared Puseyite, an ultra-Puseyite',
but as we have seen (p. 103 above), he came to regard the whole Tractarian movement as a disastrous episode in the intellectual life of the university of which its
leaders were all prominent members. 'For so long it had been given over to discussions unprofitable in themselves, and which had entirely diverted our thoughts
from the true business of the place. . . . From that moment dates the regeneration
of the University' (*Memoir*, pp. 236ff). But his personal admiration of Newman
never waned.

[4] 'Theological study is still the study of topics of defence' (p. 364).

conclusion is valueless, the principle of free inquiry has been violated.' The eighteenth century marked the beginning of a period of theological reconstruction, and its appeal to reason was altogether needful and salutary. Its defect 'was not in having too much good sense, but in having nothing besides'. Yet it did try to relate theology to life. 'The endeavour of the moralists and divines of the period to rationalize religion was in fact an effort to preserve the practical principles of moral and religious conduct for society.' Pattison's judgment upon the age of reason is ambiguous. He at once praises and blames; the century did its best to stay the rot of belief by the methods which it understood, yet theology, in the true sense of the word, 'had almost died out when it received a new impulse and a new direction from Coleridge'. The 'evidence-makers' ceased from their futile labours all at once, and Englishmen heard with as much surprise as if the doctrine were new that the Christian faith is 'the perfection of human intelligence'; whereas the eighteenth-century divines and their contemporary opponents alike assummed that 'a man's religious belief is a result which issues at the end of an intellectual process'.

The moral for his own age, Mark Pattison would have inferred, was to learn the method of a new apologetic, certainly needed, from the failures of the previous century. What the principles of this new apologetic should be are left vague, and his observations, acute as they often are, remain largely negative. In this the essay is characteristic of its author, who, although he continued to perform clerical duties, had by middle age become virtually an agnostic. Besides, tart criticism and detraction were temperamentally congenial to him, as is obvious from the *Memoir* published in 1884. Thus he pronounces the Victorian clergy to be in general 'professional quacks trading in beliefs they do not share'. That his true place is with the 'honest doubters' of his age might nevertheless be difficult to maintain in view of his own retention of the clerical office long after he had given up any positive faith. Stricter honesty and rather less care for status and emoluments would surely have led him to follow the course of men like Leslie Stephen and Henry Sidgwick. George Eliot's alleged portrait of him in *Middlemarch* is a refinement of cruelty which he himself, strangely enough for one so morbidly sensitive, appears not to have felt. But, unattractive as he may have been as a man, he had courage and foresight enough to urge, at a time when university reform had become a public cause, that the real purpose of a university is to provide neither professional qualifications nor social advantage, but to train men in the knowledge of themselves and of the world.

Chapter VIII

The Erosion of Belief

I. AN EPOCH OF CHANGE

Those aspects of nineteenth-century religious thought which we have considered so far all lay within the bounds of Christian orthodoxy. The liberal-minded may have pleaded for a less mechanical and rigid doctrine of biblical inspiration, deplored a too close insistence on traditional formularies or the niceties of dogma, and wished for the most part to put an end to the strife of ecclesiastical parties. But on the fundamentals of belief and the authority of both Scripture and Church they were staunch, however short they may have come of the more exacting standards required by Tractarians and old-style Evangelicals alike. Yet although English Christianity during the first half of the century was still largely immune to continental influences and showed little capacity of its own to strike out on new intellectual paths, it none the less was beginning to feel the mounting pressure of criticism from more than one quarter and along more than one line. No doubt educated public opinion still remained solidly Christian and predominantly Anglican, but voices were to be heard challenging the long-cherished assumptions with more and more assurance.

Scornful and openly defiant was, of course, the Utilitarian school of Bentham and James Mill. Critical too, though with some measure of sympathy, which indeed ripened with the years, was Mill's son, John Stuart. But there was another group—although the use of the word must not suggest cohesion or even a general agreement in outlook—consisting of a number of 'free-thinking' Christians, as well as sceptics and agnostics: Charles and

Sara Hennell, and Hennell's brother-in-law, Charles Bray; R. W. Mackay, author of *The Progress of the Intellect*; Mary Ann Evans—the novelist George Eliot, as she afterwards called herself—and G. H. Lewes; John Henry Newman's brother, Francis: J. A. Froude, a one-time Tractarian; and A. H. Clough, the poet. At a somewhat later date—his *First Principles* appeared in 1862—Herbert Spencer could be listed among them also. Consideration of Spencer, an important figure in his day, even if posterity has long since deprived his reputation of its former gravity, we must defer to a subsequent chapter, but some notice of the rest, a rather motley company, will be in place here, preliminary to a discussion of John Stuart Mill and the Utilitarians. But first we must endeavour to take account of the chief reasons which from 1840 onwards led to a bolder and more persistent questioning of official religion as represented by both the established Church and the dissenting bodies.

What, perhaps, more than anything else contributed to a growing uneasiness about the tenability of Christian belief was an awareness that the Bible, fount and monument of 'saving truth', might no longer possess the authority once unhesitatingly conceded to it. Precise knowledge of the methods and results of biblical criticism was uncommon enough in this country at the time, even among theologians; but it was becoming more widely realized that the customary view of inspiration, according to which every statement in Scripture is divinely guaranteed truth, could not be maintained in face of enlarging knowledge, both scientific and historical. But if the Bible were at fault on a few ascertainable points, might it not be wrong on many others? Could it be relied upon at all? Such questions were the more disconcerting in that English Christianity since the Reformation had been absolutely explicit in its appeal to Scripture as the sole authority in matters of faith. Some there were—Coleridge had been among the earliest—who were convinced that the authority of Holy Writ is not impaired so long as the nature of the inspiration rightly attributed to it is properly understood. More saw the only alternatives as lying either in retention of the old idea regardless of the objections brought against it, or else in rejection of the Bible altogether if the reason for accepting it has to be sought in a doctrine now manifestly incredible. Some, it might be, allowed to Scripture a relative degree of inspiration, but denied it

I*

as the ground of a specific system of revealed doctrine. A particular difficulty was the problem of miracles. Christianity was supposed to be based on their truth, but if they could no longer be believed in religion became a purely natural phenomenon the expansion and development of which could be explained in terms of ordinary historical processes. This had been the argument of David Friedrich Strauss, whose *Leben Jesu* (1835–36) appeared in George Eliot's English version in 1846. The question that had moved Strauss to take up his task was whether the gospel history is 'true and reliable as a whole, and in its details', or not so. His conclusion was that historically the evangelical records are not reliable, although he himself insisted that the essence of Christian faith is independent of historical criticism, however negative. Strauss's book was avidly read in this country, but public opinion was very little prepared for what it contained. Its effect was to astonish and disturb.

Even apart from the biblical issue unsophisticated belief was bound to be shaken by new knowledge in science. What this involved we shall have to look at more closely later. It is sufficient to remark here that a secular account of the world and the life of humanity within it was now juxtaposed to the immemorial teachings of a religion disputed hitherto only by the impious. The early nineteenth century, so placid-seeming to us today, was in fact an era of far-reaching change, intellectual as well as social and industrial. Such indeed was its momentum that the accustomed certainties, even for those who held on to them—still the great majority—had plainly ceased to be above the tidemark of doubt. The large-scale erosion of belief had begun.

2. FREETHINKERS

Charles Hennell (1809–50), whose book, *An Inquiry concerning the Origin of Christianity*, was published in 1838, was a Unitarian. He and his sister Sara, herself the author of a volume of *Thoughts in Aid of Faith*,[1] their brother-in-law Charles Bray, who had been brought up as a Methodist, and his wife, formed a little group of earnest and open-minded seekers after truth whose ideas and

---

[1] Mary Ann Evans was lavish in her praise of it, finding it 'quite unparalleled in the largeness and insight with which it estimates Christianity as an organized experience' (J. W. Cross, *The Life of George Eliot* (1884), ii, p. 258).

personal friendship strongly influenced the always impressionable George Eliot, undermining her allegiance to the orthodox Protestantism in which she had been nurtured. Hennell's *Inquiry* had no large circulation in England, but it was translated into German and gained the warm approval of Strauss himself, who contributed a preface for the German edition and whose own position has its analogue in Hennell's pages.[1] Hennell was by no means anti-Christian and even claimed that his work would promote a truer understanding of what Christianity really is. Thus in his preface he wrote that the Christian religion,

> regarded as a system of elevated thought and feeling will not be injured by being freed from those fables, and those views of local or temporary interest, which hung about its origin. It will, on the contrary, be placed on a surer basis; for it need no longer appeal for its support to the uncertain evidence of events which happened nearly two thousand years ago, a species of evidence necessarily attainable only by long and laborious research, impracticable to most men, and unsatisfactory and harassing even to those who have most means of pursuing it; but it will rest its claim on an evidence clearer, simpler, and always at hand—the thoughts and feelings of the human mind itself. Thus, whatever in it is really true and excellent, will meet with a ready attestation in every breast, and, in the improvement of the human mind, find an ever-increasing evidence.[2]

But Hennell's outlook is purely humanist and naturalistic, as becomes still plainer in his later work on *Christian Theism*. His philosophy entirely precludes miracle, and as a historian he sees in Jesus—of whom he speaks with much reverence—only a man whose actual personality and work were for the most part translated into legend by his followers and the generation that succeeded them.

> A true account [he says] of the life of Jesus Christ, and the spread of his religion, would be found to contain no deviation from the known laws of nature, nor to require, for their explanation, more than the operation of human motives and feelings, acted upon by the peculiar circumstances of the age and country whence the religion originated.

[1] Hennell had not read Strauss, and knew very little about the progress of German biblical scholarship, a fact which makes the originality of his own book all the more striking.

[2] *An Inquiry concerning the Origin of Christianity*, p. viii.

What is of particular interest today in view of recent discussion is the importance he attaches to Essenism as the immediate source of primitive Christianity. The book is the work of a mere amateur in its field, but in its grasp of the purpose and methods of criticism it is a landmark in the history of biblical study in this country.

Bray's *The Philosophy of Necessity* came out in 1845.[1] It was ambitiously conceived as a *magnum opus*, a definitive statement of the views to which his reading and thinking over the years had inevitably led him. He relates in his autobiography how he had arrived at 'one Truth about which I was certain, viz., that no part of the Creation had been left to chance, or what is called free-will; that the laws of mind were equally fixed or determined with those of matter, and that all instinct in beasts, and calculation in man, required that they should be so fixed'. He had therefore set himself to build up a system of ethics 'in harmony with the established fact, that everything acted in accordance with its own nature, and that there was no freedom of choice beyond this'. The reading-matter which helped to shape his ideas almost certainly included Bentham's *Deontology*, James Mill's *Analysis of the Human Mind* and George Combe's *System of Phrenology*, with its notion that the whole of a man's potential character could be deduced from the conformation of his head. As the title of Bray's book implies, nature and human life are alike the expression of a universal necessity. A cause is simply an antecedent condition. God exists only as 'the all-pervading influence which maintains the connection between all antecedents and all consequents'. Moral responsibility hence becomes a figment. What, the author had asked himself, was virtue? 'Not that which is free, spontaneous, or uncaused, but that which does the greatest amount of good, or produces most happiness.' Conduct, however, should be governed by prudence; although how this rather than fecklessness can be pursued according to his system is left unexplained, man being only a mechanism.

A work of greater interest is *The Creed of Christendom: its Foundation and Superstructure*, by another Unitarian, William Rathbone Greg (1809–81), a philanthropist and a keen if somewhat detached student of current political and social problems.

[1] Its two volumes are subtitled 'The Law of Consequences as applicable to Mental, Moral, and Social Science'. A second, much revised, edition was published in 1861.

Published in 1851, it is a significant addition to what John Morley called the 'dissolvent literature' of the time. Here, as in Hennell's book, we have an attempt to account for the origin and growth of Christianity in terms more or less naturalistic. To start with, no theory of the verbal inspiration of Scripture can possibly hold; nor does Scripture provide the materials for a dogmatic system. It is in vain even to look to it for a special divine revelation. How indeed can the human mind compass what it does not itself conceive, or by what means distinguish a divine idea from a human? Jesus was certainly not unique in the sense the churches claim him to have been, but he was a great prophet, and the lamentable thing is that Christendom has been more intent on worshipping his person than in heeding his words. 'It has made his life barren, that his essence might be called divine.'[1] Miracle, of course, is inadmissible; in any case it could not authenticate doctrine and a religion based upon it must collapse. A further and serious difficulty for the modern mind is that of recovering the historic truth about Jesus. The gospels being in large part legend have little value as a record of events, while the apostles understood him only imperfectly and transmitted his teachings inaccurately. Had his original doctrine been in fact better preserved the Church would have spread more slowly than it did, since the very corruption of his teaching aided its reception. Apart then from Jesus's moral example—still shining, despite the inadequacies of tradition—what has Christianity to offer? Prayer, although it is the expression of a natural impulse, cannot alter God's will. A future life is something we may hope for but cannot prove, and our sense of freedom must be set against the background of universal law. The tone of Greg's work is consistently reverent, but its conclusions, as orthodox belief would have judged them, are entirely negative.

Another attack on 'miraculous' religion had been delivered the year previously by Robert William MacKay (1803–82), a man of considerable scholarship, in a lengthy publication entitled *The Progress of the Intellect as Exemplified in the Religious Development of the Greeks and Hebrews* (1850). For the ancient mind miracles were possible and even commonplace, in that it knew nothing of the order of nature as disclosed by modern science. Toward any rational conception of life the Hebrews made little progress, and

[1] *The Creed of Christendom*, p. 241.

their religious outlook must be appraised accordingly. But if the world we know is an embodiment of law why should we expect the unknown to be capricious and inexplicable? God today is revealed through the regular rather than the irregular, the predictable rather than the unpredictable. Miracle therefore has ceased to have any evidential value. But this is not mere loss. The progress of the intellect in matters of religion is away from superstition and towards a reasoned faith. This may and will exceed knowledge, but should always be subject to its control. MacKay's effort was not without use in its day as a contribution to the historical study of religious phenomena. It showed how the beliefs and practices of different religions often resemble one another and in course of time take on new forms. But the author's overall position could best be described as a Christian humanism in which the idea of God is scarcely more than the symbol of an ethical ideal; and as such George Eliot welcomed it in *The Westminster Review* of January 1851. A later book of MacKay's— it appeared in 1863[1]—was *The Tübingen School and its Antecedents: a Review of the History and Present Condition of Modern Theology*, in which he sought to acquaint a public much agitated by the *Essays and Reviews* controversy with the history and principles of scientific biblical criticism. It is well-informed and discerning in its assessment of the then recent developments in Germany, but offered no reassurance to the many who saw in criticism only an insidious move against the foundations of faith.

3 . GEORGE ELIOT AND OTHERS

All these writers are today figures but dimly descried. George Eliot, by contrast, occupies a commanding place in Victorian literature and as a novelist enjoys now perhaps a greater prestige than any of her contemporaries. But her work in fiction is not our present concern. Her interest in religion, as in scientific questions, was lifelong, but she soon passed from the narrow Evangelicalism of her youth, through a phase of 'radical' Christianity, to agnosticism and positivism. At the age of twenty-three, and to her father's grief, she gave up church attendance as incompatible with her

---

[1] *The Progress of the Intellect* had been followed in 1854 by *A Sketch of the Rise and Progress of Christianity*. In his personal philosophical outlook MacKay was a Kantian; but he was also a devoted student of Plato.

changed beliefs. The influence of the Hennells and Brays upon her was important, though she had also been a good deal affected by Isaac Taylor's *Ancient Christianity* (1839–40).[1] In 1844 she took over from a friend, Miss Brabant, the task of translating Strauss, a laborious business which kept her occupied for three years. But by the spring of 1846 the work was finished and in the following June published. She also applied herself to the study of Spinoza, a philosopher then still little known in England. Later, on moving to London, she became assistant to John Chapman as editor of *The Westminster*, and it was through Chapman that she met the positivist thinker, Herbert Spencer, with whom she formed a close friendship. Spencer it was who, in turn, introduced her to G. H. Lewes, her partner in life from 1854, when she accompanied him to Weimar, until his death twenty-four years later. In 1853 she gave up her editorial work and the year after brought out a translation of Feuerbach's *The Essence of Christianity*, the only book, as it happened, that she ever published under her own name. Her first venture in prose fiction, *Amos Barton*, was written in 1856 and published two years later, along with *Mr Gilfil's Love Story* and *Janet's Repentance*, as *Scenes of Clerical Life*, under the pen-name by which history knows her. Thereafter novel-writing became her life's work. But although she had by now completely abandoned Christianity her deep sympathy with and understanding of the religious sentiment remained. Years before she had written to Sara Hennell that

> agreement between intellects seems unattainable, and we turn to the *truth of feeling* as the only universal bond of union. We find that the intellectual errors which we once fancied were a mere incrustation, have grown into the living body, and we cannot in the majority of cases wrench them away without destroying vitality . . .[2]

For with George Eliot head and heart, intellectual conviction and instinctive feeling, were divided. By intellectual conviction she realized that orthodox Christianity was a myth which in the modern world had been exploded. God was inconceivable,

---

[1] Taylor had found the ascetic tendencies of early Christianity especially objectionable. Such 'artificial purity'—and here, he warned, the history of Romanism was eloquent witness—could only lead to 'a violent reaction, ending, as might have been foreseen, and as every convulsive moral struggle must, in a correspondent corruption, as well of manners as of principles'.

[2] Cross, *op. cit.*, i, p. 121.

immortality incredible. Duty, however, was peremptory and absolute, and consisted in one's obligations to one's fellow-men.[1] 'I
begin', she wrote to the Brays in January 1853, 'to feel for other
people's wants and sorrows a little more than I used to do.
Heaven help us! said the old religion; the new one, from its very
lack of that faith, will teach us all the more to help one another.'[2]
Humanity, not deity, was now the object of her conscientious
devotion, faith giving way to love of the brethren, from whom no
man was excluded. The supernatural had no place beside, still less
above, the natural. The 'highest calling and election' was '*to do
without opium*', and live through all our pain with conscious,
clear-eyed endurance'.[3] Breadth of view, tolerance, intellectual
integrity, with—of necessity—moral stoicism added, were the
virtues of the life of modern man. 'I have faith in the working out
of higher possibilities than the Catholic or any other Church has
presented, and those who have strength to wait and endure are
bound to accept no formula which their whole souls—their
intellect as well as their emotions—do not embrace with entire
reverence.'

Strauss, Feuerbach and latterly Auguste Comte had left
indelible marks on George Eliot's mind. Yet she had no time for
brash rationalism; not only were her affections too warm, even the
eye of reason could not fail to discern the grounds for a more
passionate assessment of the human condition than professed
humanism was prone to allow for. Hence the emotional and
indeed moral value of a faith which the informed intellect, for
its part, could only disown.

> Pray don't ever ask me again [she wrote to a correspondent in 1862]
> to rob a man of his religious belief, as if you thought my mind
> tended to such robbery. I have too profound a conviction of the
> efficacy that lies in all sincere faith, and the spiritual blight that comes
> with no faith, to have any negative propagandism in me.
>
> In fact [she continued] I have very little sympathy with Free-
> thinkers as a class, and have lost all interest in mere antagonism to

---

[1] See the well-known passage in F. W. H. Myer's *Essays—Modern* (1883), pp. 268f,
describing a conversation the author had with the novelist in the Fellows' Garden
at Trinity College, Cambridge. It was for him an unforgettable occasion. 'Never,
perhaps,' he remarks, 'have sterner accents affirmed the sovereignty of impersonal
and unrecompensing law.'

[2] Cross, *op. cit.*, i, p. 302.

[3] *Ibid.*, ii, p. 283.

religious doctrines. I care only to know, if possible, the lasting meaning that lies in all religious doctrine from the beginning till now.[1]

The significance of religion in the life of mankind could not be underrated, nor did the practice of religion, for all its superstitions, call for denunciation. Christianity was essentially a great moral idea, however tenuous its claim to historical authenticity. Thus she wrote of Renan's *Vie de Jésus* that it seemed to her that

> the soul of Christianity lies not at all in the facts of an individual life, but in the ideas of which that life was the meeting-point and the new starting-point. We can never have a satisfactory basis for the history of the man Jesus, but that negation does not affect the Idea of the Christ in its historical influence or its great symbolic meanings.[2]

George Henry Lewes (1817–78), the man with whom she spent her life in a morally dedicated union unacknowledged by church or law, was in temperament very different from herself. His self-confidence was boundless, his optimism unassailable. He exercised his versatile talent now as philosopher, biographer and man of science, now as dramatic critic, novelist and even actor. Pursuits so multiple suggest superficiality, possibly even charlatanism. That he was much less adept at some than at others is, however, in no way a denial of his signal abilities. His interest for us here arises from his role as a popularizer of Comtism, since he was one of the first in this country to master the positivist system. Comte's *Cours de philosophie positive* was completed in 1842, and Lewes, in his biographical history of philosophy (1845–46)—a still quite readable book—shows him as a convinced disciple and warm advocate of the new doctrines. His view of metaphysics is based on Comte's own *loi des trois états*, according to which human thought has passed through three stages of development: a theological or mythological; a metaphysical, in which spiritual entities are replaced as causal forces by abstract ideas; and a positive or scientific, in which the test of truth is empirical. 'For the first time in history', Lewes enthused, 'an explanation of the World, Society and Man is presented which is thoroughly in accordance with accurate knowledge.' Indeed 'a new era' had dawned, in which all knowledge would be formed into a homogeneous body of doctrine, 'capable of supplying a Faith and consequently a Polity'. Lewes stayed faithful to positivist

[1] *Ibid.*, p. 343.   [2] *Ibid.*, pp. 359f.

principles all his life, and in *Comte's Philosophy of the Sciences* (1853)
he gave himself single-mindedly to explaining the whole system.
The last philosophical work published during his lifetime,
Problems of Life and Mind (1874–79), revealed his ardour to be as
fresh as ever. Even among his own countrymen the French
thinker has never had a more dedicated follower.

To many minds the attraction of Comtism lay in its author's
claim to have presented the world with 'a sound Philosophy,
capable of supplying the foundation of a true Religion'. Not many
of the Victorians were ready to dispense with religion altogether,
even if they could not believe in it. Orthodoxy might be
impossible, but a cold and calculating rationalism was no food for
the sentiments. In the Religion of Humanity, on the other hand,
the balance between intellect and feeling was redressed. The latter
—the 'heart'—must, of course, have pride of place, but the former
is its necessary coadjutor and an authority with rights of its own
and an irremovable position in the scheme of things. It is noteworthy, therefore, that of Comte's apostles in England two of the
most prominent were women. For next to George Eliot in this
role was Harriet Martineau (1802–76), author of *The Positive
Philosophy of Auguste Comte*, published in the same year, 1853, as
Lewes's book. Sister of the well-known Unitarian leader, James
Martineau, she was even more explicit in her admiration of the
positivist doctrine than the great novelist herself. Her brother
retained his loyalty to Christianity, but Harriet, recognizing, in
her own choice phrases, 'the monstrous superstition in its true
character of a great fact in the history of the human race', found
herself at last 'a free rover on the broad, bright, breezy common
of the universe'.[1] Miss Martineau was not, all the same, the pure
intellect she liked to fancy herself, and her critical capacity—
W. R. Greg described her as 'dogmatic', 'hasty' and 'imperious'—
sometimes evaporated before one or other of the varying objects
of her esteem. She was a prolific writer in many kinds—fiction,
politics, economics and history, both ancient and contemporary.
Perhaps the best of her efforts, apart from the industrious
exposition of Comte, was her *Illustrations of Political Economy*
(1832–34), tales depicting the main principles of the science as then
understood. Earnest, sentimentalizing, intellectually muddled,
she is in many respects a type-figure of her period, a casualty—not

[1] *Autobiography* (1877), i, p. 116.

too serious, however—of the persistent mid-nineteenth century war of head and heart.

Another such personage, but one also who in historical retro-spect is apt to gain stature, is Francis William Newman (1805–97), a brother of the cardinal and for many years professor of Latin at University College, London. Reared as a child in an atmosphere of evangelical piety, he, like John, moved away from it, but in an opposite direction. High Churchism never attracted him, and when his evangelical fervour abated—he was at one time power-fully influenced by J. N. Darby, the founder of the Plymouth Brethren—he turned, via Thomas Arnold, to a thoroughgoing liberalism. A description of his spiritual odyssey is contained in an apologia, *Phases of Faith*, published in 1850, long before his brother's celebrated work. He began by jettisoning outright the Calvinist doctrines of his youth, especially those of the fall, total depravity and eternal reprobation, as manifestly unscriptural. But could even the authority of Scripture be maintained once reason has started to press its objections? The Bible as traditionally read presented grave difficulties, and in the light of advancing know-ledge the infallibilist claim had to be dismissed. 'It had', for example, 'become notorious to the public, that Geologists rejected the idea of a universal deluge as physically impossible.'[1] Arnold's advice was that such questions are not material to religious faith, but Newman was still too much of a biblicist himself to accept this very easily. The truth had though to be faced that the problems posed by the Bible were not only of a factual kind. More serious were the moral ones, and these were not confined entirely to the Old Testament. Could ethical values be substantiated by physical miracles like those which the New Testament alleges? Seemingly not; yet in Scripture morality and miracles go hand in hand. Once a doubt of the oracular authority of the Bible had made entry its further intrusion, it seemed, was not to be halted.

The conclusions, therefore, to which Newman found himself impelled were, first, that the moral and intellectual powers of man must be acknowledged as having a right and a duty to criticize the contents of Scripture; secondly, that when so exerted they condemn certain parts of the Bible as erroneous and immoral; and thirdly, that 'the essential infallibility of the entire Scripture is a

[1] *Phases of Faith*, p. 122.

proved falsity, not merely as to physiology and other scientific matters, but also as to morals'. The problem accordingly was how to discriminate the trustworthy from the untrustworthy within the limits of Scripture itself.[1] In his perplexity he turned to the German scholars, to Michaelis, de Wette and Neander, and discovered them fruitful. His way forward he now saw more clearly.[2] A vast amount of traditional Christianity might have to be shed, but he would still continue to think of himself as a Christian, critical indeed but in intention sincere. 'Those who believed that the apostles might err in human science, need not the less revere their moral and spiritual wisdom.'[3] The solution of the miracle problem, which he viewed as basically a moral not a scientific one, could also now be broached. Miracles, so-called, cannot be the prop of faith and might well prove its destruction. God's goodness and veracity are not in any case to be demonstrated thus. In short, religion in its spiritual essence can and must be distinguished from its incredible or obsolete accompaniments. As soon as the principle of liberalism in Christianity is admitted, with reason and conscience supplying the criteria, all unnecessary burdens placed upon belief can be discarded. Considerations of history and literary composition are not of final relevance. A Christian who understands his faith loves it for its inner *truth* alone, his creed resting where 'new discoveries in geology and in ancient inscriptions' and 'improved criticism of texts and of history' will not overturn it.

For Francis Newman was a man of a genuinely religious temper, and it is this side of him—to call it devout is not to use too strong a word—which stands out impressively in his *The Soul, its Sorrows and Aspirations*, published in 1849.[4] The true religion, he tells us, is a religion of the spirit, not of forms and institutions.

[1] *Ibid.*, pp. 110f.

[2] In 1847 Newman published an Old Testament study, *A History of the Hebrew Monarchy*, in which he acknowledged his debt to de Wette, especially for his conception of the growth and development of the Hebrew religion; for once allow that there is progress in men's ideas about God then the moral difficulties which the more primitive parts of Scripture are bound to raise can be discounted by a higher understanding. The trouble which many faced in interpreting the Old Testament sprang from the dogmatic approach, required by assent to formularies like the Thirty-nine Articles.

[3] *Phases of Faith*, p. 121.

[4] Subtitled 'An Essay towards the Natural History of the Soul as the True Basis of Theology'.

Its guiding light is personal intuition, not dogmas and definitions. By 'Soul' Newman evidently means something like Coleridge's 'Reason', the faculty for the discernment of spiritual truth. It is 'that side of human nature, upon which we are in contact with the Infinite, and God, the Infinite Personality: in the soul alone is it possible to know God'.[1] Its operation is direct, its apprehension immediate. 'Evidences', and the sort of inference based upon them, have nothing to do with it. History and literary criticism, like logic and metaphysics, no doubt have their place, for the understanding needs to be critical; but these things are not religion and no part of its fabric. Religion, first and last, is spiritual, not erudition or intellectual acumen.

> Those truths, and those only, are properly to be called Spiritual, the nature of which admits of their being directly discerned in the Soul, just as Moral truths in the Moral Sense: and *he* is a spiritual man, not who believes these at second-hand (which is a historical and dead faith), but who sees internally, and knows directly.[2]

It is through the Soul that we may know with certainty that God exists, that there is in the universe 'Mind', 'acting on some stupendous scale', though of course imperfectly understood by us. But our knowledge cannot be intellectually projected in any very satisfactory way because the language of religion is not and cannot be that of science. 'A system of Theology, constructed like a treatise on Mechanics, by fine-drawn reasoning from a few primitive axioms or experimental laws, is likely to be nothing but a sham science.'[3]

Although religious language is figurative or metaphorical not literal, this does not mean that it cannot convey truth. On the contrary, 'jealously to resist metaphor, does not testify to depth of insight'.[4] The difficulty with religious belief, the reason why in fact it has lost so much of its potency, is that it has made such inordinate demands at the purely intellectual level, requiring assent to a mass of propositions that can neither be proved nor properly grasped. But the same goes, too, for the modern theologian, intent upon his ancient languages, his texts and his

[1] Preface to the first edition, p.v.

[2] *Ibid*. The distinction is one which immediately recalls his brother's between a merely 'notional' and a 'real' assent.

[3] *The Soul, its Sorrows and Aspirations*, p. 90.

[4] *Ibid*., p. 94.

historical inquiries. 'Our misery has been that the men of thought have no religious enthusiasm, and the enthusiastically religious shrink from continuous searching thought.' Where, however, the writ of science runs faith may not encroach, although the truths of science and the truths of the soul are not in conflict. The great danger for English Christianity was bibliolatry, which 'does not consist in reverence to the Bible, however great, as long as Conscience is too dull to rise above the Bible'.[1] Such 'depressing' of conscience and the treating of 'inspired' words as 'premises for syllogisms', as 'ready-made weapons against heretics', as 'barriers against free-thought and feeling' were all too familiar. In any case three centuries of Protestantism had demonstrated that the letter would never of itself put an end to controversy nor bring enlarged wisdom or the recognition of goodness.

On the question of a future life Newman points out that all attempts at a rational proof of immortality have failed, from Plato onwards. But here again the mistake has been in confusing religion with science. The life hereafter is a religious belief, a conviction of the soul that its union with God will never be sundered, even by death. Christ's resurrection—which Newman himself, needless to say, does not believe in as a historical event—establishes nothing. It is an 'exceptional phenomenon' claimed by orthodox Christianity as a demonstration of Christ's uniqueness.

Francis Newman's position was an unusual one. He certainly was a liberal, yet to describe him as a liberal Protestant, as the expression came to be used, would be misleading. Liberal Protestantism has centred its belief on the historical figure of Jesus as the one supreme revelation of the divine. But for Newman Jesus had no special singularity. He denies his sinlessness and even accuses him of self-seeking in trying to make men believe in him regardless of their grounds for so doing,[2] whilst in his sometimes riddling answers to questions he practised a kind of deception. Jesus' teaching has, accordingly, no absolute authority, although Newman assures us that religion will not recover its 'pristine vigour' until it appeals to the soul 'as in apostolic days'. The fact that the New Testament is permeated with definite religious concepts seems not to have occurred to him. Basically his attitude was dictated by temperament. As his elder brother could not conceive a religion without forms, so he could not conceive one

[1] *Ibid.*, p. 42*n*.   [2] p. 146.

with them. Everything traditionary was 'earthy husk', in contrast
with 'heavenly spirit', although the intellectual implications of his
own type of religious affirmation he refrains from considering.
Endowed with something of the sensitivity of the mystic, he was
an out-and-out individualist, to the point, as his personal life
shows, of eccentricity. Hence the difficulty of taking him altogether
seriously. His sincerity is beyond question, but the long list of
'causes' which won his crusading ardour—women's suffrage,
pacifism, penal reform, teetotalism, opposition to blood sports,
anti-vivisection: he himself confessed to being 'anti-everything'—
suggest the crank. He was also quite without humour. John all his
life looked upon him distantly and disapprovingly, whereas
Francis, in spite of his radical differences of temper and outlook,
was by no means unappreciative of the great personal gifts of the
elder brother 'with whose name all England'— the words are his
own—'was resounding for praise or blame'; for even John was in
his way 'struggling after truth, fighting for freedom in his own
heart and mind, against Church articles and stagnancy of thought'.
But if the future cardinal's attitude was cold and occasionally
acidulous, Matthew Arnold's—disagreement with Newman had
arisen over the right way to translate Homer[1]—was suavely
contemptuous, adding to the air of absurdity from which Newman
is now hardly dissociable. But this should not be allowed to
obscure his real interest as a thinker.

However, the two classic instances of Victorian doubters
agonizing over their doubts are James Anthony Froude (1818–94)
and Arthur Hugh Clough. Froude was a younger brother of
Hurrell Froude, Newman's closest friend in the early days of the
Oxford Movement, and was always himself fascinated by the
Tractarian leader's personality. His two novels, *Shadows of the
Clouds* (1847) and *The Nemesis of Faith* (1849), feeble enough as
fiction, are significant as documents of their age, the second
especially so. *Shadows of the Clouds* is plainly autobiographical.
Its hero, Edward Fowler, is Froude thinly disguised. Indoctrinated
as a boy with the conventional orthodoxy of the day, maturity
brings insistent questioning of all received beliefs and a period of
spiritual desolation ensues. In the end, by much stoical self-
discipline, Fowler is able to reconstruct his life on the two

[1] See Arnold's *On Translating Homer* (1861), and *On Translating Homer: Last Words*
(1862), lectures which he delivered as professor of poetry at Oxford.

fundamental articles of God's providence and man's duty. If these are abandoned existence has no moral meaning. Conduct indeed is the one test of religious belief; but a multiplication of beliefs is an obstacle rather than a help to morality. The working out of the novel's plot is implausibly melodramatic, and much of the writing, particularly when the author—very obviously under the influence of Carlyle—projects his own sentiments, is turgid. *The Nemesis of Faith* is a better book, though here again the theme of a clergyman whose faith disintegrates has too many melo-dramatic accompaniments. Markham Sutherland is actually driven to the verge of suicide, but is persuaded by a Roman Catholic priest, identifiable as John Henry Newman, to enter the Church. The haven of an authoritarian religion, however, is only temporary: reason will out. Sutherland–Froude—for here also the autobiographical element is scarcely concealed—seems to have equated religion very largely with the instruction and practices of childhood and adolescence. Not unnaturally he found it wanting when challenged by experience. But the only apparent alter-native to this limited creed is sceptism elevated by Carlylean prophecy. He who had first been impressed with the irrationality of religion when writing a life of St Neot for Newman's *Lives of the English Saints* thus came round in the end—after studying Spinoza[1]—to a deterministic philosophy for which moral failures were errors, not crimes, and an assurance that reason must always prevail over religious authority, be it Church or Bible. On its publication *The Nemesis of Faith* created something of a scandal and brought Froude's Oxford career to an abrupt close. Yet what exactly the 'nemesis' of faith is does not emerge with certainty. It could be the retribution which overtakes 'the unlucky man who as a child is taught even as a portion of his creed what his grown reason must forswear'.[2] Some, on the other hand, saw in it an indictment of freethought for its regrettable moral con-sequences. Froude's ambiguity on the point seems to have resulted from a division of his mind between nostalgic affection for the religious certainties of youth and loyalty to the ration-alizing liberalism which now rendered these impossible. He was but one of many during the middle decades of the century who found themselves in a like predicament. He was more at

[1] See the appended Note to this chapter.
[2] *The Nemesis of Faith*, p. 316.

home with his historical studies, in which he showed himself a doughty champion of the Reformation as against its High Church detractors. In this realm the antagonism of head and heart could be more easily mitigated.

Arthur Hugh Clough (1819–61) came under Tractarian influence at Oxford, confessing later that for two years he had been 'like a straw drawn up the draught of a chimney'.[1] W. G. Ward had been among his more intimate friends. Religious difficulties began to trouble him, however, and in 1848 he resigned his Oriel fellowship. He offered no public explanation of his scruples, but 'pure reverence for the inner light of the spirit' was a genuine element in his character. He might indeed be said to have carried scrupulosity to excess. His self-distrust was almost morbid.

> Even in like manner [he wrote], my own personal experience is most limited, perhaps even most delusive: what have I seen, what do I know? Nor is my personal judgment a thing which I feel any great satisfaction in trusting. My reasoning powers are weak; my memory doubtful and confused; my conscience, it may be, callous and vitiated.[2]

The supposedly solid ground of religious authority was manifestly not open to him. Yet what satisfaction could the relentless pursuit of mere reason give? To authenticate Christianity by appeals to its historical origins was too problematic. Intellectual perplexity caused Clough distress because, although a sceptic, he had in him a strong vein of religious feeling. Faith he could not arrive at, but dogmatic unbelief was an alternative he shrank from. Suspense of judgment might have to be the answer:

> 'Old things need not be therefore true,'
> O brother men, nor yet the new;
> Ah! still awhile the old thought retain,
> And yet consider it again!
>
> The souls of now two thousand years
> Have laid up here their toils and fears,
> And all the earnings of their pain,
> Ah, yet consider it again!

---

[1] *Poems and Prose Remains* (1869), i, p. 14.
[2] *Ibid.*, i, p. 421.

> We! what do we see? each a space
> Of some few yards before his face;
> Does that the whole wide plain explain?
> Ah, yet consider it again!
>
> Alas! the great world goes its way,
> And takes its truth from each new day;
> They do not quit, nor can retain,
> Far less consider it again.

The age-old tradition of religion, widely interpreted—this at least was a fact, found indeed 'everywhere; but above all in our work; in life, in action, in submission, so far as action goes, in service, in experience, in patience, and in confidence'.[1] All things good, all things noble feed the human spirit; and to recognize this is, essentially, to understand the vital spirit of Christianity and of man. One ought not to try to swim against the stream. Nevertheless, Clough's attitude to Christian doctrine was negative. The actual state of Christianity denied its claim to dogmatic truth:

> Christ is not risen, no—
> He lies and moulders low;
> Christ is not risen!

Clough's nature was sensitive and reflective and with a marked tinge of melancholy. Spiritually the times were out of joint for him and the problem of faith haunts his verse continually. But although life might remain an enigma he was not without either humour or hopefulness. His 'Say not the struggle nought availeth' is too well known to need quotation here, but it is not an isolated utterance. Others in the same strain of tempered optimism could be cited, as:

> Let us look back on life; was any change,
> Any now blest expansion, but at first
> A pang, remorse-like, shot to the inmost seats
> Of moral being.[2]

[1] *Ibid.*, p. 424.
[2] *Dipsychus.*

Or

> And yet, when all is thought and said,
> The heart still overrules the head;
> Still what we hope we must believe,
> And what is given us receive;
> Must still believe, for still we hope
> That in a world of larger scope,
> What here is faithfully begun
> Will be completed, not undone.
> My child, we still must think, when we
> That ampler life together see,
> Some true result will yet appear
> Of what we are, together, here.[1]

This mood of mingled doubt and hope, of dejection and determination to put the best face on things pervades much Victorian poetry. Its most poignant expression is in Tennyson and Matthew Arnold; but Clough, far inferior as a poet to the one and less clear-headed as a thinker than the other, is perhaps more characteristic than either of the dilemma of their age.

4. JOHN STUART MILL

The intellectual standpoint most obviously antagonistic to the Christian tradition was, however, that of the Utilitarians, or Philosophical Radicals, as they have sometimes been called, and of whom John Stuart Mill (1806–72) was the most brilliant if not the most typical representative. There was in fact too much humanity in Mill for him ever to have been quite the embodiment of those rationalist principles of which professedly he was always the dedicated servant. The founder of the Utilitarian school had been Jeremy Bentham, whose ideas continued to be a guiding light for all its members. But although Bentham died in 1832 he was essentially a figure of the preceding century, and this same 'period' air pervades the work of his disciples, John Stuart Mill not excepted. In his lifetime his chief adherent and interpreter was Mill's dour father, James Mill (1773–1836), a man of powerful though rigid intellect, who in person was almost a caricature of the southerner's notion of the hardheaded Scot. Although at one

---

[1] *Through a Glass Darkly.*

time a minister of the Scottish Kirk, James Mill had developed for religion nothing but contempt and hostility, and saw to it that his son was brought up according to an educative regime from which religious influences were completely barred. 'I am', the latter wrote in his *Autobiography*, 'one of the very few examples in this country of one who has not thrown off religious belief, but never had it. I grew up in a negative state in regard to it.' The father's mind was not only prejudiced in the matter; on his own unwitting disclosure it was thoroughly ill-informed. All ages, he considered, have 'represented their gods as wicked in a constantly increasing progression', doing so, 'till they have reached the most perfect conception of wickedness which the human mind can desire, and have called this God, and prostrated themselves before it'. It was under the strict tutelage of a man holding such an opinion—the product in all likelihood merely of a jaundiced reaction from Calvinism—that the immensely impressionable John Stuart was nurtured and trained. Presumably his mother had no part in the process, for of her we never hear from him. The father's views, as such, need not detain us; but their effect on the man who in the middle years of the century was accounted the most important British philosopher of the age cannot be written off. John Stuart Mill's own lack of understanding of the religious temper and outlook evidently persisted to the end of his life, a conclusion which his three *Essays on Religion*, despite their somewhat stiff-lipped attempt at sympathy, do not mitigate.

The anti-religious character of Utilitarianism is not difficult to explain. Bentham, in whom an absolute aversion from religion was ingrained, set the tone in this as in other respects.[1] James Mill's animus against all religious ideas was partly at least a personal bias. So too was Grote's—Grote was Mill's pupil—if a little less overtly so. All of them disclose virtually no appreciation whatever of the religious sentiment as an expression of a human need and to look to any of them for a fair account of the Christianity of their day is idle, since their notion of its teaching never rises above a crude deism. Of religious belief as the projection and symbol, however tentative or partial, of a high moral ideal

---

[1] Bentham was the author of a number of works—*Church-of-Englandism and its Catechism Explained* (1818), *Not Paul but Jesus* (1821), *The Analysis of the Influence of Natural Religion on the Temporal Happiness of Mankind* (1822) (this last in collaboration with George Grote)—directly attacking religion, either in substance or in its traditional forms.

they have hardly an inkling. But personal prejudice aside, the whole interest and tenor of utilitarian thinking was opposed to religious aspirations. Its main concern was social reform, which, it was believed, could be brought about only on the basis of a scientific study of social relations. Knowledge in this sphere was expected to emulate, or at least to pursue, the successes of the physical sciences. The life of man could and should be examined as a matter of factual analysis. Religion, professing to deal with a transcendent world, offered nothing that could be scientifically investigated. It was therefore to be dismissed. Neither credal assertions about the unprovable nor worship directed to the unimaginable could any longer rightfully take the place of legislation and education as a means of human good, and indeed served only to impede its attainment. The Church was also resented and disliked as a nest of privilege and for the support it lent to an unjust and inefficient social order. Fundamentally, however, it was the utilitarian philosophy itself, as an anti-metaphysical empiricism, which was irreconcilable with religious belief. Without their being self-declared atheists the entire trend of the utilitarians' thinking ran contrary to the primary assumptions of Christian theology. For although they were not materialists in the sense of the *philosophe* d'Holbach or, later, Ernst Haeckel, their values were materialistic in that their conception of human nature and knowledge left no room for what was usually termed the 'spiritual'. They at all events were deficient in imagination and mistaken in their assessment of the place of the emotions in human life, whilst their necessitarianism—'circumstances make the man'—appeared to exclude any real freedom of individual self-determination. Thus utilitarianism was a soil in which religion could not thrive or even sprout. Nor, we might add, was it any more congenial to the arts. Its atmosphere was too desiccated, too narrowly rationalist. From the spirit of Coleridge, or of romanticism generally, it was completely remote. It is a measure of John Stuart Mill's departure from strict utilitarian orthodoxy that he was able to praise Coleridge's genius as he did, along, of course, with that fount of prudential wisdom, Bentham.

The interests of Mill for our present survey lies mainly in the fact that the doctrines he all his life professed with complete conviction do not appear wholly to have satisfied him, as they did his father and George Grote, and that he looked for some further outlet for his pent-up emotional life. But to understand Mill we must first consider what he himself has to relate in his *Autobiography*. The details of his early education need not be dwelt on: how he read Greek fluently at six years old and had got through six of Plato's Dialogues by the time he was eight, or how after the classics he went on to mathematics, history, English poetry, chemistry, logic and political economy, with philosophy in the shape of Aristotle's *Analytics* while he was scarcely in his teens. 'Anything', he wrote, 'which could be found out by thinking I was never told, until I had exhausted my efforts to find it out for myself.' Yet he denies that his abilities were abnormal. 'What I could do could assuredly be done by any boy or girl of average capacity and healthy physical constitution.' A year in France provided additional intellectual stimulus, but the climax of his education was reached with the works of Bentham, to which he was introduced by Dumont's *Traité de Législation*. This last he looked back on as an epoch in his life, the 'greatest happiness' principle bursting upon him 'with all the force of novelty'. All previous moralists he felt now to have been superseded and that with the Benthamite philosophy a new era of thought had commenced.[1] To himself he seemed even to have become 'a different being'.

> 'The Principle of utility', understood as Bentham understood it, and applied in the manner in which he applied it, fell exactly into its place as the key-stone which held together the detached and fragmentary component parts of my knowledge and belief. It gave unity to my conception of things. I now had opinions; a creed, a doctrine, a philosophy, in one among the best senses of the word, a religion; the inculcation and diffusion of which could be made the principal outward purpose of my life.

This was his moment of the initiate's zeal, and, as he realized, he could fairly be described as a 'reasoning machine'. But it was not long before he became aware of the defects of so straightened an outlook. He was all intellect; the heart seemed to have no room in him. His devotion to human welfare was less a spontaneous and practical attitude than a loftily detached option. What his high principles needed was their 'natural aliment, poetical culture'; the dissolvent power of mere rational analysis

[1] See *Dissertations* (1859), i, p. 403.

had been applied too far. He had started with 'a well-equipped ship and a rudder', but without 'a sail'. By the autumn of 1826 this sense of the radical deficiency in his makeup had turned into an emotional crisis which very nearly prostrated him. What the conscious issue was he afterwards stated in explicit terms:

> Suppose that all your objects in life were realized; that all the changes in institutions and opinions which you are looking forward to, could be completely effected at this very instant: would this be a great joy and happiness to you? And an irrepressible self-consciousness answered: 'No'.

So much precocious reasoning and analysing had been a worm at the root of the passions and virtues alike. Desire and pleasure had lost their savour. The breakdown continued for about a year, but restoration began with the discovery of poetry, especially Wordsworth's: 'What made Wordsworth's poems a medicine for my state of mind was that they expressed, not mere outward beauty'—this might have been too intellectual an experience— 'but states of feeling, and of thought coloured by feeling, under the excitement of beauty. They seemed to be the only culture of the feelings which I was in quest of.' The outcome was not by any means a drastic qualification of the Benthamite doctrine but a realization that happiness can only be attained by not making it the direct aim of living, and that it is, rather, a byproduct of worthwhile activities, such as promote the good of mankind. Moreover the 'internal culture of the individual' was also important, as against the 'ordering of outward circumstances' alone. 'The cultivation of the feelings became one of the cardinal points in my ethical and philosophical creed.' The reading of Wordsworth was now supplemented by the study of other contemporary authors: Coleridge and his followers—Maurice for one—Goethe, Comte, Carlyle. With Carlyle he formed a close but astringent friendship, and his praise of Maurice's ability, although the theologian's views in themselves could only strike him as a kind of mental perversion, was, as we have seen, unstinting. Mill had not dismantled his earlier beliefs, but he had woken up to their limitations. His regard for the eighteenth century was unabated, but he recognized that his own age provided a needed reaction and off-set to it.

The famous *System of Logic*, Mill's first major work, was

published in 1843, although completed two years previously. In it he was plainly following in his father's footsteps, as an uncompromising exponent of the empiricist philosophy. All knowledge, he holds, originates in sensation, which in turn is constructed from units of sense-impression. When the mental processes are examined it is found that they depend upon associations, a theory that James Mill had borrowed from Hartley.[1] But to reduce knowledge ultimately to sensations clearly posed difficulties. What is their organizing principle, if 'experience' is to have unity and continuity, when the 'self', as a metaphysical entity, has been excluded? 'Association', on the other hand, is not in itself an explanation. Again, if the only data of experience are sensations what exactly is it we can be said to 'know', unless we are for ever held within the circle of our own ideas? The problem obviously worried Mill, yet he would in no way qualify his dictum that 'of the outward world we know absolutely nothing, except the sensations which we experience from it'. Thus exterior reality becomes no more than the unknown and unknowable cause or occasion of our private sensations. The result would appear to be sheer individualism and subjectivism, a position which he is clearly not content with. Nevertheless, in spite of its difficulties, the *Logic* became, as Leslie Stephen said, 'the sacred Scripture of the Liberal intellectuals'.[2] More, in fact, than a technical treatise, it was a manifesto. The author's aim was polemical: to overthrow the defences of all 'intuitionist' thinkers, whose methods, in utilitarian eyes, were sinister because *a priori*. To combat this deeply entrenched philosophy, upon which the foes of enlightenment always fell back, was the great intellectual challenge of the times. No concessions could be made; even the certainties of mathematics were in the final resort empirically grounded. What we call causation is, as Hume had argued, only a matter of invariable succession. The role of the knowing mind is reduced to a minimum.

In the sixth book of the *Logic*, on 'The Logic of the Moral Sciences', Mill turns his attention to the larger, and to him the far more interesting, questions of ethics, politics and history. His

[1] David Hartley's *Observations on Man* (1749) was an attempt—subsequent to Hume, but influenced chiefly by Locke—to explain all mental development by the association of psychic elements, on the principle that complex states may have a quite different character from that of their simple constituents.

[2] *The English Utilitarians* (1900), iii, p. 76.

concern here is whether 'human nature' is itself capable of scientific analysis; whether indeed morality, along with the principles of social organization and historical development, is also a science. For this it would have to be shown that it exhibits fixed laws capable of demonstration. But what if man is a free agent? The question was one to be faced at the very start, and Mill does not shirk it. Volitions and actions, he contends, are always the effects of causes. Given, that is, the motives which are present in the individual's mind, as too his character and disposition, then the manner in which he will act may be unerringly inferred. Mill admits that this doctrine is repugnant to the upholders of free-will, but asks what there is derogatory to human dignity in the view that volitions and actions are 'the invariable consequents of antecedent states of mind'. Rather is it in the notion of an external causality or 'necessity' constraining the individual to act in one way instead of in another. When a man acts he 'chooses' in accordance with the motives by which he himself is inwardly moved. Our characters are not formed *for* us—'a great error', Mill judges—but *by* us. The power to alter character is thus 'to a certain extent' ours.[1] Though effects are to be traced to causes a man yet can permit himself to be determined by one cause more than by another. The cause–effect sequence, however, is strong enough for a science of human nature to be worked out. It will not be an exact science, but it can be constituted of approximate truths on the basis of general laws. What states of mind and 'associations' really are we are unable, of course, to say; at any rate we have no right, with Comte, to label them simply as physiological. It is sufficient for a *science* that it is a body of knowledge expressed in terms of law. Finally, the science of human nature—'ethology', as Mill calls it—is of paramount importance to the one to which all others lead.

Mill's ethical theory is elaborated in *Utilitarianism* (1863). Again it is the Benthamite position which is his starting-point, and as before the author is not quite comfortable in maintaining it. He is determined to adhere, that is, to the basic utilitarian principle, but at the same time he wants it to serve a higher end.

---

[1] 'Its being, in the ultimate resort, formed for him, is not inconsistent with its being, in part, formed *by* him as one of the intermediate agents' (*A System of Logic*, Bk vi, sect. 2). What, Mill thinks, is sound in the doctrine of free-will is its insistence on a truth which the necessitarian neglects, namely 'the power of the mind to co-operate in the formation of its own character.'

Actions, he continues to suppose, are right in proportion as they tend to promote happiness, wrong as they fail to do so; but he concedes that the pleasure principle appears to many people unworthy as a *moral* criterion, and indeed so far allows the objection as to introduce a qualitative difference between sorts of pleasure: some—those of the intellect, conspicuously—are more valuable and to be desired than others. In short, the mere quantity of pleasure, on a true reckoning, is of less importance than its quality. 'It is better to be a human being dissatisfied than a pig satisfied; better to be Socrates dissatisfied than a fool satisfied.'[1] And the quality of a pleasure is to be estimated only by those best able to do so. All the same a pleasure is a pleasure and if the quest of the pleasurable is made the standard of action then self-interest will provide the motive force, be the nature of the pleasure noble or ignoble. Once more Mill feels the point of the objection and endeavours to turn it by presenting the highest pleasure as the promotion of that of others. Thus, he believes, selfishness can be transformed into altruism. But what if one's own and the general happiness do not so easily coincide? Is one not, in that case, to pursue the latter *without* reference to the former? Mill, however, will not permit himself to stray so far from his original position and insists that in advancing other people's happiness we also create our own. Such at least is the theory. But he knew enough about human nature to realize that sustained altruism needs some more potent stimulus than a disinterested concern for one's neighbour's welfare, that it demands of it a conviction more akin to religious faith. Only the religion of altruism must be a humanistic not a supernatural one, a creed based on education and sound opinion, not on a supposed divine revelation. Man has to learn to acquire a feeling of unity with his fellow-creatures, making it an integral element of conscience, as spontaneous as 'the horror of crime to an ordinarily well brought up young person'. Hence virtue becomes a habit and deliberate thought of pleasure does not arise—an admirable sentiment, to be sure, but scarcely in line with the simple, hard-headed doctrine of Mill's master. The neo-utilitarian has here in truth approached the threshold of Christianity, and it is to his carefully stated views on the religious issue that we must now turn.

These are set forth in the posthumous volume of *Essays on*

[1] *Utilitarianism* (Everyman edn), p. 9.

Religion,[1] the first essay dealing with 'Nature' the second with 'The Utility of Religion' and the third with 'Theism'. Their intrinsic value is still substantial, but to the student of Mill himself they are of special interest. For here is a man plainly struggling to admit to himself the importance of a fact which, on the showing of a doctrine he had spent his life in propagating, had no importance at all. Yet he treats the subject throughout in a spirit of frigid detachment, entirely in the manner of the eighteenth century. Of religion as experienced by the believer he appears to sense nothing. The ethos of worship and prayer, the enthusiasm of a conviction that does not derive from logic, the impulse which sustains faith despite lack of evidence or even in face of contrary evidence, of these things Mill seems unaware or uncomprehending. Religion for him is a matter only of statements, propositions, true or false, capable or incapable of verification. These he reviews and considers and judges as though feeling and the needs of action had no bearing on them whatever. Faith is dissected on the study table and found to be unscientific, gravely wanting in the authenticity that belongs to rational demonstration. A Schleiermacher or indeed a Coleridge might never, so far as he is concerned, have written a word. Yet Mill cannot simply write off religion, as did Bentham, or his own father. Something about it holds him and worries him, as though he suspected, deep in his mind, that there might possibly be some realm of truth which his philosophy has failed to map out.

The first of the *Essays*, that on 'Nature', scrutinizes the ancient principle of *naturam sequi*, which in modern times had been extolled by Rousseau, the *laissez-faire* economists and the poet Wordsworth. In one sense, Mill notes, it means 'all the powers existing in either the outer or the inner world and everything which takes place by means of those powers'. In another it signifies, not everything which happens but only what takes place 'without the agency, voluntary and intentional, or otherwise, of man'.[2] With these connotations the term refers merely to nature as a matter of fact, but its employment in ethics seems to invoke a

---

[1] Published in 1874, with an introductory note by Mill's step-daughter, Helen Taylor. The first two, she tells us, were written between the years 1850 and 1858, the third—'the last considerable work which he completed', summing up 'the deliberations of a life-time'—many years later, between 1868 and 1870.

[2] *Essays on Religion*, p. 8.

third, by which nature stands not just for what is but for what ought to be. However, those who use the expression do not intend these differing senses to be exclusive; on the contrary, they think that nature does afford some external criterion of what we should do. For them what *is* constitutes the rule and standard of what *ought* to be. Yet this is precisely the question that needs explaining, for nature, on any candid view, seems anything but a model for men to adopt in determining their own actions. She is altogether mighty and wonderful, but does she evoke feelings of moral approval? For the truth is, alas, that 'next to the greatness of these cosmic forces, the quality which most forcibly strikes every one who does not avert his eyes from it is their perfect and absolute recklessness. They go straight to their end, without regarding what or whom they crush on the road'. Nearly all the things, says Mill, which men are hanged or imprisoned for doing to one another are nature's everyday performances. Natural phenomena are simply non-moral in every respect. But he does not leave his indictment there. Even nature's much-vaunted 'order' is an illusion. 'All which people are accustomed to deprecate as "disorder" and its consequences, is precisely a counterpart of Nature's ways. Anarchy and the Reign of Terror are overmatched in injustice, ruin and death, by a hurricane and a pestilence.'[1]

The theme is one certainly on which Mill can let his temperamental pessimism have its head; but the conclusion to be drawn is that on no account can it be religious or moral—as has so often been claimed—'to guide our actions by the analogy of the course of nature'. Not even our natural instincts are a safe conductor, for 'naturally' men are dirty, selfish and dishonest. 'There is hardly a single point of excellence belonging to human character, which is not decidedly repugnant to the untutored feelings of human nature.'[2] The theological inference, if one be made, is obvious, therefore: God, as the author of nature, cannot be both omnipotent and benevolent. 'If the maker of the world *can* all that he will, he wills misery.'[3] Where men have maintained a faith in divine benevolence the divine omnipotence has in fact gone by the board. Accordingly,

[1] *Ibid.*, p. 31.
[2] *Ibid.*, p. 46.
[3] *Ibid.*, p. 37.

whatsoever, in nature, gives indication of beneficent design proves this beneficence to be armed only with limited power; and the duty of man is to co-operate with the beneficent powers, not by imitating but by perpetually striving to amend the course of nature, and bringing that part of it over which we can exert control, more nearly into conformity with a high standard of justice and goodness.[1]

The possible implications of the fact that man, who can thus pass moral judgment on nature, is himself part of nature Mill does not ponder.

In the second essay the author raises the question of the utility of religion. If religion is true there can be no doubt of its usefulness, which indeed had no need to be asserted until the truth-claims of religion had largely ceased to convince. But the present is 'an age of weak beliefs': men are more determined by their wish to believe than by any logical assessment of the evidence. Wishful thinking is not necessarily selfish, be it said; yet whether 'all this straining to prop up beliefs which require so great an expense of intellectual toil and ingenuity to keep them standing, yields any sufficient return in human well being' is something the honest mind is bound to cogitate. That religion may be morally useful without being 'intellectually sustainable' is evident; but does this moral value depend directly upon dogmas? That it does do so is something repeatedly urged, but it is clear also that morality is powerfully inculcated by other means as well—by authority, education and public opinion. Among the ancient Greeks, for example, social morality was quite independent of religion. If the latter has been a prop to morals this was for circumstantial rather than intrinsic reasons, and Mill points out how religious writers and preachers have never tired of complaining of what little effect religious motives have on men's lives and conduct.[2] The truth of morality remains, however, even though the supernatural authority for it becomes increasingly dubious. Are not moral truths, he asks, strong enough in their own evidence for mankind to believe in them, although without any higher origin than 'wise and noble hearts'?

What then is there in human nature that prompts the need for religion? Mill does not think fear to be the answer. Much more is it the sense of *mystery*, in which the imagination plays a

[1] *Ibid.*, p. 65.
[2] *Ibid.*, p. 90.

commanding part. Poetry is one expression of this, religion another. But religion, as distinguished from poetry, comes of the craving to know whether the products of the imagination have some corresponding reality in another world. The satisfaction of human longing can, however, be had without going beyond the boundaries of this present world. Man's lot here can be indefinitely bettered, and although the effort may tax us, 'the idea that Socrates, or Howard, or Washington, or Antoninus, or Christ, would have sympathized with us' should be a great encouragement. But if we understand the essence of religion as 'the strong and earnest direction of the emotions and desires toward an ideal object, recognized as of the highest excellence, and as rightfully paramount over all selfish objects of desire', we ought also to ask ourselves whether this condition is not fulfilled by the 'Religion of Humanity' as eminently as by the supernatural faiths, 'even in their best manifestations, and far more so than in any of the others'.[1] But that humanism, as we today would call it, is a superior religion to the traditional ones Mill finds it impossible to deny. In the first place, it is disinterested: it does not look for future rewards in a way that can only promote selfishness,[2] whilst secondly, it does not depend on the intellectual contortions involved in ascribing absolute perfection to the author and ruler of 'so clumsily made and capriciously governed a creation as this planet and the life of its inhabitants'. The author of the Sermon on the Mount is certainly a much more benignant being than the Author of Nature, but unfortunately the believer in the Christian revelation is obliged to see in the same being the author of both. Again, it is free of the moral as well as the intellectual difficulties which religion constantly poses: how God could make a hell, or why so precious a gift as salvation should have been withheld from so many. Finally, as to the religious promise of a future life, improvement in the conditions of earthly existence will render the expectation less alluring: 'When mankind cease to need a future existence as a consolation for the sufferings of the present, it will have lost its chief value for them.'[3]

[1] *Ibid.*, p. 109.

[2] 'Even the Christ of the Gospels holds out the direct promise of reward from heaven as a primary inducement to the noble and beautiful beneficence towards our fellow creatures which he so impressively inculcates' (*ibid.*, p. 111).

[3] *Ibid.*, p. 119.

The essay on 'Theism' is the weightiest of all. Mill's attitude, needless to say, is consistently detached and argumentative. He is concerned with religious doctrines simply as 'scientific theorems', and asks what evidence they appeal to which science could recognize as such. The initial inquiry accordingly relates to the existence and attributes of God and raises the issue of the classic proofs. The argument to a First Cause does not impress him. Experience does not support it: the principle of causation is inapplicable to the material universe as a whole but only to its changeable phenomena.

> No cause is needed for the existence of that which has no beginning; and both Matter and Force (whatever metaphysical theory we may give of the one or the other) have had, so far as our experience can teach us, no beginning—which cannot be said of Mind.[1]

But if there is nothing in the nature of mind which in itself implies a creator then the demand for '*a priori* Intelligence' becomes unnecessary. Similar arguments from the 'general consent' of mankind and 'consciousness' do not afford any real basis for belief in God. 'It is not legitimate to assume that in the order of the Universe, whatever is desirable is true.' It is only when Mill reaches the argument from 'marks of design in nature' that he detects firmer ground. Here, he suggests, is something genuinely scientific in that it relies for its force on data of observation. 'Certain qualities it is alleged, are found to be characteristic of such things as are made by an intelligent mind for a purpose. The order of Nature, or some considerable parts of it, exhibit these qualities in a remarkable degree.' Does this then justify the conclusion of a designing Intelligence? Mill's reply is a tentative Yes: 'In the present state of our knowledge, the adaptations afford a large balance of probability in favour of' the idea.[2] Thus in spite of what he earlier has said about nature's 'disorder' he still finds enough order—sufficient evidence, in fact, of the most remarkable contrivance of means to ends—to make him feel that purposive design in the universe is *not* excluded. Since writing the essay on 'Nature', however, Mill had read Darwin, whose speculations he at once realized were not to be ignored. The Darwinian theory, 'if admitted', he observes, 'would be in no way

[1] *Ibid.*, p. 153.
[2] p. 174.

whatever inconsistent with Creation'. But it must be acknowledged that it would greatly attenuate the evidence for it.

All things considered, therefore, Mill can allow the existence of God as creator and designer, but not with the attribute of omnipotence. The deity's power, although great, is limited, and 'any idea of God more captivating than this comes only from human wishes, or from the teaching of either real or imaginary Revelation.'[1] Whether a revelation is real depends, again, on evidences, commonly distinguished as either external or internal. Internal evidences cover such indications as the revelation itself may be thought to supply concerning its divine origin—the excellency of its precepts, for example, or its adaptibility to human needs. These, Mill concedes, are important, but in the main only negatively so: they give us grounds for rejecting a revelation as divine, but not for its acceptance. As for the external evidences—miracles, in a word—Hume's objections are cogent. Mill discusses this problem at length, but in the end dismisses miracles both as having no claim to the character of historical fact and as wholly invalid when adduced in support of an alleged divine self-disclosure.

Of Christianity itself Mill speaks with a grudging praise. Even through its darkest and most corrupt periods, he recalls, it has maintained, in the image of one person, a standard of the highest human excellence; 'for it is Christ, rather than God, whom Christianity has held up to believers as the pattern of perfection for humanity'. Whatever else may be taken away from us by rational criticism, Christ, a unique figure, is still left.

> About the life and sayings of Jesus there is a stamp of personal originality combined with profundity of insight, which if we abandon the idle expectation of finding scientific precision where something very different was aimed at, must place the Prophet of Nazareth, even in the estimation of those who have no belief in his inspiration, in the very front rank of the men of sublime genius of whom our species can boast.[1]

Mill goes even further, entertaining the possibility that Christ actually was what he supposed himself to be—not God indeed, for this he made no claim at all to be—but 'a man charged with a

---

[1] *Ibid.*, pp. 194f.
[2] *Ibid.*, p. 254.

special, express and unique commission from God to lead mankind to truth and virtue'.

That Mill's conclusions on religion, at the end of a life dedicated to the service of reason, should amount to no more than a barely tenable theism, along with an unfeigned admiration for the moral doctrine and example of Jesus Christ, will strike the orthodox Christian as a meagre alternative to the traditional faith. Yet for Mill, considering his upbringing and the intellectual principles to which he was committed from his youth onwards, the concession is far from negligible. Through the many pages of dry analysis and argument there is discernible a nostalgic gleam, a half-wish that it *might* be true, in spite of the cumulative criticism which renders religion in its customary shape quite incredible. Mill, we may say, is also to be ranked among that impressive body of Victorians for whom the erosion of belief by reason, by science and by the pressure of changing social circumstances left them with a sense of deprivation and loss. The age of secularism had dawned; facts destructive of the old securities had to be faced and accepted. But the ties of the past, for all the promise of the future, were still strong enough for their breaking to be painful.

NOTE
The Influence of Spinoza

To the freethinkers of the age the discovery of Spinoza brought a veritable inspiration. Thus Coleridge, describing in Chapter 10 of the *Autobiographia Literaria* his state of mind at Nether Stowey and the growth of his mature opinions, tells us that although 'his whole heart remained with Paul and John', 'his head was with Spinoza'. It was the great seventeenth-century thinker also who helped to free the young George Eliot from the 'Procrustean bed of dogma' and to realize that 'nothing but gloomy and sad superstition forbids enjoyment', and that 'blessedness is not the reward of virtue, but is virtue itself'. In the spring of 1846 she even embarked on a translation of the *Tractatus Logico-Politicus*, finding it 'such a rest for her mind' after her labours on Strauss. George Eliot was among the pioneers of Spinozistic studies in this country, since at that time Spinoza's writings were still very little known here. (Three years previously G. H. Lewes had written an essay on Spinoza for *The Westminster Review*, claiming it, with justice, as the first attempt to vindicate this often misjudged philosopher before the English public.) George Eliot gave up the translation after her father's death in 1849, explaining to Charles Bray her feeling that what was wanted in English was not a translation of Spinoza's actual works but a true estimate of his life and system. 'After one has rendered the Latin faithfully into English, one feels that there is another yet more difficult process of translation for the reader to effect, and that the only mode of making Spinoza accessible to a large number of readers is to study his books, then shut them up and give an analysis' (Cross, *Life of George Eliot*, i, p. 238). The *Ethics*, an English version of which was also undertaken by her, was in 1856 abandoned; at least it was never published, presumably for the same reason. Froude was drawn to the rationalist philosopher by the splendour—especially in its contrast with the puerilities of popular mediaeval hagiography—of the *amor intellectualis Dei*. His article on Spinoza in *The Cambridge and Oxford Review* for October, 1857 represents him not only as the committed foe of all religious bigotry and superstition but as both the source of the 'purest and loftiest religious philosophy' of modern times and an example of the human mind in its highest development. The Spinozistic creed was in fact religion in its true essence: 'The love of God is the extinction of all other loves and all other desires. To know God, as far as man can know him, is power, self-government, and peace.' It was virtue and blessedness. (See *Studies on Great Subjects*, i, pp. 386f.). Another devotee was William Hale White (1831–1913)—'Mark Rutherford' —who published a standard translation of the *Ethics* in 1883. White's feeling, under Spinoza's guidance, that he was not a mere transient, outside interpreter of the universe, but had 'a relationship with infinity'—nay, was truly 'a part of the infinite intellect of God'—gave massive consolation for the loss of more traditional religious convictions. (See White's *Pages from a Journal* (1900), pp. 32–58).

Chapter IX

Religion, Science and Philosophy

1. THE BIBLE AND GEOLOGY

The seventeenth and eighteenth centuries had been an era of scientific advance and consolidation. By 1700 natural philosophy, as it was then called, had reached a stage which made the Newtonian synthesis possible. Thereafter science enjoyed growing prestige as a body of truths about the physical universe which were beyond sectarian dispute and could be taken for granted by all men of good sense. Moreover, that these truths might in any important way conflict with sound religion was scarcely considered. On the contrary, throughout the eighteenth century it was the generally accepted view that science had established a realm of facts which religion may gladly accept as illustrative of the ways of God. Nature was to be read as a book of divine authorship. In the words of Addison's well-known hymn:

> The spacious firmament on high,
> With all the blue ethereal sky,
> And spangl'd heavens, a shining frame,
> Their great Original proclaim.

Thus religion and science were in mutual support. And such continued to be the prevalent view in the opening years of the nineteenth century, when the writings of William Paley in this country were at the height of their popularity. But as the decades passed a change of outlook was becoming evident. Not only was scientific knowledge itself rapidly increasing, it was determining the very ethos of civilization to a degree hitherto unparalleled. The scientific spirit now permeated thought in all its ranges. Poetry and imaginative prose responded to it. Ruskin judged that he might himself have become the best geologist of his day and chided Wordsworth for failing to understand 'that to break a rock with a hammer in search of crystal may sometimes be an act not disgraceful to human nature, and that to dissect a flower may sometimes be as proper as to dream over it'.[1] It was impossible that in the circumstances religion should be oblivious of science's presence or not become apprehensive of what its expanding influence and authority might portend for beliefs long rooted in holy Scripture. Could Genesis come to terms with the new geology? Were miracles compatible with the reign of natural law? In the past, no doubt, there had been scientists who despised religious creeds, as there had been theists who denied them. Laplace had assured the Emperor Napoleon that for his calculations there was no need for the hypothesis of God. But such men and such attitudes were exceptional. The great Newton had been a devout Christian, for whom the providence of God was as certain as the principles of natural philosophy. Cuvier, foremost among the biologists of his time, and Owen, whose fame as an anatomist was surpassed by none, maintained the fixity of animal species in the manner the Bible seemed plainly to teach. But with the development of a conception of the natural order as autonomous, continuous and uniform, the acts of God, whether in originally creating or in providentially governing, became harder to discern. Hence the appeal to natural phenomena in evidence of the divine existence and attributes began to lose its former cogency.

The issue between religion and science was first clearly posed by geology. Between 1800 and 1834 four different series of Bampton lectures had dealt with the subject, and three of them, Faber's *Horae Mosaicae* (1800), Nares's *A View of the Evidences of Christianity at the close of the Pretended Age of Reason* (1805) and Bidlake's *The Truth and Consistency of Divine Revelation, with some Remarks on the contrary extremes of Infidelity and Enthusiasm* (1811), were strongly critical of the claims being made for geological study, either rejecting outright the facts alleged or else contending that they demanded another interpretation—for example, the presence of marine deposits on mountain-tops could be

[1] *Modern Painters* (1843–60), iii, xvii, p. 7.

explained by the Deluge. But always the clinching argument was that to question the accuracy of Scripture in any matter is to impugn divine revelation itself. Frederick Nolan in 1833—writing, that is, after the appearance of Lyell's *Principles of Geology*—was less intransigent; he allowed that the aim of the biblical authors was to teach religion not science, but had sufficient confidence in Moses' personal inspiration to believe that no serious discrepancy could arise between what the prophet was moved to write and what science long after might discover.[1] The apparent implications of geologically important advances—continued, however, to exercise the minds of educated Christians. In 1829 the Earl of Bridgewater, an eccentric cleric, bequeathed the sum of £8,000 to the President of the Royal Society for the sponsoring of a number of apologetic treatises. These were duly produced between the years 1833 and 1840, the best of them being William Whewell's *Astronomy and General Physics considered with reference to Natural Theology*, and William Buckland's *Geology and Mineralogy*, although the latter was felt to have made some dangerous concessions to the scientific position. Buckland, a clergyman who later became dean of Westminster, was at the time professor of mineralogy at Oxford and a man of some ability.[2] But most of these *Bridgewater Treatises*, as they were called—there were eight of them in all—were in content thin enough. Four of the authors were physicians seeking to prove intelligent purpose in nature from physiological data; the rest were divines, and included the famous Scottish church leader, Thomas Chalmers. Doctors and divines alike approached their task with outdated presuppositions, having nothing better to offer than the physico-theology of the preceding century, with its deistic notion of an external, 'watchmaker' God.

The difficulty in these years was to square the statements of Genesis, till then regarded as inerrant, with the time scale required by the geologists; for whereas Scripture spoke of the mere 'days' of creation the new geology reckoned in terms of millions of years. Must not one or other of them be wrong? Or could it be that the 'days' of Genesis would have to be understood figuratively? There also was the problem of the Flood. When did it occur

[1] See *The Anatomy of Revelation and Science Established* (1833).
[2] His opposite number at Cambridge was Adam Sedgwick, a bitter opponent of evolutionary views.

and how far was it universal? To the mind of an age that took the verbal inspiration of the Bible for granted such questions seemed to touch the very heart of faith. Philip Gosse, himself a scientist as well as a member of the Plymouth Brethren, believed that the Almighty had created the rocks with the fossils already in them, presumably as a trial of men's belief.[1] Much nonsense indeed was talked and written on these matters and attempts to arrive at a more reasonable conclusion were met with denunciation and abuse, not always from clergymen and pious layfolk. Buckland especially came in for opprobrious treatment by the press and in a stream of hostile pamphlets. The dean of York, William Cockburn, was his unrelenting opponent in this war of words. The latter as late as 1844 was still hammering away at the unfortunate Oxford professor, deploring that the ancient seat of learning and orthodoxy should continue to house a man who in spite of his clerical office worked only to promote infidelity.

The details of these disputes are both amusing and lamentable, but it would be pointless to dwell on them. Traditional religion had run up against new knowledge in the secular sphere and many of its cherished ideas had received a painful knock. British Protestantism was inveterately biblicist and took it as matter of course that the statements of holy writ could not be false. There seemed thus to be a head-on collision, and in the situation the theologians,—as too some scientists—still wearing the intellectual blinkers of an older time, could for the most part see nothing to avert disaster except a downright denial that what science was now saying could possibly be true.

Unfortunately for them the new findings were not to be disposed of by clamorous negations. Solid work had been done and signal discoveries made: the names in particular of Werner, Hutton and William Smith are still honourably remembered. Pre-eminent, however, was the achievement of Sir Charles Lyell, by whom the science of geology had been placed at last on a systematic basis. The importance of Lyell's work, on the long view, is that second only to Darwin's it effectually brought the whole realm of nature under the conception of developmental

---

[1] Other questions that troubled Gosse were whether Adam had been created with a navel—he gave the title *Omphalos* to a book he published in 1857—or whether the trees in the Garden of Eden, when cut down, showed the usual signs of growth. But Gosse's speculations were widely regarded as foolish in his own day.

law. It was in a genuine sense epochal, for biological evolution is really no more, in essence, than the extension to the organic world of principles which Lyell held to be dominant in the in-organic. Lyell himself, we may note, was somewhat slow to concede this; which explains his equivocal attitude to Lamarck, whose speculations he found at once fascinating and repellent. But he was reluctant to contemplate the possibility that man himself was descended from lower forms of life. When more than thirty years after the first appearance of the *Principles* he published his second major work, *Geological Evidences of the Antiquity of Man* (1863), Darwin's statement of the evolutionary theory had already caused a *furore* and the influence of the younger man's ideas was traceable in it. Nevertheless Lyell's fear of the implications of the theory—and he saw them plainly enough—disappointed Darwin, whose regard for Lyell's judgment was of the highest.

2. THE THEORY OF EVOLUTION

Long before *The Origin of Species*, however, a curious and much-talked of book of anonymous authorship had called attention to the evolutionary principle in the natural order. This was *Vestiges of the Natural History of Creation*, which appeared in 1844. The seal of its anonymity was not finally broken until 1884, when the fact that the writer was a certain Robert Chambers (1802–71) became publicly known. Chambers was a Scottish journalist and a man of eclectic interests, who with his brother William founded the publishing house of W. and R. Chambers, also giving his name to *Chambers's Encyclopaedia*. A prolific author, he was in no way a professional scientist and much of the biological informa-tion conveyed in the book, the sales of which were enormous—four editions were printed in six months—was wildly and even ludicrously inaccurate. Competent biologists were embarrassed at it. Thomas Huxley was incensed at 'the prodigious ignorance and thoroughly unscientific habit of mind manifested by the writer'.[1] Darwin praised it from the literary angle, but dismissed its content as worthless. Richard Owen, on the other hand, took a more sympathetic view of it, perhaps not surprisingly. Yet a success the book undoubtedly was, in so far as it aroused great popular interest. Its merit was its readability, which eased the

[1] F. Darwin, *The Life of Charles Darwin* (1887), ii, p. 188.

impact of its basic concept that once it be admitted that the system of the universe is subject to natural law it follows that the introduction of new species into the world 'must have been brought about in the manner of law also'. The idea, of course, was not new. Erasmus Darwin—Charles's grandfather—and Lamarck had both raised the hypothesis of a general modification of species by natural causes, but their suggestions had gained little public notice. Chambers's *Vestiges*, for all its shortcomings, deserves credit for having stated a principle of great scientific importance in an arresting and interesting way. It only remained for an abler intelligence and more thorough research to restate it with the support of the requisite factual evidence.

The belief that the 'Almighty Author' of nature made the progenitors of all exisiting species by 'some sort of personal or immediate creation' Chambers rejected as absurd. God truly is creative—'the Eternal One' had 'arranged for everything before-hand'—but he afterwards had entrusted the process of the whole to laws of his own appointing. Chambers buttressed his evolutionism with arguments not at the time familiar, such as the survival of rudimentary structures, the known development of the individual embryo, the geographical distribution of organisms and the unity of structural type among species; and he himself was prepared to believe that the organic was developed from the inorganic without special divine intervention. He thought it possible, however, that nature sometimes moves forward not by single steps only but by a leap, an opinion which orthodox Darwinism subsequently discountenanced. In any case there was nothing in the evolutionary idea as he saw it which was inimical to theism; on the contrary, it supported the argument from design in a form altogether superior to Paley's.

As a serious contribution to science *The Vestiges of the Natural History of Creation* did not bear examination; yet in the history of ideas it is in its way something of a landmark, even though dwarfed by the great literary event of 1859—the publication, after years of careful preparation, of *The Origin of Species*.[1] Nevertheless, when the reader turns to the later work its jejune forerunner is

---

[1] There is a draft plan of the book dating from as early as July 1842. This is of interest as showing both that evolution by natural selection had already occurred to Darwin as a principle needing a factual basis and that he also was concerned to prove intelligent design in nature, were such possible.

soon forgotten. Indeed it is given to few works in any field of study to have the revolutionary effect of Charles Darwin's book. Its immediate consequence, from our point of view, was that the tension between science and religious belief was to enter a new and acute phase. The power of the book lay not only in the intrinsic significance of its presiding idea, which, as we have noted, had already been anticipated, but in the mass of recorded data by which the thesis was sustained. At the time of its appearance the author was fifty and had devoted a full twenty years of his life to its gestation. The enterprise was a triumph of constructive thinking, the implications of which were to affect the entire outlook of the civilized world. But it had its critical and destructive side also. Whatever objections biologists of an older school might bring against it—and many of them, like Owen, did object to it on purely scientific grounds: all species, it was argued, were permanent[1]—its rudest challenge was felt to be to the accepted doctrines of religion. Genesis says that the world was created in six days and evidently means that the various kinds of living things as known today were produced in exactly that space of time. Darwin, on the other hand, when he observed how gardeners and pigeon-fanciers could produce new varieties by cross-breeding, had lighted on the idea that a process of purely natural selection might well be the explanation of all varieties whatsoever. Prolonged research had both confirmed him in the principle and provided him with the needed evidence. Thus the evolution of nature could be thought of as an immanent development requiring no impulsion or control from without. In the struggle for existence it was some physical capacity like strength or speed or protective colouring which ensured survival. Such creatures as had it continued and multiplied, those that had it not perished and the species died out. In a word, it was the *fittest* which survived. Special creativity by an 'external' purposive intelligence seemed no longer to be a necessary postulate.

The book was denounced in pulpits up and down the land as an impious absurdity. Current journals were filled with articles and

[1] John Morley remarked how 'one group of scientific men fought another group over the origin of species' (*Recollections* (1917), i, p. 13), while in 1860 Thomas Huxley, Darwin's most committed partisan, conceded that supporters of the Darwinian views were 'numerically extremely insignificant' (Francis Darwin, *op. cit.*, ii, p. 186). See C. E. Raven, *Science, Religion and the Future* (1943), pp. 35ff.

correspondence about it, most of them condemning it as irreligious. Darwin himself was certainly not a religious man: his spiritual sensitivity seems in fact to have become atrophied over the years; but he was no atheist. It was simply that he doubted 'the right of the human mind to draw so tremendous a conclusion' as that of divine existence. In any event his book was not intended as a criticism of belief, this being quite outside his purview. *The Origin of Species* is even prefixed with a quotation from Bishop Butler, and its closing words invoke the language of theism:

> Authors of the highest eminence seem to be fully satisfied with the view that each species has been independently created. To my mind it accords better with what we know of the laws imposed on matter by the Creator, that the production and extinction of the past and present inhabitants of the world should have been due to secondary causes, like those determining the birth and death of the individual. ... There is grandeur in this view of life, with its several powers having been originally breathed by the Creator into a few forms, or even one.[1]

He himself regarded 'the impossibility of conceiving that this great and wondrous universe arose through chance' as one of the chief arguments for the existence of God.

Darwin's personal opinions, however, did nothing to assuage his critics' anger. For what the theory indicated, if consistently adopted, was the pithecoid origin of the human race. Lyell, as we have seen, shrank from this prospect, and even Alfred Russell Wallace, a keen supporter of Darwinism whose own essay *On the Tendency of Varieties to depart indefinitely from the Original Type* follows an identical line of reasoning, held that the problem of human kind demands special treatment. In 1871, with the publication of *The Descent of Man*, Darwin explicitly drew the reprobated inference. Yet he did so with something also of apology to theological susceptibilities.

> I am aware [he wrote] that the conclusions arrived at in this book will be denounced by some as irreligious. But he who denounces them is bound to show why it is more irreligious to explain the

---

[1] When asked by Tennyson whether his theory told against Christianity Darwin replied: 'No, certainly not' (Hallam Tennyson, *Alfred Lord Tennyson: a Memoir*, ii, p. 57).

origin of man as a distinct species by descent from some lower form, than to explain the birth of an individual through the law of ordinary reproduction.[1]

Moreover, by the time this second most important of Darwin's works saw the light, public opinion had gone far towards assimilating the evolutionary concept. Vituperation and abuse had proved futile, and the theory had now become part of the changed intellectual landscape.

But in the early 'sixties, when the idea first struck the public mind, 'Darwinism' to many was practically a synonym for unbelief. More offensive even than its overt questioning of a Bible truth was its seeming humiliation of man himself, whose origins were now to be sought among the beasts of the field. Further, though species themselves may persist, their individual members were 'to be envisaged rather as transitory embodiments of relatively abiding types than as the supremely important realities for the sake of which the whole process exists';[2] and this presumably applied also to humanity. The disgust and contempt with which a theory having such implications was widely received among churchmen is illustrated by the well-known story of the passage of arms between Bishop Samuel Wilberforce and Thomas Huxley at the 1860 meeting of the British Association at Oxford, the bishop having already subjected Darwin's book to virulent attack in an article in *The Quarterly Review*. What exactly was said on that famous occasion is not altogether clear, since accounts of it vary. But Wilberforce, it is related, after again trouncing the theory, turned to Huxley and 'with smiling insolence begged to know whether it was through his grandfather or his grandmother that he claimed to be descended from a monkey'. On this Huxley whispered to his neighbour, 'The Lord hath delivered him into my hands', and then, rising to his feet, answered the bishop—according to J. R. Green's version—with the words:

I asserted—and I repeat—that a man has no reason to be ashamed of having an ape for his grandfather. If there were an ancestor whom I should feel shame in recalling it would rather be a *man*—a man of restless and versatile intellect—who, not content with an equivocal success in his own sphere of activity, plunges into scientific questions with which he has no real acquaintance, only to obscure them by an

[1] *The Descent of Man* (1901 ed), p. 937.
[2] C. C. J. Webb, *Religious Thought in England since 1850*, p. 13.

aimless rhetoric, and distract the attention of his hearers from the real point at issue by eloquent digressions and skilled appeals to religious prejudice.[1]

Yet just as some biologists opposed Darwinism from the start so a number of distinguished churchmen did not follow the Bishop of Oxford's suit. F. J. A. Hort, for example, intellectually one of the most keen-sighted men of his day, welcomed the theory. In March, 1860 he wrote to B. F. Westcott: 'Have you read Darwin? How I should like a talk with you about it! In spite of difficulties, I am inclined to think it unanswerable. In any case it is a treat to read such a book.'[2] Frederick Temple, a contributor to *Essays and Reviews* who was later to become Archbishop of Canterbury, saw a place for Darwin's teaching in a progressive theology as making the creation more wonderful than ever, in that he showed 'not a number of isolated creations, but all creation knit together into a complete whole.'[3] It was a great improvement, he judged, on Paley.

> To the many partial designs which Paley's *Natural Theology* points out, and which still remain what they were, the doctrine of Evolution adds the design of a perpetual progress. . . . [It] leaves the argument for an intelligent Creator and Governor of the earth stronger than it was before.[4]

Dean Church, Tractarian as he was, realized nevertheless that it was useless and mistaken merely to condemn the Darwinian theory.

> I owe [he wrote] my first interest in the subject to the once famous *Vestiges*,[5] and I remember thinking at the time it came out, that the line taken against it was unphilosophical and unsatisfactory. . . . Mr Darwin's book is *the* book of science which has produced most impression here of any which has appeared for many years. . . . One wishes such a book to be more explicit. But it is wonderful 'shortness of thought' to treat the theory itself as incompatible with ideas of a higher and spiritual order.[6]

[1] L. Huxley, *The Life and Letters of T. H. Huxley* (1900), i, p. 185. Huxley himself denied using the word 'equivocal'. Wilberforce, it should be said, had consulted Professor Owen beforehand and doubtless would have felt entirely justified in relying on so eminent an authority. Cp. Owen Chadwick, *The Victorian Church*, Part ii (1970), pp. 9–11.

[2] F. A. Hort, *The Life and Letters of F. J. A. Hort*, i, p. 414.

[3] See E. G. Sandford, *Frederick Temple: an Appreciation* (1907), p. 301.

[4] *The Relations of Religion and Science* (1884), pp. 117, 122.

[5] Church had reviewed it in *The Guardian*.

[6] M. C. Church, *The Life and Letters of Dean Church* (1895), p. 153.

A fortnight later he added:

> The more I think of it, the more I feel persuaded of the 'shortness of thought' which would make out of what is in itself a purely physical hypothesis in the mode of creation or origination (in which it seems to me very difficult at present to imagine our *knowing* anything), to be incompatible with moral and religious ideas of a very different order. But I am afraid that this is the present way of thinking among our religious people: and so the theory does not get fair discussion, either for or against, because there is on both sides an irresistible tacit reference to other interests in the minds of the disputants.[1]

In 1863 Charles Kingsley told Maurice that 'Darwin is conquering everywhere ... by the mere force of truth and fact'.[2] Even H. P. Liddon, for all his profound conservatism, was not prepared quite to turn his back on the theory, which although (as he thought) by no means proven, was still 'not inconsistent with belief in the original act of creation which is essential to Theism'. Evolution, he conceded, was from a theistic point of view 'merely one way of describing what we can observe of God's continuous action upon the physical world'.[3]

Meantime Darwin's ideas were being aggressively propagated by some fellow-biologists. Of these Thomas Henry Huxley (1825–95) was the most formidable. Although lacking Darwin's great originality of insight, he was a man of letters as well as of science. His role, which he discharged with surpassing competence, was that of a disciple and popularizer, writing always clearly and forcefully and often with a scathing wit. His declared aim was 'to smite all humbugs, however big; to give a nobler tone to science; to set an example of abstinence from petty personal controversies, and of toleration for everything but lying'.[4] Not surprisingly, his career was spattered with controversies, since he was naturally pugnacious. Theologians like Dean Wace, for example, suffered much at his hands. Gladstone, too, came off decidedly the worse in one of these verbal contests, concerning the ethics of a gospel miracle.

---

[1] *Ibid.*, p. 157. Church's correspondent was the noted American biologist, Dr Asa Gray, himself a convinced Christian.

[2] Mrs C. Kingsley, *Charles Kingsley, his Letters and Memories of his Life* (1877), ii, p. 155.

[3] *Some Elements of Religion* (1872), p. 56. On the impact of the evolutionary theory on the churches see Chadwick, *op. cit.*, pp. 23–35.

[4] L. Huxley, *op. cit.*, i, p. 151.

Huxley described his own position as agnostic, a word of his own invention. He did not, that is, categorically deny divine existence; he simply did not know it to be a fact. It was the same with personal immortality, that very special article of Victorian religious faith: he could neither affirm nor deny it. 'I see no reason', he wrote to Kingsley, 'for believing in it, but, on the other hand, I have no means of disproving it. Pray understand that I have no *a priori* objections to the doctrine. Give me such evidence as would justify me in believing anything else, and I will believe that.'[1] On a subsequent occasion he confessed to the same correspondent that he had 'never had the least sympathy with the *a priori* reasons against orthodoxy', and that he had 'by nature and disposition the greatest possible antipathy to all the atheistic and infidel school'.[2] Kingsley happened to be a personal friend of Huxley's, to whom the latter would doubtless wish, in this matter, to show his most amenable side. Yet in an essay on 'Agnosticism' he stated that 'greatly to the surprise of many of my friends, I have always advocated the reading of the Bible, and the diffusion of the study of that most remarkable collection of books among the people'. He dilated, however, on the superiority of the Bible's teaching to that of the sects, whether ancient or modern, as on the fact 'that the Bible contains within itself the refutation of nine-tenths of the mixture of sophistical metaphysics and old-world superstition which has been piled round it by the so-called Christians of later times'. Nevertheless his own professed standard of truth was always that of science, the trouble with religion —which he was apt to identify only with its formal doctrines— being that it could not be verified. Nor could he appreciate its language, the personalism of which offended him.

> Whether astronomy or geology [he again is writing to Kingsley] can or cannot be made to agree with the statements as to matters of fact laid down in Genesis—whether the Gospels are historically true or not—are matters of comparatively small moment in the face of the impassable gulf between the anthropomorphism (however refined) of theology and the passionless impersonality of the unknown and unknowable which science shows everywhere underlying the thin veil of phenomena.[3]

[1] *Ibid.*, i, p. 217.
[2] *Ibid.*, i, p. 241.
[3] *Ibid.*, i, p. 239.

Yet Huxley was not a secularist in the modern sense. Not only was the problem of religion and science of unflagging concern to him, he was by no means himself without a certain religious feeling, shaped though this was by the Protestant prejudices of his time and social milieu. In another and very remarkable letter to Charles Kingsley, written at the time of the death of his own eldest child, he declared:

> I have the firmest belief that the Divine Government (if we may use such a phrase) is wholly just. The absolute justice of the system of things is as clear to me as any scientific fact. The ledger of the Almighty is strictly kept, and every one of us has the balance of his operations paid over to him at every moment of his existence.[1]

On the other hand, in his famous Romanes lecture of 1893, he pressed the view that ethical progress and natural evolution do not go hand in hand and that nature is, as the poet had said, 'red in tooth and claw'. But the dark view of the natural order which he there takes he did not, it seems, quite consistently hold. 'One thing', he once confessed, 'which weighs with me against pessimism and tells for a benevolent author of the universe is my enjoyment of scenery and music. I do not see how they can have helped in the struggle for existence. They are gratuitous gifts.'

Another ardent Darwinian was John Tyndall, whose own position was quite frankly materialist. He was unable to believe in anything of which a model could not be made. Matter itself, he was satisfied, contained the promise and potency of all terrestrial life, of whatever form or quality. Consciousness was only its byproduct. Yet religion could be entertained so long as it was not permitted 'to intrude on the region of objective *knowledge*, over which it holds no command', since it was 'capable of adding, in the region of *poetry* and *emotion*, inward completeness and dignity to man'.[2] W. K. Clifford, professor of applied mathematics at University College, London, who in his youth had been a devout High Churchman, was less compromising even than this. Nature, including man, is a pure mechanism, and talk of the will influencing matter he thought sheer nonsense. The emergence of life itself is in all probability attributable to a series of

[1] *Ibid.*, i, 219.
[2] *Fragments of Science* (1879 ed.), ii, p. 198.

coincidences and thus a thing of chance. There is no such entity as the soul and morality is a social development originating from a 'tribal conscience'. Human progress is and always has been dependent on the advance of scientific knowledge and in a world dominated by such knowledge religion is an anachronism. Yet another of Darwin's converts was G. J. Romanes, whose own early religion had been evangelical. A correspondence between Darwin and himself seems to have been the turning-point and by 1875 Romanes was convinced that Darwinism had disproved Christianity. The upshot was the appearance in 1878 of *A Candid Examination of Theism*, in which he argued that belief in God is unwarrantable, as having no scientific ground. But to do so went against the grain of his personal feelings and he confessed that with the virtual negation of the divine the universe for him had 'lost its soul of loveliness'.

> When at times I think, as think at times I must, of the appalling contrast between the hallowed glory of that creed which once was mine, and the lonely mystery of existence as now I find it—at such times I shall ever feel it impossible to avoid the sharpest pang of which my nature is susceptible.[1]

The words are eloquent of the anguished disillusionment which many a Victorian, bred to the view that Christianity provides the one sure basis of moral living, must have endured when confronted by what reason declared to be the inescapable truth. For many in these years science appeared as religion's foe, and a foe bound to win. In Romanes's own instance, however, negation was not the end of the road and at the time of his premature death in 1894 he left notes for another book qualifying his previous conclusions. These were published in the following year in an edition, entitled *Thoughts on Religion*, by Charles Gore, to whom his widow had consigned them.

3. HERBERT SPENCER

But it was in Herbert Spencer (1820–1903) that evolution had its boldest theorist, a thinker who took over the principle as the key to an all-embracing system of philosophy. Meagrely though

---

[1] *A Candid Examination of Theism*, p. 114.

posterity may now estimate this ambitious enterprise, of its author's intellectual courage, hardihood and expansiveness of vision there can be no question. In early life a railway engineer, Spencer might have been expected to show a mainly practical bent, but it was to speculative thought that he came to dedicate his entire energy. Although from 1848 to 1853 he was sub-editor of the *Economist*, and for some years after a regular contributor to *The Westminster Review*, philosophical study occupied more and more of his time until by 1860 the scheme of the Synthetic Philosophy had been fully devised. The rest of his long life was to witness its gradual realization. It had been preceded by a number of preliminary studies such as the books on *Social Statics* (1851) and *Over-legislation* (1854). His *Principles of Psychology*, which first appeared in 1855, was itself, in the revised edition of 1870–72, to form an integral part of the completed system, the other components being *First Principles* (1862), *Principles of Biology* (1864–67), *Principles of Sociology* (1876–96) and *Principles of Ethics* (1892–93). Yet despite this formidable output he remained always more or less of an amateur. Max Müller, for example, described him as 'a writer without any background—I say on almost every page, "There he has discovered London again".'[1] Henry Sidgwick, the Cambridge philosopher, who as a young man had been attracted to Spencer's position, was afterwards 'appalled by the grotesque and chaotic confusion' of his metaphysics and dismissed his ethical doctrine as 'crude and superficial'.[2] These deficiencies, far from proving a hindrance to Spencer's popularity, may very well have stimulated it. He was nothing if not a plain man's philosopher, offering a vast range of plausible opinions to an age in search of a world view based on the idea which Darwin had so impressively demonstrated. Spencer's writings had all the appearance of being scientific, and the extension of the evolutionary method to the study of politics and society appealed strongly to the type of progressive thinker whose idealism demands the prop of seemingly hard fact. Yet Spencer also was a dogmatist, and although for a time this in itself told in his favour, it later destroyed his intellectual credit beyond recovery. Today he is unread and all but forgotten.

The basis of Spencer's philosophy is his much-criticized

---

[1] Mrs Max Müller, *The Life and Letters of Max Müller* (1902), ii, p. 188.
[2] A. Sidgwick, *Henry Sidgwick: a Memoir* (1906), pp. 277, 344.

division between the Knowable and the Unknowable, a distinction taken directly from Mansel's Bampton lectures and thus ultimately from Hamilton's philosophy of the conditioned. But according to Spencer the unconditioned must be conceived as positive, not negative. To prove the relativity of knowledge is at the same time to postulate the existence of something beyond the relative; and because all existence, as such, is positive, all consciousness is necessarily a positive consciousness of existence. What therefore is conceived as existing beyond knowledge cannot be thought of only as negative of the knowable. Although it eludes any distinct consciousness it at least is something more and other than the limited or conditioned; something, accordingly, of which we have 'a positive though vague consciousness'. In other words, the very relativity of knowledge involves the indefinite consciousness of that which transcends definite knowledge. For the definite is such only because of its origin in the indefinite, which persists throughout the variations of definite thought: all definition implies something which falls to be defined, and which, while still undefined, nevertheless is real. Hence Spencer's conclusion is that:

> Our consciousness of the unconditioned being literally the unconditioned consciousness, or raw material of thought to which in thinking we give definite forms, it follows that an ever-present sense of real existence is the very basis of our intelligence. As we can in successive mental acts get rid of all particular conditions and replace them by others, but cannot get rid of that undifferentiated substance of consciousness which is conditioned anew in every thought; there ever remains with us a sense of that which exists persistently and independently of conditions.[1]

The latent contradiction here is readily detectable, for if we can affirm of a thing that it exists then it is not completely unknown. Not only have we, as Spencer maintains, an indefinite consciousness of reality as the ground and guarantee, so to speak, of whatever is definitely known, but reality itself is precisely that which our knowledge progressively defines. In his view the idea that we have an indefinite consciousness of reality *in addition* to the definite consciousness which constitutes knowledge is the one safeguard against scepticism. But if scepticism is thus avoided it

[1] *First Principles*, sect. 26.

is only at the price of complete agnosticism. Either existence, although unknown, is yet capable of being known, or else, if it truly is knowable, nothing whatsoever can be said about it. The result in that case will be nescience, an intellectual vacuum—a strange basis indeed for the grand design of a 'synthetic philosophy'. The fact is that Spencer's unknowable is neither unknowable nor wholly unknown, but merely serves as the postulated substratum of phenomena. His failure to see this is typical of the logical blind spots which occur throughout his writings.

The *First Principles* discloses the guidelines of all Spencer's subsequent theorizing, but the metaphysical foundation is laid for the sake only of what is to be built later, and is otherwise of little importance to him. His real concern is to follow the workings of the principle of evolution from the simplest to the most complex forms, thus progressing from biology to psychology, sociology and ethics. This design is vastly more ambitious than anything Darwin ever envisaged. The latter's interest was confined to the origin of species; of the origin of life itself he had nothing to say. Spencer, on the other hand, believed that he could explain all things by the single law of the persistence of force or the conservation of energy, which he posited both as the ultimate presupposition of science and as implicated in each and all of the most general forms and antitheses of consciousness. Evolution, that is, is simply 'the law of the continuous redistribution of matter and motion'. To this principle he accordingly looks for the proof of all lesser or subordinate principles that claim acceptance as expressing duly ascertained knowledge. 'The persistence of force . . . being the basis of experience, must be the basis of any scientific organization of experience. To this an ultimate analysis brings us down; and on this a rational synthesis must be built up.'[1] But Spencer significantly adds that 'by persistence of force, we really mean the persistence of some cause which transcends our knowledge and conception'. In other words, the foundation of knowledge again is nescience. A single principle is made the pivot for sustaining a grandiose scheme of scientific knowledge compassing the whole of reality. Yet surprisingly the step from the inorganic to the organic is left unaccounted for. Spencer excused himself on the grounds that what comes after is the more

[1] *Ibid.*, sect. 62.

urgent consideration. Nevertheless, for one so confident of the omnicompetence of his method the omission is glaring.

The application of the evolutionary principle to human psychology shows, in Spencer's judgment, that the development of mental functions parallels that of organic. Ideas which appear to be innate or intuitive are, like certain types of mental reaction, to be traced to heredity. Society likewise is an organism and social institutions are to be seen as the outcome of a process embodying two opposing tendencies: the state and the individual. Capacity for initiative, Spencer holds, lies with the individual, whose aggressive instincts must be curbed. Conduct, on a properly naturalistic assessment, simply means the adjustment of the organism to its environing conditions. That which secures the most nearly perfect adjustment is at once the most acceptable to society and—at least in the long run—the most satisfactory to the individual. Moral concepts arise from the experience of the race, conscience (as we call it) originating in social custom, whether restrictive or permissive. A hedonistic element—'pleasure promotes function'—has to be recognized; but the law of evolution ensures that actions which are found to be pleasurable will also be such as to possess survival value. A perfect balance of egoism and altruism, achieved when moral conduct becomes a purely 'natural' functioning and the sense of duty as such disappears, will, of course, be realized only in some future and utopian stage of social development.[1] Finally, the world's religions also take their place within the evolutionary scheme and are interpretable as expressions of man's efforts to transcend the ordinary bounds of experience. Spencer himself combined an intellectual agnosticism with feelings of mystery and awe at the thought of the Unknowable, an attitude which he regards as the true essence of religion. For the Unknowable, inscrutable though it is, will be apprehended by the thinking man as the ultimate source of all things.

In his day Spencer's name was one to conjure with, and the fact that his Synthetic Philosophy has long since ceased to arouse interest should not blind us to the importance it had for very many of his contemporaries. His attempt to synthesize the entire field of knowledge, although doomed to failure, was as audacious

---

[1] See *The Data of Ethics*, published separately in 1879 but later used to form part one of the first volume of *The Principles of Ethics*.

as Auguste Comte's.[1] His sociology gave impetus to that study in its earlier phases, but with increased knowledge, especially in the field of social anthropology, it inevitably came to be superseded. His attempt to effect a reconciliation between science and religion on the proposition that both have a common underlying faith in the existence of some ultimate cause of phenomena, some profound mystery which lies at the heart of the universe and from which all things proceed, was imaginative enough. His contemporary success, however, was the measure of his eventual eclipse. As a thinker he was wholly of his age and without the originality or the vision that could out-top it. When his age passed away and new intellectual forces took the ascendant his system fell into abeyance. At any rate all that is left of it is his naturalistic ethics.

4. THE NEO-HEGELIANS

For Spencer was confident that the ethical life of man could be sufficiently explained by the principle of evolutionary naturalism. The synthetic philosophy is not expressly atheistic, but theism has no place in it: the ultimate is unknown and unknowable. His contemporary, Henry Sidgwick (1838–1900), on the other hand, although he himself gave up orthodox Christianity as intellectually untenable—his change of convictions being

[1] Spencer, like Comte, who also took all knowledge for his province, was a positivist. Philosophy he sees as nothing other than the system of the sciences, or knowledge taken as a coherent whole, the function of science being to organize and unify by analysis and synthesis. 'Knowledge of the lowest kind is *un-unified* knowledge; science is *partially-unified* knowledge; philosophy is *completely-unified* knowledge' (*First Principles*, sect 37). The principle on which he attempts to schematize the sciences is that of their relative degree of abstractness or concreteness. A science is concrete in proportion as it deals with a thing in respect of the full actuality of its being, abstract in proportion as it disengages the properties and relations of things and treats of them in isolation. The concrete, abstract-concrete or abstract. Spencer does not indeed follow Comte in arranging them in a hierarchy or serial order, but he does emphasize their mutual dependence and influence, and the farther they advance the more evident does their interdependence become. Their means of coordination is that of increasing generalization, the most general principle of all— i.e. the persistence of force—being used to reinterpret the conclusions reached by each science separately. The sciences thus diverge and reunite. 'They inosculate; they severally send off and receive connecting growths; and their intercommunion has been becoming more frequent, more intricate, more wildly ramified. . . . There has all along been higher specialization, that there might be a larger generalization; and a deeper analysis, that there might be a better synthesis' (*The Genesis of Science*, p. 29).

marked by his resignation in 1869 of his fellowship at Trinity[1] —was persuaded none the less that a naturalistic ethics is inadequate to human needs. Spencer's doctrines had appealed to him as a young man, but, as we have seen, he was later repelled by their manifest defects, when viewed from the standpoint of either metaphysics or morals. His own most considerable work was *The Methods of Ethics*, first published in 1874, in which he takes up the argument on behalf of intuitionism, one of the three 'methods' he chooses to examine, the others being egoism and utilitarianism. Egoism, Sidgwick points out, seeks to justify an action from its contribution to the greatest happiness of the agent himself, utilitarianism from its contribution to the greatest happiness of all who are affected by it. Intuitionism, on the other hand, in whatever form, recognizes ultimate ends beyond mere felicity and ethical rules other than those which enjoin the maximization of the happiness of the greatest number. Ordinary men, quite plainly, accept ends or rules 'as desirable apart from the happiness they promote'—namely, the disinterested pursuit of virtue or knowledge or beauty. Yet it has also to be recognized, Sidgwick holds, that the injunctions of common sense are apt to be vague and indefinite, at times conflicting and often allowing of exceptions. They do not supply, therefore, a sufficient basis for rational conduct, even though they do tend to further the general happiness. Sidgwick admits a measure of psychological hedonism, believing that any action can to some extent be justified by showing that it promotes the agent's personal happiness; yet the egoistic principle, if consistently followed, seems repugnant to the moral sentiment. Utilitarianism, that is, can certainly offer a rationally coherent account of the moral consciousness; but the question remains whether the reasonableness of self-love can really explain what is felt to be the special character of moral obligation. Moreover, what proof is there that the general happiness and the individual's own are in fact coincident? Sidgwick concludes that only belief in God will render such a coincidence possible and give to human conduct an effective principle of unity.

Although a searching critic of naturalism, Sidgwick did not

---

[1] Sidgwick retained his lectureship in moral philosophy and in 1883 was appointed Knightbridge professor in that subject. With the eventual removal of religious tests at the university his college re-elected him to a fellowship on the foundation.

himself produce a completed system of philosophy.[1] This was more rigorously attempted by his contemporary, Thomas Hill Green (1836–82), a fellow of Balliol College, Oxford, and Whyte's professor of moral philosophy in the university from 1878 until his death. Green's doctrine was worked out in strong opposition to the empiricism, naturalism and agnosticism of his day. 'He it was', said Scott Holland, 'who shook us all free from the bondage of cramping philosophies and sent us out once again on the high pilgrimage towards Ideal Truth.'[2] Lord Bryce, who also had been Green's contemporary at Oxford, regarded him as 'the most powerful ethical and most stimulating intellectual influence upon the minds of the ablest youth of the university', not least upon the more religiously inclined, in spite of his own wide departure from orthodox Christianity.[3] Green was, of course, a convinced exponent of the idealist philosophy, yet he was not a mere camp-follower of Hegel, whose name appears a good deal less frequently in his pages than does that of Kant. He was, moreover, considerably affected by the 'personal idealism' of Hermann Lotze of Göttingen, whose fame and influence were now reaching out beyond his native Germany.[4] Although among the foremost British thinkers of the century, Green's ultimate influence was somewhat diminished by the clumsiness of his literary style and by the fact that the relative shortness of his life prevented his achieving a really full and mature expression of his ideas. His *Prolegomena to Ethics*, published in 1883, is the most important of his writings.

Green's approach to philosophical problems was epistemo-

[1] See D. G. James, *Henry Sidgwick: Science and Faith in Victorian England* (1970).
[2] *A Bundle of Memories* (1915), p. 145. Cp. the same author's *Lombard Street in Lent* (rev. ed.), Introduction: 'Philosophically the change in Oxford thought and temper came about mainly through the overpowering influence of T. H. Green. He broke for us the sway of individualistic Sensationalism. He released us from the sphere of agnostic mechanism. He gave us back the language of self-sacrifice, and taught us how we belonged to one another in the one life of high idealism.'
[3] *Studies in Contemporary Biography* (1903), p. 99.
[4] See R. L. Nettleship, *Thomas Hill Green: A Memoir*, p. 192. And cp. p. 196n. Green had studied Lotze's works in their original tongue, but it was not until the appearance in 1887 of an English translation of *Mikrokosmos* that his views became at all well known. The subsequent 'personal idealist' phase in English philosophy owed much to him, Hastings Rashdall—a notable representative—praising him as 'the one philosopher of our time who is at once a thinker of the highest rank and wholly and unexceptionally Christian in his thoughts' (*Contentio Veritatis* 1902, p. 43).

logical. Experience and reality, he held, were one, experience being possible only because both knowledge and its object have a common principle or nature. Any postulated existence which could be distinguished from and opposed to knowledge would *eo ipso* have been so far qualified as necessarily to fall within its sphere. Thus even were it admitted that consciousness is conditional upon material being—matter and motion, that is—in the sense that, as known objects of consciousness, they are required to explain particular mental facts or functions, nevertheless consciousness cannot itself originate from them as though they had a reality prior to it and apart from it. Matter and motion, as known, express relations between constituent elements of experience and are insufficient therefore, in themselves, to explain the possibility of experience as a consequence of reality.[1] Any separation of the process of experience from the facts experienced is thus untenable.

> It renders knowledge, as of fact or reality, inexplicable. It leaves us without an answer to the question, how the order of relations, which the mind sets up, comes to produce those relations of the material world which are assumed to be of a wholly different origin and nature.[2]
>
> It is not that first there is nature, and then there comes to be an experience and knowledge of it. Intelligence, experience, knowledge, are no more a result of nature than nature of them. If it is true that there could be no intelligence without nature, it is equally true that there could be no nature without intelligence.[3]

But although Green's reassertion of the Kantian principle of the synthesizing activity of the mind itself may lead in the end to the Hegelian concept of infinite Spirit, his interest in religion detered him from equating this with the sum total of finite spirits. Green disliked the way in which the traditional theism contrasts God's being with that of the world and finite spirits, and preferred himself to think of man's spiritual life as a *participation* in the divine. But neither would he identify God with humanity in its spiritual development or with the idea of human knowledge as a completed whole. At any rate the human spirit could be said to be *identical* with God only 'in the sense that He *is* all which the

[1] *Prolegomena to Ethics*, sect. 9.
[2] *Ibid.*, sect. 34.
[3] sect. 36.

human spirit is capable of becoming'. God should rather be thought of as infinite and eternal Subject whose own perfect knowledge 'reproduces itself' progressively in finite subjects under the necessary modification imposed by the constitution of the human organism. As to why God, the all-perfect, should have made this imperfect world has never been answered, and in Green's view never would be.

> We know not why the world should be; we only know that there it is. In like manner we know not why the eternal subject of that world, as the spirit of mankind, or as the particular self of this or that man in whom the spirit of mankind operates. We can only say that, upon the best analysis we can make of our experience, it seems that so it does.[1]

Green was typically a Victorian in his concern for belief in the immortality of the soul, defending the idea on the grounds that the destructability of thought is a contradiction in terms, destruction having no meaning except in relation to thought.[2] How indeed the continuance of personal life after death might be maintained he did not claim to understand, but he believed such a faith to be in no way incongruous with the basic principles of his philosophy. There may be reason, he thought, for holding that 'there are capacities of the human spirit not realizable in persons under the conditions of any society that we know or can possibly conceive, or that may be capable of existing on earth'. Hence the probably justifiable supposition that the personal life, which in history or on earth is inevitably subject to conditions that thwart its development, is hereafter to be continued in a society which, although unattainable through the senses, nonetheless shares in and advances any measure of perfection attainable by man under known conditions. In any case the negative conviction must remain 'that a capacity which is working except as personal, cannot be realized in any impersonal modes of being'.[3]

There is little doubt that Green's teaching proved the most stimulating philosophical influence in this country during the latter half of the nineteenth century, especially through its critique of the presuppositions of scientific naturalism. Man, he assured his generation, is not an isolated creature in an alien

---

[1] *Ibid.*, sect. 100.
[2] *The Works of T. H. Green*, ed. R. L. Nettleship (1885–88), iii, p. 159.
[3] *Op. cit.*, iii, p. 195.

universe, and the merely physical aspect of his being cannot be cited as the true cause of his actions. Green's arguments, however, are not always well stated and his language is frequently ambiguous, faults which afterwards were to reduce his standing with professional philosophers. Had he been less anxious to avoid controversy, for he had no taste for polemics, he might have given his ideas clearer shape. He was particularly scrupulous in avoiding religious controversy, although unable himself to accept traditional Christian doctrine, being content to believe that God is the sum of all perfections and the essence of religion as a consistent faith in the ideal. But orthodoxy was undoubtedly heartened by his example at a time when its very foundations seemed threatened. Anglican theology in the last quarter of the century probably owed more to him than to any other thinker since Maurice.

The impact upon British philosophy of Green's contemporary and friend, Edward Caird (1835–1908), occurred somewhat later, his revised and expanded study of Kant appearing only in 1889. Less original than Green, he was much his superior as a teacher and writer, possessing a brilliant gift for exposition. But as with the former the real weight of his achievement has to be reckoned in personal rather than in literary terms, first—and perhaps mainly—as professor of moral philosophy at Glasgow, and subsequently as master of Balliol. The idealist philosophy—and his own profound debt to Hegel he readily acknowledged[1]—was, he too believed, the necessary because only effective counterbalance to the growing pressure of naturalism and materialism. If the gulf between religion and science was not to widen further—and the naïve common sense of the Scottish school (already undermined by Hume) plainly could not bridge it—then reflection must seek a synthesis in which the opposing forces could be reconciled at a higher level. Hegel, Caird judged, had rightly perceived that the world of intelligence and freedom could not fundamentally be other than that of nature and necessity; on the contrary, it was 'only the same world seen in a new light, or subjected to a further interpretation'.[2] The spiritual world must

---

[1] Caird denied, however, that he was a disciple of Hegel, holding that any attempt simply to import a foreign philosophy *en bloc* was bound to fail. See his preface to *Essays in Philosophical Criticism*, ed. A. Seth and R. B. Haldane (1883).

[2] *Hegel* (Blackwood's Philosophical Classics), (1883), p. 125.

therefore be looked for *within* the natural and not simply, as with
the traditional supernaturalism, beyond it.

To the attainment of this higher view Kant, in Caird's estimation, had made an invaluable contribution, although in precisely
what respect had not always been understood. The misunderstanding originated with Kant himself, in his unresolved dualism
of phenomena and noumena. For what these represent are really
no more than different stages in the progress of knowledge itself,
the unknown and unknowable *Ding an sich* being a mere irrational
residuum of which a truly critical philosophy would strive to rid
itself. Dismiss the 'thing-in-itself' and it becomes evident that
'objectivity' exists only for a self-conscious subject and that
between subject and object there is an intrinsic relationship, a
subsisting unity-in-difference. No doubt life as we usually think
of it moves back and forth between these two terms, regarded as
essentially distinct and even mutually opposed. Nevertheless 'we
are forced to seek the secret of their being in a higher principle, of
whose unity they in their action and reaction are the manifestations, which they presuppose as their beginning and to which
they point as their end'.[1] Science, of course, is held to be
exclusively concerned with the object, yet in its task of discovering
and correlating universal laws it implicitly acknowledges the
existence of an intelligible order which cannot be detached from
the thought that comprehends it.

The reality which is 'at once the source of being to all things
that are, and of knowing to all things that know' is what Caird
understands by God. As such, however, not all men are aware of it.
Religion has passed through a long process of evolution, the main
phases of which admit of fairly clear distinction. The first is that
of 'objective religion', in which man's thinking about the divine
is conditioned entirely by experience of his external environment.
Man at first looks outward, not inward, and can form no idea of
anything to which he cannot give 'a local habitation and a name'.
The gods, like himself, must have being in time and space. The
second phase, that of 'subjective religion', is one in which God is
conceived as a 'subject', and as such is 'brought under the
limitations . . . of a human understanding'.[2] God now is thought
of as a spiritual being of a different order from both the world and

[1] *The Evolution of Religion* (1893), i, pp. 65, 67.
[2] *Ibid.*, i, p. 193.

man and as revealing himself above all in conscience. In the final stage, that of 'absolute religion', subject and object are recognized as essentially related and as standing in an ultimate unity. They are grounded, that is, in a Being 'who is at once the source, the sustaining power, and the end of our spiritual lives',[1] and who is disclosed to us alike in nature and in human history.

With the later developments of British absolute idealism, in the work of Francis Herbert Bradley (1846–1924) and Bernard Bosanquet (1848–1923) it is hardly to our present purpose to deal. Both were academic philosophers whose writings either fall outside our period or had virtually no significant influence on contemporary theological thought.[2] Both, however, discuss religion at some length, holding it, at least on their own interpretation, in high regard. Where they parted company with anything resembling Christian conceptions was in their denial that, metaphysically speaking, personality can be judged as ultimately real. Bradley, in *Appearance and Reality*, argued that the very idea of a 'self' is so shot through with contradictions as to provide no acceptable clue to the nature of the ultimate reality, the sole criterion of which must be non-contradiction. If God were conceived as personal in the usual sense of personality he could not possibly be the ultimate. The Absolute, in other words, is not and cannot be God.[3] Reality therefore must be 'suprapersonal'.[4] A view such as this inevitably determines Bradley's account of religion itself, since if religion, as its apologists claim, is a practical attitude or feeling then plainly it is bound to have an object, and between this object and the person thus confronting it there must be a relationship. But religion, like God himself, —paradoxically, in view of the meaning of the word—is *above* relatedness, for 'short of the Absolute God cannot rest, and

---

[1] *Ibid.*, i, p. 195.

[2] Bradley was appointed to a fellowship at Merton College, Oxford, in 1870 and retained it to the end of his life, which was virtually that of a recluse. *Appearance and Reality* was published in 1893 (2nd ed., 1902) and *Essays on Truth and Reality in* 1914. He was awarded the Order of Merit in 1914. Bosanquet, who had been much influenced by Green and Nettleship, was a fellow of University College, Oxford. From 1903 to 1908 he occupied the chair of moral philosophy at St Andrews. The best known of his numerous writings are the two series of Gifford lectures, *The Principle of Individuality and Value* (1912) and *The Value and Destiny of the Individual* (1913). His express views on religion are contained in his essay *What Religion Is* (1920).

[3] *Appearance and Reality*, p. 335.

[4] *Ibid.*, p. 531.

having reached that goal, he is lost and religion with him'.[1] Alternatively religion could be seen as 'the attempt to express the complete reality of goodness through every aspect of our being. And, so far as this goes, it is at once something more, and something higher, than philosophy'.[2] In any case metaphysics cannot be used as a prop for Christianity, although in *Essays on Truth and Reality* Bradley concedes that a religious belief might be founded otherwise than on metaphysics, 'and metaphysics is able in some sense to justify that creed'. In fact in this later book he shows himself by no means unappreciative of the merely partial and imperfect truths of religion, holding that 'the demand for a theoretical consistency which mutilates the substance of religion, starts from error in principle and leads in the result to practical discord or sterility'.[3] Evidently upon this subject Bradley was not wholly sure of his position or was diffident of stating it openly. God may have to be thought of as 'appearance', but still he possesses a higher degree of reality than anything else we know. 'There is nothing', Bradley is even ready to say, 'more real than what comes to us in religion'.[4]

With Bradley's ideas Bosanquet's are very largely in line, but there are differences also, probably attributable to the two men's diversity of temperament. Bosanquet believed that as between the philosophy of the Absolute and the Christian religion, particularly in the matter of the doctrine of a future life, there is a sufficient affinity to allow them to draw sustenance from one another.[5] Religion indeed, like other activities of the spirit, is necessary if man is to transcend the constricting and impoverishing limits of the individual self. Yet, as C. C. J. Webb puts it, Bosanquet's philosophy 'wears an air of almost inhuman serenity while dismissing much that has been precious to many generations of our spiritual forefathers, and is still precious to multitudes of men', whereas in Bradley's, on the other hand, we find 'a very

[1] p. 447.

[2] *Ibid.*, p. 453.

[3] *Essays on Truth and Reality*, p. 432.

[4] *Appearance and Reality*, p. 449. Cp. *Essays on Truth and Reality*, p. 449: If I am forced to take reality as having . . . only one sense . . . nothing to me in this sense is real except the Universe as a whole: for I cannot take God as including or as equivalent to the whole Universe. . . . But if . . . I am allowed to hold degrees in reality . . . God to me is now so much more real than you or myself that to compare God's reality with ours would be ridiculous.'

[5] See his 'Are we Agnostics?', in *The Civilization of Christendom* (1893), p. 141.

human melancholy, as of one who, with all his devotion to his chosen task of following the argument withersoever it may lead him, is yet profoundly convinced that there are inexorable limits set to Philosophy's power of satisfying the human spirit, and acutely sensible of the discontent which must thus remain to her votaries when she has done all that she can do to reward their faithful services'.[1]

5. PERSONAL IDEALISM

The distinguished Unitarian teacher James Martineau (1805–1900), whose long life spanned nearly the whole century, is not to be classed along the neo-Hegelians, but in the task he set himself of explaining the world and mankind in spiritual terms he is fairly to be considered in idealist company. For while he neither adopted absolutist philosophical principles nor pursued its method he was at one with the Hegelians in his strong opposition to scientific agnosticism. His most important publications, *Types of Ethical Theory* (1885), *A Study of Religion* (1888) and *The Seat of Authority in Religion* (1890), were the product of his old age, but they embody teaching which he had been imparting for many years before, both orally and in magazine articles, chiefly in the *Prospective*, *National* and *Westminster* reviews.[2] His main targets were the doctrines of Spencer and Tyndall, whose monism and naturalism were inadequate to meet the full facts of human existence. As against the theory of the 'atomists' he held that

> to suppose that by pulverizing the world into its least particles, and contemplating its components where they are next to nothing, we shall hit on something ultimate beyond which there is no problem, is the strangest of illusions. [The atomist] must, in spite of his contempt for final causes, himself proceed upon a pre-conceived world-plan, and guide his own intellect, as step by step, he fits it to the universe by the very process which he declares to be absent from the universe itself.[3]

In the preface to *Types of Ethical Theory* he affords by contrast a brief sketch of his own intellectual development. He began his study of philosophy only after having first been trained as a

[1] *Divine Personality and Human Life* (1920), p. 253.

[2] His collected *Essays, Reviews and Addresses* were issued in a four-volume edition dated 1890–91.

[3] *The Contemporary Review*, February 1876, pp. 340, 345.

civil engineer. 'I had', he says, 'nothing to take with me into logical and ethical problems but the maxims and postulates of physical knowledge', and so found himself 'shut up in the habit of interpreting the human phenomena by the analogy of external nature'. Thus 'steeped in the "empirical" and "necessarian" mode of thought' he served out 'successive terms of willing captivity to Locke and Hartley, to Collins, Edwards, and Priestly, to Bentham and James Mill'. A change of mind, however, began to show itself in 1834, in a review of Bentham's *Deontology*.[1] The familiar utilitarian arguments were now losing their cogency for him, thanks less to any intellectual persuasion from without than to reflection on his own inner life.

> It was the irresistible pleading of the moral consciousness which first drove me to rebel against the limits of the merely scientific conception. It became incredible to me that nothing was possible except the actual; and the naturalistic uniformity could no longer escape some breach in its closed barrier to make room for the ethical alternative ... This involved the surrender of determinism and a revision of the doctrine of causation.[2]

Thenceforward his task was to be to elucidate the full meaning of the ideas of will and conscience. The former he saw as the type *par excellence* of causality, in man and in God; the latter, whose authoritative judgments are a voice divine, as the testimony of man's freedom, the evidence that personality is not wholly enmeshed in the causal nexus, necessary as this is to the maintenance of nature's order. For natural causation must also itself be referred to the divine will as its ground, the only true causes in the universe being God and rational entities: 'force' in the scientific sense—'will *minus* purpose'—is merely an abstraction and does not really exist. Martineau's religious philosophy revives in fact the teleological conceptions of an older theology, though in a more thoroughgoing way. Science, he believes, illustrates the presence of rational ends in nature, just as the moral consciousness indicates the presence within us of a moral order which in turn discloses

---

[1] See J. Estlin Carpenter, *James Martineau* (1905), p. 148. 'Sum up', Bentham had said, 'the values of all the *pleasures* on the one side, and those of all the pains on the other. The balance, if it be on the side of pleasure, will give the *good* tendency of the act upon the whole . . .; if on the side of pain, the *bad* tendency of it upon the whole' (*Introduction to the Principles of Morals and Legislation*, repr. 1907, p. 31).

[2] *Types of Ethical Theory*, pp. xxiif.

the transcendent holiness of God. Thus a sound philosophy will postulate an adequate spiritual cause for both the cosmos and the ethical experience of conscience, so linking the religion of nature with that of the moral personality.[1]

The working-out of Martineau's metaphysical theory was greatly facilitated by a period of study in Germany from 1848 to 1849, mainly under the direction of Trendelenburg and in the field of ancient Greek philosophy. The effect of this he describes as 'a new intellectual birth'. 'The metaphysic of the world had come home to me, and never again could I say that phenomena, in their clusters and claims, were all, or find myself in a universe with no categories but the like and the unlike, the synchronous and the successive'.[2] Its eventual outcome, in the long series of occasional essays as well as the books of his final years, was a restatement of ethical theism in terms which took full account of the antitheistic assumptions of contemporary science and the new philosophies based on it. Despite the author's liberal Unitarianism, Christian opinion of whatever denominational colour gladly applauded him as a formidable champion of the basic affirmations of the common faith.

In his theology Martineau remained loyal to the traditional teaching of his sect until about 1832. With the publication in 1836 of his first book, *The Rationale of Religious Inquiry*, his shift of position became evident. Reason was to be his guiding principle, and 'no seeming inspiration' could establish anything contrary to it. 'The last appeal in all research into religious truth must be the judgments of the human mind.'[3] Even so he still held belief in the gospel miracles to be a test of Christian conviction, a view he later rescinded. As the years passed he became more radical in outlook. The advances in New Testament criticism made by the German scholars impressed him deeply, and before long he came to accept the principal positions of the Tübingen

---

[1] In all ethical judgments Martineau discerns a preference: one chooses the higher rather than the lower, and it is conscience which decides, regardless of prudential consequences. For conscience, as distinct from prudence, 'is concerned with quite another order of differences; differences of inherent excellence and authority, which by their very nature must be cognisable *prior* to action, and accordingly not learned by experiment, but read off by *insight*, presenting themselves to consciousness as premonitions, not as the sequel of conduct' (*op. cit.*, p. 186).

[2] *Ibid.*, p. xiv.

[3] *The Rationale of Religious Inquiry*, p. 125.

school.[1] But his adoption of a liberal standpoint meant also a discarding of the old intellectualism and notably the determinism he had inherited from Joseph Priestly. Will and emotion were taken to play a larger part in the shaping of faith as an act and disposition of the whole personality. But this in turn necessitated a change in the conception of divine revelation and therefore of the seat of authority in religion. No longer was he content to think of revelation as a supernatural communication of specific truths, of which Scripture is the infallible record; nor of prophecy and miracle as an external guarantee of its veracity. Rather, if personality is the highest value known to man it is to be expected that revelation will be made through personal media and that the real criterion of divine truth is provided by the heart and conscience. In short, if a man would know the will and purpose of God let him first search the depths of his own nature. The primal authority in religion is experience itself, the inner witness of moral feeling and perception. In Jesus Christ, the supreme revelation, the character of God is disclosed under human conditions such as all men can understand.

Thus Martineau became convinced, in the light of his own religious development, that a theology tending more and more to be critical and even sceptical in tone might well mean not a weakening but a positive reinforcement of inward assurance, and he points out in a letter of 1840 to the American theologian, W. E. Channing, how 'there is a simultaneous increase, in the very same class of minds, of theological doubt and of devotional affection; there is far less *belief*, yet more *faith*, than there was twenty years ago'.[2] The kind of apologetic the age needed was one which largely abandoned the old and now tenuous appeal to extrinsic 'evidences' in order to rely on that 'profounder sense of the intrinsically divine character of Christianity' which the more thoughtful among younger men were beginning to feel. It was an apologetic Martineau himself consistently aimed at and no English theologian of his age had a deeper apprehension of what the changing intellectual climate demanded or was more far-sighted in his attempt to meet it.

The case against materialism and naturalism was further

[1] Cp. 'The creed and heresies of early Christianity', published in *The Westminster Review*, 1853.
[2] Quoted by J. Estlin Carpenter, *op. cit.*, pp. 183–8.

L*

elaborated, however, in the works of the 'personal idealist' school at the close of the century, which principally included Arthur James Balfour (1848–1930), the statesman—afterwards Earl Balfour—James Ward (1843–1925), naturalist, psychologist and philosopher, who was professor of logic and mental philosophy at Cambridge from 1897 until his death, and Hastings Rashdall (1858–1924), a fellow of New College, Oxford, and later dean of Carlisle. The first named, in his *The Foundations of Belief* (1895) and Gifford lectures on *Theism and Humanism* (1914), stressed the importance of the non-rational *causes* as well as the rational *grounds* of belief. In the formation of men's beliefs, he argued, the general psychological 'climate' inevitably counts for much and tends in fact to condition the attitude of scientists no less than of religious believers. The problem as he saw it is how non-intelligent nature can possibly be held to have produced an evaluating intelligence unless, behind and controlling it, there is an ultimate 'purpose' which itself is intelligent. All philosophies which deny such a purpose are 'intrinsically incoherent'. 'In the order of causation they base reason upon unreason. In the order of logic they involve conclusions which discredit their own premises.'[1] Nor does the Darwinian theory bring us nearer to an explanation.

> Why should faculties designed only to help primitive man or his animal progenitors successfully to breed and feed, be fitted to solve philosophical problems so useless and so remote? Why, indeed, do such problems occur to us? Why do we long for their solution?

Reflective agnosticism cannot be combined with scientific naturalism, since it is itself the product of a process which naturalism discredits.[2] More, naturalism fails to account even for the valid pursuit of natural science.

> Here, if anywhere, we might suppose ourselves independent of theology. Here, if anywhere, we might expect to be able to acquiesce without embarrassment in the negations of naturalism. But when once we have realized the scientific truth that at the roots of every rational process there lies an irrational one; that reason, from a scientific point of view, is itself a natural product; and that the whole material on which it works is due to causes, physical, physiological

[1] *Theism and Humanism*, pp. 257ff.
[2] *Ibid.*, p. 259.

and social, which it neither creates nor controls, we shall ... be driven in mere self-defence to hold that, behind these non-rational forces, and above them, guiding them by slow degrees, and, as it were, with difficulty, to a rational issue, stands the Supreme Reason in whom we must believe, if we are to believe anything.[1]

Ward, a professional philosopher as compared with Balfour, dealt with the same problem, but on more systematic lines and in a way which clearly shows the influence of the 'personal' idealism of Hermann Lotze. In the first series of his Gifford lectures, published in 1899 under the title *Naturalism and Agnosticism*, he insists on a distinction being drawn between natural science proper and naturalism as a philosophy. Mechanics, for example, deals only with the quantitative aspects of physical phenomena, whereas a mechanistic theory of nature aspires 'to resolve the actual world into an actual mechanism'.[2] The scientist *qua* scientist must be content to regard the laws of mechanics as resting on an abstract and selective methodology, valid within their limits though these laws are; what he is not entitled to assume is that of themselves they provide a sufficient account of reality as it is. But if materialistic monism is unwarranted so too is a bare mind–matter dualism: the object of knowledge can stand in relation to the knowing subject only because it is not itself heterogeneous to the subject. Indeed in Ward's view all entities are in some sense spiritual and the philosophy he himself propounds, more especially in the second series of Gifford lectures, *The Realm of Ends*, dating from 1911, is a spiritualist pluralism. It is a philosophy, he claims, founded on experience.

The world is taken simply as we find it, as a plurality of active individuals unified only in and through their mutual interactions. These interactions again are interpreted throughout on the analogy of social transactions, as a *mutuum commercium*; that is to say, as based on cognition and conation.[3]

Ward admits that it would be possible to look no further than this plurality of finite centres of experience, particularly as the so-called proofs of divine existence are open to damaging criticism. Nevertheless the concept of God supplies a principle

[1] *The Foundations of Belief*, pp. 322f.
[2] *Naturalism and Agnosticism*, i, viii (ed. 1906, p. x).
[3] *The Realm of Ends*, p. 225.

of unity which pluralism must otherwise lack; whilst those of creation and conservation help also to explain the existence of a multiplicity of beings.

> Without the idea of a Supreme and Ultimate Being, least inadequately conceived as personal, transcending the world, as the ground of its being, and yet immanent in it, as it is his idea—the world may well remain for ever that *rerum concordia discors*, which at present we find it.[1]

Hastings Rashdall, along with G. F. Stout and F. C. S. Schiller, was a contributor in 1902 to a volume of essays expressly entitled *Personal Idealism*,[2] his own dealing with the subject, 'Personality in God and Man'. Subsequent statements of his views on the philosophical grounds of belief included the essay on 'The basis of theism' in *Contentio Veritatis*[3] and a series of Cambridge University lectures delivered in 1908 and printed the year after as *Philosophy and Religion*. Rashdall, who followed Ward closely, denied that materialism is a possible doctrine, in that all that we know of the matter implies mind. On the other hand, matter does not exist solely as an object for man's transitory and incomplete knowledge. But if it cannot exist apart from mind then inferentially there must be a universal Mind in which and for which all things exist. As for naturalism it has to be said that in our experience of external nature what we encounter is not causality but, as Hume had pointed out, only succession, the uniformity of nature being a postulate of physical science, not a necessity of thought. The idea of causality really derives from our consciousness of volition, but events not caused by human volition indicate the operation of a will or wills other than human, although the systematic unity of nature suggests a single will. Further, 'if the ultimate Reality be thought of as a rational Will, analogous to the will which each of us is conscious of himself having or being, He is no longer the Unknown or the Unknowable, but the God of Religion, who has revealed Himself in the consciousness of man, "made in the image of God" '.[4] However—and the proviso is very characteristic of Rashdall's moralism—the mutual indepen-

[1] *Ibid.*, p. 421.
[2] Ed. H. Sturt.
[3] The other contributors were W. R. Inge, A. J. Carlyle, W. C. Allen and H. L. Wild.
[4] *Philosophy and Religion*, p. 54.

dence of divine and human personality must be clearly maintained, despite the truth that all human persons are of God's creating. Individuals are in no sense 'lost' in God or absorbed into his being—Rashdall had no sympathy with mysticism—nor was God himself to be thought of as 'superpersonal' if the term be meant to denote some kind of existence in fact lower than that of persons, 'as a force, an unconscious substance, or merely a name for the totality of things'.[1]

Philosophical idealism, both in its absolutist and in its personalist forms, was a sustained attempt to dispel the growing fear that science had turned the universe into a soulless mechanism. In this at least it resembles the Ritschlian movement in contemporary European theology, hostile though Ritschl himself was to all such metaphysical would be aids,[2] for Ritschlianism's basic aim was to uphold man's freedom amid the enveloping determinisms of nature. The fault of absolute idealism, from the Christian standpoint, was its conclusion that although reality is to be explained in terms of mind, personal distinctions obtain only of the world of 'appearance' and thus have no ultimate validity or even meaning. Personal idealism, it is fair to say, stood in the main for an unequivocal theism[3] as against any sort of all-dissolving monism, but its exponents were not always very rigorous in their arguments and in retrospect their systems emerge as not much more than individual statements of faith. As philosophies they are type-products of their time and now chiefly of historical interest. Not that the issue between science and religion has been demonstrably resolved one way or the other. The truth is that scientists and philosophers alike prefer to

[1] *Ibid.*, p. 55.

[2] Ritschl, little enough of a philosopher, relied for the philosophical grounds of his theism on Kant and Lotze, and could be described loosely as a personal idealist. His *Theologie und Metaphysik*, first published in 1881, is the most explicit account he ever rendered of his own philosophical position. But it is mainly a polemic against absolutism.

[3] J. McT. E. McTaggart, a fellow of Trinity College, Cambridge from 1891 to 1925, combined both Hegelianism and personal idealism in a highly idiosyncratic doctrine—an atheistic spiritual pluralism. 'If all reality', he thought, 'is a harmonious system of selves, it is perhaps itself sufficiently godlike to dispense with God' (*Some Dogmas of Religion*, 1906, p. 250). In terms of his own definition of religion as 'an emotion resting on a conviction of a harmony between ourselves and the universe at large' (*op. cit.*, p. 3) McTaggart was himself an intensely religious man. Truth, however, he seemed to envisage only as a kind of dream, personal and barely communicable.

devote their attention to specific problems sooner than advance comprehensive world views in which theology can at once recognize either an enemy or an ally. But that theology, the former queen of the sciences, should find herself alone on a deserted battlefield is far from being proof that the campaign has gone in her favour.

Chapter X

Liberal Theology and the Biblical Question

1. 'ESSAYS AND REVIEWS'

The publication in February 1860 of *Essays and Reviews*, the joint undertaking of six clerics and a layman, the majority of them Oxford men, proved in the event to be a turning-point in the history of theological opinion in England. At the time it caused a sensation, although this (with the book's uninviting title) was not immediate. Spring and summer, in fact, passed by and very little attention was aroused. It was only later that the storm of controversy broke, and when at last it did, 'addresses, memorials, and remonstrances against the mischievous tendencies of the book poured in upon the Archbishops and Bishops', whilst the luckless authors were denounced as 'traitors to their sacred calling' and as 'guilty of moral dishonesty'.[1] The leader of the opposition was that most able and energetic of the occupants of the contemporary episcopal bench, Samuel Wilberforce of Oxford. Our concern here, however, is with the contents of this literary enterprise, not with its reception by the public.[2] The several contributors wrote independently of one another, and in a brief prefatory note stated that each was responsible solely for his own chosen subject. But the significance of the volume lay in its general tone and tendency, which were undoubtedly meant by all the authors to be a challenge to accepted views and especially the complacent ignorance which in many instances alone sustained them. They

[1] R. E. Prothero, *The Life and Correspondence of Dean Stanley* (1893), ii, pp. 30f.
[2] On this see Chadwick, *The Victorian Church*, Part ii, pp. 75–90.

themselves described their work modestly enough as 'an attempt to illustrate the advantages derivable to the cause of moral and religious truth, from a free handling, in a becoming spirit, of subjects peculiarly liable to suffer by the repetition of conventional language, and from traditional methods of treatment'. Benjamin Jowett, then Regius professor of Greek at Oxford, and author of the longest and perhaps most important of the essays, gave in a letter to his friend, A. P. Stanley, a firmer hint of their common intention:

> [Our] object is to say what we think freely within the limits of the Church of England. ... We do not wish to do anything rash, or irritating to the public or the University, but we are determined not to submit to this abominable system of terrorism, which prevents the statement of the plainest facts, and makes true theology or theological education impossible.[1]

The immediate promoter of the scheme was Henry Bristow Wilson, vicar of Great Staughton, Huntingdonshire, and a former Bampton lecturer, the supporting contributors being Frederick Temple, headmaster of Rugby and subsequently archbishop of Canterbury;[2] Rowland Williams, rector of Broadchalke, Wiltshire, and vice-principal and professor of Hebrew at Lampeter—classicist, orientalist and theologian; Baden Powell, Savilian professor of geometry at Oxford; Charles Wycliffe Goodwin, an Egyptologist and the one layman among them; Mark Pattison, tutor of Lincoln College, Oxford, a man we have already noted as a dedicated scholar, if an enigmatic personality; and lastly Jowett himself, not as yet elevated to the headship of his college, but one who for long was to be the eminent representative of a type of churchmanship whose features his contemporaries found it difficult to determine: 'He stood', said Leslie Stephen, 'at the

---

[1] E. Abbott and L. Campbell, *The Life and Letters of Benjamin Jowett*, i, p. 275. Stanley himself declined to participate, not merely from a dislike of composite publications.

[2] In a speech to Rugby masters in the following year Temple explained that the book owed its origin 'to some conversation between Mr Jowett and myself, as far back as eight or nine years ago, on the great amount of reticence in every class of society in regard to religious views—the melancholy unwillingness of people to state honestly their opinions on points of doctrine. We thought it might encourage free and honest discussion of biblical topics, if we were to combine with some others to publish a volume of essays ... one stipulation being made, that nothing should be written which was inconsistent with the position of a minister of our Church' (E. G. Sandford, ed., *Memoirs of Archbishop Temple* (1906), ii, p. 225.

parting of many ways, and wrote "No thoroughfare" upon them all.' In sum, this book, like the equally notorious *Tract 90* before it, staked 'a claim to hold new and dangerous opinions within the pale of the Church of England'.[1] Churchmen at large saw it as an attempt to discredit Scripture and subvert the creed; yet today it reads as no more than a collection of theological and critical commonplaces, somewhat truculently voiced.

The opening essay, 'The Education of the World', was Temple's, and had already served its turn as a university sermon: the marks of pulpit oratory are obvious, as in its overworked and in any case dubious analogy between the history of mankind and the life of the individual. The record of the human race, it is argued, discloses three stages, corresponding to childhood, youth and maturity. Childhood needs a 'Rule', youth an 'Example', adulthood 'Principles'; and these are met by, respectively, the Law, the Son of Man and the gift of the Spirit. According to this view the ancient Greeks and Romans were but 'children', whereas the modern world has reached maturity. The principles of living are to be found in Scripture; hence 'the immediate work' of our day is the study of the Bible, since it is 'utterly impossible . . . in the manhood of the world to imagine any other instructor of mankind'. But the Bible must be studied with the mind of a grown man.

> Every day makes it more and more evident that the thorough study of the Bible, the investigation of what it teaches and what it does not teach, the determination of the degree of authority to be ascribed to the different books, if any degrees are to be admitted, must take the lead of all other studies.

Were geology to prove that the first chapters of Genesis cannot be read literally, or historical investigation to show that inspiration, though protective of doctrine, did not preclude occasional inaccuracies, or criticism reveal interpolations or forgeries, the results should still be welcome. New knowledge will of itself do no harm; on the contrary, 'he is guilty of high treason against the faith, who fears the result of any investigation, whether philosophical, or scientific, or historical'.[2] The tendency of modern times has been to modify the dogmatism of ancient

---

[1] F. Warre Cornish, *A History of the English Church in the Nineteenth Century*, ii, p. 128.

[2] *Essays and Reviews*, p. 54.

Christianity by substituting the spirit for the letter and practical religion for precise definitions of truth.

Temple's contribution was in substance entirely innocuous, even if so sane a critic as Connop Thirlwall, in his episcopal charge of 1863, discovered in it 'the broadest room for an assault upon the foundations of historical Christianity', deeming it to have handed all authority in religion to private judgment. The second essay, Rowland Williams's, cut more deeply. Some years before he had published a volume of sermons entitled *Rational Godliness*, in which his views on the biblical question were clearly indicated: a human element in Scripture has to be recognized; divine revelation had been progressive and by no means confined to a single race of men; prophecy was not simply predictive. The prevailing notion of inspiration had had, he thought, the unfortunate effect of removing God altogether from the sphere of daily life, so leaving religion as an alien thing without analogy in nature or parallel in history. The biblical writings are inspired, but in varying measure, and in any case the province of inspiration is that of religious not scientific truth. The problem of the miraculous is not to be settled merely on a principle; alleged miracles must be judged on their particular merits and with regard to the relevant circumstances, which include the cultural environment. Williams's contribution to *Essays and Reviews*, on 'Bunsen's Biblical Researches', dealt specifically with the work of the eminent Prussian diplomat in the field of biblical criticism.[1]

> Bunsen's enduring glory [he wrote] is neither to have paltered with his conscience nor shrunk from the difficulties of the problem, but to have brought a vast erudition, in the light of a Christian conscience, to unroll tangled records, tracing frankly the spirit of God elsewhere, but honouring chiefly the tradition of His Hebrew Sanctuary.[2]

The essay is not, however, confined to personal econiums. Historical study, it argues, is not to be warned off the biblical terrain.

[1] Baron von Bunsen, who had been Prussian ambassador at the Court of St James's from 1841 to 1854, was a man of wide learning as well as deep personal piety. His book, *God in History*, was in course of publication when *Essays and Reviews* appeared. He also was the author of a 'modern' translation of the Bible and of a history of ancient Egypt.

[2] *Essays and Reviews*, p. 62.

We cannot encourage a remorseless criticism of Gentile histories and escape its contagion when we approach Hebrew annals; nor acknowledge a Providence in theory, without owning that it may have comprehended sanctities elsewhere.

Williams's statements, considering the times, were provocative and doubtless were intended to be. The conclusions, then novel, of continental biblical scholars were detailed: the 'Books of Moses' were a compilation of only gradual growth; the 'Child' of Isaiah vii was in fact to be born in the reign of Ahaz; chapters xl to lxvi of the same book are not the work of the prophet of that name but are of anonymous authorship and of a much later date, the celebrated fifty-third chapter having probably been written by Baruch as a portrait of Jeremiah; the Book of Daniel is not authentic history and belongs not to the sixth but to the second century B.C.; the Epistle to the Hebrews is not Pauline, nor the Second Epistle of Peter genuine. In the light of criticism a new theory of inspiration had become imperative, the facts demonstrating both that the Israelites of old were not infallible and that for a right understanding of Scripture the Spirit is ever necessary. The further proposition, that 'if such a Spirit did not dwell in the Church, the Bible would not be inspired, for the Bible is, before all things, the written voice of the congregation'[1], gave great offence; as too did the opinion that the sacrosanct doctrine of justification by faith might better be taken to mean 'peace of mind or a sense of divine approval arising from trust in God' than 'a fiction of merit by transfer'. Again, much of the language of the scriptures is that of imaginative poetry rather than factual prose, and the 'dulness which turns symbol and poetry into materialism' is only to be deplored. It was for such views that Williams was afterwards condemned in the Court of Arches.

Baden Powell's, the third in order of the essays, bore the title 'On the Study of the Evidences of Christianity', but concentrated on miracles. A fellow of the Royal Society, the author had for many years been keenly interested in the relations of science and religious belief and had not long previously published a book on *The Order of Nature*, in which his ideas on the subject of the miraculous were clearly stated.[2] He was himself convinced that

---

[1] *Ibid.*, p. 92.
[2] Some broader aspects of the matter had been discussed by him in an earlier work, *Revelation and Science*.

the orderliness of nature testifies the control of a divine intelligence, but the very fact of such order precludes those breaches of it which the allegation of miracle demands. The essay follows up this argument by seeking to show how unsatisfactory is the kind of defence which apologists for miracle usually erect. But whatever the strength of his case Powell's way of presenting it leaves no favourable impression. His style is opaque, his phrasing clumsy and his use of italics unsparing. Yet the gist of it is plain. Miracle implies an 'arbitrary interposition' if the phenomenon is not in principle to be explained in terms of natural law and thus lose evidential value. With the advance of science the incidence of the miraculous is certain therefore to disappear.

> The boundaries of nature exist only where our *present* knowledge places them; the discoveries of tomorrow will alter and enlarge them. The inevitable progress of research must, within a longer or shorter period, unravel all that seems most marvellous, and what is at present least understood will become as familiarly known to the science of the future as those points which a few centuries ago were involved in equal obscurity, but are now thoroughly understood.[1]

The probative force of miracles, on which in the past so much stress was laid, has to be judged by reference to the mental outlook of those to whom it is offered, and with changing times such appeals lose their cogency. Instead of buttressing faith, as formerly, miracle now needs faith to render it credible. If Christianity in an age of science is to be effectively defended its spiritual truth must be separated from physical portents. Powell summarizes his argument as follows:

> An alleged miracle can only be regarded in one of two ways:—either (1) abstractly as a physical event, and therefore to be investigated by reason and physical evidence, and referred to physical causes, possibly to *known* causes, but at all events to some higher cause or law, ... or (2) as connected with religious doctrine, regarded in a sacred light, asserted on the authority of inspiration. In this case it ceases to be capable of investigation by reason, or to own its dominion; it is accepted on religious grounds, and can appeal only to the principle and influence of faith.

His overall conclusion is that 'advancing knowledge, while it asserts the dominion of science in physical things, confirms that of faith in spiritual; we thus neither impugn the generalizations

[1] *Essays and Reviews*, p. 130.

of philosophy nor allow them to invade the dominions of faith, and admit that what is not a subject for a problem may hold its place in a creed'.[1] The distinction thus made between science and religion was one which the future was to render increasingly common as the only way of securing an anchorage for faith without inhibiting the progress of knowledge. But at the same time, and in so far as his meaning was comprehended, Powell was thought to have questioned Christianity's divine credentials. On this score alone Thirlwall, for example, deemed the essay the most balefully significant in the whole book.[2] The pity is that the author did not make a better job of what he aimed to do. If his critics were unable to produce a successful refutation their ineptitude was no measure of his own skill. But for his sudden death he too would have found himself before the courts. As it was, Jowett's prosecutors at Oxford merely observed that Powell, 'after denying Miracles', had been 'removed to a higher tribunal'.

The fourth paper, '*Séances historiques de Genève*: the National Church', by Wilson, provoked more hostile comment than perhaps any other. Apart from Jowett's it was the longest, and it occupied the central position. Its purpose was to state what in the writer's view the Church of England, as the national Church, ought properly to be. The *séances* referred to had been an evangelical Christian conference lately held at Geneva, but the essay had very little to do with it, save in borrowing the term *multitudinisme*, used by one of the speakers there. This Wilson applied to his concept of the nature and function of a national ecclesiastical establishment, which in his view ought certainly to be 'multitudinist'. The idea had already been explored in the essayist's own Bampton lectures of 1851 on *The Communion of Saints*, in which he had contended both for the provisional character of dogmatic statements in theology and for a substantial broadening of the Church's comprehensiveness. On the first point he claimed that 'all dogmatic statements must be held to be modalized by greater or less probability'.[3] Fixity in such statements is not to be expected and is dangerous when insisted upon. Dogma cannot be

---

[1] *Ibid.*, p. 152.

[2] Baden Powell was alone, as it happened, among the seven contributors to refer to Darwin's *Origin of Species*. He praised it for having demonstrated 'the grand principle of the self-evolving power of nature'.

[3] The precise expression is from the same writer's essay, 'Schemes of Christian Comprehension', which he contributed to a collection of *Oxford Essays* in 1857.

made to supply any effective basis for unity among Christians; formularies may be and are varyingly interpreted and none can be taken as legally binding. The true bond of union is a moral one. As to the second point, it is evident that by the time he wrote his *Essays and Reviews* paper Wilson had changed his opinion on the matter of clerical subscription since the day, nearly twenty years previously, when he had been one of the four college tutors to protest against *Tract 90*. He now urged its abolition on the ground that there should not be a dual standard of belief, one for the clergy and another for the laity. Only with complete doctrinal freedom would the Church be able to move with the times and so fulfil its service to the nation. At present, 'while the civil side of the nation is fluid, the ecclesiastical side of it is fixed'; on which Thirlwall's comment was that 'a Church, without any basis of a common faith, is not only an experiment new in practice and of doubtful success, but an idea new in theory, and not easy to conceive'.[1]

On the subject of biblical inspiration Wilson refused to identify the Word of God with the Bible simply as such. The letter of Scripture contains the Word, but is not to be equated with it. He pointed out that the sixth of the Thirty-nine Articles itself gives no definition of inspiration nor even speaks of Scripture as supernaturally inspired. Instead it permits us to accept 'literally, or allegorically, or as a parable, or poetry, or legend, the story of the serpent tempter, of an ass speaking with a man's voice, or an arresting of the earth's motion, of waters standing in a solid heap, of witches, and a variety of apparitions'. There are differing kinds of truth, of which myth or legend may quite fittingly be the vehicle. 'We do not apply the term "untrue" to parable, fable, or proverb, although their words correspond with ideas, not with natural facts; as little should we do so, when narratives have been the spontaneous product of true ideas, and are capable of reproducing them.' What matters in the sacred narrative is its spiritual meaning, beside which questions of precise historicity are secondary. And the same holds true of the rest of the symbolism of religion, the sacraments included. The forms are human, the content divine; and both aspects are to be recognized. There was no need then to be exigent in particulars. 'Jesus Christ has

[1] From his episcopal Charge of 1863. See *Remains, Literary and Theological* (1877–8), ii, pp. 46f.

not revealed His religion as a theology of the intellect, nor as an historical faith; and it is a stifling of the true Christian life, both in the individual and in the Church, to require of many men a unanimity of speculative doctrine, which can never exist.'

C. W. Goodwin's dissertation on the Mosaic cosmogony argues that the creation stories in the Bible have nothing in common with modern scientific hypotheses, and the efforts of such apologists as Dr Buckland, Archdeacon Pratt and Hugh Miller, author of the popular *Testimony of the Rocks*, to 'harmonize' Genesis and geology were merely misguided. 'It would have been well', says the writer, 'if theologians had made up their minds to accept frankly the principle that those things for the discovery of which man had faculties specially provided are not fit objects of divine revelation.'[1] Physical science continued to pursue its own paths unconcernedly, whereas theology, the science whose object is the dealings of God with man as a moral being, maintained 'but a shivering existence, shouldered and jostled by the sturdy growths of modern thought' and lamenting the hostility it encountered.

Why should this be, unless because theologians persist in clinging to theories of God's procedure towards man, which have long been seen to be untenable? If, relinquishing theories, they should be content to enquire from the history of man what this procedure has actually been, the so-called difficulties of theology would, for the most part, vanish of themselves.

The essay of Mark Pattison, unobtrusively entitled 'Tendencies of Religious Thought in England 1688–1750', is the best in the book, excepting Jowett's. It is not ostensibly polemical and in form is simply a review of the religious ideas characteristic of a selected period of recent history; though as such it is of significance as the work of a pioneer in this type of study.[2] Pattison admits that the period in question had usually been written off as a time of decay in religion, licentiousness in morals, public corruption and profaneness of language—'an age whose poetry was without

---

[1] *Essays and Reviews*, pp. 251f.

[2] Pattison was a fastidious scholar and the bulk of his published work is not large. His study of Isaac Casaubon appeared in 1875 and the volume on Milton, in the 'English Men of Letters' series, in 1879. What was to be his most important undertaking, a life of Scaliger, remained a fragment only (see *Essays*, ed. H. Nettleship, 1889, i).

romance, whose philosophy was without insight, and whose
public men were without character'. History, however, is not to
be treated in this way; an age should be critically studied, not
summarily judged. 'We have not yet learned, in this country, to
write our ecclesiastical history on any better footing than that of
praising up the party, in or out of the Church, to which we happen
to belong.'[1] But the historian is aware of continuities and if the
position of the Church today is to be understood then what has
gone before, over preceding generations, must be duly appreciated. In the previous century interest in Christianity seemed to
turn only on its provability, and what use to make of it when
proved was little considered. Similarly the only quality of
Scripture dwelt upon was its credibility. Yet evidences, as they
were called, 'stir no feeling' and the mind preoccupied with them
'knows nothing of the spiritual intuition, of which it renounces
at once the difficulties and the consolations'. Even so, serious
inquiry into the nature of the authority by which these evidences
are furnished was entirely neglected. Indeed, anything like a
genuine theology, as distinct from defensive argumentation, had
all but died out 'when it received a new impulse and a new direction from Coleridge'; thereafter 'the evidence-makers ceased from
their futile labours all at once'. Englishmen had heard 'with as
much surprise as if the doctrine was new' that the Christian faith
was 'the perfection of human intelligence'. Taught by Coleridge,
the present age was coming to realize that faith is not the end
product of a process of abstract reasoning, but rather a 'devout
condition of the entire inner man', although Pattison observes
that 'theological study is still the study of topics of defence'.[2]

The appeal to reason has of course its proper use and function,
in theology as in other disciplines, but reason is more than 'the
rational consent of the sensible and unprejudiced'. The Deists
and their opponents alike had made this mistake. In fact, 'the
defect of the eighteenth century theology was not in having too
much good sense, but in having nothing besides'. Its aim, allow-
ably, had been practical—to maintain the principles of moral and
religious conduct for society—and so far it had merited praise.
But its conceptions were too narrow. The nineteenth century
must learn from its predecessor's errors, for what is needed now

[1] *Essays and Reviews*, p. 308.
[2] *Ibid.*, p. 364.

is the impartiality of science, not the bias of mere special pleading. 'If theological argument forgets the judge and assumes the advocate, or betrays the least bias to one side, the conclusion is valueless, the principle of free enquiry has been violated.'[1]

Pursuit of the historical method alone, Pattison thinks, will induce such impartiality and prevent theology from becoming for the Church of England what it already is for the Roman, 'an unmeaning frostwork of dogma, out of all relation to the actual history of man.' The truth was that even the existing situation afforded little encouragement for a critical observer.

> Whoever would take the religious literature of the present day as a whole, and endeavour to make out clearly on what basis Revelation is supposed by it to rest, whether on Authority, on the Inward Light, Reason, self-evidencing Scripture, or on the combination of the four, or some of them, and in what proportions, would probably find that he had undertaken a perplexing but not altogether profitless enquiry.

The implication of Pattison's dry comments was not lost on contemporary opinion: their tone was negative. His work, accordingly, for all its apparent detachment, was lumped with the rest as unconstructive and essentially inimical to orthodox faith. The author remarked long afterwards that his attempt to present the English public with a philosophical monograph on a special phase of English thought was 'singularly unsuccessful. To judge from the reviews, it never occurred to any of our public instructors that such a conception was possible'.[2]

> So wholly extinct [he concluded] is scientific theology in the Church of England that the English public could not recognize such a thing as a neutral and philosophic enquiry into the causes of the form of thought existing at any period. Our clergy know only of pamphlets which must be for or against one of the parties in the Church.

The concluding essay was Jowett's. But this calls to be considered within the wider context of the writer's standing and influence as a theologian and biblical exegete.

[1] *Ibid.*, pp. 365f.
[2] *Memoirs*, p. 314.

2. BENJAMIN JOWETT

The facts of Jowett's career are soon recounted. One of the outstanding classical scholars of the century, he was born in London
in 1817 and educated at St Paul's School and Balliol College,
Oxford, of which he became a fellow in 1838 and tutor in 1840.
Two years later he was ordained. Disappointed of the headship
of the college in 1854, he was elected in the following year to the
Regius professorship of Greek in the university. Master of Balliol
at last in 1870, on death of the man (Robert Scott) who had
received the preferment sixteen years earlier, he shortly afterwards
brought out his translation in four volumes of the *Dialogues of
Plato*, which, despite the somewhat carping criticism to which it
has often been subjected, is the literary achievement whereon his
fame as a scholar largely rests. Versions of Thucydides and the
Politics of Aristotle appeared in 1881 and 1885 respectively, but
neither will bear comparison with work on Plato. A great educator as well as a distinguished scholar, Jowett will be remembered
as one of the makers of modern Oxford. He died in 1893.

Long before the publication of *Essays and Reviews* Jowett had
been known for the exceeding broadness of his theological
opinions. German influence had contributed to this: he was well
versed, especially for an Englishman of his time, in Kant and
Hegel, although he never himself became a Hegelian to the
extent of accepting the complete idealist system. But along with
T. H. Green he was mainly responsible for 'that naturalization
of Hegelian thought in England which was so marked a feature
of the close of the nineteenth century'.[1] Indeed, he was Green's
precursor in this regard.[2] He was, moreover, familiar with the
work of Schleiermacher and F. C. Baur. The latter on St Paul
particularly impressed him. 'Baur's', he told A. P. Stanley,
'appears to me the ablest book I ever read on St Paul's Epistles:
a remarkable combination of Philological and Metaphysical
power, without the intrusion of Modern Philosophy.'[3] Whatever
one thinks of the justice of this last observation, it is clear that
Jowett realized how much contemporary biblical criticism, as
developed in Germany and especially at Tübingen, had to teach

[1] A. E. Taylor, in *D.N.B. 1922–1930*, p. 102.

[2] Jowett was also, it should be recalled, Edward Caird's tutor. See the article on
Caird in *D.N.B.*, Second Supplement, pp. 291–5.

[3] Geoffrey Faber, *Jowett* (1957), p. 212.

the English student, hitherto insulated from such influences by the blind veneration in which, in this country, the very letter of Scripture was usually held. Jowett's own theological position— at least in his own mind; it never perhaps was very plain to others —was becoming more clearly defined between 1846 and 1848, and in the former year he again wrote to Stanley about an enterprise which the two of them had long contemplated: a series of commentaries on the New Testament.

> I propose [he said] to divide it into two portions: (a) the Gospels, and (b) the Acts and Epistles, to be preceded respectively by two long prefaces, the first containing the hypothesis of the Gospels, and a theory of inspiration to be deduced from it; the second to contain the 'subjective mind' of the Apostolic Age, *historisch-psychologisch dargestellt*. I think it should also contain essays. . . .[1]

In the event, Stanley undertook the commentary on Corinthians, completing the task by 1849, while Jowett tackled Thessalonians, Galatians and Romans, writing, however, much more slowly than his partner, the superficiality of whose own contribution is obvious. But after much interruption caused by the university reform issue, the work was at length finished and in the summer of 1855 published. Jowett's part in the collaboration is easily the weightier. Stanley's treatment is historical, after the 'picturesque' manner for which he had a *flair*—'critical notes', he admitted, 'were not his vocation'.[2] Besides, in addition to the actual commentary, Jowett had in a second volume included a number of *Essays and Dissertations*, dealing with the larger, doctrinal aspect of his subject, a supplement which retains some value even today. But although these chapters are a stage in the advance of liberal theology in England, to the reading public at the time of their appearance they were far from welcome and did more than anything else in the entire three volumes to provoke that 'storm of acrimonious controversy' described by Stanley's biographer.

It was the essay 'On Atonement and Satisfaction' which occasioned most displeasure. A true exegesis, the author maintains, must be determined by the given passage's original meaning, so far as this can be ascertained. As a rule it has been obscured by

[1] E. Abbott and L. Campbell, *op. cit.*, i, pp. 100f.
[2] R. E. Prothero, *op. cit.*, i, p. 474.

layers of subsequent theologizing, so that the task of the modern exegete has become as difficult as it is necessary. And no doctrine has suffered more from wrong-headed and even morally repulsive explanations than that of Christ's atoning sacrifice.

> God is represented as angry with us for what we never did; He is ready to inflict disproportionate punishment on us for what we are; He is satisfied by the sufferings of His Son in our stead.

The imperfection of human law is transferred to the divine, and the death of Christ explained by analogy of the ancient rite of sacrifice, 'a victim laid upon the altar to appease the wrath of God'. What was needed was a return to the simplicity of the Bible itself.

> I shall endeavour [Jowett wrote] to show: 1, that these conceptions of the work of Christ have no foundation in Scripture; 2, that their growth may be traced in ecclesiastical history; 3, that the only sacrifice, atonement, or satisfaction, with which Christ has to do, is a moral and spiritual one; not the pouring out of blood upon the earth, but the living sacrifice 'to do thy will, O God'; in which the believer has part as well as his Lord; and about the meaning of which there can be no more question in our day, than there was in the first ages.

In view of the place which the doctrine of the atonement still held in Victorian Protestantism and the manner in which it was generally interpreted, it is little wonder that Jowett's comments struck his readers as a betrayal of the gospel. His language on this subject had in fact an unwonted vehemence. 'No slave's mind', he declared, 'was ever reduced so low as to justify the most disproportionate severity inflicted on himself; neither has God so made His creatures that they will lie down and die, even beneath the hand of Him who gave them life.' Further, he was well aware that the doctrine in its familiar forms was no recent excrescence of belief, but 'the growth of above a thousand years; rooted in language, disguised in figures of speech, fortified by logic', and thus had come to seem a part of the human mind itself. 'One cannot but fear whether it be still possible so to teach Christ as not to cast a shadow on the holiness and truth of God.' A restatement of the doctrine would necessarily place Christ's death within the context of his life. Too precise a definition ought in any case to be avoided: 'In theology the less we define the better';

and the reality of the atonement is something greater far than the theories invented to explain it. Nothing should be done to divest the doctrine of its essentially moral meaning.

The essay on 'The Imputation of the Sin of Adam' dealt briefly but hardly less trenchantly with another of orthodoxy's basic tenets, original sin. On this belief whole systems of theology had been erected. But what in truth was its own foundation? When looked at critically its New Testament grounds—a couple of not unobscure passages in St Paul[1]—would be seen to be insufficient to bear the immense doctrinal superstructure built upon them. The apostle was simply employing modes of expression native to his own age and religious tradition but not to be used as intellectual currency good for any time and place. Instead of merely reproducing his words a serious attempt should be made to fathom his meaning. When Paul uses a figure of speech 'a figure of speech it remains still', an allegory appropriate to the circumstances, though with a signification that can be determined. 'It means that "God hath made of one blood all the nations of the earth"; and that "he hath concluded all under sin, that he may have mercy upon all".' We are one in a common evil nature, which, if not actually derived from Adam's sin, exists as really as if it were. 'It means that we shall be made one in Christ, by the grace of God, in a measure here, more fully and perfectly in another world. It means that Christ is the natural head of the human race, the author of its spiritual life.'[2] In short, Jowett tries to see the apostle Paul not as a mere storehouse of theological builder's materials but as a man of his period whose teaching, when stripped of its adventitious elements, nevertheless has spiritual import for all periods.

The only other dissertation that calls for notice here is that on 'Natural Religion', a discussion prompted by St Paul's condemnation of the heathen. It is characteristic of the 'large' outlook that had been forming in the author's mind over the years. His feeling is that no sharp distinction between nature and supernature, between natural religion and revealed, can be drawn. Man's apprehension of God from the light of nature is the presupposition of any accepted revelation, and the traditional

[1] Romans v, 12–21; I Corinthians xv, 21, 22, 45–49.
[2] *Commentary on Thessalonians, Galatians, and Romans, with Essays and Dissertations,* ii, pp. 315f.

division between the two is the result only of an abstract conceptualizing which has outlasted any usefulness it had. Nowhere has God left himself without witness and his self-disclosure is not to be confined to a single historic channel. Jowett's implication clearly is that Judaism and Christianity are themselves historical phenomena, subject to the forces which shape all such phenomena. He does not, however, wish to imply that because the Jewish-Christian tradition can be seen by the critical historian to belong to a specific context and to have incorporated elements originating elsewhere that this tradition has no special and even unique significance and value. Quite the contrary; but the question at issue—inescapable in the modern world—is one of approach, of intellectual attitude. Religion is the expression of a people's mind and character, and to study Christianity comparatively is the only fruitful way to comprehend it. Other religions, therefore, are not to be dismissed as heathen darkness, since even in their crudest forms they somewhere evidence the divine activity. In one aspect the religious impulse and the forms it assumes are natural; but in another supernatural. Nature and history—all history—are the spheres in which God works. Christians today cannot in this matter judge as uncompromisingly as did the authors of Scripture.

It is hardly surprising that Jowett's orthodox critics should have accused him of denying to the Bible, or at least to the Old Testament, any special inspiration. Of the latter he had said:

> It is not natural, nor perhaps possible, to us to cease to use the figures in which 'holy men of old' spoke of that which belonged to their peace. But it is well that we should sometimes remind ourselves, that 'all these things are a shadow, but the body is of Christ'.[1]

He had himself learned Hebrew, but seems to have made no great progress in the language, and with the Hebrew Scriptures his sympathies, Hellenist that he was, were less than perfect.

His general attitude to the Bible was set forth at length—it is a composition of some one hundred pages—in the *Essays and Reviews* chapter 'On the Interpretation of Scripture'. This had been designed to take its place in the *Commentary*, but was finished too late for inclusion. In its new setting it became 'the book's centre of gravity',[2] and is the one contribution, excepting

[1] *Ibid.*, p. 307.
[2] Basil Wiley, *More Nineteenth Century Studies* (1956), p. 154.

only Pattison's, which would bear reprinting today. The writer's meaning is always transparently clear, his tone cool and candid.

> As the time has come [he states] when it is no longer possible to ignore the results of criticism, it is of importance that Christianity should be seen to be in harmony with them. That objections to some received views should be valid, and yet that they should be always held up as the objections of infidels, is a mischief to the Christian cause . . . It would be a strange and incredible thing that the Gospel, which at first made war only on the vices of mankind, should now be opposed to one of the highest and rarest of human virtues—the love of truth.

The Christian religion was in a false position when all the tendencies of knowledge were opposed to it; a position, therefore, which could not be maintained for much longer and could only end in the withdrawal of the educated classes from the influences of religion, a state of things which Jowett dreaded the more because he felt it to be approaching. Might it not come to pass 'that in Protestant countries reconciliation is as hopeless as Protestants commonly believe to be the case in Catholic'? But theological reconstruction will have to be founded in a proper knowledge and understanding of the Scriptures, and this means adopting the historical perspective, with all that it entails. The would-be interpreter must set himself to rediscover the original meaning; no easy task, admittedly, but a necessary one if varying interpretations are not to proliferate. This demands historical sympathy, the ability to transfer oneself to another age, 'to imagine that he is a disciple of Christ or Paul' and 'to disengage himself from all that follows'.[1] He should especially be aware of invoking the assumptions and imposing the standards of a later age. Critical procedures must be employed to establish points of date and authorship, and figurative language be taken for what it is and not as if it were that of logical statement. To a presentday reader such stipulations are merely trite, but it should be remembered that in 1860 they certainly were not so. The canon that historical science must work in freedom had first to be secured. What Jowett in particular objected to was the narrowing and hardening of the idea of inspiration into a settled dogma. The word, 'from being used in a general way to express what may be

---

[1] *Essays and Reviews*, p. 408.

called the prophetic spirit of Scripture, has passed within the last two centuries into a sort of technical term'. What inspiration really connotes can be discovered only within the Bible itself, and a valid theory will have to meet the requirements of the historical understanding, the broad principle of which is *Interpret the Scripture like any other book* even though there are many respects in which Scripture is unlike any other book, as a sound interpretation will readily show.

> No other science of Hermeneutics is possible but an inductive one . . . based on the language and thought and narrations of the sacred writers. Fundamentally it is a matter of common sense, and the method creates itself as we proceed. But it has to be borne in mind that the Bible is the only book in the world written in different styles and at many different times, which is in the hands of persons of all degrees of knowledge and education.

Once the general method of serious biblical study has been indicated secondary considerations fall into line. Great tact and insight are required in the interpreter, the most formidable difficulty of all perhaps being to enter into the meaning of the words of Christ himself, 'so gentle, so human, so divine, neither adding to them nor marrying their simplicity'. But any attempt, in the allegorical or typological manner, to unearth hidden and mysterious meanings is misguided. We have no business, under the guise of reverence, to make the Bible mean just what we please. Finally, the interpreter of Scripture will feel as he proceeds 'that the continuous growth of revelation which he traces in the Old and New Testament is a part of a larger whole extending over the earth and reaching to another world.' The outcome of applying the new principles of study will thus inevitably be seen in theology, in which the sort of distinctions made on the basis of the old interpretations must fade away. Not only will doctrines be differently stated and defended, there will be more caution, more reserve than formerly in dealing with doctrinal issues at all.

The whole essay was typical of its author—moderate, critical, but with a deep underlying religious sentiment. 'Much depends on the manner in which things are said . . . There is an aspect of truth which may always be put forward so as to find a way to the hearts of men.' Jowett was himself confident that Christianity could be reconciled with the intellectual demands of a scientific age; but it would be a Christianity a good deal lightened of its theological obesity. The paper nevertheless was his last publication in the theological field. As the years went by he had other more pressing or more congenial concerns to occupy him. But it is probable also that the uproar which the book caused disillusioned him as to at any rate the more immediate prospects of theological liberalism in the established Church. His own belief rested in an 'essential' Christianity, consisting chiefly in the Christian life itself. This, however, could be further qualified as 'the re-enactment within the soul of the life and death of Christ', meaning thereby death to the world and sin and rebirth in a union with God such as Christ himself had known. There exists, besides, an 'absolute' morality to which Plato and the gospel alike bear witness. On the other hand, the souls' immortality may in the end signify no more than a present consciousness of God, whilst even the divine personality could resolve itself simply into an 'idea'. Miracles and metaphysical dogmas will become things of the past. A faith, in any case, built on historical events of untrustworthy report cannot subsist, for 'holiness has its sources elsewhere than in history'. So spoke the older Jowett, though in private; and it is evident that his mind have moved far beyond the acknowledged positions of 1860.

What then of *Essays and Reviews* as a whole? Challenging to conventional religious ideas it was designed to be, but the outcome surpassed even its author's expectations. Dean Church, ever judicious, thought it 'a reckless book' but with 'many good and true things in it'.[1] Time, it has to be said, has entirely vindicated its overall standpoint. The essayists were right in sensing that the difficulties in which orthodox belief seemed likely to founder were in large measure the result of an untenable theory of biblical inspiration. The question of scriptural authority, its nature and its force, had to be faced and to this end the science of historical criticism, applied in the manner already familiar in the German universities, was the necessary instrument. Yet these writers, in some instances, had themselves only imperfectly assimilated the historical spirit and seemed more iconoclastic than they really were. But the book, whatever its faults, was opportune. What it said needed saying. The prevailing theological outlook in Britain, sustained by reactionary influences both High Church

[1] M. C. Church, *The Life of R. W. Church*, p. 155.

and Low, would in Germany have been old-fashioned a generation earlier. But the tendencies of the time were irreversible and had to be met with something more than a cry of dismay. *Essays and Reviews* gave liberalism a place in English theology from which it could not in future be dislodged and might extend a continuously widening influence. This achievement was in the main Jowett's. Lacking his contribution the volume, though little less sensational, would have been also less impressive. Yet behind the seven writers is discernible, too, the broad figure of Coleridge, interpreting dogma in terms of moral and spiritual reality. Williams, Baden Powell—who quotes the famous saying on 'Evidences'— Wilson, Pattison and Jowett himself all reflect the gleams of his luminous intelligence.

3. FURTHER CONTROVERSY: COLENSO ON THE PENTATEUCH

Essays and Reviews attracted public notice only after the appearance of an article relating to it in the October issue of the rather *avant-garde Westminster Review* by one Frederick Harrison, a youngish man of twenty-nine and an agnostic.[1] It was headed 'Neo-Christianity' and its aim was to mock. What, the writer asked, had happened to traditional faith when clergymen in responsible positions could reject most of its basic articles, leaving only (as he put it) 'a revised Atonement, a transcendental Fall, a practical Salvation, and an idealized Damnation'? Such a reduced creed might suffice for learned divines but not for the ordinary man who could never accept that the Bible is 'a medley of late compilers', full of errors and untruths, 'and yet remains withal the Book of Life'. Orthodoxy had been sold from within, a group of eminent 'believers' having given clear proof of their unbelief. Yet these singular apologists, in words addressed to the public at large, presumed to assert that Christian dogma still possessed authority. Harrison's squib had a greater effect than probably he himself expected. The evangelical *Record* took up the cry and denounced the seven writers as 'Septem contra Christum'. The bishop of Oxford, with characteristic verve and self-assurance, responded in *The Quarterly Review* of January 1861. 'It is the doctrine', he pronounced, 'of Tract 90 carried into a new region and development, and goes far beyond it in intellec-

---

[1] He died in 1923, at the age of ninety-one.

tual eccentricity.'[1] The essayists' attempt to combine the advocacy of doctrines so negative with the status and emoluments of Church of England clergymen he repudiated as 'moral dishonesty'. But one telling quip he did get in: 'They believe too much not to believe more, and they disbelieve too much not to disbelieve everything.' Other writers in other periodicals reinforced the bishop's strain. Powell's viewpoint especially, according to a commentator in *The Guardian*, was 'for all practical purposes . . . indistinguishable from atheism'. But not all the discussion was hostile. Stanley, in *The Edinburgh Review* for April 1861, came out manfully against the clamour. The writers, mistakenly or not, had sought to place Christianity 'beyond the reach of accidents', whether of science or of criticism and to rest its claims on 'those moral and spiritual truths which, after all, are what have really won an entrance for it into the heart'. Of his friend Jowett in particular he observed that he stood 'confessedly master of the situation in the eyes of the rising generation of English students and theologians'.

The archbishop of Canterbury was pressed by Samuel Wilberforce to issue a pastoral letter (which he himself had considerately drafted) expressing the disapproval of the entire episcopate. Then Convocation, awake again and vigorous after its one hundred and thirty-five years' quiescence, was also urged to take action, the upper house witnessing the strange alliance of Wilberforce and the *quondam* 'heretic' Hampden in support of threatened faith. Although no immediate censure was adopted, several bishops insisted on carrying matters further, and at length, in June 1864, the bishop of Oxford moved to invite the Lower House to concur with the Upper in the judgment:

> That this Synod, having appointed Committees of the Upper and Lower House to examine and report upon the volume entitled *Essays and Reviews* . . . doth hereby synodically condemn the said volume as containing teaching contrary to the doctrine received by the United Church of England and Ireland, in common with the whole Catholic Church of Christ.

The motion was carried, in a by no means full house, with only two dissentients—Tait, who had concurred in the Privy Council

[1] Ironically H. B. Wilson had been one of the four Oxford tutors who twenty years previously had protested against the liberty of interpretation which the author of that notorious document had in their view so signally abused.

judgment, and Jackson of Lincoln. Thirlwall absented himself.[1] Meanwhile legal action had been taken against two of the contributors, Wilson and Williams, who were indicted for heresy in the Court of Arches, the adverse judgments of which were subsequently reversed, however, by the Judicial Committee of the Privy Council, to the dismay of all conservative churchmen.[2] In giving judgment the Lord Chancellor, Westbury, declared that in matters on which the Church had prescribed no rule 'there is so far freedom of opinion that they may be discussed without penal consequences'; nor did he and his colleagues feel at liberty 'to ascribe to the Church any rule or teaching which we do not find expressly and distinctly stated, or which is not plainly involved in or to be collected from that which is written'.[3] Powell would almost certainly have been prosecuted but for his untimely death. Jowett, at first served with a monition to appear before the vice-chancellor of his university, suffered in the event the more material indignity of being denied a long overdue increase in his professorial salary.[4] Mark Pattison, for his part, did not again fail of his college rectorship, although even his own supporters had serious reservations about his election.[5] But the disappointment of 1851 had done much to poison a nature always prone to feed on its own disillusionment. Eventually the storm passed and Temple—such ever have been the vagaries of preferment in the established Church—lived to become Primate of All England, though not without a lasting sense of embarrassment for his indiscretion in 1860.

Attempts to answer *Essays and Reviews* more constructively than by mere denunciation and legal process were numerous. But the quantity of such apologetic was no guarantee of its effectiveness. The bulk of it was feeble, the two most noteworthy of these publications being composite volumes, the one, edited by William

[1] The voting in the Lower House, with a total membership of 145, was 39 to 16.

[2] The two archbishops, Longley of Canterbury and Thompson of York, and the bishop of London sat as assessors.

[3] High Churchmen and Low Churchmen alike, under the joint leadership—*mirabile dictu*—of Dr Pusey and Lord Shaftesbury, united to protest against it 'for the love of God', an address to the archbishops to that effect being signed by 11,000 clergymen.

[4] The chair of Greek was worth no more than its traditional £40 per annum until the dean and chapter of Christ Church, in September 1865, at last saw fit to raise it to £500.

[5] See V. H. H. Green, *Oxford Common Room*, p. 201. A candid friend wrote to inform Pattison that he could not guess what his (Pattison's) reglion was.

Thompson, then bishop of Gloucester, called *Aids to Faith*, the other, edited by Samuel Wilberforce, simply *Replies to Essays and Reviews*. The former, which contained papers on 'Inspiration' (by Harold Browne, Norrisian professor of divinity at Cambridge) and on 'The Study of the Evidences of Christianity' (by W. L. Fitzgerald, bishop of Cork, Cloyne and Ross)—both of them putting up reasoned arguments on behalf of orthodox positions—was much the better. For the *Replies* was only a poorish effort; the essay by C. A. Heurtley, Lady Margaret professor of divinity at Oxford, defending miracle against Baden Powell's assault, is the strongest in the book; whereas the editor's preface reveals the astonishing fact that the writer had never even read the volume he was so vociferously criticizing. But what is most likely to surprise any modern student of the period who may happen to light upon these long-forgotten apologies, representative as they are of the official, not to say popular, religious outlook of the time, is the all but total failure of the contributors—men eminent in their day—to measure or even recognize the intellectual forces by which the old-fashioned orthodoxy would so soon be shattered. In particular the attitude to the Bible is throughout purely literalist and for these defenders of the faith the advances already achieved in scientific biblical study in Germany might never have been made.[1] The intellectual isolation of English theology at that date could not have been more signally demonstrated.

But even the *Essays and Reviews* affair, coming so soon upon the wonder and dismay occasioned by *The Origin of Species*, did not monopolize the attention of offended orthodoxy during this unhappy decade. Further alarm was caused by the appearance in 1862–63 of the first two parts of a work entitled *The Pentateuch and Book of Joshua Critically Examined*, by John William Colenso, a Cornishman who since 1853 had been bishop of Natal.[2] A former

---

[1] According to Bishop Lee of Manchester 'the very foundations of our faith, the very basis of our hopes, the very nearest and dearest of our consolations are taken from us when one line in that Sacred Volume on which we base everything is declared to be unfaithful or untrustworthy' (See *The Guardian*, 1863, pp. 302, 323). Bishop Christopher Wordsworth, in his contribution to the *Replies*, stated categorically that inspiration means that 'the Bible must be interpreted as a book written by a Being to whom all things are present, and who contemplates all things at once in the panoramic view of his own Omniscience' (p. 456).

[2] The book was not finally completed until 1879. For an account of Colenso's chequered career the reader is referred to P. Hinchcliff, *John William Colenso* (1964) and H. L. Farrer, *The Life of Bishop Gray* (ed. C. N. Gray, 1883).

second wrangler at Cambridge, he had taught mathematics at St John's College and afterwards at Harrow School, when Dr Longley, later archbishop of Canterbury, was headmaster. His *magnum opus* on the Old Testament had been preceded a year earlier by a *Commentary on the Epistle to the Romans*, the unsoundness of which upon the doctrines both of the atonement and of eternal punishment had already seriously disturbed Colenso's metropolitan, Bishop Gray of Cape Town. Colenso, however, was a man of courage reinforced by obstinacy and of honesty unmollified by tact. His views on the Pentateuch, to which contemporary German scholarship lent substance, were quite unprecedented for an English bishop of that time. Indeed it was the abruptness of their presentation which really upset clerical opinion, more even than their positive content, objectionable though this was. He argued that little if any of the Pentateuch as it has come down to us could be assigned to the Mosaic age, that Moses himself was a figure of dubious historicity and that Joshua must be relegated to the realm of legend. He observed, too, that Genesis contains duplicate and incompatible accounts of the creation, deluge and other events, contended that much of the so-called 'Law of Moses' was the work of priests not earlier than the Captivity, whilst the Book of Deuteronomy belonged in fact to the reign of Manasseh in the seventh century B.C., and dismissed Chronicles as a late and tendentious compilation unreliable as history. As for the actual composition of the Pentateuch, the reader was told that Samuel, whom Colenso regards as one of its principal authors, 'appears to have adopted the form of history, based upon the floating legends and traditions of the time, filling up the narrative —as we may believe—perhaps to a large extent out of his own imagination, when those traditions failed him.' Moreover, Colenso had applied his mathematical talent to introduce elaborate arithmetical calculations concerning such things as the measurements of the tabernacle and the camp in the wilderness, the size of armies and the growth of population. The sacred writers' accuracy in these matters was proof, in the bishop's forthright opinion, that the sphere of inspiration is not that of scientific history. Yet neither did he doubt that although the Bible itself, as a literary compilation, is 'not God's Word', that Word could be 'heard in the Bible, by all who will humbly and devoutly listen for it'.

The religious press condemned these utterances with prompt

unanimity as impugning the truth of Holy Writ, always the most sensitive spot in an Englishman's religion. Colenso's own brother-in-law, Bishop M'Dougall of Labuan, read them as an 'attack' upon the Pentateuch and a denial of its inspiration. 'He says, in short, that he can believe in a miracle, but cannot believe in a bad sum and false arithmetical statements; and so he falls foul of the Book of Numbers especially.'[1] The upshot of this new assault upon traditional ideas was, first, the despatch of a letter to Colenso, dated 9 February 1863 and signed by all forty-one English bishops (Thirlwall alone dissenting), advising Colenso to resign his office. His refusal to do so resulted in his being tried by Bishop Gray, a strong Tractarian, in the November of the same year, a process which ended in a sentence of deposition a few weeks later. Having ignored the summons to attend the court, Colenso himself appealed to the Privy Council, whose Judicial Committee, again under Lord Westbury, found that the Bishop of Cape Town had for certain technical reasons no coercive jurisdiction and that the judgment of deposition was therefore null and void in law. Thus despite the sentence of excommunication passed upon him by his metropolitan in December 1865 and the all but total opposition of the clergy of his province and diocese, the bishop of Natal was able to retain the temporalities of his see until his death in 1883, although in the meantime a bishop of Maritzburg had been consecrated by Gray—without the queen's mandate—to succour the needs of a flock which now declined its legal pastor's spiritual ministrations.

Colenso's excursion into biblical criticism had been prompted by the human conditions of the mission-field itself; to the naïve question of Zulu lads, 'Is all that true?' his heart had answered, he said, 'in the words of the Prophet, Shall a man speak lies in the name of the Lord?'; and although it left something to be desired in the way of scholarly finesse it had served a purpose in compelling churchmen to take a more realistic view of the Bible as a historical document. In Jowett's words, set down long after the events of 1865: 'He has made an epoch in criticism by his straightforwardness. No one now talks of verbal inspiration. He was attacked bitterly, but the recollection of the attacks has passed away; the effect of his writings, though they are no longer read, is permanent.'[2]

---

[1] R. T. Davidson and W. Benham, *The Life of Archibald Campbell Tait* (1891), i, pp. 334f.

[2] Abbott and Campbell, *op. cit.*, ii, p. 65.

4. BIBLICAL STUDY AT THE UNIVERSITIES

The initial reaction of public opinion in this country to critical biblical study—the 'higher criticism', as it came to be called—was thus far from favourable. The upshot had been controversy, denunciation by authority and legal prosecution. But the progress of scholarship could not be halted indefinitely. When indignation and fear at last subsided reason resumed its sway. By 1884 Mandell Creighton, in his inaugural address as Dixie professor of ecclesiastical history at Cambridge, could state it virtually as a truism that the traditions of theological learning had been thoroughly leavened by the historical spirit: 'Theology has become historical, and it does not demand that history should become theological.'[1] But the credit for this change of view rests mainly with the small group of scholars sometimes known as the Cambridge school, of whom it has been said that they raised English theology, and particularly English New Testament scholarship, from a condition of intellectual nullity up to the level of the best German work, while they infused into it a characteristic English spirit of caution and sobriety.[2] The three leading figures were those of Brooke Foss Westcott (1825–1901), James Barber Lightfoot (1829–89), and Fenton John Anthony Hort (1828–92). The first two had been at school together at Birmingham under Prince Lee, later bishop of Manchester, the last at Rugby under Tait. Wescott was Regius professor of divinity at Cambridge from 1870 to 1890; Lightfoot held professorships there from 1861 until 1879, when he became bishop of Durham, an office in which Westcott himself was to succeed him; whilst Hort likewise held senior posts in the same university from 1878 till his death. All three had experienced the fecund influence of F. D. Maurice, with his qualities of moderation and depth and his belief in the power of words. None of them aimed at popular appeal, and Westcott had more than a little of the Maurician obscurity. All of them, Hort especially, maintained the strictest standards of scholarly integrity, as they understood it.

In this triumvirate Lightfoot's pre-eminence is that of a historian, a pupil of his, H. C. G. Moule, who too became bishop

---

[1] *Historical Lectures and Addresses*, p. 2.

[2] Hastings Rashdall, *Principles and Precepts*, ed. H. D. A. Major and F. L. Cross (1927), p. 164.

of Durham, testifying in particular to his 'unfailing thoroughness of knowledge and unsurpassable clearness of exposition and instruction'.[1] As a biblical scholar he ranks with the first of his age, but in dogmatic or speculative theology he had slight interest. Indeed Hort considered him 'not speculative enough to be a leader of thought'.[2] His approach was always historical, and even in his New Testament commentaries—*Galatians* appeared in 1865, *Philippians* three years later, and *Colossians* in 1875—he is less reliable when he leaves the terrain of textual and historical criticism for that of exegesis.[3] These books were originally planned as part of a series of New Testament studies in which, in addition to Lightfoot's own work on St Paul, Westcott would deal with the Johannine writings, and Hort with the Synoptic gospels, Acts and the epistles of James, Peter and Jude, although the scheme was not fully carried out owing to the extremely slow rate of production to which Hort's stringent requirements reduced him.[4] The Galatians commentary did more perhaps than anything else to overthrow the theory of F. C. Baur and the Tübingen school, which had assigned most of the New Testament writings to the second century, Lightfoot's procedure resting on a learning no less massive than the Germans' and a caution they had too often disdained. To the Philippians commentary he had appended a long essay on the primitive Christian ministry, in which he expounded the view that the three orders of bishops, priests and deacons emerged only gradually 'as the Church assumed a more settled form, and the higher but temporary offices, such as the apostolate, fell away'; supposing also that it was the diaconate which was first established, followed by the presbyterate (on the model of the Jewish elders), whose members, in the gentile Churches, bore the alternative designation of

---

[1] J. B. Harford and F. C. Macdonald, *Handley C. G. Moule, Bishop of Durham* (1922), p. 19.

[2] A. F. Hort, *Life and Letters of F. J. A. Hort*, ii, 89.

[3] Lightfoot had the prescience of the great scholar. 'If', he wrote, 'we could only recover letters that ordinary people wrote to each other without any thought of being literary, we should have the greatest possible help to the understanding of the New Testament generally' (quoted in G. Milligan, *Selections from the Greek Papyri*, p. xx). The truth of this view has been fully confirmed by discoveries since Lightfoot's day.

[4] The Apocalypse was edited by E. W. Benson, later archbishop of Canterbury and a lifelong friend of both Westcott and Lightfoot, with whom he had been at school at Birmingham.

'bishops'. The subsequent exaltation of a single bishop in each *ecclesia* he thought to have been necessitated by practical require-ments. But Lightfoot's principal achievement was his edition of *The Apostolic Fathers*,[1] a veritable landmark in the history of patristic study. His work on the Ignatian question, in which, after subjecting the whole controversy to a judicious investigation, he pronounced in favour of the seven letters referred to by Eusebius, constitutes his most important contribution to early Church history. But mention is due also of his authoritative article on Eusebius himself in Smith's *Dictionary of Christian Biography*. Five volumes of essays, sermons and notes were pub-lished after his death.[2]

Lightfoot's acceptance of the bishopric of Durham—he had some years previously declined that of Lichfield—was probably a mistake; his true place was the university and had he stayed at Cambridge scholarship would almost certainly have been enriched by further products of his learning.[3] But of his personal dedication to the new and very different work imposed on him by his northern industrial diocese there was never any doubt.

Hort was a scholar in whom great erudition informed a keenly critical intelligence. His own criteria were even more exacting than those of his two colleagues. But the result was a paucity of output that can only be regretted. The work by which he is remembered is, of course, his edition of the New Testament in the original Greek, in which he collaborated with Westcott.[4] The two scholars were able to make use of the immense accumulation of new knowledge which the precursors in this field had by then

---

[1] Part I: *Clement of Rome*, 1890 (this two-volume edition superseded the single-volume edition of 1877); Part II: *Ignatius*, 1885 (3 vols).

[2] Lightfoot also replied, in a series of articles first published in *The Contemporary Review* and later reprinted in book form, to an imposing-seeming work in three volumes and of anonymous authorship which completed publication in 1874 under the title *Supernatural Religion*. He did so less, however, with the intent of refuting its arguments than of exposing its inaccuracies. The writer (subsequently identified as W. R. Cassels) defended a non-miraculous Christianity based on the teaching of Jesus *minus* its Pauline interpretations. He was particularly critical of the rationale of miracle put forward in the Bampton lectures of J. B. Mozley and H. L. Mansel.

[3] As Church remarked: 'To be the foremost teacher of Christian learning at Cambridge at such a time as this is to hold a critical post, which is, in its way, alone and without its fellow, even in the highest places of the Church' (M. C. Church, *op. cit.*, p. 325).

[4] They worked independently, comparing their findings afterwards. See A. F. Hort, *op. cit.*, ii, pp. 243ff.

rendered available, thousands of Greek New Testament manuscripts as well as versions in numerous languages having already
been examined, dated and grouped in 'families'. The outcome of
their own investigations had led them to set aside, first, the bulk
of the readings of later manuscripts as deriving only from a
fourth century Syrian revision and hence worthless for the
reconstruction of the true text; secondly, a number of mainly
'Western' readings found chiefly in Codex Bezae (D) and the Old
Latin and other versions, which they regarded as early but in
general to be attributed to a corruption of the original; and
thirdly, an 'Alexandrian' type of text—one, that is, supported
largely by authors and manuscripts associated with Alexandria—
suspected of over-corruption by scribes in the course of its
transmission, in favour of a 'neutral' text which, although not
actually preserved in any surviving Greek manuscript or version
in its original purity, found its nearest embodiment in the great
Vatican unicial (B) of the fourth century, supported by the Sinai
codex (‫א‬), then at St Petersburg. The Introduction to the work
was from Hort's pen and remains a masterly accomplishment,
whatever the progress in New Testament textual study since his
day. The translators of the *Revised Standard Version* of 1946,
although adopting a more eclectic principle in determining the
text they themselves intended to employ, nevertheless thought it
'really extraordinary' how frequently they concurred in following
in the wake of the earlier scholars.

Hort's range of interests was wide, his intellectual training
having included both classics and natural science. Indeed he
examined in the natural sciences tripos at Cambridge the same
year (1871–72) in which he delivered the Hulsean lectures, *The
Way, the Truth, the Life*.[1] The only work of his to appear during
his lifetime, apart from the Greek New Testament, was his *Two
Dissertations* on the Nicene creed, in which he showed that the
symbol bearing this name was in fact the ancient creed of
Jerusalem as revised by St Cyril, *c.* 360. His other posthumous

[1] Published posthumously in 1908. At one time Hort even thought of replying to
Darwin's *Origin of Species*, not with any aim of rebutting its thesis—as he told Westcott, he was inclined to think it unanswerable, for all its difficulties—but in order to
criticize it on particulars and to supply further illustrations. The scientific question
he deemed 'a very complicated one—far more complicated than Darwin seems to
have any idea' (F. A. Hort, *op. cit.*, i, pp. 415, 433). His project was not realized,
but that he should seriously have entertained it indicates the scope of his learning.

volume comprised a series of lectures delivered in 1888–89 under the title *The Christian Ecclesia* (1897). Himself a High Churchman of sorts, he is concerned here to examine the meaning of the word *ekklesia* in the light of Scripture.[1] The Christian Church originated with the apostolic band as constituted after St Peter's confession, and Hort believes the idea of a universal Ecclesia underlay the application of the term to the local communities, though it was not to be identified with that of the Kingdom of God as such. In any case the 'unit' of the Church is the individual. 'The one Ecclesia includes all members of all partial Ecclesiae; but its relations to them all are direct, not mediate.'[2]

Infinitely painstaking though Hort was, the minutiae of scholarship did not absorb his whole attention, the 'attainment of truth in matters of historical or linguistic fact' being, he held, 'always not an end but a means'.[3] Caution, however, was of his very nature. He declined an invitation to contribute to *Essays and Reviews* on the grounds that

> at present very many orthodox but rational men are being unawares acted on by influences which will assuredly bear fruit in due time, if the process is allowed to go quietly; but I cannot help feeling that a premature crisis would frighten many back into the merest traditionalism. And as a mere matter of prudence, it seems to me questionable to set up a broad conspicuous target for the Philistines to shoot at, unless there is some very decided advantage to be gained.

All the same, when the volume was published he judged its authors 'to believe very much more of truth than their (so-called) orthodox opponents, and to be incomparably greater lovers of truth'; and he wholly deplored 'the violent and indiscriminate agitation' directed against it and of any resultant official policy that might 'deter men of thought and learning from entering the ministry of the Church' or 'impel generous minds into antagonism to the Christian faith'.[4] For his part he averred to havin 'ag strong sense of the Divine purpose, guiding all the parts of the New Test-

---

[1] 'I have', he confessed, 'a deeply rooted agreement with High Churchmen as to the Church, ministry and Sacraments' (A. F. Hort, *op. cit.*, i, p. 400). All three scholars had begun their careers as Evangelicals. But Westcott became critical of Evangelicalism, and Hort, who considered its characteristic doctrines 'perverted rather than untrue', liked to speak of himself as 'a staunch sacerdotalist', in contrast with Lightfoot (*ibid.*, ii, p. 86).

[2] *The Christian Ecclesia*, p. 168.

[3] *A. F. Hort, op. cit.*, ii, pp. 53f.

[4] *Ibid.*, i, 400, pp. 428f.

ament', but could not see 'how the exact limits of such guidance can be ascertained except by unbiased *a posteriori* criticism'.[1]

Hort contributed largely to the making of the Revised Version of the Bible. He attended meetings of the Revisers' committee regularly over ten years and was an unfailing source of exact and detailed information. For the New Testament, however, the committee did not adopt the Westcott–Hort text outright, paying greater regard to the *textus receptus* than the two Cambridge scholars would themselves have wished. Even so the result, published in May 1881,[2] was not pleasing to the conservative, as was shown by Dean Burgon's attack on it in *The Quarterly Review*. Although the Revisers' aim had been to produce a version which would be 'alike literal and idiomatic, faithful to each thought of the original, and yet in the expression of it harmonious and free', it was criticized, perhaps inevitably when compared with the Authorized Version of 1611, on grounds of style. But in accuracy it was much the superior, the marginal readings being especially valuable, and it served its purpose well until at length displaced by the *Revised Standard Version*, based as that is on wider knowledge.[3]

The mention of Westcott's name brings us to the member of the Cambridge group who was most in touch with the general public and able thus to exercise a broader influence, although purely as a scholar he is less impressive than the others. His work in the field of primitive Christianity lacks the qualities which have perpetuated Lightfoot's, and he had not Hort's critical acumen. immensely conscientious, he was over-conservative and in interpreting the Greek built too much on existing knowledge, which he was apt to consider final. And he was without the truly great scholar's foresight of future possibilities. But as a theologian he had depth and imaginative force, if not always clarity.[4] As a

---

[1] *Ibid.*, i, p. 420.

[2] The Old Testament translation did not appear until May 1885, and that of the Apocrypha not until 1896.

[3] It is arguable that the whole undertaking was at the time premature. Armitage Robinson considered it to have been made a generation too soon. See G. R. Eden and F. C. Macdonald (edd.), *Lightfoot of Durham* (1932), p. 126, and cp. A. F. Hort, *op. cit.*, ii, p. 128.

[4] E. W. Benson found his manner 'at once bewildering and fatiguing' (A. C. Benson, *The Leaves of the Tree*, p. 125). Westcott said himself that 'to some I am a cloud; and I do not see how to help it' (A. Westcott, *The Life and Letters of Brooke Foss Westcott* (1903), ii, p. 24).

preacher he was among the most powerful of his day,[1] whilst his activities in the sphere of social and industrial problems won him national fame.[2] He was essentially a religious leader, with a strong mystical bent, if the word be taken in its popular sense, although he personally disliked it.[3] His principal theological writings, apart from his commentaries on the fourth gospel (1881) and the Johannine epistles (1883) and on Hebrews (1889) and Ephesians (1906), are the three volumes: *Religious Thought in the West* (1891), a collection of essays which includes two of special note, 'Origen and the Beginnings of Religious Philosophy' and 'Benjamin Whichcote'—the latter, a study of the Cambridge Platonist, being particularly characteristic; *The Gospel of Life* (1892), an outline of Christian doctrine and his nearest attempt at a systematic theology; and the Westminster Abbey sermons of 1885–86 which make up *Christus Consummator: Some Aspects of the Work and Person of Christ in Relation to Modern Thought* (1886). His concern for social questions is shown in *Social Aspects of Christianity* (1887) and *The Incarnation and the Common Life* (1893).

Religious faith Westcott saw as ultimately a matter of insight, a 'mystical' apprehension of those 'eternal realities which lie beneath and beyond the changeful shows of life'.[4] Certainly 'if we try to establish by argument the existence of a spiritual Being whom we may reverence and love, our intellectual proofs break down'. On the contrary, 'the Being to which they guide us is less than the Being for whom we look and in whom we trust'.[5] Science and history are lavish sources of purely human knowledge, but only revelation will add 'that element of infinity' which gives 'characteristic permanence to every work and thought',[6] although it is knowledge which supplies the material that faith uses. 'If we go back to the three fundamental conceptions, self, the world, God, we shall notice one feature that is common

[1] But not the most illuminating. Rather, it has been said, 'his words moved you strangely, because they moved him' (G. R. Eden, *Great Christians*, ed. R. S. Forman (1933), p. 578. Cp. H. Scott Holland, *Personal Studies* (1905), p. 132).
[2] See appended Note to Chapter XIII below.
[3] 'I don't think', he once wrote, 'I have ever used the word 'mystics'; it is so hopelessly vague, and it suggests an esoteric teaching which is wholly foreign to the Christian. But from Cambridge days I have read the writings of many who are called mystics with much profit' (A. Westcott, *op. cit.*, ii, p. 309).
[4] *Christian Aspects of Life* (1897), p. 201.
[5] *The Gospel of Life*, p. 34.
[6] *Ibid.*, p. 89.

to them. In fashioning each we enter the future and the unseen, and act without hesitation on the conclusions which we have formed.' Hence experience itself compels us to look beyond experience. When Westcott quotes Whichcote, that 'reason is not laid aside nor discharged, much less is it confounded by any of the materials of religion, but awakened, excited, employed, directed, and improved by it; for the understanding is that faculty whereby man is made capable of God and apprehensive of Him',[1] he is stating a presiding truth of his own mind.

In his theological sympathies Westcott, like Maurice and unlike the Tractarians, was much more a Greek than a Latin, as is clearly brought out in the essays on Origen and Dionysius the Areopagite.[2] Origen, in contrast with Augustine, stood 'in the meeting-place of struggling thoughts' and knew that 'he had that to speak which could harmonize and satisfy every spiritual aspiration of man: an answer to the despair of the West, which saw in man's good an unattainable ideal; an answer to the despair of the East, which saw in man's way a vain delusion'. Augustine, on the other hand, faced with the barbarian invasions, 'was called upon to pronounce sentence on the old world, and to vindicate Christianity from the charge of social disintegration. One was the interpreter of a universal hope; the other was the interpreter of a secular overthrow'.[3] It was not too much indeed to say that a work remained for Greek divinity in the nineteenth century hardly less pregnant with results than that wrought by the Greek classics in the fifteenth.

Revelation Westcott held to be in its essence absolute but in its human apprehension relative.[4] That it should thus be both might appear inconsistent; but the answer to the problem lies in the special nature of the incarnation, which has the resurrection for its culmination. 'Since we have to consider a final revelation given to man . . . such a revelation must come through a true human

[1] *Sermons*, iii, pp. 17f. See *Religious Thought in the West*, p. 383.

[2] *Religious Thought in the West*, pp. 142–252. Tractarian theology carried a markedly Augustinian strain, while its doctrine of the Church was Cyprianic. Hort observed that 'the total absence of any specific influence of Greek theology upon the Oxford Movement, notwithstanding the extensive reading in the Fathers possessed by its more learned chiefs, is a very striking fact' (A. F. Hort, *op. cit.*, ii, p. 38). See D. Newsome, *Bishop Westcott and the Platonic Tradition* (Bishop Westcott Memorial Lecture, 1968).

[3] *Religious Thought in the West*, p. 249.

[4] *The Gospel of Life*, p. xxiii.

life.' But the Son of man was also Son of God. 'The Incarnation and the Resurrection reconcile the two characteristics of our faith—they establish the right of Christianity to be called historical, they establish its right to be called absolute.' These twin mysteries furnish the basis for a spiritual religion which is also intensely human, one which 'at every moment introduces the infinite and the unseen into a vital connection with the things of earth'. This last phrase is significant. Westcott's 'incarnationalist' theology, like Charles Gore's later, provided, if not the immediate stimulus, at least the ultimate rationale of his Christian socialism. 'The Incarnation', he wrote, 'binds all action, all experience, all creation to God; and supplies at once the motive and the power of service.'[1]

As with Maurice so with Westcott, the gospel proclaims the unity—actual, not merely potential—of the whole of humanity in Christ; and the consequent solidarity of man and man entails a mutual obligation. Somewhat surprisingly, it was this aspect of Auguste Comte's system which led him to regard positivism with a measure of sympathy.[2] At all events it brought to notice features of Christian truth more or less hidden since the eclipse of Greek theology by Latin, and in its way was itself a testimony to Christianity. The great difference of course was that the latter 'does not pause where Positivism pauses, in the visible order'.[3] Westcott was also deeply impressed by Maurice's *Social Morality*, as he acknowledged in the preface to his own *Social Aspects of Christianity*.[4] His view of socialism, moreover, was, like Maurice's, ethical rather than political: socialism was the antidote to individualism, the principle of self-interest. 'Individualism regards humanity as made up of disconnected or warring atoms; Socialism regards it as an organic whole, a vital unity formed by the combination of contributory members mutually interdependent.[5] But anything in

[1] *Ibid.*, p. xxi.

[2] See the articles by Westcott in *The Contemporary Review*, December 1867 and July 1868. The second of these was re-published as an appendix to *The Gospel of the Resurrection* (7th ed, pp. 249–76).

[3] *The Gospel of the Resurrection* (18—), p. 273. 'Comte's view of Humanity as organic outweighed his agnosticism, in Westcott's mind' (C. E. Osborne, *Christian Ideas of Political History*, p. 264).

[4] Westcott's admiration for Maurice grew with the years, although he himself scarcely realized the degree of affinity between his own thinking and Maurice's until he read the latter's *Life*. Cp. A. Westcott, *op. cit.*, ii, p. 160. See also J. Clayton, *Bishop Westcott* (1906), with an appendix by Llewelyn Davies, and above, p. 214.

[5] See his 1890 (Hull) Church Congress paper, reprinted in *The Incarnation and the Common Life*, pp. 223–47.

the nature of a revolutionary ideology, or even political radicalism, was totally at variance with his cautious, aloof and fundamentally conservative nature.[1]

The new critical approach to the understanding of early Christianity, especially in relation to its pagan environment, was well exemplified in the work of a scholar who seems never to have won quite the recognition, at least in England, which his merits warranted: Edwin Hatch (1835–89), reader in ecclesiastical history and fellow of Pembroke College, Oxford. A man of very independent views, whom Sanday considered to be 'bolder and more disinterested than even the great Cambridge trio', he was probably too much of a liberal for most churchmen of his time. He wrote a good deal, his most permanent achievement being a *Concordance to the Septuagint*, completed by H. A. Redpath after his death.[2] But the volumes which aroused the widest interest were two sets of lectures, his Bamptons on *The Organization of the Early Christian Church* (1881), which attracted attention in Germany and were translated into German by Harnack in 1883, and the still more controversial Hibberts on *The Influence of Greek Ideas on Christianity* (1889).[3] The thesis of the latter is that the gospel, largely identified with the Sermon on the Mount, had been transformed under the influence of Greek speculative thought from a way of life into a body of *credenda*.

> The Nicene Creed is a statement partly of historical facts and partly of dogmatic inferences; the metaphysical terms which it contains would probably have been unintelligible to the first disciples; ethics have no place in it. The one belongs to a world of Syrian peasants, the other to a world of Greek philosophers.[4]

It was in fact precisely the argument for which Harnack supplied massive documentation in his *Dogmengeschichte*, in the preface to the English version of which he referred to the Oxford

---

[1] As President of the Christian Social Union, founded by Scott Holland and others in 1889, he declared: 'The Union affirms a principle, enforces an obligation, confesses a Divine Presence. It has no programme of immediate reforms' (*Christian Aspects of Life*, p. 252).

[2] His *Essays in Biblical Greek* came out in 1889.

[3] Edited by A. M. Fairbairn. A German edition by E. Preuschl, with additions by Harnack, was published in 1892. The original English edition by F. C. Grant, was reprinted in 1957.

[4] *The Influence of Greek Ideas on Christianity*, p. 1.

scholar's work as already giving 'the most ample proof of the conception of the early history of dogma which is set forth in the following pages'. Hatch's conclusion was that since the Hellenistic influence had introduced into Christianity Greek rhetoric, logic and metaphysics, 'a large part of what are sometimes called Christian doctrines, and many usages which have prevailed and continue to prevail in the Christian Church, are in their essence Greek still'.[1] But the fact posed a question, namely the relation of these Greek elements in Christianity to the nature of Christianity itself. Was what was absent from the religion in its primitive form non-essential, or was it the duty of each succeeding age at once to accept the developments of the past, and to do its part in bringing on the developments of the future?

After Hatch's death the pre-eminent figure in Oxford New Testament scholarship was William Sanday (1843–1920), at first Dean Ireland's professor at Oriel and then, from 1895, Lady Margaret professor at Christ Church. Over the years his view changed from conservative to moderate liberal, and he later—in 1914—was to join issue with Bishop Gore on the right of the 'Modernist' cleric to minister in the Church of England, claiming that what he called 'a sound and right Modernism' was entirely permissible: 'The Saviour of mankind extends His arms towards the cultivated modern man just as He does towards the simple believer.'[2] The bulk of Sanday's publications belongs to the early years of the present century and includes principally his article on the life of Christ in Hastings' *Dictionary of the Bible*,[3] reprinted in volume form in 1907 as *The Life of Christ in Recent Research*, and the lectures which he delivered in 1904 at Union Theological Seminary, New York, and subsequently published as *The Criticism of the Fourth Gospel*. In the latter he confessed to having to part company with those younger critics, German and French, who (as he thought) approached the critical problem of the fourth gospel with a 'reduced' conception of Christianity akin to ancient Ebionism or Arianism and so automatically ruled out the gospel either as a dogmatic authority or as a record of historical events.[4] But the work which properly falls within our period and which

[1] *Ibid.*, p. 350.

[2] *Bishop Gore's Challenge to Criticism* (1914), pp. 30f.

[3] Hastings' *Dictionary* started publication in 1898 and the whole enterprise was completed six years later. Its standpoint was a temperate conservatism.

[4] *The Criticism of the Fourth Gospel* (1905), p. 29.

established its author's reputation as a teacher as well as a scholar is the Bampton lectures on *Inspiration*, published in 1893. In this Sanday aims to show wherein, granting modern critical assumptions and methods, the spiritual authority of the Bible still lies. That the application of such methods has led to some negative results he admits, but the Bible's authority derives from its 'inspiration', a term, therefore, whose proper meaning it is all-important to examine. The traditional view, that Scripture as a whole and in all its parts is the Word of God, quickly leads to the notion of inspiration as 'something dead and mechanical'. Criticism, on the other hand, leaves room for an 'inductive' theory, based on an attempt to investigate the consciousness of the biblical writers themselves. Yet the measure of inspiration is eventually more than this: the isolated efforts gravitate towards a common goal and form part of a larger scheme. 'We may study the operations not only of these individual minds but of the central Mind',[1] that 'Higher Providence' the workings of which are detected, for example, in the writing down of prophetic utterances in the Old Testament or the preservation of occasional letters in the New so as to provide a basis for Christian theology. Also to be noted is the 'Law of Parsimony' by which all revelation is adjusted to the condition of its recipients. The 'All or Nothing' idea—that the Bible's inspiration is either 'verbal' or else non-existent—is a wholly false antithesis. Inspiration is real, but it has to be sought and tested by the means under which all truth is realized.

Old Testament studies in Oxford had been retarded rather than promoted by the occupant of the chair of Hebrew, Dr Pusey, who throughout his long career had maintained an unbudging traditionalism. Thus his massive commentary on *Daniel* (1863), as a serious study of its subject, is now negligible. But his successor, S. R. Driver (1846–1914), who understood and accepted the main positions adopted by the best continental scholarship, soon swept away the accumulated dust and established himself, with his *Introduction to the Literature of the Old Testament*, as the foremost authority in England in this domain. And with him must be placed T. K. Cheyne (1841–1915), a man, however, of far less critical reserve who, as his later work proves—especially his Bampton lectures of 1891 on *The Historical Origin and Religious*

[1] *Inspiration*, p. 402.

Ideas of the Psalter and the articles contributed by him to his own *Encyclopaedia Biblica* (1899–1903)—was prepared to travel as far as current radicalism would take him. In Cambridge Westcott had been succeeded in the Regius professorship by H. B. Swete (1835–1917), a biblical scholar of a generally conservative outlook and now remembered chiefly for his work on the text of the Septuagint and for his resourcefulness in organizing the studies of other people.[1]

Thus in the forty years that had elapsed since the publication of *Essays and Reviews* a great change had been wrought in the attitude of at any rate the theologically educated towards what had hitherto been a sacrosanct authority, the only ground and standard of true religion. Suggestions of a more discerning approach to the Bible and its problems had here and there been voiced earlier, though with little positive result, having for the most part been scouted as 'German rationalism'. But *Essays and Reviews* had thrown down a challenge that could no longer be ignored. Interpret the Scripture, Jowett had said, like any other book, and the task of doing so was henceforth gradually to be assumed, if with reluctance and caution. The outcome was a view of the Bible in its historical setting as a highly diversified collection of ancient writings from many different hands and periods. The 'Higher Criticism' did not trench directly upon dogmatic questions—its field of interest was simply that of objective historical inquiry—but its concern with the human conditions under which divine revelation has been received almost inevitably gave rise to misgivings about the extent to which the divine might on the critics' own showing turn out to be the all too human. This indeed had been precisely its effect on the French Catholic, Ernest Renan. But in English Protestantism, traditionalist though it was, compromise proved easier than in Catholicism, and by the close of the century theology had found means of coming to terms with criticism and even of welcoming it for the new light it could be claimed to have shed on the nature and course of divine revelation itself. Nor did the historical study of the Bible foreclose the question of its inspiration; it only suggested that what was inspired was not so much writings as writers. Yet the truth could hardly be hidden that the dogmatic systems

---

[1] It was largely through Swete's enterprise that *The Journal of Theological Studies* was founded in 1899.

inherited from the past had been built upon entirely different presuppositions from those which the modern critical scholar entertains. How far then would such systems continue to stand after their foundations had shifted? And when once it was acknowledged that the hope of salvation is in part at least a projection of human longing what further qualifications of it might not in the end prove necessary? These were questions to which varying answers were already being given. But one thing seemed plain: the old certitude was no more. The authority of the Bible itself had to be explained and defended. Theology, in becoming more liberal, was sapping the assurance of faith.

Chapter XI

Literature and Dogma

I. THE POETS

To appreciate fully the Victorians' concern over the problem of religious belief one must look beyond the theologians and philosophers to the writers of imaginative literature, to the poets and novelists of the age. In an epoch when the Christian creed is still very largely taken for granted explicit reference to it by authors whose purpose is not directly religious and didactic is rare. The literature belonging to the early part of our period is of such a kind. Dickens and Thackeray, like Fielding or Miss Austen before them, although they might lampoon certain types of demonstrative religiosity, evince no theological curiosity and to all showing accept Christianity, as to both its doctrines and its moral principles, without question. With the writers of the next generation, however, it is otherwise. In the mid-century and after, Tennyson and Browning, Matthew Arnold and Arthur Hugh Clough, George Eliot and George Meredith, as, finally, Thomas Hardy and Mrs Humphrey Ward—the latter admittedly at a much lower level of imaginative evocation—are all acutely aware that religious faith, at least in its traditional form, constitutes a grave problem. They question and they doubt, and in varying degrees worry about their doubts and questionings. At the same time an attitude of mere secular indifference is also unusual: to criticize religion is obviously not to ignore it. But the nineteenth century, far more than any preceding era, was making belief in Christianity increasingly difficult for the intellectually sensitive. To some indeed unbelief itself had become a moral necessity.

The Victorian age saw the novel attain its maturity. Although in the main it lacked sophistication as an art form, it had the advantage over verse and even the prose drama in its capacity to depict the manifold actuality of life. But its function as a medium for the informed presentation of moral and social issues was of somewhat tardy growth and at first its role was simply to entertain, without any *arrière-pensée*. On the other hand the use of poetry for the higher ends of edification was both recognized and demanded. The poet, accordingly, was also a prophet, even if in the eyes of the orthodox he might turn out to be a false one, preaching strange doctrine. For many, throughout a great part of the century, this prophetic function was most signally discharged by Wordsworth. The Wordsworthian faith in Nature, with its assurance of a 'central peace subsisting at the heart of endless agitation' could, it was found, sustain the spirit in an 'iron time' when science and industrialism seemed to be turning the dogmas of institutional religion into a meaningless anachronism. Thus typically of those who now looked to Wordsworth for spiritual consolation, William Hale White, in *The Autobiography of Mark Rutherford*, could write that the poet's 'real God is not the God of the Church, but the God of the hills, the abstraction Nature, and to this my reverence was transferred. Instead of an object of worship which was altogether artificial, remote, never coming into genuine contact with me, I had now one which I thought to be real, one in which literally I could live and move and have my being, all actual fact present before my eyes'. Wordsworth, he continues, 'unconsciously did for me what every religious reformer has done—he recreated my Supreme Divinity; substituting a new and living spirit for the old deity, once alive but now hardened into an idol'. It was all the more embarrassing, therefore, to Wordsworth's agnostic admirers when in later life he aligned himself openly with orthodox Christianity as taught by the Church of England. Yet the poet's religious development was a slow and even tortuous process, starting in the Anglicanism of his early upbringing and passing through Godwinian rationalism —Coleridge thought him 'at least a semi-atheist' while under Godwin's spell—and the nature mysticism of his poetic prime, before returning to a sincerely confessed belief in God's 'pure word by miracle revealed'.

The question is how far, during the great period of his creativity, did Wordsworth depart from a basically orthodox creed. It is hard to believe that his return to orthodoxy followed immediately on his disillusionment with the Godwinian doctrines, and that that

> . . . sense sublime
> Of something far more deeply interfused

of which he speaks so movingly in *Tintern Abbey* was only a way of describing his restored belief in Christian theism. Later indeed the charge of 'Spinosism' was apt to nettle him and he denied that there was anything 'of this kind in the *Excursion*'. But the poems of earlier date, from *Tintern Abbey* to the *Ode on Immortality*, disclose nothing that could be identified with a distinctively Christian conviction. It is not simply that they do not allude to the central dogmas of the faith, but that the whole attitude of mind expressed in them is quite different from the Christian. The medium of revelation of the spirit

> . . . that impels
> All thinking things, all objects of all thought,
> And rolls through all things

is nature alone. A religious truth imparted through unique historical persons and events has no relevant place in a mysticism of this sort, resting as it does on visionary insight, when

> What we see of forms and images
> Which float along our minds, and what we feel
> Of active or recognizable thought,
> Prospectiveness, or intellect, or will,
> Not only is not worthy to be deemed
> Our being, to be prized as what we are,
> But is the very littleness of life.

Such consciousness the poet could then

> . . . deem but accidents,
> Relapses from the one interior life
> That lives in all things.

By this interior life man had mystical communion, through the natural world, with the all-pervading spirit of the universe. For

> . . . whether we be young or old,
> Our destiny, our being's heart and home
> Is with infinitude, and only there.

This, then, was the faith which spoke so powerfully to the typical Victorian doubter, consoling him for the loss of his traditional convictions. Thus, when Mark Rutherford tells of the change wrought in him by his reading of the *Lyrical Ballads* as only comparable with that wrought in St Paul when confronted with 'the Divine apparition'[1] the reference is appropriately religious; although Matthew Arnold, himself a devout Wordsworthian, also warned his readers to be on their guard against 'the exhibitors and extollers of a scientific system of thought in Wordworth, the poet's cast of mind not being scientific or even systematic. What he had to offer was a potent religious *feeling*, at odds alike with rationalism and industrialism, but unencumbered with impossible *credenda*. Eventually, however, Wordsworth himself came to look for something more in religion. The 'power of solitude' had ceased to be self-sufficing and he once again felt the need of the fellowship of believers and the traditional institutions of the historic faith. It was a change of mind which the literary critics have generally united in deploring. No doubt with reason, for his increasingly rigid conservatism in religion as in politics was attended by a commensurate decline in poetic inspiration: it was not the errant imagination but an assiduous study of church history which was the generative force behind *Ecclesiastical Sonnets*. And the 1840 revision of *The Prelude* shows a consistent attempt to expunge any trace of the regrettable 'Spinosism' of his earlier years.

Wordsworth's successor in the laureateship was Alfred Tennyson, *In Memoriam* having appeared on the eve of his appointment to the office. The poem was the outcome of seventeen years of brooding on the death of his friend Arthur Hallam. Yet it is not only an elegy, an expression—the finest, possibly, of its kind in English—of a profound personal grief, but a philosophy of life and death in verse. To the public of the day it appealed strongly, on both counts, and is the basis of the author's claim to be regarded seriously as a thinker. Certainly he proves himself, for a layman, unusually well informed on scientific matters. Astronomy had been an early love of his, and Laplace's nebular theory had already found mention in *The Princess*:

[1] *Autobiography*, pp. 18–21.

> This world was once a fluid haze of light,
> Till toward the centre set the starry tides,
> And eddied into suns, that wheeling cast
> The planets: then the monster, then the man.

More interesting, however, are the poet's anticipations of Darwin. *The Palace of Art* (1832) had once included among its later excised stanzas the following:

> 'From shape to shape at first within the womb
> The brain is moulded', she began.
> 'And thro' all phases of all thought I come
> Unto the perfect man.
> All nature widens upward. Evermore
> The simple essence lower lies,
> More complex is more perfect, owning more
> Discourse, more widely wise.[1]

Lyell's *Principles of Geology* had been closely studied, the sound of streams, for example, suggesting to the poet how they

> Draw down Aeonian hills, and sow
> The dust of continents to be.

Other reading comprised Herschel's *Preliminary Discourse on the Study of Natural Philosophy* (1830) and the anonymous *Vestiges of the Natural History of Creation*. The latter in particular would seem to have furnished material for *In Memoriam*, although it is not unlikely that Tennyson's own grasp of the evolutionary principle in biology antedated Chambers's best-selling book.[2] Thus whereas to so many *The Origin of Species*, on its first publication, brought only astonishment and dismay, the poet was already facing the possible implications for a spiritual faith of the concept of a Nature bleakly indifferent to all human values, and for an appreciation of the arguments of *In Memoriam* the extent of Tennyson's reflections on the problems which science was more and more pressing upon the consideration of the religious believer must be recognized. The poetic form which such reflections took comprise, of course, some of the best-known stanzas in the whole work.

[1] Quoted in Hallam, Lord Tennyson's *Memoir* of the poet (1899 ed), p. 101.
[2] *Ibid.*, p. 186.

Are God and Nature then at strife,
   That Nature lends such evil dreams?
   So careful of the type she seems,
So careless of the single life;

That I, considering everywhere
   Her secret meaning in her deeds,
   And finding that of fifty seeds
She often brings but one to bear,

I falter where I firmly trod,
   And falling with my weight of cares
   Upon the great world's altar-stairs
That slope thro' darkness up to God,

I stretch lame hands of faith, and grope,
   And gather dust and chaff, and call
   To what I feel is Lord of all,
And faintly trust the larger hope.

       *   *   *

'So careful of the type?' but no.
   From scarped cliff and quarried stone
   She cries, 'A thousand types are gone:
I care for nothing, all shall go.

'Thou makest thine appeal to me;
   I bring to life, I bring to death:
   The spirit does but mean the breath:
I know no more.' And he, shall he,

Man, her last work, who seem'd so fair,
   Such splendid purpose in his eyes,
   Who roll'd the psalm to wintry skies,
Who built him fanes of fruitless prayer,

Who trusted God was love indeed
   And love Creation's final law—
   Tho' Nature, red in tooth and claw
With ravine, shriek'd against his creed—

Who lov'd, who suffer'd countless ills,
   Who battl'd for the True, the Just,
   Be blown about the desert dust,
Or seal'd within the iron hills?

> No more? A monster, then, a dream,
> A discord. Dragons of the prime,
> That tare each other in their slime,
> Were mellow music match'd with him.
>
> O life as futile, then, as frail!
> O for thy voice to soothe and bless!
> What hope of answer, or redress?
> Behind the veil, behind the veil?

In Memoriam is the utterance of a mind torn by doubt of whether life has any moral meaning whatsoever; a doubt made all the heavier by the sorrow of a desolating bereavement. Any death could raise the same question, but the death at the pathetically early age of twenty-two of a man of great promise whom Tennyson loved with a rare intensity rendered it inescapable. The poet felt himself like 'an infant crying in the night'. To his bitter personal problem there seemed no answer—none assuredly in the commonly accepted creed. Yet in the long course of his meditations he gropingly finds an answer. It is not the full Christian answer by any means, despite the apparent confidence of the famous opening stanzas. For *In Memoriam*, although Tennyson's contemporaries were pleased to read it as such, is not a Christian poem and the questions which the poet wrestles with, under the crushing weight of his own near despair, are questions of basic import. The issue is not whether the Christian doctrine is true, or generally acceptable as true—the debate of the liberal theologians —but whether existence will admit of any spiritual interpretation at all, whether there is any possible assurance

> That nothing walks with aimless feet;
> That not one life shall be destroy'd,
> Or cast as rubbish to the void,
> When God hath made the pile complete.

In the end the poet follows the beckonings of his own heart rather than linger with the cold misgivings of reason:

> If e'er when faith had fall'n asleep,
> I heard a voice 'Believe no more'
> And heard an ever-breaking shore
> That tumbl'd in the godless deep;

> A warmth within the breast would melt
>   The freezing reason's colder part,
>   And like a man in wrath the heart
> Stood up and answer'd 'I have felt.'

But one notes how the poet clings to the truth of his experience when he adds:

> No, like a child in doubt and fear,
>   Then was I as a child that cries,
>   But crying knows his father near . . .

Hence the only positive conclusion, painfully reached, was that

> What I am beheld again
>   What is, and no man understands;
>   And out of darkness came the hands
> That reach thro' Nature, moulding man.

No doubt even with this expression of faith, hard won though it was, the mid-nineteenth century public was satisfied, and the poet's evident assurance gave his work a large measure of its popularity. It helped indeed to reassure his readers. Yet it is a good deal less a poem of belief than of scepticism, and in this respect was a mirror to its times. Such is brought out clearly in a letter of Henry Sidgwick to Hallam, Lord Tennyson, when the latter was preparing the *Memoir* of his father. The poem moved him, Sidgwick said, by its disclosure of a region deeper than the differences between theism and Christianity, a region where agnosticism and faith finally confront each other. With the passing of the years this great issue had become acute. The freedom of thought for which, in the 1860s, he and others had fought had not brought with it any well-reasoned confidence.

It brings us face to face with atheistic science; the faith in God and Immortality, which we had been struggling to clear from superstition, suddenly seems to be *in the air*: and in seeking for a firm basis for this faith we find ourselves in the midst of the 'fight with death' which *In Memoriam* so powerfully presents.

What the poem did for him in this struggle was to strengthen 'the ineffaceable and ineradicable conviction that *humanity* will not and cannot acquiesce in a godless world: the "man in men" will not do this, whatever individual men may do'.[1] And here surely is where the poem's value lies—apart, that is, from the beauty of its visual imagery and the music of its verse. Although there was little enough of the academic philosopher or theologian in Tennyson he was a man genuinely religious by nature, and it was the conflict within him between his longing for a viable faith and the growing doubts to which he and his age were prey that gave the work an appeal far beyond the pathos of the actual circumstances in which it originated. The doubt itself is the thing, and the well-known Prologue fails to carry conviction through its own over-assertion. Whatever in the outcome Tennyson may have found, it was nearer to the vague, uncertain 'Power in darkness whom we guess' than to the 'Strong Son of God, immortal Love' of the Christian doctrinal tradition. As R. H. Hutton observed, 'the lines of [Tennyson's] theology were in harmony with the great central lines of Christian thought; but in coming down to detail it soon passed into a region where all was wistful, and dogma disappeared in a haze of radiant twilight'.[2]

Tennyson's religious attitude is, then, one of faith riddled by doubt. Robert Browning, that other poetic idol of the Victorian reading public, was possessed of a very different temperament, extroverted and naturally sanguine. He was more disposed, therefore, to trust his reason to yield positive conclusions. He was also better read than Tennyson in the general literature of the day and certainly more conversant with the theological. Too much has been made of a line in *Pippa Passes*, lifted out of its context; Browning's optimism was not so crass. But he was nonetheless confident that God *is* in his heaven and that in the final assessment all must be well with the world, a belief he retained from his nonconformist upbringing. Indeed as a young man he was 'passionately religious', according to Dowden, although his verse hardly conveys the impression of personal religious feeling. He later outgrew the narrowness of early Victorian dissent, which could scarcely have fostered sympathy with such diverse human types as he portrays in his verse. Yet his sympathies did not extend to Anglican ritualism and he rather arrogantly dismisses Puseyism as 'a kind of child's play

---

[1] See *Enoch Arden and In Memoriam*, ed. Hallam, Lord Tennyson (1908), pp. 200f.
[2] *Aspects of Religious and Scientific Thought* (ed. E. M. Roscoe, 1899), p. 408.

which unfortunately had religion for its object'.[1] His knowledge
of the Bible was considerable, as *Saul* and *A Death in the Desert*
testify; but as he grew older dogmatic Christianity meant less and
less to him, his own religion assuming—to cite Dowden again—
'the non-historical form of a Humanitarian Theism courageously
accepted, not as an account of the Unknowable, but as the best
provisional conception which we are competent to form'.[2] The
poem most readily comparable with *In Memoriam* in its subject-
matter is *La Saisiaz*, published in 1878, commemorating a friend
who died suddenly while staying with the Brownings at a villa
(called La Saisiaz) near Geneva. The author's direct concern here
is with the questions of God, the soul and the life hereafter. The
first part tells the story, the rest unfolds the argument. 'Was
ending ending once and always, when you died?', he asks himself,
and the reply he gives follows not church teachings but his own
reasoning. The existence of God and the soul he postulates, but
submits that if consciousness ends with physical death then life
presents a baffling problem. Assume, however, that consciousness
continues and the here and now takes on a very different aspect.

> Without the want,
> Life, now human, would be brutish: just the hope, however scant,
> Makes the actual life worth leading; take the hope therein away,
> All we have to do is surely not endure another day.
> This life has its hopes for this life, hopes that promise joy:
>   life done—
> Out of all the hopes, how many had complete fulfilment? None.
> 'But the soul is not the body': and the breath is not the flute;
> Both together make the music: either marred and all is mute.

The point of view is a purely personal one, but it comprises the
whole interest of the poem. To its author—and surprisingly for
those who persisted in thinking of Browning as the ever un-
conquerable optimist—

> Sorrow did and joy did nowise, life well weighed—preponderate.
> By necessity ordained thus? I shall bear as best I can,
> By a cause all-good, all-wise, all-potent? No, as I am a man!

[1] E. Dowden, *The Life of Robert Browning* (1904), p. 86.
[2] *Ibid.*, p. 364.

But on the supposition of a future life the present can be borne, suffering itself giving assurance of an ultimate gain. The poet then proceeds with his argument in the form of a dialogue between 'Fancy', or intuitive feeling, and 'Reason', contending that life in this world is not only best explained as a probation but that probation demands such conditions as in fact obtain here. The very uncertainty of a future existence, with rewards and punishments, brings to men's actions a moral dimension they would not otherwise have. Moreover, if the future life with its presumed higher faculties and greater happiness were not in doubt, would we not hasten its coming, to the detriment of our present responsibilities? The conclusion is one of 'hope—no more than hope—no less than hope'. As a piece of reasoning in verse *La Saisiaz* is arresting if unconvincing, although apart from its argument the verse is nugatory. What Browning really had to say could have been better said in prose.

Browning's humanitarianism comes out most clearly where he is most truly himself, in depicting human nature. It was 'Men and Women' who held his attention always. The dramatic mode of expression was also his most successful and his sense of absolute values has telling utterance in three of his best-known pieces, the dramatic monologues *Fra Lippo Lippi*, *Andrea del Sarto* and *Abt Vogler*. Thus in the last-named he can say—and it is perhaps his own confession of faith—

> The high that proved too high, the heroic for earth too hard,
> The passion that left the ground to lose itself in the sky.
> Music sent up to God by the lover and the bard;
> Enough that He heard it once: we shall hear it by and by.

If what Tennyson gives us is belief struggling to overcome doubt and Browning a hopeful activism—as G. K. Chesterton put it, 'he offered the cosmos as an adventure rather than a scheme'—Matthew Arnold is distinctively the poet of faith in retreat: that faith whose sea (like the English Channel on a moonlit night) was

> once at the full, and round earth's shore
> Lay like the folds of a bright girdle furl'd';

whereas now he hears—typical nineteenth century intellectual that he is—only

> Its melancholy, long, withdrawing roar,
> Retreating to the breath
> Of the night-wind down the vast edges drear
> And naked shingles of the world.

Arnold's considered views on the problem of Christianity we shall have to take note of, and at some length, later in this chapter. But whatever his reasoned opinions may have been his instinctive feelings are expressed in his verse. They are both negative and regretful. The poet felt himself to be

> Standing between two worlds, one dead,
> The other powerless to be born.

Some renewing power was needed to take the place of the old religious certainties, but its arrival was delayed. The age was one of criticism, necessary but disintegrating, and Arnold could not contemplate it with much of either joy or hope; hence the attraction for him of the author of *Obermann*, Senancour, who provided him with the subject-matter of two poems and of an essay published originally in *The Academy* for October 1869 and reprinted in the third series of *Essays in Criticism*.[1] For the Swiss writer also had sensed that 'ground tone of human agony' which an epoch of relentless change had thrown up. This mood of nostalgia for a vanished or a vanishing past for which neither present nor future could offer any greatly compensating substitute pervades all Arnold's verse. Such a consistent note of disappointment and disillusionment was bound to limit his stature as a poet, but it is also unquestionably the source of his special appeal and the reason why many today find him the most satisfying of all the Victorian verse-writers. Certainly he was no optimist on the score of his age's material progress, which, without the guidance of adequate spiritual values, promised only a desolate 'iron age' of vulgarized standards and diminished ideals. But where were such values to be discovered? The problem of modern civilization is intractable through its very complexity. The classical world, by contrast, was simple and the necessary distinctions could be easily drawn. But in face of modern difficulties no such enlightenment is to be had. This mood of near-defeatism, of all but paralysed action, is perfectly caught in *Empedocles on Etna*, in which through the lips of the ancient philosopher the modern

[1] Boston, 1910.

poet himself speaks. Although excluded from the 1853 edition of Arnold's *Poems*—it had appeared in that of the previous year[1]—and not republished until 1867, it remained one of his favourite pieces.[2]

It is not surprising, therefore, that the elegaic strain should have been the mode in which Arnold was most successful as a poet. Others—Milton, Gray, Shelley, Tennyson—have written great elegies, but no poet is so much an elegiast by temperament as is Arnold. The subject of his verse may be a particular individual: in *Rugby Chapel* his father, in *A Southern Night* his brother, in *Westminster Abbey* and *Thyrsis*—his finest single work—his friends A. P. Stanley and A. H. Clough respectively; but the personal sorrow in each case is the occasion for a lament of wider import, a drooping reflection on human destiny. The fitting attitude, the poet believes, if one is 'to possess one's soul'—a favourite phrase of his—is resignation—a lesson which Nature herself teaches:

> Yet, Fausta, the mute turf we tread,
> The solemn hills around us spread,
> This stream which falls incessantly,
> The strange-scrawl'd rocks, the lonely sky,
> If I might lend their life a voice,
> Seem to bear rather than rejoice.

Hence

> Be passionate hopes not ill resign'd
> For quiet, and a fearless mind.

[1] *Empedocles on Etna, and Other Poems.*

[2] In a letter dated 12 November 1867 Arnold denied that Empedocles's musings were to be taken as expressing his (Arnold's) own thoughts. 'Empedocles', he wrote, 'was composed fifteen years ago, when I had been much studying the remains of the early Greek religious philosophers, as they are called; he greatly impressed me and I desired to gather up and draw out as a whole the hints which his remains offered. Traces of an impatience with the language and assumptions of the popular theology of the day may very likely be visible in my work, and I have now, and no doubt had still more then, a sympathy with the figure Empedocles presents to the imagination; but neither then nor now would my creed, if I wished or were able to draw it out in black and white, be by any means identical with that contained in the preachment of Empedocles.' On the other hand J. Campbell Shairp—Principal Shairp—had written to Clough in the summer of 1849: 'I saw the said Hero—Matt—the day I left London. . . . He was working at an "Empedocles"—which seemed to be not much about the man who leapt in the crater—but his name & outward circumstances are used for the drapery of his own thoughts.' The two statements are not necessarily contradictory. See C. B. Tinker and H. F. Lowry, *The Poetry of Matthew Arnold* (1940), pp. 287ff.

Arnold's resignation is, however, a stoic virtue. It is not merely an escape from 'the hopeless tangle of the age' but an honest acceptance of the obligations which circumstances impose, even though in the end the individual will always know himself to be alone, beating where he must not pass, and seeking where he shall not find.

With Algernon Charles Swinburne, whose *Poems and Ballads* made their sensational debut in 1866 (*A Song before Sunrise* came five years later) not only is Christian dogma explicitly rejected— 'Glory to Man in the highest!' the poet cries, 'for Man is the master of things'—but its morality as well. The temper now is one of open revolt against established institutions and indeed anything savouring of an ethic of restraint. All the same it is difficult to take Swinburne quite seriously as a thinker. A master of language himself, language too often mastered him and he was apt to fall back on mere posturing. His readers, at first at least, were scandalized. They need not have been: he was only trying to make their flesh creep. A voluminous writer, critic as well as poet, he fails through overstatement and his opinions, after their first audacious impact, seemed as facile as his rather too fluent verse.

2. THE HERO AS PROPHET: THOMAS CARLYLE

At his best Swinburne is a musician in words, but the Victorians, as we have observed, expected their poets not only to sing but to prophesy. Certainly in an era of waning faith the man of letters was looked to for the spiritual and moral guidance which the times demanded; and in the century's middle years none fulfilled the role more impressively—to himself as well as to his readers— than did Thomas Carlyle (1795–1881). James Martineau spoke of his 'pentecostal power' and of his having given 'the first clear expression to the struggling heart of a desolate yet aspiring time, making a clean breast of many stifled unbeliefs and noble hatred':[1] and there is no question but that 'the best growler of the day', as Maurice bluntly called him, was a voice crying in the wilderness to very many young men of the period, distrustful as they were of the too-long canvassed verities of the Christian creed yet anxious for some new light in the gathering darkness. 'I, for one,'

---

[1] *Essays, Reviews, and Addresses*, i, p. 226.

said J. A. Froude, 'was saved by Carlyle's writings from Positivism, or Romanticism, or Atheism, or any other of the creeds or no creeds which in those years were whirling about us in Oxford like leaves in an autumn storm.'[1] Indeed in this latter half of our own century, when few, one surmises, who are not professed students of Carlyle's epoch open his books, his former prestige may seem wellnigh unintelligible. Thus when Maurice, again, deplored 'his silly rant about the great bosom of Nature',[2] we may feel that for once at any rate he had hit the nail squarely on the head. Yet Maurice had a very genuine respect for Carlyle and esteemed his friendship highly, whilst Dean Hutton, always a reliable judge, records that 'for many years before his death Carlyle was to England what his great hero, Goethe, was to Germany—the aged seer whose personal judgments on men and things were eagerly sought after, and eagerly chronicled and retailed'.[3]

In his earlier days—until, that is, the publication in 1851 of his *Life of John Sterling*—Carlyle was generally regarded as a religious writer. But the sympathy he there displayed with Sterling's own doubts, and indeed the negative character of the book as a whole, made it plain that the author's personal standpoint was far removed from orthodox Christianity. In *Heroes and Hero-Worship* (1840) he had declared a man's religion to be the chief fact about him, but what Carlyle understood by religion was even then something different from the teachings of the churches, which appealed to him little. Not that he well understood them. The mere fact that religious institutions were by their nature traditional was, as Tulloch remarks, equivalent to saying that they were dead.[4] But neither did he consider religion, even according to his own conception of it, to be all spirit and no embodiment. 'We inherit', he says, 'not only Life, but all the garniture and form of Life.' The garniture and forms of Christianity, however, in which he saw too much of 'Hebrew old-clothes', were not to his liking. The fault of Christian institutions was that they were no longer an adequate expression of the ideal

[1] *Thomas Carlyle* (1882–84), *London Life*, i, p. 295.
[2] F. Maurice, *op. cit.*, i, pp. 282f.
[3] *Modern Guides of English Thought* (1887), p. 1.
[4] *Movements of Religious Thought in Britain during the Nineteenth Century*, p. 200.

which once animated them. Hence they had become superstition, and to superstition he desired only a speedy end.

> What can it profit any mortal to adopt locutions and imaginations which do *not* correspond to fact; which no sane mortal can deliberately adopt in his soul as true: which the most orthodox of mortals can only, and this after infinite essentially *impious* effort to put out the eyes of the mind, persuade himself to 'believe that he believes'.[1]

The efforts of a Coleridge, 'sublime man' though he had been, to revive such ancient forms were futile. Yet religious symbols are both inevitable and right: the world itself is a symbol of God, and duty God's call.

> Various enough have been such symbols, which we call religious, as men stood in this stage or another, and could worse or better body forth the godlike; some symbols with a transient intrinsic worth, many with only an extrinsic.

Nay, he continues:

> If thou ask to what height man has carried it in this manner, look on our divinest symbol, on Jesus of Nazareth, and his life and biography, and what followed therefrom. Higher has human thought not yet reached: this is Christianity and Christendom: a symbol of quite perennial character; whose significance will ever demand to be anew enquired into and anew made manifest.[2]

He could, it seems, when so minded, go further still in affirming the positive value of historic Christianity:

> Cheerfully recognizing, gratefully approving whatever Voltaire had proved, or any other man has proved, or shall prove, the Christian Religion, once here cannot pass away; that, as in Scripture, so also in the heart of man, is written 'The gates of hell shall not prevail against it.'[3]

Yet of the supernatural or miraculous he was entirely incredulous, and the Christian dogmas he scornfully repudiated. Little wonder is it that to his contemporaries the prophet's utterance, for all its profundity, remained enigmatic.

[1] *The Life of Sterling*, i, ch. 7.
[2] *Sartor Resartus*, Bk III, ch. iii.
[3] See essay on Voltaire in *Critical and Miscellaneous Essays* (1872), i, p. 409.

While still a young man Carlyle had become detached from the religion of his upbringing by 'grave positive doubts'. The mind of the eighteenth century, much as he might dislike it, was nevertheless a fact he could not blink. Voltaire, Diderot, Gibbon had not written in vain. But they were an essentially negative force and he looked for something that would serve him better. Wordsworth, rather strangely, did not help him as he had so many others. He was perhaps too close a figure, in place more even than time. Carlyle always needed distance for admiration. The year 1819 he records as one of deep despondency for him. But the 'Spiritual New-Birth', or 'Baphometic Fire-baptism', was not long delayed; and it came primarily through the inspiration of German literature—then little known in this country—and especially of Goethe. His first encounter was with Schiller, of whom he wrote a *Life* (1823–24); but Schiller, who lacked the prophetic qualities which Carlyle demanded, was not of sufficient magnitude to hold him. Novalis and Richter were more promising, but even as early as 1823 Goethe was to him 'the only living model of a great writer'.[1] Years later he wrote to his brother that the sage of Weimar was his 'evangelist'. 'His works, if you study them with due earnestness, are the day-spring visiting us in the dark night.'[2] Goethe possessed the required stature and spoke with the true oracular voice. Art was not enough, for 'in these days prophecy (well understood), not poetry, is the thing wanted. How can we *sing* and *paint* when we cannot yet *believe* and *see?*' On the other hand the difference between the two men, in temper and outlook, was all but total. The most striking aspect of Goethe's mind, according to Carlyle himself, was its calmness and beauty.[3] Nothing of the sort could ever have been said of his Scottish disciple, an irascible Puritan. But Carlyle had also both a keen intelligence and the sensibility of a poet; and Goethe's poetic genius was beyond all cavil, while as a thinker he had reflected deeply on the intricate problems of modern life. The great German was, in short, 'one to whom Experience had given true wisdom, and the Melodies Eternal a perfect utterance for his wisdom'. Goethe saw life steadily and whole, with such a

[1] *Early Letters of T. Carlyle* (ed. C. E. Norton, 1886), ii, p. 191.
[2] Froude, *op. cit.*, *Early Life*, ii, p. 260.
[3] See the essay on Goethe in *Critical and Miscellaneous Essays*, i, p. 287.

calm version as the young Carlyle desiderated to compensate for the loss of old and impossible beliefs. For a religion of some kind was a necessity to him; a religion, as he put it in *Past and Present*, that would consist 'not in the many things [a man] is in doubt of and tries to believe, but in the few he is assured of, and has no need of effort for believing'. In contrast with 'earnest Methodisms, introspections, agonizing inquiries, never so morbid'—not to mention 'spectral Puseyisms'—Goethe offered a spiritual faith shorn of outworn dogmas; a faith, that is, which a man of reason could maintain despite the negating rationalisms, utilitarianism and machine-worship of a soulless age.

But why after all had Carlyle not looked nearer home for guidance, namely to Coleridge at Hampstead, as so many were doing? For Coleridge was himself a recognized fount of German influence and had certainly found a way out of 'black materialism' and 'revolutionary deluges'. Apart, of course, from the fact that Carlyle was not a man ever to join a throng, the notorious comments on Coleridge in the *Life of Sterling* must be presumed to supply the reason. Coleridge 'had skirted the howling deserts of Infidelity' indeed, but had not the courage to press resolutely across them to firmer lands beyond; he 'preferred to create logical fatamorganas for himself on this hither side, and laboriously solace himself with these'.[1] No 'hocus-pocus' of reasoning versus understanding would avail to make the incredible credible. If Carlyle were to believe in God it would have to be a God of his own conceiving, or rather imagining, since although his thought was for ever turning on broadly philosophical issues he seldom expressed himself in technical philosophical language, which he distrusted. 'In the perfect state all Thought were but the picture and inspiring symbol of Action; Philosophy, except as Poetry and Religion, would have no Being.' Carlyle's deity is described nevertheless in suitably unanthropomorphic terms. As Sterling had once objected, under an abstract use of the name of God lay the conception only of a 'formless Infinite', a 'high inscrutable Necessity', as the 'mysterious impersonal base of all Existence', to which it was the sum of wisdom and virtue to submit. There is no doubt that in fashioning this philosophical pseudo-religion Carlyle had been largely aided by Goethe, with

[1] *The Life of Sterling*, i, ch. 8.

some contribution from Fichte also.[1] And it was through the imagination much more than the speculative reason that Carlyle reached it. Here Goethe's poetry—such things, notably, as the song of the Earth-Spirit in *Faust* and the opening hymn of *Gott und Welt*—was a predominant influence; for Carlyle's divinity, like Goethe's, is immanent: a spirit of potency working in and through the universe, having nature as its living garment but revealing itself in full articulation only in man. It was this 'natural supernaturalism' which alone satisfied both his intellect and his deep-rooted religious sentiment, enabling him to reconcile acceptance of the irrefutable truths of science with the fear that if the world is really no more than a mechanism the profoundest longings of man's heart, the dynamic of his moral action, have no meaning.[2]

Carlyle, however, preached his vaguely pantheistic gospel with all the fervour of a Covenanting minister. It is a brew of strange ingredients: Old Testament prophecy, Norse mythology, Scotch Calvinism, German metaphysic. He had even undergone

---

[1] The influence of Fichte came not from the philosopher's earlier, technical writings but from his later and more popular, such as *Das Wesen des Gelehrten*, published in 1794. Carlyle was neither by training nor by cast of mind an analytic thinker, and what he looked for in the German author was not analysis but stimulus for the imagination. His references to Fichte in *The State of German Literature*, dating from 1827 and thus one of his own earliest publications, show plainly enough whence the inspiration for his theological musings came. 'According to Fichte', he writes, 'there is a "Divine Idea" pervading the visible Universe, which visible Universe is indeed but its symbol and sensible manifestation, having in itself no meaning, or even true existence independent of it. To the mass of men this Divine Idea of the world lies hidden: yet to discern it, to seize it, and live wholly in it, is the condition of all genuine virtue, knowledge, freedom; and the end, therefore, of all spiritual effort in every age. Literary men are the appointed interpreters of this Divive Idea; a perpetual priesthood, we might say, standing forth, generation after generation, as the dispensers and living types of God's everlasting wisdom, to show it in their writings and actions, in such particular form as their own particular times require it in. For each age, by the law of its nature, is different from every other age, and demands a different representation of the Divine Idea, the essence of which is the same in all; so that the literary man of one century is only by mediation and reinterpretation applicable to the wants of another. But in every century, every man who labours, be it in what province he may, to teach others, must first have possessed himself of the Divine Idea, or, at least, be with his whole heart and his whole soul striving after it' (*Critical and Miscellaneous Essays*, i, pp. 68f.).

[2] 'That the Supernatural differs not from the Natural is a great Truth,which the last century (especially in France) has been engaged in demonstrating. The Philosophers went far wrong, however, in this, that instead of raising the natural to the supernatural, they strove to sink the supernatural to the natural. The gist of my whole way of thought is to do not the latter but the former' (Froude, *op. cit.*, *Early Life*, ii, p. 330).

a conversion experience, described by him with characteristic sound and fury, in the second book of *Sartor Resartus*:

> There rushed like a stream of fire over my whole soul; and I shook base Fear away from me forever. I was strong, of unknown strength; a spirit, almost a god. Ever from that time the temper of my misery was changed: not Fear or whining Sorrow was it, but Indignation and grim fire-eyed Defiance. 'Thus had the EVERLASTING NO (*das Ewige Nein*) pealed authoritatively through all the recesses of my Being, of my ME; and then it was that my whole ME stood up, in native God-created majesty, and with emphasis recorded its Protest'[1]

Later in the same work and in the same vein of high-pitched expostulation he can invoke Nature as God:

> How thou fermentest and elaboratest in they great fermenting vat and laboratory of an Atmosphere, of a World, O Nature!—Or what is Nature? Ha! why do I not name thee God? Art not thou the 'living Garment of God'? O Heavens, is it, in very deed, HE, then, that ever speaks through thee; that lives and moves in thee, that lives and moves in me?

Traditional Christian beliefs are thrown into the cauldron of the author's rhetoric, to reappear transformed:

> Reader, even Christian Reader, as thy title goes, hast thou any notion of Heaven and Hell? I rather apprehend, not. Often as the words are on our tongue, they have got a fabulous or semi-fabulous character for most of us, and pass on like a kind of transient similitude, like a sound signifying little.
>
> Yet it is well worth while for us to know, once and always, that they are not a similitude, nor a fable nor semi-fable; that they are an everlasting highest fact! 'No Lake of Sicilian or other sulphur burns now anywhere in these ages', sayest thou? Well, and if there did not! Believe that there does not; believe if it thou wilt, nay hold by it as a real increase, a rise to higher stages, to wider horizons and empires. All this has vanished, or has not vanished; believe as thou wilt as to all this. But that an Infinite of Practical Importance, speaking with strict arithmetical exactness, an *Infinite*, has vanished or can vanish from the Life of any Man: this thou shalt not believe.[2]

[1] *Ibid.*, Ch. vii.
[2] *Past and Present*, Part II, ch. ii.

What positive conceptions emerge, then, from Carlyle's turgid pages? His own age took him with a deadly seriousness. His pulpit thunder was reassuring. 'God' might well be a difficult notion when framed in the creeds, but the modern prophet's invocation of the 'Immensities' and 'Eternities' conveyed a hope-inspiring sense of the universe not as a mere cold mechanism but as life and purpose justifying the human struggle. The visible world, he taught, is the symbol of an invisible divine Power working its ends for the ultimate benefit of the human race. Thus there is an eternal moral order which mankind must reverence and obey. Not personal happiness—leastwise on some hedonistic calculation, some 'pleasure-principle'—but duty, the doing of God's will on earth, is paramount. 'Love not Pleasure; love God. This is the everlasting Yea, wherein all contradiction is solved: wherein whoso walks and works, it is well with him.' If a man find 'Blessedness' he can do without happiness; but wrong must in the long run bring retribution, for right is might, whatever temporary successes evil may win. Yet the impression persists that for Carlyle might itself is proof of right, although, to be fair to him, he states categorically that 'if the thing is unjust, thou hast not succeeded'. 'In all battles', he tells us in *Past and Present*, 'if you await the issue, each fighter has prospered according to his right. His right and his might, at the close of account, were one and the same. He has fought with all his might, and in exact proportion to all his right has he prevailed.'

It is not easy for us today to see the Cheyne Row oracle as his contemporaries saw him. His tortured prose style is an all but insuperable obstacle to any attempt to read him continuously, except as a deliberate task. The constant railing against this and that, the jibes and the jeers, the heavy irony, the vividness wrapped in vagueness have the effect in the end only of rant and the reader's attention flags. Carlyle—it is hard to resist the conclusion —was an egomaniac, a wouldbe man of action at perpetual odds with the times but by temperament as by circumstance unable to fulfil the heroic role—of a Cromwell or a Frederick—for which, in his own dream-world, he cast himself. The outcome of his frustration was self-contradiction. He must have a God and a Providence, but the creeds are incredible and the Church dead. The universe is a miracle, but miracles never happen. Nature is divine, but what does nature know of duty? Science is truth, but what has it to do with the existence of 'the eternal Unnameable'? Man himself is godlike, but his follies are unending. The toiling masses call for pity, but democracy is contemptible. Only the isolated Hero, the rare Great Man, is left to be admired; and the reader at once guesses that in this select gallery the author has already assigned himself a forward place. It is scarcely surprising that of all the eminent Victorians Carlyle should now be one of the least remembered; posterity is impatient of a bore.

3. THE CRITIC AS THEOLOGIAN: MATTHEW ARNOLD

Matthew Arnold, of whose verse we have already spoken, was in almost every respect the antithesis of Carlyle. Yet in their religious philosophy they are in some ways akin, for Arnold's 'Eternal not ourselves which makes for righteousness' could also well describe Carlyle's divinity. So diverse are they, however, in mode of expression that at first glance they appear to have nothing in common.[1] Where they stand together, along with so many of their earnest-minded contemporaries, is in having abandoned the traditional dogmatic beliefs whilst at the same time strongly asserting a spiritual interpretation of life and the world along with those fixed moral valuations which this alone seemed to substantiate. But whereas the one fulminates and denounces, the other suavely reasons, not without occasional ironic banter. Arnold's role in prose was that of critic much more than preacher: he revered his father's memory deeply, but did not inherit his temper or outlook. Yet the son also was conscious of a mission to edify and 'improve', indeed to be a moral leader. Where he is distinctive is in the means by which he would accomplish it. He intends to be detached, candid, critical; and criticism, on Arnold's lips, was a word of large meaning. It certainly meant more than literary criticism. He defined it, rather, as 'the endeavour, in all branches of knowledge, theology, philosophy, history, art,

[1] Much of the difference between the two men is patent in a single reference of Arnold's in *Culture and Anarchy*, to 'Mr Carlyle' as 'a man of genius to whom we have all at one time or other been indebted for refreshment and stimulus'. Later, however, he could refer to him as a 'moral desperado' and deplore 'that regular Carlylean strain which we all know by heart and which the clear-headed among us have so utter a contempt for' (*Letters of Matthew Arnold to Arthur Hugh Clough* (1932), ed. H. F. Lowry, pp. 111 and 151).

science, to see the object as in itself it really is'.[1] So defined it becomes virtually a synonym for *culture*, itself to be understood as 'a study of perfection'—something greater far, therefore, than a mere scientific passion for knowing. Knowledge, of course, is indispensable; but knowledge is a matter not of mere fact-hunting or unmotivated curiosity but of 'getting to know, on all the matters which most concern us, the best which has been thought and said in the world, and through this knowledge, turning a stream of fresh thought upon our stock notions and habits'. Culture, in fine, rests on nothing less than belief in 'making reason and the will of God prevail'.

It is not necessary here to recall in detail the argument of *Culture and Anarchy*.[2] But it is a work in which the author plainly declares his sense of mission. The quest of perfection in all things demands detachment, or, in Professor E. K. Brown's phrase, 'a strategy of disinterestedness'.[3] Understanding requires the object of contemplation to be seen 'as in itself it really is', without the bias, of one kind or of another, which falsifies perspectives and results in misjudgment. The anarchy which it is Arnold's aim to expose is the outcome of confused and uncriticized standards, a confusion pre-eminently visible in Anglo-Saxon society. But this necessary disinterestedness does not exclude commitment, moral engagement. In all his prose writings Arnold sought 'to get at' the English public—'such a public as it is and such a work as one wants to do with it'. In a word, he sought, like Carlyle, to preach; but his gospel is culture, 'sweetness and light'. On this Arnold at once enlarges:

> There is a view in which all the love of our neighbour, the impulses towards action, help, and beneficence, the desire for removing human error, clearing human confusion, and diminishing human misery, the noble aspiration to leave the world better and happier than we found it—motives eminently such as are called social— come in as part of the grounds of culture, and the main and pre-eminent part.[4]

[1] See the lectures *On Translating Homer* (1861).

[2] Subtitled 'An Essay in Political and Social Criticism', it was first published in 1869.

[3] See *Matthew Arnold. A Study in Conflict* (1948). Brown thinks the 'commitment' in Arnold negatived the 'detachment'. But this is a very questionable thesis. The abiding interest of Arnold's criticism is his success in achieving both.

[4] *Culture and Anarchy* (popular edition, 1909), pp. 5f.

What culture promotes is 'the harmonious perfection of our whole being', as it also reveals 'how worthy and divine a thing is the religious side of man', even though it is not the totality of man. Religion is in fact a vital constituent of culture, its culminating part; and the separation of religion from culture—the excess of 'Hebraism'—misrepresents, and hence weakens, religion itself. 'The worth of what a man thinks about God and the objects of religion depends on what a man *is*; and what a man *is* depends upon his having more or less reached the measure of a perfect and total man.'

Religion was in truth the apex of Arnold's whole edifice of thought. As to his father so to him, it mattered more than anything else, and his criticism, his political and social ideas, his work as an educationist are all orientated towards it. But if religion were thus of paramount importance, a thing necessary to the life of rational man, no less certain was it that the orthodox Christianity of the day was no longer available to a man of critical intelligence. This was Matthew Arnold's own dilemma, to the resolution of which he devoted much of his best effort in prose. Supernatural Christianity, he was convinced, would have to be discarded. On the European continent it already was well on the way to being so, in full consciousness; but the process had begun even in 'provincial' Britain, although the partisans of traditional religion were still unaware how decisively the whole force of progressive and liberal opinion in other countries had pronounced against Christianity. In his own essays on religious philosophy—and there are few such writings of the time which can be read today with a like interest and stimulus—he set out to present the public with a revised Christianity from which the incredible and the irrelevant, supernatural miracles and abstruse dogma, had been pruned away; a Christianity preserving the essential values but acceptable to the modern mind, impatient as that now was both of miraculous portents and of metaphysical puzzles. He assuredly did not wish to unsettle the beliefs of people who were content to hold to what they had always been taught. Let them continue, he says, in their simple faith. Nor was he concerned with the 'Liberal secularists', to whom the values of religion are in themselves of no consequence. Nor again was he interested in the merely frivolous. Those, however, whom he did seek to address were persons who,

won to the modern spirit by habits of intellectual seriousness, cannot receive what sets these habits at nought, and will not try to force
themselves to do so, but who have stood near enough to the Christian religion to feel the attraction which a thing so very great, when
one stands really near to it, cannot but exercise, and who have some
familiarity with the Bible and some practice in using it.[1]

He saw his enterprise as thus conservative and religious, an
attempt to meet the spiritual needs of the modern man who
neither wishes to abandon Christianity nor is able to swallow its
formal doctrines. It is embodied in four notable volumes: *St Paul
and Protestantism* (1870), *Literature and Dogma* (1873), *God and the
Bible* (1875) and *Last Essays on Church and Religion* (1877). Of these
the second is the most arresting, but all of them call for some
remark.

St Paul and Protestantism, a part of which first appeared in *The
Cornhill Magazine* in 1869, is a critique of the theology of Protestant Christianity as familiarly stated. Arnold points out that the
Protestant position rests almost entirely on the teaching of St Paul,
although Spinoza and latterly Coleridge had shown how erro-
neously have selected Pauline texts been used by it. Protestantism
maintains that Paul's doctrines derive their sanction from his
miraculous conversion, an occurrence which in the apostle's own
judgment (so it is claimed) gave them their authority. In other
words, it treats his ideas as though they constitute a coherent
scheme of scientific knowledge about the relations of God and
man. Yet such a system when constructed is dead. Paul himself
wrote out of a living experience and his language has to be taken
in the context of that experience. So to approach it is to adopt the
method of 'culture', the only appropriate method. Taken thus the
apostle's words no longer bear the rigorous interpretation which
Protestant doctrine imposes on them and his role as, in Renan's
phrase, 'the doctor of Protestantism' is accordingly ended. But the
new Paul, Arnold thinks, will be a far more intelligible figure to
all who care for the true values of Christianity, since a 'miraculous'
conversion adds nothing to whatever force those values already
possess of themselves. For what the Apostle is really concerned
with is righteousness. Paul was a Hebrew and to the Hebrews the
aim and end of all religion—namely, access to God—meant in
practice access to the source of the *moral* order. 'It was the great-

[1] *God and the Bible*, Preface, p. xxiii.

ness of the Hebrew race that it felt the authority of this order, its preciousness and its beneficence, so strongly.'[1] Paul's intensely Hebraic religious sense, joined with his native power of intellect, enabled him to perceive and pursue a moral ideal, alike in thought and action, with extraordinary force and closeness. He had, of course, his mystical side and 'nothing is so natural to the mystic, as in rich single words, such as *faith*, *light*, *love*, to sum up and take for granted, without especially enumerating them, all good moral principles and habits'.[2] But the apostle's mysticism never for once blunts the edge of his moral sensibility or lessens his emphasis on the finer moral virtues: meekness, humbleness of mind, gentleness, unwearing forbearance, or the crowning emotion of charity, the very 'bond of perfectness'; as he also possesses a profound awareness of what a modern would call the *solidarity* of mankind, 'the joint interest . . . which binds humanity together', involving 'the duty of respecting every one's part in life, and of doing justice to his efforts to fulfil that part'.

Whereas, then, the Paul which Protestantism portrays is the author of abstruse and unverifiable doctrines—a theurgy of election, justification, substitution and imputed righteousness— the figure discerned by one who approaches him with an open mind will be dealing with the verifiable facts of life and experience. By an adroit manipulation of texts Paul no doubt can be made to give his authority to such a theurgy, but to an unbiased reader it is evident that what chiefly concerns him is an ethic. Intellectually he had no option but to adopt the mental frame of reference of his time; but to maintain this was not his real interest. His basic concern was the 'voluntary, rational, and human world' of righteousness, of moral choice and moral effort. To this the mystical, divine world provided the necessary background, and he could pass naturally from the one world to the other. But righteousness remains his constant theme and his religious concepts are always made to serve it. The ideas of calling, justification and sanctification, essential to Protestant theology, are to him secondary. The primary order of ideas is expressed in such phrases as 'dying with Christ',[3] 'resurrection from the dead',[4]

---

[1] *St Paul and Protestantism* (1896 ed), p. 23.
[2] *Ibid.*, p. 24.
[3] Col. ii, 20.
[4] Phil. iii, 11.

and 'growing into Christ'.[1] His originality as a thinker lies in his effort to find a moral significance for all aspects of the religious life, however mystical. Thus the resurrection he was striving after, for himself and for others, was a *present* resurrection to righteousness. 'And when, through identifying ourselves with Christ, we reach Christ's righteousness, then eternal life begins for us.'[2] But the metaphorical character of Paul's language, like the ethical preoccupation of his thought, popular Protestantism has never understood. Consequently it turns an imaginative literary utterance into pseudo-science.

This pseudo-science is the theology that has its starting-point in a notion of God as a 'magnified and non-natural man, appeased by a sacrifice and remitting in consideration of it his wrath against those who had offended him'. The doctrines of justification and election are placed in relation to this. Hence the classic formularies of historic Calvinism, notable indeed for their seriousness, but a seriousness 'too mixed with the alloy of mundane strife and hatred to be religious feeling':

> Not a trace of delicacy of perception, or of philosophic thinking; the mere rigidness and contentiousness of the controversialist and political dissenter; a Calvanism exaggerated till it is simply repelling; and to complete the whole, a machinery of covenants, conditions, bargains and parties-contractors, such as could have proceeded from no one but the born Anglo-Saxon man of business.[3]

But all this is not the creation of St Paul and it is alien to his mind. Calvinism is intent, in the end, not upon the moral life but upon 'fleeing the wrath to come'; whilst Methodism, hardly less assiduous in holding to what it supposes is the teaching of the great apostle, is chiefly moved by the hope of eternal bliss. Both alike assign all activity to God and mere passivity to man, although for Paul righteousness requires effort and its achievement is possible for such as really strive after it.

The fatal weakness of Protestant theology, whether Calvinist or Methodist, is in Arnold's view its assumption that belief can be substantiated by either fear or hope. That an idea has scientific validity only experience can demonstrate. Paul is superior to

[1] Eph. iv, 15.
[2] *St Paul and Protestantism*, p. 59.
[3] *Ibid.*, p. 12.

his Protestant interpreters in founding his own beliefs on experience, from which he derives 'the conception of the law of *righteousness*, the very law and ground of human nature so far as this nature is moral'; for when the apostle starts by affirming the grandeur and necessity of the law of righteousness 'science has no difficulty in going along with him'. Here evidently Arnold is himself making a large assumption; for how can science affirm the *grandeur* of the moral law? Is it at all the function of science to attempt such final evaluations? But he would probably have replied that, as Lionel Trilling puts it, the definition is accurate and 'the mark of a scientific truth, like that of a moral truth, is that great teachers the most unlike are in agreement on the matter'.[1]

St Paul and Protestantism was not by any means Arnold's first venture into the field of religious philosophy. During his tenure of the chair of poetry at Oxford he had written articles on religious matters for *Macmillan's Magazine*. He was greatly interested in the Colenso controversy, for example, and had made a significant contribution to the public debate thereon. At the time he was a good deal influenced by his study of Spinoza, of whose 'positive and verifying atmosphere' he had written to Clough as far back as 1849 or 1850. In an article in *Macmillan's* for January 1863 he dealt with 'The Bishop and the Philosopher', contrasting Colenso's dry and technical treatment of the biblical question with Spinoza's, who, unlike both the bishop and the bishop's critics, knew how to distinguish religion from mere history, some of which may anyway be false. For the philosopher, Arnold points out, the centre of the religious life is where it should be, and he does not allow it to be shifted to peripheral matters. A little later, in a lecture of 1864 on 'The Function of Criticism', he again refers to the Colenso affair and the hostility which his own comments on it had evoked. He confesses to disliking religious controversy, but must maintain his own view that there is truth of science and truth of religion, and that the former does not become the latter till it is made religious. In the 1869 edition of *Essays in Criticism* direct reference to Colenso is omitted, Arnold includes a lengthy chapter on 'Spinoza and the Bible', in which his personal opinions on the fundamentals of the biblical question are plainly indicated.

[1] *Matthew Arnold* (1939), p. 331.

The proposition that the truths of science and religion are separate and that the essence of all religion is moral are the themes of *Literature and Dogma*, one of the most persuasive of Arnold's writings and a work still eminently worth study. The problem, he says in his preface, is to find for the Bible and Christianity a basis in something verifiable instead of merely assumed. To the understanding of the former the theology of the churches and sects has become a hindrance rather than a help. Such a new basis— an experimental one—is indispensable if Scripture and the religion it teaches are to reach the people. The right procedure derives, again, from the idea of culture as 'the acquainting ourselves with the best that has been known and said in the world, and thus with the history of the human spirit'.[1] And this, in regard to the Bible, means 'getting the power, through reading, to estimate the proportion and relation in what we read'; a task never so necessary, Arnold considers, as in the England of his own day, nor perhaps so difficult. But the difficulty must be faced because the necessity is urgent. Literature is to be distinguished from dogma, the imaginative from the factual or scientific. And the Bible being literature, it is to be judged in the way that literature should be judged, 'without any turmoil of controversial reasonings'.

In the chapter on 'Religion Given' Arnold looks for the ground of Old Testament religion and finds it, not, for certain, in any enterprise of metaphysical speculation, but in the conviction that 'Righteousness tendeth to life'. This conviction is expressed in the concept of God, whose being is apprehended simply as a fact of experience. The term 'God' may be incurably ambiguous, but morality 'represents for everybody a thoroughly definite and ascertained idea'. God in the Old Testament is in fact 'the Eternal not ourselves which makes for righteousness', and any antithesis between the ethical and the religious is false.

> Ethical means *practical*, it relates to practice or conduct passing into habit or disposition. Religious also means *practical*, but practical in a still higher degree; and the right antithesis to both ethical and religious, is the same as the right antithesis to practical: namely, *theoretical*.[2]

[1] *Literature and Dogma* (popular ed, 1884), p. xix.
[2] *Ibid.*, p. 15.

A theology which is independent of or anterior to the ethical is, Arnold believes, wholly misconceived and has no warrant from the Bible. This, however, is not to say that religion and morality are indistinguishable. Religion as a binding and a transforming force is ethics heightened, enkindled, lit up by feeling. Hence its true equivalent is not simply morality, but 'morality touched by emotion'.[1] And for this the proper word is 'righteousness'.

The language of the Bible, in so far as it is literary and not scientific, is wholly fitted to convey this meaning; for

> if the object be one not fully to be grasped, and one to inspire emotion, the language of figure and feeling will satisfy us better about it, will cover more of what we seek to express, than the language of literal fact and science. The language of science about it will be *below* what we feel to be the truth.[2]

Nevertheless, behind this figurative language and the consciousness which it articulates, what scientific or factual basis might there be? It is a question which inevitably forces itself upon us; but we have to be content with a very unpretending answer. For science, Arnold thinks, 'God is simply the stream of tendency by which all things seek to fulfil the law of their being.' As a definition this may, he agrees, seem meagre, but as compared with expressions such as 'a personal First Cause' or 'the moral and intelligent Governor of the universe' it stays within the orbit of the certain and verifiable, which alone is what science requires. However, the religious consciousness of Israel, in the course of its development, did not rest there and proceeded to add *Aberglaube*, 'extra-beliefs', and in particular the belief in the coming of a divinely appointed 'Messiah' who would restore Israel's political fortunes. Extra-belief no doubt displays the poetry of life and to that extent is justified. But it has its dangers; for it is taken as science, which it is not. The Messianic idea, an idea profoundly poetical and inspiring, had been taken as science in the age when Jesus Christ came; and it is the more important to mark that it was so, because similar ideas have performed the same function in popular religion since.

In 'Religion New-Given' Arnold discusses the New Testament and Christianity, and observes at once how the then current

[1] *Ibid.*, p. 16.
[2] *Ibid.*, p. 31.

'political' form of Messianism was not fulfilled in Jesus. What Jesus taught was something new, the true 'method' and 'secret' of righteousness. Judgment and justice themselves, as Israel in general conceived them, had, Arnold maintains, something 'exterior' in them, whereas what was wanted was more 'inwardness', more 'feeling', as it had indeed already been provided by adding mercy and humbleness to judgment and justice. Jesus' method was repentance or change of heart, 'the setting up a great unceasing inward movement of attention and verification' in matters of conduct; his secret, renunciation—the understanding that he who will save his life shall lose it, while he that will lose his life shall save it. Jesus himself was the embodiment of mildness and 'sweet reasonableness' (*epieikeia*)—qualities which, with self-renouncement, he made his followers realize to be their own 'best selves', and the attainment of them something in the highest degree requisite and natural, on which man's whole happiness depends. Because of this Jesus may appropriately be called the Son of God, as having with unique insight revealed the true character of God's righteousness. This was the *Christ* whom St Paul discovered and to whom personal devotion was the faith that justifies.

Yet even in the case of religion new-given *Aberglaube* reasserted itself. Miracles, and above all those of Jesus' own resurrection and ascension, to be followed by his second advent, were from the beginning firm elements in the disciples' faith; and legend, too, was soon added. These were the things which popular religion drew from the records of Jesus as the essentials of belief. They were expressed in a short formulary, the Apostles' Creed, in which, says Arnold, we may be said to have 'the popular science of Christianity'. Yet even this was insufficient to satisfy the demands of ingenious questioners, who accordingly gave us the so-called Nicene Creed, which is 'the learned science of Christianity'. Finally, bring to this learned science 'a strong dash of violent and vindictive temper' and you have the Athanasian Creed. And the irony is that all three creeds, along with the whole body of orthodox theology, are founded upon words 'which Jesus in all probability never uttered'. The 'proofs' of this historic Christianity have, of course, been prophecy and miracle; but the *Zeitgeist* is now against both. The so-called prophecies of Christ, with the 'supernatural prescience' they imply, have ceased to stand; literary history and criticism have undermined them. So too with miracles.

> That miracles, when fully believed, are felt by men in general to be a source of authority, it is absurd to deny. But the belief is losing its strength. . . . Whether we attack them, or whether we defend them, does not much matter. The human race, as its experience widens, is turning away from them. And for this reason: *it sees, as its experience widens, how they arise.*[1]

Our popular religion, Arnold adds, 'at present conceives the birth, ministry and death of Christ, as altogether steeped in prodigy, brimful of miracle;—*and miracles do not happen*'.[2] In *God and the Bible*, a sequel to *Literature and Dogma*, he enlarges on the same theme, by way of answering criticisms. He had in the earlier book treated it, he claims, only with 'brevity and moderation'. That there is no complete induction *against* miracles he admits; but there is an incomplete induction, enough to satisfy the mind that the evidence against them is untrustworthy and that we are really dealing with fairy-tales. Indeed he presses the point:

> That they *do not* happen—that what are called miracles are not what the believers in them fancy, but have a natural history of which we can follow the course—the slow action of experience, we say, more and more shows; and shows, too, that there is no exception to be made in favour of the Bible-miracles.

Christianity must, in fact, stand—if it is to stand—by its 'natural truth'. Miracles will have to go the way of clericalism and tradition; 'and the important thing is, not that the world should be acute enough to see this, but that a great and progressive part of the world should be capable of seeing this and yet holding fast to Christianity'.

So likewise with the idea of God. In *St Paul and Protestantism* Arnold says that the licence of affirmation about God and his proceedings in which the religious world indulges is increasingly met by the demand for verification. Calvinism talks of God 'as if he were a man in the next street', whose operations it intimately knew. But assertions in scientific language must bear the test of

[1] *Ibid.*, p. 96.
[2] *Ibid.*, p. 12.

scientific examination. The notion of God as 'a magnified and non-natural man' will no longer suffice when critically examined. To satisfy what three-fourths of our being demands he must, rather, be the power 'which makes for righteousness'. But the one-fourth of our being, concerned with art and science, with beauty and exact knowledge, has also to be considered.

> For the total man, therefore, the truer conception of God is as the Eternal Power, not ourselves, by which all things fulfil the law of our being as far as our being is aesthetic and intellective, as well as so far as it is moral.[1]

That a surrender of the customary 'personal' view of God will, in the minds of many ordinary people, mean that all is in fact lost in religion, Arnold admits. But his reply is simple:

> We say, that unless we can verify this, it is impossible to build religion successfully upon it; and it cannot be verified. Even if it could be shown that there is a low degree of probability for it, we say that it is a grave and fatal error to imagine that religion can be built on what has a low degree of probability. However, we do not think it can be said that there is ever a low degree of probability for the assertion that God is a person who thinks and loves, properly and naturally though we may make him such in the language of feeling; the assertion deals with what is utterly beyond us. But we maintain that, starting from what may be verified about God—that he is the Eternal which makes for righteousness—and reading the Bible with this idea to govern us, we have here the elements for a religion more serious, potent, awe-inspiring and profound, than any which the world has yet seen.[2]

It will not indeed be the religion which now prevails, the religion which has been made to stand on its apex instead of its base—righteousness on ecclesiastical dogma instead of ecclesiastical dogma on righteousness—but who can suppose that religion does not and ought not to change?

Traditional religion, then, to quote from Arnold's essay on 'The Study of Poetry', had materialized itself in the fact, or the 'supposed fact'; it had attached its emotion to the fact, which now

---

[1] *St Paul and Protestantism*, p. 230.
[2] *God and the Bible*, p. 57.

was failing it.[1] But he at once adds that for poetry the *idea* is everything. 'Poetry attaches its emotion to the idea; the idea *is* the fact.' The real strength and value of religion, therefore, as Arnold himself sees it, lies not in its supposed factualness but in its unconscious poetry. Its truth is truth of imagination, not of science. If men today cannot do with Christianity as it is—and the advance of science and historical criticism prevent them from doing so, once the issue has been squarely faced—neither can they do without it. Christianity has enabled mankind to deal with personal conduct—'an immense matter, at least three-fourths of human life'; but physical science is incapable of this. The myths and legends of Christianity may, as alleged facts, be incredible, wholly unable to withstand 'the habit of increased intellectual seriousness' by which religion is inevitably being transformed. But intellectual seriousness is not alone sufficient for human life. Religion *as poetry* has a vital part to play. 'More and more mankind will discover that we have to turn to poetry to interpret life for us, to console us, to sustain us.'[2] The demands of the rational intellect, in religion as in all else, must be met: facts that are not facts will have to be exposed. Religion cannot of course dispense with science; but the scientific data of religion are the proven facts of moral experience, and moral experience is best illuminated by poetry. Accordingly dogma has its role in Christianity still, not as pseudo-science but as symbolism. 'It is a great error to think that whatever is thus perceived to be poetry ceases to be available in religion. The noblest races are those which know how to make the most serious use of poetry.'[3] Even ideas and phrases that time has rendered obsolete or unmeaning may still be reverenced as an attempt on man's part to articulate feelings towards things of which in the end no adequate account can possibly be given.

For all his inability to accept the old theology in the old way and his dislike (and bemused incomprehension) of metaphysics in religion, as well as for the haziness and ambiguity of his own language when trying to convey positively what he himself

---

[1] *Essays in Criticism: Second Series* (1888), 1938 ed, p. 1.

[2] *Ibid.*, p. 2.

[3] *Last Essays on Church and Religion* (1903 ed.), p. 27. Besides its important preface this volume comprises four magazine articles: 'Bishop Butler and the Zeit-Geist', 'The Church of England', 'A Last Word on the Burials' Bill' and 'A Psychological Parallel', all of them published in 1876 in either the *Contemporary* or *Macmillan's*.

believed,[1] Matthew Arnold was a man of sincere religious feeling and concern. His critical intelligence obliged him to confront the intellectual problem which religion poses, but, poet that he was as well as critic, he was ever sensitive to the poetry of religion. Moreover, if poetry is 'a criticism of life' religion too is to be recognized as such: it is an evaluation of life as men actually live it. With secularist aims he had no sympathy. The attitude of a W. K. Clifford filled him with mocking contempt; for Clifford and his like talked about religion but did not understand it, nor in truth 'the great facts of life' out of which it grows. Arnold believed profoundly in the importance of religion and in the special virtues of Christianity. To the Church of England, that 'great national society for the promotion of goodness', he was always devoted. But his dilemma was that of many Victorian intellectuals; he was loath to contemplate, and indeed could barely conceive, a Western civilization, moulded as it has been by centuries of Christian thought and feeling, in which Christianity would no longer have any significant place.[2] Yet what he admired and reverenced and desired to see perpetuated failed nevertheless, in its publicly recognized form, to command the allegiance of his reason. Faith and culture, therefore, would have to reach mutual adjustment at a wholly new level if continuity were to be preserved. He thus in a way was attempting to do for

[1] Arnold's religious views were scathingly criticized by F. H. Bradley in the latter's *Ethical Studies*. Morality, Bradley pointed out, may be a characteristic of religion, but there is no concluding from this that religion and morality are one and the same. On the contrary, religion is more than morality. 'In the religious consciousness we find the belief, however vague and indistinct, in an object, a not-self; an object, further, which is real. An ideal which is not real, which is only in our heads, can not be the object of religion' (*op. cit.*, 2nd ed, 1927, p. 316). To define religion as morality 'touched by emotion' tells us nothing, since all morality, in one sense or another, is 'touched by emotion' (p. 281). Arnold's phrase is therefore a mere tautology. Equally vacuous, in Bradley's judgment, was the definition, 'the Eternal not ourselves that makes for righteousness'. One might as well term the habit of washing as 'the Eternal not ourselves that makes for cleanliness' (p. 283)! Nor could he approve Arnold's notion of verification. 'We hear the word "verifiable" from Mr Arnold pretty often. What is it to verify? Has Mr Arnold put "such a tyro's question" to himself?' (p. 283*n*). But whatever the force of Bradley's objections, Arnold, as a religious thinker, has some warm admirers still. See, e.g., R. B. Braithwaite, *An Empiricist's View of the Nature of Religious Belief* (1955).

[2] 'I believe, then, that the real God, the real Jesus, will continue to command allegiance ... I believe that Christianity will survive because of its natural truth. Those who fancied that they had done with it, those who had thrown it aside because what was presented to them under its name was so unreceivable, will have to return to it again, and to learn it better' (*Last Essays*, p. xxx).

his own generation what Coleridge had done for his father's. The God of orthodox trinitarianism would have to be translated into 'the Eternal not ourselves', of which nothing could be said but that it makes 'for righteousness', and for the proof and verification of which one must look to the moral consciousness alone. That the deliverances of conscience, however, come not from any transcendent source but are part of man's 'instinct' and habit— his latent impulses, his inherited norms of conduct—was a possibility Arnold did not face. Had he done so could he have prevented the metamorphosis of his ethical deism into an overtly secular humanism, for which the Christian tradition must in time have only a minimal relevance?

Chapter XII

Scottish Developments

I. THOMAS ERSKINE OF LINLATHEN

The dominant event in the life of the national church of Scotland during the nineteenth century—and the religious tradition in that country has been considerably more homogeneous than in England—was the great Disruption of 1843, itself the outcome of a decade of acute controversy. No account of these occurrences need be given here. It is sufficient to recall that when the General Assembly met in that fateful year 451 ministers out of a total of 1,203 left the Establishment. The cause of the division was not doctrinal but administrative: the issue of lay patronage. The leading opponent of the system, abolished in 1690 but restored in 1712, was Scotland's pre-eminent divine, Thomas Chalmers, an Evangelical of strong convictions and abounding energy. But Chalmers was not himself a theologian of any distinction, while the party that he led was identified with an unbending Calvinist orthodoxy. Moreover, internal dissension resulting in open schism and its long aftermath of reconstitution and settlement—for the new Free Church, to begin with, had no material resources whatever: everything had to be acquired and organized from scratch—was by no means conducive to theological innovation or exploratory scholarship.[1] In times of external stress the old certainties are clung to with a determination all the greater. Yet it would be a mistake to suppose that Scottish churchmen, then or earlier, had no impulse at all to freer ways of thinking. The religious situation north of the border was not indeed what it was in England, and no revival of theological interest took place there

[1] For the history of the period see J. R. Fleming, *A History of the Church in Scotland 1843–1874* (1927).

comparable with that of the Oxford liberals or their Tractarian opponents. But intellectual concern was not entirely quiescent and three men in particular—Erskine, McLeod Campbell and Irving—are in their differing ways of special note. McLeod Campbell's work on the atonement remains a landmark in the history of Presbyterian thought.

Erskine's first book was published in 1820, but many years before this tendencies of a more speculative kind had already appeared, represented by such men—professors at Edinburgh university—as Sir John Leslie and Thomas Brown, neither of whom had much sympathy with the reigning theology and who therefore were held in suspicion by the Church, especially its evangelical wing. Thus strong opposition was aroused by Leslie's appointment in 1805 to the chair of mathematics. A 'naturalistic' outlook similar to his—the view, namely, that nature rather than divine revelation is man's surest guide in living the moral life— was also associated with the contributors to the 'progressive' *Edinburgh Review*, founded in 1802. To all such free-thinking the Evangelicals in the Establishment were hostile, and their organ, *The Christian Instructor*, complained often and bitterly of the prevalence of 'modern heresies', an example of which, as the journal was at pains to make clear to its readers, were the opinions of Mr Erskine of Linlathen.

Thomas Erskine (1788–1870), a layman and laird of a country estate near Dundee inherited by him on the death of his brother, was trained for the law, but his life interest was religion, as to which he displayed a remarkable originality of mind. Not that his views themselves were novel; but in him their growth was spontaneous, since Erskine was not a particularly learned man and his knowledge of the history of Christian doctrine seems always to have been limited. That he was quite unaware of contemporary developments in German theology is pretty certain. Yet such an authority as Pfleiderer, commenting on the views of both Erskine and Campbell—the two men were close friends—considered them to have made 'the best contribution to dogmatics which British theology has produced in the present century', and this simply by 'their own absorbing study of the Bible'.[1] Moreover, Erskine

---

[1] *The Development of Theology in Germany since Kant and its Progress in Great Britain since 1825* (1890), p. 382. As a result of their work the doctrine of salvation, the author thinks, was 'converted from forensic externality to ethical inwardness and a truth of direct religious experience'.

seems never to have been influenced, directly at least, by Coleridge, the age's great spiritual mentor. But Erskine's own influence on Maurice, although the latter did not come to know him personally until 1847, when he paid a first visit to Linlathen, was profound. Back in 1831, soon after the appearance of Erskine's *The Brazen Serpent* (1830), he wrote to one of his sisters of how 'unspeakably comfortable' the book had been to him. 'The peculiarities of his system may be true or not, but I am certain a light has fallen through him on the Scriptures, which I hope I shall never lose, and the chief tendency I feel he has awakened in my mind is to search them more and more.'[1] Especially was he impressed by Erskine's conception of humanity redeemed and renewed in Christ as its head, and his concomitant refusal to press the dire consequences of Adam's fall as the proper basis of a theology. When their personal acquaintance had ripened Maurice spoke of him as 'the best man I think I ever knew'.[2] His own *Priests and Kings of the Old Testament* was dedicated to him.

Of Erskine's singularity many others, like Principals Shairp and Tulloch, have testified. What in particular struck Shairp was his 'entire openness of mind, his readiness to hear whatever could be urged against his own deepest convictions, the willingness with which he welcomed any difficulties felt by others, and the candour with which he answered them from his own experience and storehouse of reflections'.[3] Tulloch says that although 'religious conversation of the ordinary sort is proverbially difficult', with Erskine it was a 'natural effluence'. 'One felt the deep sincerity of the man', and that he himself 'had laid hold of the Divine in his own heart whether he understood it rightly or not'.[4] For the religious controversy which was so much a feature of the time he had no taste at all. Spiritual truth did not emerge from polemical exchanges, and to discuss theological questions merely in the abstract he considered futile. Argument, he would say, was too commonly the enemy of *light*. His own attitude was consistently that of the earnest student, the modest seeker after truth and understanding. With heavy-fisted theological pugilists like Dr Andrew Thomson, whose pulpit drubbings he was obliged to

---

[1] F. Maurice, *Life of F. D. Maurice*, i, p. 121.
[2] *Ibid.*, i, p. 533.
[3] Quoted in W. Hanna, *Letters of Thomas Erskine* (1877), ii, p. 369.
[4] Tulloch, *Movements of Religious Thought*, p. 130.

suffer, he had nothing in common. Nor did the ecclesiastical conflict which ended in the Disruption move him. Church causes involving party rivalry were simply not of his world. Religion to him was essentially an interior matter: a concern of the soul, a commitment of the moral will. Temperamentally he was introspective and given to meditation: the works of William Law had provided much of his spiritual nourishment. 'He reached the truth, or what he believed to be the truth, not so much by enlarging his knowledge, or by exercising any critical or argumentative powers, as by patient thoughtfulness and generalization from his own experience.'[1] Little wonder is it that he and the Dr Thomsons of the age were as the poles apart. Yet not a few who admired him as a man could not follow him as a thinker. Thus Mrs Oliphant saw him as 'the prophet of a creed which nobody could define'.[2] Others, like Bishop Ewing, were conscious of the difficulty of conveying the sense and quality of Erskine's very personal thinking. A very reliable witness speaks of him as

> one of those it is most natural to think of in the mysterious world that lies beyond the grave. He was never at home in this world, there was something in him that demanded a different atmosphere from ours. His realities lay all in the region we are tempted to consider unreal; the visible and tangible universe seemed to have no soil in which he could take root.[3]

Erskine's earliest published work bore the characteristic title *Remarks on the Internal Evidence for the Truth of Revealed Religion.* In view of its date (1820) it is of unusual interest and importance, since it preceded Coleridge's *Aids to Reflection* by a quinquennium. In youth Erskine had had his doubts; but these, as he tells us, had been overcome by 'the patient study of the Gospel narrative and of its place in the history of the world', in particular 'the perception of a light in it which entirely satisfied his reason and conscience'. These last words are a clue to his whole thought. Erskine, like Coleridge, could never endorse the assumption of those who, in accord with Dr Chalmers, maintained that once the Christian revelation is accepted on its historical evidence it is impious to scrutinize it at the bar of reason and conscience.

---

[1] *Ibid.*, p. 131.
[2] See her *Memoir of Principal Tulloch* (1888), p. 111.
[3] Julia Wedgewood, *Nineteenth Century Teachers* (1909), p. 78.

Religion, he felt bound to believe, must commend itself as in-herently reasonable and conducive to moral living; as worthy, in fact, of the God to whom its worship is addressed. This con-viction, as regards the prevailing orthodoxy, meant for him a parting of the ways. Dogma propounded simply on authority, even the authority of the Scriptures, was inadmissable, or rather unintelligible, until inwardly assimilated and transmuted into character. It is of the nature of Christian truth to persuade, to move the believer by evidence internally weighed, not to coerce by external compulsions.

> The reasonableness of a religion seems to me [he tells his readers] to consist in there being a direct and natural connection between a believing of the doctrines which it inculcates, and a being formed by these to the character it recommends. If the belief of the doctrines has no tendency to train a disciple in a more exact and willing discharge of its moral obligations, there is evidently a very strong probability against the truth of that religion. . . . What is the history of another world to me, unless it have some intelligible relation to my duties and happiness?[1]

Yet he is here saying no more than what the Tractarians, and Newman particularly, were to say a few years later, namely that a belief should be real and not merely 'notional'. Doctrines, that is, if *believed* and not just assented to, must move the heart and will; which in turn implies that they must have gained the support also of reason and conscience. 'All that a man learns from the Bible without its awakening within him a living consciousness of its truth, might as well not be learned.'[2] Erskine was in no way minimizing the need or the fact of a truth which is *given*, but the use of the outward was to foster and educate the inward. Newman's adverse reaction to Erskine's views is curious, therefore. For it was specifically Erskine whom he attacked in *Tract 73* on the score of 'rationalism'. The offence in Newman's eyes, as in those of the divines of Erskine's own communion, was the seeming assump-tion that revelation can be judged by sinful men.[3] But Erskine's

---

[1] *Remarks on the Internal Evidence of the Truth of Revealed Religion*, p. 58.

[2] See H. F. Henderson, *Erskine of Linlathen* (1899), p. 23.

[3] Newman, looking back in 1883 on the reception of Erskine's writings amongst the Oxford Evangelicals, wrote (in an unpublished letter): 'I knew, when young, Mr Erskine's publications well. I thought them able and persuasive; but I found the more thoughtful Evangelicals of Oxford did not quite trust them. This was about

contention was simply that unless the truths of revelation can
be genuinely apprehended—made one by the believer with the
longings of his own heart and the searchings of his own mind—
they remain only an alien quantity, never effective because never
understood in any real sense.

Erskine was but stating the conditions of his own experience
as a Christian. A layman, living in seclusion, he saw the
institutional religion of his day from a distance, its paramount
concerns scarcely troubling him. He was not steeped in School
theology and knew little of doctrinal history. Faith, first and last,
was a deeply felt personal commitment; and as he felt so did he
speak.

> I must [he insists] discern in the history itself, a light and truth
> which will meet the demands both of my reason and conscience. In
> fact, however true the history may be, it cannot be any moral or
> spiritual benefit to me, until I apprehend its truth and meaning.
> This, and nothing less than this, is what I require, not only in this
> great concern, but in all others.

The basis of his reasoning is thus the Christian *consciousness*. An
orthodoxy which could no longer stimulate and shape this
consciousness was otiose, for doctrine is to be judged only as it
can serve this end. From the dogmatist's standpoint Erskine's
position doubtless appeared rationalistic, for he teaches that
human responsibility cannot be excluded from the knowledge of
God and his ways. What Erskine most certainly is not is a
rationalist of the eighteenth-century stamp, or even after the
fashion of Whately. Religion as he comprehends it is not a matter
of credal propositions buttressed by 'evidences' and arguments
but a motion of the heart or at least of that 'reason' which mere
rationalism fails to appreciate.

The characteristic of Erskine's thought is its subjectivity.
Truth in the abstract is not truth in any sense that will satisfy the
man who seeks faith. The doctrine of the trinity, for example,
considered simply as a theory of the divine being, might very well

---

the year 1823 or 1824. A dozen years later I wrote against them or one of them in the
Tracts for the Times, and certainly my impression still is that their tendency is
anti-dogmatic, substituting for faith in mysteries the acceptance of a "manifestation"
of divine attributes, which was level to the reason. But I speak from memory. I have
always heard him spoken of with great respect as a man of earnest and original
mind' (Newman MSS, Birmingham. Copied letters, 83:1. To G. F. Edwards, January 2, 1883. The present writer is indebted for this quotation to Dr D. G. Rowell).

be justified speculatively. But until it is related to redemption it signifies little and the ordinary man would be likely, when confronted with it, only to feel 'that Christianity holds out a premium for believing improbabilities'. Put it, however, within the context of the divine love and it becomes an illuminating belief, a constraining influence.

In his later books Erskine turned to some specific problems of Christian theology. Two years after the *Remarks* he published *An Essay on Faith* and in 1828 *The Unconditional Freeness of the Gospel*.[1] This last came as a clear challenge to prevailing teaching on pardon, salvation and eternal life. Against the view that pardon is offered to the sinner only on condition of faith Erskine maintains that God's forgiveness has already been declared—that it is a fact and not merely a possibility; all men actually have it and do not need to purchase it. As he states in one of his letters:

> You know that I consider the proclamation of pardon through the blood of Christ, as an act already past in favour of every human being, to be essentially the Gospel. ... When it is supposed that this pardon is not passed into an act of favour of any individual until he believes it, no one can have peace from the Gospel until he is confident he is a believer; and further, his attention is entirely or chiefly directed to that quality of belief in himself, so that his joy is not in God's character but his own.[2]

But pardon has to be distinguished from salvation. To equate salvation with justification, according to the common doctrine, is an error. To be effective for the life of the individual pardon must be accepted. Salvation is a positive state of the soul, a healing of its spiritual diseases, a renewal of its spiritual vitality. For this the believer must exert and discipline himself, a view which, as Erskine replied to his critics, implies the very opposite of antinomianism.[3] Similarly eternal life is not only a heavenly existence hereafter but rather the communication here and now of the life of God to the soul. Indeed the very idea of heaven as localized is a misconception. Properly it is 'the name for a state conformed to the will of God', with hell as its antithesis.[4]

---

[1] *The Brazen Serpent* appeared in 1831, *The Doctrine of Election* in 1837.

[2] Hanna, *op. cit.*, i, pp. 167f.

[3] *The Unconditional Freeness of the Gospel*, p. 25.

[4] 'Eternal life is living in the love of God; eternal death is living in self; so that a man may be in eternal life or in eternal death for ten minutes, as he changes from the one state to the other' (Hanna, *op. cit.*, ii, p. 240. Cp. p. 238).

But behind Erskine's salvation doctrine there lies the whole conception of the divine as a beneficent power in the lives of ordinary people.

> Our systems make God a mere bundle of doctrines, but He is the Great One, with whom we have to do in everything. . . . Religion is for the most part a covert atheism, and there is a general shrinking from anything like an indication that there is a real Power and a real Being at work around us.[1]

Theology, he felt, had become, instead of a pointer to the living God, a mere intellectual scheme, or, even worse, material for scholastic controversy. What concerned him was the life of faith, the abiding sense of the nearness of the presence of God, as one to be trusted and ever to be learned from. The notion of this life as a 'probation' offended him. Few religious phrases, he considered, had such a power of darkening men's minds concerning their true relation to God as this. 'We are not in a state of trial: we are in a process of education directed by that eternal purpose of love which brought us into being.' Hence every event, even death itself, becomes a manifestation of God's eternal purpose. 'On the probation system, Christ appears as the deliverer from a condemnation; on the education system, he appears as the deliverer from sin itself.'[2] The corollary was that if man is continually being taught by God theological systems have no final fixity: they must develop, progress. The essence of religious and ecclesiastical authority is educative. But the principle of infallibilism is not to be contemplated: an infallible Church, 'if it could be, would destroy all God's real purpose with man, *which is to educate him,* and to make him feel that he is being educated—to awaken perception in the man himself—a growing perception of what is true and right, which is of the very essence of all spiritual discipline'.[3]

Central to Erskine's teaching is the Maurician concept of Christ as head of the human race. The Lord had come once, manifested eighteen hundred years ago, but 'both before and since that time he has been, as it were, diffused throughout humanity, lying at the bottom of every man as the basis of his being. . . . Christ the Head was latent in humanity as the Head, but

[1] *The Unconditional Freeness of the Gospel*, p. 142.
[2] Quoted Henderson, *op. cit.*, pp. 128f.
[3] See Tulloch, *op. cit.*, p. 132.

O

the Head did not come out and show itself to the senses until the personal Christ appeared in the flesh'.[1] He is 'the sustaining head, to the power of whose pervading presence through all the members of the human race the actual existence of every member of the race is alone to be attributed'.[2] The immediate witness to this truth is the conscience, which 'in each man is the Christ in each man'. In every one of us there is 'a continual inflowing of the Logos'. It is in virtue of Christ being in all men, that conscience is universal in man.[3]

Erskine had no intention of attacking traditional doctrine, but his viewpoint was sufficiently new at the time to antagonize church opinion. Dr Chalmers himself often expressed his admiration of Erskine's writings, but in this he was not voicing the common judgment, which unhappily was more certainly articulated in Thomson's polemic. Had Erskine been a minister he would probably have suffered the fate of his friend McLeod Campbell, or of the unfortunate Mr Thomas Wright, the parish minister of Borthwick.

2. TRADITIONALISM BREACHED: MCLEOD CAMPBELL AND ROBERTSON SMITH

John McLeod Campbell's is the outstanding name in Scottish theology during the last century and at once evokes the memory of a *cause célèbre* of a kind unparalleled south of the border, at least in modern times. Campbell (1800–72) was minister of Row, near Cardross on the Gareloch. A 'Moderate' by upbringing, he was of a studious disposition, disinclined to party affiliations and assiduous in his pastoral duties. As a parish minister, however, he was soon struck by the perfunctory attitude of most of his flock towards religion and attributed it to the lack of any individual sense of God's goodwill and favour. What was needed was a personal assurance of faith, a conviction of the objective fact of the divine love for all men. But how could any man be sure that God loves him unless he knew it as a truth that Christ died, not merely for an elect few, but for all? Assurance being essential for holiness, Christ's atonement must have been

[1] See Hanna, *op. cit.*, ii, p. 357.
[2] *The Brazen Serpent*, p. 42.
[3] Hanna, *op. cit.*, ii, pp. 353f.

universal. Whether or not Campbell's preaching had made his meaning clear—and in many minds there undoubtedly was genuine confusion as to what precisely he was saying—the more rigid Calvinism of his day at once scented heresy. The objections to his teaching were, on the one hand, that it denied the possibility of a fall from grace, and, on the other, that it was antinomian. The upshot was that Campbell and some sympathizers—such as Robert Story, minister of Roseneath—were arraigned before the church courts and convicted of disseminating false doctrine. In the General Assembly of 1831 both Moderates and Evangelicals united in condemning Campbell and he was forthwith expelled from the ministry. In his defence he had pleaded that his teaching was not inconsistent with a fair and reasonable interpretation of the Westminster Confession, but that even if this were not so he still had the right of appeal to Scripture itself as the higher authority.

> If you show me [he declared] that anything I have taught is inconsistent with the Word of God, I shall give it up, and allow you to regard it as a heresy. . . . If a Confession of Faith were something to stint or stop the Church's growth in light and knowledge, and to say, 'Thus far shalt thou go and no further', then a Confession of Faith would be the greatest curse that ever befell a church. Therefore I distinctly hold that no minister treats the Confession of Faith right if he does not come with it, as a party, to the Word of God, and to acknowledge no other tribunal in matters of heresy than the Word of God. In matters of doctrine no lower authority can be recognized than that of God.[1]

Divine truth, in short, cannot be for ever fixed in formularies and those who seek it must in the end return to the original fount itself.

Not indeed that Campbell himself was free of the dogmatic spirit. He was not in favour of latitude in interpreting doctrine; his own strong conviction of being in the right prevented it. He referred disparagingly during his defence to the 'charity' which is tolerant of wide ranging opinions and regards 'speaking dogmatically as necessarily an evil'.[2] The remainder of his life—he afterwards ministered to an independent congregation in

---

[1] Quoted from Campbell's speech before the bar of the Synod of Glasgow and Ayr in Tulloch, *op. cit.*, p. 152.

[2] D. Campbell, *Memorials of J. McL. Campbell* (1877), i, p. 80. See Tulloch, pp. 153f.

Glasgow—was devoted to theological study and reflection, the outcome of which was his famous work on *The Nature of the Atonement and its Relation to the Remission of Sins and Eternal Life*, first published in 1856.[1] Although it makes somewhat difficult reading today it must still be regarded as one of the most important contributions to dogmatic theology which its century produced. In so far as its author sought to overthrow the old legal and forensic view the tendency of the book was liberalizing. Theology, Campbell maintained, is useless unless spiritually fruitful, and for this it has to have its roots in life. The great atonement doctrine, however, had long been treated abstractly and legalistically, in virtual isolation from the other fundamentals of the Christian creed. The present need, if the religious value of the doctrine is to be conserved, is to recover the relationship between Christ's death and his incarnation.

Campbell's starting-point is the Fatherhood of God, as the sole ground of the atonement: the divine forgiveness is the presupposition of any theology of reconciliation. Were man himself able to atone for sin then fittingly enough forgiveness would follow; whereas if it is God who provides the atonement forgiveness must *precede* it, the actual atoning act being the manifestation of God's forgiving love, not its cause. This, Campbell argues, is the authentic Scriptural teaching: '*God so loved the world, that He gave His only begotten Son, that whosoever believeth on Him, should not perish, but have everlasting life.*' The attention of theologians, he points out, has been too much confined to the doctrine's retrospective aspect. It certainly is the case that having violated God's moral law men are sinners under a standing condemnation, a truth terrible to contemplate. Yet Christ's sufferings ought not to be regarded only as penal.

> Let my readers endeavour to realize the thought. The sufferer suffers what he suffers just through seeing sin and sinners with God's eyes, and feeling in reference to them with God's heart. Is such a suffering a punishment? There can be but one answer.... I find myself shut up to the conclusion, that while Christ suffered for our sins as an atoning sacrifice, what He suffered was not—because from its nature it could not be—a punishment.[2]

[1] A new edition was issued in 1959.
[2] *The Nature of the Atonement* (6th ed), p. 101.

In essence the atonement is the means by which God has bridged the gulf between man's actual condition as a sinner and what, in the fulfilment of the divine purpose, he was intended to be. Christ's suffering, therefore, was not a mere punishment but 'the living manifestation of the Son's perfect sympathy in the Father's condemnation of sin'. In other words, he revealed to mankind what sin means to an all-holy God.

> That oneness of mind with the Father, which towards man took the form of the condemnation of sin, would in the Son's dealing with the Father in relation to our sins, take the form of a perfect confession of our sins. This confession as to its own nature must have been a perfect Amen in humanity to the judgment of God on the sin of man.[1]

The suffering is itself a revelation of that divine righteousness which condemns sin and hence is not just its consequence. Its role is positive, a demonstration of God's love. Thus the atonement, so far from being the legal transaction commonly represented, has a profound moral and spiritual significance in view of the relation of all men to God as their Father.

> There is [Campbell urges] much less spiritual apprehension necessary to the faith that God punishes sin, than to the faith that our sins do truly grieve God. Therefore men more easily believe that Christ's sufferings show how God can punish sin, than that these sufferings are the divine feelings in relation to sin, made visible to us by being present in suffering flesh. Yet, however the former may terrify, the latter alone can purify.[2]

But at no time does Campbell try to attenuate the divine wrath. In his dealing with God on our behalf Christ must, he says, be thought of as dealing also with this, sin's due. But if Christ alone is able to make the perfect confession of man's sin, in that a perfect confession demands perfect holiness, then the truth of the incarnation is fundamental. Further, Christ's intercession is the complement of his confession and forms part of his sacrifice.

> In itself the intercession of Christ was the perfect expression of that forgiveness which He cherished toward those who were returning hatred for His love. But it was also the form His love must take if He would obtain redemption for us. Made under the pressure of the

[1] *Ibid.*, pp 116f.
[2] p. 140.

perfect sense of the evil of our state, that intercession was full of the Saviour's peculiar sorrow and suffering . . . : its power as an *element of atonement* we must see, if we consider that it was the voice of the divine love coming from humanity, offering for man a pure intercession for the will of God.[1]

The Lord's death, therefore, was the perfect culmination of his work; for only to the perfectly holy could death 'have its perfect meaning as the wages of sin' and the withdrawal of God's gift of life. 'Death filled with that moral and spiritual meaning in relation to God and His righteous law which it had as tasted by Christ, and passed through in the spirit of sonship, was the perfecting of the atonement.'

On the relation of the atonement to eternal life Campbell is insistent that Christ's attitude to sin must be reflected in men. Only so will his reconciling work avail for us. But Christ's righteousness is not simply *imputed*, in the manner of a legal fiction. Rather is it that in him men confront the true possibilities of their own humanity. Such righteousness as he showed 'could never have been accounted of in our favour, or be recognized as "ours", apart from our capacity of partaking in it.' What Christ's work really effects is deliverance from sin itself, for when we allow the atonement 'to inform us by its own light why we needed it, and what its true value to us is, the punishment of sin will fall into its proper place as testifying to the existence of an evil greater than itself, even *sins*, from which greater evil it is the *direct* object of the atonement to deliver us—deliverance from punishment being a secondary result'.[2] Christ indeed is the head and representative of humanity, and his own righteousness is to be transmitted to the redeemed human race. Men die with him in order to rise again to a higher life.

There is no need here to discuss Campbell's theory in detail. R. C. Moberly, whose own views as expressed half a century later in *Atonement and Personality* (1901) follow up the same line of thought, criticizes it as more successful in discerning the nature of the relation of Christ to God than of men to Christ.[3] Could Christ's relation to God in respect of human sin, he asked, be rightly described as a 'perfect confession'? What exactly was

[1] *Ibid.*, pp. 127f.
[2] *Ibid.*, p. 261.
[3] *Atonement and Personality*, p. 402.

Campbell's scriptural authority for so calling it? But the point of interest to the historian is the import of the book itself. In regard to Calvinist orthodoxy the author was trying to pour new wine into old bottles, struggling to save the traditional language whilst infusing into it a new meaning. For him the heart of the atonement was its moral appeal: the spectacle of suffering willingly borne for the sake of others. Herein it was a revelation both of God's nature and of man's. But this implies, as Campbell's opponents were quick to observe, a very different principle from that embodied in the doctrine usually taught. In the Church of England, the censuring of views like Campbell's would have been unthinkable; in still Calvinist Scotland it was otherwise.

Campbell, moreover, was not the only divine at that time to give offence to orthodoxy. Two contemporaries, men of lesser intellectual calibre admittedly, were likewise deposed from office for their faulty beliefs: Edward Irving and Thomas Wright of Borthwick, near Dalkeith. In fact it was the same General Assembly, that of 1831, which expelled Campbell, that began proceedings against Irving, although the latter's actual deposition was not effected until two years later. His talents, let it at once be said, were markedly different from either Campbell's or Erskine's. A graduate of Edinburgh university, he had spent some time in teaching when Thomas Chalmers took him on as his assistant at St John's, Glasgow, a post which secured him the freedom of a well-known pulpit. However, no independent charge in Scotland came his way and when offered the ministry of the Caledonian church in London he at once took it. Though not an original thinker or a man of learning Irving was highly impressive as an orator and his preaching soon drew a large and eclectic audience. His *Orations*, published in 1823, the second year of his London ministry, displayed—to quote Tulloch—'grandeur of imagination, richness of poetical and spiritual conception, and fulness of vivid feeling, rather than any glow of higher insight, penetrating to the deeper problems of religion'.[1] As delivered, with all their author's fiery eloquence, they aroused great interest and a larger church became necessary.

It was about this time also that he made McLeod Campbell's acquaintance, having already become a warm admirer of Coleridge, to whom he dedicated one of his most arresting

[1] Tulloch, *op, cit.*, p. 156.

sermons. Both men exerted a widening influence on his mind, Campbell's views on the atonement especially attracting him. His own theology was 'incarnationalist' and he did not think of the death of Christ as a mystery to be contemplated apart from what to him was the more fundamental doctrine. But in stressing the reality of Christ's manhood—'bone of our bone and flesh of our flesh'—he used some unguarded turns of phrase. Christ, he preached, had completely identified himself with sinful humanity, not, of course, to the extent of actually sharing its sinfulness, but as having nevertheless its innate tendency to sin. If the Lord had been kept from sin it was only 'by the indwelling of the Holy Ghost'. The idea was startling enough to prompt the cry of 'Heresy', and unfortunately Irving had neither the critical acumen nor a sufficient knowledge of the history of doctrine to guide him safely along a slippery path. Further, he had become closely associated with a pentecostal religious movement that had arisen in the Gareloch district, where such signs of the Spirit as the gifts of tongues and healing were gaining a good deal of publicity, mainly adverse. Irving was so entirely caught up in the enthusiasm as to lose all sense of proportion, and under his inspiration similar phenomena—'Bedlam and Chaos' was Carlyle's description—occurred in his London church. His Scottish presbytery, however, was not disposed to tolerate his eccentricities farther and his dismissal followed. Irving, as it happened, had not much longer to live—a year only; but in that time he renewed his London ministry, under prophetic guidance, it was claimed, thus starting the sect of the so-called Catholic Apostolic Church, at first known popularly as the 'Irvingites'. That Irving lacked mental ballast is plain; his ideas were confused and he became less and less open to reasonable counsel and persuasion. But he undoubtedly was a man of intense religious imagination, with a rare power to kindle to the loyalty of disciples. Coleridge spoke of him, with truth, as 'a mighty wrestler in the cause of spiritual religion and Gospel morality'. In his way he was a portent, for although he was far from being a liberal or at all responsive to the more progressive trends of his day he clearly proved the need for something other and more than the desiccated orthodoxy which then prevailed.

The affair of Thomas Wright, a friend of Sir Walter Scott's, did not reach its crisis until a few years after the Campbell and Irving disputes, but once again the unhappy outcome was the deposition of the offender on a charge of heresy. Yet many of the books for which he was condemned—none of them works of technical theology but manuals of devotion—had appeared much earlier and at first without occasioning any unfavourable criticism. A private prayer book, *The Morning and Evening Sacrifice,* had secured a good circulation and was generally approved. Similar volumes, seemingly inoffensive, bore such titles as *The Last Supper, Farewell to Time* and *A Manual of Conduct.* All were published anonymously. Then a three-volume work called *The True Plan of a Living Temple* appeared in 1830. This was a rather different venture, not so much a practical aid as a compendium of highly personal religious reflections, and the impression it created was from the first dubious. As usual *The Christian Instructor* sniffed false doctrine, and whilst praising the book for its literary qualities denounced its theology as 'not only defective, but positively pernicious'. Certainly the latter pointed a new direction in religious thinking, little in accord with Calvinist standards. The author's criterion was that of moral fruits: Christianity is a means of producing good among men and overcoming vice and disorder. The fundamental gospel truth is that of the Fatherhood of God, who loves and pities all his children. Suffering there must be, as part of the divine method of dealing with men, a necessary element in 'the true plan of the living temple', but its aim is corrective, never vindictive. The whole tone of the book was in fact humanitarian, even 'secular'. Calvinism (and Calvin himself was here dubbed 'the prince of dogmatists'), fanaticism and 'enthusiasm' were not to the author's taste; reason, a personal ethic and social progress were. All the same its critics, though detecting far more of nature in it than of grace, could scarcely indite it for any specifically heretical teaching, and since the writer was shielded by his anonymity nothing was done. In time, however, his identity leaked out and the agitation against *The True Plan* was revived. Elderly and personally unobtrusive as Wright was, the Church authorities gave him short shrift. The time for enlarging theological horizons in the Scottish establishment had plainly not yet arrived.

This unfortunately was again demonstrated, a generation or so later, in the instance of William Robertson Smith (1846–94) of the Free Church, an eminent and indeed isolated biblical scholar whose views were well in advance of current teaching. An

Aberdonian by birth, Smith was educated at Aberdeen university and New College, Edinburgh, where he studied under the noted Old Testament scholar, A. B. Davidson (1831–1903). He also spent some time in Germany as a pupil of Albrecht Ritschl at Göttingen. The scientific study of the Bible had long been *de rigueur* in German Protestant theological faculties and Smith's naturally inquiring mind encountered no problem whatever in adopting the critical standpoint. In 1870, having only just completed his formal theological training, he was elected to the chair of oriental languages and Old Testament exegesis at the Free Church college at Aberdeen, and in his inaugural lecture on 'What History teaches us to look for in the Bible' gave clear indication of his own position. The higher criticism, he explained, did not mean negative criticism, but simply 'the fair and honest looking at the Bible as a historical record, the attempt to reach the actual historical setting'. It was a process, he thought, which could be dangerous to faith only if begun without faith, when it was forgotten that the biblical history is 'no profane history, but the story of God's saving self-manifestation'.

A couple of years later he was back again at Göttingen, this time studying Arabic with Lagarde and making the personal acquaintance of the greatest biblical scholar of the day, Julius Wellhausen. Then came the fateful invitation to contribute a series of articles to the forthcoming edition of the *Encyclopaedia Britannica*, a task of the difficulties of which he was by no means unaware. But retarded though the critical study of the Bible might be in Scotland, or even in England, where the *Essays and Reviews* uproar was still fresh in the public mind, in Germany, with the work of men like Kuenen, Graf and Nöldeke, it had been advancing by strides. The young Aberdonian professor was in fact one of the very few men in the country who were abreast of recent developments or had the professional equipment for pursuing them farther. The second volume of the Encyclopaedia carried an entry of his under 'Angel' and the third a more considerable one under 'Bible', in which he frankly set out the conclusions relating to the origins of the Pentateuch, the authorship of the psalms, the real nature of Old Testament prophecy and the literary composition of the gospels which were then commonly accepted by critical scholars. The content of both articles drew disapproving comment, however, and in 1876 a committee of the

Free Church Assembly was appointed to investigate the matter. Its report the following year was hostile. Smith, astonished at such a reception of what seemed to him no more than the commonplaces of an established science, responded by demanding a formal trial by 'libel' (i.e. indictment) for his allegedly heretical opinions. The resulting proceedings, as was to be expected, were complicated and long drawn out. Much more appeared to be at stake in the eyes of Free Church divines than issues of technical scholarship. If the Bible were truly the foundation of Christian faith then to treat it in such a manner as to impugn its inspiration and inerrant authority was a threat to religion itself. That Robertson Smith personally saw no discrepancy between his opinions as a scholar and his beliefs and responsibilities as a minister of the Church did not suffice for an answer. Many were gravely disturbed by the fact of such statements being set forth in an authoritative work of reference for the general reader.

In 1876 Smith virtually gave up teaching, but the successive volumes of the *Britannica* continued to bear articles from his pen. He also contributed, in 1879, a paper on totemism ('Animal Worship and Animal Tribes') to *The Cambridge Journal of Philology*. All alike were objected to as suggesting that the Bible is not of divine authorship and does not present a reliable statement of divine truth. The formal indictment was indeed withdrawn, but it was replaced by a vote in the Assembly of no confidence, with the result that in June 1881 he was dismissed from his chair at Aberdeen.[1]

Smith now removed to Edinburgh and took over much of the editorial responsibility for the *Britannica*, and it was largely through his efforts that the whole enterprise was brought to a successful outcome in 1888. Many more articles of his own were included: e.g. on 'Levites', 'Messiah', 'Prophet', 'Priest', 'Sacrifice' and 'Tithes', besides entries on particular Old Testament books. Meanwhile he continued his Semitic studies and travelled in Egypt, Syria and Palestine. In 1883 he was appointed professor of Arabic at Cambridge, which was to be his home for the rest of his life. A few years later he succeeded William Wright in the

---

[1] For the details of the case see J. S. Black and G. Chrystal, *The Life of William Robertson Smith* (1912) and P. Carnegie Simpson, *The Life of Principal Rainy* (1909). Rainy was Smith's leading opponent in the Assembly, although himself a man of moderate and not extreme views.

Adams chair of Arabic, at the same time bringing out his *The Religion of the Semites: Fundamental Institutions* (1889; 2nd ed, 1894), based on lectures he had given at Aberdeen. A second and much revised edition of a book on *The Old Testament in the Jewish Church* was published in 1892.

Smith's importance was that rather of a popularizer of new learning than an original contributor thereto. But although he sought to place the Old Testament within the wider context of Semitic religious culture generally he was far from satisfied with a purely naturalistic account of Hebrew development and con-demned the views of 'those who are compelled by a false Philo-sophy of Revelation to see in the Old Testament nothing more than the highest point of the general tendencies of Semitic religion'.[1] As he stated in *The Prophets of Israel* (1882):

> There is a positive element in all religion, an element which we have learned from those who went before us. If what is so learned is true, we must ultimately come back to a point in history where it was new truth, acquired ... by some particular man or circle of men who, as they did not learn it from their predecessors, must have got it by personal revelation from God himself. To deny that Christianity can ultimately be traced back to such acts of revelation ... involves in the last resort a denial that there is a true religion at all, or that religion is anything more than a mere subjective feeling.

But he realized that new methods of presenting the truth were necessary. Theology had become backward-looking and defensive:

> Our whole theological literature, even when not apologetical in subject, is impregnated with an apologetical flavour; the most popular commentaries, the most current works of doctrine, do little or nothing to carry theology forward to new results, and direct all their energy to the refutation of attacks from without.[2]

The trial for heresy of a prominent scholar and sincere Christian teacher is to presentday ways of thinking repugnant and absurd. But Smith's case, however inconvenient to himself, was not simply a waste of time and energy. His own carefully worded statement, eloquent and logical, forced the biblical question upon public attention and gave rise to nationwide discussion.

[1] J. S. Black and G. Chrystal, *op. cit.*, pp. 536f.
[2] *Lectures and Essays* (1912), p. 315.

Issues had been brought to the fore which could not now be ignored or suppressed. Younger churchmen were bound to take account of them and ponder their implications. Criticism had so challenged orthodoxy as to make a complacent relapse into the old assumptions impossible. Within a few days of the vote which ended Smith's academic career in Scotland some three hundred of his friends and well-wishers together adopted a resolution declaring that 'the decision of the Assembly leaves all Free Church ministers and office-bearers free to pursue the critical questions raised by Professor W. R. Smith', and pledged themselves 'to do our best to protect any man who pursues these studies legitimately'.

All the same liberty of critical biblical scholarship in the Free Church was not immediately won. On two subsequent occasions decisions were forced upon the General Assembly. The first involved Dr Marcus Dods, who in 1889 was elected professor of New Testament studies at New College. Excellent scholar though he was, his views on biblical inspiration and inerrancy were highly distasteful to the conservatives, especially that section of them commonly known as 'the Highland host'. A like dissatisfaction was voiced—in the same quarter, needless to say—with the teaching of Dr A. B. Bruce at Glasgow. The Assembly's College committee examined the opinions attributed to both men and found them open to censure on a number of points, but not so far at fault as to justify proceedings against them. The assembly took no action therefore, although it reaffirmed in unqualified terms the central articles of the Church's belief and deplored any attempts to undermine them. In particular the Assembly emphasized the infallible truth and divine authority of Scripture and deplored the use of language which seemed to maximize the element of human ignorance and error in the scriptural record. Bruce specifically was admonished for his statements on the inspiration of the gospels and other matters, including Jesus' own teaching. But neither professor was condemned, nor was the doctrine of verbal inerrancy expressly asserted. Churchmen might dislike the tone of the new biblical scholarship, but they were not prepared to inhibit its inquiries by a formal decision. This was made finally plain when in 1902 the Assembly declined to institute proceedings against George Adam Smith's *Modern Criticism and the Preaching of the Old Testament*.

3. RENEWAL AND REACTION

But if recognition of the right of the Church's ministers to apply scientific methods to the study of the Bible was in Scotland somewhat slow and thus possibly the cause, for a time, of a certain hesitation among Scottish divines to embark on the kind of biblical study which south of the border was making steady if cautious advance, the traditional Scottish flair for systematic and philosophical theology was by no means repressed. In this field the century's two outstanding names are those of the brothers John and Edward Caird, with whom the idealist reaction against empiricism, begun by T. H. Green at Oxford, assumed an expressly Christian form. John, the elder of the two, was born in 1820 and graduated at Glasgow university. His first ministerial charge, at Newton-on-Ayr, was followed by two years of work in Edinburgh, where his gifts as a preacher received the stimulus of a well-educated congregation. From 1849 until 1857 he was parish minister of Errol in Perthshire, devoting his leisure time to theological study and to mastering the German language. It was while here that he preached before the queen at Balmoral his famous sermon on 'Religion in the Common Life', a discourse which in published form sold in large numbers and won from Dean Stanley superlative praise as 'the greatest single sermon of the century'. He returned to Glasgow in the same year (1857) to minister at the Park Church, and in 1862 was appointed professor of theology at the university, which had already conferred on him an honorary doctorate in divinity. Academic work suited him well and he was active on many sides of university life, displaying a remarkable business capacity, a keen interest in promoting higher education for women and a sincere readiness to implement the changes proposed by the universities commissions of 1876 and 1887. In 1878 he delivered the Croall lectures at Edinburgh, revising and enlarging them for publication in 1880 as *An Introduction to the Philosophy of Religion*. A book on Spinoza for Blackwood's series of 'Philosophical Classics' came later (1888), and in 1890 he was appointed Gifford lecturer at Glasgow. The first course, of twelve lectures, was supplemented a few years afterwards by a second of eight, during which, however, he was taken ill. He never made a complete recovery and died in the summer of 1898. The lectures were published in 1900, with a prefatory memoir by his brother Edward, under the title *Funda-mental Principles of Christianity*, two other posthumous collections of his writings having appeared the year before: *University Sermons, 1873–1898* and *University Addresses*.

The inspiration behind the philosophy of both men was, as we have seen,[1] that of Hegel, although the Hegelian influence is less pronounced in the elder. Hegel's grand intention had been to support and defend Christianity by rationalizing it within the framework of an all-comprehending metaphysical system; though whether the sort of interpretation thus put upon it was not, religiously speaking, the kiss of death is a question that was soon to be asked. His contention was that theology depicts religious truth in the guise of a representation or figure (*Vorstellung*), whereas it is the task of speculative thought—and for Hegel speculation was the breath of life—to translate such figures and representations into philosophical concepts (*Begriffe*). But the impression which Hegel left on nineteenth-century theology varied greatly. In John Caird it is seen at its most constructive and conservative. Caird believed profoundly in the value and capacity of reason and its entire appropriateness to the knowledge of God. As his brother wrote in the memoir referred to above, 'the conviction that God can be known and is known, and that in the deepest sense all our knowledge is knowledge of Him, was the corner-stone of his theology'. Undoubtedly John Caird—more theologian than philosopher—like Edward—himself more philo-sopher than theologian—was instinctively drawn to Hegelianism, especially through his implicit trust in the power of the human in-telligence to penetrate all mysteries. He refused to immunize religion against rational criticism by identifying it with feeling or the moral consciousness or aesthetic intuition. On the other hand, if, as his brother points out, a Hegelianized Christianity meant sub-stituting a theory of reality for reality itself, or taking man for 'a mere modus of the divine', or regarding God as 'the poetic sub-stantiation of an abstraction', or denying the essential truth of the ordinary Christian consciousness in favour of a metaphysical doctrine, then Caird was no Hegelian.[2] The lectures on the philosophy of religion, although evidently the work of a man of strongly philosophical bent, are the utterance also of a genuine

[1] See above, ch. IX.
[2] *Fundamental Principles of Christianity*, i, pp. lxxviif.

religious feeling: 'the words of Scripture and the dialectical evolution of thought' pass into each other 'without any conscious-ness of a break or incongruity'. Indeed, as Caird saw it, religion to the sophisticated intelligence naturally seeks philosophical articulation, so that as between philosophy and theology, faith and reason, there is no basic discrepancy. 'Christianity and idealism were the very poles of [his] thinking, and the latter seemed to him the necessary means for interpreting the former.'[1] The point of view is, of course, the antithesis of that maintained by Mansel in his Bampton lectures, or in their differing ways by Caird's great German contemporary, Ritschl, and in our time by Karl Barth.[2] If he committed an error, his brother comments, it was rather that he followed Hegel too assiduously 'in believing that the whole structure of dogma, as it has been developed by the Church, could be interpreted by philosophical reflection, without any essential change'.[3]

Nevertheless, John evinced a deeper regard for the positive doctrinal inheritance of Christianity than did his brother. While he opposes the drawing of any sharp distinction between natural and revealed religion inasmuch (he claims) as it is Christianity which explains natural religion to itself, he also is convinced that there is not a single doctrine of natural religion which, once it falls within the context of Christian experience, is not in some measure transformed by it. As a Hegelian he believes in the 'unity' of God and man and that it is in humanity that the divine is disclosed, but not to the extent of minimizing what is singular and specific in the Christian revelation.

If in the religious history of mankind we can discover indications of a progressive development, it is not by leaving out of view what is peculiar to Christianity, those ideas which constitute its spiritual glory and excellence, and taking account only of that which we see or suppose to be common to it with the earliest and rudest nature worship, that we can discover the real meaning of that history: for it is just that in which Christianity differs from all the pre-Christian religions which realizes, for the first time, the true idea of religion. As the absolute and only perfect form of that idea, Christianity,

---

[1] *Ibid.*, p. cxli.
[2] 'An agnostic apology for Christianity, in which security for the faith was sought in the incapacity of man to criticize it, seemed to my brother like calling in the devil to protect the sanctuary' (*Ibid.*, pp. liif.).
[3] *Ibid.*, p. lxxvi.

whilst it explains the latent significance of all that was true in the imperfect religions, at the same time transcends, and in transcending, transmutes and annuls or supersedes them.[1]

Thus the distinctively Christian idea of God finds expression in the doctrine of the Trinity.[2] Again, for the Christian 'there is something unique in the Person of Christ', however true it be that he is the representative of humanity; and such a 'participation' in the being and life of God can be predicted of him as to distinguish him from all other members of the human race. His was pre-eminently a human consciousness 'possessed and suffused by the very spirit and life of the living God'. Even the concept of God's moral personality requires, Caird thinks, to be underwritten by that of the Christian doctrine of the Logos or Son of God as 'a self-revealing principle or personality within the very essence of the Godhead'. The idea of God as an 'isolated, self-identical infinite, complete and self-contained in the abstract unity of His own being', a purely metaphysical Absolute, would of itself give no entry to that which we recognize as the highest element of a spiritual nature: namely, love.

In his teaching on the atonement Caird followed McLeod Campbell, upon whom, in 1868, he proposed the conferring by Glasgow university of the degree of D.D. Christ, he held, by virtue both of his embodiment of the ideal of spiritual perfection and of his loving us 'with a love so absolute as to identify Himself with us', making our good and evil his own, was possessed of such 'a capacity of shame and sorrow and anguish', such 'a possibility of bearing the burden of human guilt and wretchedness', as humanity, enfeebled by sin, could never bear of itself. And from this Caird passes to the still larger idea of the divine *possibility* itself. Not only can the sinless suffer for sin; there are, he contends, sufferings for sin which only the sinless can undergo in fullest measure. It is in the nature of things 'that a moral and spiritual evil should be expunged or cancelled by a suffering which is itself moral and spiritual'.[3] Of the historic life of Christ he maintained that the particular facts are of less account than the underlying ideas. 'A true idea is true independently of the facts and events that first suggested it.' Even if many of the details

---

[1] *Ibid.*, p. 27.
[2] *Ibid.*, p. 58.
[3] *Fundamental Principles of Christianity*, ii, p. 223.

of Jesus' mission and teaching should fail to stand the test of scientific criticism, even indeed if the whole gospel record were lost, yet 'the ideas and doctrines concerning the nature of God and the hopes and destinies of humanity, which had their historic origin in that life, would be recognized as true in themselves, and as having an indestructible evidence in the reason and conscience of man'.[1] Hence—a further unmistakably Hegelian touch—the actual increase in the depth and richness of experience, of the spiritual *knowledge* of Christ, which has come to the Church over the ages, will also explain the 'apparent paradox' of ascribing higher opportunities of knowledge than his own immediate followers possessed to those in after times who never knew him in the flesh.

Edward Caird, professor of moral philosophy at Glasgow from 1866 until 1893, when he succeeded Jowett at Balliol, was, as we have remarked, much more consciously a philosopher than a theologian, and the sense of tension between the idealist meta-physic and traditional Christian theology which marks his brother's thought no longer occurs. One of the most eminent British philosophers of his century, his most important publica-tions were the volume on *The Critical Philosophy of Immanuel Kant* and the two series of Gifford lectures, although the little book on Hegel in Blackwood's 'Philosophical Classics', dating from 1883, ranks yet as one of the best of all introductions to its subject. Caird believed intently in the necessary union of philosophy and religion, holding that Christianity was ideally constituted to express certain basic philosophical principles; which for him meant preponderantly, though not exclusively, those of the Hegelian system, especially as touching the relations of God and the world and the concept of *Versöhnung* or reconciliation. The history of religion, as he sought to demonstrate in the first series of Giffords, *The Evolution of Religion*, displays a continuous process of develop-ment from lower to higher; a process indeed in which he is confident of finding religion's vindication. God is a spiritual principle manifested in all nature and history; and but for nature and history, regarded as a development having its ultimate goal and culminating expression in the life of man as a spiritual being, divine revelation could have no meaning.

[1] *Ibid.*, pp. 241f.

Whilst Caird was teaching at Glasgow the 'common-sense' Scottish philosophy continued to hold its own and Hegelian idealism made headway only with difficulty. Love of controversy, however, was not in Caird's nature and he seldom if ever attacked opposing positions directly. He was content to propound his personal views, satisfied that in good time they would make their impact. Similarly, although in theology he was markedly more liberal and detached from the traditional formularies than were the great majority of his contemporaries among Scottish church-men, he was never iconoclastic in his treatment of popular religious beliefs. But the effect of his doctrine, in academic circles at least, was undoubtedly to weaken the old dogmatism. In truth the teaching of both the Caird brothers did more to bring about a change in Scottish theological attitudes than any other single factor. For they both realized—Edward most certainly—that a new intellectual climate was forming in which Calvinist principles would no longer thrive. Christian belief itself was under threat from the new forces of scientific naturalism and materialism and had to be re-equipped to meet them. The Reformation standpoint had been right in its day, but in the vastly altered world of nine-teenth-century science and of philosophies claiming to be scientific at the expense of spiritual valuations only an idealism which itself was fully abreast of the times would suffice to bring to Christian truth its needed metaphysical aid.

To defend theology on strictly rational grounds was also the great endeavour of that tough-minded thinker, Robert Flint (1838–1910), professor of divinity at Edinburgh university. Flint's confidence in reason as the pillar of faith was unshakable. In *Theism*, published in 1877, he declared that belief should not outstrip knowledge, holding that if a man has no *reason* to believe there is a God then he has no right to do so. 'Belief is inseparable from knowledge and ought to be precisely co-extensive with knowledge', a maxim at the opposite pole to Ritschlianism. For whereas Ritschl denounced natural theology as a sham in failing to express God's will for men as sinners, Flint saw in it the foundation of all other theology, in the same way that natural law is the foundation of all political and ethical science. No heathen religion or philosophy has ever been without the truths of natural religion, and to teach a faith that denigrates reason or relies blindly on authority Flint dismisses as 'a foolish procedure', incapable of justifying the ways of God to men. The conspicuous fault of the Reformers was in their ascribing to Scripture a position inconsistent with adequate recognition of either the rights of reason or the evidences of God in creation, providence or the nature of man himself.

> The evidences or proofs of God's existence are countless. They are to be found in all the forces, laws, and arrangements of nature— in every material object, every organism, every intellect and heart. At the same time they concur and coalesce into a single all-comprehensive argument, which is just the sum of the indications of God given by the physical universe, the minds of men, and human history. Nothing short of that is the full proof.[1]

Yet the mind can only rise to the apprehension of God by a process which involves all the essentials of its own constitution, especially the will, from consciousness of which the very idea of causality is in fact derived. 'If we did not know ourselves as causes, we could not know God as a cause; and we know ourselves as causes only in so far as we know ourselves as wills.' But in the end the logical understanding is paramount. 'The whole duty of man as to belief is to believe and disbelieve according to evidence, and neither to believe nor disbelieve when evidence fails him.'[2]

But if Flint's view directly negatives Ritschl's as to the place of metaphysics in religion so too, on the other hand, did his estimate of mysticism. Mysticism, like anything else, may have its defects, but it has been of immense service to religion and 'no worthy theologian will deny profound obligations to the great masters of mystic theology'.[3] In the Catholic tradition mysticism has held a prominent place, possibly even too prominent, since it has been made to subserve ecclesiastical interests. But the disregard of it in Protestantism has been a fault. However, Flint's assessment of the role in Christianity of both reason and the mystical temper never lessened his concern for its biblical foundations. The critical study of the Bible he thought in no way profane or unwarranted, although the kind of rationalist assumptions which would exclude miracle could very well be dangerous. Dogmatics must be rooted in Scripture, from which

[1] *Theism*, pp. 62f.
[2] *Ibid.*, p. 358.
[3] See especially his *On Theological, Biblical and Other Subjects* (1905).

alone it draws its truths and of which the central theme is that 'mediatorial principle' which reached its ultimate realization in an atoning death. Christian theology throughout is but a demonstration of Christ's mediating function, apart from which the human race could expect only that 'eternal death' in which, by nature, it already lies. Finally, in respect of the intellectual climate of the age, Darwinism had done nothing, Flint judged, to render theism less credible than formerly. Creation is the sole possible theory of the absolute origin of things: evolution must assume it or else hold that the universe is self-existent. The evolutionary theory is concerned with process only. 'Nothing can be conceived of as subject to evolution which is not of a finite and composite nature. Nothing can be evolved out of a finite and composite existence which was not previously involved in it. And what gives to anything its limits and constitution must be more perfect than itself'.[1]

A theologian of a very different stamp was Alexander Balmain Bruce (1831–99), professor of apologetics and New Testament exegesis at Free Church Hall, Glasgow, and the most pronounced liberal of his time in Scottish Presbyterianism. Bruce was without the technical equipment of a front-rank scholar, nor had he massive learning. With much in the Church's traditional doctrine he lacked sympathy on account of what he regarded as its legalism. Above all, he felt, the Christ of the synoptic gospels had been supplanted by the metaphysical abstractions of ecclesiastical dogma: what was needed was a recovered knowledge of the 'Son of Man' as the only authentic revelation of God. Apologetics was necessary—and Bruce himself was the author of a well-known treatise thereon[2]—but he despaired of any successful defence of traditionalist positions. The apologist's proper task is to present the Christianity of Christ himself, in the assurance that its intrinsic worth must convince any man of good will.[3] Yet Bruce was not a critical theologian, his attitude to the gospels is at times almost naïvely conservative, and his statements are

[1] *Theism*, pp. 390f.

[2] *Apologetics; or Christianity Defensively Stated* (1893).

[3] Of his own aim Bruce wrote: '[The author] regards himself as a defender of the catholic faith, not as a hired advocate or special pleader for a particular theological system. He distinguishes between religion and theology, between faith and opinion, between essential doctrines and the debatable dogmas of the schools' (*Apologetics*, 3rd ed., p. 37).

not always self-consistent; although it has to be recognized that his opinions shifted over the years and that as between an early and popular book like *The Training of the Twelve* (1871) and his last work, the article on 'Jesus' which he contributed to Cheyne's *Encyclopaedia Biblica*, there is a very perceptible movement away from the orthodox standpoint. The fact is that while Bruce personally believed in Christ's divinity, which he held to be in full accord with the teaching of the gospels, he was increasingly unhappy about its classical formulation. From this dilemma he tried to extricate himself by recourse to what is virtually Ritschlianism. Thus in *Apologetics* he writes that:

> All we really know of God in spirit and in very truth we know through Jesus; but only on condition that we truly know Jesus Himself as revealed to us in the pages of the evangelic history. Knowledge of the historical Jesus is the foundation at once of a sound Christian theology and of a thoroughly healthy Christian life.[1]

Against those who would minimalize the historical basis of Christianity Bruce brings a moral argument:

> If the Jesus of the Gospels really lived as there described, I have a right to condemn nonconformity to His image in others, and am under obligation to aim at conformity thereto in my own conduct. What He was we ought to be, what He was we can approximately be. But if the Jesus of the Gospels be a devout imagination then the right to reform and the obligation to conform cease. The fair Son of Man belongs to the serene region of poetry.[2]

For the modern Christian consciousness, as for that of the early Church, Jesus Christ possesses 'the religious value of God', an affirmation which always eludes the precise categories of a philosophical definition. On the other hand Bruce had no doubt that a Christianity without dogma would be an impossibility and that a creed is a practical necessity for the Church's continuing existence as a social force. To describe him, therefore, as a liberal in the sense which the epithet came increasingly to acquire during the final years of the last century and the first of the present could be misleading. He seems never seriously to have questioned

[1] p. 350.
[2] *Ibid.*, p. 352.

that Jesus is in some ultimate way a supernatural figure to whom even the character of omniscience is not improperly ascribed.

Clearly there were tensions in Bruce's thought which he did not fully resolve and which became more acute as he grew older. In *The Chief End of Revelation*, published in 1881, he voices his impatience with the customary appeal to miracle and prophecy as primary evidence for the truth of Christianity, although for his part he doubts neither the authenticity of the one nor the predictive significance of the other. But a distinction has to be drawn between '*doctrines* of faith and theological *dogmas*', and he desiderates a 'simplified creed' retaining only the essentials of belief. The supreme miracle in any case was that of Christ himself: the moral miracle of his perfect holiness, which it was natural should have 'physical relations and aspects'.[1] In *The Kingdom of Christ* (1889) his attitude towards both 'ecclesiasticism' and 'sacramentarianism' and rigid credal orthodoxy hardened. He has no hesitation in describing Jesus as 'the absolutely true and full manifestation of the Divine Being', if he also can speak, somewhat ambiguously, of Christ and God being 'one in spirit'. But he finds nothing in the synoptics at least which attributes to Jesus a divine sonship in any metaphysical sense that is clear and indisputable. Again, the gospel teaches 'a rudimentary, moral and religious Trinity', but not 'the developed, metaphysical, and speculative Trinity of theology'. Further, the divinity of Christ has to be understood ethically, the heart of what he revealed being God's Fatherhood and, in his own person, 'the prototype of sonship'. The Kingdom (as with Ritschl) is a moral quantity, the unobtrusive but certain growth of which is best appreciated in the light of Mark's parable of the seed growing secretly. Eschatological imagery cannot be taken at face value and the Son's declared ignorance of the day of his second coming makes it highly unlikely that he foretold an early Parousia.

In 1896 and the year following Bruce delivered the Gifford lectures at Glasgow, taking as his subjects *The Providential Order of the World* and *The Moral Order of the World*. The evolutionary theory of human origins he readily accepted and was prepared to concede that in the course of evolution mind may well have arisen from matter. The incarnation is appraised in ethical terms: the entry of God into human experience makes him 'a moral

[1] See *The Miraculous Element in the Gospels* (1886).

hero', a burden-bearer for his own children, a sharer in the sorrow and pain that overtakes the good because of the world's moral evil. The noble army of martyrs have the comfort of knowing that the Eternal Spirit is at their head, and Christ is the visible human embodiment of the Spirit's leadership. The second series treats of the relation of God and man, pursuing the Maurician theme that man as such stands indefeasibly in a relation of sonship to God. 'All men indiscriminately are God's sons.' Religious faith is simply the recognition of this in the light of 'the Galilean gospel'. The standpoint of the *Encyclopaedia Biblica* article is throughout detached: the author reviews the biblical data but avoids theological inferences. In Mark we see 'the real man Jesus, without the aureole of faith around his head'. 'For modern criticism the story, even in the most heroic version, is not pure truth, but truth mixed with doubtful legend.' Nevertheless Jesus' spiritual intuitions are 'pure truth valid for all ages'. The ultimate conclusion is that God, man and the moral ideal could not have been more truly or happily conceived than in Christianity. But whether the 'divinity' of Jesus signifies anything beyond the sum of his moral perfections is not said. What is said goes no further than the affirmations of Harnack or Sabatier.

Against the background of the Scottish Presbyterianism of his day Bruce appears a somewhat isolated figure, not easy to classify. At the other side of the picture stand two conservatives, colleagues together at the Free Church college in Glasgow: James Orr (1844–1913) and James Denney (1856–1917). Orr at all events was a diehard whose hostility to critical and liberal trends deepened with the years. Denney, although prominent as a biblical scholar, likewise lacked sympathy with the changes which to a growing number of churchmen now seemed inevitable. But he denied that he held the old-fashioned doctrine of verbal inspiration and was ready to allow that in a pre-scientific age the myth presented in the opening chapters of Genesis was an appropriate medium of revelation. Orr, on the other hand, in *The Problem of Old Testament Criticism*, published as late as 1906, launched an all-out attack on the main positions in Old Testament analysis as then held. A formidable controversialist and able writer, his view of the Bible, although he too disclaimed any 'mechanical' theory of inspiration, was that of a bygone generation. Yet he did recognize that in the gospel record of Jesus' sayings the end is gained if the meaning be preserved, whatever variations may occur in the actual form of the words. Orr is seen in a better light, however, as a systematic theologian. His volume on *The Progress of Dogma* (1901), as was to be expected, is very critical of Harnack, but in its positive aspect offers a clear and informative exposition of its subject. His understanding of the great historic tradition of Christian theology is, moreover, superior to Bruce's. His best work is probably his volume of Kerr lectures, *The Christian View of God and His World* (1893), on any showing a worthy addition to the modern literature of dogmatic theology. Orr shared Flint's trust in reason—God's existence, if a truth, must challenge rational comprehension—endorsed the role of metaphysics in religion and was appreciative of mysticism. Natural theology, with its long-established place in Christian thought, is, he judged, both possible and necessary and the believer has no reason to regret that theism can be demonstrated apart from revelation. Further, man as a creature is undoubtedly a child of God, whose image sin has not wholly defaced. Thus between the human spirit and the divine mind there is an essential kinship. In accord with this conviction Orr believed the incarnation to possess a wider significance than that purely of a remedy for sin. Its ultimate end was the 'perfecting' of humanity. Regarding the atonement he will not separate fact from theory: if the fact be a fact it can be understood. Orr's refusal to accept the evolutionary account of human origins stemmed from his fears as to its consequences for Christian belief as a whole. But he was optimistic that as between the best-attested results of science and the familiar biblical story no irreconcilable antagonism need subsist.

Denney's work as a biblical and dogmatic theologian is best seen in his books on the atonement: *The Death of Christ* (1902), its sequel, *The Atonement and the Modern Mind* (1903), and the post-humously published Cunningham lectures, *The Christian Doctrine of Reconciliation* (1917). The basis of these studies is a close examination of the New Testament beliefs and the interpretations put upon them by Christian thinkers since. On this he rests his own restatement, convinced that precise formulation is what the doctrine still calls for. He was in full agreement with Orr, that is, on the unsatisfactoriness of merely asserting the *fact* of the atonement without any attempt at explaining it: the question what exactly it was that Christ's death effected is one which cannot rightly be evaded. And the answer he himself gives is an unhesitating reaffirmation of the classic Protestant doctrine of penal substitution: Christ, bearing in himself the condemnation of man's sin, had suffered and died in man's stead. Denney disliked the word 'representative' in this context, as implying action on the part rather of man than of God, whereas the truth is that God, out of his very love, had given Christ for man. And because sin deserves punishment such substitution was inevitably penal. In Denney's earlier writings this aspect of the atonement is especially marked; in the later it is the divine love itself which receives the prominence. Sin, as he insists, is a terrible reality, but it is not the final reality. The ultimate is 'a love which submits to all that sin can do, yet does not deny itself, but loves the sinful through it all'.

Denney's theology of the incarnation is clearly set out in his early *Studies in Theology* (1894), a course of lectures delivered in the United States of America. Here he follows the ancient patristic line in using the Logos doctrine as the key to the meaning of personality, in mankind generally as in the incarnate himself. Thus the Logos made flesh became the personal centre not of a life alien to man, but of one truly and essentially human. It is through personality as such that man's relatedness to God subsists. What might be considered the sheer paradox of the incarnation, the antithesis of divine and human, is accordingly diminished: 'In whatever sense personality is to be ascribed to the Word, that same personality is the centre of the life which began at Bethlehem.' But if in this book Denney identifies himself with the movement of thought which eventuated in the Definition of Chalcedon—a formulary he resolutely defends— a subsequent work, *Jesus and the Gospel*, dating from 1908, shows an unexpected change of front. The traditional Christology now appears to him less than adequate to convey the reality of Christ as presented in the gospels and he finds the Athanasian doctrine incapable of a satisfactory interpretation. At the same time he by no means commits himself to a 'liberal' view and his own thinking remains somewhat obscure. At any rate he had scant sympathy with Ritschlianism, of which the 1894 volume is sharply critical. Ritschl's rejection of natural theology he could not countenance, whilst a Christology founded on the concept of the *Werthurtheil* or value judgment only harboured a dangerous ambiguity.[1] Indeed one of the most remarkable features of the Scottish theological tradition is the way in which it has maintained its conviction that the human mind has the capacity for a rational knowledge of God and his ways.

Although both Orr and Denney were pronounced conservatives at a time when conservatism was fast losing ground they were less of an anachronism in Scotland than they would have been south of the border. For the kind of 'modernism' which became influential in the Church of England during the first quarter of the present century and which is best represented by such men as Hastings Rashdall, J. F. Bethune-Baker and Percy Gardner, won little support in the Church of Scotland or the Free Church. At least the point of view indicated in W. A. Curtis's inaugural lecture at the beginning of the 1903–4 session at Aberdeen university proved to be a more or less isolated one. Orthodoxy might be critical, as in the work of H. R. Mackintosh, but its essential traditionalism was never in doubt. The Protestantism of the Westminster Confession, however, had retreated into the past. The teachers of the new era bore a different stamp. Mackintosh himself, George Galloway and John Oman, W. P. Paterson and D. S. Cairns, Donald and John Baillie—to such as these the English-speaking theological world still gladly acknowledges its debt.

[1] Cp. *Studies in Theology*, p. 14: 'Though Jesus has for the Christian consciousness the religious value of God, He has for the scientific consciousness only the common real value of man. He is, in truth and reality, to the neutral consideration of science, mere man like any other; it is only the *Werthurtheil* the subjective estimate of the pious Christian, that gives him the value of God.' Orr, too, thought Ritschlianism theologically unsound. See *The Ritschlian Theology* (1897).

Chapter XIII

Critical Orthodoxy

I. THE 'LUX MUNDI' GROUP

The publication in 1889 of *Lux Mundi*, like that of *Essays and Reviews* thirty years earlier, has been described as a landmark in the history of English theological thought.[1] At the least the volume marked 'a new era in Anglican thought'.[2] The joint production of a group of High Churchmen, it was a clear departure from the rigidly conservative Tractarianism represented until his death in 1882 by Dr Pusey and by Henry Parry Liddon (1829–90), canon of St Paul's and the indefatigable chronicler of the former's life. Liddon had held his canonry since 1870, in which year he also was given the Dean Ireland chair of exegesis at Oxford, and was famed as a preacher attracting large audiences. Earlier he had strongly opposed attempts to minimize the use of the Athanasian creed in public worship,[3] whilst in his Bampton lectures on *The Divinity of Our Lord*, published in 1867, he had sought to maintain the strictest standard of orthodoxy and without the slightest concession to the difficulties then being raised by biblical criticism. On the credal issue he saw the Church already 'on an inclined plane, leading swiftly and certainly towards Socinianism tempered by indifference'.

> Surrender in this case [he was writing to Samuel Wilberforce] opens the floodgates. It establishes, in an instance of capital importance,

---

[1] S. C. Carpenter, *Church and People 1789–1889* (1933), p. 537.

[2] A. M. Ramsey, *From Gore to Temple*, (1960), p. vii

[3] The attitude of Broad Churchmen to the formulary was exactly expressed by Archbishop Tait: 'I believe that this Creed has done more to alienate the minds of intellectual men from the Church of England than all other causes' (R. T. Davidson and W. Benham, *op. cit.* ii, p. 129). Hort considered that its clauses 'substitute geometry for life' (A. F. Hort, *op. cit.*, ii, p. 140).

the principle of Prayer Book revision. It will constitute an *a fortiori* argument for revising the Baptismal, Ordination and Visitation of the Sick Services in the sense of the anti-Sacramental Puritans. This done, it will authorize the eternal elimination of all direct adoration of Christ, our Eternal God, in order to satisfy the Socinian school in our midst . . . For myself, I see no future when the first step on the road to spiritual ruin shall have been fairly taken by the English Church.[1]

'A particular intellectual presentation of Truth', he said, 'may be modified, but nothing of the kind is possible with an article of the Christian Faith.'[2] To him it seemed that originality, of which his own work was destitute, could only mean novelty, and novelty in turn heresy.

The appearance of *Lux Mundi* was certainly a blow to Liddon and may well have hastened his death some months later. The book's editor, Charles Gore (1853–1932), was himself highly regarded by the older man, who had been largely responsible for securing his appointment as principal of Pusey House, Oxford, an institution founded as a memorial to the great Tractarian. That Gore, therefore, should have gone so far in propagating opinions which Pusey would have judged a betrayal of the orthodox faith and Liddon himself could only deplore is proof of the new outlook which the heirs of the Tractarians believed that changing times and the advance of knowledge had made inevitable.[3] Dean Church, always the most openminded of the High Churchmen of his generation, had written to Liddon in the same year with the intent of reassuring him: 'Ever since I could think at all I have felt that these anxious and disturbing questions would one day be put to us; and that we were not quite prepared, or preparing, to meet them effectively; adding:

---

[1] J. O. Johnson, *The Life and Letters of Henry Parry Liddon* (1904), pp. 157f.
[2] *Ibid.*, p. 366.
[3] What distressed Liddon was the book's 'rationalizing and pelagianizing tone'. He was not alone in so thinking. An attack on *Lux Mundi* in Convocation was led by that last-ditch defender of traditionalism, Archdeacon Denison, but with little success. The theological atmosphere had changed much since the condemnation of *Essays and Reviews*. The new volume was not a sell-out to infidelity, although it did signify a fresh approach to the problems of religious belief and one for which precedents, it was pointed out, could be found in the thought of the Cambridge Platonists, certain of the Laudian divines, St Bonaventura and the medieval Franciscans and ultimately Origen and Clement of Alexandria.

It seems to me that our apologetic and counter-criticism had let itself be too much governed by the lines of attack and that we have not adequately attempted to face things for ourselves, and in our own way, in order not merely to refute but to construct something positive on our own side.[1]

To construct something positive was the set purpose of all those in whose thinking there was a confluence of two theological streams, the Coleridgean-Maurician and the Tractarian. Their standpoint was made plain by Gore in his editorial preface: the enterprise was 'an attempt on behalf of the Christian Creed in the way of explanation'; and the authors were agreed that if the true meaning of the faith is to be made sufficiently conspicuous such explanation was needful. Whilst they had not written as mere ' "guessers at the truth", but as servants of the Catholic Creed and Church, aiming only at interpreting the faith they had received', they shared the conviction that

the epoch in which we live is one of profound transformation, intellectual and social, abounding in new needs, new points of view, new questions; and certain therefore to involve great changes in the outlying departments of theology, where it is linked on to other sciences, and to necessitate some general restatement of its claim and meaning.

What the current conditions demanded was a new development in theological thinking. This should be neither an innovation or heresy, nor 'the hardening and narrowing process of further defining or multiplying dogmas'. The whole collection of essays was very deliberately the work of writers with common pre-suppositions and a common goal and thus avoided the somewhat haphazard character which had marred the *Essays and Reviews* enterprise. As a group of Oxford teachers—Arthur Lyttleton, master of Selwyn, was the only Cambridge man among them and even he had for a time been a tutor at Keble—they had had many occasions over the preceding years not only to meet and discuss[2] but to confer upon specific means of 'commending the faith to the acceptance of others' and of trying to put it 'into

[1] M. Church, *op. cit.*, p. 341.

[2] The book was planned at Longworth rectory, near Oxford, the home of one of the contributors, J. R. Illingworth, which for some years had been the meeting-place of Gore's 'Holy Party'—i.e. the *Lux Mundi* group. It was here, too, that the essays were read and criticized before publication.

its right relation to modern intellectual and moral problems'—a phrase which, in seeming to reverse the right order of procedure, was to give offence to some readers. It is noteworthy that in the book's contents table the authorship of the several essays is not specified, the list of contributors being inserted before the preface and each paper taking its due place in a sequence of numbered chapters.

Lux Mundi is subtitled 'A series of studies in the Religion of the Incarnation', and this declared interest was in keeping with the already settled trend of English theology, associated alike with the Tractarian teaching and with Coleridge, Maurice and the Cambridge theologians, towards readjusting the balance between the incarnation and the atonement as the focal points in a scheme of Christian doctrine. What in general the authors were concerned to emphasize was both the intrinsic importance and the ramifying implications of the claim that in Christ the Son of God had assumed human nature. The tendency of Evangelicalism had been to isolate the atonement from other aspects of Christian belief. Thus Lyttelton in his own essay on the atonement especially stresses the close connection between Christ's death and his resurrection and ascension. It had been

> the fault of much popular theology to think only of our deliverance from wrath by the sacrificial death of Christ, and to neglect the infinitely important continuation of the process thus begun. The Gospel is a religion of life, the call to a life of communion with God by means of the grace which flows from the mediation of the risen and ascended Saviour.[1]

The sixth chapter, by R. C. Moberly (1845–1903), headed 'The Incarnation as the Basis of Dogma', and the fifth, by J. R. Illingworth (1848–1915), 'The Incarnation in relation to Development', were particularly interested in connecting the dogma with the modern principle of evolution.[2] Henry Scott Holland (1847–1918), a colleague of Liddon's at St Paul's, wrote on 'Faith'; Aubrey Moore (1848–90), very strikingly, on 'The Christian Doctrine of God'; Illingworth again on 'The Problem of Pain', in its bearing

---

[1] *Lux Mundi*, p. 301.
[2] Of the actual content of the dogma the authors had little indeed to say. As A. M. Fairbairn remarked: 'Curiously the Incarnation is the very thing the book does not, in any more than the most nominal sense, either discuss or construe' (*The Place of Christ in Modern Theology* 1893, p. 451*n*).

on faith; E. S. Talbot (1844–1934), warden of Keble, later bishop of Winchester, on 'The Preparation in History for Christ'; Walter Lock (1846–1933), afterwards warden of Keble, on 'The Church'; Francis Paget (1851–1911), Regius professor of pastoral theology and a canon of Christ Church, on 'Sacraments'; W. J. H. Campion on 'Christianity and Politics'; and R. L. Ottley (1856–1933) on 'Christian Ethics'. The editor himself wrote on 'The Holy Spirit and Inspiration', an essay which provoked more comment than any other. Gore also contributed a lengthy preface to the book's tenth edition, which appeared—for such was its circulation—in the following year. In this he sought to meet objections and underline the authors' united purpose of succouring 'a distressed faith'. What was needed was not compromise but readjustment, 'a reconciliation which shall at once set the scientific and critical movement, so far as it is simply scientific and critical, free from the peril of irreligion, and the religious movement free from the imputation of hostility to new knowledge'.[1]

The unity of standpoint among all the contributors was enhanced by the pervasive philosophical influence of T. H. Green, whose pupils some of them had been. Mark Pattison indeed had noted how the philosopher's honey had been carried off to the Tractarian hive, evidently considering that they had no right to it.[2] But the fact that the younger generation of High Churchmen could thus turn for intellectual guidance to one who, although at the time the *dernier cri* in philosophy, was himself by no means an orthodox believer indicates how ready they were to seek new aids for the communication of the old faith.[3] Moreover, neo-idealism seemed to accord well with the Alexandrian type of theology which they also found attractive. Scott Holland's regard for Green, strengthened by ties of close personal friendship, was especially high. But the positive influence of idealist theories was, as we shall observe, most evident in Illingworth, particularly in his later writings.

The opening essay was Scott Holland's on 'Faith' and is a work of considerable originality, anticipating the 'personalism' which was soon to become familiar in religious philosophy. Holland sees

[1] *Lux Mundi*, p. xii.

[2] *Memoirs*, p. 167.

[3] Green's own concept of God was of 'a Being in whom we exist, with whom we are in principle one: with whom the human spirit is identical, in the sense that He *is* all which the human spirit is capable of becoming' (*Prolegomena to Ethics*, sect. 187).

faith as an 'elemental energy of the soul' encompassing the entire body of man's activities. Hence the difficulty of examining and defining it in isolation, since 'the deepest and most radical elements of man's being are the hardest to unearth'. It grounds itself, solely and wholly, on an inner and vital relation of the soul to its source. Faith verifies itself only in actions and can best be described as 'a struggling and fluctuating effort in man to win for himself a valid hold upon things that exist under the conditions of eternity'. Religion is simply its articulate utterance:

> The Christian Creed only lifts into clear daylight, and endows with perfect expression, this elemental and universal verity, when it asserts that at the very core of each man's being lies, and lives, and moves, and works, the creative energy of the Divine Will.

Nevertheless the life of faith precedes any conscious expression of itself in religion, and the secular life can continue as if faith were unnecessary to it: 'Its own practical activity is complete and free, whether it discovers its hidden principle or not.' What faith does in religion is to confess life, all life, as holy: 'God-given, God-inspired, God-directed.' Accordingly faith is not opposed to reason; it is only that it exists at a deeper level than any of the capacities of which it makes use. Reason is one of faith's essential components, though not, of course, its entire essence. 'When, therefore, the self puts out its primitive power, it will do actions which satisfy reason, indeed, but which reason cannot exhaustively analyse, or interpret, since the entire force of reason, if it were all brought into action, would still be only a partial contribution to the effect.'

But although faith is identified as 'a simple adhesion of the soul to God' it has, in its objective expression, a history of its own. The record of this is in the Bible and the dogmatic creeds, both of which derive their significance from belief in Christ; for faith, first and last, is 'a spiritual cohesion of person with person'. The formularies, for all their difficulties and complications, are the product of faith: 'The creeds only record that certain questions have, as a fact, been asked. Could our world be what it is, and not have asked them?' The articulation of faith has been shaped, that is, by the needs and complexities of man's actual existence. Yet it is always to the personal life that dogmas relate, which is why they differ from scientific generalizations. To claim that the

Christian dogma is final is really no more than to assert the finality of Christianity itself. 'If we are in a position to have any faith in Jesus Christ, then we must suppose that we have arrived at this one centre to all possible experiences, the one focus under which all insights fall.'

Holland's contribution to *Lux Mundi* remained one of the best of his works. His other publications consisted of collections of sermons, *Logic and Life* (1882), *Creed and Character* (1887) and *On Behalf of Belief* (1888) being perhaps the most noteworthy.[1] His theological position as a whole was conservative. For all his sympathy, in certain regards, with Roman Catholic Modernism—he always spoke of Tyrrell's writings with profound admiration—he could follow it in neither its historical scepticism nor its philosophical pragmatism. The Christian experience, he believed, has its solid basis in historical fact; but he also was insistent that the facts can properly be known only in terms of spiritual and moral experience. The fourth gospel appealed to him as pre-eminently the gospel of fact *and* experience. It was this same belief in the mutual dependence of fact and experience, faith and life, which led him to Christian socialism, an important and characteristic side of his thought and career.[2]

The second essay in *Lux Mundi* was that of Aubrey Moore, a theologian who had also read widely in both philosophy and natural science and whose death at the age of forty-two was a loss to Oxford and to the Church of England. On the subject of the Christian doctrine of God he sought to show how far modern philosophy and science might enrich as well as modify the traditional theism. The religious and the philosophical conceptions of deity differ, but are mutually necessary. 'Religion demands as the very condition of its existence a God who transcends the universe; philosophy as imperatively requires His immanence in nature.' Christian trinitarianism makes possible the satisfaction of each requirement. The one absolutely impossible conception to the modern mind, for which evolution has become a basic category, is the deist notion of an occasional celestial visitor.

[1] Mention should be made of his article on Justin Martyr in *The Dictionary of Christian Biography* (1882); the Romanes lecture on 'The Optimism of Butler's "Analogy" ' (1908); and the posthumous *The Philosophy of Faith and the Fourth Gospel*, ed. W. Richmond, (1920). A selection of his writings is contained in the present author's *Henry Scott Holland* (1962).

[2] See the appended Note to this chapter.

Science had pushed the deist's God farther and farther away, and at the moment when it seemed as if He would be thrust out altogether, Darwin appeared, and under the guise of a foe did the work of a friend. It has conferred upon philosophy and religion an inestimable benefit, by shewing us that we must choose between two alternatives. Either God is everywhere present, or He is nowhere. He cannot be here and not there.[1]

The immanence of God in all things is the great spiritual lesson which science now teaches; and it wholly fits the ancient doctrines of the Logos and the Trinity. The author optimistically concludes that

all and more than all that philosophy and science can demand, as to the immanence of reason in the universe, and the rational coherence of all its parts, is included in the Christian teaching: nothing which religion requires as to God's separateness from the world which He has made, is left unsatisfied.

Moore's argument that the 'higher pantheism' and the religion of Christ are not wholly incompatible is resumed by John Illingworth in the essay on 'The Incarnation and Development'. A key idea in contemporary thought is the principle of evolution; the question to be asked by the theologian, therefore, is its bearing on the central doctrine of Christianity, since great scientific discoveries are not merely new facts to be assimilated but involve new perspectives. Here the Fathers of the early Church are of assistance, having seen in the incarnation the climax and keystone of the whole visible creation, an idea also shared by the medieval schoolmen: the incarnation, says Aquinas, is the exaltation of human nature and the consummation of the universe. It is true that the modern scientific view of the origins and progress of life appears at first to be inimical to final causes; but at a deeper level evolution seems rather to underwrite the teleological principle and to give to the evidence of design in nature a firmer basis. 'Under scientific guidance, we have acquired a more real, as distinct from a merely notional apprehension of the manifold adaptations of structure to function, which the universe presents.'[2] This more thoroughgoing conception of teleology is in perfect harmony with the Christian creed. In addition it teaches the further

[1] *Lux Mundi*, p. 99.
[2] *Ibid.*, p. 191.

doctrine of the indwelling presence of the eternal Reason in all things of his creation. For science has a religious as well as a theological importance, constituting as it does the element of truth in that higher pantheism which the modern mind finds so amenable. No good, however, is to be had from attempts to limit the sphere of scientific advance. 'If the remaining barriers between reason and unreason, or between lifelessness and life should one day vanish, we shall need to readjust the focus of our spiritual eye to the enlarged vision, but nothing more.' Yet man himself has a unique power of initiation. Always dissatisfied with his actual achievement he presses forward to something new. Modern philosophy has helped us to grasp more fully the significance of individuality, originality and personality in man, whose capacity for self-adaptation means that the human species is virtually permanent. Hence as touching the personality of Christ it may be said that the incarnation has introduced a new species into the world, 'a Divine man transcending past humanity, as humanity transcended the rest of the animal creation, and communicating His vital energy by a spiritual process to subsequent generations of men'.[1] To the objection that the incarnation traverses experience by importing an alien factor, the miraculous, the answer is that Christianity does not rest its claim solely on its miracles. These, to many minds, are comforting; but the real basis and true verification of Christianity is in present experience. It is in fact the only power which has regenerated personal life, 'and that beyond the circle even of its professed adherents, the light of it far outshining the lamp which has held its flame'.

Illingworth's philosophical position, as expressed in his book on *Divine Immanence* (1898), was a moderate idealism. Matter and spirit, he says, are known only in combination, with the result that neither can be known completely. Yet they represent distinct and distinguishable phases of experience. As we encounter it the spirit is, of course, always embodied; but it uses matter for its purposes and must be judged to have a certain primacy. Among such uses one of the most striking has been the religious. Primitive religion always finds divinity in nature, and even where mythology is outgrown the religious influence of the external world remains as strong as ever. A survey of religious ideas, Christian and non-Christian, leads to the conclusion that basically

[1] *Ibid.*, p. 207.

438

man's religious consciousness is one and points to a spiritual reality behind all things. Herein indeed is that 'natural' religion which Christianity presupposes. If we ask how the divine Spirit is related to matter the answer, Illingworth replies, can at once be anticipated by considering our own reality as personal beings. Man's consciousness transcends the material being with which it is associated, but also is in some way immanent in it. Similarly with God: 'The divine presence which we recognize in nature will be the presence of a Spirit, which infinitely transcends the material order, yet sustains and indwells it the while.'[1] To the question whether the universe is God's body or his work different answers may no doubt be given; but the Christian is entitled to urge that the trinitarian conception—to Christian faith a primary truth of revelation—is intellectually the most satisfactory since it embraces an immanence of both kinds and so 'harmonizes with the entire analogy of our personal experience'. For according to this doctrine the Logos, the second Person of the Trinity, is the essential, adequate and eternal manifestation of the first, as, in the case of man himself, is the body to personality. He is also immanent, in a secondary sense, in his whole creation, as are we in our works; only with the obvious difference that we as finite and transient beings are there only 'impersonally' present, 'whereas He must be conceived as ever present to sustain and animate the universe, which thus becomes a living manifestation of Himself'. Whether personality as humanly understood can in all strictness be referred to God Illingworth regards as a debatable question. He would not himself object to speaking of divine personality as *supra*personal, so long as this includes 'the essential attributes of personality',[2] although he is also disposed to consider human personality as imperfect, a replica—no more—in the finite of the divine archetypal personality,[3] the psychological elements of thought, desire and will in man being a reflection of the triune personality in God. Illingworth, we may add, realized well

[1] *Divine Immanence*, p. 72. In his last volume, *Divine Transcendence* (1911), Illingworth sought to modify the immanentist tendency of his earlier work. God, he points out, cannot be immanent in a world he does not transcend, nor transcendent over the world unless he is immanent within it.

[2] *Op. cit.*, p. 158. The whole problem of personality in man and God he discusses at length in his Bampton lectures, *Personality, Human and Divine* (1894), where he develops the argument that God, as trinitarian theology describes him, is in fact the perfection of human personality.

[3] *Personality, Human and Divine*, p. 216.

enough that a radical immanentism would impair the uniqueness of the incarnation, a course very far from his own intentions. He was convinced of the truth of the historical revelation on which he believed all Christian doctrine must be founded (in matters of criticism he was decidedly conservative), and he resolutely defended miracles inasmuch as the incarnation—*ex hypothesi* a unique event—was not miraculous in any sense to which objection could fairly be taken: 'If the Incarnation was a fact, and Jesus Christ was what He claimed to be, His miracles, so far from being improbable, will appear as the most natural things in the world.'[1]

Moberly's chapter on the incarnation as the basis of dogma opens with a plea for dogmatic truth. The principle of dogma is not to be attacked or defended on *a priori* grounds, the only real question being the truth of what is affirmed, which is a matter of evidence. Acceptance of dogma is in itself entirely reasonable, since its claims to authority and finality are in the case of Christianity the necessary outcome of the facts accepted in it. The facts themselves are all-important and the truth they convey has a completeness which scientific theory cannot parallel.

> The Christian Creed does not simply enunciate so many abstract principles of natural or supernatural life or governance. It introduces us straight to a supreme Person, Himself the beginning and the end, the author and upholder of all. Such a doctrine may be false, but it cannot be a fragment.[2]

For the believer every aspect of experience endorses his belief. 'There is no part or element of life which does not to him perpetually elucidate and confirm the knowledge which has been given him.' In the evidence for the incarnation—'either a fact or a fiction'—the vital datum is the resurrection, a historical event that is not a mere happening but 'an eternal counsel and infinite act of God'. The dogma of the incarnation is the Church's answer to the question, inevitable in the light of its primal experience, 'What think ye of Christ?' The decisions of the early councils represent no more than a growth in intellectual precision through encounter with error, the creed in its whole substance being the direct outcome of the fact of the incarnation. Further,

---

[1] *Divine Immanence*, p. 88. See A. M. Ramsey, *From Gore to Temple*, p. 20.
[2] *Op. cit.*, p. 228.

dogma is to be distinguished from theological speculation. The theology of one age may be discredited and superseded in another. It may develop and it may err. Indeed so far as language is concerned even the creeds are obviously human. The so-called damnatory clauses of the Athanasian are no doubt open to misunderstanding, but nevertheless are justifiable. The formulary is addressed not to outsiders but to believers, to encourage and to warn. For thought and life are not to be separated, and Christian dogmatism is but devotion to truth for truth's sake.

The essay clearly stood for the integrity of the received faith, and the author's later work is no less firmly rooted in the Catholic tradition. Thus *Ministerial Priesthood* (1897), without presuming to challenge Lightfoot's competence as a historian, does question the Cambridge scholar's implied doctrine of the Christian ministry in his famous essay,[1] a view resting, in Moberly's judgment, on some very disputable assumptions. Lightfoot, he wrote,

> insists, truly in the main, upon the Church's essential existence as spiritual. But he uses this truth to deny the reality of her proper existence as bodily; and then, being forced to deal with her existence as bodily, he treats it, not ... as the living, proper method and utterance of Spirit, but as a lower, politic, condescending, accidental necessity.[2]

Lightfoot further assumes, he thinks, that the words 'sacrifice' and 'priesthood' legitimately carry only the meaning put upon them in the Old Testament, and takes it for granted—confusing 'representative' with 'delegate'—that the representative character of the ministry requires that any and every member of the Church implicitly possesses the right to minister. His own theory of the priesthood, unlike (he claims) either the Roman or the Protestant conceptions, is that it is essentially a function of the Church, which itself derives from that of the exalted Christ ('If Christ is a priest, the Church is priestly'),[3] specialized and personified in certain representative instruments.

> From this representative leadership in all external enactment of worship and sacrament . . . it follows also, on the inward and spiritual side, that those who outwardly represent the priesthood of the

---

[1] See above, pp. 347f.
[2] *Ministerial Priesthood*, 2nd ed., p. 43.
[3] *Ibid.*, p. 251.

Church must no less specially represent its true inwardness. The priest is not a priest in the act of divine worship only. His personal relation to the priestliness of the Church is something which has been conferred on him once for all, and which dominates everything that he does, or is.[1]

Ministerial Priesthood was followed in 1901 by *Atonement and Personality*, a work still to be accounted a major product of Anglican divinity: 'a study in systematic theology such as had not been produced for many years within the Church of England'.[2] Here again Moberly's standpoint is that of tradition, whilst differing from the teaching of the Congregationalist R. W. Dale's well-known book published in 1875. Dale, he thought, had made the common evangelical mistake of failing to relate Christ's death to the work of the Holy Spirit and the life of the Church. He was also critical of Dale's idea of the cross as involving penal suffering, with Christ's having submitted to the 'actual penalty of sin.' His own thesis is virtually McLeod Campbell's, that of the 'perfect penitent'. Its statement, more elaborate than Campbell's, is prefaced by an examination of the terms 'punishment', 'penitence' and 'forgiveness'. Punishment denotes retribution, but it issues in penitence. Complete penitence, however, is impossible for a sinner, since 'the reality of sin in the self blunts the self's power of utter anthithesis to sin'.[3] Yet complete penitence is inherently necessary. In other words, 'penitence, in the perfectness of its full meaning, is not even conceivably possible, except it be to be personally sinless'.[4] Such sinlessness is found only in the humanity of Christ, 'identically God', 'inclusively man'. 'Only He, who knew in Himself the measure of the holiness of God, could realize also, in the human nature He had made His own, the full depth of the alienation of sin from God, the real character of the penal averting of God's face.' What Christ offered the Father was not an expiatory sacrifice but humanity perfectly penitent and righteous, wholly in accord with and responsive to 'the essential character of Deity'.[5] By the cross atonement was wrought as an eternal, objective, historical fact, consummated adequately and once for all. But since forgiveness is 'inchoate' until the one

[1] *Ibid.*, pp. 259f.
[2] J. K. Mozley, *Some Tendencies in British Theology* (1951), p. 25.
[3] *Atonement and Personality*, p. 42.
[4] *Ibid.*, p. 117.
[5] *Ibid.*, p. 404.

forgiven becomes righteous, the objective reality must in turn be subjectively apprehended. This the Holy Spirit makes possible, the result being a 'transfiguring' in which at last, for the first time, self becomes fully self and the meaning of human personality is consumated and realized.[1]

Moberly's treatment of his great theme is a masterly expression of Christian sentiment, yet it met with a good deal of criticism, especially in regard to his view of penitence and forgiveness and his alleged confusion of the doctrine's objective and subjective aspects.[2] Lyttelton's account of the atonement also adopts the *motif* of representation rather than (although not to the exclusion of) propitiation. Sin gives rise to that sense of alienation from God which the ritual of sacrifice endeavours to overcome, and the most complete and typical form of the sacrificial idea was embodied in the Mosaic system. Yet even this was only a partial expedient, something external and provisional. The death of the sinless Christ alone answers to the demands of the conviction of sin and of the desire for forgiveness. That death, in the perspective of the New Testament, was a propitiatory sacrifice. Man could offer nothing acceptable; the offering had to be made by Christ, whom it behoved to die, the punishment being willingly accepted by him as an acknowledgement of the due reward of sin. But propitiation is not the only element; on the manward side Christ acted as humanity's representative by virtue of his assumption of complete human nature. Thus there was 'nothing artificial in His sin-bearing, for His human nature was so real and so perfect that He was involved, so to speak, in all the consequences of sin'. Hence 'only as His brethren, because He has united us to Him, are we enabled to plead the sacrifice which He has offered'. In its attempt to combine two distinct ideas the essay is not, however, altogether a success. The author, anxious to omit nothing upon which traditional faith and piety have fastened, whilst at the same time correcting the errors by which atonement theology has so often been marred, fails to shape his own views into a consistent whole. But he at least tried to render a more comprehensive account of the doctrine, and one more satisfying ethically.

---

[1] *Ibid.*, p. 153.

[2] See, e.g., Hastings Rashdall's observations in *The Journal of Theological Studies*, iii (1901), pp. 178–211. Moberly's argument was in essence repeated by his son, W. H. Moberly, in an essay in *Foundations*, ed. B. H. Streeter, published in 1912.

To return, however, to *Lux Mundi*. Upon the remaining essays, other than Gore's, we need not dwell. In 'The Preparation of Christianity for Christ' Talbot sought to do what Temple had attempted in *Essays and Reviews*. Modern historical study, he thinks, has served less to diminish than to emphasize 'the wonder of an apparently unique convergence of lines of preparation' in the Hebrew and the Greek traditions respectively. Lock's paper on the Church approaches its subject empirically, seeing in it the final satisfaction of the social need of cooperation for life, knowledge and worship, a need which the complexity of modern civilization has served only to accentuate. Paget on the sacraments urges the prominence of the sacramental principle in the gospels and its immense subsequent importance for Christian thought and piety, pointing out, at the experiential level, the correspondence between the ministry of the sacraments and the diverse elements which compose the nature of man himself. Campion, on Christianity and politics, describes the Christian role in society as at once consecrating and purifying. The Christian view of political order rests on a conception of man and his destiny: family, State and Church are each and all places of training for a 'perfected common life in the City of God'. It is this heavenly City, moreover, which 'judges and corrects the splendour of earthly States'. Ottley's essay on Christian ethics, concluding the volume, aims within its compass at providing something of a formal treatise, in view of 'the absence of books of a genuine English growth'. In an appendix the writer expressed his belief that 'every transaction between man and man is to be regarded as *personal*, and therefore *ethical*. . . . To reason rightly on social problems we must ever have regard to *personality*. . . . Our problem is how to supersede the technical and legal relation by the personal'—one that remains no less pressing or difficult today, nearly a century later.

2. CHARLES GORE

The contribution which aroused most interest, as also, in some minds, the most disquiet, was the editor's own, on 'The Holy Spirit and Inspiration'. Gore's was the task of confronting the issue, by then inescapable, of the implications of biblical criticism for the historic faith. The array of patristic learning was on the face of it reassuring, however. The writer's opening theme is the life-giving work of the Holy Spirit: in nature (the 'body' of which the Spirit is the 'breath'), in man (created for divine sonship, 'for the life of the spirit'), in man's recovery from the sin into which he had fallen (the Spirit is at work in the righteous 'remnant' of God's chosen), in Christ (the perfect realization of man's destiny), and in the Church, the special and covenanted sphere of the Spirit's regular and uniform operation, 'the home where, in spite of sin and imperfection, is kept alive the picture of what the Christian life is'. Of the work of the Holy Spirit within the Church four characteristics are to be noted. It is social, for man cannot realize himself in isolation; but at the same time it nourishes individuality, the very idea of the Spirit's gift being that of an intenser because more individualized life. The Spirit is also to be understood as consecrating the whole of nature, material existence as well as spiritual; whilst his way of procedure is always gradual: 'He lifts man little by little, He condescends to man's infirmity.' In the Church the Spirit is personally present and continuously active.

The second section of the essay deals with the theology of the Holy Spirit, of whose being and action we have through revelation a real if limited knowledge. As simply stating the orthodox doctrine it calls for no special comment. The third and last section discloses the author's main purpose: to discuss the meaning and scope of the term inspiration when applied to Scripture. Gore begins by pointing out the danger of not consistently relating the idea to the rest of the Spirit's work in the Church. Indeed, 'it is becoming more difficult to believe in the Bible without believing in the Church'. When a man believes in Christ 'he will find himself in a position where alike the authority of his Master and the *communis sensus* of the society he belongs to, give into his hand certain documents and declare them inspired'. But the doctrine of inspiration is an article of the faith, not one of its bases, although as such an *article* it has a necessary place. The difficulties occur when one asks what exactly is meant by it. The question can be answered only by actual study of the Scriptures. These in the case of the Jews are 'a national literature marked by an unparalleled unity of purpose and character, a spiritual fabric which in its result we cannot but recognize as the action of the Divine Spirit'; and in the case of the Christian Church a uniquely authoritative interpretation of Christ to the world. Practically, 'to believe in the inspiration of the Holy Scriptures is to put ourselves to school with every part of the Old Testament, as of the New', despite evident imperfections and limitations. The problem, however, is in determining how far these latter—the human factor—may detract from the Bible's divine authority. Revelation, we claim, is conveyed in a historical process, but is a certain idealization or heightened dramatization of that process, as recorded, compatible with the aims of imparting truth? Can the concept of inspiration allow for the presence even of primitive myths? In reply Gore points out that the Church is not restrained by not having committed itself to a dogmatic definition of inspiration, a fact which he regards as fortunate and even providential.

A serious obstacle to the acceptance of modern criticism might, on the other hand, be made of Christ's own evident belief in the traditional Jewish view of the authorship of Scripture: his assumption, for example, that David was the author of Psalm 110 or that Jonah really had lived and been swallowed by a great fish. The difficulty can be met, Gore thinks, on the supposition that the Son of God, in becoming incarnate, 'emptied himself' of, or temporarily laid aside, certain of his divine attributes, among them his omniscience, thus submitting to the intellectual limitations of the time and circumstances in which he had chosen to manifest himself. In Gore's own words: 'He willed so to restrain the beams of His Deity as to observe the limits of the science of His age, and He puts Himself in the same relation to its historical knowledge.'[1] Here, almost in an aside, was that speculative doctrine of the *kenosis* which he was to elaborate in subsequent works, notably the Bampton lectures of 1891, *The Incarnation of the Son of God*, and the *Dissertations on Subjects connected with the Incarnation*, published in 1895; and to it we must return in a moment.[2] Meantime we are to remark Gore's general conclusion

---

[1] *Lux Mundi*, p. 360.

[2] So called from the Greek word *kenoō*, used in Phil. ii, 7 (*heauton ekenōsen*, lit. 'he emptied himself'). Kenotic theories of the incarnation have been designed to explain what actually was involved in the Son of God's becoming man. The expression seems to have first been used by Ernst Sartorius in 1832, the idea denoted by it rapidly gaining favour among Lutheran theologians, who taught that the Son, in order to assume humanity, relinquished such attributes of deity as omnipotence and omniscience and with them his exercise of cosmic sovereignty. Thus G. Thomasius (*Beiträge z. kirchlichen Christologie*, 1845) held that the Logos laid aside the fulness of his divine nature in all respects touching his self-manifestation to men. See also the same author's *Christi Person and Werke*, 1853; and F. Loofs, in *Realencyclopädie f. protestantische Theologie und Kirche* (3. Aufl.), x, pp. 246–63.

in the essay that although it is impossible to maintain the historicity of the Old Testament at all points, and although Jesus himself spoke as a Jew of his century, yet to represent the New Testament history as 'idealized' (and hence to some extent falsified) cannot be admitted 'without results disastrous to the Christian Creed'. There the absolute coincidence of idea and fact was vital. The Church must then insist that although the New Testament may contain errors of detail the history, in a general sense, is nevertheless entirely trustworthy. Upon this Gore was to remain adamant to the end.[1]

The Bampton lectures show their author at his best.[2] Their ground theme is that nature and grace are not antithetic, and the view that the supernatural is the unnatural is wholly mistaken. 'In whatever sense men believe in God, they believe that nature is God's ordinance, and nature's laws, and the knowledge of nature as far as it goes, the knowledge of God'.[3] Christ, therefore, who according to the Church's faith and doctrine is a supernatural person, is yet himself completely in harmony with nature and is in truth its fulfilment. Redemption does not repudiate creation. 'Nature as a whole, moral and physical, demands Him to accomplish its yearnings and to restore its order.'[4] This had been the assurance of the ancient Greek Fathers, who insisted that the incarnation was on the lines of God's inherence in nature and that in Christ God's presence was only intensified. So in speaking of the incarnation as 'the crown of natural development in the universe' one would not be resorting to novel language. The God who reveals himself in nature, in the advance from inorganic to organic and from animal life to rational, offers his culminating self-disclosure in Christ, to whom all that precedes leads up. Seen thus he is no affront to reason: 'The first volume of the divine author in fact postulates a second.' It appears indeed as perfectly intelligible that God should take man's nature as the

---

[1] Thus in 1929 he wrote: 'As far as historical evidence, strictly considered, goes, the Gospels supply us with the firm foundation for the belief in Jesus which appears in the Epistles and in the Creeds of the Church' (W. R. Matthews (ed.), *Dogma*, p. 80).

[2] The Gifford lectures, *The Philosophy of the Good Life*, published in 1930, have by some been ranked as his finest work, and as the final statement of their author's own deepest convictions they may well be judged so. But the prevailing intellectual climate had changed greatly in the interval and the later book was less opportune and perhaps less forceful than the earlier.

[3] *The Incarnation of the Son of God*, p. 29.

[4] *Ibid.*, p. 39.

medium of his own self-revelation, without either annihilating manhood or compromising the Godhead. The claim, moreover, that Christ is supernatural is relative to what is considered natural, each new stage of life appearing supernatural from the point of view below it. Moral life is supernatural from the standpoint of the physical; and similarly Christ is supernatural as seen by man. But there is also discontinuity as well as continuity; for Christ not only is the consummation of nature, he is its restoration as well, after the ravages of sin.

Yet even here there is a manifest 'order' in things. Sin is essentially lawlessness, a violation of man's true nature, and must be seen as such if the 'naturalness' of Christ is to be appreciated. Approached in this way miracle loses its arbitrariness and alleged unnaturalness. It appears not as a contradiction of nature but as a vindication of its 'true, divine orderliness', previously obscured by sin. For a miracle is 'an event in physical nature which makes unmistakably plain the presence and direct action of God working for a moral end'. The incarnate Son of God could not therefore have been otherwise than miraculous. Science itself teaches that there is emergence, novelty, in nature; and on the Christian hypothesis Christ is a new creature whose coming must be expected to have exhibited new phenomena. God violates nature's superficial uniformity in the interests of a deeper law, of a profounder understanding of what nature itself really is.

This section of Gore's book points, in fact, the direction Anglican thought on the incarnation was to take for some years to come.[1] The evolutionary principle clearly provides a leading motive and what Gore here has to say, were it taken by itself, would appear entirely in line with the current immanentist idealism. But so to take it would be to misrepresent him seriously. Gore was not by any means uninfluenced by T. H. Green, but he was at no time strongly drawn to idealism, in this differing markedly from his friend Illingworth.[2] The prophetic, sin-conscious, sin-denouncing strain in his thinking was too potent to allow him to assimilate Christ to the natural order as commonly conceived by philosophers. But here his purpose is not so much to

[1] See A. M. Ramsey, *op. cit.*, p. 18.
[2] Only at one place in his published work did Gore acknowledge a debt to Green, in *Belief in God* (1921), p. viii. Green's influence on Gore, in the present writer's view, lay in the field of social ethics, although it is evident that virtually all Anglican theology during the years 1890 to 1920 took up a broadly idealist position.

stress the singularity of Christ and his discontinuity with the natural, as the apologetic one of showing that in the perspective of the Christian dogma 'the Word made flesh', although unique, does not represent a mere heteronomy which the reason cannot assimilate. He is unique indeed even on the humanitarian plane; but in his uniqueness he is not isolated, having set in motion 'a new development, which is the movement of the redeemed humanity'. And of this last Christ is the centre, 'the Head with the body, the Bridegroom with the bride'.[1]

It was Gore's aside, in the *Lux Mundi* essay, on the problem of Christ's human knowledge which especially distressed Liddon, for whom the gospel history implied without a doubt that 'the knowledge infused into the human soul of Jesus was ordinarily and practically equivalent to omniscience'.[2] This, however, was an idea which Gore found objectionable. Since Christ was God in manhood it is certain that he at all times *possessed* the divine as well as the human consciousness and nature. But Gore also considered that the self-sacrifice of the incarnation lay particularly in Christ's refraining to exercise what he possessed in order that he might live under the conditions of a true manhood. There were genuinely things which on earth he did not know.[3] That the concept of the 'self-emptying' of deity involved theoretical problems Gore realized. To the question, for example, of the Son's cosmic functions he felt he could give only 'a very hesitating and partial answer'. On the one hand, as the Christian theological tradition had consistently maintained, the work of the Son could in no way have been interrupted by the incarnation; on the other, the Son in becoming incarnate, must reasonably be held to have accepted the limitations of humanity as an essential element in his self-sacrifice.

In the Bamptons these matters are dealt with only briefly, in an appended note. Gore's developed theory of the *kenosis* is set out with fulness in the *Dissertations*. He was himself well aware—much more so than any of the older school of High Churchmen—that New Testament criticism had raised the whole issue of the gospel's historicity and that a modern theologian is bound to view Christ's manhood in a historical perspective. In this regard 'much

[1] *The Incarnation of the Son of God*, pp. 51f.
[2] *The Divinity of Our Lord*, 14th ed, p. 474.
[3] *The Incarnation of the Son of God*, pp. 265f.

of the patristic and all of the medieval theology' was inadequate.[1] From the pen of so adept a patristic scholar such words carried weight and in conservative quarters gave offence. Gore's use of the kenotic idea had indeed been immediately anticipated by at least two Anglican theologians—in standpoint far apart from each other—T. K. Cheyne and A. J. Mason.[2] But it was he who unquestionably gave it currency and, we may say, considering his personal standing in the Church of England, respectability. Gore was a High Churchman, an 'Anglo-Catholic', yet one also who held that the Church, whilst preserving continuity in doctrine, should be free to 're-express its theological mind, as it has so often already done, in view of fresh developments in the intellectual, moral and social life of man',[3] a conviction he had made plain in *Lux Mundi*. A turn of phrase Gore was wont to use was that in the incarnation Christ had 'abandoned (or surrendered) his prerogatives', or at any rate the exercise of them. He perhaps was being deliberately imprecise.[4] All he wanted to ensure was that, under the conditions of the mortal incarnate life the divine Son 'did, and as it would appear habitually—doubtless by a voluntary action of his own self-limiting and self-restraining love—cease from the exercise of those functions and powers, including the divine omniscience, which would have been incompatible with a truly human experience'.[5] The Godhead, as he chose to put it, was 'energizing' under the conditions and limitations of manhood. But on the cosmic functions of the Logos Gore continued to maintain what he deemed a proper reserve. Such functions, 'in another sphere, had of course been exercised during the earthly life, but the humiliation and self-limitation of the incarnate state was, it must be supposed, wholly consonant with them. What in fact really concerned Gore was the *moral* force of the kenotic principle. Given this he was, it seems, prepared to let the metaphysical difficulties go unanswered, as constituting a problem essentially unanswerable.

[1] *Dissertations on Subjects connected with the Incarnation*, p. 9.

[2] See Cheyne's Bampton lectures on *The Origin and Religious Content of the Psalter* (1889), p. 25, and Mason's *The Faith of the Gospel* (1887), pp. 152–9 (1905 edn.).

[3] *Dissertations*, p. 213.

[4] In the original edition of the *Dissertations* Gore had spoken of 'a real abandonment of divine prerogatives *and attributes* by the Eternal Son within a certain sphere' (p. 206, italics ours). His modification of the wording in the second edition evidently indicates his awareness of the metaphysical difficulties it could have raised.

[5] *Dissertations*, p. 95.

To attempt to deal with the large volume of criticism which Gore's theory provoked during the earlier years of the present century, when kenotist Christianity was still in the forefront of theological discussion, would take us beyond our period.[1] Suffice it to say that much of it was directed against its dubious scriptural basis, particularly the famous passage in Philippians, the language of which, as D. M. Baillie urged, is that of poetry more than metaphysics.[2] Hastings Rashdall considered the theory to demand so complete a break in the consciousness of the Son as to render it ridiculous to say that it is consistent with the Word's being unchanged.[3] Gore's phraseology, with his seemingly reckless use of words like 'abandonment' and 'surrender', was also found to be open to objection. This in particular was William Sanday's point.[4] The difficulties which the kenotic argument presents may well have been lessened by Weston,[5] Forsyth[6] and Mackintosh.[7] But William Temple, in *Christus Veritas* (1924), could still look on kenotic theories as 'intolerable' and reject the principle as involving 'something dangerously close to mythology'.[8] Creed, however, is less ready to condemn, and whilst not arguing expressly for kenoticism he nevertheless commits himself to the opinion that 'if we take seriously both the human conditions of the life of Jesus and the theory of His personal identity and continuity with the eternal Word, then a kenotic Christology seems to be indispensable'.[9] What Gore did was to compel theologians to take the human conditions of Jesus' life seriously, and no Christology could nowadays gain attention which, whatever else it might succeed in doing, failed in this.[10]

[1] In 1938 J. M. Creed wrote that 'though kenotic doctrine is no longer so much in favour as it was, I should think it probable that a majority today of those among us who have a Christology which they are prepared to state and defend, are still kenoticists' (*The Divinity of Jesus Christ*, p. 75). O. C. Quick, in *Doctrines of the Creed* (1938), stoutly upholds the principle.

[2] *God was in Christ* (1948), p. 94.

[3] *God and Man*, ed. H. D. A. Major and F. L. Cross (1930), p. 95.

[4] *Christologies, Ancient and Modern* (1910), pp. 76f.

[5] Frank Weston, *The One Christ* (1907).

[6] P. T. Forsyth, *The Person and Place of Christ* (1909).

[7] H. R. Mackintosh, *The Person of Jesus Christ* (1912).

[8] See especially *op. cit.*, pp. 161ff.

[9] *Op. cit.*, p. 136.

[10] See K. E. Kirk's Charles Gore Memorial Lecture, *The Coherence of Christian Doctrines* (1950), p. 9.

One other but a signal contribution by Gore to theological debate at the turn of the century remains to be noted: his study of eucharistic doctrine in *The Body of Christ*, published in 1901. On this subject it remains one of the best works by an English divine, and Dr E. L. Mascall is right in deploring the undeserved neglect into which it has fallen.[1] That the eucharist is 'the extension of the incarnation is an idea, he claims, not only Tractarian but patristic, and he himself willingly adopts it. But it would be truer to the turn of Gore's thought to refer the expression to the Church itself, or at all events to the sacraments in general, with the eucharist as the special medium or focus of the divine presence.[2] The sacramental principle, he holds, is consonant with the entire procedure of God in creation and redemption, as also in the twofold nature of man, compounded as he is of body and spirit (the body being the spirit's organ).[3] Opposition of body and spirit can draw no sanction from the New Testament. Gore further considers that between the incarnation and the sacraments there is an analogy of fundamental principle, even though it may not admit of being carried out in detail. In communion it is the whole Christ who is received, not merely 'the Spirit for our spirits, or the teaching for our intellects'. Touching the eucharistic sacrifice Gore strongly denies any repetition of Calvary. Its true meaning is determined by its relation to the offering of the glorified Christ in heaven.

> The sacrifice of the Son of Man once offered in death has been accepted in glory. In the power of that sacrifice Christ ever lives, our high priest and perpetual intercessor, the continually accepted propitiation of our sins unto the end of time. All that we need to do and can do is to make thankful commemoration, in His way and by His Spirit, of His redemptive sufferings, and to unite ourselves to His perpetual intercession when He presents Himself for us in the heavenly places, or as He makes Himself present among us in our eucharistic worship.[4]

[1] See *Corpus Christi* (1953), p. 138.

[2] Cp. *The Incarnation of the Son of God*, p. 218: 'For this primarily the Church exists: to be the Spirit-bearing body, and that is to be the bearer of Christ, the great "Christopher", perpetuating, in a new, but not less real way, the presence of the Son of Man in the world.'

[3] *The Body of Christ*, p. 40.

[4] *Ibid.*, p. 183.

The description of his theological and ecclesiastical standpoint which seems best to have satisfied Gore himself is that of 'liberal Catholicism', an expression he frequently employed.[1] But by it he meant nothing idiosyncratic or exotic. He was a liberal Catholic simply because he was a member of the Church of England, an Anglican. Anglicanism as he understood it was but a convenient name for liberal Catholicism as it had developed under the historic conditions, political and cultural, of the English people.[2] There was, he judged, no doubt about what the English Church had stood for since the Reformation, when it inherited the ancient faith and order of Christendom, other than a Catholicism reformed and preserved in accordance with the teaching of Scripture. This was his firm conviction throughout life. The spiritual test was necessary as the guarantee of liberty against the pressures of ecclesiastical authority and an inordinate dogmatism. But the Church of England did not attempt to make 'the Bible and the Bible only' the fixed norm of its doctrine. History also plays its part: Catholicism, that is, is identifiable as a historical tradition within which Scripture has been interpreted in terms of a continuing experience under varying circumstances. Of this experience the Catholic creeds and the decisions of the ecumenical councils are at once the embodiment and the safeguard. That Bible, creeds and councils are in essential agreement Gore did not for a moment doubt and any attempt to separate them he steadfastly opposed. On the other hand the claims of reason, of which the best Anglican divinity at all periods has never been oblivious, had also to be met. In the sixteenth century and after the English Church had opened her arms alike to the new learning, to the new appeal to Scripture, to the freedom of historical criticism and to the duty of private judgment.[3] Anglican Catholicism believed

[1] See J. Carpenter, *Gore: a Study of Liberal Catholic Thought* (1960), Ch. 2. For the use of the term in a Roman Catholic context see Appendix III below.

[2] 'I have always maintained that we in the Church of England represent a liberal Catholicism' (*The Basis of Anglican Fellowship in Faith and Organization*, 1914, p. 4. Cp. p. 23).

[3] In the earliest of his published works, a paper on 'The Nature of Faith and the Condition of its Exercise', privately printed and circulated in 1878, he had written: 'The Church of England truly adopts a *via media* in that she will side neither with those who, in confidence of the powers of the unaided reason, would have each man his own pope; nor with those who, in despair of their own capacity to find out truth at all for themselves, would submit their reason once and for all, by a single act, to an external, infallible voice. She will not acquiesce in this Manichaean severance of reason and authority' (p. 28).

in freedom as a principle and thus was bound to repudiate an absolutist authoritarianism of whatever kind. 'True authority does not issue edicts to suppress men's personal judgment or render its action unnecessary, but is like the authority of a parent, which invigorates and encourages, even while it restrains and guides the growth of our individuality.'[1]

To some Anglicans of more ultramontane sympathies—Lord Halifax, for example—Gore seemed indeed too much a Protestant, if not a 'modernist'. Were the charge meant to imply only the exercise of personal responsibility in the matter of faith he would certainly not have rejected it. But to the type of liberalism which in his opinion tampered with the Catholic creeds he was implacably hostile.[2] Intransigence towards modernism became in fact increasingly characteristic of his policy as a diocesan bishop. On the substantial historicity of the events in which Christianity originated, as presented in the New Testament, he was ever insistent. Doctrines of an overtly metaphysical or symbolic nature might admit of differing modes of interpretation, but not the historical affirmations; and to the end Gore made the historical claims of Christianity the foundation of his apologetic method. Among such claims were the literal truth of Christ's virgin birth and bodily resurrection, express assent to which he deemed an obligation incumbent at least upon the clergy.[3] For these doctrines, to his mind, could not be taken in any merely figurative sense, although he conceded that the ascension may be placed in a rather different category, the idea of Christ's *upward* motion to his final, heavenly state being necessarily symbolical, since heaven itself is not a locality. But the virgin birth and the resurrection had been actual historical occurrences, fully capable of description

---

[1] *Roman Catholic Claims* (11th ed.), p. 54. This book was first published in 1884. A second, enlarged edition appeared in 1889.

[2] 'There must', he wrote in 1903, 'be no compromise as regards the Creeds. . . . If those who live in an atmosphere of intellectual criticism become incapable of such sincere public profession of belief as the Creed contains, the Church must look to recruit her ministry from classes still capable of a more simple and unhesitating faith' (*Report of the Church Congress of 1903*, p. 17). Later, when bishop of Birmingham, he declared: 'I have taken occasion before now to make it evident that, as far as I can secure it, I will admit no one into this diocese, or into Holy Orders, to minister for the congregation, who does not *ex animo* believe the Creeds' (*The New Theology and the Old Religion*, 1907, p. 162).

[3] 'Our Church leaves lay folk to their own discretion, but it does make specific requirements on the clergy, its officers' (*The Basis of Anglican Fellowship*, p. 7). Cp. *The Clergy and the Creeds* (1887), p. 28.

in the language of ordinary experience. To object to them on the
a priori ground of the incredibility of miracle seemed to him
totally illegitimate inasmuch as nature is not a closed system
excluding all possibility of intrusion from without. Christian
philosophy recognizes the reign of law, but law may pertain to a
higher or a lower order of things; and in the interest of the higher
the divine action may fittingly abrogate the lower. He who
imposes law may also suspend or transcend it. In any case 'the
point of a divine miracle, as the Bible conceives it, is not to be a
mere portent, but a sure indication that the moral will of God is
supreme in the world'.[1]

As time went by Gore appeared more and more of a conservative: a Catholic assuredly, although never of the 'Romanizing'
kind; but a liberal, at least as measured by the criteria of the
Churchmen's (later the Modern Churchmen's) Union, by no
means. He even seemed a conservative by the standards of a
younger school of High Churchmen more open to the influences
of what he himself regarded as a dangerously radical type of New
Testament criticism, a school whose religious philosophy,
accordingly, was based less upon the assumed authenticity of
Christ's historical claims than upon the pragmatic value of the
Christian experience itself. However, Gore's influence upon
Anglican opinion throughout the first quarter of the present
century was greater than that of any other living divine. W. R.
Inge, a thinker of a very different mental cast and an always
abrasive critic of Anglo-Catholicism, deemed him 'one of the most
powerful spiritual forces in our generation', a view in no way
exaggerative.[2] Gore combined a wealth of theological learning
with great independence of judgment, intense moral fervour and
the strength of a personality never deterred by opposition. He was
a teacher, prophet and natural leader of men, and among his
successors in the Church of England only William Temple is to be
compared with him.

3. LIBERALISM, ANGLICAN AND FREE CHURCH

'A devout Christian', it has been said, 'may be a Liberal Protestant
or a Liberal Catholic; he can hardly be a Liberal without any

[1] *Belief in God* (1921), p. 238.
[2] *Outspoken Essays: First Series* (1919), p. 134. The essay on 'Bishop Gore and the
Church of England' was written in 1908.

qualification.'[1] Liberalism in western Christianity is bound, that is, to qualify one or the other of its two divergent traditions. Gore and his fellow-contributors to *Lux Mundi* represented a liberalizing of the High Church or 'Catholic' strain in the Church of England; but what of the Low Church or Evangelical? How far did it show itself responsive to the demands of the changed and changing cultural environment? The Evangelical party had never been noted for its interest in or concern for theological learning or the relations between Christian thought and contemporary science and scholarship. On the contrary, its aims were strictly practical and the religious atmosphere it tended to create (and certainly found congenial) was predominantly emotional. Intellectual curiosity in religious matters is eschewed as misleading and purposeless. An old-fashioned orthodoxy, centred on the doctrine of the atonement as a penal substitutionary sacrifice, was all, theologically speaking, that it had to offer. This included a largely Old Testament theism, a naïve supernaturalism, a literalist view of the Bible and an eschatology which admitted heaven and hell but not purgatory. The evangelical idea of salvation was still prevailingly individualist.[2] Such attitudes would not yield readily to new influences from outside the traditional religious sphere.

Nevertheless the party was not quite without its scholars; and of them one of the most learned was Henry Wace (1836–1924), dean of Canterbury, an authority on the sixteenth-century Protestant Reformers and a hard-hitting controversialist.[3] Another was the Church historian, H. M. Gwatkin (1844–1914), whose work on the early Church, and especially the Arian controversy, is still of real value.[4] Yet another respected figure was H. C. G. Moule (1841–1920), a fellow of Trinity College, Cambridge, and a former pupil of Lightfoot's, who after holding the Norrisian professorship of divinity succeeded Westcott as bishop of Durham.[5] But his theological conservatism, seemingly impervious

[1] W. R. Inge, *Vale* (1934), p. 74.

[2] Even Queen Victoria disapproved of 'ultra-Evangelicals' as narrow-minded. See W. F. Monypenny and G. E. Buckle, *The Life of Benjamin Disraeli*, ii, p. 45.

[3] His editing (with W. Smith) of *The Dictionary of Christian Biography* (1880–86) was carried out with admirable impartiality and complete competence.

[4] Notably *Studies of Arianism* (1882), *The Arian Controversy* (1889) and *Early Church History to 313* (1909).

[5] He was also first principal of the Evangelical theological college at Cambridge, Ridley Hall, founded in 1881.

to every current trend, never wavered, and his outlook remained that of a bygone age. The Oxford Evangelical, F. J. Chavasse, afterwards a much-respected bishop of Liverpool, although less of a scholar than Moule, was more open-minded, realizing that critical theories of the Bible's literary history could not be refuted by being ignored and that evolution might after all have some relevance to theology. But the day of Liberal Evangelicalism, as represented by such men as V. F. Storr and, somewhat later, C. E. Raven, had not yet dawned.

It is probable, however, that the real roots of liberal Evangelicalism lay in what had already become known, as far back as the 1850s, as the 'Broad Church', a term first used, it would seem, by W. J. Conybeare in an article in *The Edinburgh Review* for 1853. Maurice, although a man of broad views, sharply repudiated the label when applied to himself. Jowett, on the other hand, could very well have been classed as such, and his friend Stanley would have welcomed the name. 'Broad' too was the standpoint of the Cambridge historian, Sir James Seeley, whose *Ecce Homo*, published anonymously in 1865, aroused a good deal of attention. The book was reviewed by Dean Church in *The Guardian* of 7 February 1866, and was commended as 'a protest against the stiffness of all cast-iron systems, and a warning against trusting what is worn out'.[1] Gladstone too gave it fairly favourable notice. Seeley's aim was to depict the central figure of the gospels in a way that a historian as distinct from a theologian might see it, although the attempt was read by many as intending to reduce Christ to purely human status, despite the fact that the author did not deny Jesus' miraculous powers. Perhaps the common opinion was expressed by Westcott when he complained that 'it is this so-called morality as "the sum of the Gospel" which makes Christianity so powerless now'.[2] A sequel, entitled *Natural Religion*, appeared in 1882, but did not repeat its predecessor's popular success. Its argument is the familiar one that nature provides a truer revelation of God's presence and purpose than does miracle. Another professed liberal was E. A. Abbott, whose *The Kernel and the Husk*, was published (like *Ecce Homo*, anonymously) in 1886. Abbott defended the practice of clergymen who, whilst personally in doubt on certain doctrines, continued to

---

[1] *Occasional Papers*, ii, pp. 133ff.
[2] A. Westcott, *op. cit.*, ii, p. 289.

affirm them in the course of public worship. The priest reciting the offices, he contended, was stating not his private convictions but the formal teaching of the Church.

A distinguished Broad Church bishop was William Boyd Carpenter (1841–1918), whose 1887 Bampton lectures on *The Permanent Elements in Religion* were a plea for the serious study of comparative religion, not least as a means of testing the truth of the Christian faith itself. The ethical criterion in all instances must, he thought, be held supreme, and judged by this the Christian religion had done more than any other to promote morality. Unfortunately in the past, all too often, orthodoxy had been preferred to ethics.

> The eager and shallow dogmatist who worshipped not God, but clung vehemently and immorally to his creed, demanded intellectual assent. Heedless of the need of intellectual honesty, or of the ethical significance of the creed, he saw no alternative between the declaration of assent to a theological proposition and the eternal damnation of a human soul. He made it possible for men to say, and to say it with a measure of truth, that orthodoxy was the sin against the Holy Ghost.[1]

In his Donnellan lectures at Dublin on *The Witness of Religious Experience* (1914) he noted in such experience the three stages of dependence, fellowship and progress, each associated, in Christianity, with men's relations with the Father, the Son and the Holy Spirit respectively. In this process the religious consciousness becomes a faculty of spiritual verification. Yet the experience of Christ himself was unique. 'He is outside the religion of those storm centres which sin, self-reproach, remorse, and rooted selfishness occasion in others. . . . He is a pattern after which all may strive, but he is not a type whose counterpart can be found in any human being.'[2] In 1898 Boyd Carpenter founded a clergy training college at Ripon, of which diocese he was bishop, with the express purpose of training ordinands in accordance with liberal ideals. It later moved to Oxford where, however, under the name of Ripon Hall, its record has sometimes been such as to raise doubts of how far liberalism can be 'institutionlized' without producing the very faults which it decries when visible elsewhere.[3]

---

[1] *The Permanent Elements in Religion*, p. 276.
[2] *The Witness of Religious Experience*, pp. 89f.
[3] See H. D. A. Major, *The Life and Letters of William Boyd Carpenter* (1925), ch. viii.

The question of free-thinking clerics using traditional formularies was provocatively raised by Henry Sidgwick in an article
in *The International Journal of Ethics* of April 1896 on 'The Ethics
of Conformity'. It was an issue he had had to face in his own
career, and one on which for conscience' sake he had many
years previously resigned his fellowship at Trinity College,
Cambridge. His argument was that a degree of latitude could be
permitted to the laity, but in the case of clergymen assent to
statements which they do not personally believe is dishonest and
to be condemned. Some months later, and in the same journal, an
answer was given by Hastings Rashdall, then a tutor of New
College, Oxford. This article was a plea for greater freedom of
interpretation and in the matter of conformity the right of
individual judgment. Some disparity between personal belief and
formal profession is, he contended, all but inevitable and is
recognized to be so by men of all parties; nor was this to be
regretted: reinterpretation of ancient formulae is necessary if the
life of the Church is to continue, a principle applying to the creed
as well as to the Articles. On the particular problem of the
virgin birth, always a test case, he pointed out that it was not in
the original creed of Niceae and is not in fact essential to the
doctrine of the incarnation.

Rashdall's main publications in philosophy and theology fall
outside our period, but he had already gained high reputation as a
historian with his impressive volumes on *The Universities of
Europe in the Middle Ages* (1895). His position as a theological
liberal was made evident in a collection of university sermons
published in 1898 with the title *Doctrine and Development*. This he
described as an effort at theological reconstruction, while denying
that 'liberal' theology meant only 'vague and indefinite' theology.
All theology arises, he believes, from the attempt to set the
facts of the moral and religious consciousness in due relation
to science and history. The place of development must be
conceded and with it the obsoleteness of not a little of the
teaching of the past. Theories of verbal inspiration are plainly no
longer tenable; but also difficult for the modern mind are theories
of the atonement which in their day seemed proper to an Anselm
or a Luther but which are felt now to be objectionable on moral
grounds. Already indeed was Rashdall defending that Abelardian
doctrine which was to form the thesis of his subsequent Bampton

lectures, *The Idea of Atonement in Christian Theology* (1915), that the death of Christ—'the culminating act of a self-sacrificing *life*'[1]—has its essential meaning in the example which it sets us. He also, in a sermon of 1889, anticipated Gore's discussion of the limitation of Christ's knowledge and indicated the need for a type of kenotic theory which in certain directions went beyond Gore's own. He did not think kenoticism incompatible with Catholic doctrine but stressed that 'we should in all our teaching put the simpler presentations—the moral, the spiritual, the personal aspects—of Christ's divinity foremost'.[2] In an address on the doctrine of the Trinity given in Balliol College chapel on Trinity Sunday 1894 he sketches his characteristic 'Sabellian' view—for which he claims the authority of Augustine and Aquinas—that in the context of trinitarian theology the word 'person' requires a meaning very different from its usual modern acceptation. Those who framed what are still the acknowledged orthodox formulae could have had no such idea in mind, whereas most people today, 'at least in their orthodox moments, when they are trying to realize to themselves the doctrine of the Holy Trinity, think of the three Persons as three distinct beings, three consciousnesses, three minds, three wills'.[3] God is not three personalities, but three 'essential' properties or activities, distinguishable as Power, Wisdom and Will (or Love) respectively.[4]

Rashdall was firmly convinced both of the possibility of a natural theology and its necessity if Christian teaching is to have a sound foundation. His position hereon is set out in the essay 'The Ultimate Basis of Theism' which he in 1902 contributed to *Contentio Veritatis*, a volume of composite authorship broadly representative of the liberal standpoint; as too in that on 'Personality Human and Divine' included in a symposium, edited by Henry Stout and entitled *Personal Idealism*, which appeared in the same year.[5] It is a Green-inspired idealism, but one which emphasizes the reality and importance of individual persons or

---

[1] *Doctrine and Development*, p. 129.

[2] *Ibid.*, p. 55.

[3] *Ibid.*, pp. 23f.

[4] Rashdall's interpretation of Augustine's and Aquinas's trinitarianism has since, however, been challenged. See, e.g., E. J. Bicknell in *Essays Catholic and Critical* (3rd ed., 1929), pp. 148–50. Cp. Ramsey, *From Gore to Temple*, pp. 185ff.

[5] See also Rashdall's 'open' lectures at Cambridge, *Philosophy and Religion*, published in 1909.

spirits. Rashdall argues the existence of God in a manner reminiscent of Berkeley. The world depends on mind, but not on
finite minds. One must assume therefore a *divine* mind, an infinite
intelligence creative of both material and spiritual reality. There
are, of course, difficulties in the way of ascribing personality to
God, yet personality is the highest category we know and if God
is mind he must be so *sensu eminentiori*. Also as a Person coexisting
with other persons he cannot be identified with the all-inclusive
Absolute: consciousnesses are mutually exclusive. Accordingly
God is limited to the extent at least of not including his creation.
As rational and moral he represents the power of good in the
universe and thus gives assurance of the final defeat of evil.
Rashdall's theism is therefore ethical to its roots. With mysticism
he had no sympathy and any apologetic appeal to 'religious
experience'—a type of argument coming into favour among his
contemporaries—he distrusted as too subjective and tending to
irrationalism.

By the close of the century Rashdall was already prominent as a
leader of liberal opinion in the Church of England, and throughout the next two decades his pre-eminence in this respect was
unquestionable, his standing indeed among Anglican liberals
being analogous to that of Gore among High Churchmen. The
place of his lifelong friend, William Ralph Inge (1860–1954),
famous later as dean of St Paul's—the 'gloomy dean' of popular
journalism, was more equivocal. In many ways Inge was emphatically not a liberal. Politically and socially his attitudes were not
only conservative but anti-democratic. Democracy, he was wont
to observe, 'dissolves communities into individuals and collects
them again into mobs'.[1] Towards socialism his feelings were
hostile and he had scant sympathy even with Gore's diluted and
Christianized form of it. 'The position of a Church which would
sell itself to the Labour party would be truly ignominious.'[2] A
thoroughgoing Platonist, he would have favoured the rule of an
intellectual *élite*, though one preferably schooled at Eton. Himself
of no party ecclesiastically, he did not share the regret of Harnack
and other liberal Protestants at the 'intellectualizing' of Christianity
by Hellenism. For the Anglo-Catholics with their supposed
concern for what he called 'ecclesiastical millinery' he had

[1] *Outspoken Essays: First Series*, p. 11.
[2] *Ibid.*, p. 131.

461

only contempt. He was a 'modernist' after his fashion, but of modernism as it showed itself in the Roman Catholic Church at the beginning of this century he was sharply critical. Its treatment of the New Testament, especially at the hands of Loisy, he thought destructive: 'What more, it may well be asked, have rationalist opponents of Christianity ever said, in their efforts to tear up the Christian religion by the roots, than we find here admitted by Catholic apologists?'[1] And to its pragmatist philosophy his reaction was one of distaste and suspicion: 'Any assertion about fact which commends itself to the will and affections and which is proved by experience to furnish nutriment to the spiritual life, may [in Modernist eyes] be adhered to without scruple.' Like Rashdall, Inge was an 'intellectualist' in his religious philosophy, but Rashdall's dislike of mysticism was the opposite of his own thinking, in which mystical experience, rather broadly interpreted, occupied a central place.

At the time (1889) of his appointment as tutor of Hertford College, Oxford, where he at first had Rashdall for a colleague, he had formed no very definite philosophical or theological opinions of his own. He as yet had only slight acquaintance with the literature of mysticism and had read nothing of Plotinus, whose thought was years later to provide the subject of his most considerable work, the Gifford lectures of 1917–18.[2] It was in fact during this Oxford period that he took up the serious study of Neo-Platonism, and in 1896 determined to make a name for himself as an authority on Christian mysticism as well as an essayist and a preacher.[3] The outcome was his Bampton lectures, published in 1899.[4] The treatment adopted is historical and expository and such indications as are given of the author's personal views hardly amount to a philosophy of mysticism. However the pattern of Inge's later thinking is already emerging: a kind of intuitional rationalism for which the mystical experience becomes an expression, not of mere subjective emotion, but of the entire personality, with reason as its controlling principle. It could be said that for Inge mysticism was a philosophy of the spirit, resting on an apprehension of absolute values. As he

[1] *Ibid.*, pp. 152f.
[2] *The Philosophy of Plotinus* (2 vols, 1918).
[3] See Adam Fox, *Dean Inge* (1960), p. 60.
[4] *Christian Mysticism* (reissued 1912).

phrased it in one of his later writings: 'The goal of philosophy is the same as the goal of religion—perfect knowledge of the Perfect.'[1]

Like Rashdall, Inge contributed to *Contentio Veritatis*, with an essay on 'The Person of Christ' and another on 'The Sacraments'. The former is the more satisfactory of the two—of sacramentalism Inge never acquired any real understanding—and is indeed one of the best of his shorter writings, well thought out and lucid in statement. It is imbued with his sense of religion as a matter essentially present and practical. Religion, he says, may relate to both history and science, but its interest is in neither.

> Religion, when it confines itself to its own province, never speaks in the past tense. It is concerned only with what is, not with what was. History as history is not its business. And abstract science, which concerns itself with relations which prevail between phenomena, without reference to ultimate truth, is not its business either. ... Errors in history, or errors in science, do not save or damn. Errors in religion are always due to what Plato calls 'the lie in the soul'.... What is the truth, in the spiritual order, which it is intended to protect by the doctrines of the virgin birth, resurrection and ascension? The answer is plain: it is the identification of the man Christ Jesus with the Word of God.[2]

Inge remains a thinker not easy to place. An individualist, he disliked institutionalism in religion and despised its familiar manifestations. On the other hand, his antipathy for mere emotionalism was if anything even stronger. His orthodox belief in the incarnation was never qualified by immanentist or 'adoptionist' theories, nor severed from its moorings—despite his Platonism—in the historical figure of Jesus of Nazareth. Nor again was the name of modernist very congenial to him except in so far as it stood for liberality of mind and a critical discrimination. He believed, rather, in the age-old values of European civilization and in the virtues of knowledge and the rational understanding whilst holding steadfastly to the conviction that divine truth is ever accessible to the enlightened spirit.[3]

[1] *Contemporary British Philosophy*, Series I (ed. H. J. Muirhead, 1925), p. 191.

[2] *Contentio Veritatis*, pp. 90f.

[3] See his presidential address to the 1925 annual conference of the Churchmen's Union, published in *The Modern Churchman* in the September of that year. Inge was president of the Union from 1924 until 1934.

In the Church of England, then, on one side and on another, the traditional positions were being increasingly modified if not abandoned. But what of the Nonconformists, or the Free Churches as they were now coming to be called? How did they welcome the new trends? Evangelical piety had as a rule been distrustful of exposing religion to worldly culture, yet could the immunity any longer be preserved? Apart from the very small Unitarian sect Protestant dissent was throughout the greater part of the century inconspicuous for its contributions to theological or philosophical thought. Its concerns were practical, its spiritual tone more pietistic than intellectual or scholarly. In so far, however, as any real theological interest existed it was to be found among the Congregationalists, and towards the end of our period the Congregational Union counted some distinguished teachers in its membership.

First in seniority was Robert William Dale (1829–1895), a famed preacher and educationalist and pastor of the well-known Carr's Lane Chapel in Birmingham. Dale deplored the persistent lack of interest shown in systematic theology not only among pastoral ministers but, less excusably, in the theological colleges. To this he attributed 'very much of the poverty and confusion of theological thought, very much of the religious uncertainty, and some of the more serious defects in the practical religious life' of Victorian nonconformity.[1] Dale's own one major undertaking in this field was his volume on *The Atonement*, based on a series of public lectures and published in 1875. Taking his stand on a progressive but fundamentally orthodox evangelicalism, he was concerned to maintain, as against the views of such men as Jowett or the American theologian, Horace Bushnell, the juridical significance of Christ's atoning death while at the same time trying to avoid the all too familiar legalism. Particularly impressive is his handling of the New Testament data.[2] On the axiom that punishment is 'pain and loss inflicted for the violation of a law'[3] Dale concludes that a sound doctrine of atonement will not exclude the penal element. Christ, however, vindicated the law of righteousness, 'not by inflicting suffering on the sinner, but by enduring

---

[1] See A. W. W. Dale, *The Life of R. W. Dale of Birmingham* (1898), p. 573.

[2] Cp. R. C. Moberly's comments in *Atonement and Personality*, p. 389.

[3] *The Atonement*, p. 61.

suffering Himself'.[1] He received the due penalty of sin, that is, by actually submitting to the authority of the *principle* which such penalty expresses.[2] But although Dale insists on the priority of a 'legal' or 'objective' view he allows that it does not represent the whole truth. Christ's death was also a demonstration of God's love by which 'a real change is wrought in us, a change by which we are reconciled to God'. Further, Dale rejects any idea of an imputation of sin to Christ—'a legal fiction'—and dismisses as mere rhetoric the notion of a ransom paid by the divine mercy to the divine justice. Christ's sufferings were not, in the strict sense, the penalties of sin at all, but, as pains freely endured, were accepted by God as the equivalent thereto—a theory suggesting the influence of Grotius.[3]

A more distinctively liberal thinker was Dale's learned Scottish contemporary, Andrew Martin Fairbairn (1838–1912), principal of the Airedale Theological College, Bradford, from 1877 to 1886 and subsequently of Mansfield College, Oxford. As a young man Fairbairn had studied in Germany and had been affected by the teaching of Dorner, Tholock and Hengstenberg. His chief works are *The Place of Christ in Modern Theology*, published in 1893, and *The Philosophy of the Christian Religion*, dedicated to R. W. Dale, which appeared some nine years later and contained his mature reflexions on the nature and meaning of Christianity. He was also the author of a perceptive if controversial study, *Catholicism, Roman and Anglican* (1899). By theology Fairbairn understood 'the science of the living God and of His work in and for a living world',[4] and its focal theme is the person and achievement of Christ. Christ, he urges, is not to be thought of, in the manner of much contemporary liberal Protestantism, only as an historical individual whose biography has its ready material in the gospels. On the contrary, he is 'even more intellectually real than historically actual', and the Christian dogma concerning him stands for 'a whole order of thought, a way of regarding the universe, of conceiving God and man in themselves and in their mutual relations'. Thus in its widest aspect it is more symbolical

---

[1] *Ibid.*, p. 383.

[2] p. 423.

[3] Cp. G. B. Stevens, *The Christian Doctrine of Salvation* (1905), p. 190, where the author calls attention to the resemblances between Dale's teaching and that of Grotius' *Defensio Fidei Catholicae de Satisfactione Christi*.

[4] *The Place of Christ in Modern Theology*, p. 403.

than factual, although it is 'a symbol which owes all its reality to its being a fact transfigured and sublimed'.[1] Christology, that is, covers both historic fact and speculative interpretation, since one who fulfils universal functions cannot be described and dismissed as if he were no more than a particular individual. Whatever may be said in criticism of the classical formularies, doubtless over-speculative and possibly defective in logic, it must be acknowledged that their purpose was to make the person of Christ representative of 'the natures, relations, inter-activities, community and difference in attribute and being, of God and man'. Had they not existed from an early date something very like them, Fairbairn believed, would have had to be devised later to explain the course things have taken. This task of interpreting Christ and the place he holds and the functions he has fulfilled in the life of man, collective and individual, is what Christian theology is essentially about. Where, however, the Church has most obviously defaulted has been in its failure to interpret Christ *ethically* with sufficient insight and consistency. There is nothing in all its history more tragic than its persistence in confining heresy to speculative opinion rather than practical morality. 'If Christ be rightly interpreted, the worst sins against God are those most injurious to man.'[2]

Fairbairn's own theory of the incarnation was kenoticist in the manner of the Lutheran Thomasius, drawing a distinction between the metaphysical and the ethical attributes of divinity, the former alone being laid aside (as it were) with the assumption of humanity. Some such doctrine he, like Gore, held to be entirely necessary if the real manhood of Christ is to be grasped by the imagination. And at the purely historical level he was confident—in the light of subsequent developments in New Testament study over-confident—that 'for the Christian theologian, the most significant and assured result of the critical process is, that he can now stand face to face with the historical Christ, and conceive God as He conceived Him'.[3] Fairbairn even believed that such a book as Renan's best-selling *Vie de Jésus*, superficial as it was, had at least served to show that Christianity is to be explained 'not through abstract principles, tendencies, differences, conciliations,

---

[1] *The Philosophy of the Christian Religion*, p. 16.
[2] *Ibid.*, p. 565.
[3] *The Place of Christ in Modern Theology*, p. viii.

but through its creative Personality'.[1] The pity was, of course, that this same creative personality had been as much thwarted as aided by the institutions, often grossly political, in which Christianity has been historically embodied. Nevertheless the Christian religion could not in its development through the ages have avoided the effects of the changing environment. 'In other words, the religion grew because it lived, and it lived because it carried within it an immanent and architechtonic idea, which governed it and yet was essentially its own.'[2]

Two other Congregationalist divines whose reputations as theologians were already founded by the close of the century were Peter Taylor Forsyth (1848–1921), who was appointed principal of Hackney College, Hampstead, in 1901, and Alfred Edward Garvie (1862–1945), principal of New College (which had incorporated Hackney) from 1924 to 1933. Forsyth, who always perhaps had more of the preacher in him than the academic scholar, had in early life followed the liberal trend, having been influenced first by Hegelianism and then by Ritschl, whose pupil at Goettingen he was for a time. Later, however, under pressure of a deepening sense of man's need of redemption, his liberalism became less and less obtrusive, and the atonement more than the incarnation occupied the central place in his teaching. 'There is in the Incarnation', he now wrote, 'that which puts us at once at the moral heart of reality—the Son made sin rather than the Son made flesh. The Incarnation has no religious value but as the background of the atonement.'[3] Revelation, he believed, can truly be found only in redemption. But the body of Forsyth's work—and notably *The Person and Place of Jesus Christ* (1909), *The Work of Christ* (1910) and *The Principle of Authority* (1913)—belong properly to the theological history of the present century.[4] The

[1] *Ibid.*, p. 279.
[2] p. 518. Fairbairn distinguished two types of churches, according to whether they are controlled by a 'political' or a 'theological' interest. The former seemed to him to confine the divine action by rules, beyond which it is only 'irregular, illicit or unconvenanted', whereas the Church really is the visible image of Christ, who 'is too large to be confined within the institutions of men, they too hard and narrow to be equal to His penetrative and expansive grace' (*The Place of Christ in Modern Theology*, pp. 154f.).
[3] *Positive Preaching and the Modern Mind* (1907), p. 182.
[4] Forsyth can hardly be described as a systematic theologian, but his thought had a remarkable consistency. J. K. Mozley said of him that no theologian of the day had 'fewer loose ends' in this respect (*The Doctrine of the Atonement*, 1915, p. 182).

R

same is true of Garvie, although his study of Ritschlianism, *The Ritschlian Theology*, published in 1899, at once established him as a leading authority on the subject in the English-speaking world. As the lifelong exponent of a solid though wide-minded Protestant orthodoxy he tended in his later years to devote his time and energies increasingly to active church work, becoming in turn chairman of the Congregational Union of England, and Wales (1920), president of the National Free Church Council (1924), vice-chairman of the Lausanne Conference on Faith and Order (1927) and moderator of the Free Church Federal Council (1928).

Thus with our survey concluded we may ask what overall impression of the period remains. 'It is one of the hardest tasks in the world', observed Matthew Arnold, 'to make new intellectual ideas harmonize truly with the religious life, to place them in the right light for that life. The moments in which such a change is accomplished are epochs in religious history.' That the latter half of the nineteenth century was of this kind is hardly to be doubted. At all events immense efforts had been made to effect a harmony. Scientific methods, in the investigation whether of nature or of human history, had been tried and developed with so over-whelming a success in their yield of positive knowledge that if religion were to retain its place in Western culture the concepts traditionally associated with it would have to undergo more or less drastic revision. Beliefs whose forms at least had come down unchanged from the era of the Reformation, from the middle ages or from antiquity itself could no longer retain their grasp upon the modern educated mind without some resolute attempt by churchmen to shape them to the new conditions. What Arnold was fond of calling the *Zeitgeist* had made demands which only those who were most obdurately set in the old ways—identifying them with eternal truth—thought it possible to resist. In general the movement towards intellectual reconciliation could be described as liberal, and if it affected the Protestant churches more than Catholicism this was because of Protestantism's inherent nature, which biblicist authoritarianism could not permanently mask. In England indeed, as to only a somewhat lesser degree in Scotland, the feeling now was one of broad optimism. The first shock of the impact of criticism had been severe, but the orthodox teaching had regained confidence. Bishop Mandell Creighton, for instance, writing in 1896, stated that 'for my part I believe the attack on Christianity is intellectually repulsed'.[1] And of those who led the counter-attack Gore himself was not the last to be assured of victory. The vastness of the universe, in space and in time, had become a commonplace; the theory of evolution, with its particular implications for the origin and status of the human race, had apparently been assimilated; the critical approach to history, and especially the sacred history of the Bible, was an assumption which scholarship had no need to defend; and that the religious experience of mankind as a whole, however devious or defective its forms as judged by Christian standards, witnessed to the reality and manifold providence of the one God, was an idea by now willingly affirmed. In short, although the Catholic faith, in its vital centre, still held, orthodoxy had become critical and even non-believers were rarely hostile.[2]

Yet, looking back to that time, the historian of thought can scarcely but feel that the optimism was somewhat too shining and that self-complacency—a fault of orthodoxies in all ages—was already evident. The changes which the preceding half-century had wrought were by no means concluded. Thus the open conflict between religion and science might to some extent have been silenced, but scientific and technological progress has since gone far to create an intellectual and social climate in which religious supernaturalism has not been able to thrive. Again, the compromise between theology and historical criticism which by the beginning of this century had been not only conceded but welcomed by men like Gore and Sanday, proved to be unstable and the attempt to justify tradition on the grounds of history alone quickly ran into difficulties. Yet again, developing study of the varied patterns of human behaviour, individual and social, have tended to weaken the claim of Christianity to a unique character and authority. Instead it has fallen into ever clearer perspective as a phase, limited and determined by time and circumstance, of man's age-old effort to establish his identity and shape his destiny. The fate of metaphysical beliefs is not that they are proved to be untrue but that they gradually forfeit their meaning and relevance.

[1] Louise Creighton, *The Life and Letters of Mandell Creighton* (1904), ii, p. 191.

[2] Cp. Herbert Spencer's admission: 'Religious creeds, which in one way or another occupy the sphere that material interpretation seeks to occupy and fails the more it seeks, I have come to regard with a sympathy based on community of need' (*Autobiography*, ii, p. 471).

They are valuable and significant so long only as they retain adherents. But their survival, unfortunately, is not decided by the ingenuity of their apologists. At the outset of the nineteenth century the religion of the Christian churches still provided an intellectual and moral frame of reference which even the religiously indifferent in the main admitted. At its end this frame of reference had lost credibility. The liberal compromise was of course—and ere long—to receive a sharp challenge from a form of neo-orthodoxy. But the moderate success of that challenge has been in the nature of a reaction, and like all reactions was the product of the very forces it has sought to repel.

NOTE

Church and Society

The year of the publication of *Lux Mundi*, 1889, was that also of the founding of the Christian Social Union, an event largely brought about by Scott Holland. Brooke Foss Westcott was chosen as the Union's president, and Holland himself as chairman of committee, its headquarters being a mission house run by Canon A. J. Mason at Tower Hill, London. The aims of the organization were stated to be:

> (i) To claim for the Christian Law the ultimate authority to rule social practice; (ii) To study in common how to apply the moral truths and principles of Christianity to the social and economic difficulties of the present time; and (iii) To present Christ in practical life as the Living Master and King, the enemy of wrong and selfishness, the power of righteousness and love.

Holland was insistent that its churchly character be made plain from the start: 'Your fervid socialist Nothingarian' was to be excluded. In his view political problems were giving place to those of large-scale industry.

> It is [he wrote] the condition of industry which is absorbing all attention and all anxieties. It is the needs and necessities of industry which are the motive powers now at work to mould and direct the fortunes of human society. It is the intolerable situation in which our industrial population now finds itself, that must force upon us a reconsideration of the economic principles and methods which have such disastrous and terrible results.

But how the problem was to be tackled depended on one's conception of humanity itself and of human need. Secular ideals would not suffice; Christ, 'the Man', was the solution of all human problems. 'We look into the face of Jesus Christ as into a mirror in which we can see what manner of thing man originally and actually is intended to be' (*Our Neighbours*, 1911, p. 143). But the difficulty lay in the application of Christian principles to the complex order of human society as it is, a fact which Holland, like William Temple and others since, realized well enough. The Ricardonian idea of the 'autonomy' of economic laws was morally unacceptable, yet Christian opinion wavered between accepting it on scientific and rejecting it on ethical grounds.

> We go a certain distance with the science, and then, when things get ugly and squeeze, we suddenly introduce moral considerations, and human kindness, and charity. And then, again, this seems weak, and we pull up short and go back to tough economic principle ... When our economy is caught in a tangle, we fly off to our morality. When our morality lands us in a social problem, we take refuge in some naked economic law.

So he wrote in a preface he contributed to a book on *Christian Economics* by his friend, Canon Wilfrid Richmond, published in 1890, but went on to commend the way in which the author had resolved this seeming dilemma. 'The ethical principle does not appear as outside the economic, entering on the scene merely as a sentiment to check, and to limit, and to correct it; but it is itself the intelligent and constructive force which builds up, from within, the scientific principles. The economic laws are exhibited, not as arbitrarily limited by moral considerations, but as themselves the issue of moral considerations' (see Stephen Paget, *Henry Scott Holland: Memoir and Letters*, 1921, pp. 172f.).

It was to this conviction that the Christian Social Union was dedicated. Particular enterprises and works of charity like those with which Stewart Headlam's Guild of St Matthew (1877) was associated were admirable in themselves but hardly adequate as an expression of Christian social responsibility. (Cp. Maurice Reckitt, *Maurice to Temple: A Century of Social Movement in the Church of England*, 1947, pp. 136f.: 'While Headlam strove to vindicate the outcast and to defy their oppressors, Holland sought to interpret the signs of the times and to win men to his own understanding of what that interpretation required.') What was needed was the more radical purpose of Christianizing (or at least moralizing) the social structure itself. Scott Holland was wholehearted in his belief in the Church's social mission, which he preached up and down the country, always with much rhetorical brilliancy. Gore indeed remarked: 'I sometimes was tempted to wonder whether his brilliant oratory and sparkling wit did not so delight his audience with a sort of physical joy as to conceal from them what severe doctrine and what unpalatable conclusions were really being pressed upon them' (Paget, p. 248). But the Union was not concerned only with social theory. It engaged in a good deal of practical activity as well. Yet its real task was to promote a Christian social philosophy as the basis for action. In this Holland's periodical, *The Commonwealth*, the first issue of which came out in January 1896, played a leading role. Much of its content was provided by Holland himself, who found the work suited to his temperament and talents. His own political opinions were in a broad sense socialist; at any rate he was dissatisfied with the official Liberalism of the day. He thought it out of touch with 'Labour'. 'The rich Liberal capitalist is not necessarily more in sympathy with the workers than the rich Tory capitalist. Parliament is still made up for the most part of wealthy men.' He was alienated, moreover, by what he and his friends considered the anti-church attitudes of the Liberal party in many matters. What was required was a wider recognition than Liberalism showed of the importance of the corporate life, of the social significance of the masses as such, and of the need for 'socialistic humanitarianism'. Gore, however, emphatically denied that the policy of the Christian Social Union itself was socialist except in the general sense of countering *laisser-faire* individualism. It did not advocate state ownership 'or tie its members to any particular platform of constructive politics' (Paget, p. 242). But Holland himself was probably ahead of Gore in this respect. He certainly believed in state controls, so long as they were freely accepted. He even praised Marxism for challenging 'the political Economists with a social philosophy as scientific as their own'. But a satisfactory doctrine of society could not be devised without liberal recourse to ethical categories, and here secular socialism, in Holland's view, failed. The questions were: 'How far can Socialism claim the sanction of Jesus Christ? Within what limit? When does it overstep that sanction? What would our Lord really say, if it is true that He would not say all that these others put in His mouth? What, in fact, constitutes Christian Citizenship?' (*Our Neighbours*, p. 10). They are questions still awaiting conclusive answer.

Appendix I

The Gorham Judgment

Whether the Book of Common Prayer does or does not teach that the baptized are as such regenerate was the issue at stake in the famous Gorham case of 1849–50. In 1847 Bishop Phillpotts of Exeter, a High Churchman, refused to institute the Rev. George Cornelius Gorham, at the time vicar of St Just-in-Penwith in Cornwall, to the Devon living of Bramford Speke on the ground that as a professed Calvinist in theology he denied the doctrine of the Church of England in holding that the grace of regeneration is not, strictly speaking, conferred by the baptismal rite but is given either 'preveniently' or subsequently at conversion. The bishop had himself conducted a lengthy examination of Gorham and had found the answers to the questions he put to him unsatisfactory. Gorham took his case to the Court of Arches, which, however, upheld the bishop's decision. Thereupon he appealed to the Judicial Committee of the Privy Council, which had not before dealt with a doctrinal or indeed ecclesiastical matter and which now found in the appellant's favour. The Committee did not itself claim authority to determine questions of faith or competence to settle what the doctrine of the Church of England ought in any particular instance to be. Its duty, it declared, extended only to the consideration of what is by law established to be the Church's doctrine upon 'the true and legal construction of her Articles and Formularies'. Gorham's argument was that the Church does not expressly teach that—in the words of his chief supporter, the Rev. William Goode—'an adult is not necessarily in a state of spiritual regeneration because he was baptized as an infant';[1]

[1] *The Doctrine of the Church of England as to the effects of Baptism in the case of Infants* (1849).

and it was this view that the Judicial Committee endorsed. As to what the teaching of the Church is the Committee relied for information mainly upon the Articles.

> Devotional expressions involving assertions [it maintained] must not as of course be taken to bear an absolute and unconditional sense. There are other points of doctrine respecting the Sacrament of Baptism which we are of opinion are . . . capable of being understood in different senses; and consequently we think that, as to them, the points which were left undetermined by the Articles are not decided by the Rubrics and Formularies, and that upon these points, all ministers of the Church, having duly made the subscriptions required by law (and taking Holy Scripture for their guide) are at liberty honestly to exercise their private judgment without offence or censure.

Gorham's view, the Committee considered, might be contrary to the opinions entertained by many learned and pious persons, but if it could not be shown that it is contrary to the doctrine of the Church of England as by law established, then there was no legal ground for refusing him institution to the living to which he was lawfully presented. This verdict, which constituted an obvious piece of 'case law', was a severe blow for the Tractarian party. A largely secular authority had pronounced upon a doctrinal issue that had always been to them a matter of high spiritual and theological concern.

In spite of the prolonged discussions to which the controversy had given rise, and Phillpotts had throughout been aided by the learning of Dr Pusey, much misunderstanding had been caused. The upholders of baptismal regeneration did not deny that a baptized person might not in fact be in a state of grace and thus require, as Pusey phrased it, 'a solid and entire conversion, notwithstanding the gift of God in Baptism';[1] and this would appear to be no less than what Goode had been contending for as 'the great and all-important doctrine'. Moreover, Pusey himself seems never to have supplied any very clear and definite answer as to what precisely should be understood by baptismal regeneration. It was J. B. Mozley, in his book on the Baptismal controversy, who brought to the subject some much-needed light, and his conclusion was that the Judicial Committee's judgment had been the right one, and that there was nothing inconsistent

[1] H. P. Liddon, *The Life of E. B. Pusey*, iii, p. 236.

with Church teaching in denying that baptism necessarily and
invariably involves regeneration. The difficulty was, as he pointed
out, that the practice of infant baptism had arisen in the early
Church 'in combination with the idea of an institution primarily
for adults'[1] and never since then had any step been taken to remove
the infant from the basis of the adult in baptism. The early Church
fathers and the medieval schoolmen had both maintained that
the infant as such receives the grace of baptism inasmuch as
it offers no impediment to it. It was the Reformers who insisted
that baptism is conditional and that infants and adults alike
receive grace subject to faith and repentance. But the Reformation
baptismal theology followed one or other of two different lines:
either baptism, in the case of infants, is *anticipatory* of a grace to be
given later, when as an adult the recipient actually comes to
believe and repent; or else the child himself receives an infused
or implanted faith (*fides infusa*) *before* baptism. (St Thomas had
taught that justifying faith, necessary for the right reception of
the sacrament, is given *in* baptism; in which event, however, it
can only be regarded as itself part of baptism instead of its antecedent condition.) But Mozley felt himself bound to admit that
Scripture is silent with respect to infants as recipients of baptismal
grace. Hence it follows that 'though the doctors of antiquity give
one plan of this omitted ground' and the doctors of the Reformation another, neither of them could, 'according to the rule of faith
adopted by our Church, compel our acceptance, and that therefore, according to the rule of our Church, the regeneration of
infants is not an article of faith', which was simply what the
Gorham judgment had stated.

Mozley allowed that according to the Prayer Book all baptized
infants are regenerate, but maintained that the term itself had
not been free of ambiguity even in ancient times. Thus in a
'poetical, rhetorical, or hypothetical' sense the word could be
referred, both in the Old Testament and in the New, to the
'People of God' as a whole—to the Jewish nation, that is, or to the
Church of Christ, 'by supposition regarded as being what certain
individuals of it really are'. In a more 'technical or conventional'
sense it could be referred simply to the outward and visible sign,
the rite itself. A third, a 'doctrinal' sense, covered the general
statement that regeneration is 'the grace of baptism', or that

[1] *A Review of the Baptismal Controversy* (1862).

adults are regenerate in baptism upon the conditions of faith and repentance, or that all infants are regenerate in baptism.[1] But it had always to be borne in mind that when the early Church spoke of baptism it did so in language used primarily of a rite for adults. The objection to Pusey's doctrine, Mozley considered, was the combination in it of the requirements at once of full regeneration— i.e. actual goodness—and the extension of the term to include all baptized infants. This, however, was to demand too much, and Pusey had never satisfactorily explained his meaning. So to insist on the inclusive connotation of the word that the sense of actual conversion of heart 'has to be apologized for' Mozley deemed to be a departure from the best traditions of Anglican theology.[2] 'Is it reasonable', he asked, 'to suppose that a moral habit can be imparted to a human being by a particular outward rite?' This might be less startling in the case of infants because the germ and commencement of life is in itself a kind of mystery. But we must feel great difficulty in the idea of a moral habit being formed by an external rite in the grown and mature man. 'Such an effect of the sacrament comes into direct collision with the reasonable modes of thinking of which we find ourselves possessed.'[3] And he adds— in a way, furthermore, very characteristic of the moral emphasis which was always so strong in Tractarian teaching: '*The* acceptable thing in the sight of God is actual holiness and goodness; where this is had, no defect of ritual can possibly interfere with the individual's favour in His sight.'

---

[1] *Ibid.*, p. 177.
[2] *Ibid.*, p. 173.
[3] *Ibid.*, p. 128.

Appendix II

Liberal Catholicism

The nineteenth-century Liberal Catholic movement, in England as on the European continent, was an attempt to bridge what seemed to its adherents to be a disastrously widening gulf between the doctrines of the Roman Catholic Church and the intellectual, social and political attitudes of the modern world. Its leader in this country was Sir John (afterwards Lord) Acton (1843–1902), its literary organ *The Rambler* periodical (in 1862 renamed *The Home and Foreign Review*), started in 1848 by John Moore Capes, a converted Anglican clergyman, and concluding, under Acton's own editorship, in 1864. Indeed the story of English Liberal Catholicism is virtually that of *The Rambler* and its encounters, increasingly serious, with ecclesiastical authority. The periodical's aim was to urge, in the words of Wilfrid Ward, 'the necessity of absolute freedom and candour in scientific, historical, and critical investigation, irrespective of results.'[1] Whether the truth told for or against Catholic polemics, it was not to be withheld. Acton himself, a man of cosmopolitan upbringing and culture,[2] was an hereditary Catholic, his family— Shropshire baronets of ancient lineage—having embraced Catholicism during the preceding century, but his associations and interests were rather with the new generation of converts, of whom Newman was the most illustrious instance, than with the

---

[1] *The Life and Times of Cardinal Wiseman* (1897), ii, p. 227.
[2] His paternal grandfather had been prime minister of the Kingdom of Naples, his mother, Marie de Dalberg, was heiress of the Dalbergs of Herrnsheim, barons of the Holy Roman Empire. A great-uncle on his mother's side had been the last archbishop-elector of Mainz. He himself married Countess Marie von Arco-Valley. He spoke and wrote German, French and Italian fluently.

'old' Catholics, conservative in outlook and socially withdrawn. He had studied for a time under Dupanloup in Paris, then at Oscott, where Nicholas Wiseman, later archbishop of Westminster and a cardinal, was the college's president, and finally in Munich under the eminent German scholar, Johann Ignaz von Döllinger, with whom he established a relation amounting to discipleship. A political career had from the first been open to him (for a while he represented the Irish borough of Carlow at Westminster), but religion, particularly in its intellectual and ethical aspects, was his life. An admirer of Montalembert and the contemporary French liberals—'the men', he said, 'with whom I must agree'— he believed passionately in the liberty of the conscience. A Christian, he held, 'must seek to extend as much as possible the field in which he is responsible only to his conscience'.[1] Freedom, in truth, was for Acton a basic spiritual principle, demanding expression alike in scientific inquiry and in political action. Thus hostility to Ultramontanism, of which in England such men as Manning and Ward were the self-chosen apostles and which he saw as the enemy of both political and intellectual liberty, became almost an obsession with him and led in the end to an unhappy disagreement even with the trusted Döllinger, himself by no means an Ultramontane. He was bitterly opposed to the promulgation of papal infallibility at the Vatican Council and believed after the event that Rome had slipped into heresy. Yet he never broke with the Church, although the antagonism he displayed towards the policies of Pius IX certainly brought him near to excommunication. In accepting the Vatican decrees he described his decision as 'an act of pure obedience' only, 'not grounded on the removal of my motives of opposition' to them.

With the years Acton's moral rigorism, as reflected in his judgments on history, became extreme. The passage from the Catholicism of the Fathers to that of the modern popes had been accomplished, he declared, by wilful falsehood. 'The whole structure of traditions, laws and doctrines that supports the theory of infallibility, and the practical despotism of the Popes, stands on a basis of fraud.' The notion that the security of religion could be attained by the suppression of truth and the encouragement of error appalled him. Christianity and Catholicism stood for the

[1] Cambridge University Library Additional MSS (Acton Papers) 5751 (quoted by Josef L. Altholz, *The Liberal Catholic Movement in England*, p. 56).

479

truth and had nothing to fear from any agency for whom this was the first objective. 'Our Church stands, and our faith should stand, not on the virtues of men, but on the surer ground of an institution and a guidance that are divine. Therefore I rest unshaken in the belief that nothing which the inmost depths of history shall disclose in time can ever bring to the Catholic just cause of shame or fear.'[1] Anyone, like Mandell Creighton in his *History of the Papacy during the Reformation,* who ventured to excuse or pass over the sins of the Church's leaders and responsible representatives, met with violent denunciation: 'In Christendom time and place do not excuse.' The principles of public morality, he insisted, are as definite as those of the morality of private life. In the end Acton felt himself more and more to be alone, understood neither within his church nor without it, and accordingly with little or no influence. He thus tended to turn inward into himself, immersing himself in study and in the task of planning and editing *The Cambridge Modern History*—he had been appointed to the Regius professorship of history at Cambridge in 1895. His proposed *opus magnum*, a *History of Liberty*, although laboriously prepared, remained unwritten except for the two sketches 'The History of Freedom in Antiquity' and 'The History of Freedom in Christianity', originally (1877) delivered as addresses to members of the Bridgnorth (Shropshire) Institution. and printed in his posthumous *History of Freedom and Other Essays* (1907). In fact Acton published no book. The various works under his name which appeared after his death—*Historical Essays and Studies* (1907), *Lectures on Modern History* (1908), *Lectures on the French Revolution* (1910), as well as the volume just mentioned, together with *The Letters of Lord Acton to Mary Gladstone* (1904)—are collections of essays and lectures delivered or written on divers occasions and assembled and edited by other hands.[2]

Acton began his close connection with *The Rambler* in 1858, in response to a felt need to give periodical expression to his views and even to provide him with an incentive to write at all. He was confident that the sort of article he would be able to contribute to it would accord him a position of influence among his fellow-Catholics and a platform from which he also could address edu-

[1] From a letter of Acton's to *The Times* newspaper, 24 November, 1874.

[2] The volumes of essays and lectures by J. N. Figgis and R. V. Laurence, the letters by H. Paul.

cated Protestant opinion. When he commenced writing for it the periodical, which had already been running for ten years, assumed a tone both more political and more liberal. Capes, who had been its first editor, had aimed to serve the interests of the new Oxford converts, especially the laymen. The cultural backwardness of the traditionary Catholics distressed him and he believed the new men, of which he himself was one, would bring to the Roman Catholic community in England fresh spiritual and intellectual vitality. To discuss theology as such was not his intention, but on the other hand not to advert to matters having theological implications was scarcely feasible. Among these 'mixed' questions social issues were well to the fore, especially the disparity of wealth, Capes himself contributing the bulk of the 'copy' besides determining the journal's general policy. But as *The Rambler*'s theological bias also became increasingly evident criticism grew, notably when its editor, in July 1849, voiced his opinion that the claims of Rome could be decided not by the certainty of faith but on a balance of probabilities. After 1852, however, Capes' health having deteriorated, the direction of the periodical was mainly in the hands of Richard Simpson, a convert of 1845 and a man of wide-ranging interests as well as a deep though undemonstrative personal piety. Simpson's editorial 'line' soon proved itself more venturesome than his predecessor's. He spoke out openly, for example, on the subject of the Thomist philosophy.

> We think [he wrote] that no greater injury can be done to the cause of those who would promote the study of St Thomas and the schoolmen, as theologians, than any attempt to identify their philosophical speculations with the truth of Catholicism, or to claim for their *modes* of reasoning on religious topics anything more than an historical, as distinguished from a logical and necessary connection.[1]

Again, he disliked the polemical attitude all too frequently adopted by Catholics, as merely alienating to educated Protestants.[2] Above all he sought to advance intellectual freedom among Catholics themselves. 'It is our firm belief that in these days the Catholic cause will be best subserved by the study of facts. . . . Theology is

[1] *The Rambler* (2nd ser.), ii. (Nov. 1854), p. 450.
[2] *The Rambler* (2nd ser.), iii, (April 1855) ('The True Principle of Religious Controversy'), p. 256.

no longer the dominant science that it was during the middle ages; and the authority of the syllogism of Aristotle has received a counterpoise in the inductive method laid down by Bacon.'[1] Catholic historians should make it their business to go back to original authorities and refrain from concealing embarrassing truths. Indeed the whole practice of circumscribing truth for the sake of piety offended him, and the popular appetite for modern 'miracles' he deplored as morbid.[2] The desire to know and tell the truth was as religious a motive as the concern to give edification.

Simpson and Acton together made *The Rambler* into one of the most intellectually lively periodicals in England, fully justifying Matthew Arnold's remark, after its demise in 1864, that 'perhaps in no organ of criticism in this country was there so much knowledge, so much play of mind'.[3] Simpson preferred to write on historical, philosophical and literary subjects; Acton, who had a high admiration for his colleague's talents, concentrated on politics and reviews of foreign literature. The latter's article, 'Political Thoughts on the Church', provided his readers with a forthright statement of his views as to the Church's role in politics.[4] Freedom again is the keynote. 'The Christian notion of conscience', he wrote, 'imperatively demands a corresponding measure of personal liberty. The feeling of duty and responsibility to God is the only arbiter of a Christian's actions. With this no human authority can be permitted to interfere.' The Church could not rightly tolerate any species of government in which this right was not recognized and was indeed bound to be the 'irreconcilable enemy' of state despotism in whatever form. In regard to Catholic scholarship both he and Simpson could only regret its manifest lack of knowledge of contemporary biblical criticism. 'It is the absence', Acton confessed, 'of scientific method and of original

---

[1] *The Rambler* (2nd ser.), viii (July 1857), p. 76.

[2] *The Rambler* (2nd ser.), viii (Sept. 1857), p. 197. 'He who falsifies history falsifies the express teaching of the Supreme Judge. Nothing can be weaker than the ecclesiastical historian's concealment of ancient corruptions for fear of giving scandal' *The Rambler* (2nd ser.), ix (June 1858), p. 424.

[3] 'The Function of Criticism at the Present Time', in *Essays in Criticism* (1865). Max Müller thought it 'one of the best edited of our quarterlys' (see Wilfrid Ward, *The Life of John Henry Cardinal Newman*, i, pp. 538f.).

[4] *The Rambler* (2nd ser.), xi (Jan. 1859). 'I would have', he told Simpson, 'a complete body of principles for the conduct of English Catholics in political affairs, and if I live and do well, I will gradually unfold them. The Catholics want political education' (see Abbot [later Cardinal] Gasquet, *Lord Acton and his Circle*, 1906, p. 4).

learning in nearly all even of our best writers that makes it impossible for me to be really interested in their writings.'[1] Careful study of the sources, genesis and growth of the Church's doctrines was an essential equipment for the modern theologian. On the theory of biological evolution, then in the forefront of public discussion, Simpson showed exceptional impartiality. The theory, he considered, should not be confounded with the facts: it was a hypothesis only. But Catholics ought to recognize that the theological doctrine of creation and the scientific concept of natural law are not incompatible: 'Creation is not a miraculous interference with the laws of nature, but the very institution of those laws.'[2] Certainly Catholics ought to encourage and not resist free discussion and should eschew any tendency 'to force all thought into the mold of the average mediocrity'. An account of *Essays and Reviews*, a publication of which Acton himself thought rather lightly, was assigned to another 'liberal' contributor—formerly an Anglican—Henry N. Oxenham, who, however, stressed what he saw as the inevitably erosive effect of biblical criticism on religious belief. In any case scientific study of the Bible must mean re-examination of the idea of revelation itself: 'And we do not regret that it should be so. It will demand from us a firmer grasp of ascertained principles, a wider range of speculation, a nicer discrimination of what is essential and what is accidental, a more generous estimate of an adversary's position, and bolder proclamation of our own.'[3]

The attitude of Newman towards *The Rambler* was equivocal. As to principle he agreed with its policy, but he had clear misgivings about its practical application. Newman was always studiously respectful of authority. That the Ultramontanes detested the periodical did not at all worry him, but the opinion of the bishops was another matter, and this *The Rambler* flouted. 'I have all the pains in the world', Acton wrote to Simpson, 'to keep Newman in good humour. He is so much riled at what he pleasantly calls your habit of pea-shooting at any dignitary who looks out of the window as you pass along the road, that I am

---

[1] Gasquet, *op. cit.*, p. 56.

[2] 'Darwin on the Origin of Species', in *The Rambler* (new ser.), ii (March 1860), p. 372.

[3] *The Rambler* (new series), iv (March 1861) ('The Neo-Protestantism of Oxford'), p. 298f.

afraid he will not stand by us if we are censured.'[1] The bishops for their part looked to Newman to exert a moderating influence on the liberals, somewhat to his own embarrassment. He admired Acton, liked Simpson and feared the consequences of *The Rambler*'s suppression, were it to occur. Reluctantly he himself took over the editorship from Simpson in 1859, but without success. No change of policy was disclosed and he was responsible for only two numbers. Both to satisfy the episcopate and not repudiate his friends was hardly possible, and when his own diocesan, Ullathorne, suggested his giving up the task he at once complied, although again with reluctance in view of his concern for the educated laity and the service which a journal like *The Rambler* could render them. Newman's withdrawal grieved Acton, for whom Newman was the one safe bridge between the liberal position and the Ultramontanes.

Acton's own first issue appeared in September 1859. His intention was to specialize in politics, but Simpson was also to carry on as a principal contributor, and there was to be no question of a theological censor to appease authority. The debate about the temporal power of the papacy received a good deal of attention. That the papal states were ill-governed Acton was well enough aware, but he nevertheless was prepared to defend the Holy See's territorial integrity as necessary for the pope's independence in spiritual matters, although he realized that territorially the latter's position was becoming precarious. As for the state of Catholicism at home Acton confessed himself disturbed by the growth of a dubious sort of 'devotionalism': devotion without intellectual discipline could be dangerous, piety providing 'a respectable cloak for all kinds of errors and false tendencies'. Simpson was no less uneasy over the tendency to confuse supplementary and optional beliefs with the substance of revelation. If Christians felt modern science to be a peril to faith it was because they had always 'fought for more than the Christian dogma', failing to recognize that 'all except the central core of revealed truth is human addition, and therefore fallible, changeable, and obnoxious to decay'. It was a fault to defend 'the accidental and temporary vestment of truth' with as much obstinacy as the truth itself'.[2]

[1] Gasquet, *op. cit.*, p. 192.
[2] *The Rambler* (new series), v (July 1861) ('Reason and Faith') p. 182.

A crisis occurred in the affairs of *The Rambler* (by now under its new name of the *Home and Foreign*) when in January 1864 it presented its readers with an enthusiastic account of the recent congress of Catholic scholars which Döllinger had organized in Munich. Döllinger's own paper, on 'The Past and Present of Theology', was hailed by Acton as 'the dawn of a new era' in Catholic theological thinking. However, in a Brief of December 1863 addressed to the archbishop of Munich Pius IX had already severely criticized the congress's aims, the 'liberal' idea of distinguishing between the Church's actual dogma and its transient theological interpretations being specifically censured. Although the language of the Brief was for the most part loftily vague, there could be no mistaking the pope's mind, which very soon became only too plain with the publication of the encyclical *Quanta Cura* and the accompanying 'syllabus of errors'. Liberal Catholicism had in fact received a grave setback, as Acton realized. But as he would neither compromise with his principles nor defy authority he felt he had no option but to bring the review to an end. The last issue appeared in April 1864 and contained his famous article, 'Conflicts with Rome', in which he stated with profound regret that the 'amity and sympathy' which he personally believed to exist between the methods of science and those employed by the Church were by the 'enemies' of the Church denied and by its friends not yet understood. 'Long disowned by a large part of our Episcopate', such amity and sympathy were now rejected by the Holy See, and the issue was one 'vital to a *Review* which, in ceasing to uphold them, would surrender the whole reason for its existence'.[1] With the promulgation in 1870 of the Vatican decree on papal infallibility liberal Catholicism came to an end. Acton had bitterly opposed the Council's decision, even having published an open letter to a German bishop urging the minority party to continue its resistance. 'No layman', it has been said, 'ever played such a part in Church matters, and no Catholic more narrowly missed excommunication.'[2] His eventual submission was but a token of his obedience to a spiritual authority whose ultimate right he never questioned, whatever his conscientious judgment might be as to the human media through which it was exercised. 'Our Church stands, and our faith should stand, not on the virtues of

[1] *The History of Freedom and Other Essays*, p. 489.
[2] Shane Leslie, *Henry Edward Manning: His Life and Labours* (1921), p. 220.

men, but on the surer ground of an institution and a guidance that are divine.'

The extent to which the *Rambler*'s promoters were theologically liberal is open to debate. Upon the rights of historical criticism to investigate tradition they were firm. At the same time they were confident that the Church's dogmatic teaching represents an unshakable truth. The dogmas are infallible and binding, the theological commentary on them not so. Thus as between faith and knowledge a clear line could be drawn, and if each kept to its proper sphere no clash need ever arise. According to Simpson:

> A detailed review of the contents of the creeds and definitions would show that their subject matter is all outside the sphere of phenomena, which is the realm of science. The Trinity, the Incarnation, the Fall and the Redemption, Grace, the Sacraments, the authority of the Church, the inspiration of Scripture, the immortality of the soul, the resurrection of the body, heaven and hell, offer no hold for scientific experiments. The philosopher may theorize upon them in a way that offends faith; but it will be only theory, not science. He will have once more proved the venerable truism, that without revelation we have no demonstration of any Christian doctrine, that each dogma becomes a mere guess, and there-fore as susceptible of denial as of affirmation.[1]

But can the problems of faith and reason, science and religion, be settled quite so easily? In defence of the liberal Catholics it may be pointed out that they were active at a time when the conflict between traditional religious belief and the new knowledge was still concentrated in a relatively small area, namely the bearing upon Genesis of geology and the theory of evolution. Biblical criticism, especially in regard to the New Testament, had not yet made its full impact, and in truth Acton himself was inclined to underrate the theological significance of criticism altogether. In so far as he and his friends did consider it they took the view that Protestant biblicism would turn out to be in a more precarious position than Catholicism, with its reliance on tradition and Church. It is hardly surprising, therefore, that the Modernists, in the early years of the present century, derived little or nothing from the ideas of the liberal Catholics. The Modernists were faced with an intellectual situation more complex and more urgent than

[1] *The Rambler* (new series), v (September 1861), p. 327.

that which had confronted their forerunners. Their problems were such in fact that any real attempt at solving them would have had to do much more than recall the arguments of a half-century before. Moreover, the fate of the liberal Catholic movement was scarcely of encouragement to this new generation of thinkers and scholars and to have appealed openly to the liberals' example would have been to invite the disaster in which, as it was, they themselves were soon to founder. The standpoint of *L'Évangile et l'Église* or *Christianity at the Cross-Roads* was, besides, utterly remote from the liberal position. Simpson's views, with their concern to distinguish a 'central core' of belief from its passing theological embodiments sounded a Modernist note, but Simpson himself, unlike Loisy or Tyrrell, was convinced that this central core included the dogmas of the faith. Indeed it is arguable that the Modernist conception of development was a solvent of all doctrinal fixity. Von Hügel, it might have been supposed, would have been in general sympathy with the opinions of *The Rambler*, but it appears that he had never read it.[1] Modernism belongs properly to the religious history of the twentieth century, not only as an ecclesiastical movement but in its theological temper and outlook likewise, and it is best to be studied in the light of Vatican II than in that of the liberal Catholicism extinguished by Vatican I.

[1] Cp. W. Ward, *W. G. Ward and the Catholic Revival*, p. 363.

Appendix III

Gladstone on Church and State

The most fully articulated contribution to the nineteenth-century discussion of the relations of Church and State was an early work of W. E. Gladstone's, *The State in its Relation with the Church*, first published in 1838 and again, in a much enlarged (fourth) edition, in 1841. Gladstone's book, especially in this latter edition, makes heavy reading, but of the strength of the convictions which lay behind it—and the author at the time was only twenty-nine—there can be no question. They were convictions which had been shaping in his mind for some years previously—he had even at one time contemplated ordination—and it is arguable that he adhered to them, in the form at least of an ideal, to the end of his life. Certainly, as Morley remarks, his intensity of interest in Church affairs never for an instance slackened.[1] A long career in politics meant, of course, a considerable chastening of the rigorism of his views, but, in the words of Sir Philip Magnus, 'the right relationship between two societies—the one eternal and divine, the other mortal and mundane—which has troubled the conscience of Europe for two thousand years, continued to torment Gladstone and to plunge his mind into a seething ferment of restlessness'.[2] Disraeli used to say of his great political opponent that he was 'never a man of the world'.

The author's mode of procedure is analytical, involving an inquiry into the nature of the State itself. The testimony of Scripture he willingly recognizes, but finds it insufficient and inconclusive, since the Old Testament does not distinguish the

[1] John Morley, *The Life of William Ewart Gladstone* (1903), ii, p. 158. Cp. *ibid.*, iii, p. 471.
[2] *Gladstone* (1954), p. 440.

differing *functions* of Church and State, whilst the New Testament is hardly of relevance since it was written 'at a time when there was no case of a nation of persons professedly Christian'.[1] Other considerations—pragmatic or historical—are likewise indecisive. Our guide, accordingly, must be the light of nature, by which the 'grounds and proofs of the principle of public religion' may be well enough discerned, although not without some help, so far as it allows, from divine revelation. It requires an examination of 'the moral character and capacities of nations and rulers', from which it can be seen that 'the whole idea of their duty' is founded upon 'that will which gave them their existence'.[2] Gladstone begins, however, by asserting the theological doctrine of the fall of man and its consequences. These, he points out, would have been even more disastrous but for God's intermediate provisions for mitigating them—intermediate because only preparatory for his great act of final redemption in Christ. Among them are to be counted the institutions of the common life: family, tribe and nation. Thus an altruistic motive and a scheme of duties are supplied which so far limit human selfishness. Even so, in a sinful world the institutions of men's collective life are themselves productive of evil results, in greed, injustice and aggression, more than would have been committed by 'the feebler means of its members as individuals'.[3] For this reason some agency is needed by which the abuse of collective power, as well as individual wrongdoing, can be rebuked. Hence the role of publicly acknowledged religion not only as a single factor but as 'a consecrating principle' within the nation's life as a whole. For religion teaches that power is held in trust to God and is rightly exercised only in conformity with his laws. This does not mean that all forms of human association ought similarly to make an explicit profession of religion, but only such as are general, natural and permanent, notably the family and the State. For family and State share alike the basic characters of being 'parts of the dispensation into which [man] is providentially born', of being 'parallel to his entire existence', and of being both manifold in their functions and unlimited in their claims upon him. Above all they have a *moral* status in that 'they require in a high degree moral motives and restraints for the right

[1] *The State in its Relation with the Church* (ed. 1841), i, p. 40.
[2] *Ibid.*, i, p. 45.
[3] p. 61.

discharge of the obligations subsisting under them' and 'distinctly contemplate moral ends'.[1]

Gladstone proceeds to specify why the State needs religion no less than the family. As an institution which is general, natural and permanent 'there is no limit of quantity to the obligations of the individual towards it'. It is, in other words, a *moral* and not merely an economic entity 'inasmuch as its laws and institutions, and the acts done under them, are intimately connected with the formation of our moral habits, our modes of thought, and that state of our affections, and inasmuch as its influences pervade the whole scheme and system of our being'.[2] The individual indeed is what he is largely through his membership of a nation or state (terms which Gladstone uses for the most part interchangeably). In short, by speaking of the State as moral the author means that of its nature it assumes moral responsibilities under an acknowledged moral law and that it cannot be morally indifferent. It has, of course, responsibilities which are sub-moral and which are 'first in time and necessity', but its concern is not restricted to matters of sheer utility, however pressing and engrossing. Further, from its moral responsibility it has, like the individual, the obligation to profess and promote a religion, providing 'that worship which shall publicly sanctify its acts'.[3] How far and in what manner this public patronage of religion will be extended depends, naturally enough, upon the given circumstances; but the principle itself is unaffected.

By religion Gladstone understands (as he makes clear) one specific religion. The State cannot afford its patronage to two or more, with their diverse and perhaps inconsistent claims. But this implies that the State is capable of recognizing truth in the religious sphere, even though unable to attend to the details of theology. On the other hand, although one religion be singled out for express recognition, others are properly to be tolerated. The form which the State's recognition will take includes the acknowledgement of God by worship and prayer, the avowed submission of its laws and actions to the divine commandments, and the diffusion of religion throughout the body of the nation.[4] Glad-

[1] *Ibid.*, p. 94.
[2] p. 86.
[3] p. 105.
[4] pp. 110f. Cp. i, pp. 244f.

stone sees Christianity, that is, as 'a principle of life intended to govern and pervade the whole of human life'. As itself a principle of common life it should govern and pervade the common life in both family and State.[1] But although the State and the Church thus have common and co-ordinate ends they also importantly differ, as to objectives as well as to means. 'The State and the Church', we read, 'have both of them moral agencies. But the State aims at character through conduct: the Church at conduct through character; in harmony with which, the State forbids more than enjoins, the Church enjoins more than forbids.'[2]

The essentials of Gladstone's theory are set out in the first part of the work, and it is here that the student of nineteenth-century religious thought will focus his attention; the remainder of the book, concerned for the most part with Church-State relations as they existed at the time of its writing, is now of slight interest. The author's other (and also voluminous) work on the subject, *Church Principles considered in their Results*, published in 1840, is likewise subordinate, although more overtly theological in content.[3] It made virtually no impression on public opinion, for not only is Gladstone's literary style ponderous, the book was scouted as the product of a mere theological amateur. Again, although Gladstone sympathized with the religious standpoint of the Tractarians he was not himself identified with a Church party and wrote from an angle of deliberate independence, a fact which, regrettably, was of no help in winning him an audience.

What strikes the modern reader of *The State in its Relations with the Church* is the archaism of its outlook. Indeed it was archaic in its own day. Gladstone was then a strong Tory and the thesis of his book was in total contrast with that enunciated in Arnold's *Principles of Church Reform*. Its affinity, as we have remarked, is much more with Coleridge's doctrine, except that Gladstone works out his theory with greater consistency than does Coleridge, whose own *Church and State* is really no more than a brilliantly suggestive (and provocative) sketch. In the light of Gladstone's

[1] *Ibid.*, p. 115.

[2] *Ibid.*

[3] William Palmer's *Treatise on the Church of Christ* (1838) was a major influence on Gladstone's thinking. 'It gave me', he said, 'at once the dear, definite and strong conception of the Church' *op. cit.* p. 162). He judged it to be the most powerful and least assailable defence of the Anglican position to have been attempted since the sixteenth century (Morley, *op. cit.*, i, p. 168*n*).

later career as leader of the Liberal party his early writings seemed insignificant and came to be forgotten. As touching the relationship of Church and State, however, it does not appear that his convictions ever underwent fundamental change, although he realized increasingly how impracticable they were. At heart, as has frequently been observed by twentieth-century commentators, and despite his own rather sententious references to 'liberal principles', he was himself a traditionalist with very little affection for the type of free-thinking radicalism with which the word liberal was associated in minds more sensitive to the intellectual climate of the times.[1]

[1] See A. R. Vidler, *The Orb and the Cross* (1945), ch. VII.

Index

Other Novels by Bob Williams:

EXCELSIOR
OZARK FLATS
GOOD LUCK ON YOUR DOWNWARD JOURNEY

END PAPERS: *MAP OF MACKINAC ISLAND*
This map of roads and trails of the island marks the historic sites —
from the British Landing to Arch Rock, with trails into the upper island
and the famous Lake Shore Boulevard which circles the island along
the shoreline.

—Photo, courtesy The Town Crier

The Island House

A Tale of Mackinac Island

BY
BOB WILLIAMS

For Thelma –
Bob Williams

JAMES D. THUESON, PUBLISHER
Minneapolis

ISBN: 0-911506-22-5

JAMES D. THUESON, PUBLISHER
Box 14474
Minneapolis, MN 55414

Dedicated to family and friends who have given me so many fond memories of our visits to Mackinac Island; to all those with The Island House who have been so gracious to us over the years; and to the people of Mackinac Island for allowing us to consider it our Island Home.

CHAPTER 1

Tuesday July 5, 1938

It was a Mackinac morning. There was still a chill in the air, even on the day after the Fourth of July. Young Ben Butler and his mother, Katie, finished unloading the suitcases from the trunk of their 1937 Oldsmobile while his kid sister, Blair, and her friend and classmate, Annabelle Shepherd, struggled with the heavy bags, half-carrying and half-dragging them from the parking area to the sidewalk near the dock. A ferryboat from the Arnold Line would not arrive at St. Ignace for another half hour, but everyone was rushing as though the ferry to Mackinac Island was ready to pull away from the pier. Other vacationers were also unloading baggage and purchasing tickets for the half-hour boat ride to the island under an overcast sky on this summer morning. More tourists, families, couples and honeymooners, were now parking their cars and heading for the line at the ticket booth.

Katie Butler slammed the door shut on the empty trunk of the Olds. Then she dug into her handbag and gave her good-looking young son a ten-dollar bill.

"Here, you go buy the round-trip tickets while I park the car," she told him. "And tell Blair and Annabelle to watch the luggage until I get back."

"Sure, Mom," Ben answered obediently. "You sure you don't want me to park the car for you?" he asked.

"No. You just take care of the girls — and the luggage."

Katie smiled. Sixteen-year-olds who just learned to drive never missed an opportunity to get behind the wheel. Because her husband, Harris Butler, had not made the trip from Minnesota, she had even let Ben drive for short stretches across Wisconsin and Upper Michigan. Business kept Harris back home in Excelsior, just outside of Minneapolis, and Katie had appreciated Ben assuming some of the responsibilities of being the "man of the house" on this trip in the absence of his father. Ben was already six feet tall, taller than most men, but Katie was the head of the household in the Butler family. The attractive brunette, with flecks of grey in her hair, would be forty-three years old on July 13. She was self-sufficient and financially independent, but as she swung the car into a parking space along the Lake Huron shoreline, she had to admit to herself that despite their differences, she missed Harris and would be glad when he arrived later in the week.

The thought also crossed Katie's mind that she should enjoy Ben as much as possible on this summer vacation. After all, he was about to enter his senior year of high school and then it would be on to college and a summer job in between. He was already working for her weekly newspaper back home but Katie had insisted he take the time off for this trip to Mackinac Island. Yes, their family vacations with Ben were numbered and she'd better make the most of this one. Teen-agers somehow lost interest in such vacations with the family as new interests came into their lives: summer jobs, activities with friends at home they didn't want to miss out on, and with boys Ben's age — girls. Up to now, girls had been on the periphery of Ben's young life. He had good friends and classmates in school who were girls, some quite attractive. He had sung with them in choir and in operettas, too. But Ben's interests seemed to be centered around sports and music and scouting, at least up until now. Katie would make this next week a special one for Ben and herself. She knew it was inevitable that Ben's interests would change and it bothered her. After all, young men were very vulnerable. And nobody knew that better than Katie Butler.

Back near the pier, Blair and Annabelle sat on a couple of suitcases, waiting for Katie to return from the nearby parking lot while Ben purchased the tickets for the short voyage from St. Ignace to Mackinac Island. The two twelve-year-old girls were glad Katie had made them wear sweaters this July morning. It was cold. But because they insisted on wearing shorts, their bare legs had goosebumps. They shivered as they guarded the luggage and watched the activity of vacationers and tourists around them. They had driven into the historic town of St. Ignace from Manistique, Michigan, halfway across the Upper Peninsula where they had all shared a two-room cabin along U.S. Highway 2 last night. It had been cold and damp in the cabin, too. When they got up early, everything seemed clammy — the bedsheets, the towels and their clothing. Ben even had to take a towel to wipe off the car windows before they drove off. Their motor trip had begun just twenty-four hours ago when they left their home in Excelsior. Blair and Annabelle had watched the countryside go by from the back seat as her mother drove across the state of Wisconsin. They had picnicked along the shores of the Flambeau River and everyone in the car barked like a dog, including Katie Butler, when they crossed the bridge at Bark River. Then they all laughed. With all the fun and games, yesterday had still been a long day and the enthusiasm, so high at the beginning of the trip, dispersed as the day wore on. Excitement began to grow again this morning, however, on the ride into St. Ignace.

Through it all, Blair had another member of the family and a trusted friend with her. It was her teddy bear, a beloved brown, furry friend who shared her inner-most thoughts at night, who was a marvelous listener and comfort to her in sad times, and who was hugged for joy in the good times of her young life. She had received the teddy bear from her brother, Ben, at Christmastime when she was a young child and couldn't pronounce the words, teddy bear. As a result, her favorite companion had become Tebby, a name that had stuck with him to this day. And although he was beginning to show signs of wear and the stuffing had been somewhat displaced, Tebby was still Blair's very best friend. She had other teddy bears left back in her bedroom in Excelsior, but Tebby had been snuggled in the back seat of the car through the long trip to St. Ignace. He had been held so tightly that he must have felt Blair's heart pounding as they entered the old town which guarded the straits between Lake Huron and Lake Michigan.

They had stopped to have a pancake breakfast in downtown St. Ignace and Blair's mother had bought an edition of *The Detroit Free Press* to read over coffee. Headlines, photos and stories chronicled Howard Hughes' new record-breaking flight around the world, 14,824 miles in ninety-one hours and seventeen minutes, cutting in half the time that former record-holder, aviator Wiley Post, set back in 1931.

This trip to Mackinac Island was the first real vacation trip in Annabelle Shepherd's whole life. She lived with her mother and dad and a younger sister, Betty, back in Excelsior, only a couple of blocks from Blair's house. Her father worked at the Hennepin County Court House in Minneapolis and commuted by bus to the city, some fifty-five minutes away. Their modest home was simply not in the same class as the Butler's large, three-story home located on Excelsior's West Lake Street overlooking historic Lake Minnetonka. Mrs. Shepherd was pleased that Annabelle had become "best friends" with Blair. But her father seemed irritated over the friendship and a little resentful of the affluence of the Butler family. Annabelle and Blair had just completed the sixth grade in Miss Anna Toftner's class. Their teacher was a pretty red-head who had taken a liking to Blair because of the youngster's intense interest in books and grammar. Annabelle had been on a few trips to Northern Minnesota with her family, but nothing like this. Why, it took a whole day or more just to get to where they were going.

"How big is the ship?" Annabelle asked Blair as they sat guarding the luggage.

"It's really not a ship," Blair explained. "It's a ferryboat that maybe holds a hundred people." Actually, each of the four ferryboats in the fleet could carry about five hundred passengers.

"Am I going to get seasick?" she asked anxiously.

"I don't think so," Blair assured her. "I never have," she added. If the truth were known, she was speaking from limited experience. Last summer had been her family's first trip to the island.

The two girls stared out on Lake Huron, looking for a sign of the incoming ferry. The waves rolling into shore were much larger than anything the girls had ever seen back home at Lake Minnetonka. The water looked cold and gray and the lake gulls circled overhead as if they were looking over the morning visitors and vacationers. Although the lake was reasonably quiet this morning, there was plenty of activity alongside the docking area. A weather-worn farmer with a sun-tanned face and wearing an old straw hat, was unloading a truckload of hay. His teenage son was stacking the bales on low, four-wheeled carts to be taken on board the morning ferry for delivery to the island. Other deliveries to the dock had been made hours ago, as evidenced by the dollies of fresh bread and cases of bottles of milk awaiting their daily shipment to the island, too. Although the island was a half-hour's ride away, there was a smell of horse manure present. It was not surprising. Six large work horses were tethered across the way, patiently waiting to be transported to their new home and job on Mackinac Island.

It was pleasant here this morning, Blair thought. In all the excitement of starting out on a long trip and seeing the sights along the way, she had forgotten just how pleasant it had been. And she realized there hadn't been a single argument on the entire journey, mostly because there was no one with whom her mother could argue. Blair and her brother, Ben, were used to hearing disagreements between their parents over the years. Serious disagreements. Most of the arguments involved money and position in the community, and Katie almost always won. After all, she controlled the money in the family and owned the community newspaper. There had been more arguing than usual these last couple of years, mostly over Harris' new job. It was the first time in a long, long while that Katie had not had her own way. Yet, Blair was sure that her mother and dad loved each other and that her mom missed having him on the trip. Ben wasn't so sure. He was just enough older to comprehend the seriousness of those family squabbles and over the years had tried to understand both sides of the agruments between his parents. At the moment, he leaned toward his mother's side of the controversy. After all, the newspaper had been in the family since the 1880's and it seemed almost disloyal for his father to leave the publishing business for a selling job. Still, Ben missed his dad and he would be glad when he arrived on the island before the weekend. Then he remembered that his father would also be bringing Grandma Markham, too.

Those thoughts brought the same kind of exciting anticipation Ben had last night when they stayed in the tourist cabin court near Manistique. The long ride was almost over then, and tomorrow would bring them to Mackinac Island and a whole week of vacation. The girls had not been too happy about being alone in a strange cabin, even though Ben and his mother shared the adjoining room with twin beds on the other side of the wall. They were too excited to go to sleep. Blair and Annabelle talked about when they might have the chance to wear their party dresses they had brought along on the trip. And Ben could hear their conversation through the thin walls of the cabin.

"I've got this brand new panty-waist and a new camisole that goes over the shoulders and has white garters," Blair said.

"Do you think it will be cool enough for stockings?" Annabelle asked as they lay quietly in bed in the dark cabin.

"I don't know," Blair replied. "Last year it got cold at night."

Ben and his mother were in the adjoining room and each smiled as they overheard the conversation of the girls. Ben laughed.

"I don't know what Blair is worried about," he whispered. "She actually likes the cold weather. After all, she was Klondike Princess when she was in the fifth grade, and even in the summertime, she's spent a lot of time in the Morse Brothers ice house with a girlfriend. The girlfriend's grandfather owned the ice company and she and Blair had spent hours cooling themselves off in the huge ice barn where straw-covered ice was preserved all summer long.

By the time Blair and Annabelle got around to talking about boys, Ben had slipped off to sleep in the room next door. The conversation was reduced to a whisper as the two girls talked about....sex, of which neither Blair or Annabelle knew very much. Their mothers had always avoided the subject and Blair received her first sex education from a cousin after Blair had her first menstrual period when she was in the fifth grade. She hadn't been sure how to break the news to her mother, and finally told her that she had hurt herself on the turning poles of a jungle gym in the school yard. Katie didn't seize the chance to give her a quick "birds and bees" lecture, but did tell her what to expect each month and how to deal with it. It was all so embarrassing. And reading the racy parts of her mother's copy of *Gone With The Wind* hadn't really helped much in the way of sex information, either.

"I'm glad Ben came along," Annabelle said in the quiet of the dark room. "I thought he was going to bring his buddy."

"Willy?" Blair paused. "He wanted to bring him but Ben said he had to work."

"Maybe he'll show us some of the sights around the island," Annabelle hoped.

"We don't need him to do that," Blair assured her. "We can do all of that without him."

"Just the same, it's nice to have an older man along."

"He's no older man," Blair corrected her. "He's only my brother. He's just sixteen."

Ben had been day-dreaming about last night when the sharp blast of the steam whistle from the ferryboat cut through the overcast to announce its arrival. With tickets in his hand, Ben rushed back from the booth shouting orders to the girls.

"You take your own luggage, Blair," he said hurriedly. "And you carry that brown suitcase of yours and that straw bag over there, Annabelle." Ben began to move his mother's suitcases toward the gates on the nearby dock as the ferryboat pulled into port to unload its passengers from the island before taking on the vacationers waiting at the gate for the trip back. Black smoke curled out of the single smokestack as the white double-decker with blue trim cut back its engines and slid quietly up to the pier. Only a handful of early-morning passengers from the island were aboard, waiting to get off at the St. Ignace docks. There was one last burst of engine noise as the ship's pilot put the ferry into reverse to bring it to an abrupt halt.

Katie Butler hurried along the sidewalk lined with green shrubs toward the docks. She was dressed in a natural-colored gabardine slack suit and wore low-heel shoes, and she could feel the first hint of a warm sun trying to break through the cloudy sky. If Harris were here, she knew what he would say. "It'll burn off by noon."

Billy Lachine had risen early, just as the sun had edged over the east bluffs of Mackinac Island and brightened his small room on the second floor of the Ashby rooming house off Huron Street. The handsome young man had already biked around the island along the Lake Shore Road next to the shoreline. He took his usual morning bike ride at a leisurely pace — not trying to set any speed records — out past Devil's Kitchen, beyond the British Landing to the far end of the historic island at Point Aux Pins. Then he biked along the opposite site of the island, below the shadows of the east bluffs and Arch Rock and passed the Moral Rearmament complex on his way back into town. It had taken the eighteen-year-old about forty-five minutes to pedal the nine miles along the lakeshore route. As he returned to the residential section of the island, he left Huron Street and headed for the waterfront, across the street from the oldest hotel on the island, the Island House. Billy still had a half-hour before he reported for work at the hotel where he served as a part-time desk clerk, bellhop, dock porter and sort-of-handyman. The hotel was ninety years old and the handyman chores took up most of the youth's time each summer day, making repairs. But this morning, he still had time to stop at the docks before breakfast to check on his most proud possession — in fact, his only real possession — his sailboat.

The sailboat, a 26-foot Herreshoff, would have been the pride of any marina. At one time, it had been in service at the United States Naval Academy and eventually found its way to Michigan and Lake Huron where it was acquired by Billy's father. Two years ago, just before his death, the elder Lachine had given the sailboat to his son. Now Billy carried on the tradition and love for sailing of the Lachine family. His only relative was a distant cousin who now lived in Sault Ste. Marie. Billy had grown up on this island where his dad had worked on ferryboats all his life. His mother had died of influenza when he was twelve. Billy had gone to school in an historic building that would eventually become known as the Indian Dormitory. Because there were no automobiles allowed on the island, young Billy never learned to drive a car. But he knew how to sail a boat and he not only sailed at every opportunity, but loved to have anyone who was interested go sailing with him.

Everything seemed to be in order on his sailboat this morning so he decided to get up to the hotel and have some breakfast before he started work. His job benefits included a room at Ashby's, a nearby rooming house, his meals at the hotel, and ten dollars a week — plus tips. The young man hurriedly left the dock and started across the street toward the twin trees that marked the sidewalk entrance to the hotel. Back on the waterfront, his sailboat wobbled in the waves alongside of the dock. On the transom of the stern was painted its strange name, *La Tortue Grande*.

The Butler residence back in the little town of Excelsior, Minnesota, was an imposing house. The tall stucco home looked out over Gideon's Bay of Lake Minnetonka which surrounded the west and north sides of the town, some twenty miles west of Minneapolis. The Butlers had lived in the house for about fourteen years now and both Ben and Blair had never known any other home. They had never known any other town, either. Excelsior was at one time very much like Mackinac Island was now. Back in the 1880's and 1890's and even for a short time after the turn of the century, Excelsior was the hub of the Minnetonka resort area which had been carved out of a Minnesota wilderness. But its summer hotels and visitors had vanished long ago and now its only claim to fame was as the home of the Excelsior Amusement Park which was built on the shores of Excelsior Bay in 1925.

Out in front of the Butler home, an occasional outboard motor was all that broke the silence of Gideon's Bay as Harris Butler fixed his own breakfast before leaving for work. Harris was a man in his early forties. He was known for his pleasant manner and, despite his receding hair-line, women still found him attractive. His marriage to Katie had been a rocky one. She was an ambitious woman, ambitious for him. She wanted him to be editor and publisher of her late father's newspapers, to be a man of standing in his community, and a figure in state, if not national, politics. She felt he looked the part, and had the brains, and could do it if he would only listen to her. Harris dismissed her arguments, thinking she was just seeking wider social acceptance. As far as Harris was concerned, Katie and her family already had all of the social prominence they could want. Her brother, Jamie, had inherited his father's daily newspapers, and Katie had been given the three weekly publications. And, of course, the family's wealth had not hurt their social standing, either. Harris, however, liked to talk to people and was instantly liked by just about everyone he met. But he liked to talk to people about things, not ideas. He would rather sell newspaper machinery than to write editorials.

Harris fell in love with Katie when they were students at the University of Minnesota, just before the World War. He met her at a sorority dance. To him, she was incredibly beautiful — a fun-loving "new woman." She obviously was out of his league, but to his amazement, she stole him away from her sorority sister and became his steady date. She was already making plans for him when he was graduated and although she still had two years more of classwork, Katie decided they should get married and settle in Excelsior. She was not a little shocked when he enlisted in the navy and went off to war. It had not been part of her plan. Nevertheless, she was convinced that he was what she wanted. She wrote to him almost daily, finished school, and they were married in the spring of 1919 at Trinity Episcopal Chapel in Excelsior.

Harris had gone to work for Emmett Markham, Katie's father, at *The Minnetonka Record*. At first, he sold advertising space and helped with the layouts. He began writing editorials and covering the basic news events such as village council meetings and school board events in 1923 and was made managing editor in 1925. Emmett Markham was an excellent newspaperman and a good teacher, and Harris gave it all an honest try out of loyalty to his father-in-law. But even Emmett had urged him to get into something he enjoyed if he couldn't hack the newspaper business. After nearly ten years of editing and bickering with Katie about running for office, he decided to quit newspapering and begin to sell things, big things, like road building equipment and farm machinery — anything to get him doing something he fully liked and understood. Shortly after Harris disclosed his intentions to Katie, Emmett suffered a stroke and died. For Katie's sake, Harris postponed his plans and stayed on as editor and publisher of the *Record*.

Two years ago, he received an offer from International Harvester to sell their new combination reaper and thresher. It was exactly what he wanted and in a rare moment of domestic courage, he reported his decision to Katie.

"What do you mean, you're going to leave the paper?" she demanded. "You promised me when Dad died that you had given up all that foolishness about becoming a salesman."

"I told you then that I wouldn't leave the paper — at least for a couple of years." He tried to reason with her. "The couple of years have gone by, Kate, and *The Record* is doing fine. It will probably do even better without me. I'm not that good a newspaperman."

"The hell with whether you're a good newspaperman or not," Katie fumed. "I want my husband to be the publisher of the newspaper in this town. I don't want to be married to some salesman!"

Harris smiled over his morning coffee as he remembered that confrontation two years ago. But he had been determined not to back down this time. And he remembered his answer.

"I'm afraid you're already married to one, dear. I start work in two weeks."

Harris thought about these things this morning, mostly because he had been thinking about Katie and the kids. They'd only been gone for a day and he already missed them terribly. He usually saw plenty of his daughter, but he was now looking forward to spending some time at Mackinac Island with Ben. When Ben was a youngster, Harris had spent a lot of time with him, back in the days when they carved model airplanes out of balsa-wood kits, the World War Spads and the racing monoplanes of Wiley Post and Roscoe Turner. Nowadays, Ben seemed to be closer to his mother and more interested in journalism and the newspaper than Harris ever was. Harris would make sure there was some time for Ben while he was on the island. He wished it were Thursday so he and Katie's mother, Hillary, could start the long drive to Mackinac Island. Whatever had come between him and Katie, Harris was still sure of one thing. Katie brought out what sensual qualities he had, and he loved her.

He dunked his toast in the coffee and paged through the morning Tribune to the sports section. Sportswriters were still mulling over Joe Louis' smashing victory over the German, Max Schmeling, in two minutes and four seconds of the first round in Yankee Stadium. It was the shortest heavyweight match in history. Minneapolis Miller right-fielder Ted Williams was named to the American Association All Star team and Johnny Vandermeer pitched his second no-hitter in a row for the Cincinnati Reds. He had blanked the Brooklyn Dodgers, 6-0, but not until after he had loaded the bases in the final inning. Then he got Dodger Leo Durocher to fly out to end the game.

The sports news was much better than the headlines on the front page.

WARPLANES CROSS FROM SPAIN — DROP BOMBS IN FRANCE
JAP PLANES BOMB CANTON IN CHINA
BRITISH SHIPPERS ATTACKED BY SPANISH INSURGENTS
GERMAN JEWS IN PANIC AS MOBS WRECK SHOPS

The only encouraging international news on the front page read:

Great Britain gave Germany a clear signal Monday to bring the whole Berlin-Rome Axis into accord with the western Europe democracies as King George VI and Queen Elizabeth ended a triumphant state visit to France.

Even then, Harris had an uneasy feeling in the pit of his stomach. Thank God Ben is only sixteen, he thought.

Back on the docks at St. Ignace, Katie and the children were already aboard *The Chippewa* as the purser called out one last "All Aboard!" Then there was the rumble of the metal gangplank being hauled on board, and the blasts of the ferryboat's steam whistle announced its departure for Mackinac Island.

CHAPTER 2

Tuesday, July 5

The history of the Straits of Mackinac started with St. Ignace back in 1634 when Jean Nicolet became the first white man to voyage into the area the Indians called Michilimackinac. French explorer, Pierre Esperit Radisson, canoed through the Straits some twenty years later. But it was Father Jacques Marquette, a young French Jesuit missionary, who in 1671, established an Indian mission on the tiny southeast corner of the Upper Peninsula which looked across the Straits to what would also become the state of Michigan. The French had already brought the Roman Catholic Church to Canada and Father Marquette's first mission was to the north at Sault Ste. Marie. A few years later he came to the Straits, naming his new mission St. Ignace in honor of St. Ignatius Loyola, credited with founding the Jesuit order. The Indians were mostly from the Huron and Ottawa tribes. To the west were the Sioux, known as the Dakotas, and the Chippewa, also called the Ojibway. While Father Marquette went about preaching Christianity to the Indians, French fur-traders arrived on the scene to roam the Great Lakes region already claimed by France.

Today, the names of those early French explorers and missionaries are a reminder of the glorious history of Michilimackinac, the Great Lakes, and beyond. As Father Marquette spread the Roman Catholic religion, he was joined by the French explorer, Louis Jolliet, and together they set out to find the Mississippi River and finally determined that its path led to the Gulf of Mexico. Robert Cavelier de LaSalle had spent time at the fort at St. Ignace, too, and had brought with him a member of the Belgian clergy whose name would be well-remembered in Minnesota — Father Louis Hennepin. LaSalle had built the first large sailing vessel, *The Griffin*, to sail on the Great Lakes. In 1682 his explorations took him to the mouth of the Mississippi River where he claimed the land for King Louis XIV and named the territory "Louisiana" in his honor. There were more familiar names. The French officer, Captain Cadillac, served as commandant of the fort at St. Ignace and founded the city of Detroit. Another such commandant's name was given to another Great Lakes city — the French explorer, Daniel Greysolon Duluth.

Standing on the deck of the ferry, Katie Butler looked back on the gray of St. Ignace as the boat pulled out of the harbor. She could see cars coming down the hill from the south into the old town, and more traffic along the lakeshore main street running all the way into the bluffs to the north. The shoreline scene of the old community diminished and as it faded in the distance, Katie turned to see where the kids were at that moment. The two girls had apparently gone below to get in out of the chilly air. But young Ben was leaning on the rail at the bow of the ferryboat, looking out on Lake Huron and toward Mackinac Island which loomed off in the distance. Katie never worried about Ben, but she often wondered just what he was thinking about when he was off by himself as he was now. Back home he would sit alone and fish for hours out on the dock on Gideon's Bay in front of their house. If he had any problems, he never said anything to his mother. And Katie never remembered Harris saying anything about such talks with his son. It wasn't that Ben was always quiet and reserved. He made friends with other young people and kids in the neighborhood — the Palmers, Anne Bisbee, Dick Dyer, and of course, all the youngsters in that neighborhood over on First Street, especially his best friend, Willy Westin.

Katie was a good mother and enjoyed her children. Yet, she was eager for Ben to finish high school and go on to college to study journalism. After all, those weekly newspapers were just waiting for him. And it seemed especially important to Katie that Ben take over the family business which Harris had seemingly forsaken.

Ben, too, was thinking about home as he looked out over the bow of the ferry. He was disappointed that Willy had not been able to make the trip. Katie had told each of her children they could invite a friend to Mackinac Island and Willy was really the only one Ben cared to ask. It had been easy for Ben to get off work at the *Record* office, where he served as a printer's devil during the summer. After all, his folks owned the newspaper. But it was different for Willy. He had a job working in a lakeside refreshment stand at the foot of Water Street in Excelsior where he and Tommy Pappas cooked hamburgers and hot dogs and opened bottles of pop all day long. The job paid $8 a week and all they could eat. There wasn't any choice for Willy. He and his family needed the money. There was no way he could take off for a whole week — without pay.

"My family's goin' to Mackinac Island again this summer," Ben announced back in June as he and Willy were on their way down to the Lake Theater in Excelsior to see the Friday night movie. "And my mom says that Blair and I can each invite a friend to go along." Then he quickly added, "Free."

They started down the hill on Second Street towards Arnold's Drug Store on the busiest corner of the main street, kicking stones off the sidewalk. "Would you like to come along, Will?"

"I'd like to, Ben, but I can't," Willy said, disappointed. "I just started this job at the stand down by the lake for Mr. Pappas and I can't ask for a whole week off. There's just Tommy and me running the place — seven days a week." He paused. "It really sounds like fun — but, naw, I couldn't get off work."

The two teen-agers stopped at Arnold's Drug to pick up their nickel candy bars. Ben always bought his favorite, a Three Musketeers. Willy's usual was a Snickers. They had been through this same Friday night ritual since 1931. Candy at Arnold's, then the movies. And even though these two were going to be seniors in high school in the fall, they still clung to their childhood habits. They would sit in the theater in seats ten rows back, on the right side of the aisle. It seemed as though they had been sitting in that same location all of their lives. And what memories. They had seen Gary Cooper and Franchot Tone in

Lives of a Bengal Lancer, Charles Laughton and Clark Gable in *Mutiny On The Bounty*, Shirley Temple in a whole series of films, from *Little Miss Marker* to *Captain January*, and all of the Tarzan movies starring Johnny Weissmuller and Maureen O'Sullivan. Tonight they were to see a brand new film — Mickey Rooney and Lewis Stone in *Judge Hardy's Children*.

The boys crossed the main street to the theater half-way up the block and paid their dimes for theater tickets. They were the first ones in the theater. At least nobody had taken their seats.

After the movie, they walked home in the warm dark night, talking about Andy Hardy — and themselves.

"I know how Andy felt when his dad wouldn't let him use the car," Ben said. "Most of the time, my folks won't let me drive unless one of them's with me."

"Big deal," Willy told him. "We don't even own a car."

"And that Polly sure is pretty," Ben reminisced about the movie.

"Yeah," Willy agreed. "Andy's got more nerve than most of us."

"Of course there are some good-looking girls in our class," Ben thought out loud, "but they're more like....like friends." They walked along in silence for a minute. "But that Polly. Now she's somethin' else."

"Her name is really Ann Rutherford," Will added.

"Ann Rutherford," Ben repeated the name. "I don't know if I'll ever date anyone as good lookin' as Ann Rutherford."

The boys had reached the Butler home now and they stood out on the sidewalk under the street light and talked some more about girls and things before they realized it was getting late. Willy started down the street toward his own home two blocks away.

"You think about Mackinac, Will," Ben shouted. "I ain't askin' anyone else. So if you change your mind, you can still go."

"I don't think so, but thanks anyway."

The wind off Lake Huron was chilly now. Ben thought about going inside to look for his mother. Then he changed his mind and decided to stay where he was. He put his hands in his pocket, turned away from the wind, and leaned against the rail. The rhythm of the engines made him more conscious of the boat. The lake looked gray and cold, not as friendly as Ben's Lake Minnetonka, and the waves were three times the size of those that slapped against the dock back home. For the first time, he realized just how enormous the Great Lakes really were. There was no shoreline off in the distance, just the horizon. Off the stern in the distance, he saw a boxy, white boat plowing through the water, followed by lots of white gulls. He could see that the on-coming boat was another ferry and as it passed them a hundred yards off to the port side, he saw people waving. His own boat seemed to stand still while the foamy, gray water rushed by. He stood transfixed by the sight and began to think of other things.

He wondered what Willy was doing this morning. Probably getting ready to open that refreshment stand down by the lake. Ben had to admit to himself that he was lucky. Willy and his family were working to survive. Here he was — on a vacation trip, and most of his future already planned for him. He'd be graduated from high school in a year from now and then it would be on to the University of Minnesota to study journalism. Actually, he was looking forward to that. He had worked as a reporter, a page editor and sports editor for the school newspaper, *The Minnetonka Breezes*, and even won an award. He had also done publicity for the high school athletic teams and covered high school sports for *The Record*. Perhaps he could hook on to the reporting staff of *The Minnesota Daily* when he got to the U. of M. And he didn't have to worry about a job when he finished college, either. When he was all through with school, he'd come back to *The Record* — and eventually it would be his. Ben knew in his heart that he would like it all, his last year of school, college and a career in newspapering. He was glad he wouldn't have to go through what his father had gone through, not liking the business and all. Besides, he truly wanted to please his mother, and Katie was used to having things go just the way she planned them, without any changes.

Ben looked up. He could see the island much better, now, and it wouldn't be long before just a corner of the Grand Hotel would come into view, a promise of more to come. They'd be there in another fifteen minutes. He'd be back on Mackinac Island with all of those college students who worked there every summer. And so many pretty girls. Maybe even one as pretty as Ann Rutherford.

Hillary Markham was excited about making the trip to Mackinac Island with her son-in-law, Harris Butler. She had travelled extensively in her younger days when her husband, Emmett, was alive. But she had not left Excelsior since his death four years ago. In some ways, her daughter, Katie, was much like herself. For most of Hillary's life, she had never worried about money. Her father had been a vice president with the Minneapolis and St. Louis Railway and she had grown up during prosperous times in St. Louis. Emmett, too, had been a good provider for Hillary and their family. She had met her husband on a vacation trip to Excelsior where her family stayed in one of the hotels owned by the railroad back in the 1880's. That was what was so exciting to Hillary now. She had never been to Mackinac Island, but the thought of no automobiles, just the horse and buggy, and resort hotels and the setting brought back memories of another era in Excelsior.

Hillary was now seventy, and her once blonde hair had turned completely white some years ago. She laughed at herself this morning. It was only Tuesday and she and Harris would not leave for Mackinac until Thursday. Yet, she was already packed. She would call Harris tonight and ask him to dinner tomorrow night. Men didn't do too well in the way of meals when left alone for a few days. Perhaps she would make one of his favorite dishes, lamb chops. After all, Hillary didn't have much opportunity to cook for anyone else these days. Yes, she was looking forward to the trip to Michigan. It would give her a chance to have a good long visit with Harris while they were on the road — to talk about....things. And Katie would not be there to interfere.

Katie leaned against the railing of the ferry and realized that this short trip from the mainland to the island marked the first time she had been alone in over twenty-four hours. The girls had hurried up the metal stairway to the deck near the bow, wincing in the strong breeze as the island drew closer with each passing wave and whitecap on Lake Huron. It hardly seemed possible to Katie that her daughter was twelve years old and Ben was nearing his seventeenth birthday only a few months away. Katie remembered when Blair was born on Easter Sunday, April 4, 1926. She remembered it looked more like Christmas when she peered out of the hospital window. It was barely above freezing in Minneapolis and high winds whipped an Easter snowfall around those third-floor windows at Deaconess Hospital. The birth of two sets of twins brought great excitement and reporters from the daily newspapers to the hospital that day. But to the Butlers, little Blair's arrival was even more of a major event.

Katie shook her head in disbelief. It had been more than twelve years. And so much had happened in the meantime. Even after Ben was born, Katie continued her relationships in Minneapolis society circles. She had helped the Junior League with its annual sale for the Minneapolis Society of the Blind and chaired other charitable projects. But after Blair's birth, things changed and Katie found herself drifting from those socialite friends in Minneapolis. The trips to the Shubert Theater to see the Bainbridge Players became less frequent. She had become a housewife and mother and although she really didn't like the idea, she was very good at it.

Those last twelve years seemed to have passed by all too quickly for Katie. But in fact, a lot had happened to the world since 1926. Things were surely different today. The same year that Blair was born, Admiral Byrd and Floyd Bennett made the first flight over the North Pole; nineteen-year-old Gertrude Ederle became the first woman to swim the English Channel; and Gene Tunney took the heavyweight boxing championship away from Jack Dempsey. Lindbergh had made his historic flight across the Atlantic in 1927 and Babe Ruth hit his sixtieth homerun in Yankee Stadium. Herbert Hoover had been elected president. Then the ticker tapes on Wall Street ran two and three hours behind on October 29, 1929, to herald the coming of the depression, unemployment and bank failures. Ben Butler was only ten years old when Franklin D. Roosevelt was elected president in 1932, the same year of the kidnapping of twenty-month-old Charles Lindbergh, Jr. in Hopewell, New Jersey. Al Capone went to prison and Professor Albert Einstein was granted a visa to come to the United States from Berlin. These last few years had seen the coming and going of Public Enemy Number One, John Dillinger, the Chicago Worlds Fair, a second term for President Roosevelt, and the Hindenburg going up in flames.

But there was one aspect of the twenties important to Katie Butler.

Bootlegging. After Blair was born, Katie spent more time at home and it was so easy to buy bootleg whiskey in Excelsior — and just about anywhere in the country. With the repeal of prohibition just before Christmas of 1933, drinking became even easier and more frequent for Katie. She nipped regularly and became the only woman in town who didn't worry about being seen going into the local municipal liquor store, the bastion of drinking males. In fact, she could use a drink from the flask in her purse right now. But she decided to wait until she got to the hotel on the island. It wouldn't be very long.

The ferryboat was moving along the southwestern shoreline of Mackinac Island and Blair and Annabelle could now make out the tiny forms of people biking along the shore, dwarfed by the tall, steep, wooded cliffs that dominated Lake Huron. At first, the bikers looked like little ants moving along at such a slow pace. Now the girls could see clearly the forms of adults and children and the bicycles. Here and there, hiding in the green foliage atop the high bluffs were larger summer homes, fresh with white paint, seemingly standing guard over this peaceful island. Ben moved to the bow and watched the scene from the rail. He thought about all the things that must have happened here in the long history of the straits. His mother had brought home a stack of history books about Michigan and Mackinac Island. "If we're going to go there and enjoy it, let's find out what it's all about," she had told the family.

Mackinac Island had not always been so at peace with the world. In its early history, there was conflict in the area known as Michilimackinac even before the white men appeared on the scene. The Indian tribes of the Huron and Ottawa had been driven west from New York by the warring Iroquois. The Michilimackinac area, then claimed by the French, extended all the way to lands now in Minnesota. But the Huron and Ottawa found the Sioux and Chippewa even more unfriendly and eventually migrated back to the Straits of Mackinac. Michilimackinac was the Indian name for the three main points of the Straits — St. Ignace, the area which would become Mackinaw City, and Mackinac Island. The name Mackinac itself is derived from the early tribe of Michilimackinac Indians and means "Great Turtle," which also describes the shape of the island. The first real settlement by the French was at St. Ignace. Indians saw French fur-traders, missionaries and explorers pass through this gateway to the west and south and eventually French soldiers built a fort there in 1688. Around the turn of the century the French withdrew from the area and abandoned the fort, but then returned to construct a second Fort Michilimackinac on the south side of the Straits. In the meantime, the English were beginning to move into the area and years of conflict between France and England culminated in the French and Indian War.

In 1760, the victorious English seized control of the French holdings in America, including the Straits. But the Indian tribes were not happy with their new victors and Chief Pontiac's warriors rose up in revolt in 1763, leading to a bloody massacre at Fort Michilimackinac on the south side of the Straits. To guard against the threat of the upstart Americans, the English garrison began to move to a more strategic location, this time on Mackinac Island, in 1779. The first party arrived on the island aboard the warship, *Welcome*, and over the next two years, the entire British community was moved across the Straits to the island. Even though it all became a part of the United States of America in 1783, it wasn't until 1796 that the first United States Army troops took command of Fort Mackinac. The British won it back again in the war of 1812 but relinquished the Fort and the island for good in 1815.

Those small dots moving along the pathway on the shores of Mackinac Island were now so close that Ben could see the bicycles very clearly. The cliffs and high bluffs gave way to more sloping ground as the ferry neared the harbor. Dominating the scenery was the breathtaking sight of the Grand Hotel with its domed cupola and flags flying from its majestic open porch which looked over the Straits to greet each ferryboat full of visitors to the island. Katie had moved inside but now joined those from the top cabin or below who rushed to the open decks

and crowded the rails to see the sights as the ferry rounded the southern tip of the island and moved closer to the harbor. Katie pushed open
the heavy door to the deck and found her son standing at the rail.

"Look familiar?" she asked.

"A little," he said shyly. "I think that's the Iroquois Hotel there on
the point."

"You're right," she agreed. "It's at the opposite end of the main
street from the Island House. "And there's the Windermere Hotel —
that yellow one over there."

"The one next to it with the spirals is the Lake View," he said as he
pointed to the long white structure across the street from the Iroquois
Hotel.

They watched for the first sign of the Island House over near the
small marina where sailing sloops and motor launches were docked.

"There it is!" Ben shouted. The large white structure with two four-
story wings and an open porch was partly hidden from view by the
trees. Even Katie was getting excited now as the ferry made its final
turn into port and headed for the large docks. Part of the main street
could be seen but much of it was obscured by the lake side of the Chippewa Hotel and the U.S. Coast Guard Station. Protecting all of this in
its white splendor on the bluffs behind the harbor and main street was
historic Fort Mackinac. Old homes and cottages along the lakeshore
drive looked so serene and comfortable, and as the terrain rose away
from the shoreline and back toward the bluffs, roofs of homes peeked
through the maze of great trees. Off to the right along a high ridge
overlooking the harbor was a row of summer homes with cupolas and
open porches and flowers everywhere.

As the ferry began to slow down for its docking, Ben could see all
kinds of activity on the main pier. Horses and wagons and dray lines
were waiting to be loaded with everything from foodstuffs to sacks of
cement. Dock workers waited patiently for the incoming ferry. There
would be lots of supplies to unload this morning. And there were the
new work horses to handle, too. Other men were checking shipping
manifests and the old pier looked more like a wholesale food market
and lumberyard rolled into one.

Ben's voice had an excitement to it. "Look at the bikes! I've never
seen so many bikes!" He paused. "I've got my own money, Mom, and
the first thing I'm gonna do is rent a bike and ride around the whole
island."

Katie laughed. "That's what everybody does when they get off the boat. Rent a bike and ride around the island — even if they haven't ridden a bike in twenty years." She had a broad smile. "Maybe I'll even join you on that bike ride," she said as she put her arm around her son's shoulder.

The ferry had come to a halt now and mooring lines were being thrown to young workers on the pier. The entire dock was full of activity, noises and sounds of hundreds of conversations, all going on at the same time. Some dray wagons were already loaded and were leaving the pier with drivers squeezing their teams past other wagons and dollies of cardboard cartons and boxes and through the crowds. The clatter of the wagons and the incessant clicks of the horse shoes made many conversations indistinguishable. People standing on the docks were shouting greetings to visitors arriving on the ferry whom they had come to meet. Other young dock workers with suntanned faces and arms, waited in rolled up shirtsleeves for the passengers to leave the ferry so they could get on with the business of unloading the bales of hay brought over on this trip.

Ben could hear the horses that had made the crossing on the ferry this morning. They were getting restless as they stomped around in their close quarters and neighed their anxiety. Ben looked out on the scene. Horses! Wagons! Crowds! Bicycles!

"We're entering a whole different world, Ben," Katie said in quieter tones. "It's like turning the clock back some fifty years."

Ben agreed. Then they both looked up at the sky as the sun, if by some magic, had suddenly dispelled all of the clouds and overcast. Now there was blue sky — and a glorious summer day. Katie smiled. Harris would have been right. It burned off before noon.

The sharp sound of a steam whistle announcing the arrival of a ferry-boat out in the harbor woke Al Davis with a start. He sat up in bed quickly and glanced around the old hotel room with a slight tinge of panic. For just an instant, he didn't know where he was. Then he looked down next to him on the bed and saw the bare back of Marian

Stanhope. The rumpled sheets and blankets half covered her nude body as she lay, face down in the pillow, sound asleep in the second-floor room of the Island House. Alvin Davis suddenly realized that he didn't have any clothes on either, that he was not in his own hotel room but that of the attractive Mrs. Harvey Stanhope. It was not a new experience for the forty-year-old assistant manager of the hotel, who looked more as though he was going on thirty. With a handsome face and dark wavy hair without any signs of gray, he fancied himself as being attractive to the young college girls who invaded the island each summer to work for meager wages and tips to help them go back to school in the fall. But the truth of the matter was that most of those coeds could spot Al Davis as a phony and stayed clear of him. Mrs. Stanhope, on the other hand, knew him for what he was, but it was all right with her. She was back on the island for the second time this summer after having come up from Detroit in early June for a few days. She had met Al Davis last year when he first came to the hotel as the assistant manager. They had shared both his bed and hers in July after her husband had been called back to Detroit on business. Marian was angry with Harvey for giving in to the press of business and leaving her on the island by herself. Al Davis had helped things along by making arrangements to take Harvey Stanhope back to Mackinaw City by a charter boat. And naturally, he felt obligated to see to it that Mrs. Stanhope was taken care of. After all, she was alone on the island. Davis felt it had been an easy conquest.

Marian, however, wasn't quite as dumb as she might have appeared. Harvey, who was fifty-eight years old and sixteen years her senior, hadn't been the most amorous husband in the world. He owned a small chain of second-rate clothing stores in Michigan and he used his wife as a "live-in model" for his mediocre women's fashions, dressing her in cheap, gaudy dresses and what she called "Betty Boop" high heels. The saving grace was that Marian, who had survived the depression as a hair-dresser and part-time prostitute, knew what was going on and made the best of it. Harvey had probably treated her better than anyone in her whole life. But Harvey had suffered a stroke two years ago and although he managed to get around all right and take good care of himself, he was even less a lover than before. And Marian was smart enough to keep things in perspective and find her sex elsewhere — and discreetly. Al Davis fit the bill, perfectly. He was handsome, a good lover, and eager to please, even though the latter quality was more for his sake than for her's. So now, Marian was back again, arriving on the island last night. Harvey would join her tonight. In the meantime, Al Davis had stopped by her room early last evening to welcome her back and to have a drink. He never left.

Marion Stanhope rolled over in bed, giving him a view of her full breasts. "What's the matter, Al?"

"Nothing, Marian," he replied as he stared toward the window where the morning sun was now streaming through and warming the foot of the bed.

"I thought you told me you didn't have to work this morning," she pouted.

"I don't." He continued to look at the window. "That boat whistle just woke me up and reminded me we had a dock boy quit and go home yesterday. I have to be sure Billy is on duty or I'll have my ass in a sling."

"Aw, don't worry about it, Al," she tried to reassure him. "You're so damn good-lookin' that even when you're in trouble, you can talk your way out of anything." She tugged at his bare arm.

"Billy's a good kid," he told himself. "I'm sure he's taking care of things this morning."

Marian pulled at his arm again. "Come on, Al. This is the last chance we'll have before Harvey comes tonight."

He looked down at Marian, her platinum blonde hair a disheveled mass. She was no Jean Harlow, he thought, but not bad looking for a gal in her forties. The best thing about her, though, was she liked him — and she was very good in bed. "Old Horseface will be here today, won't he?"

"You shouldn't call him that," she said as she rolled over in bed and hid her smile.

"Well, that's what he lookes like." He paused. "Good old Horseface Harvey." Al Davis slid down on to the bed again, fit his body along Marian's back, buttocks and legs and reached over to caress her breasts. Good old Horseface, he thought.

Billy Lachine had also heard the steam whistle as the ferry entered the harbor of Mackinac Island. The sound was a signal to dock boys at all of the local resort hotels that another ferryboat was arriving and there might be those with reservations for their particular hotel stepping off the boat in a matter of minutes. Like all good dock porters, Billy was now in a rush to get to the waterfront. He crossed the expansive open porch of The Island House, found his bike on the front lawn, and pedaled off toward the municipal pier to meet the boat. He could see the ferry docking as he sped past Marquette Park, down Huron Street, past the Chippewa and Murray Hotels and then swung left to the pier, crowded with visitors, horses and wagons, and dock workers. Dock porters from the other hotels were already there, waiting for passengers to step off the ferryboat. The young men would each call out the name of his hotel in hopes that guests for their particular hostelry would be on board and need their baggage hauled. Although most of the passengers would be day visitors to the island, Billy watched the gangplank being hauled into place and wondered if there would be anyone interesting on board coming to The Island House.

CHAPTER 3

Tuesday, July 5

Mackinac Island, steeped in history, was alive with hotels from the past, and oldest of them all was the Island House. This marvelous old building was originally built by Charles O'Malley in 1848 and became the first summer hotel at Mackinac. Captain Henry Van Allen, a skipper on the Great Lakes, purchased the hotel in 1865 and the structure was later moved from the beach to its location on Huron Street across from the harbor. It was not only the oldest of the island's hotels but had gained the reputation as the best family hotel on Mackinac Island. The Van Allen's daughter, Rose Van Allen Webster, took up the ownership of the historic hotel in the early 1890's on the death of her parents. She was the wife of Col. John Webster whom she had met during the 1870's when he was stationed at Fort Mackinac. The new owner added one large wing and in 1912 added another one to complete the structure. Mrs. Webster continued to operate the Island House in the early 1900's through the World War, the flapper era of the twenties, and into the depression of the early thirties. Today, the Island House, glistening in a fresh coat of white paint, stood proud with all of its charm of the past. And like its sister hotels on the island, there was something about it, some intangible, that made every new visitor believe that a hundred years from now, this old hotel would still be here on Mackinac Island.

The Island House and the Grand were not the only hotels on the island, however. Others were recovering from the lean years of the depression and were beginning to fill up again during this peak season of the year. One of the oldest hotels on the island was the Lake View Hotel with its tall corner turrets and marvelous view of the lake from all three stories of the wood-frame structure. It had been built in 1858 but was now only one of many hotels offering accomodations to summer visitors.

Next door was the Windermere Hotel, built in 1887 as a private residence and turned into a hotel at about the turn of the century. The hotel had been owned since 1905 by the Doud family, one of the best-known and respected families on the island. Stephen and Bridget Doud had come to the island in the 1850's when Stephen made his living as a cooper. They raised a family of seven sons and a daughter and eventually, two of the sons, James and Patrick, opened Doud's Grocery Store in 1885. Patrick also went on to become a contractor on the island and built the Michigan Governor's summer mansion on Mackinac Island. The Doud's Windermere Hotel was still a favorite for many visitors and its handsome architecture caught the eye of most visitors as ferryboats moved along the shoreline toward the harbor.

Across the street from the Windermere was the Iroquois Hotel which came to be known as the Iroquois on the Beach. The building experienced a number of expansion projects over the years to accomodate the increased business of this popular hotel which had been constructed in the early 1900's by Robert H. Benjamin, another name synonymous with well-known Mackinac families. The Benjamins had come to Michigan from England through Canada in the 1880's and Mr. Benjamin had served as a sheriff and also as a postmaster at Mackinac. His son, Herbert, had come to the island with his family when he was two years old and eventually Herbert's blacksmith shop would become the busiest place in town and historically famous.

The Murray Hotel was another of the early hotels, getting its start in the 1880's. Located in the heart of the main street of Mackinac Island, the Murray faced the municipal docks and Doud's Grocery and was famous for its little front porch on the busy main street. The Chippewa

Hotel also dated back to the turn of the century. Built in 1902 by George Arnold, the hotel looked out on the harbor and faced busy Huron Street as well. In addition, there were smaller hotels — the Windsor, the Beaumont, the St. Cloud and others, plus a long list of rooming houses.

Dock porters, all young men in their teens, waited on the pier to see if there were passengers bound for their particular hotel. Because they met just about every ferry to arrive during the day, some were not too enthusiastic about their job and leaned back against the wall of the warehouse on the pier, keeping under the overhang of the roof and staying out of the sun. Some of the more energetic young porters were eager to help, even though their own hotel might not be involved. They helped other dock workers haul materials off the ferry and helped with the mooring lines. Those from the Grand were easy to single out — in their white shirts and black bow ties. But they were all friendly and most of them let passengers know they were there.

"Lake View Hotel! Lake View, anyone?"

"Grand Hotel. Baggage for the Grand right here."

A teenager from the Chippewa helped a passenger haul his luggage off the ferry and ran into another porter. "Hey, gimme some room," he shouted.

Another hotel boy shouted across the crowd. "Hey, Billy, when are you going to take us out on that tub of yours again?"

"Sunday, maybe," Billy Lachine answered as he waited on the dock to see if there were any passengers going to his hotel. "Anyone for the Island House?" Billy shouted amidst other dock porters who kept identifying themselves from the Chippewa, the Murray, the Iroquois and the rest. "Island House, anyone?"

The Butler clan, led by Katie, hauled their own baggage across the short gangplank and heard Billy's voice over near one of the storage buildings on the pier. Katie set down a suitcase on the cement and waved at the young man with the curly hair. Then she picked up the bag again and the rest of the group followed her through the crowd toward the young man still calling out, "Island House."

VIEW OF MACKINAC ISLAND
A view of the historic community of Mackinac Island and its harbor, once the hub of American fur-trading and the setting for the story of *The Island House*.

—Photo, courtesy The Town Crier

HURON STREET
Visitors, bikers, and horses and carriages are familiar sites along Mackinac Island's main thoroughfare. Fort Mackinac is seen at the top of the photo.

—Photo, courtesy The Town Crier

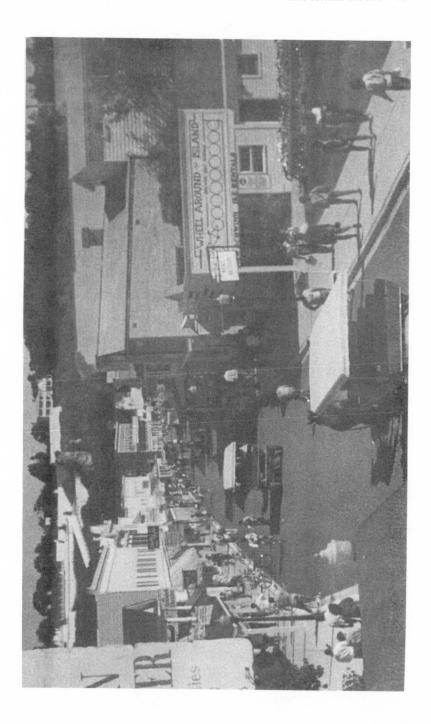

THE ISLAND HOUSE
The oldest hotel on Mackinac Island, the Island House has served visitors each summer since 1848. In 1970, the hotel began a refurbishing that is on-going today. It hosts the guests in the story of The Island House.

—*Photo, courtesy* The Town Crier

MARQUETTE PARK AND FORT MACKINAC
Lilcas bloom in Marquette Park below the famous Fort Mackinac which has guarded the straits for more than 200 years.

—*Photo, courtesy* The Town Crier

FORT MACKINAC
Now a major attraction for visitors to Mackinac Island, Fort Mackinac once garrisoned the United States Infantry shown here on the parade grounds in 1891.

—Photo, courtesy The Mackinac Island State Park Commission

THE HARBOR
A view from Fort Mackinac, overlooking the harbor and marina, the island's Huron Street, and Lake Huron on a Mackinac Island summer day.

—*Photo, courtesy* The Town Crier

THE SOUTH AMERICAN
From days gone by, the Great Lakes liner, The South American, shown in port at Mackinac Island. Now retired, it made its last visit to the island in the 1960's.

—Photo, courtesy The Town Crier

ARCH ROCK
Mackinac Island's Arch Rock not only offers a magnificent view of Lake Huron but also plays an important part in the Indian legends of the historic island.

—*Photo, courtesy Mackinac Island State Park Commission*

THE GRAND HOTEL
The world-famous structure boasts the longest open porch in the world and has stood proud atop the bluffs of Mackinac Island since 1887. Its name is synonomous with Mackinac Island.

—*Photo, courtesy* The Town Crier

TRINITY EPISCOPAL CHURCH
Trinity Church — a popular historic site on Mackinac Island, still serving the community throughout the entire year. The building dates back to 1882.

—*Photo, courtesy* The Town Crier

Billy could see the Butler party shouldering their way toward him —
an attractive dark-haired.mother, two young girls and a teen-age son.
Katie caught the dock boy's eye.

"Guests for the Island House?" he shouted above the din of the
crowd.

"Hello," Katie greeted him, with a hint of exhaustion from lugging
the suitcases off the ferry. "Can you take our bags to the Island
House?" Ben and the girls gathered around Billy Lachine.

"You leave your baggage right here, and I'll see to it that it gets up
to the hotel. Just tell me how many pieces you have."

Katie began to point with her finger and count. "There's ten
altogether," she told him. "But I'll carry this round hat bag myself.
You can bring the rest."

"No problem, Ma'am." Billy looked up toward the main street and
then turned to the Butler clan again. "You been here before?" he
asked.

"Yes — we stayed at the Island House last year," Ben answered.

"Then you know the way." He pointed toward the main street.
"Just up there and a few blocks down to your right past the park."

Katie thanked him, gathered the group around her, and started for
the main street. The dock porter looked familiar — like she had seen
him before. The dark, curly hair. The broad shoulders. There was
something about him.....

Her thoughts were interrupted by the giggling of the young girls.

"What are you feeling so good about?" she asked. Both Blair and
Annabelle looked a little sheepish.

"The boy who's going to bring our luggage up to the hotel is cute,"
Annabelle said with a shy grin.

"And he smiled at us, too," Blair added.

"Come on, you two," Katie said, amused.

The four of them walked up to Huron Street, the main street of the
crowded little town, and started down the street past Doud's Grocery
and the Chippewa Hotel toward their own hotel. They walked under a
canopy that extended all along the front of the Chippewa. Across the
street were more stores, all housed in wood-framed buildings that
looked like they had been there forever. In most, the second floors had
been made into apartments or living quarters and curtains could be
seen in the upstairs windows. At the moment, Ben felt as though he

was part of a movie set, but the scene was different. It was real. This was an honest-to-god town that had turned the clock back and was operating in a different time frame from the rest of the world. The sidewalk was crowded, and in the street, horses and buggies and bikes and pedestrians reminded Ben of the midway at the state fair back in Minnesota. Families who had just arrived to spend the day on the island were walking down the middle of the busy street, not realizing the dangers of being hit by a team of horses or a wagon. One mother pushed a four-wheeled taylor-tot through the crowd. The infant taking the ride was already exhausted with the day's events and was sound asleep. Another mother scolded her two youngsters for running in front of a taxi carriage. An overweight father in a colorful Hawaiian sport shirt almost backed into the Markham family as he snapped a photograph of his wife and kids with his new candid camera. An elderly city couple stopped to inspect a team of horses standing in the street. The dapple-gray work horses stood quietly amidst the flurry of activity on the street and brought back fond memories to the elderly couple who reminisced about their childhood days back on the farm. A couple of farmers were impressed by a dazzling team of horses from the Grand Hotel, resplendent in shiny new harnesses. The team was groomed to perfection and the two farmers nodded their heads in amazement and admiration.

Katie and her clan stopped at Marquette Park to look up at Fort Mackinac which towered over the harbor and the green park below. The girls were fascinated by all the pigeons roosting on the very top of the head of the statue. While they were standing there, Billy Lachine went by, pushing a two-wheeled cart so loaded with luggage that he could hardly manage it by himself. "Some day I'll have to try bringing up the baggage from the docks on my bike. It couldn't be any harder than this," he thought.

All the kids ooh'd and ah'd as Billy passed them. Katie shook her head in disbelief. Any one of those pieces of baggage teetering on the top of the cart could easily fall off. She was glad she had opted to carry one piece of luggage herself. The hat bag contained her liquor.

Alex Shepherd had worked in the Hennepin County Auditor's Office in downtown Minneapolis for the past four years. He had grown up in Minneapolis, went to Central High School and then on to the University of Minnesota. Despite his slight build, Alex was a strong-willed man, ultra-conservative, with a mind of his own, and after two years of college, quit because he suspected that many members of the faculty were Communists. He had been too young for military service during the World War and as a young man, had worked his way through the last few years of the Twenties at a variety of jobs — as a teamster for Northland Milk Company out of horse barns at Twenty-Eighth and Lyndale in Minneapolis; then as a streetcar conductor for the Twin City Rapid Transit Company's line from Minneapolis through the suburb of Hopkins out to Excelsior; and then as a bookkeeper in the accounting department of the streetcar company. He had met Florence Whittier while he was still a conductor on the Minneapolis to Excelsior line. She was a local Excelsior girl and he was living at the Sampson House Hotel in Excelsior. They were married in the Excelsior Methodist Church and settled down in that small town to begin their married life and raise a family.

The depression came and Alex was unemployed. He had been a conservative and a Republican all his life. Then he found himself working for the kind of government he objected to — the Public Works Administration — building a grandstand out of limestone rock at the Excelsior Commons baseball field. It was hard work and he hated every minute of it. And although it allowed Alex and his wife and two daughters, Annabelle and Betty, to survive during those dark economic days, he despised the PWA and the WPA, and the Democrats for defeating Herbert Hoover in the election of 1932. Most of all, he hated Franklin D. Roosevelt and blamed him for all that had happened over those bad years. And to add insult to injury, his birthday was the same date as FDR's — January 30.

Alex was upset with Florence this evening. She had invited Harris Butler to dinner, and if there was anyone for whom he had a passionate dislike, it was a liberal with money. Harris and Katie happened to be Democrats who owned the local newspaper, right in the middle of this Republican stronghold of a community. And they had lots of money.

"It was thoughtful of you to invite me over for dinner, Mrs. Shepherd," Harris said as he sat across from her in the small dining room of the Shepherd's modest home on Third Street, a few blocks from the Butler home.

"Call me Florence," Mrs. Shepherd cautioned him.

"Florence," Harris said hesitatingly.

Mrs. Shepherd poured coffee for Harris and Alex while their youngest daughter, Betty, helped clear the dishes from the dining room table. Florence was preparing to serve ice cream for dessert. It was a special treat in the Shepherd household. Good ice cream was too expensive to have very often and when it was served, it all had to be consumed at one sitting. There was no way to preserve it in their kitchen ice box which took a fifty-pound chunk a couple times a week from the Morse Bros. Ice Company in Excelsior. Betty had overheard her parents arguing about the ice cream before Harris arrived for dinner.

"It's only a quart of ice cream, Alex," Florence had defended herself.

"It's still too damn expensive," Alex insisted. "And besides, it's probably not even a treat for Butler. I bet they have it all the time over there on the Gold Coast." The Gold Coast was the name given by locals to those houses along West Lake Street in Excelsior. They were mostly large summer homes that looked out on to Gideon's Bay of Lake Minnetonka, and were relatively expensive.

"I see no reason why I shouldn't serve ice cream tonight," Florence said defiantly. "After all, I've known Katie for a long, long time. We went to school together and even sang in the same women's quartet together."

"I know, I know," Alex relented.

"It's the least I could do, seeing that Harris is home alone." She paused. "And Annabelle *is* on vacation with his family."

"I suppose," he mumbled as he had left the kitchen. "But I hate having to give in to those bleedin'-heart liberals," he muttered.

"Come on, Alex. We're just being neighborly." She smiled. "It has nothing to do with politics."

Young Betty Shepherd was reminded of that conversation between her parents as she took some of the dirty dishes from the dining room into the kitchen and overheard Harris.

"It's really quite neighborly of you two to take care of this bachelor who doesn't do too well for himself when his wife and family aren't around."

Florence served the French vanilla ice cream at the dining room table and asked the two men if they would like more iced tea. Harris seemed delighted with the dessert. "We don't get this too often at home," he remarked to Florence. She smiled triumphantly.

"It's from Arnold's Drug Store," she said. "They make their own ice cream there."

"Yes," Alex added. "We have it quite often. It's much better than the commercial ice creams. Much better."

Florence rolled her eyes up into her head. And out in the kitchen, Betty almost dropped a pile of dishes on the floor.

The after-dinner conversation between Harris and Alex quickly turned to politics. Alex warned Harris that the Farmer-Labor candidate, Hjalmer Peterson, would surely lose in the governor's race in the fall when the Republicans ran the up-and-coming politician, Harold Stassen, against him.

"A little young, isn't he?" needled Harris, knowing Alex's lack of faith in the growth of America.

"He's thirty-one and probably the smartest man in the state. Graduated from high school at fifteen. Believe me, he's going places," replied Alex, shaking a finger at Harris.

Alex told Harris how he had been out campaigning for Stassen and then turned to FDR's policies since winning his second term. Alex said he was worried about the national debt and what it would do to the next generation.

"Do you realize that even with a half-million-dollar cut in this year's budget, FDR is going to have a billion-dollar deficit this year and another billion next year?"

Harris was impressed. For somebody working in a county office, Alex was well-read when it came to national politics. Harris would have guessed that a county office-worker would have only been interested in his day-to-day tasks and local affairs and not so concerned with the nation's politics. He was wrong and he found it out as the possibility of war in Europe got into the conversation between the two men.

"He's gonna get us into a war in Europe if we're not careful," Alex argued about FDR. "I'm concerned for this country," he told his guest, "not for myself. After all, I have daughters. But you," he told Harris, "you should be worried. You have a son — and just about the right age, too."

"There may be something going on in Europe one of these days," Harris agreed, "but I don't think we'll get involved except for providing military goods to our friends over there." Then he told Alex something that he hadn't even discussed with Katie. "In fact, I've been in contact with a number of firms now producing military supplies and they tell me that now is the time to get in on the ground floor as a sales representative." He waited to see Alex's reaction, but there was none. "Selling to the war department would be a new challenge for me."

Alex was cool. And as the evening ended and Harris thanked Florence for the dinner and turned to leave, Alex offered one last word of caution. "Remember what I said about daughters and sons, Butler."

Harris assured Alex he'd think about it. Then he turned to Mrs. Shepherd. "Thanks again — Florence. I'll be leaving for Mackinac day after tomorrow and I'll tell Kate how kind you both were to have me over for dinner."

"It was the least we could do," Florence replied. "After all, our Annabelle is enjoying a whole week of vacation because of you and Katie." Then she added, "And you know how much we think of your Blair." Florence and Alex stood on the front steps of their home and watched as Harris started down the sidewalk for home. "Give our love to the girls," Florence called out as she waved one last time.

Back home, Harris warmed up some left-over coffee and sat up on the second-floor sun porch which overlooked the lake. He remembered he had been invited to Hillary's for supper tomorrow night and he'd better get his clothes packed for the trip tonight. He sipped the last of the coffee and thought again about the challenge of selling to the military — and how he could make so much money that he wouldn't have to be dependent on Kate. Then he thought about Ben.

As Florence Shepherd finished the supper dishes, she could see her husband through the kitchen window. Alex was on his way out back to close the garage doors, checking to make sure the keys weren't left in the 1934 Ford sedan, and to set the lawnmower back up against the garage wall. He was carrying an old Mason jar in which he would store some nails. He was thinking about Annabelle and was happy for her. Then he thought about Harris Butler and their table conversation earlier. Perhaps it was his talk with Harris, or maybe he was just jealous that Annabelle was having such a good time with the Butlers, but Alex felt so frustrated. He was not a violent man, but without hesitation, he threw the Mason jar, smashing it against the garage wall. Then he closed the doors to the garage and started back toward the house. He'd clean up the damn broken glass tomorrow.

Harvey Stanhope had called the Island House earlier in the day when he found he would arrive from Detroit earlier than expected and left a note for Marian as to when he would get to the island. Al Davis saw the note in the Stanhope key box behind the main desk and volunteered to deliver it to Mrs. Stanhope's room. The college girl working the front desk was not surprised. Earlier in the day, the chambermaid on the second floor had returned Al's set of hotel keys to the front desk after finding them in room 200 while doing her daily cleaning.

When Marian opened the door, Al stood there with the note in his hand. "We have a phone message from your husband, Mrs. Stanhope," he said properly.

"Thank you Mr. Davis." She accepted the note and started to close the door.

"May I come in for a moment?" he asked. "I hope it isn't bad news."

"Come in if you like."

She turned and started for the bathroom as Al slipped inside the room and closed the door. He noticed she was wearing a shiny rayon aqua dressing gown with palm trees across the back. Marian came back out of the bathroom reading the note.

"You all right, Marian?" he asked. "You seem a little cool."

"I'm okay." She was chewing gum. "But I don't think you should come up anymore. I'm sure you know that Harvey will be here in a few hours." She put her hand to his neck and kissed him on the cheek. "It was nice, Al, but nothin's gonna happen between us after Harvey gets here. It's 'until death do us part,' " she cautioned him, "and don't you screw it up, Al."

Al assured her there would be no problem and they talked for a minute or two before he left the room. As the assistant manager started back down the stairs he shook his head. What a body, he thought. Then he spoke out loud. "Goddamn that Horseface!"

Katie and Ben and the girls had finished an elegant dinner in the Drum and Eagle dining room of the Island House. The dinner conversation extended beyond the dessert as Katie listened to the three youngsters tell about their first day's experiences on the island. All had dressed for dinner this first evening on the island. Ben seemed a little uncomfortable in the new seersucker jacket Katie had bought for him before they left home. Annabelle wore a white dress and Blair had waited all day to put on her new pink print frock with the fresh white collar. Even Katie wore a new colorful organza dress for the occasion.

At the dinner table, the girls talked excitedly about their day — shopping in all of the gift shops along Huron Street, sitting in Marquette Park, and eating fudge they had bought from one of the many candy shops. Katie had spent part of the day getting everyone settled in their rooms. Then she had sat out on the veranda of the hotel in the afternoon and read part of Daphne du Maurier's *Rebecca*. Blair wondered what her dad was doing this evening and Katie guessed he was home alone, grumbling about having to fix his own supper for a change. Then the conversation got around to what Ben had done during his first day on the island. But Ben wasn't listening to the talk at the table. Ever since she came to take their dinner order, Ben had been watching the dark-haired waitress with the sunburned face. No one else seemed to take notice of her, but Ben couldn't keep his eyes off her as she moved in and out of the dining room and around their own table. He had made a selection from the menu but when it came time for him to give the young waitress his order, he couldn't remember what he wanted.

"Ben — we're talking to you," his mother said. "What about your first day here?" she asked.

"Oh yes." Ben gathered himself together and got back into the table conversation again, telling them how he had biked around the island in about forty-five minutes and had made friends with the young man who worked at the hotel, Billy Lachine.

"He took me down the docks this afternoon and showed me his sailboat. It's a 26-footer, Mom, the kind we talked about getting at home. You should walk down to the docks and take a look at it tomorrow. It's really swell."

The mention of the young man who had hauled their baggage from the ferry to the hotel this morning prompted Katie to think about where she had seen him before. The dark curly hair, the handsome young face. She'd seen him somewhere before — but where? The pretty, sunburned waitress brought the check to Katie after dinner. Katie dug into her purse to find her billfold.

"Where are you from?" she asked the girl in the waitress uniform.

"I'm from Ferrisville — Ferrisville, Michigan," she said proudly. "I'm going to be a freshman at Michigan State this fall." Then she added, "My folks are farmers."

"How nice." Katie didn't seem too impressed.

Earlier, the waitress had introduced herself as Janet Rachel. Katie paid the check but didn't pay much attention to her. Ben, however, thought she was beautiful. If only Willy were here, he thought. She's as beautiful as — Ann Rutherford.

The four walked out on to the veranda of the Island House and found the night air had turned chilly since they had gone to dinner. Then Katie remembered about Billy Lachine. No, she hadn't met him before, but he reminded her very much of another young man, Frank ——Frank Jennings, a college student from the neighboring community of Deephaven near Excelsior, who was home for the summer a few years ago and had done some dock work for Harris out in front of the Butler home. Now she remembered — very attractive face, black hair, and a suntanned body. The recollection brought a tingle of excitement to Katie. She had given into one of her occasional whims and had seduced young Frank Jennings on a hot July afternoon on that second-floor sun porch of the Butler home. It was not the first such encounter with a younger man for Katie.

It was not that she had planned them all. Sometimes it just happened. But in each instance, Katie knew in her heart that she was in complete control. Perhaps that's why she had enjoyed those infrequent indiscretions. She had not purposely set out to be unfaithful to Harris. It was just that he was the passive one in the marriage and Katie was the aggressor, just as she was in everything else she attempted. As a kid, she was a better swimmer than most boys in the neighborhood, she was valedictorian of her senior class at Excelsior High School, and was graduated with honors from the University of Minnesota. She had fallen in love with Harris Butler, wanted him, and married him. She still loved him, but there was a special excitement about younger men.

It was the curly hair and the classic face she thought to herself. Yes, the dock porter looked a lot like one of her young lovers of the past.

Marian Stanhope dressed for dinner and hurried out of the hotel, down the front walk through the twin trees and along Huron Street to the main pier to meet the ferry from Mackinaw City. When her husband, Harvey stepped off the boat, Marian embraced him and gave him a long, lingering kiss. Harvey was still dressed in a business suit, and the two of them walked arm in arm back to the Island House while he told her of his activities during the day and how much he had missed her these past two days. Because there was no bar in the hotel, Harvey and Marian fixed a couple of highballs in their room and took them down to the veranda to enjoy the people-watching and the sunset. Then they went inside the hotel to the main dining room to have dinner. Harvey was even glad to see the assistant manager of the hotel, Al Davis, who stopped by their table to welcome him back to the island. He invited Davis to sit down at the table and visit, and Marian seemed irritated as Al offered everyone a cigarette and then lit up a Viceroy. She hated the smoke.

It was after ten when the Stanhopes got back to room 200. It had been a long day for Harvey and he was ready to retire for the night. While Marian was slipping into a flimsy fuschia-colored rayon nightgown with black lace trim (one of Harvey's creations), Harvey was also preparing for bed, walking around the hotel room in his floppy undershorts, knee-length stockings and garters. It was while he was brushing his teeth in the bathroom that he noticed the Viceroy cigarette box in the wastebasket alongside the sink. At that moment, Harvey's love of life was replaced by a gnawing heartache. When he had finished his bedtime preparations and slipped into his pajamas, Harvey came back out of the bathroom and stood in front of the bay window and looked out on to Lake Huron. Sailboats and some small cruisers in the harbor were tossing lazily and pulling at their mooring lines. Off to the right, Harvey could look down the island's main street where lights and shadows were cast from the old-fashioned street lights. He finally turned out the light and slipped into bed where Marian was waiting for him with open arms. She gave him a long goodnight kiss.

"I love you dear," she whispered in his ear. "And I've missed you." you."

"I love you, too, dear," he told her, sadly. "I've missed you these past few days. I'm so glad to be here now."

He rolled over and saw the moonlight through the bay window and thought about the cigarette package in the bathroom. Then he lay still for a long time, clouded in sadness, and listened to the clip-clop of the horses and buggies going by before he finally fell asleep.

CHAPTER 4

Thursday, July 7.

▐t was a long drive across the state of Wisconsin. Harris Butler and his mother-in-law, Hillary Markham, had left Excelsior early this morning and had stopped at Ladysmith for coffee. They would probably get no further than the western edge of Michigan's Upper Peninsula by evening. They would make the day's drive just short of 400 miles and Harris had decided that would be just about enough for Hillary. Actually, the distance would be about all Harris could manage in one day in his blue 1937 Ford two-door sedan. It only had a 60-horsepower engine as opposed to the bigger 85 h.p. deluxe model, but it was more than sufficient for Harris who found he needed a second car in the family when he left the newspaper and started his career as a salesman. Katie wouldn't let him buy a used car. She had told him that if he wasn't going to be a publisher and editor, at least he wouldn't look like he was out of work by driving some old used car. As a result, they had selected the small Ford at Freed Motors in Excelsior and Katie paid for it. A month later, she bought the new Olds for the family car.

When Harris and Hillary stopped for coffee, he also filled the gas tank again at a Standard Oil station. Every Standard station looked the same whether it was located in Excelsior or Rhinelander — a square brick building with a tile roof and a canopy out over part of the drive and the gas pumps. The pumps themselves were tubular and perhaps seven feet tall. The top part was a holding tank made of glass with graduated marks for the gallons of gasoline visible from the outside. When the station attendant filled up the Ford, he simply drained the gas from the glass tank into the car. It took ten gallons and Harris paid the bill — two dollars. As Harris started the engine and pulled away from the station, the attendant was hand-pumping gas back up into the glassed-in area and Harris could see it foaming and churning.

Back on the road, the blue Ford would take them through the same small towns Katie and the kids had passed through just two days ago, Tony, Glen Flora, Catawba, Prentice, out of the rolling Wisconsin farm country and into the wooded lands of Tripoli and Bradley and the lake region of Rhinelander.

"I was through this area last winter on a sales trip," Harris told Hillary as they drove along U.S. Highway Eight. "We'll stop at the Rhinelander Hotel for lunch. There's an excellent dining room there."

"Whatever you say, Harris," Hillary agreed as she watched the passing Wisconsin scenery.

"I'd say another hour and we'll be there," he assured her.

"Don't worry about me. I'm just fine," the older woman said. "I'm enjoying the scenery — and the company."

Harris smiled. They had discussed just about everything since they left home: Ben and Blair, politics, Harris' future, and Katie.

"She's a good person and she loves her children," Harris said of Hillary's daughter.

"I know." Hillary smiled and then a frown crossed her face. "I know she is, but I'm sorry about the troubles you two have had concerning your job."

"She'll get used to it," he replied. "She's just not quite ready to accept the fact that I'm no longer a newspaper editor. Now I'm a salesman," he said emphatically. "And I'm happy."

"Even when Emmett was alive, she didn't want you to leave the newspaper," Hillary said. "She talked to him about it, you know."

"I know," he replied, nodding his head, "but Emmett told me to think it over and if I was really convinced that I should leave the paper, I should go ahead and do it, regardless of what Katie thought." He paused. "But when he died....." His voice trailed off. Then he became afraid that he was bringing up too many memories for Hillary.

"It's all right, Harris," she assured him. "At the moment, I'm much more concerned about Katie." She looked out the side window of the Ford. "I just wish she wouldn't drink so much."

"So do I, Hillary. So do I."

"Can't you do something about it?"

"I wish I could. Every time I talk to her or start to talk to her about it, she gets mad and shuts me up," Harris said, almost in an angry tone. "It really got worse when Emmett died. She took it pretty hard. That was the main reason I stayed on at the paper."

Harris paused, and then spoke hesitatingly. "But she's been brooding about something else. Not all the time, but something has been eating at her. Maybe it was because I wouldn't run for office. Or, maybe, she was sorry she married me."

"Oh, Harris, no. I know that's not true."

There was silence. Harris didn't mention it, but it wasn't only the drinking. Even Kate was unaware that her husband knew about the Frank Jennings affair. Thank God that Hillary didn't know. Harris, himself, would have been devastated if he had known how many more there had been.

Harris began to think about Katie and being with her on Mackinac Island. Perhaps it would be a second honeymoon. He would court her and bring her back to her old self.

Hillary changed the subject and told Harris how much she had been looking forward to the Mackinac trip. Besides the treat of vacationing with her family, Hillary began to speak of the old days when Emmett was alive — and their younger days when Excelsior and Lake Minnetonka were in their glory years as a summer resort. The conversation slowed down. There were long gaps where they didn't speak to each other at all as Harris watched the road. Finally, Hillary nodded off to sleep, dreaming about Emmett and of another time, one to which she was now returning.

It would all come alive to Hillary tomorrow morning at Mackinac Island.

Ben purchased some postcards of the island and sat out on the sunny porch of the Island House to write short messages and address the cards to those back home. He sent some to his friends along West Lake Street and one to Willy Westin for Willy and the rest of The Neighborhood. "You wouldn't believe the beautiful girls here," he wrote to Willy. "Some of them older — college girls." Then he walked down to the post office on the main street next to the theater, bought the one-cent stamps, and mailed off the cards. It was nearly eleven o'clock when he walked back along the main street toward the hotel. It was a glorious, warm, sunny day and Huron Street was already crowded with visitors who had jammed the morning ferryboats to spend the day on the island. As he came to a corner and pressed through the sight-seers at the busy intersection, Ben bumped into a girl in a white waitress uniform. When Ben turned to apologize, he recognized the pretty brunette with the sunburned face.

"I'm sorry I....." The frown turned into a smile as he realized who she was. "You're.....Janet. Janet....."

"Rachel," she broke in. "Janet Rachel. I waited on your family the other night at the Island House."

"I remember," he assured her. "I'm sorry about just now. I guess I wasn't looking where I was going."

"It's okay."

"Where are you going?" he blurted out, treating her as if she were from the old neighborhood back home. Suddenly aware of his familiar manner, he could feel his face get hot and flushed.

Janet just smiled and answered him in a soft and friendly tone. "I just finished working the breakfast shift and came up to see a friend who's working at the Chippewa Hotel. I'm off work now until dinner time and I'm on my way back to my room." She nodded toward the hotel. "I stay at the Mackinac House just a few doors beyond the Island House."

"That's where we're staying. At the Island House."

"I know," she smiled.

"C'mon, I'll walk down there with you." Ben couldn't take his eyes away from the beautiful girl he was walking with and he almost ran into an elderly man whose face and mind were buried in a map of the island. Ben was so engrossed in their conversation, comparing likes and dislikes of movies, music, food, and other things, that he barely managed an "oops" in the way of an apology.

"I don't doubt that you go without lunch if you eat as much as you say you do for breakfast," Ben said in amazement.

"I told you," she smiled, "I'm a country girl and breakfasts were always big at our house. Pancakes, eggs, bacon — the whole bit. And besides, the meals at the hotel come with the job."

"I can't even go a few hours without getting hungry," Ben said. "I'm always fixin' a sandwich or a snack or a bowl of Wheaties at home."

"You sound like my brothers," Janet said. "They're always eating something."

"Yeah, but up here, I can't fix those snacks," Ben told her. "I've spent half my money so far, just buying hot dogs and hamburgers to fill in between meals."

They both laughed as they crossed an intersection. Ben, still talking excitedly, wasn't paying attention to where he was going and slipped on some horse manure and almost fell down. It was embarrassing, but both he and Janet laughed it off.

"Only a city boy would do that," she kidded him.

It was surprising that their conversation covered so much ground in the short two-block walk.

"I came on the island the first week in June, but my roommate from Wisconsin has already gone home," Janet said. "Waitressing is hard work and the hours are long. The pay isn't very good, either, but the tips are getting better now since there are always more tourists in July." She looked around the street with the homes and the picket fences and trees as they walked along. "I love living on the island, but since my roommate left, I haven't had time to make many friends."

Ben told her he had only been on the island for two days and that he would be here with his family for about another week. It was his second year at the Island House, and already his family talked about it as though it were their second home. He suddenly blurted, "I'm thinking about coming back to the island to work next summer after I get out of high school." He seemed a little embarrassed to admit to someone who was about to go to college that he was still in high school. "Will you be coming back next year?" he asked shyly.

Janet smiled. "I don't know, yet."

Of course, he hadn't told his parents about his plan yet. The walk had taken only minutes but to Ben, it seemed as though he had talked to Janet for an hour. She seemed genuinely happy to have someone to talk to.

"I can't believe that you have been on the island for a month and aren't surrounded with all kinds of friends," Ben said.

"You've got to remember that I grew up on a farm and I'm not used to having this many people around," she said with a smile.

"I'm surprised there isn't a long line of guys waiting to ask you for a date."

"I guess I don't make friends quickly," she said. "Even when I was in my 4-H club at home, it took me a long time to get comfortable with everyone else in the club." Then she added, "I do have tomorrow off, though."

Ben was hoping she would not be busy. No. He was praying she would be free tomorrow afternoon. If she would just say she wasn't doing anything after lunch. "What do you do when you get a day off?"

"Well..." she hesitated. "When I've had a little free time, I usually bike around the island."

"How about biking around the island with me tomorrow afternoon?" Ben asked.

Janet was embarrassed. "I really wasn't hinting...."

"Naw..I mean it," Ben assured her. "I was goin' around the island anyway. Honest."

Janet smiled up at him. "Well....if you really want to...."

"Then it's settled."

She thanked him again and closed the iron gate behind her.

"Two o'clock be okay?" Ben asked as she started up the walk to the rooming house.

"Two o'clock will be just fine," she answered. Then she waved and bounded up the steps to the porch and in the front door of the large white house.

Ben turned and started back down Hurton Street and although he felt like jumping up and down and shouting for joy, he kept a look of calmness about him. He was actually going biking with that beautiful girl tomorrow. He had a date — sort of. He just wished Willy was here so he could have someone to tell about it.

Al Davis was so grateful to Billy for filling in the other morning as a dock porter that he offered to buy the young man lunch. He stopped down on the main street and bought some hot dogs and took a few beers from the coolers at the hotel. Then he and Billy went down and sat on Billy's sailboat and ate lunch under sunny skies. The teen-ager wasn't used to drinking anything stronger than Orange Crush or Coca Cola, but he downed a couple of beers and began to feel just a little giddy. The assistant manager had thanked him a number of times over the last couple of days for working the ferryboats on Tuesday. One dock boy had gone home and another had taken a job as a bell hop at another hotel. In the meantime, Al had hired a couple of new dock porters.

They talked about things — the hotel, the guests, and eventually about women. "Billy, my boy, let me tell you that women are fickle creatures," mused Al. "If you're smart, you'll never fall in love. Keep yourself free to play the field."

Al seemed to be sour on all women this afternoon. Usually he was a ladies' man, boasting about the women he'd known, but he hinted to Billy that he wasn't too satisfied with his own social and sex life these days. When they finished their late lunch, Al headed back toward the hotel. Billy had the afternoon off and stayed on the deck of his sailboat. The combination of too many beers and the hot sun prompted Billy to think about girls himself. Maybe he would get a date for tonight, begin playing the field, perhaps bike out around the island and go skinny-dipping in the lake. Hell, he could go for a swim right now. He was already in his swim trunks. He half-dived and half-fell off the boat into the chilly water of the harbor. Swam around the boat a few times and climbed back on to the deck. He needed to take a nap. The sun and the alcohol were too much for him and he went below to the cabin, stripped off his wet suit and fell into the bunk to sleep it off.

Katie had been shopping along Huron Street in the downtown area of Mackinac Island, began to feel tired and stopped at the bar for a drink. In the tavern's cool darkness, she relaxed and, for a while, felt like spending the rest of the afternoon right there. After her second drink, she began to think about herself. Was she getting old? Even worse, was she looking old? "God, I was born in the ninetenth century," she muttered half aloud.

Hearing something, the bartender scurried back from the front window. "Another one, ma'am?" he asked.

"No, thank you," Katie answered quickly. "I've got to get back to the hotel."

She paid the tab and stepped out into the sunshine. She was dressed in a matching beige gabardine shorts and halter top, had on a new pair of huraches and wore some costume jewelry. The woven leather shoes with their sling-back heels squeaked with newness as she walked down the sidewalk. When she passed the Coast Guard Station, the boats in the harbor caught her eye and she decided that now was a good time to take a look at the Herreshoff Ben had been talking about. Among the many sailboats in the harbor this afternoon, she could spot the ensign pulling on its mooring lines. She stood on the dock and looked over the 26-foot sloop. Ben was right. It was exactly the kind of sailboat they had been talking about back home. And it was in excellent shape. Katie wasn't sure but thought it would sleep two — maybe four. Brashly, she decided to take a look inside and see for herself. As she stepped down into the small passageway, it took a few seconds for her eyes to adjust to the darkness in the cabin. Then she saw Billy's sun-tanned nude body sprawled out on one of the two bunks. At that moment, Billy rolled over, opened his eyes in astonishment and grabbed for a blanket to pull over his lap.

"Oh, my God," he half-whispered as he saw Katie standing there.

She smiled, completely at ease. "It's all right. I was just inspecting your boat." She carried on the conversation as though she hadn't even noticed that Billy was nude, and as though she weren't trespassing.

"My son, Ben, was telling me about it and I thought I'd come and see for myself."

Young Billy could still feel the effects of the beers he had drunk, but he was also embarrassed. "I'm sorry, ma'am. I hadn't expected anyone else to come aboard."

"It's all right," she reassured him. "It's really my fault for looking around the boat without asking you first."

He tried to pull the blanket up a little more around his waist. He felt naked. He realized he *was* naked. "I guess you can if you want, Mrs. Butler. Go ahead and look around. There's a small galley back in there and..." He could see she was staring at him and he rattled on about the boat, unconsciously hoping his conversation would distract her.

Katie could smell the beer on his breath and noticed the sun-tanned muscles in his arms and body. She felt young again and decided then and there to seduce him. She asked him about the size of the boat, how long he had owned it, and was it easy to handle? Billy felt heady. He was trying to answer all those questions intelligently, but his mouth and his tongue didn't seem to work just right. And now, it didn't seem to bother him that he was sitting there in the bunk with no clothes on and just part of a blanket pulled over him. He hardly noticed that Katie was sitting next to him on the bunk. She touched his bare arm, then his back. He was feeling light-headed again and didn't seem to mind her hand on his thigh. He couldn't believe what was happening. He knew she was an older woman and yet, he wasn't about to say no.

Katie was in command now and got up and closed the hatch to the deck. When she turned back to face him, she was kicking off her new huraches and untying her halter top. She didn't have to ask anymore questions about the boat. She knew there would be room for two in the bunk.

Harvey and Marian had a late lunch at the Island House this afternoon and Marian had gone back to the room for a lipstick. Her husband waited for her out on the front porch of the hotel, watching visitors go by and passing the time of day with other hotel guests sitting out on the veranda. He hadn't meant to eaves-drop but couldn't help but overhear two college-girl workers as they stood on the front steps of the hotel. He recognized one who worked at the front desk. The other, apparently, was a chambermaid.

"He's been after me for about a week, now, but he always covers himself by pretending he's really not pressing," the chambermaid said.

"So what did you tell him?" the desk clerk asked.

"I keep telling him I'm not interested, but for some reason, he thinks he's attractive to every girl who works here."

Because of his stroke, part of Harvey's face was slightly paralyzed, but he half-smiled. He bet that this same conversation went on every-day someplace on the island. It was ever thus, he thought.

"So far, he hasn't bothered me in the office," the young desk clerk went on. "He keeps telling me that he can help me get ahead, though."

"Well, just be careful," the chambermaid warned. "He seems to think that just because he's the assistant manager, he owns us."

"Listen," the other girl said. "As long as there are some older women around that are his age, and available, he won't cause us any trouble."

"You're probably right," the chambermaid agreed. "Last week alone, we brought his keys back to the front desk from two different rooms."

"I'll bet he was doin' the same thing back in those Detroit hotels before he came here...."

Their voices faded as the girls moved off the steps and down the front walk, talking about what they were going to do the rest of the day. Harvey wasn't smiling anymore. He realized who they were talking about, the guy who had been so thoughtful to him and Marian. At first his heart sank. He knew his own limitations, and he also knew his wife's needs. But Al Davis.....

Then his practical mind began to work. He didn't have to sit idly by. He rationalized that he really couldn't blame her, but he didn't have to sit still for that gigolo bastard. A quiet anger had started to smoulder within Harvey and he knew what he would do now about Al Davis.

"Sorry I took so long." It was Marian. "I couldn't find that damn lipstick I wanted." She took Harvey's arm. "Come on, dear, let's go for that walk now."

Her blonde hair was brushed by the summer breeze off Lake Huron, and Harvey realized how attractive she really was. And he knew that he loved her.

Annabelle and Blair had been feeding popcorn to the pigeons in the park and then walked down along the shoreline to look at the boats and cruisers in the harbor. Out on the dock they stood in awe of a large cruiser which had pulled into port this morning. It was so big that it had a half-dozen deck chairs on the open deck and curtains on the windows in the cabin section. The girls were impressed and moved on to a couple of smaller inboard cruisers. Then they stopped to look at a sleek sailboat with a cabin. Blair wondered how anyone could stand up in a sailboat cabin and she and Annabelle knelt down on the dock, shielded their eyes from the sun and tried to look through the portholes into a darkened cabin.

"I can't see a thing," Annabelle said. "It's too dark in there."

"I know," Blair agreed as she strained to see what the inside of a sailboat cabin was like. Then her eyes adjusted a little to the light and through the glass porthole she could see a flash of silver and something moving. It was somebody's arm. No, it was somebody's legs. No, there were bare bodies in there!

"Annabelle!" she whispered in astonishment. "There's people in there with no clothes on. And I think they're.....doing something they're not supposed to."

"What?" Annabelle gasped excitedly. Annabelle looked again. "Oh, Blair! I think you're right! They're — you know — you know...."

The two girls pressed their faces against the glass, but it was apparently too dark inside for them to distinguish anything except some bare skin.

The boat lurched in the waves and the girls pulled back, looked around and promptly stood up. Then they brushed themselves off and hurried off the dock to the shoreline.

"You gonna tell what we saw?" Annabelle said.

"We're not going to tell anybody anything." Blair wasn't sure just why or why not. Then she added, "We really didn't see anything, did we?"

"I guess not." Annabelle thought for a moment. "But there was something goin' on in there, even if we couldn't see it all."

"Something," Blair repeated. She had an uneasy feeling. "But we don't know for sure just what. And we won't talk about it again."

Then the two twelve-year-olds started back toward the main street. They had never looked back or noticed that the sailboat with the darkened cabin, rolling with the waves in its moorings, had the name *La Tortue Grande*, painted across its stern.

CHAPTER 5

Friday, July 8

There was no greater place for people-watching than the veranda of the Island House. The open porch ran across the front of the main building and then along the north wing, spreading out into a greater area at the very front. Guests could sit in porch chairs and put their feet up on the freshly-painted white railing and watch the matched teams of horses going by, the bicycles, and the foot traffic. The people came in all shapes and sizes, dressed in everything from sportcoats, shirts, ties and skimmers to pedal-pushers and summer frocks. Some would stop to read the menu posted near the street for the Drum and Eagle dining room. Others gawked at the historic hotel. Young college girls in waitress uniforms hurried by on their way to work at other hotels and restaurants in the downtown section of the island. There was a constant parade of bicycles ridden by vacationers of all ages.Once in awhile, a family dog would trail along behind a bike. Yes, there was nothing like an afternoon of people-watching from the veranda of the Island House, and all under sunny skies on this lazy July day.

It had been a long drive from Excelsior to St. Ignace and Harris Butler was perfectly willing just to sit out on the veranda and watch the people go by. He and Hillary had arrived on the island about mid-morning and Katie and the kids had been down at the docks to welcome them when they arrived on the ferryboat. Harris sipped on a cold lemonade, a drink he wished Katie had chosen instead of fixing herself the glass of almost straight gin she was drinking. Katie was genuinely glad to see her husband again and delighted that her mother had braved the trip from Minnesota and come along. Harris was not only thankful finally to reach their destination, he was happy to see Katie and the kids again. He seemed especially pleased to see his son, Ben. Perhaps he was unconsciously thinking about his conversation earlier in the week with Alex Shepherd. For whatever reason, Ben looked particularly good to Harris.

Katie listened to her husband tell of the details of his drive to the island from Minnesota and of the long visit he had with her mother.

"Actually, she seemed to handle the travelling better than I did," he told his wife. "When we finally stopped last night at Escanaba, she was much fresher than I. Of course, I had driven all day and she had taken some long naps. But for her age, she was an exceptionally good traveler."

"We missed you dear," Katie told him, "but Ben did his best to be the 'man' on the trip. I'm just sorry you couldn't have been here earlier or that we couldn't stay longer."

"I'll still have almost a week, Kate," Harris replied. "It'll be time enough."

"You wouldn't have to be in such a hurry to get back to Excelsior if you were still running the newspaper," Katie interjected. "But when you're working for someone else....."

Harris had wanted to tell his wife about the possibility of taking a new job selling to the government and the War Department, but he realized that this was not the time to talk about another change. The fact that he would be making more money wouldn't change anything in Kate's mind, but it was important to Harris. He'd wait to tell her about those plans at another time. There was no use spoiling these first days on the island.

Katie also realized that if they were going to enjoy the next few days together, she'd have to go easy on the subject of Harris being a salesman and not a newspaper publisher. Just the thought of it, however, made her angry. It also eased her conscience about yesterday afternoon's encounter with young Billy on his sailboat.

"You just relax here on the porch this afternoon, dear," she told Harris, "and we'll celebrate your arrival at dinner this evening."

Harris smiled, leaned back in his porch chair and looked out on the busy street in front of the hotel where they was a constant parade of people. All kinds were passing by — some fat, some skinny; laughing youngsters and admiring grandparents; some obviously well-dressed and reasonably well-to-do; others who looked like they were regular customers of Harvey Stanhope's chain of cheap clothing stores. And always, there were young couples, walking hand in hand.

Harris looked beyond the street to the boats docked in the harbor. "I'd like to go down and look at some of those sailboats and cruisers tomorrow," he said.

"I went down to look at them yesterday and there's one in particular that Ben would like to have you see," Katie told him. "I found it very interesting."

It didn't take long for Hillary Markham to get into the flow of activity on Mackinac Island. She had only arrived with Harris this morning and had already fallen in love with the island in the short time it took to walk from the docks to the Island House just a few blocks away. The teams of horses, the wagons, carriages, the crowds and the bustle of activity along the main street of the island had quickly made Hillary feel like twenty again. Memories of her youth and of Excelsior, when it was a summer resort town with hotels and horses and carriages, flooded her mind. She would try to take it all in during the coming week and she had wasted no time. After getting settled in her room at the Island House, she had a light lunch with her daughter and son-in-law, and was off for a tour of the island with her granddaughter and Anna-belle.

Hillary and the girls stopped at a gift shop along the main street where she bought each of the girls an inexpensive gold chain bracelet with little hanging letters spelling out *Mackinac Island*.

"We looked at those yesterday, Grandma, but couldn't decide whether we wanted to spend our money right away or wait to see what else we might find," Blair said.

"Thanks, Mrs. Markham," Annabelle said with a big smile. "These are really swell."

The girls put the bracelets on immediately.

Hillary smiled. "Come on, you two. We've got some sightseeing to do." She rented a carriage and driver and the three set off for some of the points of interest in the upper parts of the island. Their driver and tour guide had taken them up past the Grand Hotel and Fort Mackinac and on to historic sites associated with Indian stories and legends. They had stopped first at Skull Cave which got its name from an incident during the days of the massacre at Fort Michilimackinac on the mainland at what was now Mackinaw City. To save his life, the English trader, Alexander Henry, had been hidden for the night in the cave atop Mackinac Island by his Ojibwa Indian friend, Wawatam. In the morning, Mr. Henry found he had been sleeping on a bed of human bones and skulls. His life had been saved, however, and the haven took the name Skull Cave.

Annabelle, Blair and her grandmother went on to Sugar Loaf, a limestone rock foundation, also said to have once been the wigwam of a great spirit of the Indians. Arch Rock, a natural formation rising nearly 150 feet above Lake Huron, had been actually formed over thousands of years through erosion by wind and water. But the girls liked the Indian legend better. It told of a young Indian maiden who was forbidden to marry a handsome Indian brave, the son of a spirit. Legend had it that her father tied her to the rock high on the bluffs of Mackinac Island and as the beautiful Indian maid wept, her tears flowed down the bluff and washed away the stone, forming Arch Rock. Of course, her lover returned to take her to his home with the spirits. Hillary was impressed with Arch Rock no matter how it came to be.

The carriage driver and guide also took the trio to a look-out point known as Robinson's Folly, high on another bluff overlooking the lake. Then he told his passengers the story of Captain Daniel Robertson, the commander of Fort Mackinac back in 1782, and of a beautiful Indian maiden who had fallen in love with him. Captain Robertson was hurled to his death from the bluff during a struggle with the maiden's jealous Indian suitor. The guide could see that the girls were impressed with the legend and didn't tell them that another story had the English captain plunging from the cliff to his death after having too much to drink.

The carriage was on its way back to the hotel, moving through town at a swifter pace now. Hillary had thoroughly enjoyed her sight-seeing tour with the girls. As the horses clip-clopped past the hotels and the hoards of visitors on the streets and sidewalks, the atmosphere took Hillary back to her younger days when her mother and father and her three brothers would arrive on a Pullman car at Excelsior, direct from St. Louis. Then they would take a taxi, very much like the carriage in which she was now riding, down the crowded main street of Excelsior to the White House Hotel. Those were carefree days for young Hillary — days of riding in monstrous sidewheel and sternwheel excursion boats, of shopping in Excelsior stores and strolling along the shoreline of Lake Minnetonka, arm in arm with Emmett. They were wonderful days of parties and excitement, of quiet times and falling in love.

Riding along Huron Street toward the hotel, Hillary found it difficult to bring herself back to reality — and to Kate and Harris. Yes, her son-in-law was very much like Emmett. He had been influenced by and learned much from her husband. But Katie! My, how women had changed from Hillary's younger days. Somewhere along the line, she had let Katie have too much. She was too demanding, too outspoken, and doing too many things that women just weren't supposed to do. Hillary admitted to herself that Katie was a good mother, and a loving person. But she wished that her daughter and Harris could resolve their differences and get on with their lives. She looked at Blair, sitting across from her in the carriage, and wondered about her grandchildren. They deserved better. Blair still had a lot of growing up to do and needed her father and mother and a home life. Ben would be going off to college in another year and yet he needed a substantial family to come home to. In many ways he was like his father, quiet and passive. Yet Hillary knew that Ben had a mind of his own and that neither Katie nor anyone else could keep him from going his own way, once he had made up his mind. She smiled. Yes, Ben was very much like his grandfather. He would be all right. Then Hillary thought about Katie again, and it pained her. She was worried about her drinking, but she was even more concerned about something else — a rumor about some affairs. She hoped that Harris would never find out. He'd be crushed.

Ben had never thought about a girl as much as he thought of Janet Rachel these past couple of days. He was attracted to her when he first saw her in the Island House dining room on that first night on the island. But since he ran into her near Marquette Park yesterday, he thought about her constantly. An excitement he had never known before had risen within him when Janet agreed to go biking with him this afternoon. The anxiety turned to sweet contentment and satisfaction when the two of them started out around the island on this sunny afternoon. They headed west, out of town, past the Windemere Hotel, beyond the old boardwalk and along the rocky shoreline. The Grand Hotel was barely visible as the West Bluffs began to rise, leaving just enough room for the narrow Lake Shore Road. Off to the west, bikers could see the historic Round Island Lighthouse which guarded the deep channel past Mackinac Island. The marvelous old structure had been a landmark for just about every kind of lake craft from sailboats to ocean-going freighters and mammoth iron ore boats. The cottages on the West Bluffs were out of sight from the roadway, and Ben and Janet pedaled on. They stopped to inspect a large cave eroded out of the rocky walls of the bluffs. It was known as Devil's Kitchen, the scene of many a campfire for college students on cold Mackinac nights. Janet and Ben parked their bikes long enough to inspect the cave and imagine all kinds of events which dated back to pre-historic days. They also drank from the Wishing Spring where legend decreed they could make a wish and in three days it would come true. The wish had to remain secret, however, and the two of them agreed not to reveal their Wishing Spring wish.

They biked on and stopped to rest at the historic site known as the British Landing at the northeast tip of the island. Nearly 125 years ago, the British discovered the site in one of the first battles of the War of 1812. Under the leadership of Captain Charles Roberts, the English had found easy access on the northwest side of the island, secretly landed during the night and moved to high ground overlooking Fort Mackinac. The location was of strategic importance to the British when they had occupied the island back in the 1780's. As a result, Captain Roberts' men hauled a cannon to the high point with its commanding position above Fort Mackinac. The American soldiers occupying the fort were taken by surprise and commanding officer, Lt. Porter Hanks, had no choice but to surrender. Two years later, the American army tried to duplicate the surprise attack at the British Landing, only to be ambushed and forced to retreat to their boats. The high ground which the British had found earlier had been named Fort George by the Englishmen. When the Americans eventually took over the island at the close of the war, they re-named the old Fort on the high ground, Fort Holmes, in honor of Major Andrew Hunter Holmes who led the assault on Fort Mackinac that failed back in 1814.

Ben and Janet sat among the rocks along the shoreline at the British Landing and talked for a while. Mostly they talked about their own homes and families and school, learning and probing into each other's past, as if time were running out on them and they must discover all they could about one another before the day was over. Ben could not believe how beautiful she was. The dark hair, the striking eyebrows, the sun-tanned face. When she smiled at him, he melted away. Her eyes seemed to see right through him. He had never had such warm feelings about anyone before and he wanted it to last as long as possible — all afternoon, forever. He was so taken by her presence at times that he didn't hear everything she was saying to him. But he didn't even care, as long as they were together. They laughed and joked and teased each other and eventually got back on the lake shore path that would take them around the island and back to town. Other bikers passed them heading in the opposite direction and most of them offered a greeting on this beautiful day. The two passed Point aux Pins.

"We're halfway around the island," Janet told Ben. "Just a little more than four miles left to go."

"It's been easy, so far," Ben said. A slight rise in the road brought a new panoramic view. "What's that over there?" he asked as they stopped.

"I think those are the St. Martin Islands," Janet said. She was right. And beyond the islands was the mainland, the northernmost point of Lake Huron.

As they rested, Ben noticed a cluster of flat-topped cumulus clouds on the horizon. "Look how fast those clouds are moving," said Ben pointing to the northwest.

"That's strange, there's hardly a breeze here and look at those clouds there," she said, pointing due north. "They're not moving at all."

Side by side they watched the formations on the northern horizon. Soon the moving clouds reached the stationary column and suddenly, a giant bolt of lightning lit up the leading edge of the moving formation from top to bottom. Ben began saying slowly under his breath, "One-Mississippi, two-Mississippi, three-Mississippi..." to count off the seconds between the lighting and the subsequent thunder clap. By multiplying the seconds by the speed of sound, he could impress Janet by calculating the distance to the storm. But the thunder never came and formations merged completely, producing a magnificent electrical storm, spectacular but soundless.

Ben's hand brushed Janet as he slid fully off his bike to stand closer to her. She took his hand and held it tightly as they watched the progress of the storm.

"It must be awfully far away, too far to hear the thunder," he said. It must be over the northern part of the upper penninsula — maybe even over Whitefish Bay in Lake Superior. Anyway, somebody's getting a lot of rain."

As the storm moved off to the northeast horizon, dropping lower in the sky, the lightning ceased and they became conscious of voices of other cyclists who had stopped to watch the show. Janet let go first and smiled at Ben. They both mounted their bikes and continued the trip around the island.

As they neared the town again, the two bikers passed the foot of Arch Rock and then came on to the flat land at the south of town where a summer retreat for the religious-related organization, Moral Rearmament, was located. Then they found themselves back on the tree-covered Huron Street with homes and small hotels and white picket fences. One island visitor said that residential scene reminded him of his home in far-off Connecticut.

The two of them pulled up in front of the Mackinac House. Janet parked her bike in the front yard and Ben leaned against the gate.

"It's been fun, Ben. In fact, it's the most fun I've had since I arrived on the island," she told him.

"I'm glad," he said. "It's been fun for me, too." He paused. "Can I see you tomorrow?" His voice sounded different. He sounded....older, more sure of himself. He could feel it as he spoke. Janet noticed it, too.

"I'd have been disappointed if you hadn't asked me," she smiled.

"Tomorrow, then."

"Tomorrow, then."

As he rode his bike back to the hotel, Ben realized that it would only be a matter of days before he'd be going home. Time was already running out for him and Janet. It had been this way for so many others on Mackinac Island.

The first church building was not erected on Mackinac until the early 1800's, but there had been missionaries visiting the island ever since those early days of French explorers and Jesuit priests. In 1670, a year before Father Marquette arrived at the Great Lakes, Father Claude Dablon had come to Mackinac to spend the winter. But it was not until two hundred years later that St. Ann's Catholic Church was built. The first Protestant clergyman to preach on the island was the Rev. David Bacon who had represented the Connecticut Missionary Society in 1802. The first Protestant Church was the Presbyterian Mission Church, constructed in 1830. The Union Congregational Church erected the Little Stone Church in 1904.

The first Episcopal clergyman to visit Mackinac Island was the Rt. Rev. Samuel B. McCoskery, Bishop of Michigan, who preached at the Presbyterian mission while on his way to Episcopal churches in Wisconsin in the summer of 1837. The bishop saw little hope for an Episcopal Church on the island, however, as the population dwindled with the breaking up of the American Fur Company and its prosperous business. Yet, Bishop McCoskery continued to pay summer visits to the island from time to time from the 1840's into the 1870's when Trinity Episcopal Church was organized and plans were made to construct a church building. There had been an Episcopal chaplain at the Fort who conducted services back in 1841, but the first rector of the new parish was appointed in 1873. He was the Rev. William G. Stonex, and after nine years of trying to decide where to locate the new church, the building site was selected below the Fort in 1882.

When the parish was organized, Bishop McCoskery had indicated he liked the name, St. Peter's Church. But an army officer living in Buffalo promised $200 toward the building if the parish were called Trinity. History records that the pledge remains unpaid. Another army officer at Fort Mackinac had promised $1,000 toward the new building if it was built below the fort. He, too, had his way, but was transferred before he could pay his pledge. It was not until August of 1907 that the Rt. Rev. Charles D. Williams consecrated the building as Trinity Church. The Rev. Percy Robinson served the parish in the early 1900s and again in the 1920s.

The present rector, the Rev. Phil Porter, had come to Trinity and Mackinac in 1928. The new rector was intelligent, sensitive, loved to read, and had a reputation for his counselling and communicating with people.

Blair Butler and her friend, Annabelle, stood on the wooden steps and looked up at the white steeple that housed the church bell of Trinity. She liked the name of the church. It was the same as her own Episcopal parish back in Excelsior where her brother served as an acolyte and where her mother and father had been married. As they entered the dark shadows of Trinity's vestibule, the girls peered into the main entrance to the church and quietly took a few steps into the rear of the nave of the building. Then they realized that there was an attractive young couple and a half-dozen other people standing near the altar rail talking to a clergyman with a round face and wearing glasses. He was the Rev. Mr. Porter. The group had just finished a rehearsal for a wedding scheduled at Trinity tomorrow afternoon. As the wedding party left, the girls stood near the rear of the church, unnoticed.

The interior was lined with narrow, horizontal lathing. There must have been ten or twelve rows of pews on either side of the center aisle, accompanied with the traditional kneeling benches. At the back of the church near where the girls were standing was a Baptismal font with the inscription, *Presented to Trinity by Children Visiting Mackinac Island in the summer of 1904.* Beautiful leaded windows bore the dedications to past parishioners: *Millie C. Highston, Died Jan. 24, 1873; Robert Van Nuys Becker, Died Oct. 4, 1858; In Memory of Sarah Bailey, Died August 26, 1876.* Blair and Annabelle went on to read the rest of them. Above the altar were the words, *The Lord is in His Holy Temple.* There was also an organ and choir stalls in the chancel, a brass altar railing, and the most beautiful lectern Blair had ever seen— in the shape of a bronze eagle with outspread wings, said to represent St. John and the soaring gospel.

The girls hardly spoke as they stood in awe of the interior of the old church.

"I think it's beautiful," Blair began to whisper.

"So do I," Annabelle agreed, holding her hands up to her mouth.

"I heard them say the wedding was tomorrow afternoon," Blair whispered back.

"Wouldn't it be fun to see it?" Annabelle said excitedly.

"I suppose we could come to it if we wanted to."

"Oh, do you think we could? We haven't been invited."

"Who would ever know if we were invited or not?" Blair asked. "We could get all dressed up. We both brought nice things to wear."

"Yes, but what about your folks?"

"We just won't tell them about it."

"Then we'll do it," Annabelle agreed.

The two girls hurried out of the old church. They would have to work out the details later.

It had been a long day for Billy Lachine who finally finished the afternoon working as a dock porter during the last couple of hours. As usual, Friday was an especially busy day as weekend visitors started arriving at noon and would continue to check into the Island House and other hotels until the last ferryboat of the day had pulled into port and docked for the night. It was probably a good thing for Billy that he had been so busy. His emotions and his thinking seemed to be all mixed up today — actually ever since he sobered up after the episode on his sailboat with Mrs. Butler yesterday afternoon. He could remember what happened but the details were a little murky. It was as though he had fantasized the affair on the boat and the memory was partially lost in swirling clouds that cleared up and then re-appeared. One fact he knew for sure. He had been intimate with a woman old enough to be his mother. Today he had made it a point to avoid Mrs. Butler at all costs. While hauling luggage up from the docks this afternoon, he had spotted her and a man — probably her husband — sitting out on the veranda of the hotel. Billy made a wide sweep to the entrance of the hotel to avoid going directly past that section of the front porch. All day long he had been trying to sort things out: Was he glad that it happened? Was he embarrassed? Was he mad at himself? Was it great — or disappointing?

He was still trying to unravel all those feelings as he left the hotel and started for his own rooming house. For someone who had always thought the best of everyone he knew, he was now having trouble with Mrs. Butler — and himself. Oh, he had been disappointed in people in the past, but the problems were minor. Never, in his wildest dreams, could he have ever imagined that what happened yesterday could possibly have involved him. Then he ran into Al Davis.

"You sick or something?" Al asked him.

"Been feeling a little shaky all day," Billy replied. "I'm on my way home now and think I'll sleep in tonight. It's been a long day."

"You really looked spooked," Al said. "Somebody give you a hard time today?"

The two talked for a few minutes and finally, Billy had to admit to Al that something had happened on the sailboat yesterday with Mrs. Butler.

"You mean you and — Mrs. Butler?" Al smiled.

"Don't talk so loud," Billy cautioned him. "I don't want anyone else to know."

"I'll be goddamned," Al said in amazement. "Congratulations, Billy."

Billy looked embarrassed. "I wish you wouldn't say that," he told Al. "I don't know what to do about it." He thought for a moment. "I don't want anybody to know about it. Honest."

"You don't have to do anything about it. And don't worry, son, I won't tell anyone." Al was smiling. "I'll be damned. Mrs. Butler."

"Please?" Billy pleaded.

"Well, Billy, if you can make time with someone twice your age, you shouldn't have any trouble around here with girls your own age."

"Aw, Al...."

"No, I mean it. Hell, if they're attracted to me, think of what a young buck like you can do," Al bragged. "Take that good-lookin' Helen Gunter who went home last week. She even came to see me in my room."

"You mean Janet's roommate? *That* Helen?" Billy asked. "She came to see you?"

"Well....." Al stammered. "I told her to. But that's the one. A little naive, I'll admit." Al smiled. "And that Janet isn't bad, either."

Billy was getting more uncomfortable. Although Janet Rachel was attractive, they had been nothing more than friends. He liked her — and her roommate. Nobody, including Janet, understood why Helen left the island to go home. Janet thought it was because Helen was homesick. Now Billy wasn't quite sure.

They talked a little while longer about women. "Some of them put up a little bit of a struggle, but you can tell when they really mean it," Al smiled.

Billy tried to change the subject. He didn't like talking with Al about women. Al was more like a father to him. They should be talking about other things — school or the future — stuff like that. Everytime Al talked about women, another little piece of that father image was chipped away. It was upsetting to Billy. Al had been good to him and had given him some responsibility at the hotel. They talked a little while longer and Al promised not to say anything to anyone about Mrs. Butler. Billy said goodnight and left.

Al went on into the hotel and after checking at the front desk, went back to the kitchen to have some supper. It had been another disappointing day for him. Marian Stanhope's husband was here now and when he ran into the couple earlier in the day, she barely acknowledged him. He had also visited with Mrs. Butler, too. He wished he'd known about her earlier. Then to make the day a complete loss, Janet Rachel didn't like some of Al's innuendoes in their conversation in the kitchen and had told him to get lost. She was alone on the island, now, which made her fair game in Al's eyes. Perhaps tomorrow he could arrange for another opportunity for them to meet.

When he finished supper, Al started back to the office behind the front desk. He would be doing the night billing until after midnght and it would give him a chance to juggle the books again. He was running short of money these days.

CHAPTER 6

Saturday, July 9

arris Butler hadn't tasted it in years, but when his son ordered oatmeal, it sounded like a good idea. The Butler family and Annabelle had decided they would breakfast at the Murray Hotel which faced the main street and the main pier, and where visitors were already disembarking for a day on the island. The sky was overcast with a thin layer of clouds which everyone at the Butler table knew would prompt a statement from Harris that "it would all burn off by noon" and they'd have a sunny day on the island. Harris sprinkled the oatmeal with a spoonful of brown sugar and poured thick cream into the bowl. While he enjoyed the early-morning meal with his family, they talked about some of their plans and activities for the day. Hillary told about the tour of the island with the girls yesterday and said she would like to do some shopping this afternoon. Perhaps Katie would go with her.

"I'm looking forward to it," Katie told her mother. "We'll take in the whole main street." She looked at the girls. "You want to come along, too?"

Blair and Annabelle looked at each other, each searching for an excuse not to go shopping. "We've already made plans to go up and look at the Grand Hotel this afternoon," Blair said quickly.

"And you, Ben?" Katie asked.

Ben seemed hesitant to speak. As usual, he felt a little intimidated whenever his mother spoke to him in that tone of voice. He looked at his dad for support and then spoke in his usual quiet tones. The pause in the conversation, however, simply focused more attention on him than was warranted by his mother's question.

"Dad mentioned something about walking up to the horse barns this morning. Neither of us knows much about horses but we thought it would be a chance for us to get away together this morning." He looked to his dad for support.

"That's right, Kate," Harris chimed in. "We talked about it last night."

"Anything else, Ben?" Katie asked.

"Well — as a matter of fact, yes." He smiled innocently. "I've got a date with Janet tonight." He looked around for approval. Harris and Hillary smiled understandingly. The girls grinned with more anticipation. But Katie was not smiling.

"You mean that....that waitress from the hotel?"

"That's right, Mom," Ben agreed. "We biked around the island yesterday and I'm going to see her tonight." Now he smiled triumphantly.

"Well, I think it's fine that you've made friends here and have a date, but I'm not so sure it's such a good idea to be dating the help at the hotel," she said.

"She's a very nice girl, Mom."

"I suppose she is, Ben, but she's undoubtedly older than you. And she's still an employee."

Harris could see that Ben was in a little trouble with his mother and came to his aid.

"I don't think we all have to vote our approval of Ben's date," he said. "I'm sure she's a very nice girl, Ben. And very pretty, too."

Katie was clearly irked but knew she was outnumbered and didn't want to cause a scene. "I just wished you would have said something before, Ben," she added. "Perhaps the hotel doesn't want its employees to socialize with the guests."

"Since when did you ever stand still for conventional rules?" Harris asked with a smile.

"She's waited on me a couple of times at the hotel and I've seen you with her, too," Hillary said to Ben. "And I think she's very attractive. I'd like to meet her personally sometime." She looked at Ben. "I trust your good judgment, dear."

"Thanks, Grandma," Ben smiled. He wanted to say that it wasn't really any big deal. They were just going to go for a walk along the boardwalk and out along the shoreline. But he had to admit to himself that it was a big deal. He hoped this was the end of the conversation because he had already made up his mind. He would see Janet tonight, regardless of whether his mother approved or not.

The breakfast table talk turned to other things and Harris quietly looked across the table at Kate and wondered whether her displeasure with Ben was more the result of her own discomfort. As usual, she looked attractive this morning, but Harris knew she was suffering a terrible hangover from last evening. She had started drinking during the usual late-afternoon get-together on the veranda of the hotel and never really stopped until she fell into bed, drunk and exhausted. It was no second honeymoon for Harris and Katie. In between, she had handled the liquor with her usual aplomb. It was only after the children had gone to bed and she and her husband were left alone on the porch that all of those tell-tale signs of being drunk began to emerge. There really wasn't any arguing between Harris and Katie. The conversation was all hers, and Harris had to admit to himself that she was right. His change of career had taken away some freedom. If he had remained a newspaper publisher, he could have set his own time schedule for coming to Mackinac Island.

Harris watched his wife finish her coffee at the breakfast table and could tell that she was giving it the old college try this morning, and he sympathized.

The Stanhopes had slept late this morning. Harvey was up and dressed before Marian was out of bed. They had decided to skip breakfast and he told her he would meet her down in the hotel dining room for brunch. He had just one business call to make on the public phone down in the lobby and he could put all of his business cares behind him for the next few days. Actually, Harvey went down the stairs, out the front door of the hotel and hurried down the street to the Chippewa Hotel to make his phone call from the lobby there in private. He put the call through the long distance operator to Detroit and a voice at the other end of the line finally answered.

"Police Department, Sergeant Vidas."

"Please connect me with Detective Phil Lafferty," Harvey asked.

"Just a minute. I'll see if he's in," came the answer. There was a pause and the sound of another phone being taken off the hook.

"Lafferty here," crackled the voice on the other end of the line.

"Phil?" Harvey hesitated and then went on. "This is Harvey Stanhope. I'm calling long distance."

"Harvey. How the hell are ya," Lafferty greeted him. "Where ya calling from?"

"I'm up at Mackinac Island, Phil, and I need a favor."

"Anything you want, Harvey. Anything you want, within reason, that is." He laughed.

Harvey knew that Phil Lafferty meant just what he said. Phil had been a street cop back in those tough times when Harvey ran a string of beauty shops and although some of Harvey's operators were doing a little soliciting on the side, he had tried to run a legitimate operation. Lafferty had made some inquiries but never pinched anyone, and ever since then, Harvey had considered him a friend. When Harvey went into the clothing business, Phil Lafferty brought his wife around to Harvey's first store and bought something for her. From that day on, Harvey always figured in a special police discount. Phil, on the other hand, always told his friend, "If you ever need help, you know who to call."

Harvey was calling now. "I want you to check out a name for me, Phil. The guy's name is Alvin Davis. He's an assistant manager of a hotel up here on the island and from his conversations and what I hear from others, he's been kicking around the hotel business in Detroit for some time. Probably in his middle thirties. A handsome bastard. And I'd be interested in knowing if you have anything on him at all." He paused, and added, "It's important, Phil."

"It shouldn't take too long, Harvey, but I can't get to too many records over the weekend," Phil's voice crackled again. "I'll try to do it for you on Monday for sure. How do I reach you?"

"You can't. There's no phone in the room, so I'll call you back Monday afternoon or Tuesday morning. I'm just fishing for some information, Phil. It's just a hunch. But it's important."

Phil Lafferty could catch the sense of urgency in Harvey's voice — even a little desperation. "No trouble at all, Harvey," he assured him. "I'll talk to you on Monday. Give my love to Marian."

"I will, Phil. Thanks."

"And don't step in the horse shit up there."

Harvey laughed and hung up. He turned and hurried out of the lobby of the Chippewa — back up the street to meet Marian for brunch. He felt better already.

Harris Butler had looked forward to spending a little time with his son and he was pleased as they walked through town to Herbert Benjamin's blacksmith shop. They had wanted to see a blacksmith at work while they were on the island and Harris and Ben watched as he finished work on a horse which had not been too cooperative. Some farriers would have used a bellyband placed under the animal to lift two of his feet off the ground to keep him still while new shoes were hammered into place. Such contraptions were never used, however, by the island's most famous blacksmith. It took him only a few minutes to pull the old shoe off the horse with a snippers and then take the old nails out of the hoof. The animal fretted while the blacksmith cleaned out the bottom of the hoof, filed it down and held the horse's front leg between his own legs as he fitted and hammered the new shoe into place. Harris and Ben were both fascinated by it all and they watched a while longer before starting back toward the center of town.

"I hope you aren't worrying about your mother's objections to Janet," Harris said after awhile. "She means well, you know. She's just looking out for her family. Your mother knows you've arrived at an age when things will be changing for you — and for us." They walked along a few more steps and Harris looked out towards Lake Huron. "It's hard for me, too, to see you growing up so quickly."

"I didn't mean to get into an argument this morning, but I can't really see what difference it makes if Janet is working at the Island House or not."

"It doesn't make any difference at all," his dad assured him. "It's the only thing that your mother could think of at the time." He paused. "It's understandable. She wants to delay your leaving the nest."

"Well, gee, I'm not running away or anything."

"I know, son, but she's bound to worry about you."

"Well, how am I going to know what to do?"

"I think your own gut feelings will tell you whether what you're doing is right for you. As far as your mother is concerned, simply be firm in your own convictions, no matter what." Harris smiled. "I know from experience."

"You know," Ben said, "I always thought you were being disloyal to the family by not staying with the newspaper. But your feelings must have told you to change jobs."

"That's right, son. It had nothing to do with loyalty, just peace of mind."

"Well, I would really like to be an editor and publisher," Ben told his father.

"If you want to be a newspaperman, I know it would make your mother — and your grandmother — very happy."

"And you?" Ben asked.

"Certainly, if it's what you really want."

They were down along the main street now and the sidewalks were getting more crowded. Vacation shoppers were in and out of stores, looking for all kinds of mementoes from the island. Visitors were buying cheap Indian head-dresses and tom-toms for their kids, billfolds and purses with *Mackinac Island* stamped on them, and everything else from toys and dolls to bracelets and necklaces and inexpensive rings. Other shoppers were pleased with more expensive clothing items and gifts they had found in the more exclusive shops. Harris and Ben edged their way along the sidewalk.

"Enjoy yourself on your date tonight," Harris advised. "I'm sure she's a nice girl. Just remember you're on vacation and in a very romantic setting. Don't take it all too seriously, Ben."

Half-kidding, Harris added, "And beware of dorms and rooming houses. People can get into a lot of trouble in such circumstances." He smiled and patted his son on the shoulder. "Just remember, girls' rooms can be very tempting. I know from experience."

"Don't worry, Dad," Ben assured him. His dad was smiling, but Ben knew when he was getting sound advice from his father.

They were nearing the Island House now.

"Thanks for this morning, Dad," Ben said. "Thanks for everything." What he didn't tell him was that his feelings about Jan were a lot more serious than his father imagined. But the "circumstance" was too much to hope for.

Blair and Annabelle didn't even know the name of the bridal couple but they were confident they would be able to get into the church for the wedding ceremony this afternoon. Blair had not said anything to her mother about the event, and the girls had made sure that Blair's folks and her grandmother had left the hotel for the downtown area of Mackinac Island before they left their room. They had put on their "dress-up" clothes. Annabelle wore the same white summer dress she had on at dinner their first night on the island. Blair wore her pink frock and even had on silk chiffon hose for this afternoon's occasion. When they were ready to go, they opened their hotel-room door just a crack and peered out into the empty hallway.

"It's all clear," Blair told her friend.

Then they stepped out into the hall, quietly closed the door behind them and instead of coming down the stairs to the lobby, headed for the fire escape stairs at the back of the old building. Once downstairs, they passed the hotel kitchen, cut through the back yard of the Yacht Club next door and eventually emerged on Huron Street, two or three doors down from the Island House. The streets were crowded with Saturday afternoon visitors and the girls went unnoticed in their walk through Marquette Park to Trinity Church.

"We're right on time," Annabelle said, as they approached the church. They had planned to arrive just before two o'clock when the guests would be crowding into the church for the start of the ceremony.

"Let's go in now," said Blair.

The girls hesitated for a moment, then each took a deep breath as they started across the street toward the front steps of the church.

Freshly-painted carriages were parked out in front of the church, waiting to take the bride and groom, the wedding party and guests to the reception following the wedding. The drivers had pulled up their rigs to the curb and were slouched in the front seats, lazily waiting for the wedding service to be over and for the guests to emerge from the old white church. The teams, freshly curried, stood patiently, occasionally shifting their weight on their legs, switching a tail or shivering their coats to chase away a pesky fly. Across the street, a crowd of vacationers and tourists visiting the island for the day had been waiting on the grassy edge of the park for a glimpse of the bride and groom.

Blair and Annabelle approached the church with great authority and stepped in stride behind a couple just starting up the steps. In the vestibule, a young usher in a tuxedo mistook the man and the woman in front of the girls as their parents and escorted the four of them into the church as though they were a family.

"So far, so good," Blair whispered to Annabelle after they had been seated. "Just try to look like you belong here."

Annabelle smiled with confidence and looked around. The church was filling up rapidly, now, and a soloist was singing, accompanied by an elderly lady at the old pump organ. Blair remembered the first time she attended a wedding back home. She was standing in the back of the church in a peach-colored dress and holding a basket of flowers. She was about to walk down the aisle as the flower girl in the wedding of one of her mother's best friends, completely unaware that what anyone was worried about was the strong possibility that Blair would wet her pants. She was only two-and-a-half years old.

Blair's thoughts were interrupted by the sound of bustling noises at the rear of the church. The bride had arrived with her father and the bridesmaids. She looked lovely in her white organza wedding gown. Blair and Annabelle didn't know it, but they were about to witness what was just about the wedding of the year in Michigan. The bride was Sarah Long, daughter of a Michigan state legislator, George S. Long, II. The music began, the bridesmaids and the bride proceeded down the aisle and the clergyman began the service.

"Dearly beloved, we are gathered together here in the sight of God, and in the face of this company, to join together this man and this woman in Holy Matrimony; which is an honorable estate....."

At the end of the service, the newlyweds left the church amid the strains of Purcell's *Trumpet Voluntary*, and handsome young ushers began guiding guests out of the church into the sunlight of a glorious Mackinac Island summer afternoon.

The girls were awestruck by the beauty and solemnity of the service. They were absolutely quiet, but their hearts were pounding, excited by the event and the fear that they might be momentarily exposed as interlopers. As they emerged from the dark confines of the church into the sunlight, Blair and Annabelle found themselves in the middle of an almost carnival-like atmosphere. Crowds lining the sidewalk across the street were waving and shouting and applauding the newly-married couple as they climbed into a carriage. Other carriages pulled up into a line at the curb to take the wedding guests to the reception at the Grand Hotel. The girls had only planned to attend the ceremony, but things seemed to be going so well that their confidence was bolstered even more.

"Whatdaya think?" Blair giggled. "Shall we try for the reception, too?"

"Gee, I don't know," Annabelle answered. "It's been so much fun and no one seems to mind."

"Well, why not?" asked Blair. "We've already seen the wedding. All they can do now is to kick us out."

The girls stepped off the curb in front of the church and climbed into an empty carriage. They were joined by two ladies and the same older couple who had preceeded them into the church. The woman reminded Blair of her grandmother. The driver prompted the handsome team of horses and the carriage lurched as it began its short trip to the Grand Hotel. The adults talked about the wedding as the carriage moved along and the girls sat quietly. At one point, one of the ladies complimented them on how nice they looked and said "wasn't the wedding fun?" The girls agreed. There was more conversation between the adults and in no time at all, the carriage pulled up to the imposing front entrance to the Grand. Doormen in bright red coats assisted each party as the carriages arrived from the church. The girls were the first to step down from the buggy and they moved quickly up the steps toward the immense open porch where the reception was already underway. As the two older ladies were helped from the carriage, one of them spoke to the couple again.

"We've enjoyed chatting with you," she said. "And your grandchildren are so delightful. They were perfect little ladies on the ride up here. You should be proud of them."

The older couple looked at each other in amazement and before they could reply, the ladies were already on their way up the steps. The gentleman spoke to his wife.

"I thought those kids were with them."

Blair and Annabelle were lost in the crowd on the porch of the Grand Hotel. They sipped punch and looked out over the Straits of Mackinac. The view was breathtaking. They would stay awhile longer and then slip out of the hotel grounds and start back towards the center of town.

"It's beautiful up here," Blair said as she looked out over the spacious grounds of the Grand.

Annabelle agreed, but couldn't help but think about Blair's mom. "She'd kill us if she knew we were here," she thought to herself.

Janet Rachel was eighteen years old and was looking forward to her freshman year at college. She had grown up on a Michigan farm and learned to be self-sufficient at a young age. Her mother and father owned three hundred and sixty acres of good farm land and the family lived in a white, two-story farm house with two bedrooms and a bath upstairs and another bedroom, along with a living room, dining room and huge kitchen downstairs. The REA had furnished them with electricity, even in the barns, but her mother still cooked on a kerosene stove. The old house had a dirt floor in the basement and big boulders and rocks for its foundation. Janet had one of the upstairs bedrooms for herself while her two brothers shared the other bedroom. On cold mornings, they would all huddle over the large, square heating register in the floor of the upstairs hall and keep warm as they dressed for school.

She was an exceptionally bright student and earned excellent grades in school. Like most farm kids, she had spent the first eight years of her eduction in a one-room schoolhouse two miles away from the farm. She and her brothers walked the two miles each way everyday and with almost perfect attendance, even in the middle of winter. After a heavy snowstorm, her father would hitch up a team to a sleigh and give them all a ride to school. It was only when her older brother had rheumatic fever one February that any of the Rachel kids missed school. He was out of school until May, but still passed at the end of the year to move up to the next grade.

Janet had been taught by three different teachers over the years in that little old school house where the enrollment at one time was down to eleven students and one year soared to 23. She had been a particularly good English grammar student, but it was when she moved into the high school in town for her freshman year that her love for grammar increased with her first two years of Latin. The school, of course, was much larger — 72 students in all — and Janet was a member of the largest graduating class in the school's history — five boys and nineteen girls. Most of the boys would stay on the farm, but some of the girls planned to go on to school to become nurses or teachers. Janet always thought she would eventually return from college and probably become a housewife and farmer, but she was now having second thoughts. Perhaps she would look to the teaching profession. Her indecision was not unusual for freshman and sophomore students who invariably changed their majors a couple of times during those first two years of college.

Slow to make friends, it took Janet a while to get used to high school where she eventually became a good student and a leader as well. As a young teenager, she had been active in 4-H Club work and along with her two older brothers, had learned to do just about everything necessary to run a farm — from the twice-a-day milking chores to hitching up a team to picking up corn cobs to feed the pigs and to burn in the cookstove. Her mother, Alice Rachel, was a typical farm woman, wife and mother: she was content to raise her children, help her husband, and listen to the radio in the evenings. She was a marvelous cook and had the advantage of an abundance of cream and butter and eggs for all those home recipes.

Janet's father, James Daniel Rachel, was an extraordinary man, an excellent father, and a very successful farmer. His accomplishments were especially impressive considering the fact that he had lost most of his left arm in a combine accident ten years ago. He had used a stick to grease the belt on the combine and his glove got caught and pulled his arm into the machinery. It took his hand off and mangled his arm to the elbow. He had walked a half-mile across a field to a neighbor's farmhouse where the housewife helped make a tourniquet and had her sons take him to the doctor's office in town, and then on to the hospital. Her father, and the rest of the family, survived the accident as well as the depression years, and Janet had earned enough money working in town so that she could become the first in the family to go on to college. Janet was determined to be independent.

The urge to stand on her own two feet and be free of depending on her family was somewhat caused by her father, a strong disciplinarian. Janet knew it had been easier for her as a daughter than for her brothers, but they had all felt the stern measures and the iron will of their father. Janet found that when she really needed the help and advice of her father, she was afraid to go to him. Instead, she used to seek out her old brother, John, for help.

She had come to Mackinac Island this year to earn her own money to help finance her first year at Michigan State. But she had found out during her first four weeks on the island that she wasn't going to make as much money as she had hoped. When her roommate suddenly left for home, Janet found herself alone on the island and not doing well financially. She was tempted to call it quits, too, and to go home, but there was something in her make-up that would not let her admit defeat and she decided she would stick it out for the entire summer. Besides, there was no opportunity for her to earn money at home.

Meeting Ben was the best thing that had happened to her since she started working at the Island House. It didn't make any difference that he was still in high school or younger than she. Janet was used to having friends and working with others of all ages, something she had learned while active in 4-H activities. Ben looked older, too. He was tall and.....sturdy. He surely wasn't skinny. She smiled as she looked in the dresser mirror of her small room, brushing her hair and putting on just a hint of lipstick before seeing Ben tonight. Strangely enough, those old suspicions about boys seemed to have faded now that she had met Ben. Things were different. Almost the way she had dreamed about them being for such a long time. Since she came to the island, she had found a new excitement in reading about love and romance in the movie magazines that she and other girls had bought at the drug store. The magazines were a luxury Janet had never enjoyed back on the farm. She read about movies she never saw — from Jeanette Mac-Donald and Nelson Eddy in *Sweethearts* to Mary Carlisle in *Touchdown Army*. She fantasized about wearing the latest fashions modeled in *Silver Screen* and *Photoplay* by glamorous stars: Loretta Young in a black woolen dress with a pencil-slim skirt and silver fox trim and wearing a felt hat; or Joan Bennett showing a tweed suit and a cashmere sweater, with suede accessories. There were the romances and rumors — Tyrone Power and Norma Shearer, Joan Crawford and Franchot Tone, and stories about Mickey Rooney whose mother said he would not get married until he was 25 years old. There were also cover photos and feature stories about her favorite — Deanna Durbin. In a recent issue of *Photoplay*, there was a photo of Deanna and Jackie Cooper and an article about Deanna starring in a new motion picture, *That Certain Age*. In an interview, the young movie star told teenagers everywhere to "be your age." "If you look too young," she was quoted, "you'll feel foolish, and if you look too old, you'll look silly."

But now Janet had the beginnings of her own romance and she was acting her age. Yes, things were different now. She didn't have to dream about Deanna. Ben was real, right here on the island, and he would be along any minute to meet her on the front steps. She had a feeling that Mackinac Island would be a lot more enjoyable than she thought it would be just a few days ago.

Ben wasn't sure just what to wear for his date with Janet but his upbringing had prompted him to put on a sport jacket and wear a shirt and tie for the occasion. He, too, smiled in the mirror of the hotel room as he tied his necktie and slid the knot up in between the collar points. He was smiling, not only because of his date with Janet, but because he was thinking of what had happened late this afternoon. He had run into his kid sister and Annabelle in the hallway as they were sneaking back to their room following the wedding reception. Blair, in her excitement, confessed to her older brother what they had done and then, realizing what she had said, pleaded not to give them away. Ben, always so proper, suprisingly thought the entire incident was absolutely great and told his sister not to worry. If they hadn't been detected through the entire afternoon, no one would possibly discover them now.

The girls that Ben and Willy dated back home from time to time were surely attractive enough and fun to be with, but they had not dominated his heart and mind the way Janet had these past few days. He had often asked Sandy Reimer to the Lake Theater on Excelsior's main street on a Sunday night. Usually, the movie date called for a stop at Wehnes' Drug Store for a Coke or Pepsi, and a walk home again to Sandy's house. It was then that Ben felt the most awkward. He wasn't sure that holding hands on the way home in the dark was a sign to him anyway, that it would be all right to kiss Sandy goodnight. But usually, he was afraid to try for fear of being turned down. He had felt a little like Andy Hardy — but not quite so lucky. It seemed that back home, the girls only took on an importance for boys like Ben and Willy when a homecoming dance or a prom date was imminent — or maybe a movie or a night at the Excelsior Amusement Park and Ballroom once in a while. But now, he had an honest-to-god date with Janet and Ben realized that his interests had taken a decided turn from Scouting to girls.

As he left the hotel, Ben could feel the excitement and the anticipation of the evening. He'd had those feelings before — like just before the start of a football or basketball game. But it was different. Before a ball game, he didn't know who was going to win. Now, as he headed for the Mackinac House, he felt euphoric. Unlike the feelings just before a game, this time he already knew he was a winner — just having a date with Janet.

When he arrived at the iron gate in front of the Mackinac House he found Janet waiting for him. She was dressed in a blouse and light sweater, a summer skirt, and the same kind of huraches his mother had been wearing on the island. They stopped in the downtown section for a Coke and then went on to the boardwalk and down along the shoreline, among the trees and grass and rocks. In the distance, they could see the blinking lights of St. Ignace across the straits. They talked about themselves for a long time, learning about each other, searching out things they had in common, and finding new feelings of excitement with their new relationship.

"I never knew anyone who had been in a 4-H club before," Ben laughed. "Did you raise one of those great big pigs, or anything?"

"A great big pig is a hog, city fellow," Janet kidded him. "No I didn't, but my brothers did. My whole family was in 4-H. Most of my projects had to do with sewing and home beautification — flower arrangements, the yard, gardening, things like that. Then most of us girls would exhibit sewing projects, and model dresses we'd made at the county fair. I never got to the state fair but my brother, John, did, and then he once showed livestock at a meeting in Chicago." Janet enjoyed remembering those 4-H days. She had been president and treasurer of her own local club. "Then we'd have field days and play softball and run races," she went on, "and sometimes we would go around to each farm to see the special projects and have a potluck supper."

"I don't think I've ever been on a farm," Ben had to admit. "I mean, did you have any horses and cows and all that?"

"Oh, sure," Janet replied. "Lots of milk cows and beef cattle, too. My father had a few Herefords — your know, the red ones with the white faces, and some Angus; they're black." She became more excited about it as she talked. "Once he bought some cattle from Colorado and he had to ask the local riding club to help him drive the twenty head from town out to the farm when the train came in."

"You ever think about marrying a farmer?" Ben asked quietly.

She thought for a moment and then became more quiet and serious. "Yes, but I guess, now, I don't want to rely on anyone else in my life. Even though my father has done fairly well as a farmer with a handicap, he still depends on others. I don't want that to happen to me. We always had enough to eat — good things, too. But we never had any money, either. Well, not much, anyway. And we never could go anywhere as a family for more than a few hours. Somebody had to stay behind to milk the cows and do the other chores."

"I admire you for what you've been through — and I admire your father even more. I'm not sure I could handle that," Ben told her. They stopped under a tree and Ben picked at the bark in the growing dusk.

"I know it's not right, but I have trouble with people who are not...."
He groped for the word. "....not.....whole. I don't mean that quite the
way it sounds. But I feel uncomfortable around people like that. I know
it's my fault, not theirs."

Janet smiled. "You're not alone, Ben. That's the way most people
feel. The only difference is that they're afraid to admit it — to others or
to themselves." They found a grassy area by the shoreline and Janet
spread out a blanket she had brought along. "I probably felt the same
way about my father when the accident first happened. Then I found
that he wasn't really any different; the same father, the same husband
and the same farmer — but without his left arm." There was a quiet
time and then Janet spoke again. "The only difference was.....he was
somewhat dependent on the rest of us after that. That's when I vowed I
would never have to depend on anyone else in my lifetime. I would
never want to be a burden to anyone."

"My life has sure been different from yours," Ben told her as he
smiled and shook his head. "I can't imagine what it must have been
like to go to a one-room school where everyone had the same teacher.
And an outdoor biffy?" They both laughed. "Even in high school — no
band and only a nine-man football team?" Ben asked.

He was amazed to find out she had never seen a big-time dance band
or a college football game or eaten a White Castle hamburger. He told
Janet how he and Willy had ushered at Memorial Stadium on the University of Minnesota campus for the last three fall seasons and watched
coach Bernie Bierman's Golden Gophers win two National Champion-
ships. They had seen great players — Bud Wilkinson, Ed Widseth,
Sheldon Beise and Andy Uram — play for the Gophers. "Usually, we
ended up ushering in the bowl end of the stadium, but once we were
assigned to the governor's box and another time we ushered in the
press box and we met Ted Husing, the famous sportscaster." Janet
didn't know much about sports, but when Ben told her how he and
Willy had been to the Orpheum Theater in downtown Minneapolis to
see Tommy Dorsey on stage, Janet sighed and said, "Dreamy!" They
had seen the first Saturday stage performance, sat through the movie,
and seen the Dorsey orchestra a second time, playing such favorites as
Marie and TD's theme song, *I'm Getting Sentimental Over You.*"

"You're the luckiest boy I ever knew!" Janet's eyes were shining.

There were so many things to tell her: about hockey games at the

Minneapolis Arena; or going to town to Dayton's Department Store on Saturdays and listening to phonograph records in their music department's sound-proof booths; or going to the University Field House to see Big Ten Basketball. That might have been Ben's favorite sport of all. He had played football as a junior at Excelsior High School, but basketball was his favorite, and he looked forward to the coming year. There would be a new coach at Excelsior. His name was Giffy O'Dell, a young coach with a winning record, and Ben was eager to play for him. Besides, most of Ben's teammates from this past year were coming back and the basketball team would be loaded with talent — Rog Hennessy, Dick Dyer, Bob Smith, Arno Windsor and John Seamans.

Ben told Janet about his best friend, Willy, and of all the kids in The Neighborhood, and about Excelsior and the Amusement Park and the lake and the swimming and the sailing and about the Butler home and how he fished out on the dock in front of his house. Janet was fascinated by it all and she could see Ben loosen up and become more natural as he talked about home and school and his friends.

"You mean you play in a drum and bugle corps?" Janet asked as he went on about the things he did back home. "In a Boy Scout drum and bugle corps?" She smiled. He hadn't meant to tell her about his Boy Scout experiences. They were important to him, but he was afraid they would sound childish to her. When they got to talking about their home towns and what they did there, however, it just seemed natural to tell her about his Scouting. "You mean you wear those shorts and handkerchiefs?" she asked.

"Yeah, we do," he defended himself with a smile, "and they're not handkerchiefs. They're neckerchiefs." He had to explain to her that at his age, he wasn't just a little Boy Scout. He was a Senior Scout now, an Explorer Scout, and there were lots of guys his age who were still active in scouting back home. "We still do a lot of camping and things like that," he told her, "and our drum corps is just about the best junior corps in the whole state. We're going to enter the state Legion competition next year," he told her enthusiastically.

Then he laughed a little. "I know I'm growing out of all that, Jan, but it's been a lot of fun — and I'll not forget those scouting days." His voice was wistful.

Janet knew better than to kid him anymore about it.

Then there was more quiet time. Only the sound of waves lapping at the rocky shore and leaves rustling in the wind off the lake. The dusk was melting into darkness of the evening.

Ben looked up at the sky. "You can see the stars now." They both stared skyward. "You know, that's something I've never told anyone — except Willy."

"What's that?" Janet asked.

"That someday I'd like to fly. Right now, I love to sail. Probably always will. But flying...." His voice trailed off.

"If you want to, you'll do it," she told him.

"I don't know....but I'd sure like to try," he said. "I never knew anybody who actually flew. My father once told me that he knew a man who actually bought an airline and went into the business with a Ford tri-motor plane and all. He failed and lost everything. But that was back in the late twenties, and now they've got DC-3's that can go 170 miles an hour and carry twenty-one passengers. Boy, I'd really like to fly one of those." Ben shook his head. "Maybe someday....."

Janet shivered in the cool of the evening and moved closer to the warmth of Ben. He could feel her body shudder again and was quick to offer his coat. "Here, let me put this around you."

For a teenager who had only dated a few times in high school — the homecoming dance and a few movies — Ben, surprisingly, felt comfortable around her and found a nice feeling in putting his coat over her shoulders. Janet moved closer and the two of them sat quietly along the shore for a long time with his arm around her. They finally agreed that perhaps it was getting late and it was time to get back to town.

"I hate to have this night end," she told him. "This is the happiest I've been since I came to Mackinac." She could see Ben's face in the moonlight. He smiled shyly, and she knew he would do nothing more than put his arm around her this night. When they stood and Ben gathered up the blanket, Janet simply put her arms around him and kissed him ever so gently on the mouth. Ben's heart was pounding, and he didn't quite know what to say, so he just held her close.

They started back along the boardwalk. It had been a marvelous evening for Janet and it left her feeling she had known Ben forever. She squeezed his hand and smiled. "I never thought I'd be dating an Eagle Scout," she kidded him. It didn't embarrass him. He simply held her hand as they walked along the silent main street of the island.

The dark quietness reminded Ben of so many western movies he had seen where the small main street was always so calm and deserted just before the big gun fight between the good guys and the bad guys. And always on Mackinac, there was the faint hint of horse manure, even when the streets were clean and the horses had been in the stables for hours. The couple walked past the park and back to Janet's place where they would make more plans to see each other tomorrow. Then they said goodnight.

CHAPTER 7

Sunday, July 10

Love divine, all loves excelling,
Joy of heaven, to earth come down!
Fix in us Thy humble dwelling.
All Thy faithful mercies crown.
Jesus, Thou art all compassion,
Pure, unbounded love Thou art;
Visit us with Thy salvation,
Enter every trembling heart.

Trinity, half-full for this morning's Communion service, was quite different from yesterday's wedding where Blair and Annabelle were among a crowded full house. Ben was almost relieved when his father told him this morning that Katie wasn't feeling well and that the rest of the family would go to church without her. The girls expressed concern but Ben had seen his father go through this time and time again, covering for Katie who usually had too much to drink the night before and wasn't up to an appearance the next morning. Ben had breakfasted with his father, his grandmother and the girls at the Island House and then took a leisurely walk to church for the mid-morning service. He was thankful that his mother was not with them. She was already upset with him over seeing Janet. It was one of the very few times Ben had displeased her — and she didn't like it. Ben was uncomfortable. He had always done what his mother had asked or suggested. But his heart told him he had no choice but to go against her wishes. Regardless of the consequences, seeing Janet again had made it all worthwhile.

The communion service was identical to the service at Trinity back home and Ben found a certain comfort in the familiar liturgy without realizing it. His mind wandered back to his days as an acolyte and as a member of the parish choir with Willy. In his younger days, he had been a serving boy at countless early morning communions, many of which were attended by only a handful of communicants. The services had forged a common bond between Ben and the parish priest however, a feeling that only Ben and Willy and other boys who served, could experience. Girls were not allowed to be acolytes. Ben wondered if Willy was singing in the choir back home this morning. It was a good parish choir, a mixture of high schoolers and middle-aged adults, vested in the traditional Anglican vestments, the black cassocks and white surplices. Willy would not believe what had happened to him these past few days, meeting Janet and all. The thoughts of Janet prompted Ben to look forward to the rest of the day and seeing her again. But it also caused some concern about his mother. His dad seemed to be understanding, and he knew he had the support of his grandmother. But his mom....

At the altar rail, Ben heard more familiar words of the liturgy.

The Blood of our Lord Jesus Christ, which was shed for thee, preserve thy body and soul into everlasting life. Drink this in remembrance that Christ's Blood was shed for thee, and be thankful.

Harris Butler was a family man and he was disappointed that Katie could not or would not make it to breakfast and church this morning.

She seemed to be all right and in a lot better shape than so many previous mornings when she could not function after one of her all-night drinking bouts. She had told Harris she just wasn't up to it this morning.

"You go on ahead, dear," she had said. "By the time you're back from church, I'll be ready for the rest of the day's activities."

"You're sure?" he had questioned.

"You go on. Just give me a little time this morning and I'll be okay," she assured him.

Harris thought about his wife as he knelt on a hard kneeling bench towards the end of the service. He had to admit to himself that for the most part, he had sat passively by and let Katie intimidate young Ben these past few years. She was over-reacting about a matter that was not that serious. Perhaps there would be a time today when the two of them could talk and maybe, just maybe, he could soften her feelings about her son and his new friend. Harris knew in his heart what part of the problem had been all along. He knew Kate was over-aggressive and that he, himself, was far too timid. When he was on the road, selling, he had great confidence in himself and had no trouble at all associating with his customers. But there was something about Kate that held him back. Without realizing it, he had always sat back and let her run things — the house, the family, the business, and even their sex life. It wasn't that Harris didn't love her and hadn't longed for her when they lay side by side in bed. But there was something about her, so dominating, that he instinctively waited for some sign from her that it was all right to make love. When he thought about it, the embarrassment tugged at his pride and he would get angry with himself. After all, he was a healthy husband with all of the natural inclinations. He guessed that in Kate's eyes, he looked like a wimp. But he really wasn't, he kept telling himself. Perhaps he had become too comfortable with the way things were.

Harris smiled as his thoughts turned to his son kneeling next to him. He had a special admiration for him right at this moment. The boy had stood up to Katie, which was more than he could say about himself. Maybe he could learn something from Ben. My God, if a sixteen-year-old could tell what was right for him, surely he could do as much for himself. And why was he so worried? He'd changed jobs once before.

One thing for sure, Harris thought. He didn't have to worry about the girls on this trip. They couldn't possibly get themselves into any trouble.

The Peace of God, which passeth all understanding, keep your hearts and minds in the knowledge and love of God, and of his Son Jesus Christ our Lord: And the Blessing of God Almighty, the Father, the Son, and the Holy Ghost, be amongst you, and remain with you always. Amen.

As the service drew to a close, Hillary looked at her grandson who was kneeling next to his father. She didn't have to follow the service in the prayer book. She knew it all by heart. This version of The Book of Common Prayer was only ten years old, adopted by the General Convention of the Episcopal Church in 1928. It had caused a furor among churchmen who were used to the prayer book of the past — one that had been ratified in 1789. Hillary had grown up with that Book of Common Prayer and the liturgy of the church had meant a great deal to her through the years. She had been disappointed this morning. She would have enjoyed attending the service with her daughter. Harris wasn't the only one who knew why Katie was not here, she thought. And Ben, dear Ben, must know about his mother's drinking. Katie could have at least made a try at coming along, Hillary felt. After all, she hadn't felt too good herself lately and a little blurred vision once in awhile was bothering her. Yet, here she was with the family. Hillary decided she had kept out of the Butler family affairs long enough. She would have to find a time now to talk with Kate about Ben. His mother might have his life planned out for him, but she couldn't live it for him.

The organ began to play the recessional hymn and the congregation stood to sing.

Lead us, O Father, in the paths of truth;
Unhelped by Thee, in error's maze we grope,
While passion stains, and folly dims our youth,
And age comes on, uncheered by faith and hope.

The congregation knelt while the acolyte snuffed out the altar candles. Then the people moved toward the entrance at the rear of the church where the Rev. Mr. Porter was standing in the vestibule, shaking hands and visiting with those leaving the church.

"Good morning, sir," the clergyman greeted Harris Butler.

"Good morning," Harris replied. "I enjoyed the service — and your sermon this morning."

"Oh, thank you." The priest smiled and looked at the girls and Ben. "Nice family."

Harris thanked him and told him they were all visiting the island from Minnesota and that their own parish back in Excelsior was another Trinity Church.

"That's interesting," the Rev. Mr. Porter replied. "I didn't know that the Long's had friends who had come that far for the wedding yesterday. Sorry I missed you in the crowd," he told Harris. "But I did see your two daughters."

Harris had no idea what the priest was talking about, but before he could answer or inqure further, others in the congregation were emerging from the church into the small entryway and Harris found himself and his young clan being edged down the steps and on to the front sidewalk. What family? Who were the Longs? And what in hell were those girls doing at a wedding yesterday afternoon? The kids had gone on ahead, but he would catch up with them and Blair would have some explaining to do to her father. Then he smiled and began to laugh out loud. He would keep it to himself. He smiled again. If Kate knew what those girls had done, she'd have a fit. Or maybe she'd think it was as funny as Harris did.

Alvin Davis had been a drifter all his life. He had made a lot of enemies wherever he'd been, but he had a likeable quality about him that also won him many friends. He'd grown up in Cedar Rapids, Iowa, where he had been an outstanding high school athlete, playing on a basketball team that went to the Iowa state tournament back in 1916.

His father had left home when he was just a youngster and he was raised by his mother. He was an only child and the pride of not only his mother but the whole neighborhood where the Davises lived. He was handsome and liked by the girls, and very good at sports, which made him popular with the boys in high school. He was also a bright student and was admired by most of his teachers. It was only after he had been in service at the end of the World War that he began to lose some of those All-American qualities. He had served as a company clerk in New Jersey while in the army and never got overseas, but he was exposed to all of the easy ways to get by in this life and he didn't stay in Cedar Rapids very long when he came out of service in 1918. He went down to St. Louis and worked as a bookkeeper in a lumber yard for a while and then drifted across Illinois, working in Belleville and Centralia, eventually ending up in Chicago. Then came the stock market crash of 1929 and Al found himself like millions of others in the big cities — standing in unemployment lines and waiting to be fed in temporary soup kitchens set up on the streets of Chicago.

Like so many others of that era, Al did almost anything in order to make a living. Once he managed a crew of young magazine salesmen who criss-crossed the state of Iowa. For a while, he taught ballroom dancing in Chicago, and then he had a sales route of Chicago bars where he sold punchboards and gambling games. For someone who was interested in sports, Al was in the right town. Even when he didn't have much money, he found some way to get free tickets to the Chicago Bears' games at Soldier Field.

It was also in Chicago where he found he had the knack to sweet-talk women into almost anything — sex, money, or a place to live. One of his many jobs took him to Minsky's burlesque theater on State Street where he made a few bucks, stole a few dollars more, and moved into the circle of burlesque performers and second-rate strippers who did the warm-ups for such stars as Margie Hart, Gypsy Rose Lee and Sally Rand. Then he moved into the hotel business and eventually went on to Detroit.

The summer of 1938 had been a successful one for Al Davis — up until now. He had not only drawn a reasonably good salary for these times as the assistant manager of the hotel, but he had bilked the unsuspecting firm for at least another thousand dollars. Besides, he had a couple of attractive bed partners, including Marian Stanhope. Now he added another prospect to his list of such candidates. This time it was that Mrs. Butler who had stopped him on the front porch of the hotel earlier this morning and asked to speak with him privately as soon as possible. He figured if Billy could win her over, it would be a snap for an experienced man like himself. He had ushered her to his back office and offered her a chair, beaming in anticipation — another conquest.

"What can I do for you, Mrs. Butler?" he asked.

"As I told you this morning, I tried to see you yesterday but you weren't available," she told him. Her voice was urgent. She had made up her mind before she left the breakfast table yesterday that she would talk to someone at the hotel and try to head off this business between Ben and the waitress. It made no difference to her whether the girl was a hayseed or a tart, she didn't want Ben to get into any girl trouble.

"Well, I hope everything's all right and that you're enjoying your stay here."

"Oh yes, yes we are," Katie smiled. "But I wanted to ask you whether the hotel has any kind of policy concerning the hired help socializing with the guests."

"Wow, this is some lady!" he thought. "Well, I don't think we have any formal policy. We....ah....of course want to accomodate our guests and wouldn't want to do anything to offend them," he said aloud.

"Well, there's something I think you ought to look into," Katie told him.

Al's charming personality quickly turned defensive. Why was she asking about hotel employees and guests? Maybe she was having second thoughts about young Billy and was about to blow the whistle on him. He tried to hold on to a friendly tone of voice while he sorted it all out. "Well....I....ah....Mrs. Butler, if one of our employees has been bothering you....."

"Oh, no, it's not that," Katie smiled. "My sixteen-year-old son has been seeing one of your waitresses — a Janet Rachel — and I wasn't sure whether he might be getting her into trouble with the management." Katie paused. "After all, he's a guest in the hotel and she's a little older and an....an...."

"Employee. Yes, Mrs. Butler." Al could see the handwriting on the wall and was relieved to know she wasn't talking about Billy or himself.

"I understand, Mrs. Butler," he assured her. "I think I can clear this whole thing up with a word or two to the Rachel girl."

Katie smiled in relief and stood up to leave. "I would appreciate that very much Mister....."

"Davis. Al Davis." He smiled back at her. "I'll speak to her today." He thought about his conversation with Billy the other day and although he didn't know all of the details, he knew enough to pursue the incident for his own interests. After all, Mrs. Butler did have nice legs. "I'm glad that's all this has amounted to," he told her. "It's reasonably easy for me to handle such problems with these college-age employees — waitresses, chambermaids, dock porters...."

Just the mention of the words, dock porters, was enough to alert Katie. Did Mr. Davis somehow know something about her little affair on the sailboat the other day? Had she picked the wrong man to talk to?

"....but I'm sure I can clear this all up," he went on. Al was back to his normal, charming self again. Even Katie was aware of his good looks. "Perhaps we can visit again about this, Mrs. Butler, and I can let you know that everything is all right."

Katie felt she had no choice. "I'd appreciate that."

"Perhaps sometime tomorrow....maybe sometime in the evening?" he asked.

"I believe we have plans to see a movie tomorrow night," she begged off.

"Possibly in the afternoon, then."

Katie felt trapped. She had the feeling he wanted to discuss something other than Janet Rachel at their next meeting. Actually, she thought, he isn't bad looking. It might even be worth another trip to the office here, just to flirt a little. But he was too old. He didn't have that youthful quality she was attracted to. Besides, he was trash. And he was waiting for her answer.

"I'm not just sure about tomorrow during the day...."

"Well, it's okay, Mrs. Butler. I'll be here during the afternoon and you're more than welcome to stop in and....talk."

"Yes, well, thank you, Mr. Davis," she replied hesitantly.

She left the back office and started down a narrow hall toward the lobby. He was tempting, but there was something wrong. Katie always liked to think she was in control of things and right now, she didn't have that feeling.

Al thought about his conversation with Mrs. Butler while he waited for Janet to finish her luncheon shift. Yes, that Mrs. Butler was surely a new prospect for him, and she had money, too. Besides, she had given him an opportunity to ask Janet to report to his office when she was through work. She had been one of those girls who had avoided him so far this summer. It was almost as though there was a conspiracy against him, and he had to admit to himself that he wasn't doing too well with the younger girls. They had successfully avoided him after hours. But things would be different now, he thought. At least with Janet Rachel.

Hillary didn't say anything to the rest of the family but she had felt just a little dizziness as she held on to Harris' arm on the way back from the service. She decided that she had simply been overdoing it lately and said she was going to her room to rest for awhile. Ben was off to change clothes and get out of the shirt, tie and sportcoat. Katie, waiting for the family, watched from the veranda as Harris and the girls stood out on the front sidewalk near the street, just far enough away so that Katie couldn't hear the conversation.

"So you decided you would what?" Harris asked incredulously.

"We just thought that the church looked so pretty and that it would be fun to see a wedding there, so we got dressed up in these and went," Blair explained as she pointed to their party dresses they had worn to church this morning.

"But you weren't invited," her father reminded her.

"We didn't think they'd mind just two more people," Annabelle chimed in.

"That's not the point," Harris said to the girls.

"We didn't think anybody would mind," Blair said. "Everybody was very nice to us — especially on the ride up to the Grand and at the reception there."

"You went to the Grand Hotel for the reception, too?"

"The carriages were right there, waiting for us when we came out of the church," Blair said.

"And they helped us get in one — so we did," Annabelle added.

Harris stood up with his hands on his waist. "I suppose you neglected to tell your mother about this, as well as me."

"We didn't tell *her*, but we did tell Ben," Blair said as she smiled at her dad.

"Oh, well, that's all right then," he replied sarcastically. "But I will make a deal with you," he added. "You be on your best behavior from now until the time we leave the island, and I won't tell your mother. She'd have a fit."

The girls smiled back. "We promise," they both agreed. Then Blair reached up and kissed her dad on the cheek. "Thanks, Dad," she said. The girls skipped off toward the entrance to the hotel, leaving Harris standing there. His face was stern, but inwardly, he was smiling. He really felt good about his kids. Then he looked up at the veranda and saw Katie waving at him. She looked great, sitting up there, and he decided that he would tell her about his proposed change in jobs. After all, he was already a salesman and a change of product shouldn't mean anything to Kate. As he started up the walk to the hotel and the front porch, he also decided he had better tell Katie about her mother. Hillary had complained of not feeling good a couple of times during the past few days and Harris had felt how tightly she held on to him this morning on their way back from church.

Katie had pulled off another miracle. She felt like hell, but she looked like a million dollars. Dressed in another garbadine slack suit and with her hair up in a turban, she stopped by her mother's room early in the afternoon after talking to Harris. She had seen the rest of the family when they returned from church, but Hillary had gone straight to her room and hadn't been seen since. Katie knocked carefully on the door to Hillary's room and heard her mother's soft voice call out, "Who is it?"

"It's me, Mom. It's Katie."

"Oh, come in, dear. The door's unlocked," came the faint voice from inside.

Katie opened the door and found her mother resting on the bed near the window which looked out on to the front-lawn court of the Island House. "Are you all right?" Katie asked.

"Oh, yes dear. I think I've overdone it these past couple of days and I felt a little faint this morning, so I thought I'd rest a bit. Sunday afternoon is a good time for resting, even when you're on a vacation."

Katie showed concern. "But you're sure you're all right?"

Hillary sat up in bed, straightened her grey hair a little, and started to get up.

"Don't get up on my account," Katie told her. "I just hadn't seen you yet today and I wanted to make sure you were feeling okay."

"I'm perfectly all right," Hillary insisted. "But I'm not so sure that you are."

"What do you mean by that?"

Hillary had decided that this was an opportune time to talk to her daughter. She'd had such talks with Katie before about various family matters and in most instances, Katie had ignored her mother's advice. Now, she decided, it was worth another try.

"What you do to your own body is your business, Katie, but I know that if you hadn't had so much to drink last night, you could have enjoyed breakfast and church with the rest of the family this morning."

"We're not going to go over all of this again, Mother. We're on vacation. And beside, it wasn't the drinking. I just didn't feel well this morning." Katie assumed that the explanation was sufficient.

"I'm no prude when it comes to having a drink," Hillary went right on. "But I think you've been overdoing it, Katie, and I think it shows. Not in your looks. God knows, you look beautiful. But it shows in your actions. I've always prided myself in not interfering in family matters of my children, but I think you have over-reacted to this thing with Ben. The boy has nothing more than a crush on a very attractive young girl. And if I were you, I think I'd let things run their course."

Thank God she didn't know about her visit with that Mr. Davis this morning, or she would be even more upset, Katie thought. But Hillary's words had put her on the defensive. "I'm not over-reacting,

Mother, and I'm not drinking too much." The words were more terse. "Harris and I have plans for Ben and we simply don't want him to make a mistake that would ruin them. That's all."

"You mean *YOU* have things planned for him," Hillary corrected her daughter with more positive tones. "Don't blame Harris for something that's all yours."

"Did Harris put you up to this?" Katie asked in a sarcastic voice. "He probably didn't have the nerve to tell me, so he had you do it. He told me you weren't feeling well just to get me in here." Katie was visibly upset now, but her mother remained calm.

"You know that's not true, dear," Hillary said, "and you also know how I feel about Harris. I don't know why you treat him the way you do sometimes."

"I might have known you'd take Harris' side, Mother," Katie said, her voice rising in anger. "If you only knew. Sometimes he deserves just what he gets."

There was no time like the present, Hillary decided. Perhaps now was the time to let her daughter know just how much she knew about their marriage. She looked Katie straight in the eye.

"He deserves better than an unfaithful wife," Hillary said quietly.

Katie was speechless. She was also defenseless. How could her mother know? How much did she know? How much did her own husband know? Had she somehow found out about the young man in the boat? The questions flashed through her mind in an instant. But dammit, she wasn't going to confession here. This might be her mother, but such accusations now made her fair game for Katie's vindictive tongue.

"Don't talk to me about unfaithfulness," Katie spit out the words. "It's all well and good for you to defend Harris and to stick up for your grandson. But you shouldn't talk about something unless you know the whole story. And you. Especially you. After all, there are some questions about your past — when you were young. Maybe not as young as Ben — but young, just the same. I mean the circumstances surrounding your first marriage — and then about Dad and the detective in Minneapolis." Katie was in deeper than she had bargained for but it was too late. She had charged head-long into her mother's past and now it was too late to back down. "Don't talk to me about unfaithfulness!'' she screamed. Then she wheeled and left the room, slamming the hotel room door behind her. She walked a few steps, then stopped, leaned back against the wall in the hallway, put her hand to her face, and began to cry. ''Oh, no,'' she sobbed. ''Oh, no, no.....''

Back in the room, Hillary stood there, white as a sheet. She knew she had hurt her daughter, but she was also crushed. She hadn't expected Katie to lash out so unfairly. Yes, it was true she had conceived her first child, her son, Jamie, when she and Emmett had been so in love that summer long, long ago. Back in St. Louis she found she was pregnant and married the boy next door to save the family name. After her husband's untimely death, Emmett had come to St. Louis, married her and took Hillary and his son back to Excelsior to live. As for the detective who was investigating a murder in Minneapolis' Ozark Flats, Hillary admitted to herself that she had a crush on him, but she never did anything more than kiss him goodnight. She may have wished for more. She couldn't remember. But she had also made a decision — that she loved Emmett and her family, which brought an abrupt end to her friendship with detective Rex Barnett. She had nothing to be ashamed of. And it was so long, long ago — before Katie was born. Her daughter could be unfair at times, but if she had known about these things before, she had never before been so cruel. All of a sudden, Hillary felt drained. She would lie down for a few hours. Perhaps she would feel better by dinnertime. Within minutes, she was asleep, dreaming about the past — and a detective.

They had agreed to meet when she finished the dinner shift and Janet was waiting for Ben along the shoreline at the foot of Arch Rock. When Ben arrived, he parked his bike in among the trees and the two of them climbed the long, steep footpath to the top of the bluff to Arch Rock.

It was growing dark and Janet was quiet throughout the climb to the top of the bluff. When they finally spread her blanket near the cliffs overlooking the lake, it was barely light enough for Ben to see that her eyes and nose were red. She had been crying.

"What's wrong, Jan," he asked with concern. "You've been so quiet — you look like you've been crying."

"I didn't think it showed," she said. "I wasn't going to tell you, but...." She burst into tears and buried her head in Ben's shoulder. Ben put his arms around her and held her. He could feel her body shaking as she sobbed and although he wanted to comfort her, he felt awkward. It reminded him of the times his kid sister had come to him for help and had cried on his shoulder. Even with Blair, he didn't now whether to speak or ask questions or to just hold her quietly. Usually, he did the latter and he decided that's what he would do now. For what seemed like a long time, they simply huddled together on the blanket.

When Janet stopped crying, Ben helped her dry her eyes with his handkerchief. "Can you tell me what this is all about?"

"I wasn't going to say anything at all," she told him, "but I have never felt so lonely or needed someone to talk to as much as I do now."

"I'm right here, Jan, and I'm a good listener. Tell me what's wrong."

"Someone made a pass at me today," she said in a matter-of-fact tone of voice.

"You mean someone whistled at you or flirted with you or asked you for a date or tried to...."

"No," she interrupted. She was more definite now. "Someone put their hands on me, Ben." She shuddered. "It was awful."

The usual calm and quiet Ben found an anger rising within him. "Who was it, Jan? What happened? When did all this happen?" He asked so many questions in a rush that she couldn't answer. Then he realized that his own anxiety was getting out of hand and he settled down again. "Can you tell me who it was, Jan?"

"Well, when I finished work this noon, Mr. Davis, the assistant manager, had asked me to stop by his office. He said he wanted to see me." She swallowed hard. "So I did, and then he said he needed to talk to me — privately — and he closed the door. I think he locked it, but I'm not sure." Ben listened intently but Janet seemed a little vague.

"We talked for a little while. He asked me how I was getting along since my roommate had left — and started to talk about how it can be lonely in strange surroundings, away from home. Then he said that I was in more than a little trouble but he thought he could work it out and

I wouldn't lose my job — if I would just be nice to him. He had walked around behind me and put his hand on my shoulder. He kept on talking and talking and the next thing I knew, he was kissing the back of my neck and had slid his hand around my waist and....started pawing me...."

Janet began sniffing again. "And that's when I broke away from him and tried to get out the door. He stood there in front of the door for a minute and told me I'd better think it over. Then he let me out." She was crying softly again.

It was Ben's face that was red, now — with anger. "That old....bastard!" Ben snapped. "That dirty old....."

"Just hold me, Ben," Janet sobbed, and the two of them sat quietly on the blanket. It was dark now, but there was enough moonlight for Ben to see her face smeared with tears. He tried to wipe the pretty face dry.

"Why would you lose your job?" Ben asked. "What could someone as nice as you have possibly done that would lose your job for you?"

The words stumbled out as Janet tried not to explain. "It really was unimportant," she finally said. She rambled on but didn't say anything and it was apparent to Ben that she wasn't making any sense and wasn't telling him what he wanted to hear.

"Come on, Jan. You've told me this much. Now tell me what Mr. Davis was talking about." He straightened her shoulders so that she was looking straight at Ben. "Now tell me."

"I shouldn't have told you any of this," she went on. "It was about you and me, Ben. Someone had complained about my being an employee and socializing with a guest of the hotel."

"What?" Ben asked incredulously. "What difference does that nake. And who could possibly care...." By the time the words had left his mouth, he already knew the answer...."My mother. My God." He thought for a moment. "Of course. She said something about it before. But I didn't think she was that serious. I can't believe she would go to the hotel management and....."

"I'm sorry, Ben."

"I'm sorry, too — for you, Jan, and for what she's put you through." He hesitated. "I know she always tries to run things but this time....."

"Please, Ben," she begged.

Ben quieted down and waited for the anger to subside. Then he looked at Janet and could see the tears on her cheeks and he gathered her in his arms.

"Don't worry, Jan. It's going to be all right." He paused to gather all of his courage and then kissed her gently. "After all, Jan, I guess I'm falling in love with you." It was the first time in his life he had ever said those words to a girl, and all he could think of now was how wonderful she was. The two of them held on to each other in the dark — on the very site where the legendary Indian maid had shed so many tears.

CHAPTER 8

Monday, July 11

For anyone taking the ferry from St. Ignace to Mackinac Island, the first glimpse of life on the island comes with the exciting view of the stately Grand Hotel, commanding one of the most beautiful scenes from atop the west bluffs of the island. The grandeur of the longest open porch in the world impresses even the most sophisticated visitors to the island. Studded with flags flapping in the breeze, the porch stretches to almost the length of three football fields. One author wrote that the summer social life of the upper echelons of the island society revolved around this majestic summer hotel and its historic background. The Grand was built in 1886 and 1887 by three transportation companies: The Michigan Central Railroad, the Detroit and Cleveland Navigation Company, and the Grand Rapids and Indiana Railroad. It first opened its doors on July 10, 1887, with the well-known families and notables from throughout the midwest attending, including the Marshall Fields, the Armours and Swifts and the Busch family. Originally known as Plank's Grand Hotel and managed by John Plank, the Grand somehow lived through a series of financial crises over the years, through the World War and the twenties. One young man from Indiana went to work at the hotel in 1919 as a desk clerk. His name was W. Stewart Woodfill and in 1933 he became the owner of the Grand. His determination led the hotel through the depression and to the national prominence it now enjoyed.

A year after Mr. Woodfill had taken over the ownership of the Grand Hotel, a new brochure had been produced by the Grand and under the title of *At the Crossroads of the Great Lakes* came these words about the island:

A little world of its own, unique and distinctive among resorts, where the simple peace of Colonial America is preserved. There are no automobiles, only horses and carriages, rolling chairs and bicycles. Ships of all kinds are on every hand. Old fortifications and historic buildings bring to mind the life of early missionaries, voyageurs and traders who made this the first outpost of civilization in the West.

From time immemorial, this has been a place apart, a sacred, glamorous and romantic spot. The island was worshipped by the Indians of all the West and used as burial grounds for their illustrious dead. The Jesuits founded here their first mission with Marquette in 1671. The French made it the capital of their Western Province, and the English came to drive them from the lakes and built a Gibraltar to rule their inland seas. Built of rock, the island is free from swamps, mosquitoes and polluted waters. The air is purest in the world, according to United States Government reports. Surely it is one of nature's beauty treasures. Broad slopes roll in green profusion, gardens, drives and beauty everywhere. Rocks look down on virgin forests. Yachts idle in the harbor and nearby islands glisten in the sun. Miles of sparkling water stretch out to meet the silver clouds, and wisps of smoke trail from steamers sailing slowly on.

Only an overnight ride from Chicago to Detroit by either railroad or steamer, Mackinic Island is easily accessible. This is the principal port of call for large lake steamers from Chicago, Duluth, Detroit, Cleveland and Buffalo. Automobile highways are paved to Mackinaw City and St. Ignace. It is from these points that railroad passengers and tourists ferry to Mackinac Island, just one-half hour away.

Of the Grand Hotel, the brochure continued:

There is dancing every afternoon in the Tea Garden, every evening in the Ballroom and every night in the Grill. Magazines and books are available for the guests without charge. Ping-pong and other games are provided. The hostess arranges bridge parties daily. There are interesting shops in the hotel, the Cocktail Lounge, medicinal baths, and brokerage office with direct wires to New York City.

The Golf Course adjoins the hotel with every tee affording a view of the Straits. Nearby is another golf course, the Country Club, also available for our guests. The swimming pool is located directly in front of the hotel in a cedar grove. Saddle horses, carriages, bicycles and rolling chairs are always available at the hotel and are particularly enjoyable on the island because of the absence of automobiles.

A price list quoted the tariff for the American Plan from $6 to $12.50 (front room with bath) per person. Green fees on the golf course were $1.50 daily and *A Michigan Sales Tax of approximately 10 cents daily per person* was added to the room rates.

Harvey Stanhope had hired a taxi late in the morning to take Marian and him to the Grand Hotel for lunch. It did not take long for the taxi driver and his twin team of brown horses to make the trip through the business district, then on to Market Street and up Cadotte Street to the Grand. Marian loved the flowers that were everywhere as they approached the Grand — thousands of tulips, geraniums and begonias.

At the entrance to the Grand, flags were flying from the magnificent open porch of white pillars and a doorman greeted them as they stepped from the carriage and mounted the steps to the main entrance of the hotel. Inside, they found their way through the lobby to the dining room where the Stanhopes were assigned a table by the window looking out on to the porch and the lake below. Black waiters wearing mess jackets were everywhere and Marian was impressed.

"You're too good to me, Harvey," Marian said as they finished their elegant lunch.

"I guess we know how to live," he told her with as broad a smile as he could muster.

"I guess we do, Honey, but ever since you got on the island you've been doing nice things for me. Goin' to the best places for dinner, takin' me to lunch here at the Grand Hotel." She stuck out her right hand to display an Alaskan diamond. "And this new ring you bought me yesterday. How come, Harvey? I really don't deserve all this." Harvey had always been good to her but he had almost overdone it these past two days. Marian was sorry she ever joined in with Al Davis's making fun of her husband by calling him "Horseface." He surely wasn't the most handsome man in the world. But he didn't deserve being called that.

"It's okay, Honey," he assured her. "We're on vacation and I just want you to know how much I love you." Harvey's toothy grin across the table was an honest reflection of how he felt about his wife. He really did love her and he was more hurt than angry over what he had learned or suspected the other night when he arrived. Maybe he simply wasn't paying enough attention to her. He reached across the table and gently patted her hand.

What he hadn't told her about was the phone call he had made to Phil Lafferty the other day. Nor had he told her of his second call to his old friend on the Detroit police force again this morning while she was up in their room, doing her platinum blonde hair with a curling iron.

"Hello, Phil. It's Harvey."

"Well, Harvey. I've been expecting your call."

"I'm sorry, Phil. I meant to call earlier but just couldn't get away."

"It's okay, friend," the voice at the other end of the line told him. "In the meantime, I ran a quick check on your Mr. Davis and whadaya know — he has a little history that's very interesting."

"Like what?" Harvey asked.

"Like being charged with embezzling funds at the Blackstone Hotel in Chicago where he worked as a night clerk three years ago. He'd also been hustling the hotel manager's young wife and they decided not to press the matter. They just fired him."

"So he doesn't have a record?" Harvey asked.

"Oh, yes," Lafferty bellowed over the phone. "They caught him altering the books at a hotel here in Detroit and he spent some time in the local workhouse." Harvey could hear Lafferty rattling the pages of the report at the other end. "Then he was accused of raping a high school girl but the charges were dropped when the parents decided they didn't want the publicity. And he was canned at another hotel here for conning a couple of women guests — one was single and the other a widow." He was quick to add. "No criminal charges, though."

"That's all?"

"Isn't that enough?" Lafferty asked with a laugh. "Apparently he's a likeable guy — but always on the fringe of trouble. He better not try to operate back here, though. We've got his picture and the department has gone so far as to list some of his habits. Hell, we even know what brand of cigarettes he smokes."

"Oh?" Harvey questioned.

"One of them fancy kinds in a box — Viceroys."

Harvey thanked his detective friend for his help and told him he'd look him up when he and Marian got back from their weekend at Mackinac. Harvey had again made the call from the lobby of the Chippewa where there was a lot of activity and nobody could hear his phone conversation. When he left the hotel he had mixed feelings about what he suspected between Marian and Al Davis. He felt sad and hurt about Marian, but he wasn't going to blame her. If anything, he was sorry for her and had decided he would try even harder to show her how much he cared for her. As for Al Davis, Harvey realized that it wasn't just anger that he felt for him. Instead, it was a new confidence, a new determination, that Mr. Davis was going to get what was coming to him.

Harvey and Marian finished their coffee to end their lunch at the Grand Hotel and he took her hand again and spoke softly across the table.

"Let's walk back down to the center of town and stop in a few shops and stores," he said. "Maybe you'll find something you like."

Marian squeezed her husband's hand. "Harv....." she hesitated. "I was bored to death while you were away." She paused. "And I...ah... fell off the wagon just a little bit. But I'm gonna make it up to you. Truly I am."

Harvey was still holding her hand and he squeezed back.

Twice this morning, Ben had stopped at the front desk to see Al Davis but he was not on duty and nowhere to be found. Ben was relieved. He wasn't sure he could go through with this, and left the hotel to stroll along the shoreline for awhile and get back his courage. Being near the lake had helped him at home when he had problems or needed to sort things out. He had spent many hours alone on the dock in front of their house on Lake Minnetonka, fishing for sunnies and working out bits and pieces of his young life in the solitude of the lake. There was something about the water that helped him think more clearly, and which gave him new strength. Although his whole weekend had been filled with such happy times with Janet, he was already beginning to dread the time when he would be leaving the island — and her. What was it going to be like back home without her? He tried to put such unpleasant thoughts out of his mind. He didn't even want to imagine not seeing her everyday. Then he thought about Davis and what he had done — or tried to do — to Jan, and the anger made him realize that he had to do something. He started back up towards the hotel and saw his grandmother sitting alone out on the veranda of the Island House, reading a book. He stopped to see her and say good morning.

"Hello Ben." Hillary looked up from her book.

"Hi, Grandma," he greeted her.

"Been for a walk down by the lake?" she asked. "I saw you coming from that direction."

"Yeah. It's quiet down there. Reminds me of home."

"Yes. There's something about the water that can affect a person; almost put a spell on you. I think it's the rhythm of the waves," she said.

The two of them sat quietly for a few minutes, looking out on the harbor. Then Ben finally spoke.

"Did you ever have trouble getting up the courage to do the right thing, Grandma?" he asked.

"I take it that you mean when the right thing wasn't always the easiest thing to do."

"Yes, Grandma. That's right. Did that ever happen to you?"

"Many times, Ben." She smiled. "Many times."

"Well, Gram — what did you do?"

Memories flashed through Hillary's mind in an instant and she remembered saying goodbye to a young police detective.

"I remember one time in particular," she told Ben. "I didn't want to do something but I knew it was right and that it had to be done. It was hard for me to do, and it made me very sad. But I knew it was right." She had a wistful smile on her face and turned to Ben. "And it all turned out all right."

Ben got up, leaned over and kissed Hillary on the cheek. "Thanks, Grandma," he said. Then he was gone.

Hillary sat there for a long time and thought about Rex Barnett and wondered what had happened to him. Then she opened her book and began reading again.

With new determination, Ben walked through the small lobby and down the narrow hall to the office in the back where Al Davis worked. He stopped outside of the door for a moment to gather his courage and then knocked on the door.

"Come in," came the voice of Al Davis.

Ben turned the knob and opened the door into the small office. Al looked surprised but smiled when he saw who it was. "Well, Butler. Come in, come in." Ben stepped inside and closed the door behind him. Al seemed to be amused that Ben would come to see him. "You didn't have to come and see me. There isn't anything I can do for you." He smiled at Ben who stepped up to Al's desk and looked him square in the face.

"You keep your hands off of Janet Rachel," Ben said.

The words caught Al by surprise. "What?"

"I said to keep away from Janet Rachel. You know what I'm talking about." Ben's heart was pounding. His voice betrayed his nervousness. And he also realized that he was scared.

Al's smile disappeared and the tone of his voice changed abruptly. "Listen, my friend. Janet may get fired. But I'm not the problem." He pointed a finger at Ben. "You're the problem."

"I'm not your friend," the young man corrected Al. "I just came to tell you to keep your hands off of her....or you'll answer to me." Ben's voice shook, but he stood his ground.

Al's voice turned mean. "Listen, you little snot-nosed kid. You get the hell out of here before I lose my temper. Why, you're not even dry behind the ears yet. I'm surprised you didn't send your mother back in here," he snarled. "She was here once, you know." Al smiled sarcastically. "I almost had to laugh — her, complaining about the help socializing with the hotel guests. Of all people, she should be the last one to come in here and complain."

Ben was a well-built young man and a good athlete, but Davis was as big and certainly more confident. Ben didn't know what Al Davis was talking about, but he didn't like the tone of his voice or the obvious disgust he was displaying for his mother and Jan. Ben's reaction was automatic, and without thinking, he reached across the desk and grabbed Davis by the shirt.

"You bast....."

Before he could finish the sentence, Davis had swung a hard right fist to Ben's face, sending the teenager reeling back across the tiny office and up against the door. Before Ben could recover, the older man was on him.

"I've dealt with kids like you all my life," he said. "All you people with money are alike. You think you can do any damn thing you please. Well, here's one guy you can't step on!"

Before Ben realized what was happening, Al had grabbed him by the neck and thrown him out the door. "And don't come cryin' to me again, sonny boy!"

The office door slammed shut and Ben found himself sitting on the floor in the hall, leaning against the wall with his head almost between his knees. He wiped his hand across his face and found blood coming from his nose. He could feel a sharp bruise on his left cheek. He didn't try to get up but just sat there, trying to gather himself together. Then he slowly stood up, shook his head, brushed himself off, and started down the hall towards the lobby. He knew he would be back again to see Al Davis.

As Ben crossed the lobby to the stairway, Billy Lachine was heading for the back hall on his way to the kitchen and he had just a glimpse of Ben wiping his bloody nose and bruised cheek with the back of his hand and then a handkerchief. He almost called out to him but before he could, Ben was out of the lobby and starting up the stairs. Billy passed Al Davis' back office and stopped. Naw. Ben Butler couldn't have been in Al's office, he thought. Maybe he ought to stop in and ask Al about it. Naw, it couldn't have anything to do with Al. Billy started back to the kitchen, but all of a sudden, he had an uneasy feeling in his stomach.

CHAPTER 9

Monday, July 11

Summer days like today brought to Janet many fond thoughts of her family back in Ferrisville. There was a lot of hard work, but the family often had fun together. There was no doubt about it. Even with the daily chores, there had been good times. Janet had been responsible for taking care of the chickens — feeding them and gathering the eggs after school. Her other major job at home was taking care of the garden. The more strenuous chores were handled by her two older brothers and her dad. They took care of the cows and pigs, the milking, the feeding and helping with the crops. Janet had to laugh at herself. She even missed the ironing these days. At home, there would be mounds of washing and ironing. Even her brothers' workshirts were ironed. And it wouldn't be long before her mother started canning — everything from pickles to pears to tomatoes. She had always helped her mother can jellies, too, from their own orchards and berry patch. With a bumper crop of cabbage came sauerkraut, made in a 50-gallon tub that was so big Janet used to stir the salt brine with a baseball bat.

The days on the farm had been long, starting at about six o'clock in the morning and going all day. Early chores were done by 7:30 and on summer mornings, she and her mother took lunch out to the fields by 9:30 or 10. At noon, her dad and the boys would come in to have dinner and listen to the radio. By late afternoon, Janet would be out to the fields again with rolls and coffee and perhaps a jug of water wrapped in cloth or newspapers to keep cool. On an especially hot summer day, her father would tell the boys to knock off early and the whole family would pile into the truck and go to the lake for a swim and a picnic. Hot dogs, something they didn't have on the farm, were a special treat.

Somehow, most everything centered around the family. Janet remembered going to visit neighbors with her family on Sunday afternoons, or roller-skating in a new barn. Once in a while, her brothers would take her along to a Saturday night dance at the city hall in town.

Right now she missed the old farm house and the kerosene lamps, and even though there was an abundance of horses and carriages on Mackinac Island, she missed the pony and the buggy and her favorite team of horses, Dick and Doc. The truth of the matter was — she was homesick.

Janet thought about her home and family as she wrote a note to her parents, telling them that everything was just fine here on the island. But everything wasn't just fine. She had troubles with her boss at the hotel and wasn't too well-liked by Mrs. Butler. If she was having this much trouble here, what was it going to be like away at college this fall? She felt alone, except for Ben. She did have Ben to talk to. In fact, she had to admit to herself that she was probably in love with him. When that realization came to her, she made up her mind that she had to go and see Mrs. Butler. She'd make her understand that there wasn't anything wrong about the relationship between her and Ben. Yes, she'd find just the right time to talk to his mother. In the meantime, she would avoid Al Davis as much as possible.

Katie sipped her coffee as she sat in her room at the Island House this morning. She was still upset about her visit to her mother's room yesterday and angry at herself for losing her temper. She had tried to make amends at dinner last night and although Hillary had accepted her apology and said that she, too, was sorry for the scene, Katie knew that all was not well between them. What made it worse was that up until yesterday, she had no idea that her mother was aware of her extra-marital adventures. Even now, she wasn't sure how she found out about them or how much she really knew. It was bad enough, however, that she knew anything at all about such matters. Katie had to admit to herself that there was no excuse for her outburst with her mother. She had simply been caught by surprise and put on the defensive, and that was not a familiar position for Katie. She had obviously hurt her mother terribly, and although she was still concerned about it this morning, she was even more worried about Hillary's state of health. She would talk with Harris about it again today.

She refilled her coffee cup from the pot which had been brought up to her room earlier. Trying not to think about her mother any further, she opened the morning paper. She found herself staring at the *Chicago Tribune*, a newspaper that was far too conservative for Katie. She would begin a news story and her thoughts would drift back to the confrontation with her mother. All that unpleasantness kept getting in the way. She finally began to read the news from abroad — most disquieting news.

Seventy-two-point headlines blared out, JAPAN WAR THREAT DEFIED BY SOVIETS, and the story went on with an account of a border dispute in northern Manchoukuo, north of Korea. In another item, the VFW had come out for peace, but not at any price. They were campaigning for a stronger army, navy and air corps. Katie shook her head in disbelief. Those nincompoops, she thought. Everytime she read such news reports, she thought of Ben and it frightened her. She went on to other news stories of the day. She smiled and wondered how Excelsior Republicans would react to the headlines, HINTS OF FDR THIRD TERM. She was pleased at a small item on the sports page which told of Patty Berg winning another golf tournament. Young Miss Berg was her kind of woman. But no woman, not even Katie, would skip the advertisements. Women's turbans were only $2 and she couldn't help but notice — *National Eagle Whiskey, The King of Blends, $1.95 a quart. Only 99 cents a pint.* She skipped over the comic strips — *Popeye, Orphan Annie, Moon Mullins, Blondie* and the rest — but stopped when she got to the movies where there were some new pictures to be seen: Humphrey Bogart in *Crime School* and Gary Cooper and Jean Arthur in *The Plainsman.* She even scanned the radio logs. At home, her radio was constantly tuned into the daily soap operas — everything from *Judy and Jane* to *Kitty Keene* and *Stella Dallas.*

One news photo caught her eye. It was of Bing Crosby and his wife, Dixie Lee, in their first family photo since their fourth son was born. It showed all the young sons: Gary, the twins, Phillip and Dennis, and the new baby, Lindsay. Katie smiled. It prompted her to think about her own family and particularly about Ben. Dear, young innocent Ben. What was she going to do about him. She was determined he would stay on course, get through school and on to college, and back to the family newspapers. Perhaps she had over-reacted to her son seeing that girl on the island. And then there was Mr. Davis. Maybe she had gone to the wrong man. He obviously knew more than he should. He had a certain attractiveness about him, Katie admitted to herself, but he was a slimy character. She would have to deal with him one way or another — for Ben's sake, of course.

Travelling on the Great Lakes dated back to the North American Indians and their canoes. Later, the French voyageurs and their over-sized canoes loaded with fur pelts gave way to sailboats and then to steamboats near the turn of the century. At first there were side-wheelers, then ocean-going steamers, and excursion ships from Detroit, Cleveland and Chicago. The Northern Steamship Company, headed by railroader James J. Hill, was one of perhaps a half-dozen steamship lines in the 1880's and 1890's, and more Great Lakes passenger ships came along in the 1900's. The railroads also brought wealthy visitors to Mackinac Island during the Victorian era. There were Pullmans, elegant dining cars, and special private railroad cars, all bringing vacationers to the island and the Straits to enjoy the pure fresh air, the fishing, the wilds of the northland, and Mackinac Island's elegant summer hotels, shopping, verandas and fashions.

Even in the 1930's, steamships still left almost daily from Chicago and Detroit and provided regular service between Mackinac Island, Duluth, Sault Ste. Marie, Milwaukee, Georgian Bay, Cleveland and Buffalo. Steamers included: the *Eastern States* and *Western States* (Detroit and Cleveland Navigation Co.); the *Seeandbee* (Cleveland and Buffalo Navigation Co.); the *Octerara, Tionesta* and *Juniata* (Great Lakes Transit Co.); and the *Alabama* (Chicago, Isle Royal and Canada Line). It was about a twenty-hour trip by steamer from Chicago or Detroit to Mackinac Island and the round trip fare (including berths and meals) was $22.50.

The round-trip railroad fare from Chicago to the island was only $16. Vacationers could leave Chicago at 6 p.m. and arrive on the island at 8:45 the next morning. Aboard the Michigan Central and the Pennsylvania Railroad companies, fares from Detroit and back were only $15.70 while the cost was $26.70 round-trip from Cleveland or $23.15 from Indianapolis and back.

Visitors to Mackinac came to enjoy the natural resources, explore the island, have lunch on the veranda, enjoy afternoon tea and fine dining in the best hotels and restaurants. Wealthy families brought their servants along and enjoyed a lengthy stay. Besides the hotels, there were beautiful homes with spacious porches and round turret corners. At Mackinac they were called summer cottages and sprang up on what would come to be known as the East and West Bluffs. Back in the 1880's, an unfurnished cottage went for anywhere from $50 to $100 for the season. Furnished cottages rented for as high as $350. And, of course, there was the 1901 ban on those new-fangled automobiles.

A reminder of those glorious days of the past had pulled into port this morning at Mackinac Island — the steamship, *The South American*. It had become popular, sailing between Duluth and Chicago and Buffalo after the turn of the century. *The South American* would be in port for a few hours today and Harris had taken Ben and the girls down to the main pier to see it. The giant luxury liner made Mackinac an important stop on its cruise through the Great Lakes each year, and Harris and the clan were allowed on board to tour part of the ship.

The tour for Harris and the kids ended on the top deck of the liner where they looked out over the harbor and pretended they were somewhere out on the Great Lakes with no land in sight. When they left the old ship, Harris took pictures of them all in front of a giant lifesaver mounted on the railing of the main deck. Each youngster posed along the rail with the words, *The South American*, imprinted on the lifesaver behind them.

After the tour of the steamer, the youngsters dispersed, leaving Harris to walk back to the hotel alone. He was pleased with the morning tour of the ship and the time he had spent with the kids. But he soon began to think about the headlines of impending war in Europe and the opportunity he had to get in on the ground floor of selling to the army — and to make a lot of money.

Just before he came to Mackinac Island, Harris had visited with Gerald P. Hagen, a fellow salesman who had left the company a few months earlier to strike out on his own. Now he was urging Harris to join him as a manufacturer's representative in selling a new product similar to one called Plexiglass.

"What the hell is that?" Harris had asked when they talked about it over coffee last June.

"It's a kind of glass — but it's unbreakable." Gerry struggled for some way to explain it. "It's transparent and weather resistant, and it won't break."

"And what is it used for, and who's going to buy it?" Harris pressed him.

"It's been on the market for a while and now it's improved. But there's more than one manufacturer of this stuff. It's light weight and strong, Harris. It's used in bombers and fighters and gun turrets and....and manufacturers with government contracts are buying it up like mad."

"And you've got the account?"

"I have the rights as a manufacturer's rep, Harris, but I can't handle it alone. I've been travelling almost seven days a week and I can't be in two places at the same time. I need someone like you. We're gonna sell it to the War Department — the Army Air Corps and the Navy and Boeing and Martin and a lot of others, Harris. And we're gonna make a bundle."

Harris was brought back to reality as he neared the Island House. He had crossed the street in the middle of the block and was almost struck down by a team of horses and a noisy dray wagon which had hurried by him. Without any automobiles on the island, he had considered the streets absolutely safe. Now he wasn't quite so sure, and he smiled to himself.

He decided that when he got home, he'd see Gerry Hagen and let him know he was willing to begin work as a partner.

Ten years ago, Marian Stanhope wouldn't have even thought about sitting out on the veranda of the Island House or anywhere else, for that matter, opening a book and actually reading. But this morning she was reading aloud to her husband about Mackinac Island history and of Dr. William Beaumont.

Dr. Beaumont was a physician and surgeon who came to the island in mid-June of 1820 as the new post surgeon at Fort Mackinac. He served there for some five years, fell in love with the island and brought his bride there where they began their family. Dr. Beaumont's work as a physician went far beyond his duties at the fort, however, and he established a private practice among the townspeople, as well. At one point, he urged that a proposed new army hospital be constructed below the fort which would have given the island civilians the use of the facility, too. The hospital eventually was built — within the confines of the fort.

Dr. Beaumont's reputation within the medical profession was enhanced through an incident on the island involving townspeople and civilians, an incident that would change the course of his life. He had served as the post surgeon for almost two years. Then one June day in 1822 he was called to the American Fur Company's store on Market Street where a nineteen-year-old French Canadian had been accidentally shot in the stomach from a shotgun blast. The doctor treated the young man's wound, broken ribs, damaged lung and stomach, and saved the voyageur from almost certain death. The young man's name was Alexis St. Martin and he was moved to the post hospital where he miraculously recovered. The stomach wound, however, would not heal, leaving a gaping hole in the abdomen. The situation prompted the inquisitive Dr. Beaumont to observe the human digestive system as no one had ever done before — and over a long period of time. As if peering through a window into St. Martin's stomach, Dr. Beaumont began experiments and recording the reactions of solids and liquids to the digestive system, even suspending pieces of food into the stomach and retrieving them again.

The good doctor completed his tour of duty at Fort Mackinac in 1825 but long after he had left the island, he was still working on the St. Martin experiment and published his historic findings to the medical profession in his *Experiments and Observations on the Gastric Juice and the Physiology of Digestion*. He eventually retired from the army and enjoyed a successful private practice in St. Louis, Missouri, where he died in 1853 at the age of 68. Ironically, the subject of his years of study, Alexis St. Martin, outlived him and died in 1880, at the age of 77.

When Marian finished the chapter about Dr. Beaumont, she turned to her husband.

"Had enough for one morning, dear?" she asked, "or would you like me to read a little while longer?"

Only a glimmer of that familiar broad smile shown on Harvey's face as he shook his head. "It's enough for now," he said quietly.

Marian closed the book and the two of them sat for a few minutes, looking out on the harbor. She was pleased with herself this morning. She had discovered she liked to read, and she was surprised at how much she learned with each new reading. She had never finished high school and simply didn't have time to read in her younger days. As an attractive 22-year-old when the war ended, she found too many things to do, too many places to go, and a lot of wealthy, older men paying attention to her. When she first went to work for Harvey as a beauty operator, she was still making money on the side from some of her former gentlemen friends. Harvey never was over-amorous and although she found it difficult at times to turn down her old customers, she learned to live with even less sex these past few years, ever since Harvey's stroke. It was almost more than Marian could handle at times and she had a string of affairs with a couple of clothing salesmen. She sensed that at times, her husband was almost encouraging her to satisfy these strong desires. That's how she rationalized her flings with Al Davis. Whether or not Harvey had any idea what was going on, she was grateful to him for his thoughtfulness and it made her love him even more. As a result, she was determined not to let Al or anyone else spoil their times here on Mackinac Island. That's why she had been reading for Harvey this morning.

"Why don't we order a buggy and go for a little ride around the island this morning?" Marian asked.

Harvey forced a half-smile. "That sounds like a wonderful idea, honey. Maybe we could stop for lunch somewhere before we come back to the hotel."

Marian brightened up. "I'll order the carriage from the front desk." She started to get out of her porch chair but Harvey reached out and put his hand on her arm.

"Don't hurry. We've got plenty of time."

"Okay, dear," she said as she settled back in her chair. "We can go anytime you're ready." She paused. "You're right. There's no hurry. No hurry at all."

"I might want to rest and take a nap this afternoon," he said as he looked out across the veranda. "It would give you a little time for yourself."

Marian could see Harvey's warm eyes and a faint smile on his face. Then he thought about Al Davis and turned away. Marian couldn't see her husband's eyes turn cold. But he knew then, he would have to do something about Mr. Davis, and soon.

"I'll take some time this afternoon," she told him. "That Mrs. Jorgenson in 105 said something about her husband playing golf and she wanted to go shopping. I promise to take a little time this afternoon — or maybe early this evening."

The two of them sat there for a while longer. Harvey was pleased. Marian was worried. She felt selfish and even more guilty about Al. She thought she had put him out of her mind but found herself wanting to see him again. She shut her eyes for a moment, shook her head, and got up.

"I'll go order the carriage," she told Harvey.

CHAPTER 10

Monday, July 11

Ben had told Janet his mother was
always late in getting started in the morning. Janet counted on that
and had come to work early in hopes of seeing her. She had seen Ben's
father and grandmother leaving the hotel and she knew that Ben was
biking around the island. And she didn't have to report for work in the
dining room of the Island House for another half hour. The timing, it
seemed, was perfect. She realized the waitress uniform she was
wearing wouldn't help her image with Ben's mother, but the time was
now and she would go ahead with her plan. She walked along the front
porch of the hotel and into a side entrance and up the stairs to the third
floor where she knocked on the door of Room 300.

"Just a minute," came Katie's voice through the door. Seconds
later, Katie opened the door and found the very pretty brunette standing in the doorway.

"Mrs. Butler?" Janet half-questioned. "I'm Janet Rachel."

"Yes, I know." Katie was dressed in a peach-colored dressing gown
and matching slippers. She wore no make up and it was obvious she

144 - The Island House

hadn't been up too long. Even so, Janet realized how attractive she was.

"May I come in?" Janet asked. "I'd like to talk with you for a moment."

She had caught Ben's mother by surprise and for a few seconds, Katie just stood there. Then she caught up to the conversation and, with a slight smile, invited Janet to come in.

It was a large bedroom which looked out towards the harbor. The front bay window also provided a view of Mackinac Island's main street and the stores, just a block away. The bathroom door was open and Janet could see a curling iron set across the corner of the wash basin. Then she looked at Katie and realized that she had been in the midst of curling her hair. The two of them stood in the middle of the room and there was a moment of awkward silence.

"I'll only stay a minute," Janet said apologetically. "I know you disapprove of Ben and me seeing each other, Mrs. Butler. Mr. Davis called me into his office yesterday. I simply wanted to tell you that you don't have to worry about Ben. We've done nothing wrong, nothing to be ashamed of. We just happen to enjoy each other's company. Is that so bad?" Janet felt calm. All the uneasiness she had felt out in the hall in front of the door had disappeared. She was actually standing up to this commanding figure — Ben's mother — but it still scared her.

The girl had spunk. Katie loved that. Inside, she was smiling, but she wasn't going to let Janet know it. "I know you must think I'm some kind of social snob," Katie said, "but I went to the hotel management because I was concerned for Ben — and you." Actually, that wasn't true, and Katie knew it. She didn't give a damn about Janet Rachel, didn't trust her, and didn't have much respect for her. What she didn't tell the girl was her fears for Ben; that he'd somehow get into more trouble than he bargained for and that the family would be faced with a farm girl from Michigan their son had knocked up. "I truly was concerned," she said again.

"I know. Mr. Davis called me into his office and told me."

"I have nothing against you, personally, dear," Katie said. "I'm sure you're a very nice girl, or Ben wouldn't be so taken with you. And you are very attractive."

"Thank you," Janet replied. She was a little embarrassed.

"But whether you believe me or not, I really have Ben's interest at heart."

"So do I," Janet agreed. She had taken on a new confidence now. Her voice was firm, but inside, her stomach was churning.

"If that's true, my dear," Katie went on, "then perhaps you can do more for him than I can." She didn't believe what she had said, but she said it for Janet's benefit.

"How's that?" Janet asked.

"By simply cutting off this relationship. Just don't see him anymore. After all, he's only sixteen years old and this is his first experience of thinking he cares about a girl." Katie shook her head and smiled a little. "He's so naive and....and so vulnerable."

"I think you underestimate your own son, Mrs. Butler." Janet's voice rose slightly. "I don't know of anyone who is more devoted to his family or wants to please them more than Ben. But I think there's a side to Ben that you apparently have overlooked. He's more understanding and wiser than you think."

Someone else telling Katie things about her own son was more than she could take. She was on the verge of losing her temper and was tempted to tell this little trollop off. Then she had a better idea. She turned and went into the bathroom and came back with a glass half-full of gin. Her voice softened. "Look, Janet. I know you like Ben and I want you to know that I'm aware Ben is maturing. It's just that I — we — have plans for him. He's going to be a newspaper publisher." Katie didn't like explaining to people — especially to Janet. But perhaps it was the best way to let the girl down easy.

"I know, Mrs. Butler. Ben told me all about it, and he's looking forward to all of that — college, the school of journalism, the newspapers — but he also has a life to live, even now, including his relationship with me."

"And just what is that relationship?" Katie snapped back. Her voice was more stern, now. The time for tactfulness was over.

"I don't know for sure," Janet said quietly. "But I think I love him."

Inside, Katie was screaming to herself: Love him? Love him? Why you little fool. You don't even know what love is.

But those words never came out. Instead, Katie forced a smile. "Look, dear. You've only known Ben for a few days — less than a week. I think you've got what I would call *a crush* on him. And I can't blame you. But believe me, it will pass. Other boys will come along, maybe right here on the island." Katie thought her voice was reassuring and convincing. She had another think coming.

"I've learned something from Ben about your family," Janet said. "It's that you each have a strong will." Janet stiffened a little, just to give herself the confidence she needed right at this moment. "If there's one thing I admire about you, Mrs. Butler, it's your determination. And I've learned something from you. I'll bet that through your whole life, if you really believed in something or if you really wanted something, you never backed down from it. Well, I believe in Ben. And I'm not backing down either."

There was a silence in the room. This time, the smile that crossed Katie's face was genuine, even in defeat. The girl had taken a page right out of her own book, her own life. The words didn't come easy.

"I guess I can't argue with that," Katie said quietly, and reluctantly.

There was more silence, broken only by Janet's bidding goodbye to Katie. When Janet shut the door after her, Katie stood in the middle of the room for a moment. Of course, she had been over-reacting, she told herself. It was obvious that Janet Rachel was a nice girl. Bright, likeable, and very attractive. No wonder Ben was taken with her. She couldn't blame him. And what must he think of his mother? Why am I doing this to him? Why am I doing this to myself? She drank the rest of the gin from the water glass and swallowed hard.

"Damn that girl!"

She walked back into the bathroom and picked up the hot iron and began to curl her hair. When she looked into the mirror, she did something she hadn't done in a long time. She began to cry.

"I love him, too," she sobbed.

If business was getting better throughout the country, it was also improving on Mackinac Island these days, and the Island House found itself operating at near capacity this very week. Hotel guests were busy with the various activities offered on the island: sight-seeing, shopping, golf, tennis and sailing. But each afternoon, the Island House veranda was filled with guests who simply wanted to watch the passing parade along the street and in the harbor, and visit with one another. It was all part of being on vacation — talking over the experiences and happenings of today and yesterday, planning for tonight or tomorrow, and making new friends. A middle-aged man and his wife had been attending a meeting of the Rural Electrification Managers at the Grand Hotel and decided to stay on the island for another day or two at the Island House. He chatted with a number of guests who had made an overnight stop at the hotel while on a bus tour of the Great Lakes from somewhere in Vermont. One young, attractive couple was there on their honeymoon and sat off at the end of the hotel porch, apart from the rest of the crowd. Harvey Stanhope sat on the porch this afternoon, listening to the conversations while Marian shopped in the downtown area of the island.

Harris Butler was visiting with a young man from Detroit.

"Where did you say you were from?" the Michigander asked.

"Minnesota. Excelsior, Minnesota," Harris told him. "It's near Minneapolis."

"You've come a long way, then, haven't you?"

"Yes. Over five hundred miles. But it's worth it to get away from it all for even a little while," Harris said. "This is our second visit to the island."

"What business did you say you were in?" the man from Michigan asked. He was short, good-looking, with an inquisitive mind and brisk, forthright actions.

"I'm a salesman," Harris told him. "Work for International Harvester. But I'm thinking of making a change. I have an opportunity to get into military service supplies."

"I thought I heard someone say you were in the newspaper business," the man from Michigan said. He talked at such a fast pace that sometimes Harris could hardly understand him.

"I was...well, we are...My wife is a newspaper publisher. She owns three weekly newspapers back in Minnesota." There were so many conversations going on at once on the hotel porch that it was hard to hear what they were saying to each other. "And you?" Harris asked. "What's your background?"

"My folks came from Poland. My father worked in a foundry," he told Harris. "Grew up in Detroit and after finishing grade school I went to work, while I was still a youngster."

As Harris and the man from Detroit talked, Harris found that his new acquaintance had married his wife, Ethel, in 1931 and had bought a caramel corn business in Detroit two years ago for six hundred dollars.

"Yes, this is our first visit to the island and we weren't sure we could afford all of this," he told Harris. "But I think the island is marvelous," he said enthusiastically. "I wouldn't mind living here myself some day. I can't get enough of that wonderful Mackinac Island fudge. Would like to come back here some day. I'm sure I could run a fudge shop. It's not so different from caramel corn. Who knows, might even run a hotel."

"That would take a lot of work and organization," Harris said. He liked the friendliness of the visitor from Detroit who exuded tremendous sincerity and energy. "My name's Butler, Harris Butler."

"I'm Harry Ryba," the man said and held out his hand to Harris.

"Well, I'm glad I met you," Harris replied, as they shook hands.

The two men talked for a little while longer and then Al Davis walked through the crowded veranda, nodding at some guests and greeting others. It was Ryba who took notice of him.

"Who's that fella, anyway?" he asked.

"That's Mr. Davis," Harris replied. "He's an assistant manager here at the hotel."

"He looks familiar," Harry Ryba said. "I've seen him somewhere before. Some place in Detroit. Can't think of who he is, though."

"I don't know him that well," Harris said. "He was here last year, too."

"It'll come to me."

After Harris left to meet his wife, Harry Ryba sat on the veranda for a while longer and then it came to him. That fella — Davis — the name rang a bell. Of course, Alvin Davis, the hotel man who had been accused of swindling and conning hotel guests in Detroit where Ryba knew the management well. Not a very trustworthy individual, he thought. And he doubted that the management here knew about Davis. Perhaps he should stop and see the hotel manager this afternoon. Yes, this afternoon.

When Ben Butler used to deliver newspapers with his friend, Willy Westin, he learned to be an avid reader. Each day when the newspaper trucks of *The Minneapolis Star*, *The Tribune* and *The Journal* rolled into the busiest corner in Excelsior and dropped their papers, the waiting paper boys would break open a bundle and go immediately to two sections of the current edition — the sports pages and the funnies. This afternoon Ben was thinking about his old newspaper delivery days and what his grandmother had told him about making hard decisions and carrying them through. Dramatically, he thought about the headlines he had peddled when Edward David Windsor had given up the throne of England to marry Mrs. Wallis Warfield Simpson: EDWARD BROADCASTS FAREWELL TODAY! MONARCH TO WED! Edward's famous radio broadcast had been reprinted on the front page of every daily newspaper starting with those famous words: *At long last I am able to say a few words of my own* and telling the world that he had abdicated in favor of *the woman I love.*

Ben felt a little silly, secretly comparing his relationship with Janet to that of the King of England. He realized that it was one of little importance to anyone but himself — and Janet — but he couldn't help but think of those headlines as he waited for Janet to finish the luncheon shift in the Island House dining room. Still he remembered how fascinated he was with those headlines — EDWARD SAILS INTO EXILE.

He couldn't believe his mother would actually go to the hotel management to try to put a stop to Janet seeing him. Now he wondered just what Mr. Davis had meant by his sneering remark about his mother — "Her, of all people. She should be the last one to come in here and complain about mixing with the help." Ben didn't know just what that meant. He'd ask his mother, except he didn't want her to know he, himself, had been to see Davis. And he had already lied to her about how he got the bruises on his face. Just the sound of that man's voice, however, told Ben that his mother had apparently done something distasteful. He saw Janet come out of the hotel and down the walk to the street.

"Hi, Ben," she called out and waved her hand.

"Hello," he replied with a smile.

"I'm sorry if I'm late. The lunch crowd stayed a little longer today and I came early, too." She looked closely at Ben's face. "How did you bruise your cheek?"

"Aw, I just fell off my bike. Nothing serious."

The two walked along the sidewalk toward her rooming house. "I've got some news," Janet said.

"Me, too. Let's hear yours first."

"Well....I went to see your mother this morning."

"You what?" Ben stopped her on the sidewalk. "You went to see *my* mother? When? Why? How did you...."

"I stopped to see her in her room before I went to work today." She paused for a minute and then smiled at Ben. "We had a very nice chat."

"Oh, Jan....I don't know if that was such a good idea."

"I do. I really think it helped," Janet said to him.

"You mean she said it was okay for us to see each other?"

"Well, not exactly. But we *did* talk and she *did* listen. I hope she doesn't think I'm just an older hussy anymore. At least she didn't throw me out of her room."

"Oh, Jan," he said. Then he smiled. "You're really determined, aren't you?" The couple walked along a little further.

"I guess so, Ben," she said. "Now tell me your news." There was an excitement in her voice and Ben liked that. It was fun to have someone eager to listen to what he had to say.

"I went to see someone myself this morning," he told her.

"Oh, who?"

"Al Davis."

Janet stopped again and faced Ben. "You went to see Mr. Davis?"

"Yes. I told him not to bother you anymore."

"Oh, Ben. You shouldn't have...."

"It's okay," he interrupted. "It was just something I had to do." He paused. "And I did it."

"I can't imagine him being very understanding," she said.

"He wasn't. I don't think I was as successful as you were with Mom, but I guess it was worth doing." Actually, Ben wasn't so sure even about that. At least Davis was aware that somebody else knew about his advances to Janet. Ben wasn't about to tell her he got kicked out of Davis' office, and he wasn't quite sure just what else he could do about all of this. Still, he wanted to reassure Janet that everything would be okay.

"I may go back to see him one more time," Ben frowned. "Although, at this late date, I'm not sure just how much good it would do."

"What late date?" Janet asked.

"We've been having such a good time these past few days, and time has gone by so quickly that I didn't realize until today that we're scheduled to leave the island the day after tomorrow."

"Oh, Ben."

"I know, Jan. I feel the same way, too. But I think we're leaving on Wednesday, the thirteenth. It's my mother's birthday and we're going to celebrate it at dinner tomorrow night."

"But Ben. It's going to be our last night. I won't see you."

Ben's eyes lit up. "I know what we'll do."

"What's that, Ben?"

"Well.....why don't you come to dinner tomorrow night — with my folks, the girls and my grandma?"

"Oh, Ben. I don't want to intrude."

"Don't worry," he told her in a reassuring voice, "It's a great idea."

"Well....if you promise me you'll check it out with your folks first. I don't want there to be a scene," she said.

"I promise," he said as he raised his right hand. "Scout's Honor."

Janet smiled. "Maybe it'll be okay," she said. "After all, she knows that both she and I have something in common."

"What's that?" Ben asked.

"I love you, too, Ben."

Ben stopped in his tracks. His face was flushed. No girl had ever said that to him before. He didn't know just what to say. She had caught him off guard. He knew that he loved her, but he wasn't quite ready to say it again right here. He felt invigorated. He felt good. He felt foolish. He wanted to say, "I love you, Jan. I love you more than anything in the world. And to think that you love me...." But the moment passed too quickly and he knew he had missed it. It was not the place or the time to tell her. Not now. There would be another time. He looked at her and smiled and squeezed her hand.

"You're something else," he said to her as he smiled.

"Why do you say that?" she asked him. "Are you embarrassed?"

"A little," he admitted.

"Don't be," she said. "I thought I would be the one who would feel funny about telling you how I felt, but it seemed so natural when I told your mom that...."

"You told that to my mom?" he interrupted. "Oh, God!"

"It's okay, Ben. Really."

"What did she say?"

"She said she had bigger plans for you."

Ben stopped and faced Janet and took her hands. "We need to talk some more, Jan, but not here."

"We have today and tomorrow and we'll get a chance to be together tomorrow night," she reminded him.

"Tomorrow night," Ben agreed. The more he thought about it, the more he was convinced he could handle it all right. But he wasn't so sure that his mother could....without a drink.

CHAPTER 11

Monday, July 11

Al Davis had finished a busy day at work and after a few beers, he was off to his room in the back of the third floor of the Island House. He was pleased with himself. He had skimmed some more money over the past weekend and although he had just about written off any meeting with Marian Stanhope, there was still a possibility that she would relent and perhaps find his room again. He certainly wouldn't be surprised. But he had some other things going for him. He hadn't given up on that waitress, the Rachel girl, and there was a new prospect on the horizon, too — Mrs. Butler. But he had checked the Butler reservation and time was running out. They were scheduled to leave the island on Wednesday.

Up in his room, Al threw his sportcoat and tie on the bed and opened a window to let the crisp evening air into the stuffy room. It had been a long day and this was a good night to catch up on some much-needed sleep. He unbuttoned his shirt, slipped off his shoes, lit up a cigarette and stretched out on the bed to relax. He had no idea that so many people were thinking about him at this very moment.

Billy Lachine had just tied up his sailboat for the night and was leaving the dock and heading for his rooming house. He could see the Island House glowing with lights from rooms across the front of the hotel and there were still small clusters of people gathering in groups along the front porch and veranda in the cool of the early evening. He was worried about Al. Not that Al couldn't take care of himself. He certainly didn't need an eighteen-year-old kid looking after him. But Billy was worried just the same. He'd been thinking about what Al said to him concerning Janet Rachel and her roommate, and he still wasn't sure just what Ben Butler was doing in that hallway that led to Al's office. Maybe he'd ask Al about it all tomorrow. Billy didn't know exactly what, but there was something going on — and he had the feeling that whatever it was, it wasn't good.

Katie, Hillary and the girls were riding in a taxi carriage up to the Grand Hotel this evening to see a movie being shown in the ballroom at nine o'clock. Katie had been mulling over the Al Davis incident. She knew he had offered a subtle proposition to her but the bastard was really doing nothing more than blackmailing her. Maybe she could fix his wagon, but maybe it wasn't worth the time. They only had two more days left on the island and the entire matter of Ben and that girl would be over. She also understood why Ben had declined to come along tonight — and it was all right with her. Ben had come to see her to ask if Janet could be included in the birthday party plans. Katie wasn't sure just why it had been so easy to say "yes." Perhaps it was reassuring just to know Ben was happy again. She felt that closeness again. She even surprised herself when she told him, "Of course it would be okay, Ben." Then she added, "In fact, I was going to suggest it anyway," she lied.

She thought about it as the taxi clattered along the way to the Grand. She hated to admit it, even to herself, but her son was changing — right here on this trip — and she already knew that he would no longer be the innocent and obedient teenager she had brought along to Mackinac Island.

She didn't blame Harris for not coming along this evening, either. They had argued this afternoon about Ben and other things. Harris was not his usual passive self, Katie told herself. He had defended Ben in a quiet, rational manner, which made her even more angry. All that had prompted a couple of extra drinks for her and some nasty name-calling on Katie's part. If that wasn't enough, he had dropped another bombshell into their lives that would have far more serious repercussions than Ben's summer romance. She simply hadn't been prepared for what had apparently been on her husband's mind for quite some time.

"I talked to Gerry Hagen just before I came up to Mackinac last week," Harris had said to Katie. "He's doing very well in his new job but it's getting too big for him and he needs help. He wants me to come in with him."

"You mean you'd leave International Harvester and go somewhere else rather than come back to our newspaper?" Katie asked while she freshened up in their room this afternoon.

"He's making twice as much money as he did before, and he thinks the possibilities are almost unlimited," Harris said.

"Isn't Gerry involved with something he's selling to the government?" Katie asked suspiciously.

"Well — yes," Harris admitted. "But now he's got his hands on a product that they're going to use in new airplanes for the Army and Navy and —"

"My God, Harris," Katie interrupted and turned to face him in the middle of the hotel room. "Don't tell me you're going to perpetuate those damn headlines I've been reading in the newspapers. Everywhere I look, I see more bombings and fighting and threats of war. Doesn't that mean anything to you?"

"Of course it does, Kate. But I'm not starting any war, and neither is Gerry. All he's doing is selling. It just happens to be something used by the military."

"It sounds terribly chancey to me," Katie said. "I should think dealing with the government is pretty risky business. After the next election, you could be out in the street."

"I don't think so, Kate. Not when you're dealing with the services. And besides, the profits are enormous," Harris said.

"Why worry about money?" she asked. "My God, we've got plenty now. Why don't you just come back to the newspaper business and enjoy yourself and your family?"

"Aw, come on, Kate. The money you're talking about is *your* money and I can never seem to forget it. But it's not just the money. There's something about the challenge of this new job that excites me. Besides, I know Gerry Hagen and he's a good salesman and he's honest. He'd make a good business partner."

Katie didn't want to hear anymore right now. She already had enough problems reconciling her differences with Ben and with her mother. Now it was Harris. "We'll talk about this later," she said to her husband as she headed for the bathroom. "I just wish to hell you could get as excited about me as you seem to be about another job."

She slammed the door to the bathroom, then leaned against it and looked in the mirror. What she saw in her face wasn't very pleasant. She had just hurt Harris again, just as she had hurt Hillary yesterday. Then everything was quiet. Harris had apparently left the hotel room. She couldn't blame him.

The team of horses clip-clopped along, pulling the carriage with Katie and Hillary and the girls towards the Grand Hotel. She'd try to make it up to Harris for this afternoon's unpleasantness. Maybe a few years in dealing with the government would make him happy to come back to the paper. She didn't want to think about it now, but she was sorry for him. He was supposed to be relaxing on this trip and so far he had been busy with Ben and the girls, traipsing around the island. He had begged off the movie tonight in favor of a quiet walk through the downtown section of the island and to bed early. She thought one more time about Davis and then turned her thoughts back to her mother and the girls riding with her in the carriage. They were almost up to the Grand now and they were looking forward to seeing the movie. It was Robert Donat and Elissa Landi in *The Count of Monte Cristo*. Perhaps she would treat them all to something in the lounge at the Grand after the movie before going back to the hotel.

Janet finished the dinner shift in the hotel dining room and met Ben for a hamburger early in the evening. They talked about what each had done during the day and their joy and enthusiasm spilled over into plans for the future.

"Maybe I could come up here and work next summer after I finish school and before I go to the University of Minnesota," Ben said.

"I don't think your folks would like that idea very much," she cautioned him.

"I suppose you're right." He smiled. "But it would be fun."

"I'm not even sure I'd come back another summer," she confided. "It takes a lot of money to go on to school..."

Both of them realized they were fantasizing about such things, and Ben searched for some other way to see her next summer. "Maybe you could come and visit at our house."

"You mean come to Excelsior?" she asked, excitedly.

"Sure, why not? We've got a big house. And my grandma lives alone."

"I don't know how you'd ever get your folks to invite me," she said.

"You just never know," Ben said. "If not, maybe I could come to see you."

Janet shook her head. "I'd love to get you out on the farm. That would really be fun."

"I think it would be, too," Ben agreed.

They talked some more and said there would be plenty of time to work something out before next summer. Surely, there had to be a way. In the meantime, they would make the most of the time they had left on the island. Then Ben took her back to her rooming house where they kissed goodnight.

When Janet got to her room on the second floor of the Mackinac House, she was exhausted. She hadn't realized until then what a long day she had put in. She slipped out of her waitress uniform and was relieved that this working day was over. She had tried to avoid Mr. Davis throughout the day and hoped that he wouldn't call her back into his office again. She was no longer worried about the threat of losing her job if she continued to see Ben. After all, she was going to have dinner with Ben's family. As for Ben's mother, Janet still had some misgivings. She was glad she had gone to Mrs. Butler and had their little talk. Perhaps Ben's mother got more out of their confrontation than she did. At least, Janet hoped, there wouldn't be any more hassle about them seeing each other. After all, they only had one night left and Ben would be gone. She didn't like it, but the questions kept creeping into the back of her mind. Will I ever see him again? Will he write to me? What am I going to do at school when he's not there? Maybe he really will invite me to come to Minnesota for a visit. I can't imagine how it will be when he's not here. Only one more night.

It was something she didn't want to think about.

It was still early in the evening when Marian decided she would take a short walk down Huron Street through the main business district of the island. Harvey said he was tired and was going up to their room to go to bed early.

Marian worried. Perhaps he wasn't feeling well and didn't want to alarm her. But she needed to get away for just a little while so she took the walk. She wasn't sure just what had lured her into the bar on main street. Perhaps it was the music and the friendly sounds of vacationers and college workers laughing and drinking. She couldn't resist and quickly found herself sitting at a corner table, sipping a cold beer. That was when she saw the familiar-looking gentleman sitting at the bar. He turned to look out over the crowd in the smokey bar and she recognized him at once. It was Harris Butler. He reminded her of some of her customers from her younger days. She had always enjoyed the company of real gentlemen, but her contact with them had been as a prostitute. She decided to turn on the charm. Marian waved to him and caught his eye. Harris slid off the bar stool and worked his way through the crowded tables to where Marian was sitting.

"Mr. Butler. What are you doing here? Haven't you had enough for one day? I've seen you coming and going with your kids all day long."

"Mrs. Stanhope," he answered. "I could ask you the same question."

"Call me Marian," she said.

"If you'll call me Harris," he replied.

"Harv — my husband went to bed early and I thought I'd take a short walk." She looked around. "It just seemed so warm and friendly in here that I couldn't resist."

"Sounds familiar," Harris said. "The same thing happened to me. My wife just left to take her mother and the girls up to the Grand to see a movie tonight. I didn't think I was quite up to that, so I begged off." Harris looked around the bar. "I guess I just needed to unwind a bit before turning in."

Harris ordered two more beers and he and Marian sat in the corner of the bar and talked about the day and about their spouses and about their lives.

"You're from Minnesota, aren't you?" Marian asked.

"That's right," Harris smiled. "And you?"

"Detroit. Lived there all my life." She paused and smiled back. "You have a nice family. I've been watching them from the veranda at the Island House."

"They're good kids," Harris agreed. "But I'm afraid my son has a crush on a waitress at the hotel."

"I know," Marian said as she smiled. "I've seen them together."

"I hope it doesn't get too serious," Harris said.

"Don't worry about it. They're young and innocent. Let them enjoy a few romantic days." Marian looked up from her beer, almost embarrassed at what she had said. For someone who enjoyed romantic notions, she hadn't experienced too many in her lifetime. Sex, yes. But romance.....

"You're probably right." Harris sipped at his beer. "They're just kids. Good kids." It seemed like such a long time ago since he had been one of those good kids. Now he found himself in a bar, talking about kids and romance with a virtual stranger. And a very attractive one at that.

Harris finally looked at his watch. The time had passed all too quickly.

"Come on," he said as he stood up. "I'll walk you back to the hotel."

Marian agreed and the two of them stepped out into the cool island air of the night and started back up the street past Marquette Park. It felt good to have someone holding on to his arm, Harris thought. Katie was far too independent for that and had stopped such practices a long time ago. Besides, Marian Stanhope was a very attractive lady. Harris could sense that she wasn't even aware of a certain sensuous aura about her. When they arrived at the Island House, it was still glistening with lights on the porch, the lobby and from many of the rooms throughout the four-story hotel. Harris and Marian walked through the lobby and up the stairs to the north wing. When they reached the second floor, the couple stopped at the head of the stairs. Harris found it an awkward moment.

"Our room is down around the corner," she said.

"Our's is up on the next floor," he nodded up the stairs.

"I'll walk you to your room," he said.

"I don't think that's a good idea," Marian whispered. "Harvey might not understand." She paused. "To tell you the truth, I'm not really that tired. But I've enjoyed our visit together downtown."

"So have I," he said softly, and smiled.

Marian put her arms around his neck and kissed Harris with a long, inviting kiss.

"I thought I was too old for that sort of thing," he said quietly.

"I don't think you're ever too old for that," she replied.

For one fleeting moment, Harris thought about taking Marian to his room. Katie would be at the movie for quite awhile yet. What's good for the goose is good for the gander, he thought. He felt a certain excitement and here was his chance to prove that he wasn't so bland after all. The moment passed quickly, but in that instant, Harris had gained a new self-confidence.

"You are a very attractive lady," he said with a smile, "but...."

Marian sensed the change. "You should know that you are handsome — and a very nice man," she told him quietly. She already knew the evening was at an end.

"Thank you," Harris replied. Then he gathered her in his arms and kissed her. "Goodnight," he whispered.

"Goodnight — and thanks," she said. Then she turned and hurried down the hall toward room 200.

What happens after we all leave the island on Wednesday? What happens to Jan? How can she avoid that hotel guy? What if he won't leave her alone? These were all questions Ben was asking himself as he waited in the lobby to see Al Davis. He was determined to try one more time to get some assurance from the assistant manager that Janet would be left alone and that she wouldn't lose her job. He wasn't sure he was doing the right thing and he lightly rubbed his hand over the bruise on the cheek to remind himself of his last meeting with Davis.

When he could wait no longer, Ben finally went to the front desk and asked again about Mr. Davis.

"Oh, he finished work quite some time ago," the desk clerk told him. "But I don't think he's left the hotel. Probably in his room."

"And what is his room number?" Ben asked politely.

"He's in 322."

"Thanks," Ben said as he headed for the stairs.

The desk clerk went back to his work and wondered why Al was so popular this evening. That was the second person who had asked for Al's room number that night.

Ben climbed the stairs to the third floor and started down the hall. He stood in front of the door for almost a minute. He could see the light under the bottom of the door and he finally took a deep breath and was about to knock when he heard someone coming down the hall. Ben looked around. There was no place to hide, but he quickly turned the corner of the hall and stood in the shadows of the dim light. Slowly and methodically, the footsteps came, past the corner and beyond. Ben recognized the man.

The man stopped in front of 322 and, like Ben, he waited for the longest time. He had thought about Al Davis throughout the day and still wasn't quite sure just how to handle him. But an anger had been festering inside of him and he eventually came to a hard decision. He had poked around in the bottom of an old trunk he had brought with him to the island. It was a long, narrow piece of luggage and little out of date. It had been designed to be carried on the running board of an automobile. At the bottom of the trunk, wrapped in an old bath towel, was the gun, a small Remington revolver. The bullets had been carefully wrapped in a white handkerchief and placed in the folds of the towel.

Now, as he stood before room 322 and looked down at the floor to see the light peaking under the door, he took the revolver out of his seersucker sportcoat pocket and looked at the gun. Then he shoved his right hand holding the gun back into his coat pocket and knocked on the door with his left hand.

Inside, Al had started to take off his shirt but when he heard the knock at the door, he smiled and buttoned the shirt part way up again, put out his cigarette, smoothed back his hair, unlocked the door and opened it. It took a few seconds for his eyes to adjust to the light before he could recognize the caller.

Standing in the dimly-lit hallway was Harvey Stanhope.

"Mr. Stanhope! What a surprise."

"May I come in?" Harvey asked as he moved through the door into Al's room.

"Sure, sure," Al replied. His voice sounded flustered. "Is there something I can do for you, Mr. Stanhope?"

"No, not really," Harvey answered. He stood in the middle of the room with great confidence. Al appeared nervous, reached to his dresser and took a cigarette out of the box of Viceroys. At that moment, Harvey almost lost his temper, but he held on and slowly pulled the gun out of his coat pocket. "But I think I can do something for you, Mr. Davis."

Al had started to light his cigarette when he saw the revolver in Harvey's hand. It was shaking, but no more than Al was at that moment. Al dropped the match on the floor and held up both hands. "Oh, my God!" he gasped. "Please, Mr. Stanhope," he pleaded, "Please, please put that gun down."

Harvey continued to point the gun at Al. "You've probably had this coming for a long time, Davis. I'm sure there are other husbands and probably a few fathers who would have loved to be in my shoes at this moment."

"You'll get caught. Somebody will hear — they'll see you," he said frantically as his cigarette fell out of his mouth. He was visibly shaking.

"I've been thinking about this all day long," Harvey said. "I couldn't make up my mind whether to shoot you or not. Just when I would make the decision to go ahead and kill you, I'd have some afterthoughts. Were you really worth it? After all, the police are going to know that I did it. At least the police in Detroit are going to know." Al could not take his eyes off the gun in Harvey's hand. "I'm not even sure right now," Harvey admitted.

"I'm not worth it, Mr. Stanhope. Really, I'm not." Al was almost crying.

"Perhaps not." He kept the gun pointed on Al. A half-smile crept across Harvey's face.

"I was wondering if the hotel management here knows about your book-juggling in Chicago and at the hotel in Detroit, Davis."

Al was getting sick to his stomach. "I'm not sure just what you mean, Mr. Stanhope," he said with as much confidence as he could muster.

"I'm talking about the incident at the Blackstone Hotel in Chicago, and the embezzling in Detroit."

"Oh, that was all a mistake and I told them I couldn't work for an outfit like that and left." He hesitated for a moment. "Nothing serious — nothing serious — honest."

"And about the women — and the rape charge?"

Al's confidence was waning, now. How in hell did this son-of-a-bitch find out about all of this?

Before Al could answer, Harvey had gone on. "I'm going to stop to see the manager of this hotel late tomorrow morning, Davis, and suggest that he check into your police record in Detroit and your association with the Blackstone in Chicago." Harvey's voice was gaining strength. "And while I'm at it, I'm going to suggest that perhaps the management here should take a look at the books of the Island House. I understand that you sometimes serve as the night auditor here, too." Harvey was just fishing, but he supposed that Al did some night book-work.

Al was actually getting ill. It was bad enough that his escapades in Chicago and Detroit had come home to roost. But the last thing he wanted was for someone here to start checking the books.

"I really don't know what you're talking about, Mr. Stanhope."

"Then you don't have anything to worry about, do you?" Harvey's face strained to break into a toothy grin. "Otherwise, I suggest that you pack up and get the hell out while you can. If you're still here tomorrow when I stop to see the manager....."

"Has this got anything to do with....." Al stopped short. He was going to try to explain away his attention to Marian, but thought better of it. He was on dangerous ground, now, but he was desperate. The grin was gone from Harvey's face, and for just an instant, he had second thoughts and brought the gun into line with Al's chest. Then he slipped the revolver back into his coat pocket and turned to leave the room. He stopped in the doorway and looked back one last time.

"You get the hell out tomorrow." His voice meant business. Then he disappeared down the darkened hallway.

Al Davis shut the door, looked around his room and shook his head. "Goddamn that Horseface! I oughta shoot *him*!"

Out in the hall, Ben stood pressed up against the wall in a dark corner. It seemed as though he had been holding his breath for an hour. He had seen the gun and had heard it all, and for a time, he thought he was about to witness a murder and wasn't quite sure what to do about it. He felt good about one thing. Mr. Davis was going to get what was coming to him. And that Mr. Stanhope. Ben had a new admiration for the man who had a hard time smiling and seemed to walk with just a slight limp. Ben's heart was still pounding, almost breaking the silence of the dark hallway.

CHAPTER 12

Tuesday, July 12

Ben and Janet had walked up the steep ramp to the South Sally Port of Fort Mackinac at mid-morning and had wandered around the old fort's grounds. They visited some of the old buildings which faced the green quadrangle and imagined what the Commissary and the Quartermaster's Storerooms had been like in days gone by, filled with medical supplies, candles, food for the mess hall, coffee, meats, produce, flour and such items as soap, muskets and uniforms.

Fort Mackinac, which overlooked Marquette Park and the island's harbor some 130 feet below and held a commanding view of the Straits of Mackinac, had seen many changes. The fort itself was the outgrowth of other forts. The first on the straits was built by the French at St. Ignace back in the early 1600's. Then came the British with their Fort Michilimackinac on the south side of the straits, built during the French and Indian War. It was 1780 before the British moved their entrenchments to Mackinac Island during the American revolution, and although the Americans won the conflict, they did not take control of Fort Mackinac and the island until 1796.

The fort changed hands again, however, during the War of 1812 with the invasion of the island at the famous British Landing. An American attempt to recapture the fort failed but the British finally gave it back in 1814 after the Treaty of Ghent had been signed.

Even though the fort would never change hands again, there were times during the next eighty years when the American garrison would be off to serve its country. In the early 1800's, soldiers were gone again to fight for the United States in the Indian wars. In 1861, they left to fight in the Civil War, and in the interim, the fort once housed Confederate prisoners. In 1875, the fort and part of the island had become the second National Park in the country's history. Twenty years later, the last U.S. Army contingent left the fort and it was turned over to the state of Michigan with the eventual formation of the Mackinac Island State Park Commission. It was Michigan's first state park.

Through it all, the island had changed from those early days of French missionaries and British soldiers to the fruitful days of the American Fur Company and the voyageurs. It changed again with the coming of the fishing industry and eventually moved into a popular vacation paradise for visiting Great Lakes excursion boats and then to one of the most popular tourist attractions in the country. Through it all, Fort Mackinac remained, and until almost the turn of the century, its primary function was soldiering. It had been the site of hours upon hours of army drills, guard duty, assemblies, of long, cold winters, of loneliness, sickness, desertion, and of many changes of command. Those same soldiers also enjoyed music and card games and chess and baseball and became part of the island's social scene with parties and dances. They hauled water, cut firewood, took care of animals, and even cultivated gardens where they grew their own food.

Hand in hand, Ben and Janet walked through the Soldiers' Barracks, the Dining Hall, the School House, the Officers' Stone Quarters and the Block Houses. They stood at the very precipice of the fort and could see Marquette Park below where visitors sat and rested in between tourist attractions. Student workers on the island gathered on the lush green grass of the park to pass some of their off-hours. Young female students stretched out to sun bathe, while young men played catch with baseballs and softballs and threw sticks for their pet dogs to retrieve. From the heights of the fort, the traffic along Huron Street, the bikes, the pedestrians, and the carriages all seemed miniature to Ben and Janet as the traffic seemingly crawled along the avenue on this busy morning. They could also see some cruisers and sailboats moored in the harbor and Ben spotted his favorite sailboat — the one belonging to Billy Lachine.

The two young people stood there for a long time, hardly speaking. They were still holding hands when Janet finally spoke.

"It's beautiful up here, isn't it?"

Ben nodded, "Yes."

"You can see the roof of the Island House from here," she said.

"Yes."

"You're awfully quiet this morning, Ben. Is there something wrong?" she asked.

In an instant, all the scenes of Mackinac Island he had experienced over this past week had flashed through his mind: his first meeting Janet; the time he'd spent with his father; his first meeting with Al Davis; last night's encounter between Mr. Stanhope and Mr. Davis; the unpleasantries of standing up to his mother; and most important of all, his time here on the island with Janet.

Janet asked him again. "Something wrong?"

His mind was back to the present now. "No. No, Jan. I guess I was just thinking about all that has happened to me — to us — in the past week. And now there's hardly any time left."

"I know," she replied. Then smiled. "But we're not going to let that spoil this last day on the island for you."

"Or for you," he added.

"I've got the day off, remember?"

The two of them watched the sights of the town below. They could hear the sounds of the horses, the clanging of the dray wagons, the urgent commands of drivers as they guided their teams, and the full sounds of the steam whistle from a ferry boat. They decided they would walk up into the inner-part of the island, left Fort Mackinac and started up the sandy road toward Fort Holmes. Even at the top of the island, there was the fresh smell of the lake, mixed with the fragrances of wild flowers everywhere. Along the trail and path through the woods there was a certain peacefulness, broken only by the sounds of the island birds and the rustle of the leaves from the soft winds.

"I'm a little nervous about coming to your mom's birthday party tonight," she told Ben.

"Don't be. She was really very gracious about it when we talked."

"I'll be nervous, anyway," she said.

"It'll be okay," he assured her. "My mom will be nice. She's really a nice person. And you have a lot of other people on your side — my dad, grandma, and, of course, the kids."

They finally reached Fort Holmes, the highest point of Mackinac Island.

"Do you know why this place is named Fort Holmes?" Jan asked.

"I know about the fort, but I don't know how it got its name," Ben told her.

"I looked up all of these historic sites when I first came to the island," she said, "and originally, it was named Fort George by the British. The Americans re-named the old fort after Andrew Hunter Holmes who was killed in the attack on the British in 1814."

"If you know so much," Ben smiled, "tell me about Skull Cave."

"Oh, that's easy. The cave dates back to the middle 1700's when some Englishman hid there to escape an Indian uprising. After spending the night in the cave, he discovered he had been sleeping on a floor of human bones — a final resting place for Indians from years ago."

The two walked along the lonely road, on to Arch Rock where they had been a few nights ago. "Now it's your turn, Ben Butler. Tell me about Arch Rock."

"That's one place I know about," he said enthusiastically, "It's one of the better-known landmarks on the island. I think the rock formation actually comes from thousands of years of erosion by the wind and water. But an Indian legend tells of an Indian maid who was forbidden to marry a young brave. When she began to cry, her tears washed away the stone, leaving Arch Rock."

Ben turned to look at Janet. The story and the talk of tears had brought tears to Janet's eyes. "Jan....what's the matter," Ben asked.

"It's all right," she said as she wiped the tears away. "I guess the story reminded me of ourselves and I realized that you were leaving tomorrow."

Ben put his arm around her and kissed her on the cheek. "I know, I know."

Janet was happy and frightened at the same time. She had never been so happy. All the romantic fantasies that she had dreamt about back on the farm could not match the joy she found in this real live romance with Ben. She hadn't realized how lonely those times were on the farm until now. She knew now that what she had thought were high school romances and special dates were nothing. The excitement of the 4-H meeting in Chicago, the thrill of her senior prom in the school gym, the all-night graduation party with the captain of the football team — those seemingly important moments in her young life were now wiped clean from her past. Ben Butler had changed everything. And now she was afraid, afraid of their time running out, afraid of losing him and being alone again. She held on to his hand tightly. She wanted him to do more than kiss her on the cheek. But she knew that at this moment, he wouldn't. And it was all right. Then she thought about the dinner they would attend in Katie's honor, and she knew that somehow, tonight would be a very special night for Ben — and herself.

The woman was plain looking. She wore practically no makeup at all but there was a certain classic look about her face which gave hints of her having been a beautiful young woman who had lived a hard life, even before the depression. At times, when she looked into a mirror, she would even admit to herself that if she worked at it, she could be much prettier. She was forty years old but looked older. She was dressed very simply in a cotton frock and wore pumps with low heels. Except for a few special occasions, she had only worn the shoes to church on Sundays. On the trip from the mainland to Mackinac Island aboard the ferry, she had worn a short white summer coat which felt good in the brisk breeze on this Tuesday afternoon. During the short trip, she had sat by herself, away from the rest of the passengers, and clutched a white purse, as if it contained her life savings. She had purchased her ticket in St. Ignace and spoke to no one while waiting for the ferry or while on the trip over. When the boat arrived on the island, she was lost in the crowd which left the ferry and stepped on to the main pier. It was her first visit to Mackinac Island and as far as she knew, she had never met a single person now living on the island. The ill-fitting dress hid what was still a slim and attractive figure of the woman as she walked along the pier towards the island's main street.

In spite of her plainness, she had a certain confidence about her, a sense of purpose. She asked a man with a horse and buggy the directions to the Island House and then walked along the crowded sidewalk in that direction. She wasn't used to so many people, but strangely enough, she felt at home. She had grown up on a farm in Wisconsin where her folks had horses as well as a dairy herd. She had married when she was sixteen and moved to a small Wisconsin town, Pembine, where her husband owned a Pure Oil gas station. He had died in a car accident shortly after their daughter was born, a little over 18 years ago, and she had decided not to go back to the farm. Instead, she stayed on in town, worked as a housekeeper and eventually got a job in a local cafe as a waitress. Then she was offered a job as a teller in the local state bank and had raised her daughter.

The woman was impressed with her first glimpse of the Island House. She stopped and looked at it in awe. It was the largest hotel she had ever seen. Then she proceeded down the sidewalk and up the front walk between the twin trees to the front steps. Inside, she went directly to the reservations desk.

"May I leave this envelope for Mr. Davis, please?" she politely asked the young man at the desk.

"Of course," he smiled at her. "He won't be in for a little while and I'm going off duty now. But I'll leave it on his desk."

"Thank you," the woman said. Then she turned and left the lobby and the Island House. When she reached the street, she stopped and looked back at the hotel for a moment. She even thought about finding the Mackinac House and even asking for Janet Rachel, but decided against it and started walking back toward the center of town. She had some time now to see a few of the sights and visit the stores along the main street. Then she would have to find out just where the boardwalk was located.

"What do you mean, you're leaving the island?" Billy Lachine asked Al as the two stood on the dock next to Billy's sailboat. The older man really didn't have any close friends on the island, and although he was not in the habit of explaining his actions to anyone, he felt some obligation to tell Billy he was leaving. So he had come down to the docks this afternoon to tell the young man.

"Can't be helped, kid. I just quit my job."

"You quit?" Billy asked. "Why?"

"Aw, some rich bag has been bitchin' about me to the manager."

"Well, didn't he stick up for you?"

"Naw, you don't know him like I do. Besides, I think he's been tapping the till and wants to use this chance to hang it on me. And I'm just not sticking around for that."

"Gee, Al, what are you going to do?"

"Think I'll go out west — maybe California."

"But you didn't do anything wrong, did you?"

"Naw, kid." Al smiled. "Sometimes it just seems to look that way. Anyway, it's probably time for me to move on, even though I liked the work, the women and the island. And I like you, Billy."

Billy wasn't sure just how to handle all of this. He tried to be nonchalant about it all, but within himself he was crushed. Al had been a good friend, sometimes even like a father.

"I'm sorry, Al," he said reluctantly. "I'm sorry to see you go."

"It's okay, Billy," Al assured him.

"You sure you can't work it out?"

"No way, Billy."

"Well — when do you leave?" Billy asked.

"Probably tonight, on the last boat. I'm all packed."

"Gosh, this has all happened so fast. I don't know what to say," Billy stammered.

"You don't have to say anything. I tried to find you at the hotel before I left but you weren't around. I figured you'd be down here on your boat. I have something for you." Al slid a gold wristwatch off his left hand and gave it to Billy. "Here, kid. You deserve this. Keep it as a gift from me."

"Aw, I can't take that," Billy resisted. He was embarrassed.

"Go ahead and take it," Al urged the young man. "I didn't steal it if that's what you're thinking. It's really a good watch. A Waltham Yankee Clipper. Keeps damn good time, too. You take it and wear it." He smiled. "It'll remind you of the good times we had together at the Island House."

"Well..."

"And you can do one more thing for me." Al reached into his inside jacket pocket and pulled out a small envelope. "Give this to Mrs. Stanhope before she leaves the island, will you?"

"Sure, Al. I sure will."

The two shook hands and said goodbye, and Al started back towards the hotel. Down at the main pier, a steamwhistle announced the departure of another ferryboat, reminding Al that he, too, would be on one of those boats before the day was over. He knew that those on the ferry felt sad about leaving the island. Everyone felt that way. The only difference was that when Al left, he knew he wasn't coming back again. At least not for a very long time. Then he put such matters out of his mind and thought about the surprise he found on his desk earlier today. It was the note which had been left by someone at the front desk, and it had caused him to change his plans and take a late ferry back to the mainland tonight.

Dear Mr. Davis,

No one knows I'm here on the island today. I'm leaving the island for the mainland on the last ferry. In the meantime, I would like to see you, but I prefer that no one knows I am here. Please meet me at the far end of the boardwalk tonight at dusk. I'll be there, I promise you.

H.G.

Al smiled. The note, of course, was from Helen Gunter, the Rachel girl's roommate who had gone home unexpectedly last month. He was pleased that she had sought him out. *I knew she really liked it, even with all that complaining,* he told himself. *It was too good to be true. Maybe they could even leave the island together, stay in a cabin court tonight on the mainland. Maybe he'd take her to California.* Even with all its problems, the day wasn't going to turn out so bad after all.

Back on the dock, Billy watched a departing ferryboat back away from the pier and leave the harbor. Al would be doing that later this evening. He looked at the envelope which he had promised to deliver to Mrs. Stanhope at the hotel. Then he looked at the wristwatch and smiled, and slipped it over his left hand. The watch was a souvenir of an affair with a lonely widow back in Detroit. It still had her husband's initials on the back.

CHAPTER 13

Tuesday, July 12

The round table had been clothed in sparkling white and the hotel had made a special effort to use its finest dinnerware for the occasion. The family gathering had sat in polished high-back chairs and not only talked about the events of the day but reminisced over all the happenings of the past week on the island. As usual, the dining room was busy with other hotel guests being served during the dinner hour.

It was a new experience for Janet to be sitting at the table with the hotel guests and being waited on by her fellow employees. It gave her an opportunity to look around the dining room and see things she never noticed before. She had worked in the room since the first week in June but had never noticed the old photographs of ships and sailboats of the Great Lakes framed on the dining room walls. One large photo showing a gathering of members of the Yacht Club must have been taken at a regatta many years ago. The Island House was still the headquarters for the annual regatta after all these years. Even though the room was old, it had apparently been redecorated this past spring before the opening of the summer season. There was no carpeting or rugs in the dining area, but the old wood floor was spotless and clean. There were fresh, green plants everywhere. A half-wall and railing separated the dining area from part of the hotel lobby and other hotel guests stopped on their way to and from their rooms to look at the activity in the dining room. At the very entrance was a table on which there was a large military field drum, painted red, white and blue, and adorned with an ornate golden American Eagle.

The family joked with Katie about the small number of candles on the birthday cake which they all enjoyed as dessert. Actually, Katie was now forty-three years old — a very attractive forty-three. When they finished their dinner and dessert, Harris suggested that they move out to the front veranda on this warm summer evening where Katie could open her birthday presents. Other guests of the hotel occupied various areas of the long front porch, but the veranda seemed to have somehow been saved especially for Katie's birthday party. In contrast to the maze of lights throughout the hotel was the darkness of Lake Huron across the way. Sailing sloops rolled lazily in the light waves of the night and a few dimly-lighted cruisers broke the blackness of the harbor. The rows of old street lamps along both sides of the main street cast dull light on a few passing carriages where the clip-clops of the teams broke the night air. Overhead, the clear July sky prompted one hotel guest to surmise that the Island House's veranda would be a wonderful place from which to watch an eclipse of the moon.

The Butler party pulled some white wooden porch chairs into a circle to watch Katie open her gifts. The first was from her husband and in a small package — a birthstone ring. It was a beautiful ruby in a solitaire gold setting. Katie loved the ring. Harris was always so thoughtful. She thought about those early days in college where she had first met him. How handsome he was, and how damn proper he was. Ben was a lot like him in that respect. Harris hadn't even kissed her on their first date and it took months before she could entice him into making love to her in her room on the second floor of a dormitory on the university campus. Katie had been the aggressor. Their relationship had never changed since that night, and she thought about it all as she admired the new birthday ring. Yes, Harris was a good husband and father and had always been kind to her parents. He had surely been loyal to her father at the newspaper and it wasn't until after Emmett's death that

Harris finally changed jobs. How he could be such a damn good salesman and still be so passive in bed was beyond her. Katie smiled. She
was pleased with the gift all right, but she was smiling as she thought
about Harris and all these things, and she just knew he would never
feel the exhilaration of an affair.

The girls had gone together and bought Katie a sweater. It was
white, with a crew neck and although it was very simple, it was elegant, and obviously expensive.

"It's a lovely sweater," Katie said enthusiastically. "And I love
white." She looked at the two beaming faces of the girls. "I hope you
didn't spend all of your vacation money on this gift," she said. "And
Annabelle — you didn't have to buy me anything."

"We wanted to," Annabelle replied.

"Yes, we looked all day today before we finally bought it."

It was true. They had scoured the Mackinac Island shops and then
dragged Harris along to see the final selection — and to pay for it.

Katie knew that Harris had paid for it, but she was pleased, and so
thankful for 12-year-olds. Blair still had a lot of growing up to do and a
long time to spend in the Butler household. At least she wouldn't be off
to college in another year like Ben, Katie thought.

While others watched Katie open her gifts and admired the presents, Hillary sat quietly and watched her daughter with great intensity.
Her mind drifted back — way back — to a Christmas Eve before Katie
was born. The year was 1894 and she and Emmett and their son,
Jamie, had come home to Excelsior from Minneapolis for the holiday.
Her folks had also arrived from St. Louis. She had kept an appointment
with old Doc Perkins late that afternoon and found she was going to
have another baby. The pregnancy had been easy, except for the last
month when the summer turned especially warm. She remembered the
day of Katie's birth and how pleased Emmett had been. She also
remembered Katie's namesake, Kitty Ging, who had befriended her
when Hillary was a lonely new resident of Minneapolis. Hillary
realized at this moment that her daughter had so many qualities of
Kitty: she was beautiful, very smart, and aggressive. That's the way

Kitty was — until she was murdered. It all came back to Hillary now as she watched Katie open the gift from her mother. In the small gift box was a gold cross and chain.

"Oh, Mother," Katie exclaimed. "It's your own cross."

"Yes, dear," Hillary said. "I want you to have it and I thought this was the appropriate time to give it to you. It's very old and here we are on Mackinac Island, almost as though we have turned the clock back to another time."

"It's beautiful," Katie said.

It was especially an appropriate time for Hillary. Emmett had given her the cross on that Christmas Eve so long ago when she told him the good news — she was pregnant with Katie.

The family kidded Katie about all of the small gift boxes she had been given this evening. Ben's was the last such present — another small package. Katie accepted it gracefully and took the joking good-naturedly. Ben's gift to his mother was another piece of jewelry; this time a small, silver sailboat for her charm bracelet.

"A souvenir of Mackinac Island," Katie said as she thanked Ben.

"I hope you like it," Ben said, almost apologetically.

"I love it," Katie told him.

"I'm so glad," her son replied. "Jan helped me pick it out for you."

Katie smiled. Inside she had felt a small sting of resentment, but it passed instantly. "You both have good taste," she said.

She had been watching Ben throughout the evening and had been particularly nice to Janet. After all, she thought to herself, he still has another year of high school, four years of college and then the newspaper. Nothing could change that now. After all, they were going home tomorrow. No, she would take it all in stride now. She really had little to worry about.

Annabelle loved the new charm for Katie's bracelet. Blair said it was nice, but wasn't as enthusiastic. A flash of silver had crossed her mind and she couldn't remember where or didn't know why. But it had given her an uneasy feeling.

Katie thought the gift-giving was over, but there was one more.

"I have something for you, too," Janet said, shyly. Then she handed Katie an envelope.

Katie opened the envelope and the birthday card to find a small snapshot inside. It was a photo of Katie and Ben, taken in front of the Island House. Katie was moved — but confused. "I don't recall this being taken," she said. "Who took the picture?"

"I did, Mrs. Butler," Janet said proudly. "I just happened to be coming up the walk as you two stood talking there by the front steps of the hotel. It was the last picture on the roll, taken nearly a week ago. I got them back this morning."

Katie was touched. "Well, it was very thoughtful. Thank you." She reached over and touched Janet's hand. It was as close as Katie could come to a compromise.

Al Davis had left his baggage on the front porch of the Island House and Billy Lachine had told him he would deliver the bags to the dock for the last ferry back to Mackinaw City. Al sensed that his walk down the near-empty mainstreet in the early darkness was like a condemned man walking his last mile to the electric chair. He would not pass this way again and he smiled in appreciation as he passed the closed fudge shops and the darkened stores. He was also filled with anticipation as he walked past the Lake View and the Windermere hotels and along the boardwalk toward the west end of the island. Today may have been the culmination of a lot of bad days for him lately, but an invitation from young Helen Gunter renewed the waning faith in his appeal as he neared the end of the boardwalk and peered beyond the basswood trees along the shoreline.

"Mr. Davis?"

An unfamiliar voice startled him. A woman's voice, all right, but not Helen Gunter's. Al whirled around in the semi-darkness and was confronted by a figure in a white jacket. His eyes adjusted to the dusk and he could see that it was not Helen. He could also see that she was holding a gun, a long-barrelled revolver, about the biggest gun Al had ever seen. And it was pointed at him.

"Mr. Al Davis?" she asked again.

"Well....ah....who are you?" he asked in a reflex action. He began to move away from her, backing towards the shoreline.

"Don't move, Mr. Davis." Her voice was polite, but it was also firm. There wasn't any question in his mind that she meant business.

Al stopped in his tracks. It was too silent. The only sound was the evening waves lapping at the shoreline. He felt he had to say something to break the silence. "Do I know you?"

"No, Mr. Davis, but I know you."

"There must be some mistake," he said in a forced friendly tone. "I was supposed to meet someone here this evening." Then he added, "Helen Gunter?" It sounded as if he were asking if she knew Helen.

"Helen isn't here tonight," she said in an even voice. "Helen isn't anywhere, Mr. Davis. Helen is dead."

Al couldn't tell whether it was the chill of the night air or the words he had just heard that ran shivers through his body. "Helen? Dead? Why I just had a note from...." he tried to explain. "She even signed it."

"The note was from me." Her face did not change expression. She paused, swallowed hard, and went on. "I'm Helen's mother."

This whole thing is unreal, Al thought to himself. Here he was, backed up against the shoreline in near darkness, and a woman whom he had never seen before, wearing a white coat and white shoes, was holding a cowboy's pistol on him. "Helen, dead?" There was more silence. "I'm sorry, Mrs. Gunter."

"I am, too. I'd like to feel sorry for you, too, Mr. Davis, because you're also going to die." The voice wavered ever so slightly, but her hands were still steady holding the gun. "You see, Helen committed suicide last week. She hung herself in the basement. She had come home from this island a few weeks ago but it was only ten days ago that she told me the real reason she left the island and came home. She had been raped. By you, Mr. Davis. After she told me, she was so ashamed that....."

There were tears in her eyes and her voice faded away. Al's heart was pumping faster than it had ever pumped before. "My God, woman. You're making a terrible mistake," he pleaded. Maybe if he could just stall her for a few more minutes, someone would come by. Or it would get so dark she couldn't see him anymore.

"It's too late for apologies," Harriet Gunter spoke again. She had regained her composure and although it was almost dark now, she could see the outline of Al Davis in the western horizon. "I've been thinking about all of this ever since the funeral and that's why I'm here now."

"Mrs. Gunter — please don't do anything you'll be sorry for. Someone's going to know you're here and that you've done this terrible thing." Al was truly panicky now.

"No one knows I'm here," she said calmly, "but I really don't care whether they do or not. You ruined a good and innocent life, Mr. Davis, and you're going to pay for it."

"It isn't the end of the world," he pleaded.

"It was for her."

Harriet Gunter squeezed the trigger and fired two shots into the dark figure standing near the water. Al Davis stepped back and then crumpled to the sand. Harriet simply put the gun back in her purse and turned away, striding through the soft sand back towards the road and the boardwalk. She never looked back, only towards the street lights up ahead on Mackinac Island's main street.

The walk back to the Mackinac House after the birthday party was a long one for Ben and Janet. They purposely passed by the rooming house without hesitation and continued down the street lined with picket fences toward the Moral Rearmament area. At the park, they veered off to the shoreline where they threw a few rocks in the lake.

"I used to come down here and shout at the lake in the darkness after work," Janet admitted.

"What for?" Ben asked.

"It seemed like a good way for my girlfriend and me to get rid of all the resentment that would build up in us during the day — from things that had gone wrong at the hotel, from rude customers, and just for the failings of life in general."

"Well, what would you say?"

"Oh, lots of things. We'd call Al Davis names and some of the customers, too. Then one of us would shout something witty and we'd both start laughing."

They laughed a little. Then they talked some more and there were more long periods of silence. Finally, they came back through the quiet lane to Janet's place where they stood in front of the iron fence for a long time.

"It was a nice party, Ben," Jan said.

"Yes. I'm glad you decided to come. I told you my mother would be just fine with all of this."

"You were right, Ben. She couldn't have been nicer."

"Yeah."

"And I love your grandmother. We had a very nice talk during dinner."

"She's a very special lady," Ben smiled.

"What time do you leave tomorrow?" she asked.

"I think about eleven in the morning."

"I'm working tomorrow and I'm not sure I can get off work," she said. The mere mention of tomorrow brought on a sadness. It seemed that neither one of them wanted to face up to the fact that this was their last night together — that they had to say goodbye. For Ben, it was a new experience. He didn't know what to say or what to do. He kept talking about the birthday dinner or other things that had happened during the day. Janet knew what to do. She would have to say goodbye, even though she didn't want it to end.

"I'd better go in now, Ben," she said. "Would you like to come up and see my room before you leave. It's right at the top of the stairs on the second floor."

"Naw, I'd better not," he said.

"Well, I think I should go in now."

The two stood close to each other and Janet put her arms around Ben's neck. "I want you to know, Ben, that this last week has been the happiest week in my whole life."

"Mine, too," he replied as he gently held her waist.

"I love you, Ben Butler," she said softly. Then she kissed him. It was a long gentle kiss and Ben held on as though his life would end with the kiss. He wasn't quite sure whether to speak or not. He didn't get the choice. Janet turned and rushed through the gate, up the walk to the steps and disappeared into the rooming house. Ben stood there for a minute or two and then started slowly back towards the hotel.

He thought again about the past week, their bike rides together, the long talks about each other, and how comfortable he felt when he was with her. He had wanted to say more things to her but this was all new to him and he wasn't quite sure just how to go about it. He should have told her that he loved her.

The birthday party for Katie was the highlight of the day for the Butler family, and the climax of the week-long vacation for Hillary. This evening's party had gone well for both Hillary and her daughter. She knew that Katie was trying hard to make amends for the harsh words the other day. Hillary understood. She had been through it all before with her daughter, and it was worth the abuse and perhaps a little heartache to have the opportunity to warn Katie about the drinking, and remind her that she was married to a very nice man. Hillary prepared for bed on this, her last night on the island, and although she was happy about this night's festivities, she wasn't feeling very good physically. She had experienced another dizzy spell and right now, as she finished wiping the cold cream off her face, her image became blurred in the bathroom mirror. She shook her head a couple of times, as if to shake away whatever it was that was obstructing her sight. But the blur was still there and she quickly finished and crawled into bed. She was afraid she knew what was happening and was a little frightened. It had happened to her before — a number of times — and her family doctor back home had told her she had suffered from a series of minor strokes. Perhaps a good night's sleep and she would feel better in the morning. Besides, she didn't want to alarm Katie and if she could hold out for a day or two more, she'd be back home where she could see her own physician. She relaxed in the darkness of her bed, telling herself how lucky she was that it wasn't a heart attack. She'd probably be fine by morning.

It was the last night on the island for Blair and Annabelle, too, but they were not content simply to go to their room and to bed. They had said their goodnights to everyone and gone to their room, all right, but they had other plans.

"Do you think it's okay?" Annabelle asked.

"Of course it's okay," Blair assured her. "It's our last night on the island. It's our last chance to walk down the main street under those old street lights and to see the lights across the lake at St. Ignace."

"But is it okay?"

"Sure it is." Blair was determined. They slipped out of their party dresses and into their play clothes. Annabelle wore culottes and a sweater. Blair threw on an old sweatshirt that had belonged to Ben, and a pair of shorts. Then they turned out the lights in their room. "Everyone will think we've gone to sleep. And besides, we won't be gone that long. We're only going to walk down to the other end of the main street and back again."

The girls slipped out of their room and down the stairs, across the deserted lobby and down the front steps to Huron Street. The streets were almost empty at this hour of the evening. All of the day visitors to the island had gone back to the mainland a long time ago, and most overnight guests were already back at their hotel or rooming house. The girls passed the main pier and continued on, going by the darkened stores and gift shops which they had practically called home for the past week. Now the buildings thinned out as they approached the Windermere Hotel and rounded the bend in the road which took them out of sight of the business district. They moved on to the board-walk and could hear the waves spashing against the shoreline and the rocks, and they looked out across the blackness of Lake Huron in search of the small, twinkling lights of far-off St. Ignace. The board-walk ended and they walked through the sand and the wet grass and the gnarled trees along the shore.

"There it is," Annabelle said with excitement. "There's St. Ignace."

"That's it," Blair agreed. "That's where we're goin' tomorrow." She blinked her eyes a few times. It was hard to see in the dark, but she was adjusting now. "That's the last time we're going to see this for another year."

"Maybe the last time forever for me," Annabelle said disappointedly. "I'm not sure if I'll ever get back here again."

"Yes you will," Blair told her. "I'll bet your folks will want to come after you tell them what a swell time we've had. And anyway, I'll ask you to come again."

"Do you think your folks will let you bring someone again?"

"I'm sure of it," Blair answered emphatically. "Well, pretty sure," she added in second-thought tones. "But what a wonderful time we've had."

"I'll say," Annabelle agreed. "This has been the best time of my whole life. Honest."

"Mine, too," Blair agreed. The two girls instinctively held hands, as if they could stay there on the beach for ever as long as they held on to each other. They heard the rustling of the leaves on the maze of trees along the shore.

"Let's skip a few rocks before we go back," Annabelle suggested.

"Sure."

The two stumbled around near the water, straining to find flat rocks to throw along the top of the waves. It was then that Blair stumbled over something at the edge of the water. At first she thought it was a log. Then she looked again, sticking her head down near the sand and the black water to see what it was.

"Annabelle."

"Find some stones?" Annabelle answered.

Blair never took her eyes off the ground. "No," she said, her voice quivering. "Somebody's here. It's a body. A man's body."

"It's what?" Annabelle shouted and rushed to her side. Even in the dark, they could see it was a body, a man's body, dressed in a suit and lying half in the water and partly on the wet sand. "Oh, my God!" Annabelle whispered.

"I think he's dead." Blair said.

"Come on," she tugged at her friend. "Let's get out of here and back to the hotel. We'd better tell somebody right away."

On the ferryboat pier, two large suitcases and a small bag which Billy had brought down earlier were still sitting in the dark next to the storage building on the pier. They belonged to Al Davis.

Back in the second-floor room at the top of the stairs, Janet was finding that the happiest week of her life was now ending with the worst night of her life. Ben was gone. She had tried not to think about it but it was impossible. She kicked off her shoes and slid out of her dress and underthings and pulled on a man's old dress shirt which she used as a nightgown. The over-sized shirt had belonged to one of her older brothers and it gave her a sense of being home. She brushed her hair and then recognized how sad her face looked in the mirror and fell face-down on her bed and began to cry.

There was a knock at the door. Janet lifted her face up from the bed and looked at the door. Then she got up, brushed her hair back with her hand, wiped her eyes and eased open the door. Ben stood in the doorway with an embarrassed smile on his face.

"I decided I'd like to see what your room looks like after all," he said apologetically.

"Ben, oh Ben," she cried out and threw her arms around him. The two stood there for a moment. Janet looked at him and laughed. Her eyes were still red from the tears.

"Well, come on in." She pulled him into the room and shut the door. Then she put her arms around him again and kissed him. Ben responded by enfolding her in his arms and holding her tight. He could feel the warmth of her body through the nightshirt, feel the firmness of her breasts. They fell on to the bed, her bare legs exposed, and for the first time, Ben touched the warmth of her smooth skin.

"I love you," she whispered.

"And I love you — very much," he said quietly.

He had forgotten the talk he had with his father about girls' rooms.

CHAPTER 14

Wednesday, July 13

There was a certain air of excitement on the island this morning. Rumors and accounts of a dead body found on the shores of the island beyond the boardwalk quickly spread among the workers on the island, from store clerks to stable boys. It was a sort of secretive kind of news, however — one that was only talked about privately with fellow employees, not with guests and visitors. There seemed to be an unwritten law on Mackinac Island that such unpleasant matters were best kept at home. A team of dray horses hauling garbage had bolted last week when a harness broke and the whipple-trees and part of the hitch began to roll up on the hind legs of the team. Frightened, the runaway team charged down a driveway and across the street, running into an empty carriage. One of the horses fell and then recovered and the team continued, out of control, on to the lawn near the shoreline and eventually stopping. Fortunately, the driver of the garbage wagon had hung on to the reins even though he was tossed backward into the garbage he was hauling. A helper had been thrown from the rig, and a passerby finally assisted in bringing the horses to a stop by grabbing a bridle and holding on. The hitch was eventually replaced and after examining the team, the driver went on his way. No one was hurt, but the potential for that team to have run over bicyclists or into a carriage full of people had been there. Within a half a day, most employees on the island knew of the incident but not a single word had been said to an island visitor and the matter went largely unnoticed.

The same kind of unwritten voluntary silence was happening this morning except at the Island House where guests having breakfast heard rumors that the assistant manager of the hotel was dead — perhaps murdered.

The Mackinac Island police department, which consisted of one town constable, had been called late last night after the girls rushed back to the hotel to announce their discovery of a body lying along the shore. As they entered the hotel, they ran right into Blair's father who was crossing the lobby on his way to his room. It didn't seem to matter that the girls had been caught out-on-the-town when they should have been asleep in their room. They were so happy to see Harris that it didn't make any difference. Half-crying, frightened and a little panicky, Blair and Annabelle spilled out the details in such rapid succession that it was difficult for Harris to understand just what it was that they saw or what had happened to them. When they finally settled down and caught their breath, Harris pieced together their story and had the hotel management call the police. Then he and Katie put the girls to bed and Katie stayed in their room to comfort them and make sure they went to sleep. She sat in one corner of the room and read until the girls finally drifted off to sleep, Blair clutching Tebby tightly.

In the meantime, Harris had hurried down the main street and to the end of the boardwalk where a small crowd of islanders had gathered. The police chief had identified the body as Alvin Davis. He had been shot twice, in the stomach and chest, and had probably been lying there on the shore for a couple of hours. The body was taken back to the fire station and a phone call was placed to the police department at St. Ignace and another to Detroit. There had not been a shooting on the island in years. In fact, there hadn't been a serious crime committed on the island in a long, long time. Most of the police reports were filled with lost articles and stolen bicycles and an occasional break-in at a store along main street. The calls to the mainland last night had brought police from St. Ignace this morning. An investigator from

Detroit was also on his way to help. The Butlers decided to keep the girls as inconspicuous as possible and ordered breakfast in their room this morning. This last day on the island would be a more sobering one in contrast to the carefree vacation days of the past week.

It had been a long bus ride for Harriet Gunter. Now she was finding familiar surroundings as the Greyhound rolled along the highway approaching the small town of Pembine. It was 6:30 a.m. and she would be home within an hour. It had been a long and uneventful ride for her since she boarded the bus in St. Ignace early this morning. She had taken the last ferryboat back to the mainland last night and although she had tried to visualize what the island had looked like to her daughter when she left there a month ago, the darkness had closed in on the straits and she was left standing on the deck in the black of night with only the moonlight flashing through the clouds. Halfway back to the mainland, Harriet had quietly dropped the revolver over the side of the ship into the blackness of the straits. At St. Ignace, she had waited patiently at the Standard Oil station for the bus which pulled into town at 12:30 in the morning. There were only a handful of passengers on board and as the bus roared out of town and headed across the Upper Peninsula, Harriet sat alone in a leather-covered seat, halfway back in the darkened bus, and leaned her head against the window. She thought about Helen and cried a little, and eventually fell asleep.

The Greyhound approached the outskirts of the little town and Harriet tried to straighten her rumpled dress and coat. She'd be getting off at the local drug store soon and would be back in her own house for breakfast. Then she'd wait to see whether the police would eventually follow her back to Pembine. It didn't matter to her if they did. In her own mind, she was quite sure she had done the right thing.

And she felt her life was over anyway.

Lt. Phil Lafferty had not had a good night last night. His Detroit Tigers had lost a close ball game to the St. Louis Browns. Of all the teams, they had lost to the winless Browns. It was embarrassing to a baseball fan and especially to a Detroit supporter to see Greenberg fan in the ninth inning and Mickey Cochrane drop the ball to let the winning run score at home plate in a close play.

Detective Lafferty scanned the morning paper at his desk in police headquarters in downtown Detroit on this July morning. Then he turned to the night records for this headquarters division and almost spilled his coffee when the name of Alvin Davis jumped out at him from the police report. Lafferty blinked his eyes and looked again — Alvin Davis, Mackinac Island, found dead last night. Death caused by two gunshot wounds in the abdomen and chest by a large caliber revolver. The St. Ignace police had called the Detroit Police Department near midnight last night because the state criminal offices were closed. And, of course, the Detroit department's records — which Lafferty had looked at only a few days ago — listed a complete rundown on Davis.

Lafferty frowned. Was his old friend, Harvey Stanhope, in trouble? He recalled his two phone conversations with Harvey last week and tried to remember anything that Harvey said or any tone in his voice that would have indicated anything at all which would point to a possible murder. He'd known Harvey since the old days and remembered those tough times of a few years back. Harvey wouldn't be so stupid as to ask for information from him and then go out and put the guy away. Naw — not Harvey. But Lafferty hadn't convinced himself and picked up the phone.

"Operator," came the female voice on the line.

"Operator, I want to place a call to a Mr. Harvey Stanhope who's staying at the Island House Hotel on Mackinac Island up state."

Ben Butler had slept late this morning and even after he awakened, he stayed in bed, looking up at the ceiling and thinking about Janet and last night. This was not a day he had been looking forward to, and now it was here. He rolled over and tried to go back to sleep for a while, as if this last day on the island would go away and time would stop if he just stayed in bed. It was only after he had dressed and wandered out into the hall of the third floor that he heard voices coming from his parents' room just two doors down — voices of not only his mom and dad, but of the girls, too. When he stopped to say good morning, he discovered they were breakfasting in the room, and it was only then that he learned of what had happened last night.

"You mean Mr. Davis — the one here at the hotel? Dead? Murdered?" Ben grew pale. "Oh, my God!" But his concern was not for Al Davis. He probably got what he had coming to him. Ben's thoughts were about someone else — someone he didn't know very well. In an instant, he was transported back to that darkened hallway, pressed up against the wall and holding his breath, watching Mr. Stanhope holding the revolver in his hand, then putting it away again as he knocked on the door of Mr. Davis' room. He remembered the conversation of that night and recalled how he had watched from the shadows as the man with the frozen face left Mr. Davis' hotel room and limped back down the hall.

"What's the matter, Ben?" his father asked him.

"Nothing, nothing," Ben replied.

"You look like you've seen a ghost," his mother said.

"No, no. Not at all," Ben said as he gathered himself together. "No. It's just that I talked to Mr. Davis just the other day."

Ben listened as the girls re-told their story of discovering the body. He became so nervous that he even asked for a cup of coffee.

"You never drink coffee, dear," Katie said to him as she poured a cup.

"Well, once in a while," he replied. Actually, he had never drunk coffee before. He listened to other conversations over the breakfast table in the room, but his mind was flooded with thoughts — not of Davis — but of Harvey Stanhope. Should he tell the police about what he had seen and heard that night in the second-floor hallway? Should he tell his folks about it? They'd surely make him go to the police. Maybe he should just say nothing. Or maybe, just maybe, he should pursue the matter a little further. If he was ever going to be a good newspaperman, this would be an excellent exercise for him. What would a good reporter do, knowing what he did? Of course. He would go to see Mr. Stanhope — this morning.

The last breakfast on Mackinac Island had been an upsetting one for Marian Stanhope. She and Harvey had just about finished eating in the hotel dining room and were sipping coffee when they heard the news of Al Davis' death. A waitress was answering questions about the incident as she served a couple at the next table. Harvey took the news calmly enough, and although Marian showed no emotion, her stomach was churning inside. As they left the dining room, Marian told him she was going back to the room for something she had forgotten, and that she would join him on the front veranda. There were no tears, but when she unlocked the door and got into the room, she lay down on the bed.

"Poor Al," she said aloud. She knew what he was, but she had enjoyed him. He had made her feel young and beautiful sometimes when she had almost given up on ever feeling that way again. He had been a sweet talker and probably not very trustworthy, but she couldn't help having a great fondness for him. She felt that he had cared for her, too. Yes, Marian felt a great loss this morning.

There was still a little packing to do before they left the island this afternoon. She went to the bathroom and freshened her face, but there seemed to be no way she could completely hide her grief. She picked up a few pieces of Harvey's clothing and folded them neatly. Then she opened his old trunk on the bed and put in a pair of his shoes in the very bottom where they wouldn't dirty any clothing. That's when she discovered the white towel neatly folded around the gun and a small package of bullets.

"Jesus!" she whispered. "He did it!" Her hands automatically went to her mouth as if to stop the words so no one else could hear. "Harvey knows!" she thought. Her heart sank, not for herself, but for dear Harvey. He'd been living with this for god knows how long, she thought. "Oh, God! What must he think?"

Marian, herself, wasn't thinking very clearly. It never occurred to her to think back on last evening. They had spent the entire night together and had played cards in the lobby and listened to the radio —

Lux Radio Theater, and *George Burns and Gracie Allen*. Marian had come up to bed early while Harvey stayed on to hear the evening news. It was the only time when she could not account for him. Elements of time and common sense were simply not part of her thinking process now, however. She carefully put the towel and gun back in their proper place in the suitcase and left the room to go to Harvey. She was only sure of one thing — that she loved her husband and wanted to protect him.

Billy Lachine sat on the front steps of the Island House in shock as he pondered the situation. He could not believe that Al was dead. Like most of Al's friends, Billy knew him for what he was, but he still liked him and considered him a friend. Although there were plenty of people who didn't like Al, Billy couldn't think of a single person capable of such violence as to actually kill another human being. Maybe that Mr. Stanhope, if he ever found out about Mrs. Stanhope and Al. But no one else. Certainly not young Ben Butler, whom Billy had seen coming away from Al's office the other day — and with a bloody nose. Right now, it was more than Billy could comprehend. He just sat there on the front steps, looking out at the lake across the way. There would be police and questions, he supposed, and then he thought of something that he probably wouldn't say anything about. He slipped off his new gold wristwatch, the one Al had given him only yesterday, and quietly slid it into his pocket.

The young clerk at the front desk had just finished telling the police about the woman wearing the white coat and white shoes who left an envelope for Al Davis yesterday afternoon. The envelope could not be found in Al's office but the police had not yet searched his room on the third floor. The clerk crooked the telephone receiver between his ear and his shoulder as he completed writing the message from a long-distance phone call. When he finished, he assured the caller that the message would be delivered immediately.

"Yes, Mr. Lafferty," the clerk said over the phone. "We'll find him right away or leave the message on the door of his room. Yes, Mr. Lafferty. Goodbye." When the clerk hung up the phone, he called a bellhop. "Danny, would you take this phone message up to room 200. It's for Mr. Stanhope and I think he's checking out today."

"I believe I saw him go out to the front porch just a little while ago," the bellhop replied. "I'll try out there first."

Ben Butler was passing the front desk during the conversation and stopped. "I'm going out to the veranda," he told the two young hotel workers. "I'll be glad to deliver it to Mr. Stanhope."

The bellhop hesitated. He didn't want to miss the possibility of getting a tip, but he didn't want to offend another hotel guest.

"You sure you know him?" the desk clerk intervened.

"Yes, I know him," Ben told the two of them. "In fact, I was just on my way out to see him."

"It's all right, Danny," the desk clerk said. "Mr. Butler will take care of it."

On the way out to the front porch, Ben had the feeling that a good newspaper man would have glanced at the contents of the folded message, but he didn't. There was practically no one on the veranda at this hour of the morning and he found Harvey Stanhope sitting near the porch rail, looking out on Lake Huron.

"Mr. Stanhope?" Ben inquired.

"Yes," Harvey answered as he turned to see who was there.

"I was on my way out here and the front desk had just received a phone message for you. I told them I'd bring it out."

"Why, thank you," Harvey replied as Ben gave him the small slip of paper.

Ben stood there for a moment while Harvey read the message. "I hope it's not bad news," Ben said, shyly.

Harvey read it a second time as if he hadn't heard Ben. Then he looked up. "Oh, no. No. It's from a friend of mine back in Detroit. He wants me to call him, that's all." Harvey half-smiled. "But thank you for bringing it out here to me."

"I was coming out, anyway," Ben said, "to see you."

Harvey looked up in surprise. "Oh?"

"Yes sir. I would like to talk to you for a minute, if you don't mind. My name's Ben Butler."

"Yes, of course," Harvey replied. "I've seen the Butler family around here all week. Actually, Mrs. Stanhope and I are leaving today."

Ben hesitated. "Sir, you seem to be leaving in a hurry. Right after.... after the murder."

"Well, now. Come sit down, Ben." Ben sat in another white wooden rocker facing Harvey. "Now what exactly do you mean by that?"

Ben wasn't so sure that he was doing the right thing now. This was more difficult than he thought it was going to be and he mustered his courage and looked straight at Harvey.

"I saw you go into Mr. Davis' room the other night," Ben told him quietly.

"Oh, so that's it," Harvey smiled as best he could.

"Yes sir." Ben swallowed hard. "And I saw you pull out your gun before you knocked on his door. I was in the hallway around the corner, in the dark."

"And what were you doing in front of Mr. Davis' room?" Harvey inquired.

"I was going to see him, sir. About my girlfriend."

"And I beat you to it," Harvey smiled again.

"I heard just about everything, sir," Ben told him.

"And after what happened last night, you put two and two together and think that I...."

"I don't know, sir," Ben broke in. "I just wanted you to know what I had seen and heard, and I'm not sure what to do about it. That's why I'm here. I haven't told anyone yet. I'm not sure whether to tell my folks or the police or what."

"I see," Harvey said. "Well, you can tell the police if you want. Or you can tell your mother or dad who will make you go to the police anyway." Harvey paused for a moment. "Fact of the matter is, I don't know who killed our Mr. Davis. But it wasn't me. My gun is upstairs, packed in my suitcase, and it hasn't been fired. The police could check that very easily."

"Yes sir," Ben nodded.

"I don't really know why you wanted to see Mr. Davis, son, but I can tell you that I didn't like him very much. I even thought about killing him. But I couldn't have gotten away with it." He held up the phone message. "That's what this phone call is about. An old friend of mine, a Detroit detective. I'm sure he wants to know what's going on up here and that I'm all right. I'll have to call him back this morning and put his mind at ease."

"Yes sir," said Ben.

"But I don't know whether I can put your mind at ease, son. I know mine is. So you just do what you have to do. I'm afraid I can't help you any more than that."

Without realizing it, Ben had been studying Harvey's eyes as the older gentleman spoke. Thoughts were racing through his young mind, trying to sort out the truth, and Ben felt he had come to a conclusion right there, right on the veranda, facing Mr. Stanhope. "What would a good newspaperman do?" he asked himself. "I guess in this case, he'd go with his gut feeling." And Ben's gut feeling was that he believed Harvey. Without even trying, his feelings were transformed into words.

"I believe you, Mr. Stanhope," he said as he got up from the porch chair.

"Thank you," Harvey looked up with that half-smile. "Thank you, son."

"Goodbye, sir." Ben shook hands, turned and left. As he passed the corner of the veranda, he passed by Marian who had been standing there, unnoticed. She had heard it all, and for the first time since she heard the news about Al Davis, she wasn't afraid for Harvey anymore. Now she was afraid for herself, and ashamed for what she had done to Harvey.

Janet had heard two distressing bits of news this morning at breakfast back in the kitchen of the Island House. Details of the discovery of Al Davis' body last night were sketchy but it was common knowledge that the young Butler girl and her friend had found him near the boardwalk. The body had been indentified by several people, including workers from the hotel. There seemed to be nothing missing, except a couple of employees mentioned that Al usually wore a gold watch which was not there. Janet thought of what an upsetting experience it must have been for those two kids, and she hoped to speak to Ben when the Butlers came down for breakfast this morning. She was sure that Ben would have the same mixed feelings that she did. The thought of murder was repugnant to her, and yet, she felt no remorse over Al Davis' death. She wondered who could be so filled with hate that he would actually take another person's life. Even Ben's concern for her and his dislike of Al Davis could not have prompted such a terrible act. No one could even suspect Ben of such a thing unless they knew about the confrontation in Mr. Davis' office a few days ago. And even if they questioned Ben, he could account for all of his time last night — first at the family birthday party and later....and oh God, if she had to, she could vouch for Ben — in her room.

But there was something else that affected Janet even more this morning than the news of the murder. Another girl working as a chambermaid in the hotel had received a letter yesterday from a friend in Wisconsin, telling her that Helen Gunter had died last week. There were not many details, but there was a rumor of suicide. The off-hand remark by the chambermaid caught Janet unprepared and all of a sudden, she felt terribly sick. Helen Gunter? Dead? It hadn't even been a month since she told Janet she was quitting her job and leaving the island to go home again. She said she was homesick, and Janet could surely understand that. But now....Janet was fighting to hold back the tears and her emotions. Even though they had been roommates for a few weeks, Janet still hadn't known Helen that well. But she was not prepared to hear of her death. The news had almost made Janet forget that Ben was leaving the island this afternoon.

CHAPTER 15

The Stanhopes had packed their bags and the bellhop had ticketed their luggage for an early afternoon ferry to Mackinac City. Harvey had come into the lobby from the veranda and placed a call to Phil Lafferty in Detroit. Marian stood by and listened.

"Phil?"

"Harvey? Is that you?"

"There was a note that I should call you, Phil."

"That's right. I saw the police reports this morning, Harvey, and thought I ought to call you. Especially after those calls you made to me last week. What the hell is going on up there?"

"Honest to God, Phil, I don't know. You probably know more about it there than we do here. But you needn't have worried, Phil. I didn't do it. Honest."

"You're sure, Harv?"

"I thought about it. But I'm clean."

"I hope so, Harvey." Phil paused. He knew that if Harvey were in trouble, he would level with him. "They're checking out some other things around here for the police up there. Something about a woman in white. But as long as you're okay, Harvey...."

"I'm okay," Harvey smiled. So did Marian. "But thanks for calling. I appreciate it," Harvey said.

After the phone call, Harvey checked out of the hotel and paid the bill. Then he and Marian took a leisurely walk through the center of town one last time and stopped at a fudge shop and bought a couple of pounds of candy to take home with them. The ferry to Mackinaw City had docked and was unloading its passengers. The Stanhopes waited on the pier with a crowd of island visitors who were also about to board for the trip back to the mainland.

"It's been a wonderful time, dear," Marian told him as she held on to his arm.

"We'll come again, honey." He patted her arm reassuringly.

"They were awfully good to us at the hotel," she said.

"Yes," he agreed. "We'll stay there again the next time we come."

Harvey thought about Al Davis for a moment and wondered just what happened last night. He thought about his confrontation with Al the other night and a half-smile crossed his face. He couldn't do it himself, but he was glad somebody else could.

Marian thought about Al as she stood on the pier. She knew him for what he was, but he didn't deserve to die.

The steam whistle aboard the ferryboat prompted both Harvey and Marian that the ship was now taking on passengers for the trip to the mainland and Mackinaw City. Billy Lachine was on duty as a dock porter this morning and had brought the Stanhope's luggage to the dock from the Island House. Harvey tipped the youth and then helped him carry their suitcases on board. Marian took one last look around the pier and started to cross the gangplank when Billy came off the boat.

"Mrs. Stanhope," he called to her.

"Yes?"

"I have a message for you."

"Oh?"

"Yes. Yesterday, Mr. Davis spoke to me and said that I should give you this envelope. He was planning on leaving the island last night."

Billy handed her the envelope and Marian quickly opened it. She unfolded the note paper which read:

Dear Marian,
Going to California. Come on out and I'll get you in the movies.
You were great, but watch out. Horseface is no dummy.

Love, Al

Marian smiled and put the note back into the small envelope, slipped it into her purse and dug out a dime which she handed to Billy. "Thank you," she said. Then she turned, crossed the gangplank in her high heels and tight-fitting dress and called out for Harvey.

As the ferry to Mackinaw City backed away from the municipal pier and made its turn to head out of the harbor, a troop of Boy Scouts rushed to the open deck to look back on the island. They had been one of a continuing contingent of Scouts who served as guides at Fort Mackinac throughout the summer, arriving every week for a tour of duty. They stayed in barracks built four years ago up near the fort. The first such group of Scouts to serve as guides came to the island from throughout the state of Michigan just nine years ago. Included in that group was an Eagle Scout from Grand Rapids. Later, he became a star football player at the University of Michigan. His name was Gerald R. Ford.

Also returning on the ferry on this day was Harry Ryba, the young man from Detroit who had sat out on the veranda of the Island House and visited with Harris Butler. He and his wife, Ethel, stood at the railing on the deck of the ferry and looked back on the scene that was fading in the distance. Someday they would be back on the island to stay, he told Ethel.

When Ben Butler arrived on the island, the coming week of vacation seemed like a long time. There would be plenty of time to do anything he wanted. He was on a holiday. But there is something about Mackinac Island that makes time go very swiftly. Janet and Ben had come to that realization last night. Now, with the Butler clan congregated on the pier, waiting for the ferryboat back to St. Ignace, Ben tried to think of where all the time had gone — and gone so quickly. Then he saw Janet walking on to the pier. She was in her waitress' uniform and had rearranged her schedule slightly so she could see Ben before he left. When he saw her, he became flustered, broke away from the group waiting for the ferry, and hurried to meet her.

"You've heard about Al Davis?" he asked.

"Yes," she replied. "I was worried that they might try to involve you. I mean — I could have told them where you were last night. And this morning, I found out that Helen Gunter — you know, my roommate here — died last week." She paused. "It's been a terrible morning."

"I'm sorry," Ben said. "I didn't think I'd see you again." He took her hand.

"I just couldn't let you leave without another goodbye," she said in her soft voice. "Not after last night." The two of them stood there, facing each other, holding hands, and offering reassuring smiles. They looked the same as they had just a week ago, but they had both changed. Everything had changed. Janet had found someone to love, someone outside of her family, outside of her old 4-H club, beyond the limits of the Ferrisville school, and beyond her expectations of the college campus. Ben had been caught even more unaware and his priorities, which had seemed to be in concert with his mother's just a few days ago, were all mixed up now. Nothing seemed to fit anymore.

"Where did the time go?" she asked.

"I don't know," said Ben. "I guess it went with the bike rides and moonlight walks and summer afternoons." He paused. "I'll write as soon as I get home."

Janet said she would also sit down tonight and put her thoughts on paper for him. "I can't stay now," she told him. "I just got off work long enough to stop for a few minutes."

He'd waited long enough. He knew his family was watching from the pier, but he nervously gathered his courage in front of them. She was leaving. He was leaving. He had never felt like this before. He'd be lost if he didn't tell her one last time. It didn't seem to make any difference that there were people walking past them, or that his family was waiting and watching. Still holding her hands, Ben could wait no longer.

"I love you Jan."

She felt like crying. Then she kissed him gently on the mouth and at the same time, reached into her purse and pressed a small envelope into his hand. "I love you, too, Ben. Goodbye," she said softly. Then she turned and left. When she reached the street, she turned to hurry toward the Island House. There were tears in her eyes. Time, which had been so fleeting during these past few days, would slow down for her now.

The family had watched from a distance. The girls, wide-eyed, gasped when Janet kissed Ben goodbye. Hillary Markham had been watching, too, and seeing Ben and Janet together brought memories of her youth and of another goodbye. The memory was bittersweet, and although Hillary knew how Ben must feel at this moment, she smiled and was happy for him.

Katie did not see the tender parting in the same way as her mother. She was relieved that they were leaving the island and this little summertime romance was over. Ben would get home and back to school and get on with his life now — back to the life Katie had planned for him. But Katie also sensed an unwanted change in her son and right now, she wasn't quite so sure of herself, either. She was afraid, and she held on to Harris' arm.

Blair and Annabelle stood in the cluster of the Butler family on the pier, waiting to board the ferryboat for the return trip to St. Ignace. A million thoughts were rushing through Blair's brain as she tried to recall every little detail of her visit to Mackinac Island. She had felt like Nancy Drew and Gloria Vanderbilt. She hated to leave. Home would be so ordinary after this week.

It had been a restless night for Blair and Annabelle last night, but by this morning, they had seemed pretty calm about discovering the dead body of Al Davis. Blair would not forget that moment on the dark beach, but it seemed to her that her folks and others were far too concerned about her and Annabelle. It hadn't seemed to bother the girls to talk with the police detective this morning, and although the authorities might have to check with them again, they were perfectly willing to allow the Butler family to leave the island. Now Blair's mind was filled with horses and buggies, with crowds of visitors, Sugar Loaf, Skull Cave and the rest. She thought of Trinity Church where she and Annabelle had crashed the wedding. Someday I'm going to get married here on the island at Trinity, she promised herself.

Those grown-up thoughts turned to a child's tears, however. Blair suddenly realized, as she was standing on the pier, that she had left the teddy bear back in the hotel room.

"Tebby!" she cried out. "I forgot Tebby! He's back at the hotel!"

Annabelle turned to Mrs. Butler. "Her teddy bear."

"I know," Katie said. "I'm not sure if there's enough time to go back and get it now." She looked around to see passengers boarding the ferry to St. Ignace.

Billy Lachine had just been paid a handsome tip by Harris for bringing the luggage down to the pier. He could see the tears in Blair's eyes as she tried to keep from crying. "What's the matter?" he asked.

"My teddy bear, Tebby," she blurted out. "I left him at the hotel." She started to cry. "I'll never see him again."

"What room were you in?" Billy asked, hurriedly. "I'll go back and get him. The boat won't leave for a few minutes and I think I can make it."

"Room 301," Blair shouted as Billy had already started back off the pier on his bike.

Minutes later, the steam whistle drowned out conversations as the Butler family boarded the ferryboat. The last passengers crossed the gangplank and Blair stood by as she watched the workmen haul the metal walkway on to the ferry. Engines began to churn and mooring lines were pulled on board. Then Blair could see Billy biking onto the pier, racing toward the departing ferry. The boat began to pull away from the dock ever so slowly.

"I've got him," Billy shouted as he jumped off the bike and ran towards the boat. "Here's Tebby," he shouted as he looked across the widening space between the dock and the ferry — perhaps a space of five or six feet. Then he tossed the brown teddy bear across the water and into Blair's arms. She grabbed the bear out of the air and clutched it tightly to her cheek, wet with tears.

"Thanks!" she shouted. "Thank you, Billy."

Billy smiled triumphantly and waved as the distance increased between the ferry and the pier. He turned and wheeled his bike off the pier and started back to the hotel. He would not forget the Butler family's visit to the island. He had also discovered a new toy. His La Tortue Grande now opened up all kinds of possibilities for him.

Harris Butler had made sure everyone was aboard the ferry and was safe. He had been someone the girls had needed last night and although he quietly stayed in the background this morning, his family sensed his steady hand through the business of Davis' death and the preparations for leaving the island. Harris had also felt a new closeness to Ben during their stay on the island. He was also feeling a terrible guilt about his momentary flirtation with Marian Stanhope and, although the experience had been exhilarating, he knew deep down in his heart that it could never be anything more — with her or any other woman except Kate. As they left the harbor, Harris thought about his future and what would happen when they returned home again. He was eager to make the plunge into his new venture with Gerry Hagen. He would have to have the courage to carry it through and Katie would just have to learn to like it. She would in time. He thought about his son. My God, if Ben could recognize when it was necessary to stand on his own two feet, surely he could, too, Harris thought.

Everyone was accounted for on the ferry except for Ben. Harris finally found his son standing alone at the railing near the stern of the ship.

"Ben, come on up front with the family," he called.

"Sure, Dad, just a minute. Okay?"

Harris had watched Ben and Janet say goodbye back on the pier and he decided to leave him alone.

Ben was thinking about Al Davis, the scuffle in his office and the threats that had been made by Mr. Stanhope. Mr. Stanhope. Ben liked him — and believed him. He was not sure, now, that he had made the right decision to keep Mr. Stanhope's visit to Davis' room just between the two of them. He wasn't sure his mother would approve. But he thought that, perhaps, his dad would. He decided to talk to him about it when they got home.

As he stood there, Ben realized he was holding the envelope which Jan had pressed into his hand when she kissed him goodbye. Hurriedly now, he opened it to find a small snapshot of her, apparently taken back on the family farm. Written on the back were the words, *I love you, Ben. Jan.*

He looked up and watched the island diminish in size as the ferry pulled out of the harbor. He could still see bikes and people and horses moving along the street. He traced the path he and Janet had taken to the white fort and noticed the steeple of St. Ann's topping the green trees. He thought about the nightly walks along the boardwalk with Jan, the talks by the lakeshore and their holding on to each other at Arch Rock. He hadn't even reached the mainland and he already

Historians in the Middle Ages

Historians
in the Middle Ages

BERYL SMALLEY

with 99 illustrations, 10 in color

Charles Scribner's Sons · New York

1 Frontispiece: Clio, Muse of
History. Medieval scholars
had a literary knowledge of
the Nine Muses from their
reading of Latin classical
texts. From a Roman
sarcophagus showing the
Muses. *Paris, Louvre*

Copyright © 1974
Thames and Hudson
Limited, London

Copyright under the
Berne Convention

All rights reserved. No part
of this book may be
reproduced in any form
without the permission of
Charles Scribner's Sons.

1 3 5 7 9 11 13 15 17 19 I\C 20 18 16 14 12 10 8 6 4 2

Printed in Great Britain
Library of Congress Catalog
Card Number 74-14155

ISBN 0-684-14121-3

Contents

For my friends at Berkeley, California

Foreword

This book has been written with the aim of helping students and general readers to read medieval histories and chronicles with pleasure. I shall use the word 'historiography' as a blanket term to signify historical writings, because medieval authors distinguished between various genres: 'history' meant one thing, 'chronicle' another, and both differed from the several forms that biography might take. The history of historiography is a rather new subject. Modern historians used to read medieval historiographers as sources for facts, opinions and attitudes; we still do. But now Crocè and his pupils have put the history of historiography on the academic map. We also try to find out what medieval writers aimed at as historiographers and how the art and skill of historiography developed through the ages.

First we need to know something about the material conditions they worked in, secondly what books they read and how their reading formed their minds as historiographers. In describing the historiographers I have had to select ruthlessly. Many old favourites have been left out. I have kept mainly to Latin historiography within the area bounded roughly by the North Sea, the Pyrenees and Naples, with one excursion into Poland (my pupil Mr B. Harónski introduced me to Master Vincent of Cracow). Crusading historiography falls into the area, since the Latin kingdom in Palestine was a colony known as 'France Overseas'. I have excluded auto-biography and hagiography, the writing of the lives and passions of saints. Medieval autobiographies are rare and untypical; lives of saints on the other hand are so numerous that they would need a book to themselves. I hope to convey some idea of the bewildering richness and variety of medieval historiography. Specialists may think that I pay too much attention to the freaks; but the student can correct me by browsing in run-of-the-mill chronicles and annals. My freaks and the great artists and thinkers may perhaps whet his appetite for the ordinary.

ISIDORVS · PRIVALON

SCRIPTORIS MISERI· PIEHAREDS MISERERE· NOLICVLPARE· PONDPENSARE MEAM·
PARVAMEL BONASINTSVP· CRIMINAMVISV· NOR·LVCICEDAT· VITE·MORS·

ISTE·RE· CTOX·

The conditions

What motives led men to write histories and chronicles in the Middle Ages? Answers will emerge in the course of this book. To prevent misunderstanding, I shall begin by excluding motives which we take for granted nowadays. Today historiography is commercialized. A textbook or pot-boiler pays for a holiday or adds to one's income; a work of scholarship helps the author to compete for posts in the job market. Enjoyment and compulsion to write come into it; but the day of the amateur scholar is past. There was no money in authorship in the Middle Ages.

The history of book production in the ancient world shows that the author made no direct profit even then, although he could count on a reading public of aristocrats and bourgeois. Publishers and booksellers existed in ancient times and earned their living in ancient cities; but the copying of books was too costly to admit of profit-sharing. A rich author would dictate his book to a slave skilled at the job. He then had it copied and circulated at his own expense. The poorer author would hand his book to a publisher, who might pay him a small sum for the manuscript; more likely he would have to pay something himself. Copyright and royalties were out of the question. A book belonged to its author for as long as it stayed in his hands. After that it was free as air. A plagiarist laid himself open to mockery and reproach – if his fraud was discovered; the victim had no legal remedy. Authors might hope for indirect reward in the form of patronage, since wealthy men of rank liked to have talented writers in their clientèle. Patronage, however, had the drawback of being precarious and degrading. The typical historian of the ancient world was a retired statesman of independent means who had left public life in disgrace or under a cloud, and then devoted himself to writing as an honourable activity in his enforced leisure. Sometimes his history took the form of memoirs; sometimes he chose a more remote period. In either case he wrote because he was rich already, not to make money. Sallust, Tacitus and the Jewish historian Flavius

2 Opposite: a monk copyist receives a supernatural reward. At the lower right he is shown lying dead, while an angel carries his soul in the form of a child to be judged by God. His good deeds are weighed in the judgment scales. The book he has copied, and to which this picture forms the frontispiece, weighs heavily in his favour. Above at the left we see St Isidore of Seville, whose *Etymologies* the monk has copied (see p. 22). The manuscript was produced at Regensburg in the mid-twelfth century. *Munich, Bayerische Staatsbibliothek, Cod. lat. 13031, f.1r*

3 Stages of book production in a monastic scriptorium. The skin is stretched on a frame and scraped with a knife to clean and smooth it (top). Then it is cut into quires. Finally, the gatherings are stitched together. From a copy of the works of St Ambrose made at Bamberg in the first half of the twelfth century. *Bamberg, Staatsbibliothek, MS Patr. 5, f.1v*

Josephus are examples. The cult of 'good fame', an indirect reward for his pains, supplied the driving motive for an ancient historian.

In the Middle Ages, between about 800 and 1200, the expenses of book production increased. The ancient papyrus roll had given way to costly parchment or vellum, prepared as quires and stitched together. They needed a hard cover to keep them from falling apart. Skilled slave-labour for copying was no longer available; the ancient bookshop had vanished. The book itself was now a precious object. It circulated as a gift or medium of exchange or as an extravagant purchase. The main centres of book production were now *scriptoria*, or writing offices, in monasteries and cathedrals. The monks or canons would sometimes employ professional scribes or artists; they often did the work of copying and illuminating themselves. The demand for books had shrunk, since the literate layman had become a rarity; readers were mainly churchmen. Court patronage survived; but most authors wrote to order or with the permission of an ecclesiastical superior rather than to please a secular prince. Historiography continued to be a spare-time occupation. The personal incentive had decreased. Christian humility forbad that the author should write in order to boost his good fame. Indeed the whole concept of authorship went by the board. An 'author' in medieval terms means 'authority'. The biblical writers and the Church Fathers ranked as 'authors' in sacred literature; the classical poets and prose-writers were their opposite numbers in profane literature. Their successors in the Middle Ages counted as mere 'writers' or 'compilers', who lacked the weight of 'authority'.

Plagiarism moved up from the vices to the virtues: one should never put in one's own weak words what had been said better already. A historiographer recording contemporary events found himself forced to be original to some extent. He tells us so and apologizes. The changed attitude to authorship put a premium on anonymity. The writer preferred not to give his name, or else he sheltered under some greater name of the past. Hence the crop of 'anonymous' and 'pseudo' authors in books on medieval thought and learning. Forgery joined plagiarism in the ranks of the virtues.

The thirteenth and fourteenth centuries saw a revolution in book production. It catered for an increased demand. More people could read and had time to read. The invention of spectacles in about 1300 prolonged reading capacity into

old age. The publisher or 'stationer' reappeared, especially in university towns. He paid professionals to produce *de luxe* copies to order, but also engaged in mass production for sale in his shop. Labour-saving methods came into use. The volume to be copied was taken apart; the 'pieces', as they were called, would be given out to separate scribes, so that a number could work on the same volume simultaneously. The scribes wrote faster. The process resulted in an uglier type of book, which more customers could afford. Royalties and copyright still had to wait for the invention of printing; but the cost of production went down and the author could reach a wider public than had been possible earlier in the Middle Ages.

The rise of medieval schools and universities brings up the question of the professional profit-motive: a teacher noted as a writer on his subject would attract more pupils. But history was not a teaching subject either in ancient or in medieval times. It was taught as a supplement to other subjects, as we shall see later. No student could enrol himself for a course or be examined in history. The minimal place given to historical works is shown in a booklist drawn up by the university authorities at Paris in 1286. They aimed at protecting masters and students from profiteering by the stationers, and each book on the list is marked with the maximum price to be charged in the shop. The compilers included all texts which masters and students would need as basic reading for their courses. Of some 140 items only three could pass as historical. The first is a compendium of Bible history, with a certain amount of pagan history, made by a

4 Three scribes are shown writing. The middle one holds an inkhorn. From an ivory relief produced in western Germany in the ninth or tenth century. *Vienna, Kunsthistorisches Museum*

Paris master, Peter Comestor, in the late twelfth century and known as the *School History*. It sometimes served as a set text for lectures on theology for beginners. The second item is *Legends of the Saints* and the third is *Lives of the Desert Fathers*. The course in theology included training in preaching and in pastoral care; hence the student needed these items as part of his equipment. Medieval history is wholly lacking, except in so far as *Legends of the Saints* stretched out to cover a few medieval saints, such as Thomas Becket. What a student chose to pay for his spare-time reading was his own business; it did not concern the university.

The history of learning amounts to a history of specialization. One branch of learning after another develops into an autonomous discipline. History was a slow developer. The first chairs in it were founded only in the sixteenth century; in the Middle Ages it was non-profit-making, non-professional and unspecialized.

The way history was presented differed from ours. We think in terms of the written word, or of the mass media for the spoken word. Ancient and medieval writers expected their books to be read aloud. Publication might take the form of reading to a circle of friends or to a larger audience, an ancient practice which was revived in the twelfth century and perhaps earlier. From the very beginning of its composition, the writer had in mind what his book would *sound* like. First, he generally dictated it: pen-driving was a chore to be avoided if help was available. Then he would have it read back to him or read it himself and make corrections. When circulated it would be read aloud. Medieval writers address their audience as 'readers' or 'hearers' interchangeably, and their punctuation often supposes that the text will be read aloud: the text of Orderic Vital's *Ecclesiastical History*, for instance, has symbols to indicate a change of pitch in the reader's voice. Even a person reading 'to himself' pronounced the words aloud and gesticulated as he read. Private reading was therefore regarded as a mental and physical exercise. We do not know, for lack of evidence, just when it became customary to run the eye along the line, relying on the eye alone instead of using both eye and ear. For the moment we have to do with writers who appealed to their public orally. This explains much that we find unfamiliar in medieval historians. A writer who appeals to the ear will try every trick of style at his command to please his audience and keep it on the *qui vive*, whether he addresses it directly or whether he imagines someone else reading aloud. The effect is 'rhetorical' (in our modern, bad sense of the word), as it was meant to be. Eleventh- and twelfth-century historians often use rhythmical prose and drop easily into verse. The most skilful translator of Latin into English cannot avoid clumsiness; the original cadences intended by the writer will not come through in translation.

Direct approach to an audience affected content as well as style. An invisible reader shuts his book with a yawn; an audience shows visible signs of boredom. A ninth-century historian called Agnellus read his history of the Church of his native city, Ravenna, to an audience of clergy and people. He is a warm and chatty person, and he tells us when he breaks off his reading for the day and whether his hearers have been attentive or bored: 'You've been hanging on my words today', or 'Yesterday you showed signs of tedium'. It was all the more pressing to tell lively anecdotes to keep one's hearers amused, as Agnellus does. Modern students are told that they must 'try to get into an author's mind'. To understand a medieval historian they must also sit in his audience. The communication is oral. The author expects them to listen to his periods and to laugh when he makes a joke to amuse them.

The medieval author also assumes that his audience will be familiar with the tradition in which he is working. His predecessors speak through his mouth, and his own reading has conditioned his ideas on what history is and on how it should be written. We need to understand his presuppositions. They go back to antiquity and to the Bible and the Fathers. We shall have to make a long journey backwards in time, to Cicero and Moses, in order to grasp how a medieval historiographer approached his material and how he presented it to his audience. The ancient and Christian traditions intermingled, but it is possible to separate them to some extent when we consider their influence on the writing of history in the Middle Ages. To put it very briefly: Latin antiquity supplied classified genres for the forms that historiography might take, rules for writing in the various genres, and models to be imitated. Medieval authors, in so far as they had a smattering of classical learning, observed or modified the ancient traditions. Their faithfulness to the ancients survived all changes in physical conditions and mental climate. The Bible and the Fathers, on the other hand, influenced the content, scope and purpose of medieval historiography.

Roman historians provided models and examples. The choice of what to read depended partly on taste and partly on the chance survival of manuscripts. Medieval scholars, with rare exceptions, could not read Greek, and they had no translations of the classical Greek historians. Of the Latins, Livy (59 BC–AD 17) was known and admired, but seldom read until he came back into fashion in the late thirteenth century. His *From the Foundation of the City* was too ambitious in scale to serve as a model. Tacitus was not read at all. Sallust (87–36 BC) stands out as the favourite. His *Catiline's Conspiracy* and *Jugurthan War* survived the shrinkage of texts studied in the schools of late antiquity, for they are historical monographs of manageable size. Sallust was valued as a stylist who wrote clear, imitable Latin.

Both the style and the method of Roman historians show the close links between history and rhetoric. There were literary conventions. The historian puts speeches into his characters' mouths: a general addresses his troops before battle, a statesman puts his case in assembly, and so on. Readers are not supposed to take these as tape-recordings or even as an accurate report of what was said: they may represent the gist of it, but their real function is to adorn the style. Medieval students delighted in Sallust's speeches and copied them eagerly. Convention allowed a certain freedom from accuracy. Dates could be dispensed with. Documentation was not called for. The writer would have broken the flow of his eloquence had he inserted copies of edicts and treaties, couched in government language. Cicero's rule that historians must tell the truth did not prescribe the truth in niggling detail.

Sallust treated history as a branch of ethics, which in turn was a branch of rhetoric. The orator was 'a *good* man, skilled in speech'. In theory he ought to use his skill to serve an honourable cause. Sallust had a moral outlook and a moral lesson. The Romans looked back to the old days when their forbears had been soldier-farmers, before prosperity and peace corrupted their descendants and led to civil strife and defeat by foreign enemies. The historian should act as a censor, pointing to good and bad examples. He must discern men's true motives. Sallust was cynical in doing so; he generally believed the worst. His books convinced medieval readers that history was moral and exemplarist in purpose and that the historian had a right both to decorate and to adorn his story. He should mount splendid, dramatic battle

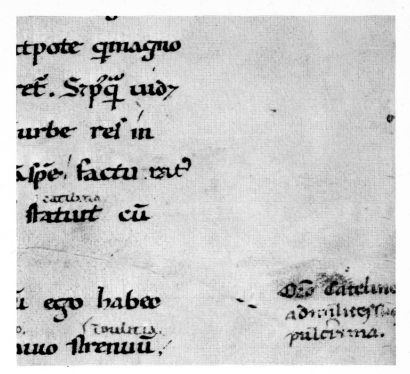

9 Marginal notes to a copy of Sallust's *Catiline Conspiracy* show that it was used as a school text for the study of rhetoric. The note shown here points to 'Catiline's very fine speech to his soldiers', encouraging them to face desperate odds. Medieval historians, mindful of their training in rhetoric, would put quotations from the speeches recorded or invented by Sallust into the mouths of their characters, especially when they described how a general addressed his troops before going into battle. This manuscript was written in the late eleventh or early twelfth century, probably in France. *London, British Museum, MS Harl. 5412, f.17r*

scenes and sieges with set speeches and all the stage properties in his repertoire.

In transmitting samples of the historical monograph, Sallust had a wholesome influence. The genre offered an alternative to the universal history or chronicle on the one hand and local history on the other. His books reinforced by example what Cicero taught on the importance of geography. Sallust described the North African background to the Jugurthan War and explained how it affected the habits and mentality of the Moorish tribes who lived there; he went on to show how these traits accounted for the Moorish victories and final defeat in their wars with Rome. *Catiline's Conspiracy* and *The Jugurthan War* bit so deep into medieval consciousness that borrowings and involuntary memories of Sallustian phrases crop up in literary histories, not to mention imitations of speeches and battle scenes, applied to the story in hand. Julius Caesar wrote a different type of monograph. His *Gallic War* and *Civil War* tell the story of his campaigns in a terse, factual way. Caesar was read and quoted, but less often than Sallust. There was less juice in Caesar; and the monks and clerks who wrote history may have felt closer to a civilian author than they could to a general.

Biography as a genre came down in Suetonius' *Lives of the Caesars* (early second century AD), which began with Julius Caesar and stopped at Domitian. This genre had rules of its own. Suetonius shows us photographs rather than cinema. A *Life* comprises the subject's early career, private life, character, physique and looks, and his public deeds as a ruler. The interaction between public and private did not interest Suetonius, nor did he trace development of character, except to show in some cases that a man might deteriorate under the strain of ruling. He did not go deeply into motive. He could be flippant: according to Suetonius, Julius Caesar decided to invade Britain partly because he was a connoisseur of pearls, which Britain produced in plenty. On moral questions, he refrained from judgment, though he supposed a common standard of right and wrong. He allows that even bad emperors could make good laws and improve judicial procedure.

Not having chosen a rhetorical genre, Suetonius thought it in order to insert record material as evidence. His book *On Grammarians and Rhetors* launched a new type of biography, the lives of literary men. It survived in fragments only, but St Jerome used it as a model for his book *On Illustrious Men*. Hence scholars as well as rulers had a right to biographies. Suetonius caters for readers of all times who say: 'I like history because I'm interested in people.' We should know less about the personal traits of medieval rulers than we do if Suetonius had not recorded that the Divine Augustus wore a woollen vest next his skin in winter. William of Malmesbury might not have told us that Henry I had a hairy chest and snored.

The *Lives of the Caesars* ran parallel to another type of biography, the eulogy or panegyric. This type, which derived from the funeral oration, was a rhetorical exercise. The eulogist praised the deceased according to rules: he exalted him by dwelling on his noble ancestors and then proceeded on traditional lines. If he were a self-made man, he had raised himself up by his own virtuous efforts. The drawback of both types was that they separated history from biography. No author would have thought of composing a *Life and Times* of his subject: that would have meant mixing up two separate genres.

Valerius Maximus provided history in the form of anecdotes or examples. His *Memorable Deeds and Sayings* (written soon after AD 40) is divided into sections which deal with various kinds of virtues and vices, such as piety and respect for the gods, and the opposite – irreligious behaviour. He subdivided each section into Roman and foreign examples. He hoped to equip the orator with a story for every occasion. This is 'packaged' history. You dip into the collection as though it were a chocolate box. Maximus strengthened the tendency to see history as assorted moral lessons (*exempla*). On the credit side, *Memorable Deeds and Sayings* spread knowledge of both important and trivial episodes in ancient history, and it served as a reference book for encyclopaedists. It became popular, too, with homilists and preachers from the twelfth century onwards. Medieval *exempla* collections were made. How far Maximus inspired them is not known; but he had set an admired precedent.

A good medieval library possessed more books on ancient history than I have mentioned here. I have kept to the main rules and models which came down to historiographers.

The Roman legacy ended with the *Etymologies* of St Isidore, bishop of Seville (d. 636). He produced the standard encyclopaedia of the Middle Ages. A scholar would normally have it to hand and look up the subjects as he needed them. The *Etymologies* come into this chapter, although Isidore was a bishop, because he compiled them from all the scraps of ancient lore available to him in Visigothic Spain in the early seventh century. Much of this information derived from late antique textbooks and reference books which disappeared during the Arab invasions. Where Isidore's sources can be traced to surviving books, he is seen up-ending all kinds of miscellaneous bits of information; but the material passed through his mind; he interpreted it in his own way.

The article on 'History' has a familiar sound with Isidorian overtones. Predictably, history is seen as a subsection of grammar, which itself is part of rhetoric. Grammar Isidore defines as 'the art of writing', and history as 'a written narrative of a certain kind'. He distinguishes history from fable and myth: fable expresses truth by means of fiction, as in Aesop's *Fables*, where animals talk and act like human beings, while poetic myth expresses truth by means of fictions about the gods (a current interpretation of myth as signifying cosmic or moral truths). History differs from these kinds of narrative in being true in itself. It is 'the narration of deeds done, by means of which the past is made known', and derives from the Greek verb 'to see' or 'to know' (a modern dictionary adds 'by enquiry', an important addition to Isidore's derivation). Isidore draws the stark conclusion: since history nar-

rates what has been seen and known for true, then it must represent an eyewitness account.

None of the ancients would write history unless he had been present and had seen what he narrated; we grasp what we see better than what we gather from hearsay. Things seen are not represented falsely.

It follows that history begins with one's personal experience. The narration of earlier events counts as mere compilation: one just copied one's sources. Isidore did not keep consistently to his narrow view of true history as eyewitness reporting. Elsewhere he classified the various kinds of historical record according to their time span instead: annals record events from year to year; history covers events which have taken place over many years. It was inconsistent of him to recommend Sallust as a historian, when Sallust did not qualify as an eyewitness, for he had not been an exact contemporary of Catiline and Jugurtha. The compiler of an encyclopaedia such as Isidore's does not always reread his articles to check whether he has contradicted himself.

A modern student will object to Isidore's definition of history for two reasons. An eyewitness account need not be historically accurate. 'They saw it happen' is no guarantee of truth, for eyewitnesses give a partial, distorted account of what happened. A second objection will be that the historian of past ages is not just a compiler. He has to discover, select, analyse and interpret his sources. To dismiss him as a mere copyist would be to abolish most historical studies as we know them. The answer is that Isidore oversimplified on his own terms: he did not find any definition of historical research in the notices on historiography which he read in his textbooks. His authorities failed him. Hence he left a confusing legacy to the Middle Ages. No thoughtful medieval scholar could have accepted that an eyewitness account was necessarily true. Canon and civil law procedure required a number of witnesses to attend in court: a witness could be bribed, or prejudiced or mistaken. Medieval historiographers generally trusted the evidence of their own eyes; but they enlarged Isidore's definition to include reports by trustworthy informants. The most scrupulous tell us whether their report is at first hand; if not, they do not vouch for its accuracy. Isidore's most misleading statements were corrected, but he certainly discouraged research on past history by limiting the 'true historian' to contemporary or near contemporary history.

Some positive points emerge from the muddle all the same. The *Etymologies* were a boon as well as a source of confusion to medieval scholars. The bishop of Seville brought a Christian seriousness to bear on the pagan precept that a historian must tell the truth. The divine command 'thou shalt not lie' and the martyr's witness to the true faith inhere in Isidore's definition of history. The medieval scholar could also quote him to justify historiography to those who dismissed it as a mere waste of time. According to Isidore, record-keeping had a practical use: it established chronology by listing the succession of rulers. Dates are useful for other than literary reasons. He also justified historiography from a moral point of view. History has a moral purpose: it teaches us to choose the good and to avoid the bad by supplying us with examples. Pagan history was a necessary supplement to Christian on both counts: the Christian looks to pagan history for both dates and examples. Isidore's list of famous historians begins with Moses, the supposed author of the Pentateuch, and the list goes on to intersperse pagan with biblical and Christian writers.

Looking back at the achievements of medieval historiographers, we may think it just as well that Isidore directed their energies to what we now call 'contemporary history'. He channelled their creative activity into the lines which they were best able to follow. To write the history of the remote past meant copying and compiling; it was not creative. A critical study of the remote past, as distinct from mere compilation of earlier sources, called for tools and equipment which were lacking in the Middle Ages. A few historians had the courage and daring to break out of the Isidorian framework in order to study the remote past. The results did not measure up to the inspiration behind them. The writer's own time and the immediate past offered more scope to his talents and more amenable material. Isidore gave him wise guidance in pointing him away from a task which was beyond his powers.

3
The Jewish-Christian legacy

Christianity is 'the religion of a book'. A Christian historiographer takes the Old and New Testaments as his starting-point. Medieval writings on history make little sense to a reader who does not know his Bible. A medieval writer will normally quote from the Scriptures; he will also refer and allude. Biblical diction and biblical stories colour his tale. He will, however, borrow style and content from the Bible rather than form. His models of form are classical, not biblical. The gulf between Oriental and Western went deep. One could try to be a good Christian; one could not turn oneself into a semite; the classical tradition of writing intervened. A Latin scholar confronted two traditions of historiography. On one side he saw his classical models and rules of composition; on the other he inherited a new time scale, a new framework and a new view of the supernatural. The two legacies amalgamated.

Let us begin with the supernatural in the biblical tradition. The reader of Roman historians would have met it before. They recorded divine intervention in human affairs in the form of omens and marvels. Even such apparent rationalists as Caesar and Sallust mentioned religious beliefs and practices as part of their stories. Modern classical scholarship has uncovered a substratum of folklore and magic in upper-class Latin culture; no one has doubted its persistence among the people. In Christian history the supernatural did not merely impinge on the story; it dominated. The divine element was definite and concrete. God was the creator of the world and the author of its history; he revealed himself in the Scriptures. The actors in Scripture were historical characters. The patriarchs and prophets, the Son of God and his Mother and the apostles had all lived on earth. They were not mythical, like the pagan gods and goddesses; their miracles authenticated their teaching; God willed it to be so. The supernatural element increased in the record of post-biblical history. Angels and devils joined the *dramatis personae*. Saints descended from heaven to warn and guide the living and to

11 Opposite: one of the four Gospels, displayed on an altar. A detail from the fifth-century mosaics on the cupola of the Baptistery of the Orthodox at Ravenna. The whole scheme of the dome illustrates the place of the Bible in the Church.

avenge their wrongs. The content of history gained a new dimension. It included heaven and hell.

The new time scale supplied a new framework. Classical authors had held varying views of time. Some imagined it as cyclical: time moved in cycles, variously calculated as the 'great year'. Everything which had happened once would happen again as the 'great year' recurred. The more common view of time in the ancient world was that it moved from past to present towards an indefinitely long future. The Christian view of time differed from both, in that the Christian gave time a beginning and an end. Time existed only between the Creation and the Last Things. Time began with Creation, as recorded by Moses in the first chapters of Genesis. It proceeded through the Old and New Testaments up to the present. It would end with Christ's second coming and Doomsday. Then time and history would give way to eternity. History, seen through Christian eyes, becomes the history of man's salvation in time.

The Bible presented history as it unrolled itself between two definite moments. It was gloriously compact. The Christian reader of any period could marvel at God's perfect plan, embracing past, present and future, although one mortal life covered but a tiny fraction of total history. God's word as set down in Scripture enables us to transcend past and present alike and to foresee their consummation on the last day. St Bonaventure, a Franciscan professor at Paris, found a poetic simile to express this traditionally Christian view of history. He puts it into the prologue to his *Breviloquium*, a compendium of theology, written in 1257. God has ordered his narrative so that it resembles 'a beautiful song', where all things flowing from his Providence can be seen:

No reader can appreciate the beauty of a song unless he looks at all the verses. In the same way, no man can appreciate the beauty of universal order and governance unless he sees it as a whole. No man lives long enough to witness all history with his own eyes; nor can he foresee the future for himself. So the Holy Spirit provides him with the book of Holy Writ, whose length tallies with the course of universal governance, whole and entire.

God opens and shuts the book; but he lets us 'look at the end' to see what will happen on the final page. Divine history is not published as a serial 'to be continued in our next number'. We have it all between two covers; only the span between our present and the end remains hidden, unless God tells us something of it by special revelation. The prophet may fore-see what is dark to the historian.

A book needs chapter division to make it readable. The Church Fathers scrutinized the Bible to discover what God had intended by way of chapters in his history of salvation. They invented new periods to serve as chapters, each one marking a stage in the fulfilment of God's plan. Periodization had to include both profane and sacred history; they could not be separated, since both belonged to the workings of divine Providence. It is well to remember that we still periodize history, even when we approach it from a secular point of view. All such divisions have drawbacks; they tend to be artificial and distorting. We use them for the simple reason that no one as yet has discovered any other way to tackle the study and teaching of history. The worst feature of periodiza-tion is that it sticks like a well-gummed label. A division of history which reflects the ideas and concerns of one genera-tion imposes its pattern long after it has lost its usefulness. All teachers of history have to struggle with the incubus – 'the Middle Ages closed down on the field of Bosworth in 1485'; 'modern history begins in England with the Tudors'. The ghost of this out-of-date chapter division still haunts us.

Periodization can sometimes act as a stimulant. The Marx-ist division of history into periods corresponding to the mode of production has led to intensive research and discussion. Fruitful criticism of this kind was inhibited in the Middle Ages by respect for authority. The saints had handed down a set of chapter divisions to be used by readers of God's history book. A medieval scholar would have thought it rash and blasphemous to tamper with tradition. It would have amounted to rewriting the holy page. If he dissented, as some did, he would fiddle with detail or suppress what struck him as untrue, instead of suggesting an alternative. Hence medi-eval historians inherited a periodization which had been invented in late antiquity and which corresponded to an early Christian outlook on history.

One kind of time scheme was religious in character. St Augustine, the 'chief doctor of the Latin Church', sponsored it with all the weight of his authority. Augustine divided world history into six ages. These represented the six ages of man, as he passes from infancy to senility. God wrote them into history from the very beginning: the six days of Creation, as told in the first chapters of Genesis, signified

12 Opposite: some of the most important events in the history of salvation are painted in roundels set into the initial letter of the opening word of Genesis in the Winchester Bible. Starting at the top, God creates Eve from the rib of Adam; Noah's ark floats on the waters of the Flood; Abraham prepares to sacrifice his son Isaac at God's command; God appears to Moses in the burning bush; John the Baptist baptizes Christ; the Christ Child lies in the manger above Mary and Joseph; finally we see the Last Judgment. All four of the first scenes presage the coming of Christ and his founding of the Christian Church. The manuscript was produced in England about 1160–70. *Winchester Cathedral Library*

both the six ages of man and the six ages of the world. God's rest on the seventh day signified that the world would end in the seventh age, which would mark the transition from time to eternity.

Augustine plotted out the course of his six ages as follows: the period from Adam to Noah represented infancy, Noah to Abraham childhood, Abraham to David youth, David to the Babylonian Captivity of the Jews manhood, Babylonian Captivity to St John the Baptist middle age; the period between the first and the second coming of Christ represented senility: it was the old age of the world. In addition, Augustine subdivided the ages, so as to link each one with its successor. Changing his metaphor, he resorted to the analogy of day and night. Each age had its morning, noon and evening within its span. The night of one age gave way to the morning of the age which followed.

The day and night scheme explains what looks puzzling about Augustine's periodization at first sight: he presented the Christian era as the age of senility, bearing all the signs of sickness associated with growing old. But in terms of day and night, it had its splendour, like the other ages. The sixth age dawned with the Baptist; the sun rose in Christ's Incarnation; the spread of Christianity coincided with midday. Augustine, living in the troubled times of the late fourth and early fifth centuries, supposed that evening would close in soon. The sixth age would give way to the seventh, when time would end. Expectation of the Last Things as due 'at any moment now' tempted Christians to look for signs of the second coming in current events. But Augustine gave them no licence to do so. He condemned speculation on the precise date of Doomsday: we must wait in readiness for the time which God has decided upon without making rash guesses.

The concept of the six ages saddled medieval historiographers with a gloomy picture of their times. Augustine taught that they were living in the old age of the world: noon had passed into evening and night drew nigh. Yet the world lingered on like some aged invalid; there is no cure for senility, however prolonged it may be. Augustine's time scheme discouraged optimism. Progress was ruled out. The individual Christian could grow in virtue by God's grace and merit salvation. There was no hope that mankind would ever improve in the mass.

Such is the resilience of human nature that the prospect of inexorable decline into death did not daunt medieval histor-

13 Opposite: St Augustine's six ages of the world are shown in a circle. They begin with the expulsion of Adam and Eve from the garden of Eden (left, above) and continue anti-clockwise to the Christian era, represented at the top by the Virgin and Child and a priest celebrating Mass. The traditional number of years for the duration of each age is written in the outer circle. An angel with outstretched arms in the centre announces the coming of the seventh age. Then time will end. This picture illustrates a prose translation in Catalan of a Provençal verse encyclopaedia composed in 1288–92. The manuscript was produced in Catalonia in the last quarter of the fourteenth century. The six ages has a long life in historical tradition. *London, British Museum, MS Yates Thompson 31, f.76r*

ians nearly so much as one might have expected. Life tasted good to some of them. Events, however sad and shocking, had absorbing interest for their recorders. One could not be indifferent to what was happening in the period before the lights would be turned off and the stage set for Doomsday. Many writers, as we shall see, conveniently forgot or ignored the sadness of their place in a time scheme which they accepted without question. The idea of the sixth age affixed itself so firmly and yet sat so lightly on medieval histori-ography for the very reason that it could not be tested or dis-proved. A religious theory generally defies the test of fact. The second time scheme inherited by medieval scholars was more vulnerable and hence more provocative.

This time scheme is called 'politico-religious'. It originated in the 'inter-testamentary period', that is the period between the last of the Old Testament books and the first of the New Testament. This period saw the desperate struggle of the Jewish people to defend their religion and preserve their national identity against their oppressors. Jewish writers tried to comfort their people and to wring hope out of despair. A natural way to stiffen resistance was to promise success to come: the Jews would be rescued by divine intervention in history. The writers conveyed their promise in a genre known as the 'apocalypse'.

An apocalypse takes the form of a vision or dream. Its pur-pose is to prophesy the final triumph of the persecuted people so as to console them in their misery. The seer, who records the vision, writes under some well-known name, so as to make it more noteworthy; he keeps his own name secret. The most famous apocalypse among Christians passed into the Old Testament canon under the name of Daniel, the hero of the story of the lions' den. The writer of this apocalypse made Daniel live in the period of the Babylonian Captivity in the reign of 'Darius the Mede'. Darius is a fictitious character, with no place in history. He stands for a type of gentile ruler over Jews. Daniel had a vision: he saw three beasts rise up from the sea, a lion, a bear and a leopard with four heads. Then a fourth beast, strongest and most terrible of all, came to chew up the three beasts with its iron teeth and trample them down with its iron claws. The fourth beast had ten horns. An eleventh horn, smaller than the ten, sprouted up among them and mastered them. Lastly Daniel saw the Ancient of Days, seated on his throne. He ordered that the fourth beast should be destroyed by burning (Dan. 7).

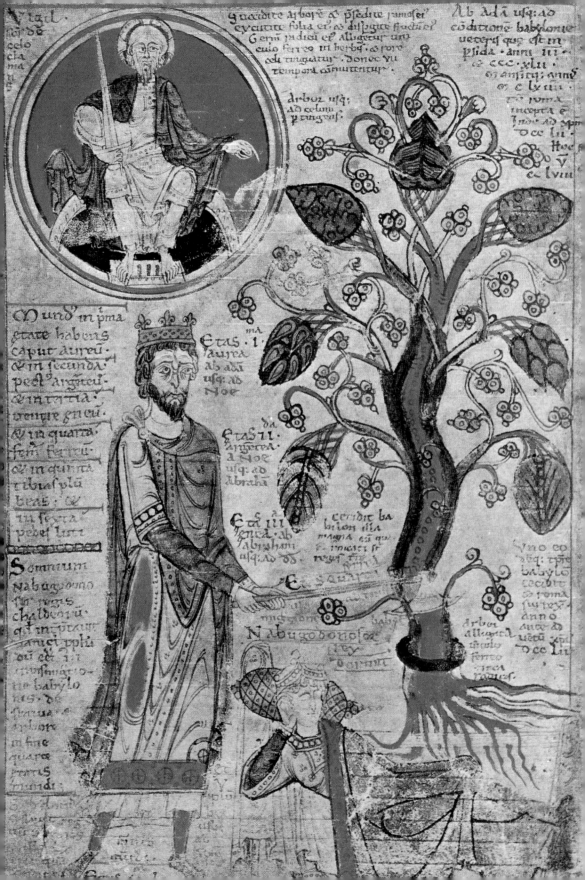

henr̄ vi mag̅n̅ Romanorum Imperator

virtutes   fortitudo   virtutes   Iusticia

fortuna rogat virtutes
et i gloriciō eay̅ set re
pullam passa est
defende minuificas

Roca for
ne

Tancred

The writer, whoever he was, probably meant his four beasts to signify the four world monarchies of which he knew: those of the Babylonians, the Medes, the Persians and the Macedonians. God would destroy the last surviving monarchy and would free His chosen people. When the Romans conquered the Greeks and set up a new world monarchy, the scope of Daniel's vision had to be stretched to include the Romans. The fourth beast now signified the Roman empire. Interpreters of the vision managed to keep the number four by joining the Medes and Persians together as 'the monarchy of the Medes and Persians'. Another passage in the book of Daniel lent itself to the same interpretation. King Nebuchadnezzar dreamed that he saw a statue which had a head of gold, breast and arms of silver, belly and thighs of brass, legs of iron and feet of iron mixed with clay. The statue was destroyed and its metals were scattered to the winds like chaff. This too signified the four world monarchies and the destruction of the last one as a prelude to the day of glory for Israel.

The theme of four world monarchies, which would rise in succession, passed into Christian historiography and supplemented the six ages as a chapter division of universal history. The destruction of the statue and of the fourth beast of the prophecy would herald the coming of Antichrist, signified by the eleventh horn on the head of the beast.

Antichrist and Daniel's ten-headed monster increased their prestige by making an appearance in the Christian Apocalypse. Medieval Latin scholars identified 'John', the author of the Book of Revelation, with St John the Evangelist and the writer of the Epistles of St John. A thirteenth-century English illuminator of Revelation brought out the identification strikingly when he set this last book of the Bible into a picture cycle showing the life and miracles of St John. We see the apostle suffering torture and exile at the hands of the emperor Domitian. He writes his book in exile on the isle of Patmos at an angel's command. Then his book unrolls itself in pictures. Finally, after the last scene of Revelation, the murder of Domitian frees him to return to continue his work of preaching the Gospel and destroying idols. The legendary setting expresses concretely the current belief that Revelation offered an authoritative version of what would happen at the end of time, vouched for in person by the Beloved Disciple.

The theme of Revelation corresponds to that of Jewish apocalyptic, here applied to Christians. John foretells in poetic

Colour plate II
THE WHEEL OF FORTUNE
(see pp. 46–7)
The theme of Fortune's Wheel is knit into the history of the emperor Henry VI (1190–97) in this illustration from the book which the poet Peter of Eboli wrote in his honour. The *Liber ad honorem Augusti* celebrates Henry's conquest of Sicily from the usurper Tancred in 1195. Henry sits crowned holding his orb and sceptre, surrounded by the Virtues, personified. They compete to offer gifts, which the emperor has deserved. Below them we see Fortune's Wheel. Tancred is shown glorying in his luck at the top and then lying at the bottom when Fortune has cast him down. His evil deeds are recorded. He has got what he deserved. Fortune in this context is supposed to reward merit and punish pride and cruelty. She can therefore be enlisted to flatter a ruler. Peter's book is meant as a eulogy. *Bern, Burgerbibliothek, Cod. 120, f.146r*

Lucuf leonium
ubi danieL miffuf fura ce ubb ...
euc poftaurfilli
pfun diuin

14, 15 Illustrations from a famous commentary on the book of Revelation by Beatus, a Spanish monk who died in 798. This manuscript from the monastery of S. Domingo de Silos in Castile was finished in 1109. Above: Daniel in the lions' den. Opposite: the vision of the four beasts. The Ancient of Days sits on his throne, whence a stream of fire proceeds. The beasts prance below him. In clockwise order from the upper left, they are the lion with eagle's wings, the four-headed leopard, the bear, and the beast whose eleventh horn (shown with a human head) masters the others. The beasts were interpreted as the four world monarchies (see also ill. 19). *London, British Museum, MS Add. 11695, f. 232r and 240r*

imagery the disasters which God will inflict on his people by means of floods, earthquakes, plagues and wicked rulers. The latter signify persecutors of the Church in general and Roman emperors in particular. Christians must take courage: the triumph of righteousness is at hand. Antichrist embodies the forces of evil in this cosmic struggle. The idea of Antichrist went back to certain Old Testament prophecies and to Jewish apocalypses, though the early Christians first gave him his name. Sometimes he took the shape of a persecuting ruler; sometimes he appeared as a beast or dragon, unleashed upon earth. He wins victories, but finally falls to the spears of the good angels.

John took over the fourth beast of Daniel's vision and presented it as an agent and forerunner of Antichrist. Like Daniel, he sees a beast rising from the sea, having ten horns on its head and upon the horns ten diadems (10:1). The ten horns still signify ten kings, who will fight for Antichrist against the righteous when the end draws near.

The fourth beast of Daniel's vision and of Revelation

36

Anno primo balcasar regis babilonis daniel sommum uidit :

ludicium sedit et libri aperti sunt fua

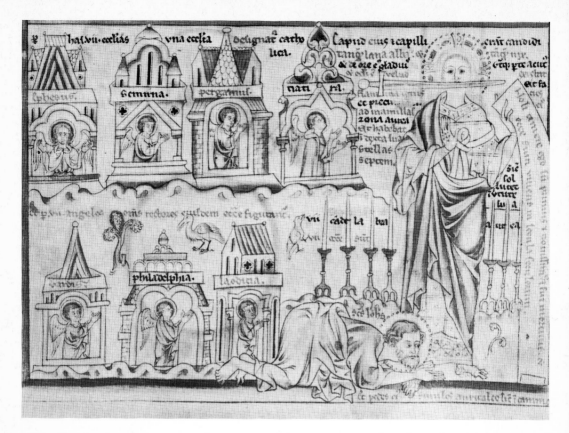

16 The Christian Apocalypse. St John falls at the feet of the Son of Man, who has a 'sharp two-edged sword' in his mouth. The seven churches of Asia to which St John is to send his message and the seven candlesticks of his vision appear at the sides of the picture (Rev. 1:9–17). From a mid-thirteenth-century English manuscript of the school of St Alban's. *Oxford, Bodleian Library, MS Auct. D.4.17, f.3r*

posed many problems. It proved to be a hardy, long-lived creature. The dream statue also persisted in standing upright, in spite of its clay-mixed feet. The beast had recurrent spells of sickness, and the statue tottered at intervals; but they failed to disappear. They survived both in fact and in theory. The division of world history into periods corresponding to the sway of four world monarchies established itself so firmly that it was still taken seriously as late as the sixteenth century. The French scholar Jean Bodin thought himself original and daring when he scrapped the idea of the four-monarchy periodization in his *Method of History* (1566).

The Jewish legacy supplied a model as well as a set of periods. The Jewish author Flavius Josephus wrote his *Antiquities of the Jews* and *The Jewish War* in the late first century AD. His books were translated from Greek into Latin; 'the Latin Josephus' became a 'must' for medieval libraries. Medieval scholars used the *Antiquities* to supplement their Old Testament. *The Jewish War* represented a monograph of the familiar classical type. It went down to the Roman conquest of Jerusalem and the dispersion of Palestinian Jewry.

ANTIXPS

ANTIXPS hElIA ET hINOC OCCIDIT

Josephus was not apocalyptic in outlook – he acquiesced in Roman rule when he could see no alternative – but his book contains vivid battle scenes and a horrifying account of the siege of Jerusalem. Medieval writers found him quotable when they wanted to describe battles and sieges.

The first Christian model of historiography on a large scale came from Eusebius, bishop of Caesarea. He finished his *Ecclesiastical History* in about 325; it was made available in a Latin paraphrase soon afterwards. Eusebius invented a new kind of historiography. No Christian before him had written the history of the Church after the end of the New Testament period. No Christian before him had harnessed universal history to polemic against the pagans. The *Ecclesiastical History* was cosmic in scope. Eusebius set himself to tell the story of divine Providence. God used the Jews directly and the gentiles indirectly for the purpose of man's salvation. Augustus Caesar brought peace to his subjects; hence he prepared them for the spread of the Gospel. The conversion of the emperor Constantine led to the recognition of Christianity as a state religion.

17 The coming of Antichrist as foretold by St John. He slaughters the saints, whose bodies lie unburied, while his servants demolish the holy city. (Rev. 11:2–9). From a manuscript of Beatus' commentary on the Apocalypse (see ills. 14, 15), made at the abbey of St Sever in Gascony in the mid-eleventh century. *Paris, Bibliothèque Nationale, MS lat. 8878, f.155r*

39

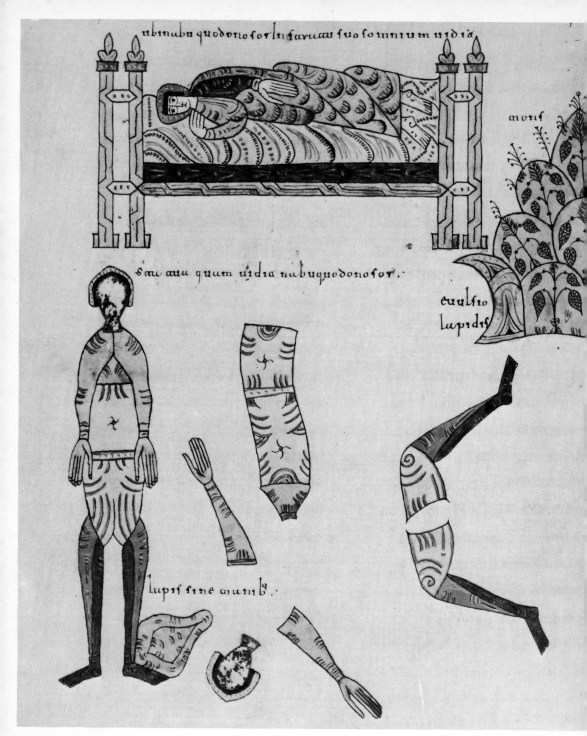

ubi nabuquodonosor in faruca suo somnium uidia

mons

sciu aiu quam uidia nabuquodonosor.

euulsio lapidis

lapris sine munib.

NEBUCHADNEZZAR'S DREAM OF THE STATUE

18, 19 Above: an illustration from the Silos Apocalypse, finished in 1109 (see ills. 14, 15). The statue is shown first whole and then broken into pieces by the stone 'cut from the mountain without hands'. The stone according to Christian interpretation signified Christ, and its destruction of the statue his final victory over the four world monarchies represented by the different parts of the statue's body.

The image lived on into the seventeenth century. Opposite: a broadsheet published at Augsburg in 1623. The statue is about to be struck by stone. The four beasts (see ill. 15) stand in the background. The eleventh horn of the fourth beast here signifies the power of the Turkish invaders. The prophecy has been brought up to date. *London, British Museum (both; above, MS Add.11695, f.224v)*

Eusebius underlined the all-embracing scope of his *Ecclesiastical History* by drawing up chronological tables to connect biblical-Christian with pagan history. His Christian readers learned from his book that true history must be universal. It was permissible to write a historical monograph; but the historiographer who aimed at something wider must comprehend the history of the whole world. Jewish, gentile and Christian history must be included, since God embraced all three in his plan. Universality became the ideal of Latin historiographers. Eusebius' notion of universality had narrow limits. His world was that of a Greek bishop of the early fourth century. It centred on the Mediterranean and shaded off to darkness outside the imperial boundaries. Medieval historians had to enlarge the area they surveyed, to correspond with the growth of the Church. The focus of history shifted, too, when the imperial provinces of North Africa and Spain fell to the Muslim invaders. The Mediterranean ceased to be the Roman *mare nostrum*, as it had been for Eusebius. Nevertheless, his limited concept of universality had a restrictive effect on medieval writers. They kept his concept in mind and enlarged or shifted their limits only when they could not avoid doing so.

The first attempt at total coverage of world history was not made by a Christian. The Persian scholar Rashēd al Din (d. 1318) compiled a history of the whole world, in so far as it was known to him. He enjoyed the patronage of a Mogul or Mongol emperor, who gave him facilities for collecting information. Rashēd's *History* includes data on places as far apart as Ireland and China. Latin efforts at universal history have a parish-pump appearance in comparison. Still the *Ecclesiastical History* corrected any tendency to mere localism.

Eusebian history was tougher and duller than the classical pagan kind. The rhetorical arguments and techniques which Latin historians used to persuade their readers to fall in with their views did not suit the bishop of Caesarea. He wanted to convince pagans as well as Christians of the truth of his story. He had an up-hill task. The victory of Christianity over pagan cults had put non-Christian intellectuals on the alert: they engaged Christians in a lively dialogue. Eusebius looked for hard proof to confute the pagans. Record evidence filled the bill: he inserted copies of documents issued by the imperial government to accredit his story of persecution followed by toleration. Copies of decrees issued by Church councils and lists of bishops supplied proof for his account of ecclesiastical history. He kept it up when he reached a period whose events he could record as an eyewitness. Now, as well as documents, we find references to his own experience. Eusebius describes persons whom he met, places which he visited and buildings which he had seen.

To insert documents meant breaking the rules of rhetorical composition. Suetonius offered a precedent; but he was writing in a less rhetorical genre than Sallust or Livy had chosen. Eusebius' departure from the classical tradition comes out clearly in one particular speech which he includes in his *History*. It is no fake speech, invented as a rhetorical flourish. Eusebius sets down a real sermon, which he preached himself on a solemn occasion, celebrating the rebuilding of the church at Tyre after public Christian worship had been authorized. His sermon belonged to the historical record. The inclusion of documentary evidence in the *Ecclesiastical History* licensed medieval writers to do the same. Following Eusebius, they would copy charters, privileges, papal bulls, letters, decrees and sermons into their histories and chronicles. The modern historian should feel grateful to the fourth-century bishop for setting the standard. Many original documents have been lost, and we rely on copies preserved by medieval historiographers.

The gravest limitation of Eusebian history appears in its title. It is a history of the Church. Secular history has its place only as a framework for ecclesiastical. A medieval historian who wanted to write about politics and battles got no help from Eusebius. Classical models still remained as the only guides to the composition of secular history. There were two

20 Chronological tables from Eusebius in the Latin translation, showing the dates of Athenian, Latin and Egyptian rulers in parallel columns. From an Italian manuscript of the fifth century. *Oxford, Bodleian Library, MS Auct. T.2.26, f.46r*

21 Orosius presents his
History Against the Pagans to
St Augustine, bishop of
Hippo. The figures are fitted
into an initial E in a twelfth-
century copy of the *History*.
*London, British Museum, MS
Burney 216, f.88v*

22 A marginal drawing in
the same manuscript
illustrates Orosius' account
of the first Roman war
against Pirrhus. An elephant
carries a cart full of soldiers.
*London, British Museum, MS
Burney 216, f.33r*

possible answers to the problem: one could try to keep
secular and ecclesiastical history distinct and write either one
or the other, or one could mix two genres. The first solution
became ever more difficult to manage, as the Church
increased in importance. Medieval historians had no alternative but to write secular and ecclesiastical history concurrently, though the two genres made uneasy bed-fellows.

St Augustine handed down a model as well as a time
scheme to later historians. That too was religious. Two
historical themes run through his *City of God*. In one,
Augustine was arguing against the pagans' objection to
Christianity: the Christian God had failed to protect the
citizens of the Roman Empire against the barbarian invaders.
Augustine answered that Christianity was not to blame for
the fall of Rome. Pagan history, he pointed out, recorded
both foreign and civil wars, famines and disasters of all
kinds. If anything, the miseries of life had been worse in the
pagan era than they were in the Christian. His second theme
was that mankind throughout the six ages of the world had
formed two cities. The city of God confronted the city of the
wicked. Abel, the just man, and Cain, his murderer, were
the prototypes. The two brothers signified the inhabitants of
the two cities for all time. They intermingled on earth, but
they would be separated at the Last Judgment. Then the city
of God would unite the saved among the quick and the
dead; the city of darkness would unite the damned.

Augustine's book represents a vision of history, not a
blueprint for historiography. His conception of the two
cities is elusive because he never identified the city of God
with the visible Church: many professing Christians
belonged to the city of darkness. His *City of God*, moreover,
was too long and rambling to share the immense popularity
of his other works in the Middle Ages. It influenced medieval
historians through the distorting medium of Augustine's
disciple Orosius.

The *History Against the Pagans* supplied the blueprint for
historiography which was missing in the *City of God*.
Orosius, a Spanish priest and admirer of St Augustine,
undertook to embody his master's ideas in a universal history.
His book, presented to Augustine in 417, gives a coarsened
version of Augustine's thought, and was popular for that
reason. The first theme of the *City of God* lent itself to
colourful treatment. Orosius painted a lurid picture of
history as a record of the crimes and follies of mankind. Both

crimes and follies, mainly committed by rulers, resulted in bloody wars. The historian mounts upon a tower and looks down from his vantage-point at the carnage spread before his eyes. To do Orosius justice, the ancient histories which he read nearly all had 'war' in their titles.

The most original part of his work was his time scheme of the four monarchies. The fourth beast of Daniel's vision represented the Roman empire; but Orosius tamed it. He thought that the empire offered the only shield against the barbarians and hoped that it would last long enough to contain their invasions. Iron teeth and claws have much to commend them, when they bite and trample down one's enemies. Orosius differed from Augustine in this warmth towards the empire. His master realized that the disappearance of Rome as a world power need not mean the end of the world; other states might replace the empire; small states might prove to be less rapacious, because they were less powerful. A careful reading of the *City of God* might have prevented medieval scholars from swallowing Orosius whole. As it was, the *History Against the Pagans* transmitted the idea that the fall of the Roman empire would usher in Antichrist. The ten horns on the head of the fourth beast of Daniel's vision signified ten kings who would divide the empire among themselves. Antichrist would come and master them, as the eleventh horn mastered the ten. His coming would bring those troubles which St John foretold in his Revelation as due to afflict the world before the second advent of Christ.

According to Orosius, his own time fell within the period of the fourth monarchy. The Roman empire was still undivided. Its division would presage Doomsday. The author was so cocksure about the meaning of history that he has been accused of 'playing God to his characters'. This further endeared him to readers who wanted to be told what to think. The *History Against the Pagans* had the merit of being comprehensive and comprehensible. It was one of the most widely read books of the Middle Ages.

Orosius wrote history as a tale of woe, and his imitators followed suit. A ninth-century bishop, Freculph of Lisieux, warns readers of his chronicle:

Almost all writers on history, especially the Greeks and Romans, begin their story with Nimrod, son of Baal, king of many peoples. Their aim is to describe the fortunes of war, the ruin of kings and the miseries of their subjects, so as to teach us that the wars of kings serve only to do them harm.

23 A marginal drawing in the same manuscript of Orosius' *History Against the Pagans* as the two details opposite shows a monster prodigy portending disaster: a child is born with two heads and a double set of limbs. *London, British Museum, MS Burney 216, f.41r*

45

Wars are cruel and futile; but rulers, being fools or criminals, never stop fighting. This is the Orosian point of view. At least, however, Orosius made history seem worth recording. His *History Against the Pagans* had an influence for good inasmuch as it reinforced Eusebius by presenting history as universal. Orosius also taught his readers that geography belonged to history. Sallust and Caesar showed the importance of geography in their monographs; Orosius introduced it on a world-wide scale (in so far as he dealt with 'the world'). He began by giving a geographical survey of the three continents known to him, Europe, Asia and Africa.

King Alfred of Wessex (d. 899) translated Orosius' *History* into English as part of his programme for educating his people. It was one of the basic texts which he thought necessary for their instruction. Since Orosius' geography centred on the Mediterranean, Alfred supplemented it by inserting data on the North Sea and Baltic areas, supplied by a sea captain. The king had taken Orosius' point that geography is a background to history.

Alfred also translated Boethius' *Consolation of Philosophy*, as another indispensable text. Boethius brings us to the last of those key concepts which medieval historians inherited from late antiquity. The *Consolation of Philosophy* is not a history book, but historians took from it the theme of Fortune's Wheel. Boethius wrote as a victim of Fortune. He had served the Arian king of Italy, Theodoric, and had had a brilliant career as a civil servant. Then Theodoric jailed him, suspecting him of taking part in an anti-Arian plot – for Boethius was a Catholic and a Roman, although he had worked for an Ostrogothic ruler. He died in prison in 524. The setting of his *Consolation* is a dialogue between himself as a prisoner and Philosophy, personified as a lady, who comforts him in his ruin. She explains that Fortune has brought him down and goes on to describe the character of Fortune, also personified as a woman. The fickle goddess turns her wheel, now spoiling and coddling her favourites, now dropping them when it pleases her mood. From rags to riches and vice versa they go. Fortune, like a woman, is 'changeable ever'. Why, asks Philosophy, should Boethius complain of her normal behaviour? The wise man will see success as transitory.

Fortune's Wheel became a cliché without losing its pathos. Boethius took care to present the goddess as an instrument of divine providence. Pride goes before a fall, as God has decreed. But her Wheel suggested a theory of causation

24 The lady Philosophy wearing an embroidered gown appears to the senator Boethius as he sits in prison behind bars. He is writing his *Consolation of Philosophy*. From a manuscript produced at Regensburg in the first quarter of the thirteenth century. *Munich, Bayerische Staatsbibliothek, MS lat. 2599, f.106v*

within the Christian framework. Orosius displayed the sweep of universal history; Boethius inserted a proximate cause for the rise and fall of dynasties, families and individuals. His Fortune deserved her popularity. The modern historian does not invoke the picture of a goddess cranking her wheel; but he still resorts to 'chance' in some cases, where no other explanation occurs to him. There is an incalculable element in court faction, which ruined Boethius, and in the feuds and lawsuits of rival families. Fortune's Wheel makes concrete the elusive, unpredictable factor in human affairs.

Hagiography, the writing of saints' lives and passions (their martyrdom), was a flourishing industry all through the Middle Ages. It lies outside the scope of this book, but the student needs to know what its rules and conventions were. The medieval historian would have read or heard *Lives* of the saints; he would often have composed or rewritten *Lives* himself. Hence the genre would influence him when he wrote his chronicle or history.

The conventions of hagiography took shape as early as the fourth century. A Greek *Life* of the hermit St Antony (d. 356) was read in the West in a Latin translation. Sulpicius Severus wrote his Latin *Life* of St Martin of Tours, a bishop and ascetic, toward 397. Here were two model *Lives*, one for a hermit and one for a bishop. Convention prescribed that the author should dedicate his *Life* to a friend, who had asked or ordered him to write. He then apologized in elegant language for not writing elegantly. The degree of elegance depended on his education. Sulpicius belonged to a literary élite and took pains over his style, so he set a high standard.

The presentation of the saint's life normally followed the rules of ancient rhetorical biography or eulogy. The hero fitted into a set pattern: he was saintly from his infancy, or else he was a sinner who was converted to sanctity. The

25 Above: the Wheel of Fortune described by Boethius. The goddess with bands covering her eyes to indicate blindness sits in the centre. A lion, the royal beast signifying pride, stands on the top wearing a crown. The three men, one of whom is losing his crown, signify the changes of fortune experienced by rulers. From a thirteenth-century French manuscript containing a French translation of the *Consolation*. *Vienna, Österreichische Nationalbibliothek, MS 2642, f.11r*

26 Right: a more elaborate representation of Fortune's Wheel. Here Fortune sits at the side of the picture, not blind but wilfully malicious, turning the wheel by means of a crank. A king, raised up in glory, sits at the top bearing symbols of wealth and enjoyment. Five men fall and rise on the wheel. Fortune's throne rests upon the earth, to signify that change is part of man's earthly condition. From a facsimile of the twelfth-century book called *Garden of Delights* ascribed to Herrad of Landsberg, now destroyed.

writer had a standard set of miracles to draw upon, such as 'the dream of the pregnant mother' foretelling the fame of her unborn son, a theme which goes back to pagan antiquity. Devils had their stock roles as tempters. Like his predecessor, the ancient eulogist, the medieval writer of a saint's *Life* omitted pettifogging details, such as dates and chronological order. Exceptions are rare. They would have broken the flow of rhetoric; worse still, they would have distracted the reader or hearer from his 'holy reading'. What did dates matter to one's veneration of a holy man?

Sulpicius' literary background led him to introduce a classical note into content as well as style. He opposed St Martin to pagan heroes and sages as the right example for Christians to follow. At the same time, he admired the virtues of good pagans, and knitted them into his story. Biblical precedents are intermixed with pagan. The saint became a hero as 'a soldier of Christ' and also a sage who taught Christian wisdom. Heroines had their parts to play: there were women martyrs, recluses, energetic abbesses.

The saint's *Life* was a semi-historical genre. Its familiarity and its well-established rules marked it out as a neighbour likely to trespass on historiography's domain. The trespass was mainly one way: historians accepted hagiographical traditions of writing more often than hagiographers borrowed from historians. The saint's *Life* offered a tempting model of dateless history.

A question may be asked at this point: why did medieval historiographers need models for their various genres? Why couldn't they write as they thought fit without having to choose a model and mould their story according to its rules? A moment's reflection will show that we still use models, beginning with school essays. New types of history develop slowly. It took a long time for old-fashioned 'political history' to make room for social and economic history, to give one example. The new type edges its way in eventually when new problems oblige us to see the past in a different light and so compel us to accept the unfamiliar. The same process can be seen in the early Middle Ages. New types of historiography were invented to eke out the older types. The classical and Christian models were supplemented by new ones, which could be copied or tailored to fit new needs. Europe after the first wave of barbarian invasions looked so different from the world of late antiquity that its history could no longer be written in the old ways.

4

The barbarian legacy
and the early Middle Ages

27 Brut the Trojan building
Stonehenge. From a
thirteenth-century French
version of the chronicle
called the *Brut. London,
British Museum, MS Egerton
3028, f.30r*

Colour plate III
HISTORY WITHOUT
HISTORICAL
PERSPECTIVE (see pp. 63–4)
Jeremiah, who began to
prophesy in 626 BC, foretold
that Jerusalem would be
conquered as a punishment
for the people's sins. His
prophecy was fulfilled in the
Babylonian capture of the
city, in 587 BC. The artist of
the Bury Bible – a monk of
Bury St Edmunds called
Hugh, working about 1135 –
shows the prophet holding a
scroll with one hand and
pointing down to the siege
of Jerusalem with the other.
The armour, mode of
warfare and fortifications
belong to the twelfth
century. *Cambridge, Corpus
Christi College, MS 2, f.245v*

The ancient world had no precedent for the history of a
barbarian people. Tacitus' *Germania* is descriptive rather than
historical. The Chosen People of the Pentateuch hardly
counted as barbarian. But the barbarian invaders of the
Roman empire moved triumphantly into historiography
just as they founded their successor-states on former imperial
territory. They produced four great historians: Jordanes
(d. 554?) for the Goths; Gregory, bishop of Tours (d. 593/4),
for the Franks; Bede (d. 735) for the English; and Paul the
Deacon (d. 799?) for the Lombards. Their histories all
survived to a greater or lesser extent. Bede's was the favourite.
Later writers quoted, abridged, and embroidered on them.

The unity of history remained unbroken: the invaders,
when converted to Christianity, fitted themselves into the
pattern of the ancient world. The Romans had set an example
in faking origins: Virgil brought Aeneas and his Trojans to
Latium to win a kingdom, so as to glorify the early Romans.
Jordanes, working on a lost history by Cassiodorus, claimed
a mixed classical and biblical origin for the Goths. They
descended from the biblical giant Magog and from the
Scythians, a people familiar to ancient historians. Gregory of
Tours contented himself with the legend that the Merovingians descended from a Frankish princess, who was raped
by a sea monster while bathing. Learned invention soon
filled the gap. The Franks traced their origin to Noah's son
Japhet, who was said to have been the forefather of the
Trojans. The Franks' Trojan ancestors wandered abroad as
refugees from Troy, and finally settled in Gaul. Bede was too
good a scholar to fake pedigrees. He simply told what he
knew of the provenance of the Angles, Saxons and Jutes and
recorded their claim to descent from the nordic gods. Paul
the Deacon, too, admitted a northern origin for the
Lombards, although he swallowed the Trojan ancestry of the
Franks, 'as our elders have handed it down to us'. In each
case the gap between origins and settlement invited fiction,
sooner or later: Brut the Trojan was said to have conquered
Britain long before the Romans came.

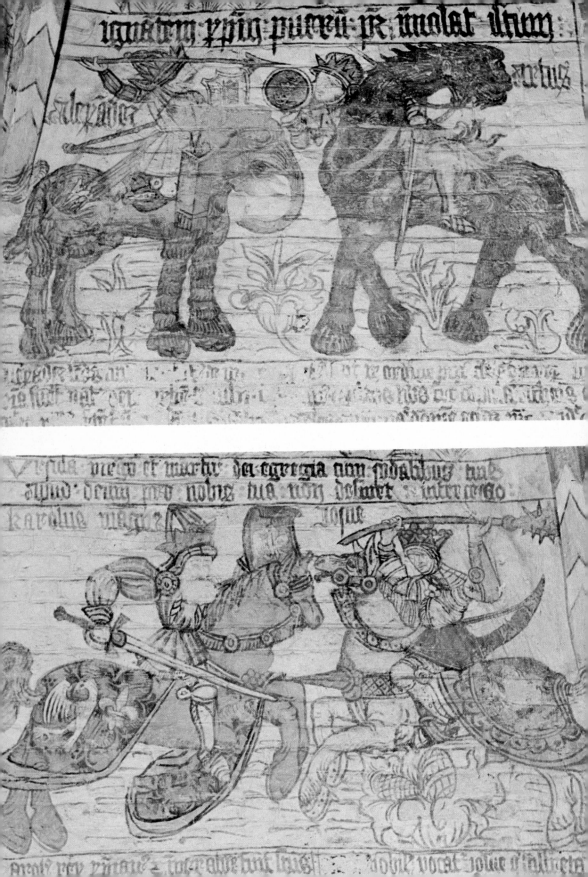

The fashion caught on, so that each town or principality which boasted of any history at all had to have its share in antiquity. The Latin king Turnus founded Tournai; Cracow derives from 'Greek Town', since the Poles were Greek by origin: their forbears had defeated Alexander the Great and then fought their way north to settle in Poland. We may gasp at these fancies; but we ought to remember that barbarian origins remain mysterious to this day. Hypotheses put forward by modern scholars have sometimes been almost as implausible as those of medieval historians.

Had the barbarian invasions brought the Roman empire to an end? That was a serious question. The end of imperial Rome would have broken continuity. More disturbing still, it would herald the coming of Antichrist, as Orosius taught. Barbarian historians had to tackle the problem. Their peoples had effectively destroyed the Roman empire in the West: could they discern continuity all the same, so as to avoid breaking with the classical past and hastening expectations of the end of time? Each of our four barbarian historians found his own answer. One solution was to look East to Byzantium. Rome survived in the East; the Byzantine emperors ruled over all the former territories of the old Roman *imperium* in theory, although in fact the new barbarian kingdoms were independent and had lost any close contact with the successors of the Caesars. Jordanes, Gregory of Tours and Paul the Deacon all took this view, while showing varying degrees of warmth or coolness towards the empire as an institution.

Dissentient voices were heard in Spain, which prepare us to understand Bede's answer to the problem. St Isidore of Seville wrote a history of Gothic Spain, in which he assumed that the Roman empire had disappeared as a world power. He accepted its division into separate kingdoms as a *fait accompli*. Its passing did not strike him as catastrophic: he seems to have thought that division into the ten kingdoms as foreseen by Daniel in his dream might last for an indefinite period. St Isidore's calm in the face of this prospect depended on his idea of the Church as a world power. The Church had replaced the empire; Christianity had spread far beyond the boundaries of ancient Rome. Isidore had witnessed the failure of Justinian's attempt to reconquer the West for Byzantium. He could not hold to the fiction that the Roman empire continued to be one and indivisible. These qualities belonged to the Church.

Colour plates IV, V
UNIVERSAL HISTORY IN
CONTEMPORARY DRESS
(see pp. 63–5)
Universal history, read as tales of heroes of all ages, is embodied in the Nine Worthies. They form a miscellaneous group, with three representatives from antiquity, three from the Bible, and three from Christendom: Hector, Alexander, Julius Caesar, David, Joshua, Judas Maccabaeus, Arthur, Charlemagne, and the crusading hero Godfrey of Bouillon. They became popular in the late Middle Ages, especially as a theme for pageantry. These wall-paintings in the church at Dronninglund in Denmark show them in fifteenth-century dress. In the detail above, Alexander the Great (seated on an elephant) confronts King Arthur; below, Charlemagne confronts Joshua.

28 The end of the fourth monarchy would herald the coming of Antichrist; hence the urgency of determining when it would end. Here Antichrist is depicted in a terrifying form as a monster riding on the back of the sea beast, Behemoth. From the Encyclopaedia of Lambert of St Omer, finished before 1120 (see also colour plate I). *Ghent, University Library, Liber floridus, f.62r*

a. Voden gen uectam.

q̅ g̅ uictam .q̅ g̅.

Wichcgils .q̅ g̅.

horfam ð hen

geft. &c &c

c. Voden g̅ Belder .q̅ g̅

Brond .q̅ g̅ frrodrega

q̅ g̅ freawmū .q̅ g̅ W

Gewritte .q̅ g̅ Ellā .q̅

q̅ g̅ Cerdic .N̅.

g. Woden g̅ frrodulge

ar .q̅ g̅ vaga .q̅ g̅ wich

deig .q̅ g̅ Vermundum.

q̅ g̅ offa .q̅ g̅ Ongelcheou .q̅

g. Comerū .q̅ g̅ Icel .q̅ g̅ Cnibbā qui g̅

kinewaldū .q̅ g̅ Crydā .q̅ g̅ Bibbā .q̅ g̅

pendam.

f. Voden g̅ Belder .q̅

Brond .q̅ g̅ Benoc.

q̅ g̅ Aloc .q̅ g̅ Ango

nuuia .q̅ g̅ Inguu

Elam .q̅ g̅ eopā .q̅ g̅ Idam. a

reges Nortðanhimbroꝛ cepiunt origin

b. geni̅ Vueolgeat .q̅ g̅ Vuitlege .q̅ psapia origins a

Voden g̅ Wegdam. q̅ g̅ Sigegarum. q̅ g̅ Sweabdegum. q̅ g̅ Sigegeat. q̅ g̅ seabaldum

q̅ g̅ seafugel .q̅ g̅ Westerfalene .q̅ g̅ Wilgils .q̅ g̅ Vscfrea .q̅ g̅ yffe .q̅ g̅ Ella.

Præ noctata serie generationum eroqua primi anglia generis reges pdicētur

sub notatur qui &u & quoto. incarnat̅ anno regnauerint p̅ illoꝛ ad

uentum inbrittanniam.

Anno ab incarnatione dn̅i. cccc . xl . ix̅ . angloꝛ siue Saxonum gens in

uitata a rege Wurtgerno trib: longis nauib: brittanniam aduehit.

apud locum q̅ dicitur ypwinesfleot. quasi ppatria pugnata . re autem uera

hanc expugnand̅ suscepe. Aduenerat aū de trib: germanie. poplis. forrioribus.

id est Saxonib: . anglis. iutis. De iutarum origine sunt Cantuarii & uectu

arii. hoc est ea gens que uectam tenet insulam . & ea que usq: hodie inpꝛ

tia occidentalium Saxonū . iutarum natio noiatur. posita cont̅ insula

uectā. De Saxonib: id est ea regione que nunc antiquoꝛ Saxonum

Bede was even more detached from the empire than Isidore. Byzantium was too remote to interest him. He accepted the six ages of the world, as handed down by tradition, but suppressed the four monarchies as a time scheme. His mind moved along the same lines as Isidore's in that he believed that religious unity transcended political. Britain had once been a province of the Roman empire. Now missionaries from Rome had converted the English and organized the Church in England as a daughter of Rome. English missionaries were converting the heathen Frisians. What did the lapse of the Roman empire matter? We shall see that it did still matter to some historians. The English and Spanish writers had buried the fourth monarchy prematurely.

Another urgent problem faced barbarian historians. Their models tended to separate sacred from secular history: could the history of a barbarian people follow such a division or must the two kinds of history be amalgamated? Barbarian history forbad the separation of its subject-matter into two parts. Conversion to Christianity, whether Catholicism or Arianism was chosen, marked a turning-point in a people's history. It affected their way of life, their institutions and their relations with their neighbours. Jordanes, Gregory of Tours and Paul the Deacon include religious history as an integral part of their stories. Bede made an attempt at separation; he concentrated on the Church, and he called his book *The Ecclesiastical History of the English People*. Secular history comes into it however. There is a larger element of the secular in Bede's *History* than there is in Eusebius'. The fortunes and preferences of English kings bore heavily on the endowment of churches and monasteries and on the careers of churchmen. The mixture of sacred and secular in historiography had come to stay.

A legacy of unresolved tension remained. Barbarian historians handled two sets of values, which clashed with each other. The writer felt proud of his people's heroic past; he loved to record the pagan warlords' splendid deeds. As a churchman, the writer could show that a successful warrior's conversion reflected glory on Christianity. The trouble was that baptism seldom led to the practice of Christian virtues. The historian found it easier to identify himself with his people, and would forgive a ruler's sins against the Church's teaching, provided that his kingdom flourished in his reign. Religion might be carried to excess in a ruler. His people

29 Opposite: the god Woden is represented as the ancestor of Anglo-Saxon kings in a treatise on the succession of kings of the Heptarchy, tracing their descent from Woden. The manuscript is written in an English hand of the early thirteenth century. Woden, shown in the centre of the picture, is conceived in the style of contemporary representations of God and of Christian kings. *Liège, University Library, MS 369 C, f.88v*

30 The beginning of book iv of Bede's *Ecclesiastical History*, from a manuscript written in southern England in the late eighth century. *London, British Museum, MS Cotton Tiberius C.II, f.94r*

might suffer if he renounced the world in order to enter a monastery or go on a pilgrimage.

To write a saint's *Life* was a less difficult assignment than to record the deeds of a king. The saint could combine wisdom with heroism in a Christian framework; but the saint was often a churchman. Few kings were canonized, and kings made history. We shall see how medieval historiographers wrestled with the problem of writing about Christian kings. Orosius' Olympian view of history held good only for the author of a universal history. To record the history of a people meant taking sides and rejoicing in victories over one's enemies. Then the Old Testament model came to the rescue. A writer could annex the role of the Israelites for his people. Their enemies joined the ranks of the gentiles, who deserved to be destroyed. All too easily, the Christian God became a tribal god, fighting on the historian's side. But particularist passion gave excitement to what would otherwise look like mere minor raids and border skirmishes.

Conditions for study of any kind worsened during the sixth and seventh centuries. The pattern of the early Middle Ages slowly emerges in the barbarian kingdoms. It centres on cathedrals and monasteries. The bishop has responsibility for teaching in his diocese. His main duty is to train his clergy. He may teach in person in his cathedral school. Many cathedrals were built in old provincial capitals of the Roman empire and might inherit a rich library: Verona, Ravenna and Lyons are examples. A conscientious bishop would encourage the copying of texts; private patronage of scribes was needed more than ever, since the public book trade had reached a standstill. Besides the cathedral, the monastery played its part in preserving culture. There were 'city monasteries', such as Fulda, St Gall and Monte Cassino. Abbots regarded their library and *scriptorium* as integral to their little 'state within a state'. Political disorder and travel difficulties did not put an end to intercourse between scholars. Cultural exchanges between the main centres of learning continued throughout Western Christendom.

New types of historiography developed to meet new needs. The most primitive form of medieval historical record was annals. They started within the modest framework of tables for reckoning the date of Easter. This is still a movable feast, but its computation has been standardized; we have only to look in our diaries. It was a question of 'do it yourself' in this early period. The mode of reckoning was stan-

ANNI · INDI · EPA · CON · CYCL · XIIII · DIES · LVN...
DNI · CTIO · CTE · CVR · ... · LVN · DOM · ...
PASC · LVN...

[medieval computistical Easter table with interlinear and marginal annotations in Latin; years running from ccccxxxiiii to ccccxlv]

31 Tables for the calculation of Easter with historical matter written into the margin and between the lines. From a German manuscript of the third quarter of the tenth century, from Einsiedeln. *Einsiedeln, Stiftsbibliothek, Cod. 29 (878)*

dardized slowly, as was the custom of counting in years from the beginning of the Christian era, 'BC' and 'AD'. Various modes of reckoning competed, and writers would sometimes use several concurrently. The movable feast of Easter determined the whole course of the Christian year, with its round of festivals and fasting. Hence monastic and minster churches needed tables which would show the date of Easter and ensure that services could be arranged beforehand. Tables were compiled to establish dates over a number of years.

A table inevitably offered blank spaces, which attracted notices of events. The computist, or someone who used his tables, would enter the record of a storm or comet or an occasion of local interest or the death of some great person. The next stage in the process of keeping annals was to have the entries copied out separately from the tables. The annals would then be kept up to date either systematically or by fits and starts. The monks of one abbey would borrow annals from another; they would make their own additions to the original and would continue it as the years passed. Their practice has worried modern scholars: to write history correctly it is necessary to isolate the original set of annals or find the common source drawn upon by the various compilers. The task has been compared to peeling an onion: a medieval set of annals always has another skin underneath. Monastic annals as a genre are uncouth, unclassical (in spite of the name) and generally derivative; but they kept historiography alive in circles where nobody felt like attempting ambitious literary history. Education and motive were lacking.

Another influential piece of record-keeping was the *Liber Pontificalis* or *Pope's Book*. The popes functioned as bishops of Rome as well as heads of the Latin Church. The former capacity is more in evidence in the early stages of their *Book*. Clerks (who in the Middle Ages were clerics as well) in the Lateran writing-office recorded the apostolic succession and added papal biographies. We refer to the *Liber Pontificalis* as a 'book' for convenience; the name is collective rather than singular in this case. It resembles a wood of trees, which thickens in some parts and thins out in others, rather than a single tree-trunk with branches. It has come down to us in a number of different versions. Its compilers in the early Middle Ages were mainly 'backroom boys' who, as papal employees, wrote anonymously. Some biographers had a propaganda purpose, in that they wished to justify papal policies *vis-à-vis* other powers, but their interests were chiefly local. The popes figure as bishops of Rome. The Romans depended on their bishops as wealthy landowners to feed the city in times of famine and to keep it habitable by looking after water supplies and drainage. The popes shouldered their responsibilities; and they also took pride in building and decorating Roman churches. To choose one papal biography as an example: the biographer of Honorius I (625–38) records his gifts and repairs to Roman churches, setting down the exact weight of precious metal spent on each of them. A later addition to Honorius' *Life* states that he installed a mill in a place called 'Trajan's Water' and that he mended the aqueduct there. No reader would guess from the *Life* that Honorius played an active part in organizing the early Church in England. That was too distant to interest his biographer.

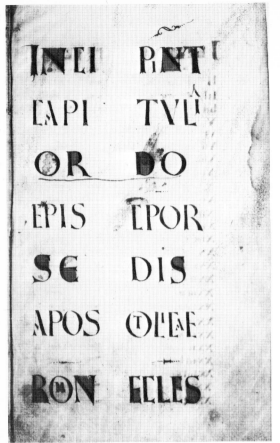

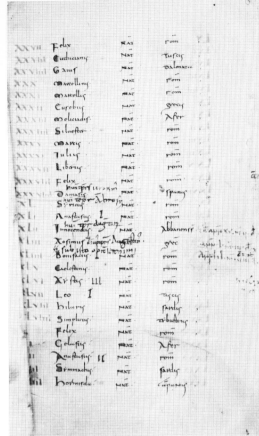

The *Liber Pontificalis* became widely known. Scholars consulted it when business brought them to the papal court. Parts of it were copied and circulated. The papal biographies suggested new ideas to historiographers whose main reading consisted of the *Lives* of saints. The early medieval popes were not saints or martyrs, but ordinary men, dealing with practical problems. Gregory I stands out as exceptional. The *Popes' Book* showed readers that it was worth while to record the doings of churchmen who had no claims to holiness. It served as a model for *Deeds* of bishops and of abbots. Paul the Deacon knew the *Popes' Book* and had it in mind when Charlemagne asked him to write a history of the bishopric of Metz. His *History of Metz* set a pattern for later historiographers. This type of history began with the foundation of the see or abbey (the account was often legendary). The writer copied such sources as he could find and went on to

32, 33 Two pages from a copy of the *Liber Pontificalis* made in the eighth or ninth century, from the abbey of St Remigius at Rheims. Above left: the title page. Above: part of the list of popes, successors of St Peter, with their places of origin. *Leyden, University Library, Cod. Voss. lat. 9.60, f.5r and 6r*

59

describe more recent happenings. He used the reigns of successive bishops or abbots as his chronological framework. The pattern made it easy for later writers to add to the story and keep it up to date.

The scope of these *Deeds* would vary according to the importance of the bishops or abbots. They might take part in the affairs of Christendom as a whole or they might be stay-at-homes. In the former case we see what world politics looked like to a local observer; in the latter we may hear more about the local town and countryside. These local historiographers bring us closer to social and economic history than do any others. No writer envisaged a history of 'the common people'. Modern scholars depend on documentary evidence rather than on literary sources when they study the history of medieval peasants. But the writer of *Deeds* had occasion to mention countrymen and townsmen, landlords and travellers, because their customs, feuds and risings and their generosity or robbery affected his community. Local history joined the historical monograph as an alternative to universal history or the history of a people. It had its secular counterpart in *Deeds* of princes or histories of a ducal family.

Secular *Deeds* bring us to a third type of centre for scholarship, the princely court. Barbarian rulers listened to tales of their heroic forbears; the interest of these stories was enlarged by what happened after their conversion to Christianity. Bede dedicated his *Ecclesiastical History of the English People* to a Northumbrian king. In France the Mayors of the Palace who replaced the last Merovingians had historians among their courtiers. Under the Frankish court of Charles Martel (d. 741) the weak beginnings of the cultural revival associated with his grandson Charlemagne (d. 814) could be seen. Charlemagne and his advisers worked hard to establish a learned clergy and to remedy the shortage of books and teachers. Their efforts bore fruit in a great output of learned writing, which started in the last years of Charlemagne's reign and continued up to the mid-ninth century. We know now that the 'Carolingian Renaissance' began earlier and took longer to get off the ground than used to be thought.

Cathedrals, abbeys and the imperial court all contributed to the revival. This association meant that upper-class laymen could share in literacy and authorship. Monastic and cathedral schools accepted external pupils. Two ninth-century historiographers, Einhard and Nithard, were both laymen. This gives

a special richness to Carolingian historiography. The reading and writing of Latin became a clerical monopoly as the ninth century passed: laymen lost either the inclination or the leisure to study. At best they figured as hearers or readers; they needed translations from Latin, and they did not write books.

The 'Dark Ages', as we ungratefully call them, added much that was new to the existing stock of genres. A historiographer of the early ninth century had a wider choice than had been available five hundred years earlier. Like an artist, he could go in for wall-painting in the form of universal chronicle or world history, or the history of a people; alternatively, he could choose to paint in miniature in the form of the story of his church or his abbey or of

34 Local monastic history. The monk Purchard kneels to present his verse *Deeds* of his abbot, Witigowo of Reichenau, to the abbot, who stands to the left of the Virgin and Child. The monks look on. At the far left a personification of the island of Reichenau supports the abbey. Purchard wrote about 994–6, adding to his local history an account of the abbot's journey to Rome with Otto III for his imperial coronation. This is a unique manuscript produced near the time of writing. *Karlsruhe, Badische Landesbibliothek, MS Aug. CCV, f.72r*

35 An example of mis-information culled from travellers' tales. Adémar of Chabannes, a chronicler of the early eleventh century living near the pilgrim centre of Limoges, illustrated his text by a sketch of the tomb of Charlemagne in the church at Aachen. Adémar got the architectural detail wrong. *Rome, Biblioteca Apostolica Vaticana, MS Vat. lat. 263, f.235r*

biography. A less enterprising writer could limit himself to keeping up the local annals.

The moment has come to mark out the main differences between medieval and modern historians. The most obvious is the medieval notion of time and space. The medieval historian's time enrolled itself between the Creation and Doomsday; it began and it would end; it moved through clearly defined periods. His space was circumscribed by the limits of ancient and biblical history in the past and by the extent of Christendom in the present. There were travellers' tales of outside peoples, but they hardly count as history. Non-Christian peoples normally entered into history only in so far as the Christian historian recorded border warfare or raids or missions to the heathen. Another obvious difference is that the medieval historian had a much smaller stock of tools for investigating the past than we have. He relied upon literary sources and hearsay. An observant author could look at ancient monuments and try to use them as evidence; but he could not bring scientific techniques to bear on what he saw, read or heard.

The main obstacle to our understanding of medieval historiography is absence of perspective. Medieval figurative art is two-dimensional. The artist paints or draws on a flat surface. The student of medieval art learns to accept the flatness as a convention: it does not spoil his appreciation of the picture. In the same way, the student of medieval historiography must learn to do without perspective in historical presentation. A medieval writer could distinguish stages in the history of salvation, but they were religious stages. He did not discern change or development in temporal history. He saw continuity in customs and institutions, where we see diversity. Roman emperors are made to talk and behave like medieval rulers. Alternatively, a writer learned in the Latin classics tended to make medieval rulers talk and behave like the Caesars. The historian did not only look back to the Old and New Testaments for parallels and precedents; he lived in an expanding Bible. The writer of a saint's *Life* felt that he was adding a new page to the Gospel story; the recorder of a warrior's deeds was continuing the tale of ancient and Old Testament heroes. Past and present interlock: ancient precedents imposed themselves on the present; the past resembled the present as the historian saw it. He had no sense of anachronism.

Neither had the medieval artist. Here, too, we find a parallel. The artist did not aim at historical correctness when he designed persons and buildings: he dressed his characters in medieval costume, or else he copied from an earlier model; sometimes he produced a mixture. The artist of the twelfth-century Bury Bible shows Jeremiah in his prophet's uniform of classical drapes, sitting on a cloud. In the lower half of the picture we watch the capture of Jerusalem, which the prophet has foretold. This scene has a twelfth-century

36 The martyrdom of St Lawrence was seen as a continuation of the Gospel story. St Lawrence carries a cross and an open book. He stands beside the gridiron, rolled into the place of his martyrdom on its wheels, on which he was burnt. On the other side stands a cabinet containing the four Gospels which he preached. A fifth-century mosaic in the Mausoleum of Galla Placidia at Ravenna.

37 Romance, legend and
history blended in tales of
'King Alexander' (d. 323 BC).
Alexander appealed to the
nobility, who saw him as the
mirror of chivalry. Marvels
of the east catered for delight
in the unknown. This
illustration to a French poem
shows both types of appeal.
On the left King Alexander
rides with his host. On the
right the knight Enoch
washes himself in a magic
fountain (shown with Gothic
covers and basins). The story
went that if anyone bathed in
its waters it could not be
found again for a year.
Alexander punished Enoch
for his disobedience by
enclosing him in a pillar.
This is one of many minia-
tures in the manuscript executed by Jehan de Grise, and
finished in 1344. *Oxford, Bodleian Library, MS 264, f.67v*

setting. Armour, costume and fortification are all depicted in the contemporary idiom. The incident has a living intensity, just because the artist sees it as taking place in the present.

Nowadays the historian thinks it his business to trace and to interpret change. He looks for continuity, too; but he regards it as a thread which runs through the changing pattern of history. Anachronism is his bugbear. Historical novels make painful reading if the characters in them wear the wrong sort of clothes or express sentiments out of keeping with their period. Our way of looking at history as a record of change contrasts with the lack of perspective shown by medieval historians. They may strike us as funny and naïve, but we must try to understand their ideas in the light of medieval conditions. Then we shall see that absence of perspective had its ground in reality.

The medieval view of past ages as all alike was rational, in that essentials had not changed. The ancient past, as it was known to the Middle Ages, had many features in common with medieval society up to the fifteenth century at least.

Production was unmechanized; the bulk of the population worked on the land; literacy was limited to a larger or smaller élite; the supernatural was ever present in one form or another; the New World was unknown. Changes and improvements in agriculture, industry and transport happened slowly in unspectacular ways. Today, the pace forces us to realize that we live in a different world from that of our grandparents' day. Nor is lack of perspective peculiar to the Middle Ages. Beginners often have difficulty in charting a time scheme before the age of discoveries or the industrial revolution. BC and AD are all the same to them. It is a privilege of children who have sophisticated parents and a chance to see historical monuments to grow up with a sense of period. Otherwise it comes gradually, if at all. Medieval men had a past where they could feel at home. We are strangers to ours. The historian has to make an effort to acclimatize himself in the Middle Ages. Then he must pack and start over again if he wants to visit the ancient world. Medieval historiographers travelled light.

38 An example of historical anachronism. Oedipus fights the sphinx. He wears late thirteenth-century armour and emerges from a contemporary castle. The picture illustrates a copy of the *Histoire universelle*, a compilation on world history from the Creation to Julius Caesar, written in French and intended to be read to a lay audience. This manuscript was produced at Acre, the capital of the Latin kingdom in Palestine, about 1285. *London, British Museum, MS Add. 15268, f.77v*

Royal biographies
c. 800–*c.* 1150

Royal biographies have one feature in common: they are propaganda pieces. The writers' purposes and techniques varied, but they all had to find a mould which would contain the unruly facts. The prince had to be presented as his biographer wished to show him to his readers or hearers.

We begin with Einhard, the biographer of Charlemagne. Einhard was a short man in stature, and he wrote a short book. It has a long history; its influence was out of proportion to its size. The author was a layman, in contrast to later biographers. The Carolingian revival of learning put a good education at the disposal of laymen who had connections with the court. Einhard was well read and well equipped to write Charlemagne's *Life*. He had served Charlemagne in the emperor's old age and then passed into the service of Charlemagne's successor, Louis the Pious. Einhard did not start from scratch, since historiography was already a state enterprise; the keeping of royal annals had begun. He was asked to write a *Life* of Charlemagne, and composed it within the years 829–36. A good Isidorian, he excuses himself for being a 'mere compiler' for the early and middle years of his hero, which fell outside the range of his memory. Recent research on the *Life* has shown that he did not shine as a compiler, being careless in handling his sources. When he reached the emperor's old age, however, he could write as an eyewitness.

Einhard might have searched in vain for a Christian model to guide him in writing the life of a secular ruler. The genre of biography familiar to him would have been *Lives* of saints, and these were quite unsuitable. A classical model lay ready to hand in Suetonius' *Lives of the Caesars*. Einhard chose Suetonius as his guide. He wrote what has been called 'the thirteenth *Life* of a Caesar' to add to Suetonius' twelve. The ninth-century biographer imitates his model's structure and style, to the extent of omitting biblical quotations and phrases. No scriptural reminiscences sully the purity of his Latin. It must have cost him an effort to avoid what a

39 Opposite: the Carolingian tradition inspired the three Saxon emperors, Otto I, II, and III. Here an Ottonian emperor sits in majesty, crowned and holding the orb and sceptre. From an ivory situla, executed about 1000, from Aachen. *Aachen, Cathedral Treasury*

40 An idealized portrait of
Charlemagne set into the
initial of the opening word
of Einhard's *Life*, from a
manuscript produced in
France in the eleventh
century. *Paris, Bibliothèque
Nationale, MS lat. 5927,
p. 280*

classicist would have regarded as contamination. Einhard
kept afloat by borrowing items as well as reproducing the
style of his Latin original. He picked out details from the
various *Lives* where he could adapt them to his account of
Charlemagne. Sometimes he had no parallel in any *Life*. The
Caesars had been literate, whereas Charlemagne began to
learn his letters too late in life to make much progress.
Einhard had no scruples about recording this barbarian trait.
He was a creative writer as well as an imitator. A convincing
portrait of the aged emperor emerges; but alas! Einhard's
choice of Suetonius makes his story a riddle to modern
historians. He followed his guide in avoiding both comment
and value judgment. We can read his silences as we like. We
do not know what he thought of Charlemagne's attitude to
the Church. He describes the emperor's piety in classical
terms, merely adding 'Christian' as an adjective to 'religion'.
The question arises: did his love of antiquity motivate him to
keep his hero's religion as close to the Caesars' as possible? Or
is there more to it? Did Einhard use his model for a more
positive end? Did he choose it as a medium to express secular
heroic values to the detriment of Christian?

The most important evidence for the second question
comes from Einhard's account of Charlemagne's coronation
by the pope at Rome on Christmas Day 800. Much has been
deduced from it. Einhard gives the initiative to the pope and
presents Charlemagne as unwilling to accept the crown. He
was taken by surprise, according to Einhard, and said that he
would not have gone to church that day, had he known what
the pope was planning to do. Perhaps Einhard implies in this
statement that Charlemagne would have preferred to take
the imperial title without benefit of clergy, thinking it
undignified for a great conqueror to be crowned by a
churchman. Perhaps he had no use for the imperial title at all.
His conquests and his inheritance gave him power and glory
enough as king; why pose as emperor? Einhard also tells us
that Charlemagne found his new title a hindrance to good
relations with the Byzantines, who objected to a Western
ruler usurping their role. All we can safely say about
Einhard's attitude is that he chose a secular model for his
biography and that he did nothing to clericalize Suetonius.
Just how secular his values were is a matter of opinion. It is
equally difficult to say how far his values reflect those of
Charlemagne. We do not know whether Charlemagne
confided in his courtier or not.

41 Einhard's love of the antique appears in the reliquary that he gave to the abbey of St Servatius at Maastricht, of which he became lay abbot in 815. This is a seventeenth-century drawing of the base of the reliquary, now lost. It was the first medieval specimen of goldsmith's work decorated with figures. An inscription in antique style set over a Roman triumphal arch records Einhard's donation. Below it a rider tramples on the forces of evil represented by a dragon. Other details represent the four Evangelists, the Annunciation and various Christian themes, all influenced by ancient models. *Paris, Bibliothèque Nationale, MS fr. 10440*

This enigmatic masterpiece influenced later biographers, but its very nature prevented them from copying it slavishly. Einhard's successors were clerks, not laymen. Hence they had a less secular outlook. Their subject-matter differed too. There was no second Charlemagne, and churchmen loomed larger in politics after he died. The break-up of his empire did not lend itself to the kind of admiring detachment which Einhard had found in Suetonius' *Lives of the Caesars*.

The break came immediately. The career of Louis the Pious, Charlemagne's son, called for pity rather than praise and thanksgiving: his troubles and humiliations made sad reading. Thegan, his first biographer, was assistant bishop of Trier and a strong partisan of Louis. He departed from the Suetonian structure in favour of a narrative form, so as to bring out the drama. Far from avoiding biblical language, he wallowed in its expressiveness. The Latin Old Testament offered an unrivalled vocabulary to convey the emotions of wrath and grief, and Thegan exploited it to the full. Instead of keeping himself in the background, as Einhard did, he bursts into exclamations and prayers. Louis' piety appealed to him as a churchman. Thegan dwelt on the emperor's humble attitude to the pope and on his moral strictness. Louis was more puritanical than his father. He never laughed or showed his white teeth in a smile even on feast days, when all around him were enjoying music and mummery. The question why so good a Christian should have suffered calamity led Thegan to broach historical analysis. He picked on a human, political cause. The emperor chose 'evil counsellors', low-born men, who betrayed him. Louis had acted against the principle of hierarchy. Great men were the natural advisers of a ruler.

The contrast between Einhard and Thegan as biographers struck their contemporary, the scholar abbot Walafrid Strabo. He edited Einhard's *Life* and added a preface, praising his learning, character and political astuteness, qualities fit to guarantee his reliability as author. Strabo excuses Thegan for writing less well than Einhard and for showing bias: Thegan had little time to spare from his duties as bishop; his love of justice and partisanship for Louis caused him to exaggerate. In Strabo's eyes, Einhard had produced the more elegant and trustworthy biography.

A younger contemporary of Thegan wrote a second *Life* of Louis the Pious. Thegan had stopped before the emperor's death in 840. The second biographer brought the tale up to date. He wrote anonymously: we know only that he was a clerk and a courtier. Modern historians call him 'The Astronomer', on account of his interest in the stars and planets. His method as a biographer puts him in a halfway-house between Thegan and Einhard. He followed Einhard in quoting less often from Scripture than Thegan. His values were more secular than Thegan's; he plays down the emperor's meekness in greeting the pope. But he was pulled two ways. The Astronomer departed from Einhard's structure in choosing a mainly narrative form for his biography. He sometimes treats himself to a purple patch, which would have offended the purists. The devil, that unclassical figure, slips into his story, stirring up Louis' sons to rebel against their father.

Another early medieval biographer tried to imitate Einhard. Asser, bishop of Sherborne, took the *Life of Charlemagne* as his model when he wrote his *Life of King Alfred* (893).

Asser did his utmost to fit the story of Alfred into Einhard's pattern, but he did not succeed. The influence of saints' *Lives* creeps in, since he wanted to present the English king as a holy man. Einhard's narrative was too dry. Asser wanted more unction and pathos. According to Asser, Alfred, like Charlemagne, learnt to write in his middle age, with the aim of teaching his people in the aftermath of the Danish wars. A biblical comparison gives solemnity to the story of Alfred's endeavours to cope with book learning. Asser likens him to the penitent thief, who was crucified with Jesus and entered late into the joys of paradise. The biographer brings himself into the picture, just as Thegan did. Asser describes how he encouraged the king to read and to collect extracts for his 'commonplace book'. The churchman's patronizing tone when writing of a layman, even of so gifted and pious a layman as Alfred, comes through his story. The result is very different from the *Life of Charlemagne*.

Einhard eluded his imitators, fortunately for the history of biography. A clerk could not write like a layman, nor would he sacrifice drama and excitement by avoiding narrative form and emotional comments on his tale. When he could not copy, he had to invent. The Einhards *manqués* were compelled to be creative.

Our next royal biographer gave up any idea of modelling himself on Einhard. Helgald, monk of Fleury-sur-Loire, wrote a *Life* of the French king, Robert the Pious, soon after Robert's death (1031). Helgald imitated the form of a saint's *Life*, and his book would have been read aloud to a religious community for edification. Robert appears as an ideal Christian king. Humble, kindly and orthodox, he protects churches and people against evildoers. So great was his virtue that he merited to work miracles. Helgald had to do some editing. By calling his *Life* an 'epitome', he covered himself for not telling everything. This allowed him to omit whatever struck him as unsuitable. He left military and political history right out. The early Capetian kings of France kept their heads above water, but only just. King Robert was not a conquering hero. His orthodoxy needed editing too. Helgald does not mention the king's matrimonial troubles and his excommunication by the pope.

Suetonius and Einhard make a sudden and welcome appearance. Helgald turned to them to fill the gap which he noticed in the *Lives* of saints. They suggested a pen portrait. The monk of Fleury had visited the court on business of his

42 A twelfth-century stained glass window in Strasbourg cathedral shows the emperor Conrad II and his son Henry III.

abbey and had met Robert in person. He drew on his memory to write a vivid description of Robert's physique and characteristics. We even hear how the king sat his horse. The portrait stands out as a triumph of observation in a conventional setting.

The empire offered grander stuff to the biographer than the French kingdom in the eleventh century. Its bounds were wider: the German emperor ruled over the duchies of Lorraine, part of Burgundy and Lombardy, while exercising a protectorate over the papacy. The peoples across his eastern border came under his influence in varying degrees. We have a biography of the emperor Conrad II, written by his court chaplain, Wipo, in 1046. Wipo wrote it for the benefit of Conrad's son, Henry III. The biographer intended to restore official imperial historiography, which had lapsed during his lifetime. His *Life of Conrad* would provide Henry III with an account of his father's policies and military campaigns. Wipo further planned to make a record of Henry's deeds for the use of future biographers. As Conrad's chaplain, Wipo could write as an eyewitness; he had good opportunities to observe and to collect data at first hand. Sometimes illness kept him away from court, and in that case he scrupulously tells us so and says that he relies on trustworthy informants.

Like Helgald, Wipo had a religious purpose; but he was more ambitious. Helgald modelled his *Life* of King Robert on a saint's *Life*, throwing in a dash of Einhard to make it more interesting. Wipo, blessed with a more splendid subject, harnessed the classical panegyric of a ruler to his purpose as a preacher. Conrad's reign lent itself to panegyric: he won battles against his enemies and he put down rebels. Wipo claimed that the glorious deeds of a Christian ruler were worth preaching as well as eulogizing. The deeds of pagan heroes and tyrants had been celebrated; so had those of the kings of Israel. What sinful sloth it was to neglect the stories of Christian kings and emperors! A ruler had charge of the public good; Conrad had fulfilled his function so well that his death evoked more public lament than had ever been heard at an emperor's death before. Wipo draws the conclusion that the biographer is also an evangelist:

Our Catholic kings, the defenders of the faith, rule without fear of error, since they keep Christ's law and the peace which he handed down to us in his Gospel. Surely, therefore, to publish their good deeds in writing is nothing less than to preach the Gospel of Christ?

He safeguarded himself by adding that the bad deeds of rulers were worth recording as a warning.

Like Helgald, Wipo had to edit his data to some extent. Conrad showed less favour to the Church than had the Saxon emperors, his predecessors. His biographer achieved a remarkable feat in raising his *Life* to so high a level. Wipo wrote seriously. He avoided details which struck him as frivolous; there is no gossip, though he tells some stories characteristic of Conrad's behaviour to point his moral. He proved that a royal biographer could add his quota to the expanding Bible of the saints.

Conrad's *Life* might have served as a model for Henry III's biographer, had he found one. It was useless to the biographer of Conrad's grandson, Henry IV. This Henry's reign contrasted with his father's and grandfather's in every way. His father died while he was still a child. A troubled minority was followed by personal tragedy and disaster to the empire. His sons turned against him. His victories proved brittle. The biographers of Louis the Pious could dwell on the fact that Louis, throughout his misfortunes, always remained a dutiful son of the Church. Henry IV, on the contrary, was excommunicated and deposed by Pope Gregory VII. Henry had himself crowned emperor by his antipope, after driving Gregory out of Rome. But it was a last resort; his antipope was just the ecclesiastical head of the imperialist party. The standard end to an emperor's reign was the glorious succession of his son and heir. Henry's heir was a rebel when the old emperor died, in the midst of such calamities that death came as a release.

It must have taken courage to write the *Life of Henry IV*. His biographer had no precedents. He could not present his subject either as a conqueror or as a holy or even a wise man, since his policies failed. No amount of editing would suffice to make his data fit the pattern. Nor would it have improved Henry's image to present him as the victim of a papal plot. That would have involved blackening Gregory VII. Gregory made many enemies; but Urban II was more politic, and opinion was veering back to the papal side when Henry died in 1106. A cautious approach to the Investiture Contest was called for.

An anonymous author undertook to apologize for the emperor. We know only that he moved in the imperial circle towards the end of Henry IV's reign and that he wrote soon after Henry's death. He had a good knowledge of the

Latin classics, of the Bible and of hagiography, so he was probably a clerk. His *Life* takes the form of a funeral lament. Henry's people mourn him; he had kept their sympathy through thick and thin. The writer calms his personal grief for his master by giving vent to his feelings. The imperial honour, exalted by Henry's forbears, had been trampled underfoot. That was cause for grief. Why did it happen? Not as a result of Henry's sins. He sowed his wild oats in his youth and afterwards lived virtuously. The Anonymous found the historical cause in the troubles of Henry's minority. Internal decay set in. Powerful men grew accustomed to snatch and grab. Peace never suited them for long, because it checked their ambitions. Hence revolt broke out as soon as the ruler had established law and order. A human cause accounted for the rebellions of Henry's sons. His enemies suborned them with promises and played off the natural resentment of youth against age.

The Anonymous went more deeply into the problem of causation than Thegan had done in his *Life of Louis the Pious*. Modern historians would like to go back further still and discover why German politics deteriorated during Henry's minority; but the work leaves them guessing. His biographer cheated a little by writing up Henry's few successes. His penitence at Canossa is represented as a diplomatic *coup*. He stole a march on his enemies by going to Gregory VII to receive absolution, exchanging a blessing for a curse, and returning to Germany to quell the rebels. It was certainly a clever move on Henry's part, though not quite as successful as the Anonymous makes out. It still remained to explain why Henry could never enjoy his victories. Defeat dogged his footsteps. The Anonymous plays down Henry's antipapal policies and does not criticize Gregory VII openly. The notion of Fortune's Wheel answered his problem. Fortune turned Henry's defeats into victories and then swiftly cast him down. German scholars put forward diverse opinions on Fortune's role in the *Life of Henry IV*. Her role can be interpreted as introducing a global view of history. Boethius' picture of the fickle goddess combined with a nordic concept of Fortune as inherent in the tribal chief, whose defeat meant loss of good luck for the whole people. Henry's troubles become all the more dreadful on this view. Another, less extreme, opinion is that the Anonymous appealed to Fortune as a subsidiary cause. He does not tell us that he means to write his book on the theme. The *Life* does not serve to illustrate Fortune's role. On the contrary, she is used simply to give pathos and drama to what might otherwise have looked like a history of petty quarrels and inconclusive fighting. She heightens our sense of tragedy. I prefer the second opinion; but in any case the Anonymous was an artist, who composed a touching tribute to Henry. Although he did not plan to write history in the strict sense of the word, he pondered the problems of causation.

Queens had their biographies, too. The most colourful is the *Encomium of Queen Emma*. *Encomium* is a modern title, but it expresses the writer's intention to praise her. Queen Emma, widow of the English King Aethelred and wife of the Danish King Cnut, commissioned a book in praise of herself and her family from a writer who was either a canon of St Omer or a monk of the neighbouring abbey of St Bertin, then in Flanders, now in the Pas-de-Calais. Emma's father was a duke of Normandy, and she spent three years of her life in Flanders. She knew that St Omer had a literary tradition: a canon or monk from there would make a good propagandist. Her career bristled with difficulties for a eulogist, especially as he was writing in her life-time, between 1040 and 1042. A queen ought to have the womanly virtues of being a loving wife and mother. Emma married twice – the second time to her first husband's deadliest enemy. She agreed as part of the bargain that her sons by Aethelred should forgo their claim to the English crown in favour of the sons she would bear to Cnut. It looked as though she was doing well for herself by neglecting her elder children. In fact they had slender chances of succeeding anyway.

The Anonymous suppressed all mention of Emma's first marriage. He gives us to understand that she was not a widow when Cnut sought her as a bride, and that her sons by Aethelred were the younger sons of her second marriage. That was why they had no claim against Cnut's offspring. Many readers might be expected to know the truth, so the Anonymous chose his wording carefully; no one could catch him out in a downright lie. The same technique was applied in other parts of his book where he had an interest in distorting the facts. He trots out the cliché in his preface that the historian must tell the truth, and then interprets it skilfully to mean 'nothing but the truth', though not 'the whole truth'. When he had no reason to mislead, he gave as correct and impartial a picture of the English scene as a foreigner, relying on hearsay, could do.

43 The Anonymous of St Omer presents his *Encomium* to Queen Emma. Her two sons Hardacnut and Edward stand beside her. From a manuscript of the mid-eleventh century which belonged to the abbey of St Augustine, Canterbury. *London, British Museum, MS Add. 33241, f.1v*

Emma herself disappears behind a cloud of rhetorical borrowings; but her eulogist could write vividly of what he had seen in person, as when he describes Cnut's generosity and devotion on his visit to St Omer. His famous pictures of naval scenes derive both from his reading of Virgil and from his powers of imaginative reconstruction. He had probably heard a description of a Viking fleet, though he may not have seen one. It caught his fancy, and there were classical precedents for describing ships. His two pictures of Viking fleets, dazzling the eye with their gilded prows and coloured boards, shine out from his pages. The centaurs and dolphins carved on the prows have slipped in from his reading; the dragons and bulls seem authentic enough, and so does the magic raven banner of the Danish fleet.

Drama, romance and brilliant writing are all absent from the *Life of Louis the Fat* by Abbot Suger of St Denis (d. 1151). We come down to humdrum life, centred on the small stage of the Île-de-France. Louis VI (1108–37) had more to his credit than Robert the Pious; he was a 'safe second-class' king. His main work for the French monarchy lay in subjecting the rebel barons of the royal domain. His forward policies in Normandy and Flanders misfired. Suger, however, was a propagandist of genius. He waved his wand over small beer and it turned into sparkling champagne. The magic came from St Denis, patron of Suger's abbey and of the French royal family. Suger was a great administrator of his abbey lands, a great church-builder and decorator and the king's right-hand man. He stressed Louis' role as lay patron and standard-bearer of St Denis. The king showed his devotion to St Denis from his boyhood onwards; he wished to be buried in the abbey church, unlike his father Philip I, who felt himself unworthy of such an honour. Suger found him a place. The *Life* ends with his burial there.

Suger gets his effect by statement rather than hyperbole. Why botch up a picture of Louis as a saint? It sufficed that he fought for St Denis, displaying the kingly virtue of 'strenuousness' in protecting his people against their enemies. The abbot exaggerates when he claims that Louis never overreached himself, but he does let him say at the end of his reign that he could have achieved more than he had. The supreme test came in 1124, when the German emperor, Henry V, threatened to invade France. Louis summoned his vassals to follow him in defence of the kingdom. Surprisingly, given the slightness of his hold, most of them either

44 Opposite: Christian rulers. The gilded copper cover of the *Golden Book* of the abbey of Prüm shows Christ in majesty worshipped by the Carolingian dynasty: Pippin and Charlemagne (above) and their descendants, Louis the Pious, Lothair, Louis the German and Charles the Bald. The rulers offer a church, a book, and charters recording donations to churches. The book is a cartulary, which includes genealogical tables of the Carolingian, Saxon and Salian kings, made about 1100. *Trier, Stadtbibliothek, Cod. 1709*

answered the summons or at least sent excuses. The emperor turned back with his tail between his legs. It appears from the German sources that he planned to make a punitive raid, not a large-scale invasion, and that he retreated partly because of a revolt in his rear. But Suger presents it as a splendid victory for the French against the Germans. St Denis had triumphed in the person of King Louis. Suger shared in his glory as abbot of St Denis and as the counsellor and biographer of his royal master.

We can see continuity and development in this sequence of royal biographers. In the first place, none of them undertakes to give us many facts and dates: these are 'not on the menu'. The practical Suger is the most generous. The classical eulogy and the Christian tradition of saints' *Lives* combined to reduce the amount of factual information required in biography. The Suetonian model permitted more precision, but it proved to be too bare for medieval taste. The rhetorical tradition defeated it. We cannot expect to find objectivity either; biographers wanted to praise or excuse. Their saving grace is that they remember the traditional advice to the historian to tell the truth and to report events as an eye-witness whenever possible. They generally keep the truth in sight, preferring to sin by omission and selection rather than by outright lying. Sudden flashes of realism light up their most conventional stories. If we judge them as propagandists, we have to admire their ingenuity. All do their best for rulers who fell short of what was expected of a Christian hero.

The development is clear and meaningful. The Church takes over biography. Einhard's Charlemagne stands alone. The ruler comes to be judged and presented to us in accordance with the standards approved by churchmen. We admire a devout emperor in Louis the Pious, a Christian king in Alfred, a saint in Robert the Pious, an evangelist in Conrad, generous donors to churches in Emma and Cnut, and the standard-bearer of St Denis in Louis VI. The unlucky Henry IV is neither anti-clerical nor anti-papal.

We see the same development when we turn from biography to less specialized kinds of historiography. The writers are churchmen, who see history through clerical glasses, but the general historian did not work to the same stereotype as the biographer. We shall find more diversity of interest and many more ways of treating the matter of history. There are surprises in store for us.

6
History, chronicle
and historical scholarship
c. 950–c. 1150

Historiography, apart from annals, stopped on the Continent between the late ninth and early tenth centuries. The wars which resulted from the break-up of the Carolingian empire and raids by Vikings, Hungarians and Saracens made literary composition difficult. Then suddenly a first-class scholar appeared in Flodoard, canon of Rheims (d. 966). Flodoard was an industrious annalist; but he also wrote a *History of the Church of Rheims* and a poem on the triumphs of Christ and his saints. Like Bede, he was a scholar-historian. Both aimed to be more enterprising than mere compilers when they studied the history of the remote past; both wrote in clear Church Latin in order to reach as wide a public as possible. Flodoard collected evidence for the early history of Rheims, drawing on oral reports, classical Latin writers and saints' *Lives*. More, he looked at archaeological remains and he copied inscriptions. The dossier which he made in preparation for writing has been discovered recently. It shows how far afield he went in his search for evidence: he procured a copy of an inscription on an altar in a church in the Vosges, because a former archbishop of Rheims had dedicated the church. A visit to Rome enabled him to transcribe epitaphs on papal tombs for his poem. On the later history of Rheims Flodoard gave a careful account of what he knew from experience.

The next surprise is what I can only call '*salon* history', incongruous as it sounds. Liudprand, Widukind and Richer were all three classicists, entertainers and partisans. They wrote in classicizing Latin. Liudprand sprinkled his Latin with Greek words and phrases. His modern English translator had the happy idea of translating them into French, which gives an effect of politeness. Widukind and Richer both prefer classical 'temples' to 'churches' and call contemporary armies 'legions'. They refrain from quoting Scripture as a rule; Liudprand uses biblical phrases only when he has to describe an ecclesiastical occasion, just as he would wear vestments in church. They seem to have no 'sense of crisis', although they

45 The emperor Otto I presents a model of the cathedral church of Magdeburg to Christ in majesty. Otto founded and endowed the archbishopric of Magdeburg to forward mission work and conquest on his eastern border. He obtained a papal bull of foundation after his imperial coronation at Rome in 962. Detail of an ivory relief from Milan or Reichenau, about 970. *New York, The Metropolitan Museum of Art, Gift of George Blumenthal, 1941*

all lived through grim events, not as onlookers, but as men committed to a point of view in politics. The fact that they recount legends does not make them naïve, any more than Livy is naïve when he tells tales of early Rome. Liudprand's dirty stories recall Voltaire.

Liudprand (d. 972) began his career as a page at the court of King Hugh of Italy, and later passed into the service of Otto I, to whom he owed his bishopric of Cremona. He called his first book *Tit for Tat*, since he wrote it partly to avenge himself on his enemies. It is dedicated to a Spanish bishop. They had met at the court of Otto in Germany, and the bishop had suggested to Liudprand that he should write a history of his own times. He explains in his preface that he aims at amusing his readers. The study of philosophy calls for recreation in the form of comedy or of pleasing histories of heroic men. Students tired of the difficult perusal of Cicero will 'find refreshment in these outpourings of mine'. His spite against his opponents in Italian factions adds to our enjoyment of his *chronique scandaleuse*. So do his snide comments: 'The Italians like to have two masters, so that they can play off one against the other.' Liudprand, though a Lombard, wanted only one master, and that was Otto. His two shorter pieces are the *Deeds of Otto*, where he praises the emperor and blackens the anti-imperialist party, and *The Embassy to Constantinople*. This is a satirical memoir of his embassy to the Byzantine court; he disliked the Greeks and their food and manners and pretensions. His mud-slinging did lasting harm. It is only recently that historians have begun to question his shocking picture of the anti-imperialist factions at Rome. Popes and women are always news: the combination has proved irresistible.

Widukind preferred battles to court intrigue. He was a monk of the Saxon abbey of Corvey, a royal foundation, and was related to the German ruling family. He dedicated his *Deeds of the Saxons* to a nun-princess, Matilda, a daughter of Otto I. It is divided into three books, each having a preface more flattering than the last. Widukind proposes to entertain Princess Matilda and to increase her glory by glorifying her ancestors. He begins with the origins of the Saxons and goes down to Otto's death in 973. We do not know when Widukind died; the dates of the various recensions of his books are still controversial; but it seems that he began to write during Otto's lifetime. His picture of the Saxons represents a blend of German heroic tradition with the

Carolingian tradition handed down by Einhard. Widukind adds his personal version of the ancient Roman tradition. Henry the Fowler and Otto I are made to look like legendary heroes. They stand out larger than life as mighty warriors and hunters, generous as 'gift-givers' to their fighting men. Widukind's portrait of Otto owes something to Suetonius and Einhard. Otto, like Augustus Caesar, turned to the business of making 'divine and human laws' after defeating his domestic and foreign enemies.

The original feature of Widukind's *Deeds* was his revival of a post-Suetonian type of Caesar. He brought in the soldier-emperors of late antiquity, who owed their creation to the army. These were not civilians like the Caesars of the *Twelve Lives*. Widukind states that first Henry the Fowler and then Otto were acclaimed emperor on the battlefield, each after his greatest victory. Their historian gives each one the imperial title after his acclamation by the army. He ignores the facts, which must have been known to a man so close to the royal house, that Henry was not crowned as emperor and that he never used the title, while Otto waited until after his coronation at Rome in 962; he did not use the title regularly before then, even after his triumphant victory on the Lechfeld in 955. Widukind goes on to ignore Otto's imperial coronation by the pope in Rome. It was a wilful omission. He certainly knew that it had happened, and had no such scruple in recording Otto's victories over the rebellious Romans. The Princess Matilda would have known of it too. Widukind covers up his omission by warning her that he does not mean to tell her the full story of her father's deeds. It seems odd that he should have omitted the coronation at Rome and yet have described Otto's coronation by the archbishop of Mainz at Aachen, when he succeeded Henry the Fowler in 936. The reason must be that Widukind disliked the Roman connection. Perhaps Einhard encouraged his feeling that a heroic war-leader ought not to be crowned by a priest, even if that priest were the successor of St Peter. Otto had earned his title on the battlefield and did not need to have it conferred on him by a churchman. The royal coronation at Aachen fitted in better: it strengthened the link between Otto and Charlemagne.

The significance of Widukind's omission has been much discussed. His text lends itself to various interpretations, just as Einhard's secular bias can have more or less importance read into it. The real point is that Widukind explored a new area of ancient history, the period of soldier-emperors. He found a setting for the Saxons which would preserve their links with the Caesars without sacrificing their glory as war-leaders.

Richer (d. *c*. 998) was a monk of St Remigius of Rheims and had studied under Gerbert, later Pope Sylvester II; Gerbert was the best master of the Latin classics available in his day. Richer dedicated his *Histories* to Gerbert as his admiring pupil, and shows his sophistication by not apologizing or explaining his purpose, as was customary. Gerbert had asked for the book and thereby showed that he regarded historiography as a civilized pursuit. One did not need to apologize for imitating Julius Caesar. Richer followed Caesar in starting with a geographical account of Gaul; then he described the manners and customs of the inhabitants and sketched their early history. He treated the history of Gaul in detail after 888, the year of the final break-up of the Carolingian empire. Unfortunately for the repute of classicizing history, Richer's credibility is low. We can see him at work and watch his method. At first he relied on the scholarly Flodoard as his source, since Flodoard's writings were to hand at Rheims; Richer says so himself. He rewrote Flodoard so as to 'improve' the plain style, messing up the content as it pleased him. When his source gave out, he was able to write as a near contemporary and then as an eye-witness; but we distrust him already. He had a political bias. Friendship and interest led him to support Hugh Capet against the last French Carolingians. Worse still, his learning led him astray. He showed off his knowledge of medicine by inventing diseases for his characters to die of. At least, he has been accused of doing so; we cannot check him. His use of Sallust *can* be checked, and the result is discreditable. His fondness for the Roman historian induced him to change the season of a siege because he wanted to quote from the *Jugurthan War*. He makes Hugh Capet 'establish laws and make decrees' on his election as king in 987. The early Capetians were not legislators. All they did in that line was to authorize land transactions. But the Roman Caesars made laws, and so did the Ottos: Hugh Capet had to wear the toga to compete with them. Modern attacks on his *Histories* would have struck Richer as the crassest kind of pedantry. Like Liudprand and Widukind, he was a gifted story-teller, especially when he described his personal adventures; he is a good entertainer.

46 Opposite: the opening page of Richer's *History*, with his dedication to Gerbert, later Pope Sylvester II. This is one of the very few autograph copies of a medieval historical text to survive; the notes and corrections are in Richer's hand as well. *Bamberg, Staatsbibliothek, MS hist. 5, f. 1r*

DOMINO A̅ BEATISSIMO PATRI GERBERTO
ARCHI EPISCOPO. RICHERVS MONACH

aliorum congressib; in uolumine regerendis. in
par sciscime. G. auctoritas seminariu dedit. q
sum̅a utilitate affert. & reru̅ materia sese multipl
pbet. eo animi nisu copleccor. qua lubentius mira benig
nitate provahor. Cuius rei initiu autem̅ o ascen
res multo ante gestis. d. m. hictemari ante te se
remoru̅ metropolitani. suis annalib. competissime an
nexui. Tantoq; superiora lector extimueris. quanto
an̅ti opuscula exordio perfecissem̅. Et hoc liqua ne
karoloru̅ aliorumq; frequens & uniuersop̅ repentio
operis utriusq; ordine rursus. Ubi eni repetitio n
aduerteret. tanto necesse error effunderit. quanto a serie ordinarii
exprimi sequeretur. Vnde & hic atq; illic seipho karoli. sepe
luloui ceuis noty efferunt. propter auctoru̅ prudens lector
progresq; uoces p̅notabit. Quoru̅ temporib. bella agalii
sepe numero patrata. uariosq; rerum tumultus. ac diuer
sas negotioru̅ rationes. ad memoria̅ reducere & scripto
p̅create p̅positu̅ e. Siqua u aalioru̅ efferant. p̅iuit
demus rationes que uicam̅ si potuerunt. ad euentussi
putet; Indicendo reusans effluere. plurima
successiue exordiens Re totius exordiu̅ narrationis
aggrediar. Breuiu̅ faci orbis diuisione. galliaq;
in partes distribueta. eoq; eius poulorum moras &
actus describere p̅positu̅ sit. EXPL P̅OLOG

† S̅ elsi ignote antiquitatis. æqueu̅ ego quoda̅ Flodoardo p̅sby
remisissi libello. me alia edere potuisse. in uerba eadem. sed aliter
habes plenissimo oratonis statu mea. res ipsa quidem
sime demonstro. Sedq; lectori fieri arbitror. amplectiat
idem̅a arcem ad uisscerim.

To add to the *salon* illusion we have a woman historian, Hrotswitha, a nun of Gandersheim in Saxony. Students of medieval drama know her for her Christian adaptations of the comedies of Terence. She also wrote a historical poem on Otto I soon after his coronation at Rome in 962. Learned authors were rare at the time; an authoress was unique. Yet there she is in the masculine company of the *Patrologia Latina*, and a scent wafts up from the pages. Hrotswitha wrote in a light, tripping style. Her verses survive in fragments only; but enough remains to show that she felt a sentimental attachment to Christian Rome. What most attracted her to Otto was his love story: he rescued Queen Adelheid from her brutal oppressor, married her and reigned with her as his empress. Hrotswitha's poem is a 'real life romance'.

To taste a contrast with these literary historians we must turn to a monastic chronicle. Benedict, monk of St Andrew's by Monte Soracte (to the north-east of Rome), whose chronicle breaks off incomplete at 972, shows what passed for Latin in less learned circles. A scandalized German scholar has described his diction as 'the lowest to which the tongue of Cicero has ever sunk'. Old-fashioned country grammar – 'them's us's' – would sound just as odd if translated into Latin. Benedict had no use for rules, and he used dialect words. His copyist may have committed some of the gaffes, but the original cannot have been perfect. The very harshness of the style suits the story. We have seen Otto through the admiring eyes of Liudprand, Hrotswitha and Widukind. Benedict tells what it felt like to be conquered by the Saxon and plundered by his men of iron. His lament for 'the Leonine City', taken over by foreigners, has a suggestion of keening. It is more poignant than literature.

Historiography loses its rarity value during the eleventh century. More monks wrote chronicles; the papal biographers broadened out; their interests ceased to be local. All the genres handed down to the Middle Ages were cultivated, and hybrids were invented. We begin to see 'types', whereas the writers we have just met were 'originals'. Their successors do not show the same extremes of polish or roughness. They are not dull, however, since they react to the new movements of the period. The rise of the towns and the crusades must wait for later chapters. Here I shall choose a sample from the polemical histories of the Investiture Contest.

As we have seen, the Contest forced Henry IV's biographer to think about causes. Bruno wrote his book *On the Saxon War* as propaganda for the opposite side. Paradoxically, the most narrowly partisan of the polemical historiographers is the most thoughtful. Bruno belonged to the cathedral clergy of Magdeburg and knew the archbishop. On the latter's death he passed into the service of the bishop of Merseberg, to whom he dedicated his war history in 1082. 'Saxony for the Saxons' is Bruno's slogan. The Saxons rebelled against the Swabian Henry IV, who tried to 'enslave' them, as they saw it. They allied with Gregory VII for political reasons, not because they were reformers. Gregory's forgiveness of Henry at Canossa struck them as double-dealing. The pope had let them down. The Saxon rebels failed to win Gregory's full support for the antiking who had been elected to oppose Henry. Bruno came to dislike the pope and his legates almost as much as the Henricians. As freedom-fighters the Saxons ought to have won their wars. Their indifferent success made Bruno reflect on causes and collect evidence. First he had to justify their rebellion, a serious matter in the German Reich. Henry was a tyrant. Why? Like Henry's biographer, Bruno pointed to the minority as a cause, though he interpreted it differently. The young king was badly brought up by flatterers; he never mended his ways. Why did the Saxons suffer reverses? Perceptively Bruno blames them for breaking their promises to their Swabian allies by making a separate peace with Henry. This mistake on the Saxons' part split the common front for good and all. The blame after Canossa lay with Gregory VII, who encouraged the rebels, only to leave them in the lurch when it suited him. To substantiate his claim, Bruno assembled *pièces justificatives* in the form of the letters which passed between the pope and the Saxon princes and prelates. Gregory excused himself for absolving Henry; the Saxons bombarded him with reproaches and appeals for his moral backing: 'Come off the fence!' Bruno was well placed to get copies of the letters because of his connections with Magdeburg and Merseberg. There were precedents for inserting documents in ecclesiastical histories and chronicles, but *On the Saxon War* is a historical monograph on the model of *The Jugurthan War*: Bruno knew his Sallust. It was less usual to copy letters into literary history. His desperation led Bruno to mix his genres. His *Saxon War* was the better for it. Polemic stimulated heart-searching and novelty.

England had a national tradition of historical record. The *Anglo-Saxon Chronicle* is unique in the West as a sustained record of events written in the vernacular. It probably began to be compiled and to circulate soon after 899. Writers at various centres copied earlier versions and made additions. One version, the 'Peterborough Chronicle', was continued after the Norman Conquest down to 1155. Anglo-Norman men of letters put much of their creative energy into historiography. That is their distinctive contribution to the revival of learning in the twelfth century. My reason for treating them skimpily here is that the English-speaking student is well provided with good introductions and translations. I shall mention only the most famous names, Orderic Vitalis and William of Malmesbury.

These two men were contemporaries: both died in the early 1140s. Orderic had the longer life; he was born in 1075 and William some twenty years later. Both took monastic vows in their youth and remained monks of their abbeys, St Evroul in Normandy and Malmesbury respectively, throughout their careers. Both came of mixed parentage. William tells us that he came of an Anglo-Norman family; Orderic had a French or Norman father and an English mother. He was born near Shrewsbury, but his father brought him as a child oblate to St Evroul so that he might serve God undistracted by his kinsfolk (that is the reason Orderic gives for his removal to a foreign land). He revisited England to collect material for his *History*. We know that he stayed at Worcester and Crowland. Both Orderic and William were dedicated scholars and book-hunters, yet we have no evidence that they ever met or that they read each other's books. As historians they were as different as chalk from cheese. Orderic's *Ecclesiastical History* conjures up a picture of Clio, Muse of history, as a big fierce woman browbeating her votary. William understood how to keep his mistress under control.

Orderic presents himself to his readers as a simple monk. He did not hold office in his abbey and had few occasions to attend church councils or go to court. The *History* ends on a note of thanksgiving: the author rejoices that he has lived all his life in religion, spiritually, if not always physically, detached from the turmoil of the world. We get the impression of a modest man, who does not force himself on our notice except to authenticate his story as an eyewitness and to show us how his career fitted into his narrative. He mentions

An. dccc.lī. Her forþferde ælfheah bisc. on pmt on ƺregoriuſ
An. dccc.lii. (mæſſe dæƺ) Her norðhymbre fordrifan anlaf
cyninƺ. ⁊ under fenƺ yric haroldes ſunu.
An. dccc.liii.
An. dccc.liiii. Her norðhymbre fordrifon yric.
⁊ eadred fenƺ to norðhymbra rice.
An. dccc.lv. Her eadred cyninƺ forðferde.
⁊ fenƺ eadwiƺ to rice eadmundes ſunu. ⁊ aflæmde S dunſtan ut of lande
An. dccc.lvi. Her forðferde wulſtan arceb.
An. dccc.lvii.
An. dccc.lviii.
An. dccc.lix. Her eadwiƺ cyninƺ forðferde. on kł octobr.
⁊ fenƺ eadgar his broðor to rice. On his daƺū hitgo
dode ƺeorne. ⁊ ƺod him ƺeuðe þ he wunode on ſibbe þa
hwile þe he leofode. ⁊ he dyde ſwa him þearf wæſ earnode

his ordination, his rare excursions outside his abbey, and his
personal reactions to disasters: in the wreck of the White
Ship (1120), when Prince William, son of Henry I, was
drowned with all his company, none of Orderic's friends or
relatives was involved; only common humanity makes him
grieve for those who died. His asides echo the usual plati-
tudes on the historian's task and the divine plan in history,
though he can let shrewd comments fall from the lips of a
seemingly gullible character. He blames robbers and spoilers
of Church – especially monastic – property in the usual way.
Hatred of cruelty in any form marks him out as being truly
sensitive. His pity for victims and his condemnation of
oppressors, even those whom he admired, are more than
mere claptrap.

Ironically enough, Clio tricked him into recording the
deeds of the Normans, the most violent and restless people of
his time. He did not start with the intention to do so. His
abbot asked him to write a history of St Evroul. He set out to
give an account on traditional lines of the founders, bene-
factors, privileges, growth, prosperity, misfortunes and
losses of his abbey. But this took him further afield. Orderic
felt obliged to include the history of Norman families whose
members had contacts with the monastery. Then he realized
that he had to write a history of the duchy, which he could
not separate from the history of all the Normans. The

47 The Peterborough version
of the *Anglo-Saxon Chronicle*
with entries for the years
951–959. Additions have
been made in blank spaces.
*Oxford, Bodleian Library, MS
Laud. misc. 636, f.36r*

Normans had conquered and settled in Neustria; Normans from the duchy conquered and founded states in southern Italy and Sicily; Duke William conquered the kingdom of England. Normans from the duchy and Italy played a leading part in the First Crusade. Bohemond of Sicily carved out a principality for himself at Antioch. Family and religious ties persisted wherever the Norman network spread. 'In for a penny, in for a pound': the *Ecclesiastical History* turned into a history of Christendom. The author worked on several parts of it concurrently, bringing it up to 1141, when he felt too tired at the age of sixty-seven to hold his pen any longer. At an earlier stage he had compiled a 'world history' from the Incarnation up to his own day to serve as a preface and make his work as comprehensive as possible.

Changes of plan as he went along necessitated digression and repetition. Orderic excuses himself when an extra long digression has led him right off the rails. The monastic mode of writing encouraged him to make a virtue of necessity. Monastic homilists proceeded by digression; it belonged to the technique of 'holy reading'. The idea that one should make a scheme before starting and keep to it when writing would have struck a monk as misguided. St Gregory says so in his *Morals on Job*, one of the most widely read books of the Middle Ages:

... if a river, as it flows along its channel, meets with open valleys on its side, into these it immediately turns the course of its current, and when they are copiously supplied, presently it pours itself back into its bed. Thus should it be with everyone who treats of the Divine Word.

The historian aimed at edification. It suited his purpose to turn aside in order to tell of a saint's life and miracles or to describe the conversion of a heathen people to Christianity.

Orderic had qualms nevertheless. He meant to write ecclesiastical history, but it encroached on secular. He tried to distinguish between the two genres and it worried him that he could not do full justice to the latter:

Skilful historians could write a memorable history of these great men and women. ... We, however, who have no experience of the courts of the world, but spend our lives in the daily rounds of the cloisters where we live, will briefly note what is relevant to our purpose.

William the Conqueror's children 'left abundant material for eloquent and learned men to compose mighty tomes'. The

History offers us more than brief notes on Anglo-Norman political history, in spite of his disclaimer. But they did not satisfy him; he thought that the story needed telling afresh in its own right and not as a mere annex to church history. The historian had inexhaustible opportunities: Orderic could not pursue all of them.

The Normans should have thanked him for the space he gave them, limited though it was. They appeared in historiography as a Christian people for the first time. Orderic's Norman predecessors had dealt with isolated aspects of Norman history; Dudo of St Quentin, for example, told a partly legendary story of the conquest of Normandy. In general non-Norman historians continued to portray Normans as ninth- and tenth-century writers had done, as cruel barbarian invaders of Christian kingdoms. Orderic had no illusions as to their national traits. He makes the Conqueror describe the men of his duchy as 'a turbulent people, ever ready to cause disturbances'. They are 'ever restless and desirous of visiting foreign lands'. Victorious abroad, they fall to cutting one another's throats as soon as a strong ruler is removed. But they excel as fighters and church builders. Orderic's lifelong sense of being an Englishman abroad was compatible with a preference for the Normans against their neighbours, Angevins, Flemish and French in the north, Greeks and Italians in the south and east. He had a standard rule of conduct to apply to churchmen; in telling secular history his prejudices overcame him. His own experience made him aware of the differences between the men of Normandy and their enemies on the border. He wrote as a partisan of the Normans.

The result was a new 'barbarian history' set into the framework of his *Ecclesiastical History*. The pagan Norsemen perform heroic feats of arms; then their prowess as Christians is recorded, though Orderic does not suppress their evil deeds. The substance of his *History* has an original element; he broke new ground.

Otherwise Orderic is 'the modern researcher's historian'. His vast, untidy narrative supplies a wealth of information on all kinds of subjects. Many details are incorrect, since his sources misled him, although he made painstaking efforts to get at the facts by reading chronicles and charters and asking questions of persons likely to know what happened. On the other hand, his classical studies do not get in his way when he records contemporary behaviour. There were no recognized types on which to model French châtelains and Norman lords of middling wealth and moderate piety. Orderic presents them as real individuals, as he observed them. We have come a long way from '*salon* history'.

Apart from its interest for local history, the *Ecclesiastical History* mirrors the history of ideas. It reflects what a Black Monk thought of the new reformed orders. Orderic disliked 'Cistercian novelties', but he tried to be fair. He is also a source for the history of political theory. He shows us what a monk of a Norman monastery expected of rulers. Strong government was essential to quell in-fighting and invasions. Orderic assumed that rebels must always be in the wrong. They put their private interest before the public good. A ruler who burdens his subjects with taxes and who snaps his fingers at clerical privilege is a lesser evil; far worse is the ruler who absents himself and neglects to discipline his barons. Orderic states a common monastic view of government; but he puts it forcibly and backs it by examples. He had plenty to hand: rebellions broke out frequently in Normandy.

The *Ecclesiastical History* is a long haul, but it rewards persevering readers by showing them how the world looked as seen from the cloisters of St Evroul. William of Malmesbury, on the contrary, is 'a modern historian's historian'. We read him as a source of facts and ideas, as we read Orderic; but we study his method too. William resembles Flodoard. He followed Flodoard unconsciously and Bede quite consciously in holding the study of the past to be a discipline in its own right: it meant far more labour than the mechanical up-ending of earlier histories and chronicles. Intensive research into the records of past ages was called for. William started with the same advantage as Orderic: the abbey library at Malmesbury housed a good store of books, since a scholar-abbot from Jumièges in Normandy had refounded it. William held the office of librarian. His duties gave him the chance to browse there and to acquire new texts for the library. He supplemented the written sources available on the history of Britain by collecting oral information both locally and on journeys round the country. He interviewed men who had seen or who had had handed down to them 'things in danger of being forgotten'. He entered a *caveat* for data which he could not verify. He tried to distinguish between legend and history. Naturally he swallowed some fiction and fable as factual, but not everything that came his way. Tall stories concerning King Arthur of Britain were circulating while he wrote. They did not deceive him – partly, it is true, because twelfth-century Welshmen struck him as unlikely to have had such valiant ancestors as the Arthur stories supposed. William made a more self-conscious effort than Orderic to judge and criticize his material.

William is more analytical and more interested in motive as a historian. He enjoys comparing a person's avowed motives for acting as he did with his real ones. To deduce motives involves guessing. William guessed, as historians still do. He worked on the principle that men normally act from motives of self-interest. We should look at their interest and not believe their professions. Pope Urban II proclaimed the First Crusade at the Council of Clermont, in order to help the Christians in the East and to win salvation for men's souls. The pope's true motives, according to William, were 'less well-known'. Urban hoped that the general confusion resulting from the crusade would enable him to recover the papal lands in Italy, which had been lost to the imperialists in the Investiture Contest. William based his interpretation on gossip or on his own view of what was probable; the Council of Clermont took place when he was still a baby or not yet born. But the guess at Urban's motives shows how he looked for historical causes.

To act 'without self-interest' seemed to William rare and wonderful. He records disinterested loyalty as the exception. Earl Robert of Gloucester supported the Empress Matilda, his half-sister, against King Stephen in the civil wars consistently, unlike her many fair-weather friends. His motive was sheer loyalty to her. Crediting readers with his own scepticism, William doubts whether they will believe his statement that the earl acted unselfishly. He doubts it all the more because they will know that the earl was his patron. He defends himself against the charge of flattery in order to prove that his statement is true. *Cui bono?*, 'to whose benefit?', remains a favourite question asked by historians when they discuss why men behaved in a certain way. William asked it and supplied the answers as a student of human nature, who looked at the seamy side first.

His sense of form was surer than Orderic's. William made a better show of separating sacred from secular history. His *Deeds of the Bishops* represents an ecclesiastical history of England, his *Deeds of the Kings* the equivalent in secular history. On reaching his own time he ran the usual risk of offending persons who were still alive if he told the truth.

Orderic, sheltered in his cloister, had less reason to fear that great men would notice what he wrote of their behaviour. William had more contact with princes. He solved his problem by writing royal biographies of the Suetonian type, which enabled him to give a detached, schematic account of rulers without judging them. He handled his model skilfully, and living individuals do come through. Some guessing was in order. We cannot test William's statement that Henry I begot large numbers of bastards to serve as a prop to his throne rather than for pleasure; but it adds a nice touch to the portrait of a cold, calculating and clever king. William painted it with loving care. His last work was a historical monograph, the *New History*. It begins with an account of Henry I's last years, leading up to the civil wars of Stephen's reign. William left it unfinished at his death in 1143. It is his best piece. Here he could exploit his knowledge as an eyewitness of events in south-west England and draw on contemporary evidence. He is careful to tell us when he was present on the occasions which he describes and when he relies on hearsay. Robert of Gloucester, Stephen's leading opponent, was the hero and recipient of the book; we are in the thick of politics.

William took seriously the precept that the historian should be impartial. He writes proudly that on account of his mixed parentage he can take an impartial view of the Norman conquest of England. Unfortunately he goes on to give the official Norman version with its bias against Harold and its blackening of the English Church. The same goes for Orderic, in spite of his awareness of being English. It was the only version to hand. William's boast witnesses to his ideal of impartiality. It was unattainable. His sources took sides, and he followed. The *New History* put his theories to the test. He invented his own version of the civil wars as he went along, having no source to guide him. He survives the test very well. The *New History* gives as fair a picture of the characters involved and the causes of the wars as could be expected from a declared partisan of Gloucester. It is a mark of his skill in the historian's craft that William puts his cards on the table. He credited students of history with the desire to read an impartial account and he tried to satisfy them by explaining where he stood, so that they could make allowances.

His gifts as a scholar justify William's popularity with modern historians: he strikes them as 'a chap like us' or 'almost a colleague'. The joy of shaking hands across the centuries may have led to some exaggeration of his modernity as an investigator of the remote past and as an interpreter of the present; but our feeling of kinship with the Malmesbury historian is real. That he possessed the crowning talent of readability adds to his appeal. So did other Anglo-Norman historians; it was a characteristic trait; even Orderic is readable in moderate doses. The difference is that William provides more scholarship as well as more entertainment.

None of the writers reviewed in this chapter bothered his head about problems of periodization. An occasional reference to the current decline in morals and the approaching end shows us that an author accepted the tradition that he was living in the sixth age of the world. Historiographers settled down to foreseeing a future of indefinite length in this last age. Both Orderic Vitalis and Henry of Huntingdon (d. c. 1155), in his *History of the English*, claim that the study of history helps to predict the future and to understand new happenings as they occur. Orderic puts it explicitly:

It sometimes happens that many events present themselves to the ignorant as unheard-of things, and new circumstances are frequently occurring in modern times on which no light can be thrown to inexperienced minds except by reference to former transactions.

The monk of St Evroul and the archdeacon of Huntingdon both assume that the historian's foresight will range over home ground. The new occurrences are not imagined as apocalyptic. Both took an interest in the prophecies ascribed to the Welsh wizard Merlin, which were circulating when they wrote. Some had already come to pass; they belonged to the genre of 'prophecy after the event', though this was not realized; others might be fulfilled in the future. But Merlin's prophecies were political, treating of human battles and conquests. The excitement which they aroused suggests lack of interest in the coming of Antichrist. Curiosity centred on battles between the English kings and their neighbours, not on the approach of Doomsday.

But Orosius had not slipped quite out of mind. His panoramic view of history was still challenging. Historiographers read the *History Against the Pagans* as an authentic source for early history, to be copied as a prelude to their account of more recent events. But a thoughtful reader would find more in it. Orosius dared him to write a new universal history, lifting his eyes to far horizons. Could one bring Orosian periodization up to date? It was time to try.

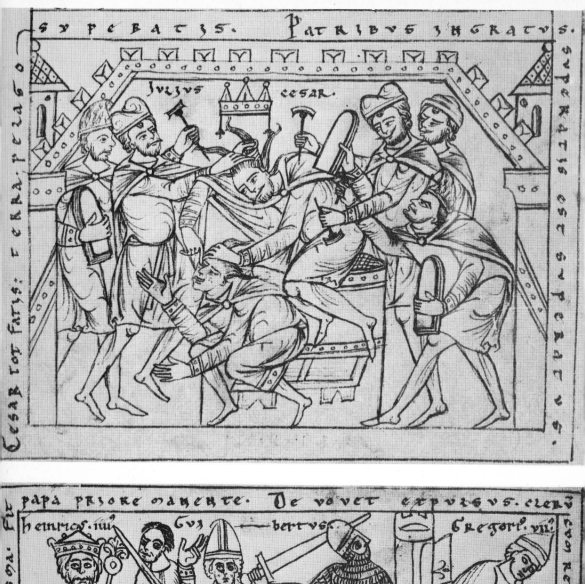

IVLIVS CESAR.

CESAR TOT FATIS. TERRA. PELAGO

SVPERATIS EST SVPERATVS.

PAPA PRIORE MANENTE. DE NOVET EXPVLSVS. CLERV

HEINRICVS. IIII° GVI BERTVS GREGORI. VII

EN FIDES SCISSA. FIT

CVM REGE FVRENTE.

HIC EXVI SEDE, PARET MVTABILIS EVI.

Universal history

Benedetto Croce rated 'reflective history' as the highest type of historiography. 'There are no periods in history, only problems.' The reflective historian examines problems. Universal history does not exist for any historian worthy of the name, because he cannot turn his mind to all aspects of history at once. Only a hack will write history at second or third hand, as one must if one tries to write universal history. While Croce's statements may be valid for modern historiography, they do not apply to that of the twelfth century. Granted that reflective history is the highest type, and that the true historian concerns himself with problems, he still cannot get away from periods. To write reflective history in the twelfth century meant reflecting on the periodization handed down by Orosius. That posed the problems. What was history if not universal? To deny its universality would have amounted to denying the truth of Christianity. But did the early time schemes of the six ages and the four monarchies provide the right framework for writing the history of the centuries between the fifth and the twelfth? Historians, chroniclers and biographers abounded; but no one had volunteered to be a new Orosius. The task bristled with difficulties.

The chief problem had its roots in the fact of change. There were philosophical reasons why 'change' meant decay. Change and decay afflict us from the moment of our conception in the womb. That belief belonged to St Augustine's philosophy of life. The parallel between the ages of the world and the life of man, with its rider that the world had reached the evening of the sixth age, made it natural to suppose that historical changes would normally be for the worse. It was easy to tell the tale of decline, easy and quite enjoyable; historiographers revelled in doling out blame. Changes for the better, on the contrary, called for explanation: how could they happen in a period of decline? Yet novelties sprang up on all sides. Some could be classified as 'bad', but not all; some were indisputably 'good', and therefore puzzling.

48, 49 Opposite: illustrations to the *History of the Two Cities* by Otto of Freising (see pp. 100–103), from a German manuscript of about 1170. The upper picture shows the murder of Julius Caesar. Roman senators, angry at his assumption of power, encourage his murderers to stab him. Caesar's death at the moment of triumph exemplifies the instability of worldly affairs. The lower picture shows recent history. Henry IV, a royal counsellor and the antipope Guibert (see p. 73) connive at the attempted murder of Pope Gregory VII, who is seen escaping from Rome. *Jena, Universitätsbibliothek, MS Bos.9.6., f.20v and 79r*

It is clear for all to see how many things, and things of great importance which are needed for this life, which are of use both to the good and to the bad, which are very beautiful in their own order, have been made and are being made both by good men and by wicked men. . . .

Hence derive in the realms of literature, art and architecture, through the countless discoveries of all sorts which men have made, so many branches of learning, so many kinds of professions, precisions in scientific research, arts of eloquence, varieties of positions and posts and innumerable investigations into the nature of this world.

What prospects these lines evoke! They were written by a Cistercian abbot called William of St Thierry, a devoted admirer of St Bernard, in his *Golden Epistle* to the Carthusian monks of Mont Dieu (1144–8). William and his friends had renounced the world; but he realized how stimulating it was to live in the world at such a time. No scholar of the early twelfth century could shut his eyes to the social, economic and intellectual changes taking place around him.

Economic developments of course led to abuses by wicked men. A churchman would disapprove of the rise of the towns and the townsmen's demand for privileges, which upset the God-given social order. Increasing wealth bred luxury and vicious fashions in clothes and hair-styles. Usury flourished. The 'varieties of positions and posts' mentioned by William of St Thierry evidently referred to the expansion of government, both ecclesiastical and secular. More sophisticated methods of extracting money from subjects led to more graft and oppression, as the officials enriched themselves. Lawyers and bureaucrats presented a new target for moralists. But who could deny that some of the new movements were 'good'? Churchmen rejoiced at the success of the First Crusade. The new religious orders, the Canons Regular of St Victor, the Cistercians or White Monks, Premonstratensians or White Canons, and communities of hermits, presented the seeker after perfection with a bewildering choice of ways to his goal. Religious reform in the early Middle Ages had been limited in scope to monks and hermits. Now the Black Monks had rivals. Members of each order claimed that its customs and ideals derived from the New Testament. More challenging still, student numbers had multiplied. There were more and better schools to provide education for a larger élite. Again, bad men abused their opportunities. Students were undisciplined; masters and students alike wasted their time on 'frivolous questions'. But study could serve the Church if it were rightly used. The schools equipped clerks to undertake pastoral care as well as deepening their understanding of Catholic doctrine.

Some scholars reflected on the fact of change, found it 'good', and gave improvement a place in their outlook on history. Hugh of St Victor (d. 1141), a Canon Regular who taught at the abbey of St Victor at Paris, had a unique and personal sense of historical development. He started from the traditional view of history as the history of salvation and drew the conclusion: the Church must encourage the growth of new institutions to meet new needs; how otherwise could she fulfil her mission on earth? 'Novelties', therefore, belonged to the divine plan. Godfrey of St Victor, one of Hugh's pupils, shared his master's optimism. His *Microcosmos*, a long theological treatise, shows how man, even fallen man, has been endowed with marvellous natural capacities to invent what he needs to live a full and civilized life on earth. Godfrey waxes as lyrical as William of St Thierry on the increased output of books on all kinds of topics.

Anselm of Havelberg, a member of the new order of White Canons, defended the Canons against accusations of innovation. He did so on historical grounds. It was not enough to argue that the way of life he had chosen derived from the Gospel; he realized that to reform means to innovate; one cannot return to the values of the past at the present time without some kind of adaptation. Therefore, Anselm argued, the Holy Spirit continues to inspire new forms of religious life, even in the last age of the world. He grasped the nettle; changes for the better can happen even in the last age.

Novelties forced themselves on the notice of another group of scholars, the canon lawyers. This was a professional matter, which intruded into their teaching and practice. Canon law was developing as fast as theology. The rules governing cases judged in the Church courts and in the papal Curia increased in number and complexity. The substratum of canon law went back to the Bible, Church councils and papal decretals (with forgeries among them); but interpretations and new rulings to meet new problems were constantly added to the original basis. Canon lawyers worked *ex officio* on the corpus of canon law, old and new. They could not overlook the differences between the law

50 Godfrey of St Victor, a pupil of Hugh, teaches at the abbey of St Victor at Paris. He holds his *Microcosmos*, which he composed about 1185. From a thirteenth-century French copy of the *Microcosmos. Paris, Bibliothèque Mazarine, MS 102, f.144r*

they handled and the practices of the early Church. The rules on clerical celibacy and property-holding, for example, had no parallels in the New Testament. But they were necessary to cope with present-day society. A canonist would approve of the fact that Christian life was increasingly regulated by the Church and increasingly tied to the papacy. Professionals take pride in their work, especially when it makes them important. The canon lawyers believed strongly in their calling. It involved making and applying changes in the courts. They were not backward-looking or nostalgic for the past. Legal developments benefited the Church, or so they assumed in their teaching of canon-law books.

The scholars I have mentioned were theologians or canonists, not historians. Hugh of St Victor was the only one who wrote a history book. His book was a manual for the use of students of Arts and theology in the form of a universal chronicle. Hugh compiled it as a book for use in teaching; he did not treat it as a means to express his views on historical development. Historiographers were more conservative and more allergic to ideas than theologians or canonists. They recorded changes and novelties, with praise or blame as the case might be. Already the Burgundian historian Ralph Glaber (d. soon after 1049) had noted the current enthusiasm for church-building: the earth seemed to be putting on white garments. But he did not discuss the relevance of this change to the old age of the world.

The six ages were taken for granted. The time scheme of the four monarchies ought to have stimulated historiographers to think and criticize. This theory could be measured against actual fact. Periods exist in the mind, whereas a monarchy is concrete. Did the fourth world monarchy, the Roman, still exist? We left it in the seventh century, prolonging its life through Byzantine rule. Some historians held that it had already been divided up among lesser kings; others ignored it. Then Charlemagne's coronation gave the Roman empire a new lease of life. It marked a shift of power. Byzantine hold on Italy weakened. As Byzantine prestige declined, the popes turned to the Franks to protect them from both the Greeks and the Lombards.

A new theory was invented in Frankish court circles to justify the revival of empire in the West. The empire had been 'transferred to the Franks from the Greeks', without ceasing to be Roman. Hence the fourth monarchy lived on. The theory of 'transfer' had internal contradictions: the

Byzantine empire survived, and indeed was acknowledged by Charlemagne; the Carolingian empire had quite different boundaries from the Roman. The Roman empire centred on the Mediterranean, the Carolingian on the Rhineland. Such petty details weighed light in the scale. The concept of empire and the imperial title outlasted the break-up of the Carolingian empire. Otto I's coronation at Rome marked a further stage in the transfer theory. The Roman empire had been 'transferred to the Germans from the Franks'. After all, this was less surprising than transfer to the Franks from the Greeks; both Franks and Germans had barbarian origins.

The Saxon and later Salian empire looked less Roman than Charlemagne's. Its boundaries stopped short to the west of Flanders and Lorraine. France, Britain, the Spanish peninsula and southern Italy lay outside it. The Saxon and Salian emperors refrained from pressing their claims as emperors over their fellow-rulers. Hence the question of status hardly arose in practice. Rulers outside the effective bounds of the empire did not regard themselves as mere kinglets, in theory subjects of the empire. What did historians make of the situation? There was a conspiracy of silence. To take an example from England: Henry of Huntingdon in his *History of the English* (written about 1145) mentions the coronation of Charlemagne as emperor, but not Otto's. He and many others dealt with the fourth monarchy by omission. Nor did they ask whether it had been divided among ten kings, as foretold in Daniel's vision, and, if so, whether this heralded the coming of Antichrist.

One historian made a timid adjustment instead of merely ignoring the transfer theory. Hugh, a monk of Fleury, who died soon after 1117, began by writing an *Ecclesiastical History* on traditional lines. The transfer of empire to Charlemagne presented no difficulty to Hugh: he counted Charlemagne and the Franks as French. He finished his *History* at the division of the Carolingian empire among the sons of Louis the Pious. Next he wrote a history of the 'modern' kings of France from the death of Charlemagne to 1108. His plan faced him with the problem of the relations between the kings of France and the German emperors. Hugh claims that the French separated themselves from the Germans after the battle of Fontenoy, won by the French king Charles the Bald in 841: 'The kingdom of the Franks has remained separate and divided from the Roman empire from that day to this.' Hugh does not deny the continued existence of the Roman empire, now ruled by Germans; he simply registers the fact that the French kingdom does not belong to it. He seems to be meeting the challenge; then he stops half-way. It was inconsistent to accept the identification of the present-day empire with the fourth monarchy: the empire had ceased to be universal on his own showing.

It fell to a German to think out the problem. Otto of Freising stands alone in his glory as a reflective historian. Exceptional qualifications and experience fitted him for the task. Otto was born about 1115. He belonged to the German nobility, Babenberg on his father's side and Staufer on his mother's. The two families feuded, in spite of the marriage alliance between Otto's parents. The disorders in his country made a deep impression on him. The young nobleman went to study in Paris, where he read Arts and theology. Here he could watch academic feuds, and here too his loyalties were divided: he admired St Bernard and yet was friendly with Bernard's opponent, Gilbert of la Porrée. Then Otto joined the Cistercian order, St Bernard's. He became abbot of Morimond and then, at little more than twenty, bishop of Freising. He owed his quick promotion to his kinsmen, but he was learned and able. As a German aristocrat, a Paris scholar, a Cistercian monk and a bishop of the Reich, Otto had an individual outlook and a probing mind. His *History of the Two Cities*, written between about 1143 and 1145, brought Orosius up to date.

The title echoes St Augustine; Otto set out to write a history of the two cities, the heavenly and the earthly, described in the *City of God*. But St Augustine was an early casualty: Otto found that he had to identify the city of God with the Church. He saw Augustine's point that good and bad Christians mingled in the Church on earth; but a historian had to treat the Church as an institution after her recognition by Constantine; he had no choice. That left him with Orosius as his model for universal history. His *Two Cities* is a history of the Church and her enemies set into the time schemes of the six ages and the four monarchies. He dealt with the history of the Church as an institution by explaining that her state was 'happier' after gaining power and wealth than it had been during the persecutions in the early days, but not morally better. He enlarged the Orosian picture by adding the history of two other institutions, study and religion (by which he meant the religious orders). These counted as part of the history of the Church.

Looking for a key to the changes that had taken place since the time of Orosius, which would enable him to plot out the whole sweep of history, Otto pointed to movement from East to West. The centres of world power, political, intellectual and religious, arose in the East and moved westward. Their history fitted into the six ages: monarchy or empire, the Church, study and religion, each had its period of rise, apogee and decline within the span of each age in turn. In Otto's eyes, monarchy or empire was not the enemy of the Church. He took over from Orosius the belief in the Roman empire's positive role; it protected the Church. Her enemies were heretics, pagans and bad Christians, whether clerics or laymen. They attacked her in all ages.

To begin with world monarchy: Otto tidied up the Orosian picture by making parallels. The dual empire of the Medes and Persians corresponded to that of the Greeks and Franks. Empire was transferred to the Franks when first Charlemagne and then Otto I revived the Roman empire. Otto of Freising regarded the Franks and the Germans as one Teutonic people. Hence the transfer from one to the other was a domestic affair. He tried to find out which people held the empire in the dark days between the break-up of Charlemagne's empire and the coronation of Otto I. Perhaps it belonged briefly to the Lombards, another Teutonic people. Clearly, however, world monarchy had moved from the Oriental dynasties to the Greeks and the Romans and thence to the Germans, who had received the empire by transfer. It was still Roman. Clearly, too, a transfer was always followed by rise, peak and decline. The fate of Charlemagne's empire resembled that of the Orientals, and that of the Greeks and the Romans; so did that of the German empire. First, in each case, came rise by conquest, then a time of prosperity, and then defeat by enemies at home and abroad. The German empire rose by conquest; it reached its peak under Henry III; it declined under Henry IV. There was no recovery this time. Henry IV's defeat represented a victory for the Church. Otto quoted a prophecy from the statue dream in Daniel (2: 33–4) forecasting the unprecedented excommunication and deposition of an emperor by a pope. But the Church's victory did not compensate for the collapse of the secular power. Disorder reigned both in the empire and in 'other kingdoms'; he instanced the civil wars between Stephen and Matilda in England to prove that 'other kingdoms' had their troubles as well as the empire. What remained but to await the coming of Antichrist? Otto did not admit that the empire had been divided among the ten kings of Daniel's vision; but he thought it was doomed to disappear. He was not quite consistent in his treatment of the Western empire as a world monarchy; he gave the Byzantine ruler the title of emperor, and he referred to 'other kingdoms' without stating that their rulers belonged to the empire of the West. Otherwise his Orosian pattern made sense in political history. The Roman empire had indeed declined; the emperors could not even keep order within their boundaries.

'Study' proved less amenable to the pattern of rise and fall. Certainly it had been transferred from the East to the West. The idea went back to Alcuin, who told Charlemagne that he must found a 'new Athens' at his capital city of Aachen. As a matter of ancient history it was clear that the Greeks had inherited the wisdom of the East and transmitted it to the Romans. Now study flourished in France and learning tended to be concentrated in the schools of Paris. It seems likely that scholars at Paris were appropriating the theory of transfer of study. It corresponded to reality, since the cathedral schools of Germany and the Rhinelands had lost their attraction; scholars made straight for Paris if they wanted to study north of the Alps. Otto of Freising probably picked up the notion while studying at Paris. Hugh of St Victor may have influenced him.

The difficulty was that if the history of study followed the pattern of political history, then study must have fallen into decline. Rise, apogee and fall followed upon transfer. Otto may have judged that the heyday of the Paris schools had passed. What he says of contemporary studies is so ambiguous that it can be interpreted either way. He does not define his view precisely, as he does when writing of empire. In any case, study had moved closer to the Atlantic seaboard, which marked the end of the known world. Geographically, the schools could expand no further, however long the process of decline might be. A fourteenth-century Oxford poet predicted that study's next move would be to 'outside peoples, far to the West': he was probably joking.

'Religion' was more troublesome still. Otto despaired of the empire. He may have disapproved of Paris doctrines and teaching methods; perhaps that explains why he became a Cistercian. He had nothing but admiration for the new ascetic movements and their saints. He tried to apply his pattern to religion. It fitted into the beginning well enough.

Religion rose in the East; the Old Testament told of holy hermits. Christian monasticism originated with the Desert Fathers. Now it had moved westward. But far from declining, it throve anew. Light shone in the darkness. The *History of the Two Cities* dwells on the mutability of human affairs as manifested in earthly institutions. Religion differed from empire and study; the saints put themselves above mutability. Their merits upheld the tottering world: 'We should expect the world to end soon, were it not supported by the prayers and good works of holy men.' Otto may have had St Bernard in mind. He had joined St Bernard's order and he wrote before the abbot of Clairvaux had dimmed his reputation as a saint and wonder-worker by preaching the Second Crusade, which came to grief.

Religion flourished as it had no business to do. It overlapped untidily with Otto's time schemes. He yielded to the evidence, a merit rare in a historian so committed to a theory. He did not force the facts to lie down on his Procrustean bed. Religion might decline in the future; it showed a strange resilience in surviving its transfer to the West. It lagged behind the pattern of rise, apogee and fall. Otto had the honesty to acknowledge his difficulty. Honesty is what a reader of his *History* has come to expect. Otto had a strong critical sense and applied it to hallowed legends; he always wanted to pay due regard to the facts which he knew. This caution appears even in his last book, which is not history but 'meta-history'. It deals exclusively with the supernatural. Otto outlines the Last Things; mutability gives way to eternity. But even here he draws his data from the Bible and the Fathers without obtruding his speculations.

Otto was an untypical historian. The *History of the Two Cities* hardly circulated outside Germany. Historiographers did not imitate his 'reflective' history. Theologians, lawyers and publicists continued to discuss the relations between the empire and papacy and between the empire and other kingdoms. The theme of the transfer of study from East to West had a long life. But no historian after Otto tried to knit the transfer theory into the pattern of universal history. None of them tackled the problem of changes for good in the old age of the world. Was it due to laziness, myopia or conservatism? It is impossible to say.

Otto himself may have scrapped his theory of universal history in later life. He had reason to do so. The emperor Frederick Barbarossa was Otto's nephew. On succeeding to the empire in 1152, Frederick planned to restore his Reich to its former glory. Propaganda played an important part in his campaign; he would publicize the glorious past of the empire in histories. Otto received a request from his nephew to send a copy of the *History of the Two Cities*. He complied with misgivings. Its account of the decline and ruin of the empire would not suit Frederick's purpose at all. The bishop of Freising excused himself for his pessimism. He wrote a preface to explain that he had written the *History* in dismal times. He also asked Rainald of Dassel, Frederick's chancellor and adviser on the propaganda campaign, to interpret the *History* to Frederick in such a way that it would not displease him. The emperor reassured the author: he had read the book and enjoyed it; but he decided to employ Otto's talents to advertise his achievements in restoring the empire. Otto was put into the position of a doctor who has diagnosed a mortal illness and then has to celebrate his patient's recovery. He set about it with a good heart.

The new book belonged to a different genre, as its title shows: *The Deeds of Frederick*. This genre made periodization unnecessary. Otto could concentrate on the illustrious story of Frederick's family and on his prowess as a young man. Then he reaches Frederick's accession. Clear morning has followed a dark, rainy night. Otto rewrites the history of the empire from the conflict between Henry IV and Gregory VII up to Frederick's accession, giving it a new slant; he brings out the rise of Frederick's family while toning down Henry IV's reverses and the decline of the empire. He tells of Frederick's successes in glowing terms. The new ruler was a righteous man; he restored the empire and worked in harmony with the Church, as his forbears had done in the good old days before the Investiture Conflict. Otto's praise must have been sincere. Frederick's early achievements in Germany and Italy could not have failed to gratify a kinsman and bishop of the imperial Church. How far did they lead him to revise his view of the pattern of universal history? We do not know. Otto continued to take an interest in events outside the empire. He exceeded his instructions by making digressions (fortunately for the value of his *Deeds*) and sometimes excused himself for not keeping to his subject. But he did not try to fit his material into the time schemes of the *Two Cities*. Empire, like religion, had upset the timetable by taking on a new lease of life. Otto contented himself with warning Frederick to beware of Fortune's Wheel. Perhaps he

51 The emperor Frederick
Barbarossa sits beside Bishop
Albert of Freising, the
successor of Otto of Freising.
From a jamb of the door of
Freising cathedral, about
1200.

thought that the revival might not last. Perhaps he also
admitted that his pattern of history needed revision. If so, he
kept his view to himself; it is still a secret.

The Deeds of Frederick breaks off unfinished at Otto's
death in 1158. He had asked his chaplain, Rahewin, to continue the book. Rahewin carried it down to 1160. His continuation shows that he was a good craftsman and a sound
historian; but the genre did not call for reflective history.

His restraint symbolizes the future of medieval historiography. Otto's successors focused increasingly on the
present, without questioning its relevance to the old time
schemes.

Nēt saraceni Nēt latini

Civil-service history

The term 'civil service' today evokes a picture of conventional men in secure jobs. A civil service existed in the twelfth century; but it was a new development in medieval government. Bureaucrats were not yet smothered by routine. In his great book on feudal society Marc Bloch argues that the rise of the salaried worker or employee marked a new stage in medieval history. The number of clerks staffing embryonic bureaucracies increased, and these 'black-coated workers' began to divide themselves into what we now call the 'administrative' and 'executive' grades of the civil service. Some worked their way up to the higher grade and got to the top, while others stayed in the lower ranks until they retired. Their employers were royal, municipal and ecclesiastical governments; all needed accountants and administrators. We have seen that William of St Thierry counted 'varieties of positions and posts' in his list of novelties perceptible in his time. The civil service offered just such a choice of career to young men in search of a livelihood, provided that they had a basic training in 'the three Rs'.

Some bureaucrats wrote history in their spare time or had leisure thrust upon them, which they used to draw up their memoirs. We might expect a civil-service historian to write in a different style from a monk. He did indeed. He had a different outlook and more direct experience. His work would often involve him in riots and other disturbances; he did not lead the sheltered life of the cloister. Our first specimen of civil-service history has the title *The Murder of Charles the Good*.

This is a precious freak of historiography. The author, Galbert of Bruges, worked as a notary for the chapter of the cathedral in his native town. He belonged to the 'executive' grade, being a clerk in minor orders, unbeneficed, as far as we know, and probably living on his perquisites and fees. The occasion for his writing was the murder in 1127 of Count Charles of Flanders while he knelt in the cathedral at prayer. His assassins were members of the powerful Erlembald

52 Opposite: civil servants. Muslim and Latin notaries at work at the royal court at Palermo. A detail from an illustration to Peter of Eboli's poem celebrating the conquest of Sicily by the emperor Henry VI in 1195 (see also colour plate II). *Bern, Burgerbibliothek, Cod. 120, f.101r*

family of servile stock. Count Charles had planned to investigate their origins and perhaps reduce them to serfdom once more. They took desperate measures to save themselves. After the murder the clan occupied the castle of Bruges, adjacent to the cathedral, and carried war into the country-side. It spread over the whole county of Flanders. Galbert must have had time on his hands, since the rebels moved the chapter archives into the castle. His normal business as a notary ceased. He resolved to keep a day-to-day record of the dreadful happenings around him. The task kept him going, and he felt a sort of compulsion, 'a little spark of charity', as he calls it. We miss the tired old excuse of writing to order. Galbert wrote on his own initiative, freshly and precisely; he had the legal precision of his calling.

Since the murdered count had no heir, a claimant to the county came forward in the person of William Clito, who was backed by the king of France. The rebels had first to be dislodged from the castle, since its possession carried control over the town. The burghers of Bruges and of the neighbour-ing town of Ghent snatched at the opportunity to wring concessions from their new lord. They clubbed together and sold their help for promises. It was a new and clever step towards winning their freedom from burdens imposed by their lord. Clito made promises at the expense of the count's vassals, whose rights to levy taxes he abolished. The burghers of Bruges and Ghent helped him to defeat the rebels after a fearsome struggle, only to rebel in their turn when he failed to honour his agreement: he had dipped his hands into other men's pockets. Clito's expulsion from Flanders brought more wars, as other claimants to the county (there were four in all) tried their luck at conquest. Galbert followed the complicated chain of events down to the restoration of peace. Then he added an introduction and some chapters of explanation to make the origins of the dispute clearer.

Galbert addressed himself to the men of Bruges and to 'all the faithful'. He had a sense of solidarity with his fellow townsmen, in spite of their misbehaviour, which he was the first to recognize. He blames the king of France, the nobles, clergy and burghers impartially; all committed crimes and blunders. He could see both sides of the question. The murderers of Count Charles were guilty of treason, and sacrilege too, and deserved their fate. On the other hand, it was natural for them to fight against the prospect of losing their status. Galbert's receptive mind saved him from being cocksure about the workings of Providence. At first he saw the troubles as God's punishment for treason against one's lord, which is forbidden in Scripture. Then the story became more complex; he admitted to being puzzled. His observation was unclouded by learning. Suetonius contributed nothing to the notary's shrewd, vivid character sketches. Galbert rose to his opportunity and innovated.

Galbert's murder story is unique. My next example, the *Annals of Genoa*, is chosen as the first of a long line of city annals and chronicles. Genoa differed from Bruges in as much as the Flemish towns owed their growing prosperity to textiles; the burghers had to safeguard their profits against their lords' efforts to hive them off by exacting dues and supervising the town government. Genoese prosperity depended on seaborne trade. The citizens turned to the sea because a mountainous hinterland hemmed them in. Genoese merchants enriched themselves by trade, by naval war against the Saracens and by piracy. A few wealthy families managed the city. The emperor was their legal overlord; but he lacked the means to interfere with them. They pushed their bishop into the background; he became a help rather than a hindrance. Business techniques in the form of accounting, investment-sharing, and insurance to offset the dangers of seafaring, developed early. Hence literacy was a 'must' for the merchants and their office workers.

The city government also called for literacy. Merchants of the wealthier families served as consuls and went on embassies to foreign powers. Caffaro, the first Genoese annalist, was a literate layman who belonged to a ruling family; he was born into the 'administrative' grade. He took part in politics and in battles too. His editor compares him to Julius Caesar: he made history as well as writing it. At the age of twenty he went on crusade with the Genoese expedition to Palestine, where he fought in sieges and visited the holy places. His *Annals* begin in 1099, a conscious choice, since the year opened a new stage in the city's history: the first communal government was formed and an unprecedented large-scale naval expedition set out. Caffaro presented his *Annals*, kept up to date, to the consuls and council of Genoa in 1152. They ordered his book to be copied at public cost: it should tell the Genoese of their city's victories for all time. He continued his record up to his eightieth year, and died in 1166.

This layman's record is written in clear, correct Latin without frills. The annalist does not efface himself. He

53 Caffaro dictates his *Annals of Genoa* to his scribe Macrobrio. Miniature on the first page of a twelfth-century *de luxe* copy of the *Annals. Paris, Bibliothèque Nationale, MS lat. 10136, f.1r*

mentions his own experience and the fact that he had access to the city archives, while keeping a discreet silence on state secrets. Where there is no need for secrecy, he gives precise details of city finances, of the measurements of buildings and of the number of galleys dispatched on forays. He makes first-hand reports on imperial and papal councils. His aim was to glorify Genoa and he admits to passing over her slacker periods briefly. It is the spirit of the parish pump; but the Genoese parish stretched over the whole Mediterranean. His ideas on politics show the practical outlook of the Italian city-states. He handles the conflict between pope and emperor in a masterly way. Genoa gained from both sides. Frederick I needed money for his Italian campaigns; he put city privileges up for sale. The Genoese received special imperial privileges, though Caffaro lets out the fact that they paid through the nose. Pope Alexander III stayed at Genoa when his quarrel with Frederick forced him to escape to France. The port was his escape route, so he paid special honour to the citizens. Caffaro wrote that the devil had stirred up discord in the Church, and left it at that. He did not state what he must have known, that from the papal point of view Frederick was an excommunicate and schismatic when he granted privileges to Genoa. Why take sides when you could batten on both? Genoa's real enemies were the Pisans, her trading rivals. Caffaro hated them much more than the Saracens, whose sea power had declined. Enemies nearer home were the country nobles, a danger to peace and naturally hostile to a mercantile commune. He had no reason to be anti-clerical; the clergy's teeth had been drawn; but his lay mind shows through when he tells of a dangerous outbreak of fire in Genoa. A monastic chronicler would have credited its control and extinction to the miraculous power of the local saints. Caffaro praises the citizens for putting it out by their own efforts.

Galbert and Caffaro have one thing in common, their *esprit de corps*. Both identify themselves with their city, Galbert during the bloodshed and misery at Bruges, Caffaro with Genoa during her brilliant rise to power. To Galbert, Bruges was 'my city right or wrong': he did recognize standards of right and wrong. Caffaro felt that they hardly came into it when Genoese interests were involved.

John of Salisbury brings us back to learned clerical circles. He was an academic ecclesiastical administrator. His long years of study in France enabled him to meet the best masters of his time. In 1147 he joined the household of Archbishop Theobald of Canterbury. John proved himself to be a skilled letter-writer and rose to be Theobald's private secretary. He has been described as a failed academic. Perhaps he would have preferred to teach in the schools, had he succeeded in finding a chair and the wherewithal to finance himself. But his duties as secretary allowed him leisure to read and write and money to buy books, though never enough to satisfy him. He also went on diplomatic business abroad, where he met former masters and fellow-students. He mixed freely with princes, prelates and popes.

Only one of John's many writings is historical in the strict sense of the word. He called it *Historia pontificalis*, which has been aptly translated as *Memoirs of the Papal Court*. John's ambition was to write ecclesiastical history after the manner of Eusebius. He read the histories available and found that none went down any further than the end of the Council of Rheims in 1148. He therefore started with the council, giving a fuller account of it than his source; he had attended it in person with his archbishop. He chose to focus his history on the papal court. It was a rational way to organize a history of the Church in the mid-twelfth century, when the Curia was becoming a centre of government for the whole of Latin Christendom. All roads led to Rome or to

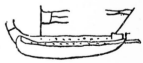

54, 55 Marginal illustrations to Caffaro's *Annals of Genoa*. Top: a butcher chopping up meat points to the record of a law which ordered slaughterhouses to be moved outside the city in the interests of hygiene. Above: a Genoese galley points to a naval expedition.

56 A Cistercian abbot, probably St Bernard of Clairvaux, is shown on the west front of the twelfth-century church of Our Lady at Maastricht.

wherever the pope might be. John was able to make digressions on Church matters in other countries in connection with appeals to Rome and so on. His *Memoirs*, as we have them, break off in 1152. He probably wrote them up from his notes in 1164. He had kept his post on the archiepiscopal staff after Theobald's death; then the quarrel between Becket and Henry II forced him to take refuge in France. His exile gave him further opportunities for writing.

The *Historia pontificalis* is the memoirs of a scholar-diplomat, who recalls his experiences and whose highly-placed friends kept him primed with news. It is free from cant and rhetoric. The speeches recorded there sound like verbatim reports from memory or from notes taken soon afterwards. John's urbane cattiness makes him good reading. He criticizes almost everyone, except his patron Theobald, and loves to report witty sayings. He had his prejudices; what diplomat has not? John was pro-French and anti-German. A churchman of blameless life, writing for a likeminded friend, Abbot Peter of la Celle, he felt free to judge the pope and cardinals severely. The visit of two papal legates to Germany gave him a welcome opportunity to score off both the legates and the Germans. However, he tried hard to be fair. His account of the Council of Rheims brought all his qualities of fairness and tact into play. It is justly famous as a scrupulous effort to present both sides of a dispute. John describes the trial of Gilbert of la Porrée, his former master, now bishop of Poitiers, on a charge of heresy sponsored by St Bernard of Clairvaux. John admired Gilbert as a man and as a scholar. He venerated St Bernard as a saint. Bernard, moreover, had written John a testimonial, without ever having set eyes on him, when John had left the schools and was looking for a post. He had personal obligations to the abbot of Clairvaux, who showed his trust in him by sending him as a messenger to Gilbert after the trial. Bernard regarded Gilbert as a dangerous teacher of error; to Gilbert, Bernard was an interfering amateur in academic questions. John does his best for them. He clears them both on the score of good intentions, sympathizing with Gilbert as an intellectual, but respecting Bernard's motives as 'zeal for God's house'. He gives a careful account of procedure at the trial, as he remembered it, and of the heresies imputed to Gilbert. Backstairs intrigue and self-interest held no secrets from him. Memoirs are always more readable when we know some of the people in the story. John's important friends and acquaintances appear in other contemporary sources, but nowhere else do they come to life so clearly.

So far our civil-servant historians have worked for municipal or ecclesiastical governments. In England, the reign of Henry II (1154–89) saw the rise of something more like a modern government machine. Henry's staff were royal servants first and foremost; but the better educated among them already had the idea that they were public servants too. Henry put new content into the ancient Roman tradition of rule. A Roman emperor wielded public power for the public good, *utilitas reipublicae*. The private interest of subjects should give way to the good of the commonwealth. Early medieval histories of rulers tended to present the king as a war-leader; churchmen normally judged him according to his record as protector of the Church. Yet the ancient notion that 'public power' was vested in the ruler was never forgotten. It lies behind Richer's false statement that Hugh Capet 'established laws and made decrees'. Richer adjusted the actions of the king to his ideas of what a ruler ought to do.

Henry II really did hold assizes, which issued administrative and judicial ordinances. He also reformed judicial procedure. His reforms had a dual purpose. They brought money to his treasury and they tightened his grip on his kingdom; at the same time they benefited free landholders by providing quicker and fairer modes of legal action. Litigants (and every landholder was a litigant in the Middle Ages) took advantage of Henry's reforms. The king showed a personal interest in improving his government. He surrounded himself with legal experts and hammered out his projects with their advice.

Civil servants have a vested interest in the establishment. Henry's men could also feel proud of it, admiring his reforms and sharing in the credit of devising and supervising the new methods. Technical treatises on government were written such as the *Dialogue of the Exchequer* and *On the Laws of England*. A good example of history as written by a retired civil servant is the *Chronicle* of Roger of Howden.

Roger took his name from his parsonage of Howden in Yorkshire. He had the title of 'Master': degrees were becoming a passport to civil service posts. He entered Henry's employment in about 1174. His work gave him an opportunity to observe the seamy as well as the more likeable side of Angevin bureaucracy. Roger served as

Justice of the Forest almost continuously between 1185 and 1190. These justices went round the country holding Courts of the Forest and fining people for poaching and other offences against forest law. Enforcement of the forest laws was the most oppressive and unpopular aspect of Angevin rule. Roger retired from service in order to go on the Third Crusade in company with a small group of northerners. On returning home in 1191, he settled down at Howden to write his book, and died in 1201/2.

The book is called a 'chronicle'. Its author did not intend to write a history with literary flourishes and analysis of causes. The chief interest of the chronicle is that Roger gave so much space to his record of government measures. He copied documents as evidence and illustrated the details of administration from his inside knowledge. This was a new type of documentation. Eusebius had inserted documents in order to prove how the Church had triumphed over her persecutors and won recognition. Monastic historiographers did the same in the interests of their community. Bruno documented his *Saxon War* in order to vindicate the Saxons. Roger of Howden wanted to hold Henry II up to admiration as a reformer; but there is also a note of sheer pleasure in his description of how royal government worked. He respected Henry's energy in devising reforms and noted his care for justice: on one occasion the king reversed a decision made by his Chief Justice because he knew that the latter had a personal grudge against the litigant. Roger took a shrewd look at foreign affairs. He understood the role of finance: Prince John's expedition to Ireland failed for the reason that John was too tight-fisted to pay his mercenaries their wages. To read through the chronicle is to see that Roger had the defects of his merits. He does not stop to reflect as he writes. Inconsistency did not bother him. His mind was a rag-bag. He veered from one side to another when he narrated a dispute; he was both pro-Henry and pro-Becket. His only constant principles or prejudices were dislike of archbishops and papal legates on the one hand, and loyalty to Henry II against rebels and foreign enemies on the other. He had the limitations of a 'second-grade administrator'.

Master Ralph of Diss in Norfolk was a grander person than Roger of Howden and more of an intellectual. He studied both Arts and theology and perhaps also taught at Paris. He made his career in the cathedral church of St Paul in London, where he held various offices and rose to the position of dean in about 1180. He functioned as dean until his death in 1202. Ralph counts as a 'supply civil servant and diplomat'; the Angevin kings employed him on commissions and embassies as a valued expert on legal and administrative matters. His office as dean, in charge of the chapter estates and head of the chapter of St Paul's, made him an administrator in his own right. He was a successful estate-manager and a realistic, sensible reformer of the chapter. The canons remembered him as 'the good dean'. Ralph's historical works consist of a short world chronicle, the *Abridgment of Chronicles*, going down to 1147, and a bigger book, *Pictures or Reflections of Histories*. This begins with the knighting of the future King Henry II in 1148 and continues until the writer's death. He prepared for it by collecting a large dossier over many years. The first draft was ready by 1190. The *Pictures of Histories* is written in annalistic form. It focuses on England, but includes notices on foreign affairs. Ralph brings himself into it, when he had taken part in the events he recorded. He was too important a person to need to obtrude himself. If he had a weakness, it was to copy in letters of advice which he had written to his friends. But then his advice had been asked for. One consulted the dean as a man whose head was screwed firmly on his shoulders.

The concept of 'public power' inspired his account of royal government. Roger of Howden described its practice; Ralph linked practice to theory. Warmly approving of its development, he copied Henry II's assizes, records of tax collection, forest laws and so on into his annals. They all go to show how Henry used his public power to benefit the commonwealth. There was no public power in Ireland to keep the peace before Henry's invasion. Public power must override private interests; Henry saw that it should. To quote a classic passage under the year 1179:

The king sought to help those of his subjects who could least help themselves, having found that the sheriffs were using the public power in their own private interests. Hence the king, in his growing anxiety for the public welfare, entrusted rights of justice to other loyal men of his realm, so that representatives of the public power should terrify delinquents when they toured the provinces . . . and that those guilty of offences against the royal majesty should incur royal anger.

Ralph goes on to specify Henry's measures to curb the power of the sheriffs in local government by sending round royal justices. He underlines Henry's care for justice throughout his kingdom and his experiments in controlling his agents. He hoped that Henry would use his public power in order to protect the weak against the strong. How far Henry actually did so is another matter. Of the three kings who come into the *Pictures*, Ralph prefers Henry, because he showed most skill in government. Richard I ranks lower, in spite of his military exploits. John had already blotted his copy-book by rebelling against his father and elder brother while still a prince.

The concept of public power, wielded for the public good, can lead on to that of the nation state. It is interesting to see whether Ralph of Diss made the step from one concept to the other or whether he had any notion of England as a nation. When Ralph describes a rebellion he stresses filial piety and loyalty to one's lord as his touchstone of conduct. He does not blame rebels as traitors to their country. His affection centred on the reigning house of Anjou rather than on England, which was only part of their dominions. He could hardly have subscribed to the xenophobic saying ascribed to an Englishman of the nineteenth century: 'Niggers begin at Calais'. Henry II and his sons would have been 'niggers' in that case. They came of mixed parentage, Norman, Angevin and French; their territories in France stretched from the Channel to the Pyrenees. Ralph, however, was prejudiced against the peoples outside France. Over her borders the uncivilized races begin: the Saxons are stony-hearted; the Austrians have dirty habits; Sicily produces tyrants. Some form of xenophobia began before what we call 'national feeling' had impinged on historiography.

A second question arises: how did Ralph's view of royal power as public power affect his presentation of the conflict between his king and his archbishop? Henry's quarrel with Thomas Becket brought up the problem of the relations between the 'two powers' of medieval political theory, *regnum* and *sacerdotium*, monarchy and clergy. As dean of St Paul's, Ralph lived through the conflict with credit, keeping in with both sides. Though Ralph stayed in England and remained on excellent terms with Henry and with Gilbert Foliot, Becket's chief opponent among the bishops, the exiled archbishop and his circle regarded him as a friend; he never incurred the reproach of being disloyal to the Church. To steer his way through the conflict was easier than to narrate it without committing himself. Ralph worked for two establishments, the Church and the Crown. They collaborated below the surface all the time; but they clashed openly some of the time. Then as now, conflict had more news value than harmony. Ralph was in a difficulty. He could not omit the events which led up to Becket's murder. The martyr was now a canonized saint: Ralph could not blame St Thomas for dying in defence of the liberties of the Church in England. On the other hand, an admirer of Henry's government could not approve of Becket's attempts at sabotage, for that was what they seemed to be.

To begin with a minor point at issue: canon law forbad churchmen to hold secular office. The reasons were moral and legal. Ecclesiastics who had cure of souls should devote themselves to their pastoral care. Legally they were forbidden to take part in any function which involved bloodshed: secular jurisdiction involved passing sentence of death or mutilation on persons convicted of felony. Still less should a churchman have custody of a castle or lead a military expedition. Yet kings rewarded their clerks with bishoprics, as a means of financing royal government out of Church revenues and feeding talent into the royal administration. The canon law ruling, if strictly enforced, would have caused a brain-drain from the civil service. Ralph saw the civil service as instituted for the public good; yet its practice went against canon law. His writings show that he wobbled on the question of principle. On the whole he thought that a bishop was justified in holding secular office, provided that he had permission from his ecclesiastical superiors. That was reasonable, since the ban could be relaxed and was enforced only occasionally.

The minor issue leads on to the major. Becket insisted on obeying the letter of canon law. On becoming archbishop, he renounced his office as royal chancellor. Then came his clash with Henry on the question of clerical privilege and ecclesiastical liberties in general, followed by his exile and murder. His shrine at Canterbury attracted pilgrims from all over Christendom.

The heroic way to present the conflict would have been to use shades of grey instead of black and white. Ralph might have taken the line that each side in the conflict was 'partly right and partly wrong'. That would have been a taxing assignment for a contemporary writer and would probably have given offence all round. Yet Ralph was more thoughtful than Roger of Howden, who slapped down incompatible

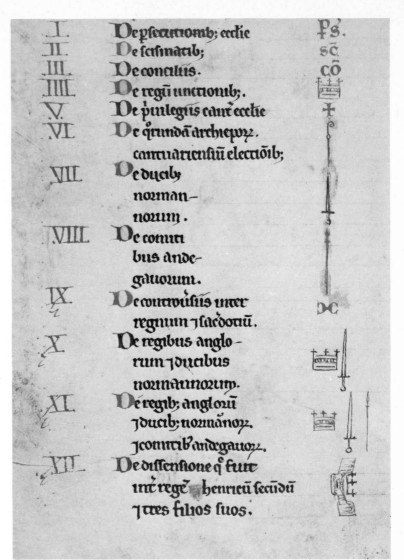

I. De psecutionib; ecclie   ps.
II. De scismatib;   sc.
III. De conciliis.   cō
IIII. De regū unctionib;.
V. De puilegiis cant ecclie
VI. De qrundā archiepor.
cantuariensiū electōib;
VII. De ducib; norman‑
norum.
VIII. De comiti‑
bus ande‑
gauorum.
IX. De controuisiis inter
regnum 7 sacdoriū.
X. De regibus anglo‑
rum 7 ducibus
normannorum.
XI. De regib; anglorū
7 ducib; normānor.
7 comitib andegauor.
XII. De dissensione q fuit
int rege henricū secūdū
7 tres filios suos.

57 A page from the copy of his historical works presented by Ralph of Diss to St Paul's, showing signs which he used to classify the subject matter in his histories. The crown, for instance, indicates matter 'on the anointing of kings', the long sword refers to the dukes of Normandy, and the symbol at the bottom, in which two hands grasp a crown, denotes the conflict between Henry II and his sons. *London, Lambeth Palace Library, MS 8, f.1r*

opinions without comment. The dean could not bring himself to be so inconsistent. He found a way out of the *impasse* by inventing a system of pigeon-holing.

His material is divided into parallel columns. One column contains what we now call 'political' history, that is, the deeds of kings. Another contains records of battles, and another ecclesiastical history – the successions of popes and bishops and church councils. Ralph allocated yet another column to conflict between secular and ecclesiastical powers. He devised special signs to put in the margin to distinguish each notice. A battle, for instance, is marked by crossed swords. He explains his method in his introduction and uses it both in his *Abridgment of Chronicles* and in his *Pictures of Histories*. The advantage of his arrangement was that juxtaposition made synthesis and judgment unnecessary. Each event could be recorded in its place. Conflicts could be narrated without prejudice to the protagonists.

Earlier historiographers had used parallel columns in order to synchronize pagan and Christian history. Ralph went further and synchronized the events of Christian history, keeping its different aspects separate from one another. He may have had other precedents for his method, but they have not survived. There may be a clue in the scrapbook of excerpts from earlier writers which Ralph had copied as a preface to his historical books. An example given by Hugh of St Victor appealed to him, and he included it in his scrapbook. Hugh advises students to keep the diverse kinds of wisdom separate. You waste your time and addle your brain if you mix them. He instances the money-changers of Paris, who keep their diverse kinds of coinage in purses divided into compartments. These handy contraptions enable them to change currency so quickly and easily that the people standing round them gape and wonder to see so many sorts of coinage coming out of the same wallet. The example must have amused Ralph; he was a financial expert himself. Perhaps he pondered Hugh's tip to students on keeping their files in order and adapted it to historical presentation.

Ralph of Diss certainly anticipates a good deal of modern historiography. Much of it has turned into a vast system of pigeon-holing. We keep our data in separate compartments; the method is time-saving and thought-saving. It has its uses as a preliminary; but we abuse the method if we make it an end in itself. We need not imitate Ralph, but we can sympathize with his dilemma and his search for a solution.

Conquest and crusade

Most people today feel uneasy about the crusades and see them as an unpleasing feature of medieval history. We have had enough of wars and especially of so-called ideological wars. The crusaders were blood-thirsty fanatics. Worse than that, some of them were 'on the make'; they used the holy wars to make unholy gains. We have to stretch our historical imagination to understand their mentality.

Another less healthy prejudice against the crusaders springs from our tendency to judge a movement by its success. The crusading movement can be written off as a failure, doomed from the start. It is a sorry record: the Latins failed to establish a permanent kingdom in Palestine; Saladin captured Jerusalem in 1187; the Latin kingdom dwindled to a coastal strip; the last stronghold at Acre fell in 1291. The Fourth Crusade of 1204 was diverted from its purpose to capture the Christian city of Constantinople. The Latin kingdom established on the site of the former Byzantine empire had disappeared by 1260. Our prejudice against the crusades as failures will weaken, however, if we think of the expeditions to Palestine as only the most far-flung of many campaigns which aimed to enlarge the bounds of Christendom. Some of these campaigns were very successful indeed. Spain was reconquered from the Moors by a joint effort: French knights crossed the Pyrenees to help the Spanish Christians and settled in the peninsula. On the eastern frontier of Germany the pagan Slavs between the Elbe and the Oder were conquered and converted.

Crusades were launched for objects other than wars against the infidel. The popes turned them against heretics too. Crusaders from northern France came south to fight against the Albigensian heretics. They also succeeded in defeating the southern nobles. The Capetian kings followed in their wake and took over the Midi. The partial Anglo-Norman conquest of Ireland could be presented as a kind of crusade, though here its victims were 'backward' Catholics, not heretics.

58 A warrior against evil. Detail of a capital on the porch of the church at Rebolledo de la Torre, in Castile, early thirteenth-century.

59 Relations between German colonists and Slavs are described in the *Sachsenspiegel*, the oldest German law-book. This illustration and the one opposite (ill. 60) come from a copy produced about 1320. Here, lords who receive enfeoffment of lands east of the river Saal in Prussia are obliged to take part in campaigns against the heathen Slavs on their borders. *Heidelberg, Universitätsbibliothek, Cod. Pal. Germ. 164, f.1v*

All these campaigns secured permanent results: they all left their mark on the map of Europe. Contemporaries could not have foreseen that the Latins would fail on one front only, in Palestine. The amazing victories of the First Crusade naturally led to the expectation that 'France Overseas' had come to stay. We have to share this confidence when we read medieval histories of the crusades.

Conquest and crusade had a liberating and stimulating effect on historiography. The novelty and excitement of the story freed its historians from dependence on ancient models. There was nothing comparable in ancient and early medieval history; the historian of the crusades had to express himself in his own way. Writing became less mannered and more spontaneous. Widening horizons gave stimulus. Historians living in a military zone had a new experience; they observed two cultures. Since the wars were intermittent and long-drawn-out, settlers in conquered territory had peaceful contacts with the enemy: it is always an eye-opener to discover that one's enemies are people and not devils.

Defeat supplied an even stronger stimulus than victory. It led to heart-searching. Saracen penetration of Palestine, the slow pace of conquest and conversion on the German border, the standstill of the Anglo-Norman venture in Ireland, all raised the question why God deserted his servants when they were fighting in his cause. Why did he delay or withhold success from the faithful? The spread of heresies within the body of Christendom, especially in the Midi, made some historians wonder who was responsible. Earlier writers had sometimes refrained from criticizing contemporaries for

60 German colonists in eastern Europe clear waste-land and build a village. An illustration from the *Sachsenspiegel* (see ill. 59, opposite). *Heidelberg, Universitätsbibliothek, Cod. Pal. Germ. 164, f.26v*

fear of offending them. Historians of the crusades were more daring, perhaps because authority functioned more weakly in a border area.

The crusades produced lay authors and vernacular histories. A laymen's literature developed. The new type of history contrasted with traditional Latin ecclesiastical historiography in many respects. At the same time, it was far removed from the vernacular epic or *chanson de geste*. These dealt mainly with fiction; a crusading history would start from facts.

The stories of 'conquest historians' are less dramatic and exotic than the crusaders', but they will help us to understand the crusading mentality. The German conquest of the Slavs will make a good starting-point. Master Adam of Bremen wrote the *Deeds of the Archbishops of Bremen* in the late eleventh century. He used the traditional genre of the history of an episcopal see as a frame for a wider story: this border city was a centre for the conquest and conversion of the heathen Slavs across the frontier. Adam inserted a geographical account of 'all Slavia', which he calls 'a very large province of Germany'. Medieval accounts of unknown territory normally included legends and marvels. Adam makes no exception to the rule; 'marvels of the East' such as Cyclops and Amazons come into his description; but he was scientific enough to add reports collected by himself and his own observations on the peoples and their countries. The Slav gods or 'idols' interested him. It was more than mere curiosity about the unfamiliar. He could see the point of view of the Slav victims of German expansion. True, he tells atrocity stories of the massacre of Christian priests, but he

does not shrink from exposing the misdeeds of Christians. Members of a newly founded mission church in Slav territory took to robbery; naturally, Adam tells us, they provoked reprisals from the Slavs.

His position in a border city sharpened his political insight: he describes a three-cornered conflict between the Slavs, the princes and the bishops. Each group had its own motives. The Slavs resisted the Germans; the bishops wanted to convert them, partly because their conversion would increase the power and wealth of the Church; the princes cared only to conquer them. If the Slavs were converted, then the princes had to share the fruits of conquest with the bishops, since bishops had a right to take tithes from Christians. Adam felt that blame for the slow pace of conversion fell on princes and prelates alike. He makes a king of Denmark say that all the Slavs could have been converted long ago, but for the greed of the Saxons in making them pay tribute when they became subjects.

The history of a see gave its writer opportunities to portray the characters of the bishops. The archbishops of Hamburg–Bremen ruled over an expanding border area; the region

61, 62 Tenth-century missionary work. Opposite: St Adalbert of Prague baptizes Prussian converts. Left: his head and body are exposed after his martyrdom by the heathen. Details from the bronze doors of Gniezno cathedral, about 1170.

offered dazzling prospects to an ambitious prelate. He could enlarge his boundaries and make himself an indispensable ally in German politics. Adam had a challenging sitter for a portrait in Archbishop Adalbert (d. 1071). He made full use of it, breathing new life into the tradition of character description. At last we have a moving picture instead of a 'still'. Adalbert's ambition turned into megalomania. Adam writes as an almost clinical observer of the onset of symptoms. He shows us the interplay of character and circumstances. The various strands in the archbishop's character are linked to his victories and reverses. Its inner unity comes through as well as the process of his *folie de grandeur*. Adam has traced an unforgettable story of a person. He might easily have looked at his subject as a moralist and resorted to the theme of Fortune's Wheel. Instead he innovated. Perhaps his unusual environment influenced him to set down his experience as an observer.

Helmold, priest of Bosau, owed much of his inspiration to Adam, though he wrote almost a century later and described the conquest at a later stage. He had read the *Deeds*, which provided him with a precedent and a source for the early history of the Slavs. Helmold's book is called the *Chronicle of the Slavs*; but the title is posthumous. The book is really a glorification of Christian missions to the heathen. Praise of the missionaries leads on to the history of military campaigns and to the rise of cities in conquered lands. Helmold dedicated his book to the canons of Lübeck, his mother church. His patron, Bishop Gerold, had advised him that this would be the best way to honour Lübeck. The first part of the *Chronicle of the Slavs* was finished in 1167/8, the second part in 1172. Adam's account of Archbishop Adalbert shows us a changing character; Helmold's book shows us a developing historian. The change in his attitude to his material is one of the most interesting features of his *Chronicle*. Like Adam, he wrote from first-hand experience; he had worked in the mission field; but his observation led him to see his story differently as it unfolded.

At first he used Adam's *Deeds*, making alterations which point to a more critical and worldly outlook. He suppressed the 'marvels' and checked Adam's ecclesiastical bias by giving more credit to the princes than the prelates in the work of conquest and conversion. He improved on his source by including archaeological evidence for the early stages: ruined churches and dykes in Slav territories bore witness to the tenth-century occupation by the Saxons, before the Slav reaction drove them back. He reminds us of Bede's use of surviving Roman remains as evidence for the Roman occupation of Britain.

The three-cornered conflict of interests described by Adam persisted in Helmold's day, and he was just as aware of it. The princes had no interest in converting the Slavs. They did not warm to the idea of the crusade against the Slavs preached by St Bernard in 1146 at the same time as he preached the Second Crusade to the Holy Land. The Slavs, according to St Bernard, were to be either 'converted or else wholly destroyed'. If 'wholly destroyed', they would not have been able to pay tribute to their conquerors. The hero of Helmold's story is his patron, Bishop Vicelin. This bishop was a true missionary; Helmold admired him. Then, after Vicelin's death, Henry the Lion, duke of Saxony, steps into his place as the leader of eastward expansion. The change of leadership marks a change in Helmold's outlook. He began to think better of armed force. Duke Henry was both heroic and greedy. At first 'he cared nothing for Christianity', in Helmold's words, 'but only for money'. Later, Henry could afford the luxury of supporting mission work, provided that he kept a tight hand on the missionaries. He was rich and successful enough as a conqueror and colonizer to go shares with the Church in exploiting the defeated peoples. Henry treated his clergy as his servants. Helmold judged that submission to the ducal will was not too high a price to pay for freedom to evangelize. He approved of those churchmen who obeyed the duke, even though it meant waiving ecclesiastical liberties.

Helmold resembled Adam in his curiosity about the Slavs. His *Chronicle* has a wider scope than the *Deeds*, in that it tells the story of three peoples, the Saxons, the Danes, who took part in the conquest, and the Slavs of the area. He portrays the virtues and vices peculiar to each people, not sparing the Saxons or the Danes. In describing the Slavs he notes what struck him as good in their customs and values: their hospitality to friends and strangers alike impressed him, though he adds that they would steal in order to find the wherewithal to feed their guests. He records the various religious observances of their tribes. Of course, he lacked a social anthropologist's understanding of their beliefs, which were primitive by his standards; but he realized that tribal customs were not uniform. Given a colonist's prejudice against the 'natives', it is surprising that he described them so objectively. He had a real sympathy for their dilemma as the conquerors' grip on them tightened; the Slavs could not escape by land or by sea. They were surrounded by enemies and had no resources left.

Helmold's sympathy for the conquered diminished as he began to rejoice at the effects of the conquest. Henry the Lion brought prosperity to his duchy by attracting settlers from foreign lands and by founding cities. The fortified port of Lübeck grew into a rich trading emporium. To Helmold it was a beautiful sight. The new prosperity delighted him. The Old Testament rears its head at this point. The conquerors resembled the children of Israel, expelling the gentiles from the Promised Land. The Slav lands between the Elbe and the Oder, if not yet flowing with milk and honey, could be made to. Settlers were clearing and draining the waste and turning it into farmland. Helmold lost interest in the fate of the Slavs. Economically, the settlers had replaced them. The natives were almost wiped out; those who escaped destruction were subjected to strict discipline. Slav vagrants were to be caught and hanged. The book ends on this colonial note, at variance with Helmold's earlier enthusiasm for mission work.

The *Chronicle* portrays individuals as well as peoples. Helmold was a student of character. He had no such giant as Archbishop Adalbert to stretch his powers; but he did his best with what was available. Bishops Gerold and Vicelin appear as the conventional type of 'the good prelate', as they may in fact have been. Gerold's successor as bishop did not fit into any type. Helmold presents him as a human mixture of good and bad qualities. Henry the Lion had foisted him on the chapter of Lübeck against the canons' wishes. Troubles followed; the Lion's protégé suffered from the canons' hostility. Helmold shows him changing, in the opposite direction to Adalbert: exile and sorrow taught him compassion for his fellow-men. Again we can enjoy a moving picture instead of a mere catalogue of personal characteristics. Secular princes are sketched in the course of the story, with their varying degrees of prowess and miscreancy. Helmold quotes the cliché that truth will offend, but only to flout the consequences: 'Blame yourself and not the mirror if you don't like what you see there.' His mirror must have shown some red faces. He became ruthless in his attitude to the natives; but he was equally so in describing their conquerors; no holds are barred.

The Anglo-Norman conquest of Ireland found a historian in Giraldus Cambrensis, or Gerald of Wales (d. 1220). Gerald was no local man, like Adam and Helmold. He was a scholar of international fame, well educated in rhetoric, law and theology. But he had local connections. He was descended from a Welsh royal house on his mother's side; his father belonged to a family of Norman Marcher lords, settled in South Wales; his relatives won estates in Ireland. Gerald was a brilliant observer, entertainer and satirist. His satire was sharpened by the failure of his ambition: he wanted to become bishop of St David's and to have the see raised to the status of archbishopric. In spite of pressure on the Angevin kings and repeated visits to the papal court, he rose to be archdeacon of St David's and no further.

Two trips to Ireland, lasting about a year each, enabled Gerald to collect material for two books, *On the Topography of Ireland* and *On the Conquest of Ireland*. The first is descriptive; the second brings the first up to date by narrating the attempted conquest of Ireland; it ends after Prince John's expedition of 1185. Gerald had accompanied the prince on the orders of John's father, Henry II. The *Conquest* was dedicated to the future King Richard I. It stands on the borderline between two types of history. It is a historical monograph, written in Latin; but Gerald felt the pull of a wider audience. He hoped that someone would translate the *Conquest* into French. He wrote in what he calls a plain modern style: his Muse jibbed at the difficult Latin of antiquity.

The *Conquest* resembles a Christmas bazaar in having something for everyone, both trash and bargains. If you want sensation you find dreams, visions, prophecies and miracles. The invaders are frightened by phantom armies, a common sight in Ireland. Gerald made use of classical rhetorical speech, which sounds especially implausible in the mouths of Anglo-Norman barons and Irish chieftains. But he also copied documents and records of councils. He provides a superb portrait gallery. His pen-picture of Henry II is unsurpassed and appears in all our textbooks.

It is interesting to compare Gerald with Adam and Helmold as a 'conquest historian'. They have much in common. We find the same ambivalent attitude to the defeated people. Gerald had reason to take the invaders' side. He hoped that an English protectorate over the Irish Church would favour reform and better discipline among the native clergy. His kinsmen, settled in Ireland as colonists, would gain by firmer military support. The Irish struck him as barbarous and inefficient; they had no idea how to manage their affairs. At the same time, like Adam and Helmold, he could sympathize with the conquered and oppressed. He reports atrocities on both sides. The difference between Gerald on the one hand and Adam and Helmold on the other springs from the nature of their stories. The Germans told a success story, slow but final. Gerald recorded a stalemate. Prince John's expedition to Ireland failed; English rule remained partial and imperfect. The Red Indians had resisted the Cowboys to some purpose. A partisan of the invaders had to explain why they lost out to the natives.

To do so he had to analyse causes. First he bows to the altar. We learn from the Old Testament and from later history that God allows no people to be totally destroyed except as a punishment for its sins. Gerald concludes that the Irish were not bad enough nor the invaders good enough to merit total defeat or victory. God had reason to punish both sides. Anyway, the four famous prophets of Irish tradition had

63 An English thirteenth-century illustration to the *Topography of Ireland* by Gerald of Wales. One man kills another with an axe, to indicate the Irish habit of feuding. *Oxford, Bodleian Library, MS Laud. Misc. 720, f.225r*

129

predicted that the English would never conquer the whole island until Doomsday was approaching. Then Gerald comes down to human causes. Henry II had to leave his conquest incomplete. His sons' rebellion recalled him and he never came back. Turning to John, Gerald again invokes God's displeasure. John had offended God by not helping the Church and he had broken his vow to go on crusade. Gerald goes on to dissect John's political errors. The prince antagonized his Irish allies by not blarneying them: you have to use blarney on the Irish; they expect it. John antagonized the Anglo-Norman and Welsh colonists too. He mocked at their old-fashioned colonial dress and customs and ignored their counsel. He ousted them and installed new men; these wanted only to enrich themselves and were slack in defending their posts. They employed mercenaries, who preferred plunder to fighting.

Then Gerald turns to the techniques of warfare. A wild chaotic country called for trained and experienced troops. Mercenaries were useless there. The Irish had succumbed to the first shock of invasion. Later they learned resistance techniques and had to be fought on their own terrain. Gerald observed that the type of warfare called for in the woods and mountains of Ireland differed from that suitable on the open plains of France, which were more familiar to the Anglo-Normans. Steady cavalry succeeded best on the open plain; light-armed contingents, trained to endure hardship, were needed in Ireland. The type of fighting differed, in that the Irish fought to kill, whereas in France the aim on both sides was to take prisoners in order to win ransom money. It followed in Gerald's view that troops for expeditions to Ireland should be recruited in the Welsh Marches. There, and only there, would you find men accustomed to living and fighting in the conditions they would experience overseas. The voice of Gerald's soldier relatives sounds louder than that of the Divine Judge when it comes to military matters. Hard advice on tactics and recruitment replaces moral considerations.

The *Conquest* ends with a blueprint for the extension of English rule in Ireland and for the government of the subject people. Gerald recommended many sensible measures, such as road-building to give access to rebel areas. He outlined a firm, paternal régime. Tribute from the natives would finance the colonial government. Like so many blueprints it gave a sound recipe for success, but the measures suggested would have cost too much for the government to carry through. A scholar had produced a plan worthy to rest in the files of any colonial office. It was not acted upon.

We have seen that conquest worked as a forcing house for historiography. The crusades supplied even stronger heat. I have chosen three of the many crusading historians available: the anonymous author of the *Deeds of the Franks*, William of Tyre and Geoffrey of Villehardouin. They number among the best-known names and they have the interest of contrast: each one represents a new kind of author or else an original treatment of an old type of history.

The Anonymous was an eyewitness of the First Crusade. He seems to have belonged to a Norman family which had settled in Sicily after the Norman conquest of the island. He joined a Sicilian contingent to the crusade led by Bohemond, the bastard son of another Norman-Sicilian noble. Bohemond was his 'lord'. The *Deeds of the Franks* begins with a short account of the Council of Clermont where Urban II proclaimed the crusade. Then comes a résumé of the various expeditions which set out from Europe to Palestine. After this prelude the Anonymous relates his own experiences as a crusader. His story gets as far as the taking of Jerusalem and the election of a king and patriarch to rule over the new kingdom of the Franks. He mentions the crusaders' victory near Ascalon in 1099; he may have died soon afterwards, since the book stops there.

He had probably begun his book during the crusaders' stay at Antioch after their capture of the city. Bohemond, who aimed to create a principality for himself, stayed at Antioch and refused to join in the march to Jerusalem. The Anonymous then transferred his allegiance to Count Raymond of Toulouse. The book was finished at Jerusalem. It emerges from the story that the author was a knight of minor rank; Bohemond trusted him, but he did not belong to the inner circle of leaders. Indeed, he had the outsider's natural distrust of diplomacy behind closed doors. It is surprising that a layman had the skill to write a history in Latin. The Latin of the *Deeds* is grammatical, though informal. The Anonymous had no literary equipment except for memories of the Bible. Perhaps, as often happened to a younger son, he was made a clerk as a small boy and received a clerical education, so as to make his way in the Church and leave the family estate to his elders. Their deaths might have released him to take up a secular career. Otherwise there is the possibility that a clerk helped him to write. In either case, he speaks to us simply and directly with a freshness of vision which is all his own.

The *Deeds of the Franks* is the first history written in Latin by a layman since Einhard and Nithard wrote in the early ninth century. (Caffaro of Genoa comes a little later.) The Anonymous is unique in his way, like Galbert of Bruges. The *Deeds* became famous as a primary source for the First Crusade; but clerical authors found the presentation too crude and rewrote it in more literary styles. The contrast with conventional histories strikes us at the very beginning. The Anonymous dispenses with a prologue and plunges straight into his story. He did not know or chose to ignore that an author was supposed to apologize for writing at all, for writing inadequately and for giving offence by his truthfulness.

Perhaps the religious purpose of the *Deeds* made the reason for writing it self-evident. The recovery of the Holy Sepulchre was a sequel to Christ's death and resurrection and to the passions of the saints. The crusade swelled the ranks of the martyrs. The Anonymous counted as martyrs all soldier-pilgrims who fell in the holy war. On the siege of Antioch he writes:

More than a thousand of our knights and foot-soldiers were martyred on one day. They ascended into heaven, rejoicing and shining white in their martyrs' robes, glorifying and magnifying our God, One and Three, in whose name they had triumphed. They cried out with one voice: 'Why dost thou not defend our blood, which we shed in thy name?'

He is alluding to a text of Revelation, where the new martyrs are bidden to rest for a while, 'until [the number of] their fellow servants and brethren, who are to be slain even as they, shall be filled up' (6:11). The Turks who were killed by the crusaders 'received everlasting death, giving up their wretched souls to the devil and Satan's ministers'. Local Palestinian martyrs appear in the sky to comfort Christ's soldiers when the Turks press them hard.

The Anonymous sets the pattern for what follows in his account of the Council of Clermont:

When the time had come which our lord Jesus Christ daily shows to the faithful, in the gospel especially, saying *If any man will come after me, let him deny himself and take up his cross and follow me*, a mighty movement spread through all the regions of Gaul.

64 The passage in the book of Revelation referred to by the anonymous author of *Deeds of the Franks*. St John sees the souls of the martyrs under the altar, calling upon God to vindicate their blood. An angel clothes them in white garments. From the Douce Apocalypse, a manuscript made for King Edward I of England and his wife Eleanor of Castile about 1270. *Oxford, Bodleian Library, MS Douce 180, p.17*

Christ's enemies and his saints were timeless and unmistakable. The writer's time scale and values are those of the child who said: 'The Bads killed Jesus, and they killed my uncle too in the War.' The very structure of the *Deeds* shows that it was intended to be read aloud as a religious piece. Each book closes with a doxology to mark the end of reading for the day.

The pious purpose goes with vivid reporting. The Anonymous understood military techniques as the average clerical writer could not do. We climb the walls of Antioch by night; the custodian of three towers has betrayed them secretly to Bohemond. The ladder breaks as we climb and we enter by a narrow gate in the wall, feeling for it in the dark. We march over waterless mountains. We smell the stench of corpses piled up in the streets. We hear the Turkish battle cry 'as they suddenly shriek, shout and gabble some devilish word in their own tongue'. The author diverts us, when we get tired of battles, by taking us to the Turkish side to hear what Turkish leaders said about the Franks. His report of their conversation recalls the scene in *Henry V* where Shakespeare makes the French nobles say rude things about the English invaders. The Turkish prince's mother plays the traditional part of the wife who foresees the consequences of her husband's plans and warns him to no avail. The Saracen lady of the *Deeds* has a remarkable knowledge of biblical prophecies and a strange ignorance of the Koran. These asides are wishful thinking; but they make good entertainment.

The Anonymous's own impressions come through when he describes the foreigners with whom he came into contact. The Greeks get short shrift; they were hereditary enemies of the Normans in Sicily. The Palestinian Christians – Syrians and Armenians for the most part – are little people, who emerge from their holes as soon as they can safely sell victuals to the crusaders at the highest price they can get. They were not warriors. The Turks were. They made worthy foes when the two warrior races, the Turks and the Franks, confronted one another. The Anonymous labels his characters to help his hearers, as in vernacular epic. They needed reminding of the character's role when the story was taken up again. All are types, of course. The Greek emperor is 'the wicked'; Bohemond is 'prudent' or 'wise' until he stays behind at Antioch, after which he becomes plain 'Bohemond'. The Turks, more easily recognizable, are called 'wicked' or 'infidel' only occasionally. It must be added that the Anonymous impartially mentions cases of cowardice and indiscipline among the Franks. His prejudices were too securely built into his mind to need propping up by the suppression of facts. Some scholars have detected a change in his attitude towards the end. He began to think more of the material as distinct from the religious rewards of his pilgrimage, telling with glee how the crusaders at last found plentiful food supplies and booty. That is rather an armchair view. An army marches on its stomach. The crusade was a war like any other. The men had gone through such hardships as to deserve their comforts when the time came.

Was the Anonymous a 'typical' second-rank crusader? Can we generalize from his outlook as expressed in the *Deeds*? I doubt it. The mere fact of his writing a history differentiates him from his companions. Maybe he reflects their naïve impressions of what the crusade was about. He was more gifted than they were, probably more thoughtful, and perhaps more religious. At least he tells us how it felt to go on crusade in the first fervour and to share in the first victories.

Turning from him to William of Tyre is like reading John of Salisbury after Galbert or Caffaro. We come back to the study and the court. Some eighty years have passed; subsequent crusades have done little to help the Latin kingdom. The story of the Latins in Palestine provokes sadness rather

than triumph. William of Tyre's *History of Deeds Done Beyond the Sea* is not original in form as was the unique *Deeds of the Franks*. It is a literary, learned history written by an archbishop. It is remarkable for having achieved as much as this kind of history could. William stands out as the mellowest and wisest historian of the Middle Ages.

William's family were colonists settled 'Overseas'. These crusading-state colonists came of landholding families, and belonged to an international network of relatives and their friends. William gives us his intellectual credentials for writing his history in an account of his journey to the West to get himself educated. He spent nearly twenty years as a

65 Bohemond's siege of Antioch on the First Crusade, from a copy of a French version of William of Tyre's *History*, produced in the capital of the dwindling crusader state at Acre, about 1280. *Lyons, Bibliothèque Municipale, MS 828, f.33r*

student in France and Italy (1145/6–65), choosing the best masters of the Liberal Arts, philosophy, theology and civil and canon law. On returning to the Latin kingdom, he received his first preferment, a prebend in the cathedral church of Tyre. The king of Jerusalem, Amalric, took a fancy to him and wished to provide him with more benefices; but certain difficulties prevented it. William rose at court. He became chancellor of the kingdom and archbishop of Tyre (1174/5). Amalric employed him as his confidential adviser and as tutor to his son. The archbishop went on diplomatic missions to Rome and Byzantium. He fell from court favour after Amalric's death, thereby missing promotion to the patriarchate of Jerusalem, which he had long hoped for. He withdrew to Tyre in disappointment in 1180. Better prospects opened at court when his friends there got the upper hand; but he died about 1185, too soon to get his promotion, and happily for him too soon also to witness Saladin's capture of Jerusalem. He had foreseen it with dread.

The *History* grew slowly out of conversations with Amalric. This king had a passion for listening to accounts of the deeds of rulers and heroic tales. He suggested that William should write up his own deeds as king of Jerusalem. The history of his reign proved to be the middle of a more comprehensive work. It was decided that William should incorporate Amalric's deeds into a general history of Overseas. So far there were histories of the separate crusades, but no general account of the kingdom. The task involved research on a large scale. William began with the Muslim conquest of Syria from the Byzantines (634–40) and worked onward. His retreat to Tyre gave him leisure for writing. He finished twenty-two books and then broke off, disgusted at the state of affairs: the plight of his country filled him with gloom. His friends, however, persuaded him to continue. He started on book twenty-three, which was interrupted by his death. His other historical work was a *History of the Princes of the East*, written at Amalric's request. It is lost; we shall never know what a thoughtful Latin made of Oriental history. His qualifications for writing were his good classical education, gained in the Western schools, his knowledge of Greek, Arabic and perhaps a little Hebrew, picked up for practical purposes, and his experience as a diplomat and statesman. He took part in the events he describes after his return from the West in 1165, and belonged to the inner power group for most of the time.

66 Opposite: a picture of the precincts of the church of the Holy Sepulchre at Jerusalem, from a guide for pilgrims written in the Cistercian monastery of Reun in the early thirteenth century. Constantine's basilica is at the top. At the bottom is the circular church of the Resurrection, with the supposed tomb of Christ in the centre surrounded by hanging lamps. Between the two, the small structure with a gable shelters the rock of Calvary. Between it and the basilica is a shrine containing the cup of the Last Supper, and to the left another shrine for the table of the Last Supper. *Vienna, Österreichische Nationalbibliothek, MS 609, f.4r*

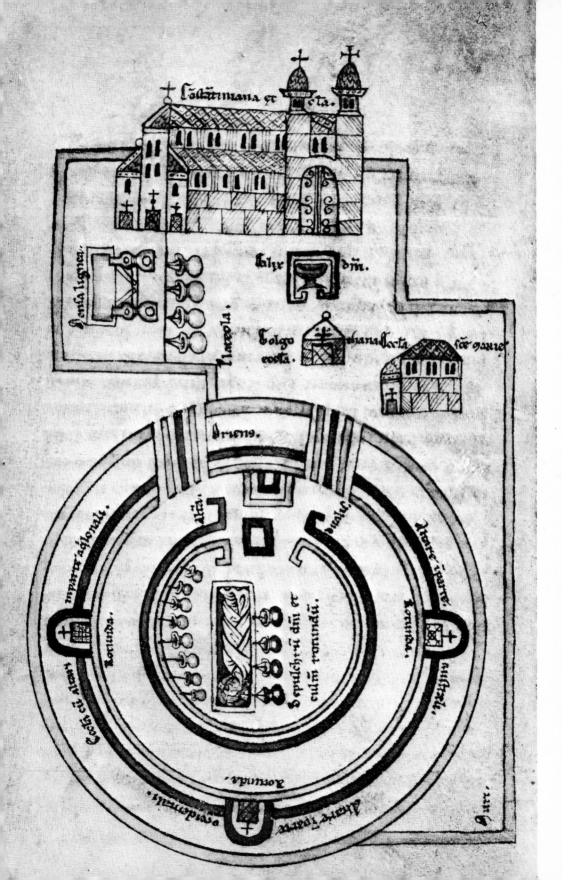

eccl̃a triniana et s̃ta.

lerz d̃m.

menſa lignea.

piſcola.

tolgo
costa.

tiana ſecta

ſc̃e garie

Oriens.

in parte aqlonali.

alta.

eucale.

Altare i parte.

eccl̃a cū altari.

Rotunda.

Rotunda.

australi.

ſepulchr̃i d̃ni et
cubiū rotundū.

Rotunda.

Mare i parte

occidentaliſ.

Turr.

William's cultural background distinguishes him from the Westerners. The Latin colonists had to live with their neighbours. There was friction with Byzantium, but also diplomatic exchanges and marriage alliances. The Greeks proved themselves to be too useful as allies to be dismissed as mere saboteurs of the crusades. Similarly there were truces and traffic with Islam. Many Saracens stayed on after the conquest. In Palestine the Latins came into touch with people at a higher rather than a more primitive level than they had reached. They appreciated Arab learning and skills. Arab doctors could provide better treatment than the Latins, especially for Oriental diseases. The ladies came to rely on 'Jews, Samaritans, Syrians and Arabs' to care for their health; their men followed suit. Their live-and-let-live attitude scandalized newcomers to Overseas. The colonists for their part felt a natural hostility to new pilgrims and settlers: 'You don't understand our problems.' The kingdom of Jerusalem belonged to them. They spent their lives in defending it, a longer time than the few months or years which sufficed for a crusade. Palestine became their home. They got used to the pinkish-grey colours of the Judaean desert and to the dark green valleys which they saw from their fortified towns and castles. Unlike many colonists, they could identify themselves with their country's past. Almost every place-name rang a bell: Mount Sinai, Bethlehem, Nazareth. These were peopled by memories from the Bible and from pagan and Christian antiquity. Interest in the history of Palestine led to more contacts with the natives. Christians would tap local knowledge in order to learn more about the holy places and the legends clustered round them. So the Latin state was more than a kingdom to the colonists settled there; they annexed it as their *patria*, their country. To go West was to go abroad. To return, as William did after his studies, was to come home.

William formulated the idea of *patria*. It gave him the emotional drive which he needed to write his long history. Love of his country has moved many a historian; but in the twelfth century it was new. *Patria* in the Middle Ages often had a religious meaning: we are wayfarers *in via*, travelling to our true *patria* in heaven. When used in a non-religious sense, it meant 'region' or 'place of birth', as on our passport forms. The Romans understood patriotism; men died for their country. Classical studies kept the ancient sense of *patria* alive; but it had no focus. Historians wrote up the deeds of a people or of a ruling house, not the story of their land. It seems odd that patriotism should have focused first on Overseas, with its mixed population, its loose government and its dicey future. Its very exposure may have sharpened the colonists' sense of possession. Love of his country is not a mere classical memory in William's *History*, but a live, anxious feeling. It comes out in his prologues, where otherwise he gives the familiar reasons for composition. He cannot allow the last hundred years to fall out of mind, because love of his country spurs him on. 'The sweetness of our native earth' must outweigh his inadequacy as a historian.

The second prologue at the beginning of his unfinished last book explains his reasons for taking up the tale. There was much to dissuade him. Nobody, he says, would wish to dwell on his country's sickness and failures, whereas it comes naturally to a historian to praise her with all his might. Just now he has nothing praiseworthy to tell. William fell back on Livy's claim to have described the purity and courage of the ancient Romans to their decadent children. Then his friends heartened him by pointing out that both Livy and Josephus had recounted disasters as well as victories when they told their stories of the Romans and the Jews. Moreover, the annalist, by virtue of his office, sets down what happened, not what he would like to have happened. So William embarked on his tale of disaster. To write of a country which was loved and threatened called for uncommon virtuosity.

His merit as a classicist is that he has mastered his ancient sources. They supply pat quotations, but not too many. He moulded the Suetonian portrait of a ruler to suit his structure: first, a narrative of the foundation of the Latin kingdom in its setting of the Muslim conquest, and then the First Crusade; second, a character sketch of each king, followed by a chronological account of his reign. He knits them together so that the ruler's character is seen to react on current events: a rash king endangered the army. The kings of Jerusalem come to life. It was not William's fault that none of them was as photogenic as Henry II. Other characters are pencilled in, and places too. William gives a geographical account and a history, going back to antiquity, of each place that he mentions. His *History* portrays a land as well as its Frankish conquerors. He worked hard to collect and sift information on what had happened when he was not present as an eyewitness. If his informants' reports varied, he set down each version, as the best he could do. He tried to write objectively, at the risk of annoying contemporaries. Mistakes in tactics or politics and irresponsible behaviour get their share of blame. Nor does he spare his own feelings. It must have cost William dear to tell how King Amalric suddenly asked him to give reasons for the doctrine of the resurrection of the body. Amalric protested that he believed the doctrine; but he wanted to know by what arguments one could prove it to a person who did not accept it on faith alone. It grieved the archbishop's very soul that a Christian prince, son of Christian parents, should question so universally accepted an article of the Creed. He tells us about the conversation nonetheless, to illustrate the king's habit of talking when he had a touch of fever and wanted company to while away the time in bed. William does full justice to the excitement and pathos of his story of Overseas. A flash of eastern magic lights up his description of a caliph's palace as it was described to him. He gives a first-hand and pathetic account of how he discovered that his pupil, the young heir to the kingdom, had contracted leprosy.

William had the defects and prejudices to be looked for in a prelate of the Church. He disliked campaigning in person and disapproved of military bishops. Hence he is at his weakest on military history. He gives bad marks to princes who whittled down ecclesiastical privileges. The archbishop naturally resented the liberties of the religious orders, and of the Knights Templar in particular, because their exemption from diocesan control created difficulties. His jealousy of the Templars prevents him from giving them due credit for their share in defending the kingdom. He is surprisingly objective in his judgments otherwise.

The problem of causation brought out William's best qualities as a historian. Pope Urban II's call to crusade brightened the darkness of troubled times and raised new hopes for Christendom. But William probed the Anonymous' account of the 'mighty movement' which launched the First Crusade. Not every crusader acted out of religious fervour. Some took the cross because their friends did, so as not to seem cowardly, some just for the fun of it, and some to avoid being dunned by their creditors; others were criminals, escaping from justice. The First Crusade succeeded in spite of these mixed motives. On reaching the year 1174, William looked back to ask himself why success had not continued: why did the present generation fail to maintain the conquests of their forbears Overseas? The obvious answer was 'moral decline'. This may have been wrong: the Franks in Palestine had grown more comfort-loving, and moralists normally equate comfort with sinfulness; it did not follow that the colonists had degenerated. But his *passe-partout* explanation did not satisfy William either. He sought other reasons in Muslim history. The first crusaders were expert soldiers, attacking a country whose natives had grown accustomed to peace and had forgotten how to defend themselves. Their enemies were disunited politically. The Muslim princes fought one another instead of obeying a superior. Almost every city had its own lord. Hence these isolated strongholds fell easily to the crusaders. Now, on the contrary, the Muslims were united under one ruler. The sultan had plenty of money, thanks to his conquests, and could pay his troops. Recruits were at hand in quantity, given the means to hire them. The present generation of Franks Overseas faced much greater odds than their forbears.

William realized that political unity and a full treasury will decide a conflict between two states. Modern historians of the Latin kingdom still subscribe to William's analysis of the causes of its fall. They refine upon his account by pointing to the special weaknesses of Latin government Overseas: the king lacked financial resources and his control over his barons grew looser during the twelfth century. General acceptance of William's theory of causes is the compliment paid to him as a historian.

Geoffrey of Villehardouin resembled the Anonymous in being a layman and a soldier. His *Conquest of Constantinople*, like the Anonymous's *Deeds of the Franks*, is an eyewitness account and a success story. Both writers planned their story in much the same way: both begin with the preaching of the crusade; they go on to describe the expedition and its victorious outcome; they round off by reporting its aftermath. There the likenesses end. Villehardouin, marshal of Champagne, was no simple knight, but a leader and organizer. He got his share in the spoils of the Fourth Crusade. After the capture of Constantinople he held the office of marshal in the new Latin empire and received the principate of Acaia in Greece for himself and his heirs.

Geoffrey wrote his book in French. The *Conquest of Constantinople* is the earliest French historical prose narrative surviving today. The absence of precedents for comparison means that the *Conquest* bristles with problems for the

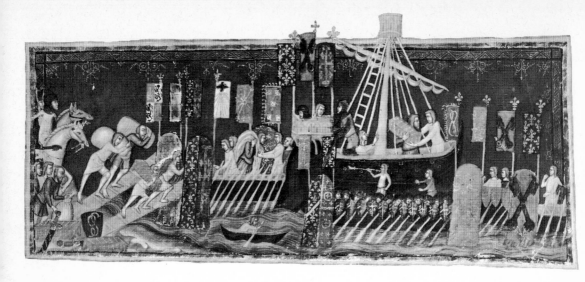

modern historian. We do not know what the author had
read. He had grasped the outlines of earlier crusading
histories and he must have listened to vernacular epics and
romances. He borrows their literary conventions, telling his
audience to 'listen carefully' and repeating 'as the book says'
to authenticate his story. But he was no romancer. He told
the true and marvellous tale of the conquest of a hitherto
impregnable city, packed full of treasure, by a small army.
Rhetoric and miracle stories would have spoilt his effect. He
had a sharp eye for military detail and he excels in conveying
a fresh direct impression of what he saw. Speechifying bored
him. Although he took part in the leaders' councils, he
contented himself with a brief summary of what was said
there and does not embroider by rhetoric.

His purpose in writing is equally open to question.
Historians of French medieval literature have classified the
Conquest as a 'failed epic'. On this view, Geoffrey planned to
write an epic on the crusaders' victory; but he ended with a
wretched anticlimax. The conquerors failed to deal with
Greek resistance in the countryside and in the smaller towns
of their empire. This view of the *Conquest* is unconvincing.
If Geoffrey had wanted to write a prose epic, he could have
stopped while the going was good. The capture of Constantinople would have made a fine ending. Moreover, an
epic should have heroes, and he does not supply them. It is
true that the doge of Venice plays an honourable role in the
Conquest; but the blind old man, though wise and courageous in Geoffrey's eyes, cannot star as a hero. We might
ascribe the star part to Geoffrey himself, but he does not
write to magnify his own exploits at the expense of others.

He mentions his name and his contribution to warfare and diplomacy without depriving his friends of glory.

A historian's view of the *Conquest* is that it was written as propaganda. Geoffrey wanted to cover up the plot which led to the diversion of the crusade to besiege and capture a Christian capital. This view is more plausible. Not all of Geoffrey's contemporaries regarded the Fourth Crusade as a glorious victory. Some saw it as a dirty business from the start. The pope had forbidden attacks on Christians; but the Venetians had the whip-hand and defied his ban. They had undertaken to provide shipping for the expedition, which set off from Venice. The crusaders could not pay the sum agreed upon; hence they had to comply with the Venetians' plans if they used the Venetian fleet. Constantinople was the main obstacle to the Venetian policy of commercial expansion. The doge and his compatriots made use of the crusaders' greed for land and booty in order to exploit a dynastic quarrel within the city. The crusade was diverted, Constantinople was taken, and a Latin empire set up there. In fact the Venetians had incurred excommunication before ever they set foot on Byzantine soil, since they had obliged the crusaders to help them to capture the Christian city of Zara in Dalmatia on their way down the Adriatic. The pope did not insist on the ban for fear of losing what little control over the crusade that he had.

Geoffrey certainly distorts his story by suppressing some known facts. He camouflages the Venetians' stake in the conquest of Constantinople and their excommunication. He gives an unfair account of the split in the crusaders' leadership. The truth was that none of the leaders had any intention of taking their troops to the Holy Land. To do so would have been romatic nonsense and would not have helped the kingdom of Acre. The intention was to strike at Saracen power at its strongest point, the naval bases in Egypt. The rank-and-file of crusaders, on the other hand, looked forward to going on an armed pilgrimage to the Holy Land of the old-fashioned type. The leaders deliberately misled their men by giving out that the expedition was going 'overseas'; its precise destination was not specified. Geoffrey tells us so honestly. The split came when it was proposed to divert the expedition to Constantinople. Some of the leaders dug their toes in. They refused to accompany the Venetians and the other crusaders. As they were too few in number to attack Egypt, the objectors set out for Palestine to do what they

68 Crusaders proceed to Constantinople by sea, from a late thirteenth-century French copy of Villehardouin. *Paris, Bibliothèque Nationale, MS fr. 12203, f.78v*

143

69 The Dominican Burchard of Monte Sion wrote a *Description of the Holy Land* in 1283 which excelled in detail and scientific precision. In this miniature from a Venetian manuscript of Burchard's work we see Christian warriors at Jerusalem. *Padua, Biblioteca del Seminario, MS 74, f.13v*

could. Geoffrey represents them as saboteurs of the crusade. He describes them as 'those who wanted to disband the army'. The 'true crusaders' were Geoffrey and his friends. He ignores the religious motives of those who scrupled to make war on their fellow-Christians. It must be admitted that he was correct in saying that they achieved little in Palestine.

It would be wrong, however, to dismiss the *Conquest* as mere propaganda. Research on the tangled story of intrigue leading up to the diversion suggests that there was no 'plot' to be covered up. The Venetians could not have plotted the diversion because they were not in a position to foresee what would happen. There were too many dangers. Hard bargaining and cunning opportunism explain their conduct better than deep scheming in advance. In any case, the Latin empire was a *fait accompli* when Geoffrey wrote the *Conquest* in 1207. The pope had recognized it. Geoffrey had no reason to apologize for the Venetians and their allies among the crusaders, though he tried to conceal the discreditable side of the diversion to Constantinople.

The most recent and probable view of the *Conquest* is simpler: the book belongs to the 'War Memoirs of a Successful General' class. Geoffrey gives us bias rather than falsification, which is what one would expect in a book of the kind. This view also disposes of the 'failed epic' theory. It comes naturally to a general to record mopping-up operations after a victory, as Geoffrey does. They are not an anticlimax to a soldier's mind; and a general can easily underrate the strength of resistance movements, as Geoffrey underrated Greek resistance to the Latins.

His memoirs are precious as a new genre, and all the more so for having been written by a layman. They show us a mind and outlook much more secular than the Anonymous's. Geoffrey takes so little interest in religion and morals that he does not even bother to criticize the clergy. Papal meddling in military matters just irritated him; clerical quarrels amused him. The two papal legates who went with the crusaders were both Cistercian abbots. One sided with 'the true crusaders', as Geoffrey calls them, the other opposed the diversion. The difference between the two abbots and legates struck Geoffrey as comic.

He has his own theory of causation: it is a simple fatalism. Whatever happens is God's will. This opinion blocked the way to any subtle analysis of causes. His secular outlook did not make for deep thinking.

We turn now to the Albigensian Crusade, directed against the heretics in southern France. These heretics left no histories or chronicles, which is not surprising. The Cathars were dualists: they believed that the devil had created the visible world. To write its history, therefore, would have been mere muckraking. Another group of heretics, known as the Waldenses (from their leader, Valdès) or 'Poor Men of Lyons', were more like Protestants in their beliefs. Perhaps they did produce a historian of their sect; if so, his work has not survived. Probably they were kept too busy disputing with Cathars and Catholics to turn their minds to history. We depend on Catholic historiographers to tell the story of the crusades against there heretics in the Midi. Fortunately for us, they approach it from very different points of view.

Our first author is a Cistercian monk, Peter of the abbey of Vaux de Cernai. His uncle, the abbot, took Peter with him when he went on the Fourth Crusade as papal legate. This was the legate branded by Geoffrey of Villehardouin as a saboteur, because he persisted in going on to the Holy Land. In 1212, when the uncle and nephew had returned, Innocent III appointed the abbot of Cernai as his legate on the Albigensian Crusade (the popes frequently used Cistercian monks to serve as legates and missionaries to the heretics). The abbot took Peter with him again. So Peter had two kinds of crusading experience. He took part in campaigns, though as a monk he did not actually fight.

The crusade against the Albigensians had a lightning success. The barons of northern France cut through the unprepared, undisciplined forces of the Midi, as a knife cuts into cheese. The southern nobles were dispossessed of their lands. The crusading leader Simon de Montfort (father of the Earl Simon who fell at the battle of Evesham) carved out a principality for himself. Peter's uncle became bishop of Carcassonne in 1214. His nephew may have stayed with him to serve him as secretary. At any rate, Peter spent most

70 Tomb-slab of Simon de Montfort, killed while he was laying siege to Toulouse in June, 1218. He was buried in the church of St Nazaire at Carcassonne.

of his time in the Midi after 1212. There he wrote his Latin *History of the Albigensian Crusades*. It breaks off at 1218. Perhaps Peter died, or perhaps he stopped writing because Simon de Montfort was killed in that year. Simon was Peter's hero. His admiration for Simon went back to the Fourth Crusade, when Simon led the contingent which made for Palestine.

The *History of the Albigensian Crusades* is a full, detailed narrative, set out in chronological order. Peter had a gift for observation and description. He has been called 'a great painter of ruins'; there were plenty to paint in the devastated area of the *terra Albigensium*. He had a soldier's delight in good fortifications. The town of Carcassonne pleased him as a citadel, even when it was still in enemy hands. We can see vividly from his comments how the unaccustomed scenery and ways of the Midi struck a northerner. If we compare him with historians of the crusades to Palestine, Peter comes closest to the anonymous author of the *Deeds of the Franks*. He regards the heretics in the same way as the Anonymous regarded the Muslims. Heretics were devilish. They deserved what they got.

71 Simon de Montfort's siege of Toulouse is represented in a thirteenth-century carving in the same church as Simon's tomb-slab (ill. 70). On the left the crusaders approach in a three-storeyed siege tower. On the right is the beleaguered city, behind a palisade. Some of its citizens, bottom right, are working a great catapult like the one that killed Simon. At the top right one of the besiegers, who has been hauled up by ropes, is hacked to pieces by the defenders; an angel receives his soul.

Peter's avowed purpose in writing is stated in a preface to part one of the *History*, addressed to Pope Innocent III. The *History* would preserve the memory of God's wonderful works: the crusaders had saved the shipwrecked Church in the Midi. Peter's unstated purpose, perhaps suggested by his superiors, was to jog the pope's elbow on behalf of Simon and his allies. Innocent had not envisaged total expropriation of the southern lords by the crusaders. The count of Toulouse appealed to Rome. It looked as though Innocent might favour him. Peter hoped to influence the pope to decide for Simon against the count of Toulouse. It was part of his propaganda to denounce the heretics and to smear the count and other southern nobles as heretics by association. Peter told the truth in stating that they had tolerated heresy on their estates; but they had more complex reasons for doing so than his *History* lets out. Some flirted with heresy; their womenfolk often did more than flirt; but his blanket accusation was unjust.

Peter used the previous history of the Midi to support his case. He traced heresy back to the Visigothic invasion and settlement in the south of France. Toulouse (the capital of the Visigoths) had been a centre of heresy ever since. It did not trouble him that the Visigoths had been Arians, not Mani-chees, or that Arianism was not a dualist creed. His statement that the counts of Toulouse had always been heretics looks odd in the light of their record as crusaders to the Holy Land. Count Raymond played a key part in the First Crusade; his heirs neglected their county in order to follow his example. In making his propaganda, however, Peter had the advantage that he genuinely believed it. He had no understanding of the southern mentality and no sense of humour. It seemed to him incredible that a Catholic could neglect his duty to suppress heresy on his domains. Therefore the counts of Toulouse were heretics. Peter over-simplified.

The same rigid orthodoxy comes out in a short Latin chronicle written by a Dominican inquisitor called William of Pelhisson (d. 1268). He was a southerner by origin; but his office as inquisitor inclined him to give no quarter to heretics. On the other hand, he shows us a different picture from Peter's. The soldier-monk came south with a con-quering army, whereas the Dominican friar had to work among the heretics and the disaffected at risk of his life. He records in simple terms his shared experiences as a member of a small community of friars. A few devout Catholics helped

t ladte se vela folece dicebant. Nec uestib;
lis utebantur nisi corijs animaliū intedū
magna necessitate. Et cum a nautis expete

ulsi fuissent: tandem sb insula qdā
modica se receperūt.ii. tanchorarū
mozsu funiumqz tphaū inmo mī

them by smuggling in food supplies when a hostile populace threatened the brothers with starvation. The pope founded a university at Toulouse in 1229 in order to combat heretical teaching. Catholic doctrine sounded so strange to the students that mocking laughter rang out in the lecture room. A tourist who visits the 'fortress churches' of Languedoc should read William's chronicle. It will show him why the Catholics had to build themselves strongholds to serve as refuges and

72 The fortress church at Albi, begun in 1282, intended to enable the Catholics to defend themselves against heretics and rebels. This view shows the wall-walk and arrow-slits.

Colour plate VIII
See caption p. 148.

73–75 The great Bible
picture book, known as the
Bible moralisée, presents the
text of the Scriptures set
beside medallions showing
both Bible history, what
happened, and its allegorical
and moral interpretation.
These roundels come from
two copies of the picture
book made in France,
probably in the 1230s.
The 'moralities' often refer to
current events. The spread of
heresy led to heart-searching
by the clergy.
Right: a lazy priest sleeps
while the heretics preach.
Centre: a heretic puts out his
tongue at a priest, who is
preaching to the people, to
illustrate the effrontery of the
heretics; they are allowed to
go about unmolested.
Far right: the Inquisition is
established to destroy heresy.
Dominican friars were put in
charge of the Inquisition at
Toulouse. Here we see a friar
interrogating a suspect and
then handing him over to the
secular arm to be imprisoned
or burnt. *Paris, Bibliothèque
Nationale, MS lat. 11560,
f.110r and 137r; and London,
British Museum, MS Harl.
1526, f.30v (far right)*

to stand up to siege. This Dominican took even less interest
in the causes of heresy than did Peter of Cernai: the devil was
cause enough for him.

The cold light of reason breaks through in our next Latin
chronicle. The author, William of Puylaurens, wrote at a
date when events could be reviewed more calmly. He was a
southerner, like Pelhisson, but not an inquisitor. Puylaurens
had the title of Master; we do not know where he studied.
He was a secular priest, employed as notary by the bishop of
Toulouse. Earlier he had probably worked on the staff of
Bishop Fulk of Toulouse, who died in 1231. Then he acted as
chaplain to the count of Toulouse. The first part of his book,
written after 1249, covers about fifty years of Midi history
from the rise of heresy down to the death of his patron, the
count of Toulouse. The second part, going down to 1273/4,
is a scrappy record, which need not concern us. Puylaurens
called his book a chronicle. It is a factual narrative without
any pretensions to style. He wrote it for a wide public, not for
an élite of scholars or lay nobles. His aim in his own words
was

to set down some of those things which I saw or heard from my
neighbours, so that men of upper, middle and lower ranks shall
understand God's judgments, by which he afflicted these lands in
consequence of the sins of their people.

We expect preacher's thunder. Not at all. Puylaurens
analysed the causes of heresy. His familiarity with southern

ways gave him a start over Peter of Cernai. The hero of his
chronicle is not the dashing Simon de Montfort, but Bishop
Fulk of Toulouse, a Cistercian and a pillar of orthodoxy, but
wise and witty. Puylaurens loves to quote his repartee. One
day, when standing on the walls of Toulouse, he heard some
heretics shout up at him that he was 'the devil's bishop'.
'Quite right,' he answered, 'you *are* devils, and I *am* your
bishop.' Puylaurens could appreciate the motive behind a
political crime. Count Raymond of Toulouse hanged his
brother, Count Baldwin. The chronicler excused Baldwin's
treachery to his brother – he joined the northerners because
Raymond had never done anything for him – but on the
other hand Raymond had a political excuse for his fratricide.
As a student of politics, Puylaurens pounces on a diplomatic
blunder; he can distinguish between propaganda and fact.
His sympathies went to the French monarchy in the long
run. The Capetians were foreigners to the Midi, but their
conquest brought law and order to a troubled country.
Puylaurens was a realist.

He diagnosed heresy as a symptom of a moral illness which
infected the whole of Midi society. The cause of the illness
was negligence: the clergy neglected their duty to teach
Catholic doctrine to the people and to set a good example.
The heretics had an appearance of goodness. Hence they
were able to gain many followers. Dissatisfaction with the
Church expressed itself in heresy. This diagnosis has had a

long life. 'The corruption of the Church' is still the commonest answer to the question: 'why did heresy make more progress in the Midi than elsewhere?' Only recently have historians begun to doubt whether the Church in the Midi was especially open to criticism and to search for other causes. Puylaurens' answer has done duty for centuries. It may be too simple; but it represents the situation as it seemed to a rational observer.

Puylaurens goes on to discuss the spread of heresy. It was a creeping disease. The sectaries worked in hiding at first; then their success emboldened them to preach openly. He explains what had puzzled newcomers to the Midi, beginning with Peter of Cernai: why did Catholics live side by side with heretics without trying to convert them or persecute them? Peter dismissed them all as heretics to a man. Puylaurens answers that the heretics' success created a vicious circle. The clergy, non-starters in the race for esteem, sank so low that no knight would make his son a clerk. Hence there was a shortage of ordinands. The bishops could not reject unworthy candidates; they 'made clerks as they could'. Clerical standards of learning and conduct deteriorated still more. A Church so poorly staffed could not discipline the laity. The knights of the Midi adhered to whichever sect caught their fancy. The heretics held their conventicles publicly and buried their followers in their own graveyards. Puylaurens' masterly account of the way heresy spread makes it easy to understand why the southern nobles feared to use force. To attack heresy would have meant disturbing the whole *status quo* and would have upset all their subjects, Catholics or sectaries. Puylaurens can convey a situation and he is adept at explanations.

Our last two historiographers are poets writing in Provençal. One began and the other continued the *Song of the Albigensian Crusade*. The first poet tells us that he was a Master of Arts and clerk called William of Tudela (in Spanish Navarre). He earned his living as a professional entertainer and reciter of verses in noble households. He began his poem about 1210 and stopped in 1213, perhaps because his patron, Count Baldwin, was killed by his brother, the count of Toulouse, in that year. There were other historical poems in the vernacular; William of Tudela says that he modelled his on a crusading story, the *Song of Antioch* (now lost). Unfortunately for the reciters, their market was limited and they had to compete with jesters and mimes,

providers of mere slapstick. One had to advertise oneself. This is William's publisher's blurb:

As soon as William started his song he hardly slept till he'd finished. It's well written and full of fine verses. Take the trouble to listen and all of you, great and small, will learn many things, well put and sensible, since the author has his belly full of good sayings. He who doesn't know the poem and hasn't felt its force has no idea what he's missing.

William calls himself 'a clever fellow' and claims to have foretold the disasters hanging over the Midi by means of geomancy, a sort of white magic:

He knew by his study of this science that the land would be burned and ravaged because of the mad beliefs which had been allowed into it, that the rich burghers would be despoiled of their goods and that the knights would depart as exiles to foreign places.

But the tale is told as 'a good yarn'; the tragic side of it only makes it more compelling. The narrator does not compromise himself. The crusaders acted savagely; but it was crazy

76 The twelfth-century tympanum of St Faith at Conques, a centre of pilgrimage for Christendom situated in the Languedoc, shows the Last Judgment and the fate of the damned. In this detail we see on the right a heretic, holding a parchment and book containing heretical doctrine. He is placed with his head below the level of the earth, and a devil shuts his mouth to prevent him from speaking.

of the southerners to let heresy spread. The real villains, in his view and doubtless in that of his audience, were the countrymen, who finished off the dying after a battle with sticks and stones in order to rob the corpses. They had no right to interfere in gentlemen's wars. William's theory of causation recalls the *Conquest of Constantinople*: what must be will be; 'what God ordains, that man cannot change.' This is history at the level of a pastime.

A better poet continued the *Song* from 1213 to 1218/19, stopping at the point when the men of Toulouse were preparing to defend their city against Prince Louis of France. He gives us a sample of 'nostalgic history', to use Croce's classification. All we know of the writer has to be deduced from his verses and qualified as 'probable'. He was a Master of Arts and a clerk, like William of Tudela; he was attached to the court of Count Raymond VII of Toulouse, whom he accompanied to the Lateran Council of 1215, when Raymond went to plead for reinstatement to his confiscated lands and rights. The poet wrote soon after 1228. Had he finished the *Song*, he might have given his name at the end. His feelings are in no doubt. He defended the southerners against the crusaders. The anonymous poet was neither a heretic nor anti-papal; he wrote as a good Catholic, believing that God took the side of those who defended their land against foreign enemies. The northerners used the crusade against heresy as an excuse for their greedy attack on the Midi; they pretended that all the southerners were heretics, which was quite untrue. Bishop Fulk of Toulouse, the hero of William of Puylaurens, appears as a mealy-mouthed hypocrite because he collaborated with the crusaders. Simon de Montfort, the hero of Peter of Cernai, had been buried with honour and praised for his holiness. The anonymous poet comments that Simon had 'earned his fame by butchering more women and children than men'.

More was at stake for the southerners than defeat, expropriation and slaughter. The northerners overturned values; a whole way of life came to an end. The poet calls his values *prix et parage*, and personifies them. *Prix* meant prowess or knightly virtue. *Parage* stood for the ranks of the southern courts, which offered due reward for prowess. The knights of the Midi tended to assemble at their lord's court instead of living mainly on their estates, since these were too fragmented to support a family. The ladies of the court attracted 'courtly love' poems. Northern courts favoured a different type of culture, less exotic and brilliant. Ruthless 'levellers' from the North destroyed *prix et parage*. Simon's death brought a moment of hope; *prix et parage* shone out again, but not for long. The next wave of invaders trod them down.

Defeat has its victories in historiography. The historians of conquest and crusade show clearly that defeat is a better teacher than success. Writers who had to tell of defeat or stalemate or the Church's failure to stop the spread of heresy were led by their theme to reflect on causation. Fanaticism gave way to cool appraisal. Moral decay and divine punishment of sin no longer sufficed as the only reasons for failure. Many of our historiographers probe more deeply. Adam of Bremen, Helmold, Gerald of Wales, William of Tyre and William of Puylaurens all look for human agencies when they record setbacks or disasters.

Emotion as well as reason belongs to the very stuff of history. It took utter defeat to bring out the full bitterness which we taste in the second part of the *Song of the Albigensian Crusade*. The conquered speak to us in some histories: Benedict of Monte Soracte described the Saxon conquest of Rome; the *Anglo-Saxon Chronicle* tells of the Danish invasions and of the Norman conquest of England. Neither can compete with the poet of the *Song* as artists in pathos.

Es hor
mais
que n
nos so
aquiu
reuau
fruois
viez l
z au
roi lo
le gros qui tante paine sofri en
tens z tante bataille forni z tre se

The thirteenth century:
an epilogue

Although the thirteenth century was not a period of experiment in historiography, the traditional genres were developed and some of them took on a new lease of life. The monastic chronicle is an outstanding example. It had its heyday in England in the thirteenth century, to the extent that it colours an Englishman's view of medieval historiography in general. An English student of medieval history is brought up on Jocelyn of Brakelonde and Matthew Paris. One represents local and the other 'world' history.

Jocelyn's *Deeds of Abbot Samson* of Bury St Edmunds in Suffolk is too well known to need description here. No writer of any time can beat Jocelyn as a portrayer of character: we come to know Abbot Samson better than any thirteenth-century English abbot, thanks to his biographer. We experience the reactions of the monks of Bury to his masterful rule. We live with them and share in their hopes and fears for the well-being of their community. The *Deeds of Abbot Samson* offers full scope to students who want to understand the workings of both local and central government in the early thirteenth century, since Jocelyn gives precious details on the relations between the king and the abbey on the one hand and between the abbey and its tenants on the other.

An anonymous writer from Bury did almost as well as Jocelyn in *The Election of Hugh*, an account of a disputed election to the abbacy of Bury towards the end of King John's reign (1199–1216). Both authors introduce us to the same quarrelsome, self-regarding community. Both describe the nervousness of the monks when the cold draught of royal anger blows through. The author of *The Election of Hugh* does not set out to portray character in the round as Jocelyn had done; he sketches in his *personae* more lightly, but persuasively. Both authors catch the excitement of the formation of parties among the brethren. The disputed election described in the second book gave the younger, more daring monks a chance to uphold the liberties of the

77 Opposite: a scene from the *Great Chronicles of France* (see p. 162). King Louis VII remonstrates with the burghers of Orleans, who want to found a commune. His counsellors back him up. From a thirteenth-century translation of the *Chronicles* by the monk Primat of St Denis (see ill. 79). *Paris, Bibliothèque Ste Geneviève, MS 782, f.26v*

abbey by demanding a free election. The older, more timid brothers and the waverers opposed them for fear of the king. The prior, a character familiar to all members of a tightly knit group at any time, was on whichever side had spoken to him last. The reader draws a sigh of relief when the abbey passes unscathed through its ordeal.

Other abbeys had their historians. To mention one only: Master Thomas of Marlborough in Wiltshire wrote a chronicle of Evesham, also in the early thirteenth century. The core of his work consists of an account of a lawsuit. Here, too, there were activists and defeatists among the monks. In spite of the length and tedium of the litigation, Thomas succeeds in holding our interest: will the abbey win its case? Eventually the appeal to Rome went in favour of Evesham. Thomas, who attended in person to plead for his abbey, was so overcome by exhaustion and joy that he fell fainting at the pope's feet.

True craftsmanship has gone into these local histories. A reader who wants to appreciate it should try his hand at writing up his own experiences of life in an institution. It is more difficult than it seems at first sight to make them sound colourful and important.

Matthew Paris (d. 1259) produced both local and 'world' history. His mammoth output surpassed anything ever attempted in a Benedictine abbey. I shall concentrate on his *Greater Chronicle*, since that is the most famous of his historical works. Its scope and volume are amazing. Scholars use it as a primary source for both English and European history. The author had his roots in the abbey of St Alban. Matthew

78 The death of Earl Gilbert Marshal in a tournament. Matthew Paris's own drawing, illustrating his *Greater Chronicle. Cambridge, Corpus Christi College, MS 16, f.147r*

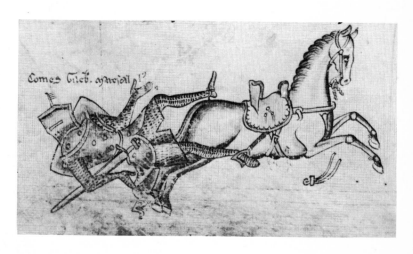

describes his fellow Benedictines as 'good brothers, whose hearts were set on prayer and hospitality'. Their duties as hosts put them in the way of collecting news. St Alban's is situated on the main road north from London; it was an ideal repository for information of all kinds. Matthew made the most of his opportunities. He had an unquenchable thirst for news and gossip, which combined with the passion of an archivist. He copied documents concerning the items he recorded, and copied so extensively that he had to find a special place for documents in his 'book of additions' to the *Chronicle*. His other gifts were a flair for writing and artistic skill. For Matthew was also an artist: he illustrated his text with bold, expressive drawings. That was a rare and personal juxtaposition. Very few authors made their own illustrations in the Middle Ages.

Matthew Paris's outstanding achievement was to put across his point of view. The vast quantity of facts which he assembled would have made his chronicle a valley of dry bones, if they had not passed through his lively mind. We see them as he did. Matthew had the nerve to let himself go. He selected, distorted, invented and commented. His chronicle presents a set of opinions and prejudices shared by other English chroniclers. Roger of Wendover, his predecessor at St Alban's, had already expressed them in a less coherent way. The great English abbeys represented an early, uncoordinated version of the 'country party' versus the 'court party' or the 'outs' versus the 'ins'. Office at court, including government office, spelled power, influence and riches. The Black Monks had no footing at court. Few became bishops in the thirteenth century. This weakened their pull at the other power centre of Christendom, the papal court. The abbeys felt the pressure of royal and papal taxation. The popes also aimed to tighten up discipline and observance in the exempt abbeys by appointing visitors, often the diocesan bishop, to enquire into the running of the house and to correct abuses.

The monks resented what they saw as exploitation and interference. They found themselves at the receiving end of the bureaucracy. Nobody likes tax-collectors, nosy parkers and money-lenders. Their being 'foreigners' added fuel to the flame; Henry III employed foreign favourites in his government. Hence monastic chroniclers tend to xenophobia and favour native opposition movements. The new orders of mendicant friars put the monks' noses out of joint too. The rise of universities left them in an intellectual back-water. Matthew's writings reflect a reaction against new movements in general. His bias is so obvious as to be self-defeating and his prejudices cancel each other out. The friars made him jealous; the reforming zeal of Robert Grosseteste, bishop of Lincoln, annoyed him. On the other hand, as an Englishman he took pride in Oxford University. Scholar-bishops and friars appealed to him so long as they kept away from St Alban's. Matthew could be careless and inaccurate as a chronicler; that is a defect. His bias stamps his personality on his story. Slapdash judgments are part of it. We must take a genius as we find him.

Matthew's *Greater Chronicle* has no rival on the continent of Europe. The monks of St Denis, however, achieved some-thing else. They became official historiographers of the French monarchy. Suger's attempts to identify his abbey with the royal house bore fruit: a royal chronicle began to be kept in the early thirteenth century, or perhaps even earlier, and was added to. A monk of St Denis called Primat trans-lated the compilation into French in 1274. The French copies, lavishly illustrated, came to be known as the *Great Chronicles of France*. England had nothing comparable. Westminster Abbey had much the same status as St Denis in the thirteenth century. Its chroniclers took the royal side in contrast to the other abbeys, which were normally opposition-minded; yet Westminster never produced an authorized royal version of English history.

The mendicant friars contributed their share to histori-ography: friaries kept annals and chronicles. The Franciscans especially breathed new life into the genre of saints' lives. Memories of their founder and disputes on the interpretation of their Rule supplied the driving force. The inspiration spilled over into *The Coming of the Friars Minor to England* by Thomas of Eccleston. Thomas studied at Paris as a secular clerk, joined the order in England about 1230, continued his studies at the Oxford Greyfriars and was later transferred to London. He finished his chronicle, which contained material collected over some twenty-five years, about 1258/9.

Thomas's chronicle is a religious piece. He divided it into homilies, to be read aloud to the friars. He wanted to rekindle the joyous simplicity and delight in poverty of the first Franciscans, true sons of St Francis. Since 'examples touch the heart more than words', he gives many examples, inserting them into his biographies of the men who played

an important part in the order in England in its early days. His chronicle gives an idealized, nostalgic picture of the first comers and of their hardships in the Oxford schools and elsewhere. An inner tension enlivens his tale. He praises their poverty, but loves to record gifts made to the friars, the addition of books to their libraries, the building of convents and their removal to larger, healthier sites. The history of any religious order had to include the history of its endowment.

Matthew Paris's opposite number in Italy was a Franciscan, Fra Salimbene, who compiled a bulky chronicle covering the period from about 1168 to 1304. His curiosity equalled Matthew's; his circumstances as a member of a mobile, international order gave him different means of quenching his thirst for new items. He could go round collecting them himself, when his superiors sent him on business or transferred him to other friaries, instead of waiting for news to come to him. Salimbene gossiped with all sorts of people, from popes down to beggars. He and Matthew have different gifts as writers. Matthew can convey a scene; Salimbene can describe an object so well that one can almost see it and touch it. He has no 'message', either religious or political, unless it be the message that a good Franciscan can enjoy just being alive. Observation concerned him more than religious observance. He was against the emperor Frederick II as a persecutor of the Church, but he had no illusions about churchmen.

79 The monk Primat presents his translation of the *Great Chronicles of France* to King Philip III. The abbot of St Denis and monks of the abbey stand behind Primat. *Paris, Bibliothèque Ste Geneviève, MS 782, f.326v*

163

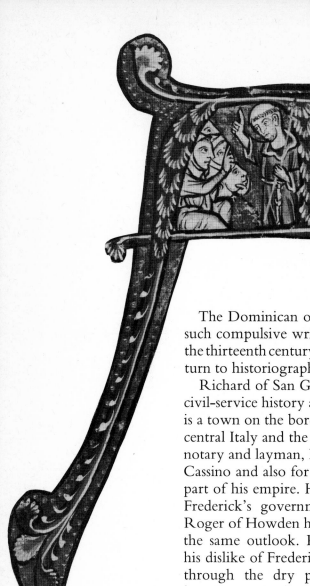

80 A Franciscan friar doctor holds a university disputation. The disputants raise fingers to make their points. One participant reflects, chin in hand. An initial from an English manuscript of the mid-thirteenth century, the Wilton Psalter. *London, Royal College of Physicians, MS 409, f.61v*

The Dominican order produced some chroniclers, but no such compulsive writer as Salimbene. Only after the turn of the thirteenth century did the Oxford scholar, Nicholas Trevet, turn to historiography as one of his many literary pursuits.

Richard of San Germano, writing in the 1230s, represents civil-service history at royal government level. San Germano is a town on the border of what used to be the papal states in central Italy and the kingdom of southern Italy and Sicily. A notary and layman, Richard worked for the abbey of Monte Cassino and also for Frederick II, who ruled the kingdom as part of his empire. He took the same professional interest in Frederick's governmental reforms as Ralph of Diss and Roger of Howden had taken in the Angevins'. He had much the same outlook. Richard's admiration for Frederick and his dislike of Frederick's opponent, Pope Gregory IX, come through the dry precision of his chronicle. Centralized bureaucracy in the interest of law and order pleased him; but he turned sour on the emperor when he sacrificed his Sicilian subjects to his imperial policy and bled them to pay for his campaigns outside the kingdom. Just as Ralph of Diss preferred Henry II to his more flashy son, so Richard of San Germano preferred Frederick the Wise as king of Sicily to the same Frederick as emperor with imperial ambitions.

No royal clerk in England took up the story of government where Roger of Howden left off. Angevin bureaucracy had passed through its heroic age. We hear of it mainly from its critics. Chroniclers approved of Edward I's reforms, but his advisers let others use them as historical material. The fact of government impinged on historiography at all levels.

Town chroniclers record the changes in local affairs and their dealings with other towns. Papal biographers deal with papal administration and finance. The merchant banker enters into history as one of its makers.

The Paris schools of the late twelfth century inspired a type of historiography which can be termed 'pulpit history'. Master Peter, chanter of Notre Dame, known as 'Peter the Chanter' (d. 1197), gathered around him a group of pupils and colleagues dedicated to preaching. They included Master Stephen Langton, who taught at Paris *c.* 1180–1206 and died as archbishop of Canterbury in 1228. The Chanter and his friends preached in person to clergy and people. They also taught in the schools that a master of the Holy Page had a duty to preach when he left Paris to take up the cure of souls elsewhere. Practical training went with the call to evangelize. It was given through the medium of lectures on the Bible. Lectures deriving from the Chanter and his circle often read like sermons or homilies. The master satirizes society: he holds up a mirror where various ranks of the hierarchy, prelates, princes and their subjects, whether clerk or lay, can see how they ought to behave and how far they fall short of the ideal. The message would carry better if the lecturer or preacher made it amusing; so he mixed grave and gay by telling stories and making jokes or pawky allusions.

This preacher's mentality conditioned the approach to history. A scholar trained in the Chanter's milieu would stress the exemplarist value of history not only in his preface, as was customary, but in his selection and presentation of events throughout his story.

James of Vitry was a devoted pupil of Peter the Chanter, whom he describes as 'a rose among thorns'. James probably came from Rheims. After studying at Paris he lived as a canon regular at St Nicolas d'Oignies. A great preacher, he helped to launch the Albigensian Crusade in 1213 and then the Fifth Crusade. His middle years were spent in the East, since he received the bishopric of Acre in 1216 and joined in the Egyptian campaign of 1218–22. The leaders of the Fifth Crusade carried out the original intention of those of the Fourth: they made for the Saracen naval bases in Egypt. Damietta was stormed after a long siege; but the crusaders could not hold it. Another crusade had failed. James returned from Overseas in 1225 and resigned his bishopric. The pope raised him to the cardinalate in 1229. He died in 1240.

81 Master Peter the Chanter is represented wearing a long clerical robe. He has a tonsure and points his fingers in the attitude of a teacher. From a manuscript produced at the German abbey of Ottobeuren on the orders of Abbot Berthold (1228–46), containing a collection of works by Master Alan of Lille, a contemporary of Peter the Chanter. *London, British Museum, MS Add. 19767, f.217r*

An eventful career had equipped him to write contemporary history, covering both East and West. The bishop of Acre had time on his hands after the loss of Damietta. He says in his preface that 'vain tales' of Oriental kings and their exploits stirred him to write a counterblast: few Latins bothered to compose histories in modern times. He would therefore spend his leisure in writing an *Eastern* and a *Western History*. His plan, as outlined in his preface, was as follows: book one would comprise a history of Jerusalem and a description of the Holy Land; book two would deal with Western history, with special reference to the religious orders and secular clergy, ending with a section on the crusades, which would describe their religious value and usefulness; in book three he would return to the East and narrate the events which had followed the Lateran Council of 1215, that is the preaching and planning of the Fifth Crusade. It appears that he was then working on book three. However, the third book is lost; perhaps it existed only in draft. The end of book two, as we have it, differs from that proposed in the preface. The author may have changed his mind and altered the book accordingly.

James of Vitry wrote as a preacher for preachers. His description of the Holy Land was added 'to supply more abundant material for preaching'. Presumably he expected it to be used in crusading sermons and in sermons intended to kindle devotion to the Holy Places. He concludes his preface by writing that his treatise will offer an example to soldiers of Christ, strengthen faith, teach good morals, refute infidels, confound wicked men, praise good men and hold them up for imitation. It would be pointless to regret that the preacher got in the historian's way. He certainly did; but without being inspired by his duty to preach, James might not have written history at all. He might have limited himself to a saint's life, letters and sermons, which are all we have from him otherwise.

The *Eastern History* begins with a 'pocket' history of the Holy Land from Old Testament times up to the Muslim occupation. James dwells on the many ills which God has inflicted on Jerusalem. The story of the Saracen invasion leads to an account of Mohammed's life and teaching, of the Koran and of the various Muslim sectaries known to the author. Another 'pocket' history, of the crusades and the Latin kingdom and of the religious orders settled there, follows on the first. James adds a geographical description of

Colour plate IX
THE TREE OF HISTORY
(see p. 182)
A tree figure illustrating Abbot Joachim of Fiore's periodization of history, probably invented by the abbot himself. God the Father, God the Son and God the Holy Spirit, shown in roundels, preside over each of the three states of world history. Noah, 'the righteous man' of the Old Testament, is shown below God the Father as a key figure of the first state. The two peoples, the Jews and the gentiles, are represented by branches, which cross at the time of Christ's Incarnation, only to merge together in unity in the third state. Joachim's tree, like that of King Nebuchadnezzar's dream (see colour plate I) bears fine foliage and fruit, which here signify good works. In the first state the Jewish branch bears more fruit than the gentile; in the second the gentile branch, signifying the Christian people, bears much more than the Jewish. In the third state, the age of the Holy Spirit, the two together bring forth a wonderful abundance of fruit. From an early thirteenth-century manuscript, probably from southern Italy. *Oxford, Corpus Christi College, MS 255A, f.4v*

Ytala pelaros tellus alis almr poetis?
Sz tibi gretos deoit hic atungere metis.

Scimr e dloli murergens ardyna mmorie
ut paceant pueds paftoribz atq colons.

82 Pulpit history in the making. A scholar studies at his desk and then teaches and preaches what he has learned. His lessons and sermons will be illustrated by historical *exempla*. From a thirteenth-century French manuscript of the *Bible moralisée* (see ills. 73–75). *Oxford, Bodleian Library, MS Bodl. 270b, f.125v*

Palestine. He concludes with the history of the Third Crusade and of subsequent events up to about 1210.

We do not know what books he had read for the section on Islam or how far he collected his data at first hand when he was based on Acre. He denounces Mohammed in pulpit language for the benefit of preachers who would use the *Eastern History* to stir up and warn the faithful against infidels. But he gathered some correct information about Muslim beliefs: the enquiring mind of the Paris scholar nudged the preacher in him. William of Tyre's *History* served as one of his sources for geography and history for the period it covered. James had to turn to other sources for the Third Crusade, which took place after William's death. His account of this Crusade brings out his inferiority to William of Tyre as a historian. James did not look deeply into problems of causation. Causes of disasters gave him a welcome opportunity to blame Christians for their sins, and that was all. He enjoyed himself when he rebuked the bathing habits of the decadent Latin colonists. The failure of the Third Crusade to recapture Jerusalem is ascribed solely to the

Colour plate X
A CHANGE IN ATTITUDE TO THE PAST (see pp. 192–3)
The Sienese painter Simone Martini (d. 1344) illuminated the frontispiece of a copy of Virgil's poems which belonged to Petrarch and has many notes in Petrarch's handwriting. Martini has dressed Virgil in a white toga and crowned him with a laurel wreath. The warrior on the left, signifying Aeneas, wears a Roman soldier's dress. It is an attempt to lift the Roman poet out of his customary medieval setting and to present him in his proper ancient setting instead. *Milan, Biblioteca Ambrosiana, Cons. I. VIII. 74, f.1v*

quarrel between the English King Richard and the French King Philip:

They say that Saladin would have surrendered all our lands if the kings had only pretended that they would join forces to invade his territories.

James reports this doubtful hypothesis without criticism.

The *Western History* is an amalgam of genres, held together by its author's purpose as a teacher and preacher. Such unity as it has depends on its concentration on the Church. A lament for the plight of the Church in the West, described in biblical similes as 'a leafless oak tree' and 'a dried-up river', parallels the lament for her sister in the East, which opens the *Eastern History*. The devil continues to poison both head and members. The Moors in Spain, heretics in Lombardy and Provence, schismatics in Greece and false brethren everywhere have afflicted the West ever since the loss of the Holy Land. Next comes a pulpit denunciation of the sins and malpractices of men and women of all ranks, illustrated by *exempla*. One might be reading a Paris lecture course of the kind which James had heard in the Chanter's school, or a set of sermons. He paints a lurid picture of the Paris schools: the scholars form a permissive, disorderly society; the same building houses a class-room upstairs and a brothel downstairs. Light breaks through the gloom when James describes the revival of preaching, both popular and learned, fostered by Peter the Chanter, though false prophets and fake relic vendors abuse their opportunities.

The *pièce de résistance* of the *Western History* follows. James gives an account of the religious revival which marked the period from the late eleventh to the early thirteenth century. He divides the religious orders into hermits and monks, tracing each of them back to the early days of the Church, and then surveys the rise of religious reform movements. We find an almost exhaustive list of orders and of institutions such as hospitals and leper-houses, drawn up by a keen and committed observer; James belonged to the order of Canons Regular. He included with approval the *Humiliati*, an order whose members sought to lead the apostolic life as laymen. Finally he introduces us to the new mendicant orders. James had seen St Francis in person outside Damietta, when the saint went on his mission to the Saracens. The *Western History* offers us the fullest religious history of the period it covers that we have from any contemporary author.

83 St Francis preaches to the Muslims. He made a great impression on James of Vitry. Detail from an altarpiece of about 1250 attributed to Margheritone of Arezzo, in the Bardi Chapel at S. Croce, Florence.

James faced the same problem that had perplexed Otto of Freising when Otto described the religious revival of his time in his *History of the Two Cities*. How could revival occur in the evening of the last age of the world? The question mattered less to James than it did to Otto, since James took little interest in periodization. He accepted that he was living in the evening of the last age. The signs of the times persuaded him that Antichrist was just round the corner. He explained the mendicant orders' return to the Gospel precepts as a mark of divine grace: God had sent the friars to defend the faithful against Antichrist.

The bishop of Acre may have felt that he had said enough about the religious orders and that the secular clergy should have their turn. The last part of the *Western History* resembles those treatises for the instruction of priests produced in increasing numbers during the thirteenth century. The genre provides basic teaching on the structure of the Church and of her institutions and sacraments. Compilers aimed at helping the priest to minister to his parishioners. Lectures on Scripture emanating from the Chanter's circle contain the same kind of matter as the manuals for priests, arranged unsystematically, since the lecturer thought fit to mention topics arising from his text. The end of the *Western History*, like the social satire of an earlier part, stems from what James had heard when he attended classes at Paris; he probably added passages from his own sermons.

James's defects as a historian are immediately obvious. He was no analyser. What happened and what existed at the moment concerned him more than why or how things came to pass. But his careful collection of facts to put at the disposal of preachers is valuable. His *Eastern History* gives the modern scholar a good idea of what a learned man with first-hand experience knew and thought of Islam. His *Western History* tells us how the same author observed and reacted to religious reform movements.

The most ornate and fanciful specimen of pulpit history comes from Poland. Master Vincent of Cracow differs from James of Vitry in many respects, but they both aim at making history 'preachable'. Vincent left his native land to study abroad, most probably in the Paris schools. He returned to Poland before 1189. If he read theology at Paris in the 1180s he could have been influenced by Peter the Chanter and Stephen Langton. That is guessing; but it would account for Vincent's didactic purpose and his determination to play up to his audience. Paris lecture techniques are easily recognizable in his chronicle.

The returned scholar became bishop of Cracow in 1207 and attended the Lateran Council of 1215 in his capacity as bishop. He resigned his see three years later in order to become a Cistercian monk in a Polish abbey, where he died in 1223. He wrote his chronicle of Poland during these last years. Though he composed it in the cloister, his experience as a scholar and bishop sets him apart from the average monastic historian.

Master Vincent began his book with a fabulous account of the origins of the Poles. He then related Polish history up to 1202. His death prevented him from going any further. The setting of the first part of the chronicle is a dinner-table conversation between two wise old men, who discuss the history of their people. Vincent chose historical characters for his *personae*. One of them was a former bishop of Cracow and the other an archbishop of Gniezno; but the fictitious nature of the dialogue is not concealed (it is made to end in 1173, by which time the two prelates had both been dead for years). Each has his own part to play. The bishop, as befits his lower rank, has the task of telling the story, and makes only a few comments. The archbishop, his ecclesiastical superior, listens to the tale and then comments on its moral significance; he draws parallels from the history of other countries and from the Bible. The commentator points his moral lessons by adducing quotations from many different types of book; he adds proverbs, *exempla*, fables, jokes and verses of hymns. One passage of the bishop's story amuses the arch-bishop so much that he roars with laughter.

When the dialogue stops, the two old men vanish and a 'valet' or serving boy tells the story. Its commentary now takes the form of a play: personified states of mind and virtues, Joy, Sorrow, Liberty, Prudence and Moderation, discuss the meaning of what they hear. The setting will surprise a reader of Vincent's chronicle; but the prologue should have prepared his mind. It assembles a larger number of assorted quotations and mixed metaphors than any other medieval prologue to a history book that I know.

The factual value of the chronicle for the origins and early history of Poland is negligible. Having no evidence, Vincent reported legends, or possibly invented them. But he becomes a priceless source after the year 1110; then we pass from myth into history, though the scantiness of other contemporary sources makes it hard to check his accuracy.

The chronicler had a clear purpose. He was a teacher and preacher like James of Vitry, but James addressed himself to Latin Christendom in general; Vincent addressed himself to the Poles. From this point of view he resembles William of Tyre rather than James. Vincent, like William, was a patriot. Love of his country inspired him to write its history. In both cases, the country was threatened with dismemberment: the Latin kingdom lay open to Saracen attack when William of Tyre was writing the last part of his book; Polish history went through cyclical crises. Unification under a single ruler would provoke a noble rebellion; the nobles, jealously independent, would break up the kingdom into principalities. The civil wars and defeat by foreign powers which followed dismemberment enabled a strong prince to gain support for establishing single rule once more. Vincent hoped that this fragile unity might be made permanent. He appealed to his readers' patriotism: 'What is done for love of one's country counts as love, not madness', he says. Solidarity is recommended as the mother of fellowship: *identitas mater est societatis*. History teaches that Poland used to be happy and strong in the good old days when the country was unified. Polish territory extended much further then than now. Present-day princes are invited to look into Vincent's chronicle as into a mirror to see their virtuous forbears, held up for imitation. As a churchman, Vincent felt bound to add that rulers would succeed all the better if they respected ecclesiastical liberties.

His chronicle won immense success. It was translated into Polish and became a textbook in Polish schools. It attracted marginal notes and commentaries, after the manner of school texts. Vincent's learned presentation suited the school-room. His chronicle, thanks to its classical allusions, had the encyclopaedic quality which the teacher needed in a set text. The teacher could refer his pupils to ancient history and myth and to classical poets as he went along. The story in itself lacked drama. Vincent could not do much with the brief annals which were all he had as sources. The decorative setting helped him out. Historians of Poland owe much to pulpit history as Vincent learned it in the Western schools. Didactic literature was a Western importation. Vincent adapted it to the needs of his people.

We may now turn from the preacher's congregations to a less specialized type of audience. The growth of an educated public led to a more widespread interest in history. Vernacular poets catered for the taste by composing histories and historical romances. The *History of William the Marshal* is a fine and well-known example of a vernacular poem on the deeds of a great English baron which serves modern historians as a primary source. Latin histories were translated into the vernacular. This gave rise to a new genre, 'history in pictures'.

Illustrated copies of histories had been few and far between before the thirteenth century. Bibles had been illustrated; but producers of histories in Latin generally contented themselves with a portrait of the author or a presentation scene to serve as a frontispiece, if they chose to illustrate the book in any way. Matthew Paris was exceptional in supplying his books with pictures. We must go to the French translations of William of Tyre's *History* if we want to find illustrations of the text. Latin and vernacular histories were presented differently. One reason for the contrast is that scholars called pictures 'the books of the laity'. Most books were written in Latin, which the layman could not understand unless he were especially well educated. He needed visual aids. It followed that a man or woman who read or heard history in the vernacular would want to see it in pictures. The need for concrete images belonged to the lay mentality. The vernacular histories which have survived are often presentation copies. A wealthy layman had a book made to order; he could afford to pay for costly illustrations. Such *de luxe* editions would be guarded as treasures and so had more chance of survival than cheaper ones.

The vogue for pictures could lead to a reversal of the functions of text and illustration. The abbey of St Mary's at York possessed a big parchment roll setting out the genealogy of the kings of England down to Edward I. It begins with the legendary story of Brutus the Trojan and his conquest of Britain. This part of the genealogy is beautifully illustrated by an artist working about 1300. The text has been reduced to several lines of writing underneath the pictures, to explain their meaning. Next the roll contains rows of 'portraits' of the kings of England with their names.

Pictures made for brighter history; but they reinforced the idea that past and present looked exactly alike. The artists who illustrated the *Great Chronicles of France* made no difference at all between the Merovingians of the fifth and sixth centuries and the Capetians of the thirteenth century when they painted costumes and court and battle scenes. The illuminator of the genealogical roll from York presents the tale of Troy in contemporary idiom. His English kings differ from one another only in their attitudes as they sit on their thrones. All wear the same type of costume as Edward I, the latest king to be depicted on the roll.

The growing interest in history inspired another type of scholar, the encyclopaedist. His task was to supply 'packaged' historical data on all periods of history known to him. A Dominican scholar called Vincent of Beauvais compiled the most extensive ever encyclopaedia of universal knowledge in about 1250. The part devoted to history, the *Speculum historiale*, alone takes up a huge folio volume in the printed edition of the *Speculum universale*. Vincent of Beauvais' history was of the world, in so far as it was known to a Westerner of the mid-thirteenth century. He refused to limit himself to the ecclesiastical and political history which formed the staple diet of medieval readers. The history of learning and of religion and mythology has its place in his *Speculum*. A whole chapter is assigned to an account of historiographers from the earliest times up to its author's own day. His interest in religion and mythology recalls James of Vitry's *Eastern* and *Western Histories*. Vincent belonged to the order of Friars Preachers, or Dominicans, and had the preacher's demand for *exempla* in mind. He differed from James in wanting to record everything that he could discover. The past appealed to him as much as the present.

Col. 1:

Il restae darius cu ecfecerur
milib; peditu. & centu milib;
equitu In acie pcedunt.; Mouebatq;
hec multitudo hostiu exercitus Ale
xandru. maxime pro pauci tate pu
citatis sue quamuis iam phde
equestnbus milib; hostiu cede
paucnunaret supeteceris. Non solu
non armata pugnar. sed &ar
uicator se etate didicisse.;
Iatq; cu instru locat uterq; utrq;
e transisen exercitus; sed ad In
cetatos ad signum belli populos
discutterent pricipes utriusq;
exercitus occurrent. Ingen
tib; uiribus conimis pugnar
conmiterat. Inqua aembo reges
& Alexander & darius uul
nerantur.; Ac arndi u certa
men conceps fuin. quo ad fu
gerer darius.; Einde cedes
psecutu securars. ibi aunc pe
ditu octogintamilia equitu
decemilia cese. capnuoru.
quadraginatamilia fuere.;
Ex macedonu uo ececidere peditu.
centu triginta. equites centu

Col. 2:

mulatu oriut. centesatuq; equi
teppeu.; Inter cumpreuos castraru
mecer & uxor. tredeci; soror. &
flie dux darii fuere.; Quartu te
depsione darius cu exec oblacer
regni dimidiae parte a Impeator
uisset.; Tercio cunctis psecutu ui
rib; socroruq; auxilus caerecens
bellu Instruturcar.; Sed du hec
darius occipir. Alexander postme
nione. ad Inuadendu psicam
classem cu copis mutacar.; Ipse
Insuhas prcnseiscit. ubi aemulosi
sibi teçib; cu Insulis uiato occur
renub; ahos elegiat. Ahos inu
ararar. Ahos pdidiar.; Extrem
urbem aemcaqssimam. & florensi
simam fiducia caethaginensiu
sibi cognatctu obsistnra oppssia
& cepir.; Eine. cilicia. rodu
atq; egyptu. parnaci fusofe p
uadiar.; Inde ad templu Iouis am
monis pegir. ut mdeocio adcep;
coposicio Ignominiae sibi po
ehs Incesti. & Infamae adulate
te macehs aboleter.; Nam apes
sictu ad se facni ipsius coneistem

Cy comence le second liure des fais le
roy phelipe dieu donne

Le premier chapitre parle coment la
cite de tours et du mans furent prises
et parle de la mort le roy henry dauitle
puis comencent les fais. teu
de lan m. En lan de lincarna
cion mil c. iiij. et xv le roy af
sembla son ost au nouuel temps
et recomenca la truerre ou
mois de may son ost fist adu
re bers nottrent et prist le frete bernart et
quatre chasteaulx qui moult fort estoient
puis vint ala cite du mans tant fist que la
prist par force de dens estoit le roy henry
qui sen sour honteusement et si auoit bien
en sa compaignie ccc cheualiers du ar
mes et tous appareilles et les chaca ius
ques au chastel de chinon qui siet en la cotree de
poitou puis retourna ala cite du mans et
fist la tour miner qui moult estoit forte et
bien estarme Quant elle fut minee siqil ne
fallout que bonter le feu on bouibois q auffi
estoit amasse que tout ne versast ceulx qui
de dens estoient la rendirent Quant le roy
ot vn pou demoure en la ville il sen parti et
fist son ost conduire bers la cite de tours sur
la rimere de loure se lou verent Quant lost
fu outre le cyoy monta acheual tout seul bne
lance en sa main et cheuaucha tant selon le
riuage come cil qui fut en grant desir de passer oul
lors comenca aregarder amont et aual pour

sauoir sil peust trouuer lieu que ne passaste en
leaue entra et comenca aversher et atasser le
parfont de la riuiere do sa lance qui tenoit et
tousiours siome salout auant mettoit en es
crire a destre et a senestre sirques tout lost vuet
passer seurement entre les enseitnes qul
mettoit si tronua en celle maniere vn passeur
par ou lexmer or oneques mais plee a nul
y peust passe et passa tout le premier deuant
toute sa tent cax la riuere qui trant estoit
denint petite en celle heure siome dieus le
bout Quant le roy et tout lost biuent qilz
estoient ainsi retraittes en vn moment et q
le roy estoit ia passe ilz cueilluent tantest a
tres et trouffefent leur hurtaois en leaue se
misterent apres le roy et passerent tous sime
ment du plus trant iusques au plus petit
¶ Quant tous furent oultre passes les eaues
rinent a reures en leur point et emplifeit
leur chanel come deuant les bourtois de la
cite qui ce miracle birent doubterent le roy
car ilz sorent bien que dieus ouuroit po lui
ceste chose admit la bestille saint jehan bap
tandis come le roy et les barons aloient en
tour la cite pour abiser dequelle partie elle
estoit plus lettiere aprandre et de ql coste
len pourroit mieulx amener les entins po
lancier aus fortereffes les ribaus de lost q
aues denoient faire la premiere oniadne
quant on assault fuent vn assault en la cite
en la prise le roy par eschielles monterent
sur les murs et prindrent la bille si spudanie
ment que ceulx de dedens ne son por midrent
onques estride le roy qui fut moult lie de
ceste aduenture bejcoteist la cite sanz rentre
fans a desmatre ceulx dedens on dehors fes
exmisons mist dedens et puis si sen parti a
tant quant il y ot demoure tant come il lui
plat ¶ Entour vn tous que ces chosz auin
drent aussi come aus octanes de la saint pere
et de saint pol moruit le roy henry dauitle
ou chastel de chinon qui en subie et estre no
ble home et assez li fut toisioux bien esther
de toutes ses emprises et en toutes les encies
res qul ot eues iusques au temps le roy
phelipe que dieus li mist en la bonde pour
feremit et pour benttier le sain saint thomas
auesesque de cantorbieu qul auoit fait mar
irer si la plus aspre auuferteux pour son

178

The *Speculum historiale* is a monument of team-work. Vincent had friar assistants to help him to collect and arrange his material. His superiors in the order tried to stop him on the reasonable ground that his gigantic enterprise cost too much money, time and labour. Vincent quietly persisted in carrying on in spite of instructions to economize. The result was the largest historical reference book of the Middle Ages. It derives from 'scissor-and-paste industry' at the highest level.

The popularity of the *Speculum* proves that it met a need for exactly that kind of book. The reader with a tough digestion could start at the beginning and plod his way through. Many more, to judge by their quotations from its pages, would dip into it or look up something that concerned them at the moment. Vincent had put an immense range of historical knowledge at the disposal of anyone who could read simple Latin and who had access to a good library. The drawback was that packaged history caused laziness, as it always will. The student has all the research done for him. He has less incentive to go to the original sources and browse among them for himself. Ideally, an encyclopaedia should serve as a guide to the original material; too often it tempts the reader to go no further. Picture histories and packaged history proved to be mixed blessings, though they spread knowledge of history over wider circles.

Here we notice a gap in thirteenth-century historiography. In all the profusion of chronicles and 'snippets' we look in vain for the old-fashioned literary history. It did not survive the early decades of the century. Various reasons suggest

86, 87 Opposite: picture history in the form of genealogy. A roll produced at the abbey of St Mary, York, about 1300 shows the arrival of Brutus in Britain, according to the legend on British origins (see p. 50). Above, he receives a wife and visits the shrine of Venus, the goddess of love. Her statue resembles images of the Virgin.

The roll goes on to illustrate the descent of English kings down to Edward I (below). The kings are portrayed in roundels. They wear the same types of costume and pose in traditional royal attitudes. *Oxford, Bodleian Library, Bodl. Roll 3*

88 The wide scope of Vincent of Beauvais' *Speculum historiale* is illustrated by a picture of the Persian King Cyrus giving orders to his troops, while a scribe sits beside him. The miniature comes at the beginning of book iv in a French fourteenth-century copy. *Oxford, Merton College, MS 2.7–10*

themselves to explain why it disappeared. There had been an element of chance in the marriage between talent and opportunity. We owe a lot of historical writing to frustrated ambition. If William of Tyre had realized his wish to become patriarch of Jerusalem, or Gerald of Wales his lifelong ambition to become archbishop of St David's, they would have left us less history. If John of Salisbury had not been driven into exile, he might never have written up his *Memoirs of the Papal Court*.

But chance and personalities are insufficient explanations. Academic developments militated against literary history. The genre 'literary history' was a child of rhetoric as taught in the Arts course. The study of rhetoric declined in the late twelfth century, and with it the means to gain a sound classical education. Students turned away from grammar and rhetoric to logic and dialectic. They skimmed over their Latin grammar and read fewer literary texts in their hurry to learn logic, natural science and philosophy. The new translations of Aristotle which were becoming available acted as a magnet in the schools.

The result was that thirteenth-century historiographers did not care to write elegant Latin. That in itself need not have lessened their competence as historians. On the contrary, the use of an unclassical style gave them freedom to express their thoughts more spontaneously. But style and content went together. Historiographers impoverished themselves when they read classical histories in extracts, as it was tempting to do, instead of soaking themselves in the originals. The ancient historians offered models of structure as well as rules of style: they taught their imitators to reflect on causation. The literary history with its classical background was more conducive to reflection than the chronicle.

To find a deeper reason for the absence of literary history we have to look at the intellectual trends of the thirteenth century. The schoolmen did not write history even in their spare time. Aristotle, their philosopher, gave them no guidance in this field. His many works contain historical allusions in plenty and he used a historical approach to problems that interested him; but he did not write any history. Theologians who studied in the schools continued to think of history as the history of salvation. As such it formed a background to their theology. Otherwise they made history serve practical ends: it had entertainment value as recreation; it provided preachers with *exempla*; it supplied precedents which could be cited in disputes on privilege and status. Thirteenth-century schoolmen put their creative effort into the discussion of problems concerning man as he is. They asked: 'What is man like in himself? What are his relations with his fellow-men? What is his relationship to God?' The answers to these questions depended less on what men had done in the past than on what they were doing now and on what the schoolmen thought they ought to do. Clio lost her appeal.

The philosopher Peter of Abano made a disparaging comment on the Muse in his *Exposition of Aristotle's Problems*, published at Padua in 1310. As a scientist Peter excluded history from scientific knowledge. His reason was that the historian, unlike the scientist, could not proceed from cause to effect or from effect to cause by inductive and deductive reasoning. Hence the composition of histories struck Peter as 'merely a laborious and pointless piling up of examples'. We cannot know what a Paris doctor of the thirteenth century would have thought of this sneer at history; it seems likely, though, that he would have regarded chroniclers as his intellectual inferiors. Master William of Puylaurens, describing the Albigensian crusade, gives a tantalizing taste of what a man trained in the schools and not obsessed by preaching could achieve when he chose to write history; but he stands alone.

Historiography met a supreme challenge just when there was no Otto of Freising to deal with it. The Calabrian abbot Joachim of Fiore (d. 1202) put forward a new time scheme and a new pattern of history. Joachim was not a historian, but a commentator on Scripture, a religious reformer and a prophet. Nevertheless, his ideas had deep implications for anyone who reflected on historical periodization. The Calabrian abbot developed the traditional Christian view that the Old Testament prefigured and foreshadowed the New. There were two dispensations in the history of man's salvation; Joachim held to that. But he went on to predict a third age in religious history. The second dispensation included a third age. The Old Testament represented the age of God the Father, the New Testament that of God the Son; the third age would be the age of the Holy Spirit, proceeding from the Father and the Son. Joachim believed that mankind was standing on the threshold of this third age; he could see the signs of what was coming.

He worked out correspondences between the ages and allowed for overlapping between them. The Old Testament corresponded to the Order of Wedlock, since the patriarchs of Israel had married, according to God's plan to people the earth. The New Testament corresponded to the Order of Clerks. The third age would be the age of monks. The hermits of the Old Testament and St John the Baptist had prepared the way for the second age. St Benedict, founder of Western monasticism, prepared the way for the monks who would characterize the third age of the world. The new order always emerged from the womb of the old. The monks of the third age would be holier and more spiritual than their predecessors. The age of the Holy Spirit would begin with the coming of a new Elias. Then twelve holy men would appear, corresponding to the twelve apostles of the Gospel. Joachim altered the traditional order by putting the coming of the first Antichrist, who would bring trials and tribulations to the faithful, before the last age. The first Antichrist would come and suffer defeat before the reign of the Holy Spirit could be established. The third age, when the Holy Spirit would reign, would last until the coming of the second Antichrist and Doomsday. Religion would be perfected in the third age and an angelic pope would rule the Church.

Pat on the heels of Joachim's prophecies came the new orders of mendicant friars. St Francis and his companions fitted into the picture of the new Elias and his twelve holy men. The emperor Frederick II fell neatly into the role of the first Antichrist. If Joachim's predictions were about to be fulfilled, then the third age must be dawning. The abbot's disciples carried his conclusions further than he would have dreamed. Works falsely ascribed to him circulated. Interest showed itself in the production of 'books of figures', where the Joachist outline of history and of its future course were shown in the form of trees with branches and captions to explain what they meant. Some of the figures go back to the early days of Joachism; others develop the abbot's ideas on extraordinary lines. Joachism spread like wildfire. Its extremist forms led to heresy, but papal condemnations failed to quench the flame. Its influence on religious prophecy lasted into the seventeenth century.

Joachim's vision of the sweep of history, in contrast to the traditional view handed down by St Augustine and Orosius, was dynamic rather than static. Joachim kept their idea that one age led up to the following age; but he opened up a prospect of a new and better era, which he inserted between the first and second coming of Antichrist. The troubles in store for us at Antichrist's first coming were to be a prelude to the reign of the Holy Spirit in this world.

The new pattern suggested by Joachim presented historiographers with an opportunity to revise their views on time schemes. He challenged them to look for signs of progress instead of remaining bogged down in the old age of the world. True, Joachim postulated religious progress only; but religious and secular history hung together. It should have been possible to pick up the threads of optimism to be found in the works of Hugh of St Victor and other twelfth-century writers. Historiographers failed to respond. The story of the abbot and his disciples and of their prophecies appealed to chroniclers as news items. They report the prophecies with varying degrees of scepticism and credulity. Salimbene went through a Joachist phase, only to be disillusioned when Frederick II did not come up to scratch as Antichrist: Frederick's death in 1250 brought little change in the world. Salimbene had no idea of planning his chronicle according to the time scheme of Joachim's three ages. Thirteenth-century chroniclers did not attempt to test the new periodization in order to decide whether it applied to their material. If anyone tested and rejected it as a useful tool to the historian, he did so in silence.

The contrast between historiographers on the one hand, and theologians and prophets on the other, is difficult to explain. Were chroniclers afraid of falling into heresy? Fear of heresy had small effect on speculation in the universities. Why should chroniclers have been especially nervous? Perhaps they refrained from speculating on the course of universal history out of common sense. Perhaps they had too little interest in ideas. Perhaps their silence is another reflection of their intellectual inferiority vis-à-vis the schoolmen. For whatever reason, they fought shy of Joachism, leaving others to discuss its merits or to refute it, as the case might be.

A modern historian may warm to this 'no nonsense' attitude on the part of thirteenth-century historiographers. We tend to regard 'prophetic history' as a pitfall, or a blind alley at best. But Joachim challenged historiographers to revise their traditional time schemes. Perhaps they showed a wise caution in keeping to tradition. In any case, they preferred caution to enterprise. The thirteenth century lacked a 'reflective' historian.

11

Conclusions

We can now consider the question, why did anyone write history when it brought him no financial or professional reward for his pains? The closest parallel to the modern professional historian in the Middle Ages seems to be the court entertainer, who composed and recited 'songs' on historical topics; he earned his living by doing so; but his 'songs' fall outside the most serious kind of historiography. It will help to answer the question if we begin at the consumers' end and ask, not why history was written, but why it was needed.

Isidore said in his *Etymologies* that record-keeping was 'useful'. That was true: rulers and corporate bodies, such as town councils and religious houses, needed to have records kept for purposes of reference and to substantiate their political and legal claims. Chronicles served as record books. Pleasure and pride in the past added to the desire to have events recorded. Members of a family or of an institution took an interest in the story of their origins and of their ancestors. The historian of a family, episcopal see, abbey, town or people expected to find interested readers or hearers. Belonging to the group himself, he would identify with his theme and his audience. It was his honour and his duty to satisfy their demands. The group might be larger or smaller. It could comprise a whole country: William of Tyre and Vincent of Cracow wrote expressly from motives of patriotism, to instruct their compatriots. If the tale were a sad one, the writer could give vent to his people's grief: the anonymous *Life of Henry IV* is a dirge for the decline of the empire; the anonymous part of the *Song of the Albigensian Crusade* is a lament for the plight of the Midi.

History also served for recreation, though this is not stated in the *Etymologies*. Hunting was the sport of kings; listening to stories was their pastime. Natural entertainers perform in all ages. We have seen them at work, from the tenth-century *salon* historians to William of Tyre amusing King Amalric and William of Tudela at the court of Count

Baldwin. A churchman could salve his conscience by pointing to the exemplarist value of history. It pertained to his office to instruct the laity: history provided a happy means to a good end. Indeed it could convey a dire warning: William of Puylaurens wrote his chronicle to show how the sins of his people had led to disaster. An element of sheer curiosity also entered into the search for news items and more rarely into the scholarly investigation of antiquities.

To choose history rather than chronicle involved thought and labour. The historian had to watch his style. He deliberately avoided a year-by-year framework, which meant that he had to plan his presentation more carefully. Yet many authors took the trouble to write history. The choice in itself marked the historian as a classicist. Desire to emulate the ancients inspired some of the best writers of the Middle Ages from the ninth to the twelfth centuries, and not least the historians. The cult of letters distinguished civilized men from mere brutes. History ranked high by ancient standards as a dignified branch of literature. 'Emulation' is a better term than 'imitation' to describe the medieval historian's attitude. His story deserved the honour of elegant narrative as much as Caesar's or Sallust's. He paid homage to his theme by adapting their techniques and language to suit his material.

The propaganda motive dominated medieval historiography, as it had Roman. Biographies show it in its crudest form: a royal biography was a propaganda piece by definition. The biographer might work to order, as the Anonymous of St Omer did for Emma in her lifetime, or he might praise the ruler after his death at the request of friends or heirs. Apart from conventional eulogy, he stressed whichever aspect of the ruler appealed to him as a lay noble or as monk or prelate. Histories, chronicles and memoirs carry propaganda of an equally obvious or at least perceptible kind. Today the word propaganda implies an intention to mislead. Originally, during the Counter Reformation, it meant 'the propagation of the faith'. We are using the word in this second sense when we describe medieval historiography as 'propagandist'. Writers often had a religious purpose uppermost in their minds, and said so. The more secular-minded advertised a cause which was dear to their hearts; thus Caffaro wrote for Genoa and Villehardouin for his fellow-crusaders. Interest and idealism shade into each other. It is always hard to separate them, and hardest of all in medieval historiography. Our authors normally wrote on behalf of an institution or fellowship. The propagandist, unless he is paid, has a personal stake in swaying public opinion. In the Middle Ages his personal interest merged into his *esprit de corps*.

One unshakable belief supported all these motives. What happened mattered and ought to be remembered. 'Despise the world and its vanities', said the preacher; 'save them from oblivion', said the scholar, who was often the same as the preacher. Historiographers acted on the second precept.

It is more difficult to estimate their achievement than to explain why they wrote. C. H. Haskins, a great medievalist, warns us that 'the historian has no business to award prizes for modernity'. A judge must know the rules of the game; that is certain. We should not blame a chronicler for not writing history, nor look in a biography for the facts and dates that we expect to find in a chronicle. But we can try to measure the distance between medieval and modern standards. There are no absolute standards in historiography; they change all the time. We can only use those which we apply to ourselves nowadays. In one respect the ideal has not changed: the historiographer must tell the truth. But how to find it? Dearth of research tools, absence of perspective and blind faith in the value of eyewitness accounts – all frustrated the medieval historiographer in his enquiries. On the question of bias, today we try to check our personal prejudices by awareness of them and by scrupulous honesty in our use of evidence. In that we score over our medieval forerunners, and in that only. To accuse them of bias would be like throwing stones in glass houses. No one can write history without having ideas about what comes into it; and ideas imply bias. What we can ask is whether an author tries to be objective. We exclude supernatural agencies as an element in causation, except in so far as belief in the supernatural has been a factor in the making of history. But the historiographer has to write of the world as he knows it. The medieval historiographer wrote of a world which included supernatural agents. Even so, he never regarded men as mere puppets. It is possible to ask of him: how far does he leave all the work to God and the devil and how far does he consider human or natural causes?

The fairest way to measure achievement is to take the point of departure. What did medieval historiographers make of their sources? They inherited a jumble of rules, models and definitions. The Romans left them guidelines which, although twisted, were indispensable to the writing of contemporary or near contemporary history. The Jewish-Christian legacy taught them to attempt universal history. This heritage put man at the centre of a cosmic drama, the history of salvation: time began with Genesis and would end at Doomsday. The historiographer therefore had to embrace the 'universe', and the whole of recorded history. It sounds a tall order; but the territory to be covered and the records of its history were limited. His task was easier than one might suppose, since Isidore told him that to write pre-contemporary history consisted of copying from earlier sources; it was mere compilation. Orosius handed down a standard model of universal history or chronicle, arranged according to the time scheme of the six ages of the world and the four world monarchies. The Roman legacy of historical monograph, biographies and eulogies fitted into the wider framework as permitted alternatives. Eusebius provided a model of Church history and Orosius presented profane history from the point of view of the Church historian. For profane history as such the classical models gave the only guidance available. Attempts were made to keep the two kinds separate; but they foundered. Ecclesiastical and secular history mingled increasingly as the Church came to play a greater part in secular life and to monopolize letters. Learned churchmen knew both their Latin classics and their Bible and used them as ingredients in varying degrees when they turned to historiography.

The mixed inheritance carried dangers. Medieval writers leaned too heavily on their authorities. Ancient and biblical characters get in the way of the story. The historiographer appropriated them and costumed them, or made his contemporaries use their language. It comes as a relief to the modern reader when they stay in the background or disappear from the scene. The Orosian periodization was accepted as a dogma and proved to be an incubus. The span of the four world monarchies sometimes provoked questions; more often it was ignored. No historiographer replaced it by any other form of periodization. Joachim of Fiore proposed a new time scheme and a new outlook on history. Historiographers left the stone unturned, either because they dared not break with tradition or because historical speculation did not appeal to them.

Men with a speculative bent made straight for the schools – monastic, cathedral or university. Otto of Freising stands alone as a scholar-historian who had ideas about history and who tested them in the light of his experience. The same reluctance to question tradition comes out in the attitude to barbarian history. Folk legends and learned inventions on the origins of peoples came down as part of the stock-in-trade. Medieval writers generally imitated instead of criticizing these fake origins; new fakes proliferated. William of Malmesbury and William of Newburgh are both famous for their scepticism on the subject of romances about early British history. The fame of these romances testifies to the general level of credulity. It was not a matter of inertia in this case, as it was in the acceptance of the Orosian time scheme. Rather, the attitude was 'me too!' Respectable peoples and towns had to have ancient or biblical ancestors, or preferably both, just as sees and abbeys often had legendary foundation stories. Local pride led to the study of history, but also to the invention of fake history.

These are small specks on the bubbling creativeness of medieval historiography. We have *salon* history, religious history of many kinds, local history, court history, pulpit history, 'country party' history, war history, colonial history, nostalgic history and even reflective history. A rich assortment of genres came down as part of the medieval inheritance, stretching from Sallust's monographs to the *Popes' Book* and Paul the Deacon's *History of Metz*. Historiographers showed a talent for adapting an old genre to new uses. The writer of a saint's life and passion saw himself as continuing the Gospel. The New Testament received some unlikely supplements in Wipo's *Life* of the tough emperor Conrad II and in the anonymous *Deeds of the Franks*. A real breakthrough came in portraiture. Suetonius' static portraits of rulers began to take on life. Adam of Bremen describes an archbishop turning into a megalomaniac. Jocelyn of Brakelonde shows how Samson's office as abbot brought out his masterful character. William of Malmesbury points to the connection between King Stephen's character and the events of his reign. Stephen was on the wrong side anyway, from William's point of view; but his defects prevented him from winning in the civil war as long as William lived to record its history. William of Tyre notes how the characters of the kings of Jerusalem affected the defence of their kingdom.

Personal memoirs are the *forte* of medieval historiography, as we have seen. In modern times memoirs have often taken the form of autobiography. This was exceptional in the Middle Ages. Guibert of Nogent, untypical and original,

Abelard and Gerald of Wales made the closest approaches to autobiography in the period between 800 and 1300. Introspection took other forms, such as prayers or meditations. The memoir writer described his experiences as a member of a group instead of focusing on his 'self': he observed and participated, but did not put himself forward in his own right. We have memoirs in pure form in Liudprand's account of his embassy to Constantinople and in the stories of Galbert of Bruges and of Geoffrey of Villehardouin; and memoirs form part of many other genres of historiography, often the best part. The reporter escaped from the temptation to imitate and he had an impetus to write freshly and directly.

Still, memoirs are not history. The historian must try to find connections between the events he describes; he must ask 'why?' as well as 'what?' and 'how?'. The best one can say for medieval historians is that they responded to shock treatment. Questions asked themselves. The Investiture Contest, the rise of towns, the growth of bureaucracy, border warfare, the crusades and the spread of heresy all posed problems. Why did Henry IV fail as an emperor? Why did the Saxon freedom fighters fail? Why the slaughter at Bruges? Was Henry II justified in restricting ecclesiastical liberties in the interests of law and order? Why did the heathen Slavs and the Irish resist for so long? Why did the kingdom of Jerusalem decline? Why did heresy spread in the Midi? These were non-questions to a disciple of Orosius. For him, history boiled down to the story of human misery; why pick on a particular episode as extraordinary? But historians minded about particular episodes which concerned them. They looked for particular causes. The old answers lay ready to hand: God punishes sin; his ways are inscrutable; Fortune turns her wheel; modern luxury softens morals and leads to defeat. Such answers struck some historians as inadequate: they left too much unexplained. The more thoughtful writers came up with shrewd, commonsense reasons. Ralph of Diss decided that some questions were better left alone; so he found an escape route by putting his data in separate compartments. At least he saw his problem.

Discernment of motive is still one of the most elusive problems which face the historian. We find it difficult enough to analyse our own. When we tackle the motives of a character in history we have no evidence, unless he or his associates stated them, and that may well have been propaganda. All we can safely say is that he had an interest in taking a certain course; but he may have had quite a different notion of where his interests lay; he may even have preferred to do what he thought was his duty; he may have been plain stupid. The problem of motive fascinated medieval historians. Guibert of Nogent in his history of the First Crusade under-lined the difficulty of establishing human motives. As the author of an autobiography, he had more experience of introspection than most historiographers. Others rushed in where he feared to tread. Again, however, shrewd common sense inspired their guesses at motives for action. It was normal to contrast what a person gave out as his reason for acting in a certain way to what he was really aiming at. Historiographers on the whole did not err on the side of being 'starry-eyed'. They were too cynical if anything: 'suspect the worst.'

Complete objectivity is impossible to achieve at all times. Medieval historiographers had an extra handicap; their best efforts went into writing contemporary or near contem-porary history, in which partiality is built into the narrative. But we do find brave attempts to stand outside and to see more than one viewpoint. Adam of Bremen and Helmold tried to understand the Slavs; John of Salisbury lent over backward to be fair to both St Bernard and Gilbert of la Porrée; William of Puylaurens succeeded in putting the southerners' point of view on heresy, explaining why it spread and why it was not resisted, without excusing the heretics. Going back to the ninth century, we find Walafrid Strabo criticizing the historian Thegan for his partiality to Louis the Pious. Signs of a wish to be objective show through medieval historiography in spite of its usually propagandist purpose. The Middle Ages produced brilliant propagandists. Surprisingly, there was room for historians too.

Finally, we expect a historian to rely on evidence and to show his hand. Footnotes are a modern invention, but it was possible to quote documentary evidence and to copy inscriptions. Suetonius did so; Eusebius made it part of the technique of writing Church history. Secular and Church history intermingled and there was cross-fertilization. The tyranny of ancient biography and of medieval hagiography tended to keep documentary evidence out of *Lives* of rulers and saints, though it did creep into them during the twelfth century. Monographs, histories and chronicles, on the other hand, increasingly supply copies of letters, charters, treaties and laws. Historiographers sometimes had a propagandist reason for inserting them; others saw documents as an integral part of the story they had to tell. They sacrificed literary elegance to their duty to be informative.

We can watch modern historiography developing gradually in the Middle Ages. Our predecessors started from a small residue of ancient histories. Many have been lost; but we have more than were obtainable in the Middle Ages. Medieval historiographers made full and imaginative use of their legacy such as it was. Sometimes it acted as a crutch; the more adventurous put it aside and walk on their own feet. This is especially true of lay writers; these had to be self-sufficient and original when book learning had become a privilege of clergy.

The history of an art or science never registers steady progress. There are always lapses, whatever standard we take as our measuring-rod. Historiography almost disappeared in the decades about 900. History as distinct from chronicle lapsed again in the thirteenth century. The twelfth-century Latin historians remained unsurpassed in the thirteenth. One can browse with pleasure in thirteenth-century chronicles, as well as reading them as source material; but one misses any awareness of history's special function. These writers are shallow compared with William of Malmesbury, Otto of Freising or William of Tyre.

The turn of the century makes a convenient stopping place. The years after 1300 saw new developments in the writing of history and new ideas about how it should be written. Monks and clerks continued to produce histories and chronicles in Latin. Secular clerks were especially busy in England. But the fourteenth century is more famous for its vernacular chroniclers. The lay historian, a soldier or a city official, comes into the foreground. He tells of events which he has seen and taken part in. We have Joinville's *Life of St Louis*, the chronicle of the Catalan general Ramon Muntaner, the Anglo-Norman *Scalachronicon*, Froissart's chronicles of the Anglo-French wars and the Villani chronicles of Florence, to mention only a few outstanding names. The German *Stadtchronik*, or town chronicle, became a major source for imperial history.

Learned Latin historiography revived. A schoolman turned to history without thinking it beneath his dignity as an academic. The Oxford Dominican friar Nicholas Trevet wrote extensively in both Latin and French. He was a polymath and history was one of his many interests. Livy came into fashion as an author. His history of Rome had been

89 A genuine sense of history, of the past as different from the present, begins to appear in the work of Giotto. In his fresco of the Flagellation, painted in the Arena Chapel at Padua about 1305, Pontius Pilate is for the first time an entirely non-medieval figure. No longer bearded and robed in dateless draperies, he is clearly a Roman, distinguished from the Jews around him. His massive head is garlanded, and his robe bears the imperial eagle in gold.

known in the earlier period, but he was little read. Now he became a favourite among the élite. Trevet led the way at Oxford at the turn of the century in his study of Livy. His commentary on Livy's *History* was sought after and read at the papal court at Avignon. The vogue reflected a serious interest in ancient history and antiquities.

The achievements of twelfth-century historians grew out of their loving study of the Latin classics, as we have seen. The early fourteenth-century revival of classical studies had the same stimulating effect on historians. A group of scholars at Padua, Livy's birthplace, took the Roman writer to themselves. They did not merely imitate his classical style. The bewildering changes in Italian history from ancient times up to their own day led them to reflect on problems of periodization. The Paduan 'prehumanists', as the group is now called, experimented with new genres and new time schemes. Albertino Mussato was probably the first historian since Otto of Freising to write 'reflective history'. He had a more secular and local approach to his subject than Otto; but they both felt the same urge to put the untidy facts of history into an intelligible order. Their originality, if nothing else, makes a link between the German Cistercian bishop and the Paduan citizen.

More decisive than these experiments, brave though they were, is the change in men's attitude to the past. The student of medieval historiography gets used to living in an intellectual world in which he can converse with Adam and Eve or Julius Caesar or Charlemagne as though they were neighbours. As soon as we know our historian, we know how he will imagine the past; it will look like the present. In the fourteenth century the sense of continuity snapped. It was no longer a question of decline from a better age. An old man in his last years can still identify with the boy that he used to be. Now, suddenly, it was as though the old man had lost his memory and recovered to find himself in a prison or mad-house. Petrarch saw that a gulf separated ancient culture from the chivalry and scholasticism of his time. Contemporary institutions struck him as 'barbarous'. He announced his discovery with the voice of genius; but it was part of a general stock-taking. To good Catholics as well as to heretics the fourteenth-century Church looked more like Babylon than the primitive community of the apostles. In ecclesiastical history as in secular the contrast between past and present loomed too large to admit of any continuous development.

The humanists did not 'rediscover the past'. It belonged to the medieval inheritance from antiquity. What they did was to discover the past *as* past. History was seen in perspective, not as a painting on a flat surface. The humanists' perspective looks faulty today. Their judgments on the past were distorted. But the attempt at perspective of any kind makes all the difference to the presentation of history. In that sense, modern historiography begins in the fourteenth century.

The new vision affected the writing of history slowly and partially. As often happens, the men who had new ideas about history did not write it, and history was left to the conservatives. We have seen that theologians and canon lawyers showed more awareness of the possibility of change for the better than did historiographers. So it was in the fourteenth century. Humanists and reformers showed more awareness of the gap between past and present than did historiographers, with few exceptions. A reader fresh from studying thirteenth-century chronicles will feel quite at home when he turns to chroniclers in the fourteenth century; he will find the same methods and the same outlook on the past. Nevertheless, he needs to watch his step and prepare himself for a change of climate. It would not do to omit Darwin's *Origin of Species* from a history of ideas, just because most of Darwin's contemporaries still believed that God created man in paradise. Even if the old conventions and time schemes lingered on in late medieval historiography, the modern reader knows that the *avant garde* had other views on history. The older notions begin to seem dull and stale. They lasted for a millennium, which is a long time in the history of ideas.

Bibliography

CHAPTERS 1–4

General and introductory reading

R. G. Collingwood, *The Idea of History* (Oxford, 1946)

B. Croce, *Theory and History of Historiography*, trans. D. Ainslie
(London, 1921)

H. Grundmann, 'Geschichtsschreibung im Mittelalter', *Deutsche
Philologie im Aufriss*, ed. W. Stammer, xxvi (1952–9), 1273–1335

B. M. Lacroix, 'The Notion of History in Early Medieval Historians',
Mediaeval Studies, x (Toronto, 1948), 219–23; and *L'Historien au
moyen âge*, Montreal and Paris 1971

A. Momigliano, 'Pagan and Christian Historiography in the Fourth
Century A.D.', *The Conflict between Paganism and Christianity in the
Fourth Century*, ed. A. Momigliano (Oxford, 1963), 79–99

J. T. Shotwell, *The History of History*, i (New York, 1939), 255–377

B. Smalley, 'Sallust in the Middle Ages', *Classical Influences on European
Culture, A.D. 500–1500*, ed. R. R. Bolgar (Cambridge, 1971)

R. W. Southern, 'Aspects of the European Tradition of Historical
Writing. 1. The Classical Tradition from Einhard to Geoffrey of
Monmouth'; '2. Hugh of St Victor and the Idea of Historical
Development'; '3. History as Prophecy', *Transactions of the Royal
Historical Society*, 5th series, xx–xxii (1970–72). To be completed by
'The Sense of the Past', forthcoming

J. W. Thompson and B. J. Holm, *A History of Historical Writing*, 2 vol.
(New York, 1942, reprint, 1967)

Texts in translation

Latin Historians and *Latin Biography*, ed. T. A. Dorey (London, 1966,
1967)

English Historical Documents, ed. D. C. Douglas, i–iii (from 1955), gives
many excerpts from English and Anglo-Norman historians and
chroniclers with introductions. The best known are translated in full
in Bohn's Antiquarian Library

CHAPTERS 5 AND 6

La Storiografia Altomedievale (Settimane di Studio del Centro Italiano di
Studio sull'Alto Medioevo, xvii, 2 vol., Spoleto, 1970) has papers in
English, French, German, Italian and Spanish on early medieval
historiography, up to the 11th century

D. A. Bullough, *'Europae Pater: Charlemagne and his achievement in
the light of recent scholarship', English Historical Review*, lxxxv
(1970), 59–105

J. Leclercq, 'Monastic historiography from Leo IX to Callistus II',
Studia Monastica, xii (1970), 57–86

Christopher Brooke, *The Twelfth Century Renaissance* (London, 1969)

R. W. Southern, *Medieval Humanism and Other Studies* (Oxford, 1970)

C. Morris, *The Discovery of the Individual 1050–1200* (London, 1972)

V. H. Galbraith, *Historical Research in Medieval England* (London, 1951)

H. Farmer, 'William of Malmesbury's Life and Works', *Journal of Ecclesiastical History*, xiii (1962), 39–54

Texts in translation

Einhard, *The Life of Charlemagne*, trans. L. Thorpe (London, 1970)

Carolingian Chronicles: Royal Frankish Annals and Knithard's Histories, trans. B. W. Scholz and B. Rogers (Michigan, 1970)

Imperial Lives and Letters of the Eleventh Century, trans. T. E. Mommsen and K. F. Morrison (Records of Civilization, New York, 1962)

Helgaud de Fleury, *Vie de Robert le Pieux*, ed. and trans. (French) R.-H. Bautier and G. Labory (Sources d'histoire médiévale, Paris, 1965)

Suger, *Vie de Louis VI le Gros*, ed. and trans. (French) H. Waquet (Classiques de l'histoire de France au Moyen âge, Paris, 1929)

Encomium Emmae Reginae, ed. and trans. Alistair Campbell (Camden 3rd series, lxxii, London, 1949)

The Works of Liudprand of Cremona, trans. F. A. Wright (London, 1930)

Richer, *Histoire de France 888–995*, ed. and trans. (French) R. Latouche (Classiques de l'histoire de France au Moyen âge, Paris, 1930–67)

The Anglo-Saxon Chronicle, a revised translation, ed. D. Whitelock (London, 1961)

The Ecclesiastical History of Orderic Vitalis, ed. and trans. M. Chibnall (Oxford, 1969–72)

The Historia Novella of William of Malmesbury, ed. and trans. K. R. Potter (London, 1955)

CHAPTER 7

A. D. von den Brincken, *Studien zur lateinischen Weltchronistik bis in das Zeitalter Otto von Freisings* (Düsseldorf, 1957)

Texts in translation

Otto of Freising, *The Two Cities*, trans. C. C. Mierow (Records of Civilization, New York, 1928)

The Deeds of Frederick Barbarossa by Otto of Freising and his Continuator Rahewin, trans. C. C. Mierow (Records of Civilization, New York, 1953)

CHAPTER 8

D. M. Stenton, 'Roger of Howden and *Benedict*', *English Historical Review*, lxviii (1953), 574–82

A History of St Paul's Cathedral and the Men associated with it, ed. W. R. Matthews and W. M. Atkins (London, 1957)

For Caffaro's Genoa, see below, chapter 9 (Boase)

Texts in translation

The Murder of Charles the Good by Galbert of Bruges, trans. J. B. Ross (Records of Civilization, New York, 1960)

John of Salisbury's Memoirs of the Papal Court, ed. and trans. M. Chibnall (London, 1956)

CHAPTER 9

A. P. Vlasto, *The Entry of the Slavs into Christendom* (Cambridge, 1970)

T. S. R. Boase, *Kingdoms and Strongholds of the Crusaders* (London, 1971) gives a bibliography which is also useful for Caffaro's Genoa (see chapter 8)

A. C. Krey, 'William of Tyre', *Speculum*, xvi (1941), 149–66

R. B. C. Huygens, 'Guillaume de Tyr étudiant. Un chapitre de son *Histoire* retrouvé', *Latomus*, xxi (1962), 811–29

B. M. Lacroix, 'Guillaume de Tyr. Unité et diversité dans la tradition latine', *Etudes d'histoire littéraire et doctrinale*, 4th series (Paris, 1968), 201–15

C. Morris, 'Villehardouin and the Conquest of Constantinople', *History*, liii (1968), 24–34

P. Belperron, *La Croisade contre les Albigeois et l'union du Languedoc à la France (1209–1249)* (Paris, 1946)

R. I. Moore, 'The Origins of Medieval Heresy', *History*, lv (1970), 21–36

Texts in translation

Adam of Bremen, *History of the Archbishops of Hamburg-Bremen*, trans. F. J. Tschan (Records of Civilization, New York, 1959)

Helmold, *The Chronicle of the Slavs*, trans. F. J. Tschan (Records of Civilization, New York, 1935)

J. J. O'Meara and A. B. Scott are preparing a new edition and translation of Gerald of Wales, *De expugnatione Hiberniae*; meanwhile on Gerald of Wales see the first version of his *Topographia*, trans. J. J. O'Meara (Dundalk, 1951)

Anonymous, *Deeds of the Franks*, ed. and trans. Rosalind Hill (London, 1962)

William of Tyre, *A History of deeds done beyond the sea*, trans. E. A. Babcock and A. C. Krey (Records of Civilization, New York, 1943)

Chronicles of the Crusades. Histoire de Saint Louis. La Conquête de Constantinople, trans. M. R. B. Shaw (London, 1967)

Pierre des Vaux de Cernai, *Histoire Albigeoise*, trans. (French) P. Guébin and H. Maisonneuve (Paris, 1951)

Chanson de la Croisade Albigeoise, trans. (French from Provençal) E. Martin-Chabot (Classiques de l'histoire de France au Moyen âge, Paris, 1931–61)

Chronique de Guillaume de Puy Laurens contenant l'histoire de l'expédition contre les Albigeois, trans. (French) C. Lagarde (Béziers, 1864)

CHAPTER 10

R. Brentano, *Two Churches: England and Italy in the Thirteenth Century* (Princeton, 1968), 306–45, compares Matthew Paris and Salimbene as chroniclers and gives bibliography

P. David, *Les Sources de l'histoire de Pologne* (Paris, 1934), 56–72, gives an account of Vincent of Cracow

B. L. Ullman, 'A Project for a New Edition of Vincent of Beauvais', *Speculum*, viii (1933), 312–26

N. G. Siraisi, 'The *Expositio Problematum Aristotelis* of Peter of Abano', *Isis*, lxi (1970), 321–39

M. E. Reeves, *The Influence of Prophecy in the Later Middle Ages* (Oxford, 1970)

Texts

The Chronicle of Jocelin of Brakelond concerning the acts of Samson, ed. and trans. H. E. Butler (London, 1949)

Matthew Paris's English History, trans. J. A. Giles (London, 1852–4)

Thomas of Eccleston and Jordan of Giano, trans. E. Gurney Salter (London, 1926)

Grandes chroniques de la France, ed. J. Viard (Paris, 1920–34)

CHAPTER 11

B. Smalley, *English Friars and Antiquity in the Early Fourteenth Century* (Oxford, 1960), chapter 12

Peter Burke, *The Renaissance Sense of the Past* (London, 1969)

D. R. Kelley, *Foundations of Modern Historical Scholarship: Language, Law and History in the French Renaissance* (New York and London, 1970)

Texts

For original texts see A. Potthast, *Bibliotheca historica medii aevi* (Berlin, 1895–6). A new edition of Potthast is in progress, *Repertorium fontium historiae medii aevi* (Rome, 1962–70)

ACKNOWLEDGMENTS

Most of the photographs from which reproductions have been made were supplied by the institutions mentioned in the captions in italic type. The publishers would also like to thank the following: Archives Photographiques, Paris 42; Giraudon 1; F. Lahaye, Maastricht 56; Mansell Collection 11, 36, 83; Marburg 39, 44, 61, 62; Nationalmuseet, Copenhagen IV, V; Yan 58, 70, 71, 72, 76. Illustrations 54 and 55 are from L. T. Belgrano, *Annali Genovesi di Caffaro*, Fonti per la storia d'Italia, vol. I, 1890.

Index

Anonymous authors are indexed under book titles. Illustration numbers are printed in *italic* type (Roman numerals indicate colour plates).